THE NEW AMERICAN COMMENTARY

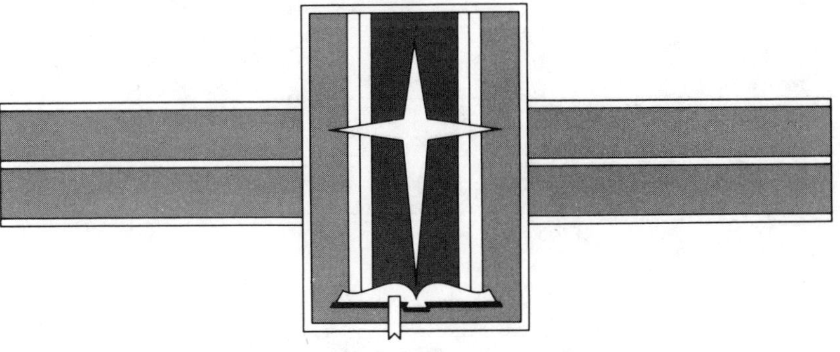

An Exegetical and Theological Exposition of Holy Scripture

THE NEW AMERICAN COMMENTARY

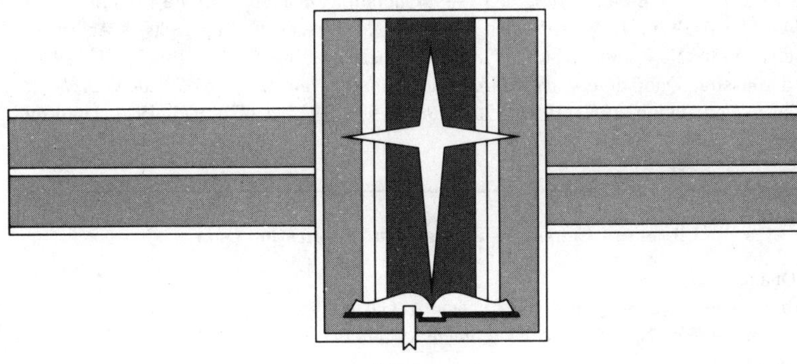

Volume
14

PROVERBS
ECCLESIASTES
SONG OF SONGS

Duane A. Garrett

BROADMAN PRESS
NASHVILLE, TENNESSEE

4201-14
ISBN: 0-8054-0114-8
Dewey Decimal Classification: 223.0
Subject Heading: BIBLE. O.T. PROVERBS, ECCLESIASTES, SONG OF SONGS
Library of Congress Catalog Number: 93-10279
Printed in the United States of America

Library of Congress Cataloging-in-Publication Data

Garrett, Duane A.
Proverbs, Ecclesiastes, Song of Songs / Duane A. Garrett.
p. cm. — (The New American Commentary ; v. 14)
Includes Index.
ISBN 0-8054-0114-8
1. Bible. O.T. Proverbs—Commentaries. 2. Bible. O.T. Ecclesiastes—Commentaries. 3. Bible. O.T. Song of Solomon—Commentaries. I. Bible. O.T. Proverbs. English. New International. 1993. II. Bible. O.T. Ecclesiastes. English. New International. 1993. III. Bible. O.T. Song of Solomon. English. New International. 1993. IV. Title. V. Series.
223′.077—dc20

To *Melissa, Kristin, and Jesse*
May they find the Wisdom of Proverbs,
the Faith of Ecclesiastes,
and the Love of Song of Songs

Editors' Preface

God's Word does not change. God's world, however, changes in every generation. These changes, in addition to new findings by scholars and a new variety of challenges to the gospel message, call for the church in each generation to interpret and apply God's Word for God's people. Thus, THE NEW AMERICAN COMMENTARY is introduced to bridge the twentieth and twenty-first centuries. This new series has been designed primarily to enable pastors, teachers, and students to read the Bible with clarity and proclaim it with power.

In one sense THE NEW AMERICAN COMMENTARY is not new, for it represents the continuation of a heritage rich in biblical and theological exposition. The title of this forty-volume set points to the continuity of this series with an important commentary project published at the end of the nineteenth century called AN AMERICAN COMMENTARY, edited by Alvah Hovey. The older series included, among other significant contributions, the outstanding volume on Matthew by John A. Broadus, from whom the publisher of the new series, Broadman Press, partly derives its name. The former series was authored and edited by scholars committed to the infallibility of Scripture, making it a solid foundation for the present project. In line with this heritage, all NAC authors affirm the divine inspiration, inerrancy, complete truthfulness, and full authority of the Bible. The perspective of the NAC is unapologetically confessional and rooted in the evangelical tradition.

Since a commentary is a fundamental tool for the expositor or teacher who seeks to interpret and apply Scripture in the church or classroom, the NAC focuses on communicating the theological structure and content of each biblical book. The writers seek to illuminate both the historical meaning and contemporary significance of Holy Scripture.

In its attempt to make a unique contribution to the Christian community, the NAC focuses on two concerns. First, the commentary emphasizes how each section of a book fits together so that the reader becomes aware of the theological unity of each book and of Scripture as a whole. The writers, however, remain aware of the Bible's inherently rich variety. Second, the NAC is produced with the conviction that the Bible primarily belongs to the church.

We believe that scholarship and the academy provide an indispensable foundation for biblical understanding and the service of Christ, but the editors and authors of this series have attempted to communicate the findings of their research in a manner that will build up the whole body of Christ. Thus, the commentary concentrates on theological exegesis, while providing practical, applicable exposition.

THE NEW AMERICAN COMMENTARY's theological focus enables the reader to see the parts as well as the whole of Scripture. The biblical books vary in content, context, literary type, and style. In addition to this rich variety, the editors and authors recognize that the doctrinal emphasis and use of the biblical books differs in various places, contexts, and cultures among God's people. These factors, as well as other concerns, have led the editors to give freedom to the writers to wrestle with the issues raised by the scholarly community surrounding each book and to determine the appropriate shape and length of the introductory materials. Moreover, each writer has developed the structure of the commentary in a way best suited for expounding the basic structure and the meaning of the biblical books for our day. Generally, discussions relating to contemporary scholarship and technical points of grammar and syntax appear in the footnotes and not in the text of the commentary. This format allows pastors and interested laypersons, scholars and teachers, and serious college and seminary students to profit from the commentary at various levels. This approach has been employed because we believe that all Christians have the privilege and responsibility to read and seek to understand the Bible for themselves.

Consistent with the desire to produce a readable, up-to-date commentary, the editors selected the *New International Version* as the standard translation for the commentary series. The selection was made primarily because of the NIV's faithfulness to the original languages and its beautiful and readable style. The authors, however, have been given the liberty to differ at places from the NIV as they develop their own translations from the Greek and Hebrew texts.

The NAC reflects the vision and leadership of those who provide oversight for Broadman Press, who in 1987 called for a new commentary series that would evidence a commitment to the inerrancy of Scripture and a faithfulness to the classic Christian tradition. While the commentary adopts an "American" name, it should be noted some writers represent countries outside the United States, giving the commentary an international perspective. The diverse group of writers includes scholars, teachers, and administrators from almost twenty different colleges and seminaries, as well as pastors, missionaries, and a layperson.

The editors and writers hope that THE NEW AMERICAN COMMENTARY will be helpful and instructive for pastors and teachers, scholars and students, for men and women in the churches who study and teach God's Word in various settings. We trust that for editors, authors, and readers alike, the commentary will be used to build up the church, encourage obedience, and bring renewal to God's people. Above all, we pray that the NAC will bring glory and honor to our Lord who has graciously redeemed us and faithfully revealed himself to us in his Holy Word.

SOLI DEO GLORIA
The Editors

Author's Preface

The modern, North American church is in crisis. For over a century it has been in battle with secularism. Recently, the evangelical revival and the resurgence of conservatism seemed to hold the promise of a return to traditional values. Instead, a disillusion is setting in as society continues to spiral further into violence, sexual immorality, financial chaos, and lovelessness. Tragically, many Christians (including pastors) seem to fare little better than the rest of society, and as such the church has no credible message. Truisms that "Christians aren't perfect, just forgiven" ring hollow.

The church needs the message of biblical wisdom. From Proverbs we must learn the essential rules of life. Teaching us to turn from the lures of easy money and easy sex and to learn again the importance of respect for authority, integrity in business, discretion in social life, and honesty in every arena, Proverbs gives practical meaning to the term "God fearing." Ecclesiastes calls us to reckon with the true meaning of our mortality and in so doing discover genuine faith. It is perhaps our strongest weapon in our contest with the empty existentialism and nihilism of the present age, and yet it goes neglected and unheeded. Song of Songs is perhaps the most desperately needed of all the wisdom books. At a time when scarcely an evangelical church is untouched by scandal, when promiscuity and infidelity are so common that society despairs of the idea that a young man or woman may maintain personal chastity, when homosexuality is all but accepted as an alternative life-style, this book, with its presentation of love between man and woman in all its joy, holiness, and richness, teaches members of the household of faith the true meaning of their sexuality. If we miss its message, we do so to our own peril.

I release this commentary with the prayer that pastors will proclaim the plain messages of Proverbs, in all their simplicity, in their pulpits. To that end, I have tried to show how the texts of Proverbs are not a hopeless chaos but that they readily fit into specific groups and collections. I similarly pray that on college campuses, in church Bible study groups, and especially in classes for young people, Christians will study Ecclesiastes and the Song of Songs in their entirety for the wholesome messages they contain.

I need to thank many people in regard to this commentary, most of all my wife, Patty, who has shown remarkable patience with this whole project. But special thanks need to go out to two men, of whom it may truly be said that without their encouragement and support, this book would not have seen the light of day. These are David Dockery and Ray Clendenen, two general editors with whom I have worked. Their positive comments and patient spirits are deeply appreciated.

Duane A. Garrett

Abbreviations

Bible Books

Gen	Isa	Luke
Exod	Jer	John
Lev	Lam	Acts
Num	Ezek	Rom
Deut	Dan	1,2 Cor
Josh	Hos	Gal
Judg	Joel	Eph
Ruth	Amos	Phil
1,2 Sam	Obad	Col
1,2 Kgs	Jonah	1,2 Thess
1,2 Chr	Mic	1,2 Tim
Ezra	Nah	Titus
Neh	Hab	Phlm
Esth	Zeph	Heb
Job	Hag	Jas
Ps (*pl.* Pss)	Zech	1,2 Pet
Prov	Mal	1,2,3 John
Eccl	Matt	Jude
Song	Mark	Rev

Commonly Used Sources and Abbreviations

AB Anchor Bible
AEL *Ancient Egyptian Literature*, M. Lichtheim
AJSL *American Journal of Semitic Languages and Literatures*
AnBib Analecta Biblica
ANET *Ancient Near Eastern Texts*, ed. J. B. Pritchard
AOAT Alter Orient und Altes Testament
AOTS *Archaeology and Old Testament Study*, ed. D. W. Thomas
ATD Das Alte Testament Deutsch
BASOR *Bulletin of the American Schools of Oriental Research*
BDB F. Brown, S. R. Driver, and C. A. Briggs, *Hebrew and English Lexicon of the Old Testament*
BHS Biblia hebraica stuttgartensia
Bib *Biblica*

BKAT Biblischer Kommentar: Altes Testament
BSac *Bibliotheca Sacra*
BSC Bible Study Commentary
BT *Bible Translator*
BZAW Beihefte zur ZAW
CAH *Cambridge Ancient History*
CB Cambridge Bible for Schools and Colleges
CBC Cambridge Bible Commentary
CBQ *Catholic Biblical Quarterly*
CHAL *Concise Hebrew and Aramaic Lexicon*, ed. William L. Holladay
CTR *Criswell Theological Review*
DOTT *Documents from Old Testament Times*, ed. D. W. Thomas
EBC Expositor's Bible Commentary
Ebib Etudes bibliques
FB Forschung zur Bibel
FOTL Forms of Old Testament Literature
GKC Gesenius' Hebrew Grammar, ed. E. Kautzsch, tr. A. E. Cowley
HAT Handbuch zum Alten Testament
HDR Harvard Dissertations in Religion
Her *Hermeneia*
HKAT Handkommentar zum Alten Testament
HSM Harvard Semitic Monographs
HT Helps for Translators
HUCA Hebrew Union College Annual
IB *Interpreter's Bible*
IBC Interpretation: A Bible Commentary for Teaching and Preaching
ICC International Critical Commentary
IDB *Interpreter's Dictionary of the Bible*, ed. G. A. Buttrick et al.
IDBSup Supplementary Volume to *IDB*
IEJ *Israel Exploration Journal*
IES Israel Exploration Society
ISBE *International Standard Bible Encyclopedia*, rev., ed. G. W. Bromiley
ITC International Theological Commentary
JAOS *Journal of the American Oriental Society*
JBL *Journal of Biblical Literature*
JNES *Journal of Near Eastern Studies*
JEA *Journal of Egyptian Archaeology*
JSOR *Journal of the Society for Oriental Research*
JSOT *Journal for the Study of the Old Testament*
JSOTSup JSOT—Supplement Series
JSS *Journal of Semitic Studies*
JTS *Journal of Theological Studies*
JTSNS *Journal of Theological Studies*, New Series

KAT	Kommentar zum Alten Testament
KB	Koehler and W. Baumgartner, *Lexicon in Veteris Testamenti libros*
LCC	Library of Christian Classics
NICOT	New International Commentary on the Old Testament
NJPS	New Jewish Publication Society Version
OTL	Old Testament Library
PCB	*Peake's Commentary on the Bible*, ed. M. Black and H. H. Rowley
POTT	*Peoples of Old Testament Times*, ed. D. J. Wiseman
RB	*Revue biblique*
RSR	*Recherches de science religieuse*
SBLDS	Society of Biblical Literature Dissertation Series
SBT	Studies in Biblical Theology
SR	*Studies in Religion/Sciences religieuses*
TDOT	*Theological Dictionary of the Old Testament*, ed. G. J. Botterweck and H. Ringgren
TJ	*Trinity Journal*
TOTC	Tyndale Old Testament Commentaries
TWAT	*Theologisches Wörterbuch zum Alten Testament*, ed. G. J. Botterweck and H. Ringgren
TynBul	*Tyndale Bulletin*
VT	*Vetus Testamentum*
WBC	Word Biblical Commentaries
WMANT	Wissenschaftliche Monographien zum Alten und Neuen Testament
ZAW	*Zeitschrift für die alttestamentliche Wissenschaft*

Contents

Proverbs

INTRODUCTION OUTLINE

1. Wisdom in the Ancient Near East
2. The Origins of Israelite Wisdom
3. An Outline of the History of Israelite Wisdom
4. Forms, Patterns, and Rhetorical Devices
   (1) Wisdom Forms
      Saying
      Admonition
      Numerical Saying
      Rhetorical Question
      Wisdom Poem
      Parental Exhortation
      Wisdom Appeal
      Controversy Speech or Disputation
      Example Story
      Confession or Reflection
      Riddle
      Allegory
      Didactic Narrative
   (2) Patterns of Wisdom Literature
      Monocolon
      Bicolon (Couplet, Distich)
      Tricolon (Triplet, Tristitch)
      Quatrain
      Pentad
      Hexad
      Larger Units
   (3) Rhetorical Devices of Proverbs
5. The Structure of the Book of Proverbs
6. On Order and Disorder in Proverbs 10:1–24:23

7. The Origin of the Book of Proverbs
   (1) History of the Redaction of Proverbs
   (2) Date
   (3) Authorship
8. The Theology of Wisdom

INTRODUCTION

The function of the Scriptures is not only to lead unbelievers to repentance and faith in Christ but also to instruct and nurture believers with truth that transforms our understanding and our lives. If this is so, then the believer must study the wisdom literature of the Bible (primarily Job, Proverbs, Ecclesiastes, and the Song of Songs); and the Christian minister must preach it, regardless of the difficulties involved, as we shall see (see Acts 20:20). In view of the current moral climate of society and even the church, we are in desperate need of the instruction offered by these books. In an age when seduction, domestic conflict, financial mismanagement, substance abuse, and dishonesty often seem to be behavioral norms, we must allow the Spirit to transform us with truths from biblical wisdom. Here we can learn to reject wrong and harmful behavior and to choose the paths that please God and bring happiness, the way of life that arises from faith in the Lord. Biblical wisdom literature, especially Proverbs, teaches how to deal with the practical, ordinary issues in life, such as social skills (Prov 27:14), financial prudence (Prov 22:26), and personal discipline (Prov 6:6-11). The results of our investigations into these matters will be well worth the effort.

Before we can read something worth understanding, we need to know what kind of material it is. Proverbs is, by universal acknowledgment, Old Testament wisdom literature. When Proverbs is compared to the literature of the Torah (Pentateuch) or the Prophets, dissimilarities are immediately apparent. It is equally obvious that Proverbs is in some way similar to Ecclesiastes and, to a lesser degree, to Job.

On the other hand, the simple assertion that Proverbs belongs to the category of wisdom literature is not without difficulties. What are the distinguishing marks of wisdom literature? How does the outlook of wisdom differ from the prophetic perspective? The definition and identification of wisdom literature is indeed the central problem of scholarly research in the area, and extensive study has produced no consensus. Even criteria such as form and style are of little help, as is apparent when comparing certain wisdom-influenced portions of narrative to the wisdom of Proverbs.[1]

[1]R. N. Whybray, *The Intellectual Tradition in the Old Testament* (Berlin: Walter de Gruyter, 1974), 1-5.

This problem reaches beyond the academic matter of settling upon a concise definition. Considering the importance of Torah, covenant history, and prophetic proclamation in the Old Testament, wisdom sometimes appears to be the stepchild of the canonical family. It is indeed significant that no major Old Testament theology has successfully integrated wisdom into a descriptive scheme of the Old Testament's theological plan and outlook. Simply put, the wisdom literature does not seem to fit in with the rest of the Old Testament.

The problem is multifaceted, involving questions concerning the literary forms of wisdom literature, identification of the "wise men" behind the literature, and the relationship with wisdom literature from other ancient Near Eastern nations. At stake is the meaning of Proverbs and the other Old Testament wisdom texts in both their historical and canonical contexts.

1. Wisdom in the Ancient Near East

Israelite wisdom literature is distinctive but not unique in form and subject matter. Throughout the ancient Near East, many analogies to Israelite wisdom (some closer than others) can be found. While none of the wisdom literature of the other nations is exactly like that of Israel (and some have even disputed whether much of the nonbiblical material can be called "wisdom" at all), similarities are so conspicuous that they cannot be ignored. More than that, the comparison of the Bible to contemporary ancient Near Eastern material has often clarified the purpose and message of the biblical text.

The history of Egyptian wisdom literature covers over two millennia, from the Old Kingdom to the Hellenistic period.[2] From the Old Kingdom (ca. 2650–2135[3]) comes the important Ptahhotep (ca. 2200?), as well as the fragmentary texts of Hardjedef and Kagemni. From the first intermediate period (ca. 2135–2040) comes the Instruction to Merikare, given by his father, an aging king.

Several important works survived from the Middle Kingdom (2040–1650), including the Instruction of Amenemhet I, the Admonitions of Ipuwer, the Dispute between a Man and His Soul, and the Eloquent Peasant. Of these, the Instruction of Amenemhet I is most relevant to Proverbs, although the others relate to Ecclesiastes and Job. Also a number of texts

---

[2]For a survey of the history of Egyptian wisdom literature, see R. J. Williams, "The Sage in Egyptian Literature," in *The Sage in Israel and the Ancient Near East*, ed. J. G. Gammie and L. G. Perdue (Winona Lake, Ind.: Eisenbrauns, 1990), 19-30.

[3]Early Egyptian chronology is not settled. I have used the dates in Miriam Lichtheim, *Ancient Egyptian Literature. Three Volumes*. Copyright © 1973-1980 Regents of the University of California. Used by permission. (See 1:xii-xiii.) All of the Egyptian wisdom literature described here can be found in Lichtheim's three volumes, hereinafter called AEL.

on the scribal trade began to appear in Egypt, including the significant work of Khety, son of Duauf, often called the Satire on Trades. These writings portrayed the profession of the scribe as the greatest of all trades.[4]

From the New Kingdom (1550–1080) comes the Instruction of Aniy as well as the Instruction of Amenemope, a work of major significance in the study of Old Testament wisdom since Proverbs 22:17–24:22 seems to be related to it.[5] Also a number of love songs closely analogous to Song of Songs appeared at this time. Later significant treatises include the Instruction of Ankhsheshonqy and the Instruction of Papyrus Insinger.[6]

A large number of Sumerian proverbs have been collected and published.[7] A few of these are moralistic in the manner of many biblical proverbs,[8] but most have a reproachful, humorous, or practical character.[9] Some material has survived in both Akkadian and Sumerian versions, including the Instructions of Shuruppak.[10] Another piece of Akkadian wisdom is the Counsels of Wisdom.[11] The "preceptive hymns," including the bilingual Hymn to Ninurta and the Shamash Hymn,[12] mix praise to a god with warnings about divine justice and thus have some affinity to the biblical wisdom Psalms and Proverbs 1–9.[13] Pessimistic literature analogous to Job or Ecclesiastes has also come out of Mesopotamia.

---

[4]Cf. J. L. Crenshaw, *Old Testament Wisdom* (Atlanta: John Knox, 1981), 223-24.

[5]See the discussion in the commentary on Prov 22:17ff.

[6]For a good study of Ankhsheshonqy, Insinger, and their relationship to other late and Hellenistic wisdom, see M. Lichtheim, *Late Egyptian Wisdom Literature in the International Context: A Study of Demotic Instructions*, Orbis Biblicus et Orientalis 52 (Göttingen: Vandenhoeck und Ruprecht, 1983).

[7]E. I. Gordon, *Sumerian Proverbs: Glimpses of Everyday Life in Ancient Mesopotamia* (Westport, Conn.: Greenwood, 1969). For a survey of the broad outlines of Sumerian wisdom, see S. N. Kramer, "The Sage in Sumerian Literature: A Composite Portrait," in *The Sage in Israel*, 31-44.

[8]Observe the moral implications of 1.18: "Possessions are sparrows in flight which can find no place to alight" (Gordon, *Sumerian Proverbs*, 50).

[9]E.g., 1.193: "A sick person is (relatively) well; it is the woman in childbirth who is (really) ill!" (Gordon, *Sumerian Proverbs*, 146) and 2.37: "You are a [s]cribe (and) you don't (even) know your own name! (You should) slap your own face!" (Gordon, *Sumerian Proverbs*, 200). Gordon classifies Sumerian proverbs according to type on pp. 17-18.

[10]For text and introductions see W. G. Lambert, *Babylonian Wisdom Literature* (London: Oxford University Press, 1960), 92-95, and ANET, 594.

[11]See Lambert, *Babylonian Wisdom*, 96-107, and ANET, 595. Warnings against the prostitute are found in lines 66-80, but the advice is more practical in orientation and does not achieve the moral depth of the biblical texts.

[12]Ibid., 118-38.

[13]E.g., Ninurta 3: "He who has intercourse with (another) man's wife, his guilt is grievous" (ibid., 119), and Shamash 97-98: "You give the unscrupulous judge experience of fetters/Him who accepts a present and yet lets justice miscarry you make bear his punishment" (ibid., 133).

A final work of note here is the Words of Ahiqar, a text found at Elephantine in Egypt and written in Aramaic.[14] It may be significant that little Ugaritic wisdom literature has been found.[15] Some proverbial material is said to have been found at Ebla.

The wisdom literature of the ancient Near East is often similar to that found in the Bible and in some cases may have influenced it. Specific parallels are discussed below.

2. The Origins of Israelite Wisdom

No scholarly consensus has emerged regarding the original social setting (*Sitz im Leben*) for wisdom instruction.[16] Three distinct groups have been proposed as the originators and transmitters of wisdom: the family, the royal scribes and counselors, and the religious scribes who studied and meditated on the Torah.

Many passages in Proverbs imply that wisdom was a family matter. The book frequently addresses its reader as "my son" and urges him to adhere to the teachings of his father and mother (e.g., 1:8). On the other hand, the attribution of many proverbs to Solomon and the biblical references to state scribes and counselors imply that the royal court may have been the source of at least the *text* of Proverbs if not much of its *content* (Prov 1:1; 25:1; 2 Sam 17:1-14; 1 Kgs 4:29-34). Religious "Torah" wisdom, however, is a later development, as discussed below.

It is important to recognize that neither family wisdom nor royal wisdom was unique to Israel. Every culture has traditional values and teachings, and the family is always the first area in which those teachings are passed down. In the ancient Near East, moreover, especially in Egypt, the royal court wisdom was well established long before Israel came into existence. Proverbial sayings and other traditional teachings were collected and studied, and court officials presented their wisdom in polished literary works.

Certainly the family was the first locus of wisdom in Israelite culture, and it continued to play an important role through Hebrew history. Unquestionably, under divine guidance a great deal of traditional family wisdom has been incorporated into the text of Proverbs. The family, rather than the school, is everywhere presented as the primary place of

---

[14]The papyrus text dates to the late fifth century, but the material is of Mesopotamian origin. It may go back to the reign of the Assyrian king Esarhaddon (680–669). See ANET, 427-30.

[15]A small Akkado-Hurrian bilingual text containing a few proverbs was found at Ras Shamra. See Lambert, *Babylonian Wisdom*, 116.

[16]B. S. Childs, *An Introduction to the Old Testament as Scripture* (Philadelphia: Fortress, 1979), 549.

training. Nevertheless, as Proverbs explicitly states, Israelite wisdom literature was a product of the royal court and its scribes. The text asserts that this tradition began in the united monarchy, under Solomon, and continued to function in the divided monarchy.[17]

Some have contended that the biblical wisdom literature arose from professional schools run by a circle of "the wise" whose social, intellectual, and theological outlook differed from that of the other leading circles in Judah and Israel, that is, priests and prophets.[18] The existence of professional schools in early Israel is argued on the basis of internal evidence from the Hebrew literature, from foreign analogies, from the complexity of the royal administration, and so forth. This position, however, has been challenged by R. N. Whybray.[19]

In Israel and throughout the ancient Near East, kings and rulers invariably surrounded themselves with counselors to assist them in formulating policy and making difficult decisions.[20] Indeed, wisdom was a *sine qua non* for the ancient ruler. He was expected to possess it himself[21] and recognize it in others. Nevertheless, no consistent evidence for the existence of a separate class of wise men as philosophic sages or academicians in pagan countries is apparent.[22] Rather, these men often combined such roles as soothsayer, counselor, cult official, exorcist, bureaucrat, and sometimes physician or architect.[23]

Although the Israelite monarchies did not have the soothsaying counselors of the pagan nations,[24] they did have numerous counselors, scribes,

---

[17]Cf. 1:1; 10:1; 25:1.

[18]Cf. J. Lindblom, "Wisdom in the Old Testament Prophets," in *Wisdom in Israel and the Ancient Near East, VTSup* 3, ed. M. Noth and D. W. Thomas (1955; reprint, Leiden: Brill, 1969), 194-97.

[19]Whybray, *Intellectual Tradition.*

[20]For a good survey of the biblical data on the giving of counsel, see P. A. H. de Boer, "The Counsellor," *VTSup* 3 (1969): 41-71.

[21]Cf. N. W. Porteus, "Royal Wisdom," *VTSup* 3 (1969): 247-56.

[22]The Bible in several places refers to the "wise men" of the nations, but not as a caste or academy. In Gen 41:8 and Exod 7:11 the "wise men and the magicians" are mentioned; this probably is a hendiadys (the expression of a single idea by using two words connected by "and"). Jeremiah 50:35 and 51:57 mention the wise men of Babylon in connection with the political leaders (princes). In Dan 2–5 the wise men are magicians. In Esth 1:13 the wise men are legal advisors. See Whybray, *Intellectual Tradition*, 15-16.

[23]Cf. R. J. Williams, "The Functions of the Sage in the Egyptian Royal Court," in *The Sage in Israel*, 95-98, and R. F. G. Sweet, "The Sage in Akkadian Literature: A Philological Study," ibid., 45-65.

[24]In times of syncretism, astrologers and mantics apparently were consulted by Hebrew kings. Cf. Hos 10:6 (read "Israel shall be ashamed of its counsel" instead of "idols"; cf. de Boer, "The Counsellor," 49-50). But soothsaying and mantic arts were not a part of canonical wisdom, either in its narrative or didactic forms. To the contrary, the magicians of the nations are everywhere lampooned in narrative wisdom. G. E. Bryce ("Omen-Wisdom in Ancient Israel," *JBL* 94 [1975]: 19-37) has attempted to show that a few of the proverbs that

priests, and other aristocratic groups in their courts. But they had no separate group that was simply identified as "the wise." Old Testament narrative literature lists various offices that were held around the royal court, but nowhere is a title, "wise man," included among them (see 2 Sam 8:16-18; 20:23-26; 1 Kgs 4:2-6).[25] In Proverbs, moreover, "wise man" refers to the moral estimate of a man's character, not to his profession.[26]

Therefore, although it is obvious that some type of teaching went on in various circles, there is little evidence for independent, professional schools in Israel. It is particularly significant that in Proverbs education is frequently said to be done by the parents (cf. also Deut 6:4-9).[27] One ramification of this is that contrary to some who needlessly confine the wisdom literature to narrow limits,[28] biblical wisdom literature goes far beyond Proverbs, Ecclesiastes, and Job (see the discussion of "Form, Patterns, and Rhetorical Devices" on p. 28).

On the other hand, the literary *Sitz im Leben* (life setting) of Proverbs (as well as Ecclesiastes) is certainly the relatively small, aristocratic circle of the royal courts. There is no reason to suppose that a commoner or group of commoners produced the Book of Proverbs, nor is there any evidence to connect it either to prophetic circles or to postexilic scribal circles. At the same time, however, one must be careful to observe that this is the *literary Sitz im Leben*. Proverbs as a literary work had its origin in the royal court, but we should not suppose that all the proverbs originated there or that they concern life and politics in the high offices of government. The majority, in fact, do not.[29]

Regarding the relationship between wisdom and the Torah, one must compare first of all the teaching of Proverbs on retribution with that found in Deuteronomy. Both strongly emphasize the concepts of retribution and reward. In both, just or right activity produces life and peace, whereas evil deeds end in self-destruction. On the other hand, in Deuteronomy the rewards or retributions come directly from the hand of God as he deals with his people according to the terms of the covenant. Proverbs, however, often

---

deal with the mannerisms of the wicked (e.g., 10:10) are not mere observations of signs of criminal behavior but are derived from priestly rules on reading omens in facial and bodily movements. Even if Bryce's position is accepted, however, this material is far removed from the astrology and mantic arts of the nations. Also, as Bryce notes, the material in Proverbs has been moralized in a way that removes it from cultic methods of omen taking.

[25]Whybray, *Intellectual Tradition*, 17-31. The proper term for the class of counselors who assisted the king was not חֲכָמִים ("wise") but שָׂרִים, "princes."

[26]Ibid., 35-45.

[27]B. K. Waltke ("The Book of Proverbs and Ancient Wisdom Literature," *BSac* 136 [1979]: 232) notes that references to the mother as teacher in Proverbs indicate that the father-son relationship is not metaphorical for teacher and pupil but is literal.

[28]Whybray, *Intellectual Tradition*, 54.

[29]See R. N. Whybray, *Wealth and Poverty in the Book of Proverbs*, JSOTSS 99 (Sheffield: JSOT Press, 1990).

views the respective benefits and sorrows of good and evil not so much as direct acts of God as the natural and almost automatic results of certain actions.[30]

The word "covenant" occurs but once in Proverbs (2:17[31]). Only rarely does Proverbs deal consciously and deliberately with the Torah. Later Jewish wisdom, however, is altogether dominated by the Torah, as is most obviously apparent in the books of Sirach (24:23) and the Wisdom of Solomon (6:17-20). This further indicates that, in contrast to the later Jewish teachers, the authors of the canonical books were primarily not religious professionals (priests or rabbis) but aristocrats. The Bible, in attributing the bulk of our material to Solomon, says this also.

3. An Outline of the History of Israelite Wisdom

What, therefore, was the historical relationship among these four socioreligious traditions—the Deuteronomic teaching, family wisdom, the royal/scribal investigations of wisdom, and the postexilic Torah wisdom? How one answers this question is to a great extent determined by how one answers other questions, such as when Deuteronomy and Proverbs were written.[32]

The bulk of Deuteronomy is Mosaic in origin (see Deut 1:1; 5:1; 27:1; 33:1; 31:9,22,24). Although the present form of the book cannot be dated precisely, Deuteronomy is here regarded as premonarchic and antedating the Book of Proverbs. Also a strong case can be made for dating Proverbs, Ecclesiastes, and Song of Songs in the early monarchy.

A history of the wisdom tradition can be outlined within the framework of these positions. We may assume that from the earliest times a tradition of teaching and transmission of wise sayings existed among the Israelite families. This no doubt included strictly religious and ethical instruction as well as "common sense" teachings on the daily problems of life.

The next stage of development was after the presentation of the covenant law of Moses. This law, particularly as it is summarized in the Book

[30]The significance of this for the theology of Proverbs is discussed more fully below.

[31]Note also that בְּרִית here refers to the marriage vow, not to the covenant between God and Israel.

[32]M. Weinfeld (*Deuteronomy and the Deuteronomic School* [Oxford: University Press, 1972], 244-74) argues that Deuteronomy arose among the scribes of Hezekiah (cf. Prov 25:1). He notes that a number of parallels exist between Proverbs and Deuteronomy (e.g., prohibition of removal of boundary stones [Deut 19:14; 27:17; Prov 22:28; 23:10]) and concludes that wisdom literature influenced the writing of Deuteronomy. But the contrary position, that the ethics of Proverbs is influenced by Deuteronomy, is equally possible. Weinfeld argues that many ethical precepts of Israelite wisdom parallel those of non-Israelite wisdom literature. But this only shows that biblical wisdom has a multitude of roots; it does not demonstrate a progression from pagan wisdom to Israelite wisdom to Deuteronomy.

of Deuteronomy, certainly would have had a profound effect on the ancient Israelite psyche and the teachings of family and folk wisdom (cf. Deut 6:7,20; Josh 4:6). It should not be assumed, however, that all subsequent family instruction would have taken the form of explicit reflections on the Torah, as are seen in Sirach. To the contrary, much of Israelite folk wisdom would have continued to concern itself with common problems of daily life as it had from the beginning and would have included few explicit references to the Torah. An analogy to this is American folk wisdom which, although often dominated by Christian morality and presuppositions, contains few allusions to the Bible or Christian theology.

The third stage was the rise of the monarchy and the beginning of the Solomonic empire. For the first time, a large upper class existed in Israel. This included landed gentry, court officials, and members of the royal family. The rise of a powerful upper class with leisure time is often accompanied by an interest in international literary culture, and this was the case there as well. The work of the "men of Hezekiah" (Prov 25:1) may be considered a continuation of this process.

The court of Solomon extended its contacts throughout the ancient world, but it was especially influenced by the court of Egypt, with which it had marital and other ties (1 Kgs 3:1; 9:16; 10:28-29).[33] Israelite court wisdom was born,[34] which combined the literary expertise of the scribes with the traditional wisdom of Israel to produce a synthesis that was both cosmopolitan[35] and genuinely Israelite. This Israelite synthesis, however, was not "secular" in outlook but was based upon Deuteronomic principles. Both Proverbs and the historical texts assert that Israelite wisdom as it is found in the canonical texts was consistent with and produced by divine revelation from the very outset.[36]

Still, the roots of Israelite wisdom in traditional family teaching and international court wisdom guaranteed that the product would not just be

[33]Cf. R. N. Whybray, *Wisdom in Proverbs* (London: SCM, 1965), 53-71. It is not necessary to agree with all of Whybray's thesis to recognize the major impact Egyptian wisdom has had on Israelite wisdom.

[34]For an analysis of texts that relate to courtly wisdom in Proverbs, see W. L. Humphreys, "The Motif of the Wise Courtier in the Book of Proverbs," in *Israelite Wisdom: Theological and Literary Essays in Honor of Samuel Terrien*, ed. J. G. Gammie et al. (Missoula, Mont.: Scholars Press, 1978), 177-90. Humphreys points out that instructions on courtly behavior are present but are fairly rare in Proverbs. I would explain this phenomenon by noting that although Proverbs as a *literary* work is a product of the royal court (hence the awareness of courtly duties), most of the material is actually derived from older clan and family wisdom.

[35]The fame of Solomon's wisdom among the nations (1 Kgs 4:34) indicates its cosmopolitan outlook and common ties to the wisdom of other nations, and this is confirmed by comparison of extant ancient Near Eastern wisdom literature to the Bible.

[36]As will be seen, redaction-critical investigations have not succeeded in overturning this perspective.

applied theology or a commentary on the law but an original work dealing with the problems in life in God's world. Proverbs is therefore practical and down-to-earth as well as conversant with the most advanced courtly wisdom of the ancient world, but its teachings are ultimately divine in origin and are entirely consistent with the orthodox faith of Israel. It achieves this without explicitly subordinating wisdom to the Sinaitic covenant, a move that would have isolated biblical wisdom both culturally and historically.

The fourth stage of this history came with the exile. The scribal tradition became exclusively tied to the temple and the priesthood, and it no longer was part of a royal court. The Jews who returned to the land were determined to keep the law and avoid another disaster like the exile. In this context the written Torah naturally became the explicit focus of attention. This process had already begun in the Canon (Ps 119), but it is fully developed in the apocryphal Wisdom of Solomon and Sirach.

Scholars often have noted the parallels between the Israelite wisdom of the canonical Old Testament and the Jewish wisdom of the intertestamental period, but the differences are more profound. The later books are a conscious reflection on the fully formed canonical books. Their identification of wisdom with the Torah sets them apart from the canonical sages. Biblical wisdom literature does not lean on other canonical books for validation. It is, in and of itself, canonical. Comparisons between biblical and intertestamental wisdom is instructive, but incorporating the latter material into "Old Testament wisdom" leads to false conclusions.

4. Form, Patterns, and Rhetorical Devices

The interpretation of individual proverbs usually does not present serious difficulties. Nevertheless, the serious reader will not be content with the apparent simplicity of the text in translation. Closer study and further reflection may reveal interpretative challenges and a richness of meaning not apparent at first. The fruitfulness of such reflection depends to some extent on an awareness of the literary tools employed by the writer. Wisdom literature, both that of Israel and of the other ancient Near Eastern nations, employs a variety of forms, patterns, and rhetorical devices. The meanings of these three terms may not be immediately transparent, and there is some overlap. Indeed, because of the lack of convention regarding terminology, it has been necessary to be somewhat arbitrary.

As used here, "form" as a descriptive category refers to the manner in which a wisdom teaching is expressed. Examples are the proverb, the admonition, and the fable. "Pattern" refers to how the lines of a single unit are related structurally (e.g., parallelism). "Rhetorical devices" such as alliteration and irony are the aspects or elements of a saying that make it memorable and readily popularized. Each of these three categories is discussed below.

(1) Wisdom Forms

The attempt to identify and isolate wisdom literature on the basis of form criticism has not been successful. That is, one cannot say that the "proverb" is the characteristic form of wisdom since a great deal of what must be reckoned as wisdom literature is not in the proverbial form.[37] Wisdom cannot be confined to certain forms, nor can certain forms be confined to wisdom literature. Nevertheless, as a matter of observation and classification, it is possible to assert that certain forms are most frequently found in wisdom literature.

The forms in which the sages communicated wisdom are as varied and complex as the groups from which the teachers themselves came. G. von Rad,[38] N. Gottwald,[39] and R. Murphy,[40] among others, have described the major forms of wisdom; and we can build on their work.

SAYING. The saying is popularly considered the basic form. The term is a translation of the Hebrew *māšāl,* which actually has a wide range of meanings.[41] There are two types of sayings: the *slogan* and the *proverb.* A reputation slogan is a brief saying or adage that epitomizes an individual's reputation in the community.

> Saul has slain his thousands, and David his tens of thousands (1 Sam 18:7; see also 1 Sam 10:11).

A derision slogan or byword is a pithy, concise, proverb-like insult or reproach.

> One who puts on his armor should not boast like one who takes it off (1 Kgs 20:11; see also Luke 4:23).

The most common form of Old Testament wisdom is the proverb. It may be defined as an ethical axiom, that is, a short, artistically constructed ethical observation or teaching. An observational proverb is a saying that describes human behavior without an *explicit* moral evaluation.

---

[37]Whybray, *Intellectual Tradition,* 72-74.

[38]G. von Rad, *Wisdom in Israel* (Nashville: Abingdon, 1972), 24-50.

[39]N. Gottwald, *The Hebrew Bible: A Socio-Literary Introduction* (Philadelphia: Fortress, 1985), 565. Gottwald prefers the term "genre" here.

[40]R. E. Murphy, *Wisdom Literature,* FOTL (Grand Rapids: Eerdmans, 1981), 172-85.

[41]Cf. A. R. Johnson, "*mashal,*" *VTSup* 3 (1969): 162-69. The root meaning of משל, as preserved in several verbal stems, is "to be like." In actual usage the noun can refer to the whole genre of wisdom literature, lengthy didactic discourse (as in Prov 1–9), slogans, reproaches and taunt songs, or an allegory. Most often, however, the word is used like the English "proverb" to refer to a pithy saying expressing some moral idea or perception.

One man pretends to be rich, yet has nothing; another pretends to be poor, yet has great wealth (Prov 13:7; see also 18:16).

A didactic proverb describes human behavior with a clear ethical-didactic purpose, that is, it includes an explicit moral evaluation.

Righteousness guards the man of integrity, but wickedness overthrows the sinner (Prov 13:6; see also 14:1).

This form is common in Proverbs. A subclass of the didactic proverb is the *better saying*, which is characterized by the presence of the word "better" (Heb. *ṭôb*, lit. "good") in the pattern "*A* is better than *B*."

Better to live in a desert than with a quarrelsome and ill-tempered wife (Prov 21:19).

ADMONITION. This is a command or prohibition written either in proverbial form (as a couplet or bicolon[42]) or as an extended discourse. A *command* in discourse form is found in Prov 6:1-5. An example of the proverb form is 16:3.

Commit to the LORD whatever you do, and your plans will succeed.

Prohibitions in discourse form occur as units (e.g., 1:10-19) or scattered among the commands of discourse admonitions (e.g., Prov 4:10-19). Prohibition proverbs are often in two parts: the prohibition proper and the reason for the prohibition (a warning of what will happen if the prohibition is violated).

Do not slander a servant to his master,
or he will curse you,
and you will pay for it
(Prov 30:10; see also 22:22-23,24-25).

NUMERICAL SAYING. A numerical saying is one that follows a numerical pattern. It often includes a list of items that have something in common.

There are three things that are too amazing for me,
four that I do not understand:
the way of an eagle in the sky,
the way of a snake on a rock,
the way of a ship on the high seas,
and the way of a man with a maiden
(Prov 30:18-19; see also vv. 21-23,24-28).

RHETORICAL QUESTION. A rhetorical question, the answer to which seems (sometimes misleadingly) obvious, is meant to draw the reader into reflection.

[42]The term "colon" refers to a line or stich of poetry. A two-line unit or couplet (or distich) is called a "bicolon"; a three-line unit, a "tricolon."

Who has gone up to heaven and come down?
Who has gathered up the wind in the hollow of his hands?
Who has wrapped up the waters in his cloak?
Who has established all the ends of the earth?
What is his name, and the name of his son?
Tell me if you know!
(Prov 30:4).

WISDOM POEM. This refers to wisdom teaching presented as a fully developed poem. Such poems often are alphabetic acrostic (e.g., Prov 31:10-31[43]).

PARENTAL EXHORTATION. This is a lengthy discourse in which a parent exhorts a child to gain wisdom, to avoid prostitutes or criminal associations, or to maintain a life of virtue.

Listen, my son, to your father's instruction
and do not forsake your mother's teaching.
. . . .
My son, if sinners entice you,
do not give in to them
(Prov 1:8-19; see also 2:1-22; 3:1-35; 31:1-9).

Parental exhortations will generally include various proverbs, admonitions, and better sayings. They open with a parental appeal, in which the parent directly addresses the child ("my son[s]") and urges heeding the parent's words. The vocative "my son(s)" can also mark off subdivisions within an exhortation (e.g., Prov 1:10; 3:11).

WISDOM APPEAL. This form is identified by the personification of Wisdom[44] as a woman who urges young men to come and learn from her.

Wisdom calls aloud in the street,
she raises her voice in the public squares;
. . . .
How long will you simple ones love your simple ways?
(Prov 1:20-33; see also 8:1-36).

CONTROVERSY SPEECH OR DISPUTATION. Although not a true dialogue (as in the Platonic dialogues), this is a series of speeches set against one another in a debate format (e.g., Job 3–41). The disputation draws the reader into the complexities of a wisdom problem.

EXAMPLE STORY. A brief story or anecdote meant to drive home a teaching on virtue is called an example story:

[43]This is the only alphabetic acrostic in the biblical wisdom books. See also Sir 51:13-20.

[44]Throughout this commentary, Wisdom written with an uppercase *W* refers to the personification "Woman Wisdom" as opposed to the abstract idea of wisdom, written with the lowercase *w*.

At the window of my house
I looked out through the lattice

. . . .

I noticed among the young men,
a youth who lacked judgment.
He was going down the street near her corner,

. . . .

She took hold of him and kissed him
and with a brazen face she said:

. . . .

Come, let's drink deep of love till morning;

. . . .

All at once he followed her

. . . .

Her house is a highway to the grave
(Prov 7:6-27; see also 24:30-34).

CONFESSION OR REFLECTION. This is a reflection on wisdom drawn from personal experience.

I am the most ignorant of men;
I do not have a man's understanding.
I have not learned wisdom,
nor have I knowledge of the Holy One
(Prov 4:3-9; 30:2-4).

The entire text of Ecclesiastes, as a genre, can be classed as a reflection, but it includes within it various other forms.

RIDDLE. A riddle is an enigmatic question meant to entertain and test the audience.

Out of the eater, something to eat; out of the strong, something sweet (Judg 14:14; see also Dan 5:12; Prov 1:6).

The ability to solve riddles was the mark of a wise man.

ALLEGORY. A descriptive narrative in which the major characters or elements symbolically describe something else is known as allegory. A *fable* is a story in which talking plants or animals represent people, often in a political context, as in Judg 9:8-15 (see also Ezek 17):

One day the trees went out to anoint a king for themselves. They said to the olive tree, "Be our king."

Other types, such as the picturesque description of the frailties of old age in Eccl 12:1-6, may be called simply *extended metaphor*.

DIDACTIC NARRATIVE. A relatively long and complex narrative, a didactic narrative is meant to drive home one or more moral lessons and is typically centered on a hero or heroine who is in a hostile or pagan setting (e.g., Gen 37–50; Dan 1–6; the Book of Esther).

(2) *Patterns of Wisdom Literature*

In addition to these *forms*, various verse *patterns* were available to the wisdom teacher. As mentioned previously, "pattern" here refers to the structuring of individual units and is analogous to (but not the same as) scansion in Western poetry. Some of the major patterns are as follows:[45]

MONOCOLON. The monocolon is a single, relatively short sentence:[46]

> An honest answer is like a kiss on the lips (Prov 24:26).
> Scatter not your sheep in untried grazing[47] (Shuruppak, old Sumerian version, V, 12).

There may be a series of one-line units, called *verbal reiteration*, in which a common word or phrase is repeated in all the lines. Beyond that common element, there may be no parallelism among the lines.

> Do not falsify the temple rations
> Do not grasp and you'll find profit
> Do not remove the servant of a god[48]
> (Amenemope chap. 5; 6:14-16).

BICOLON (COUPLET, DISTICH). By far the most common pattern in Proverbs, the bicolon is a development of the common Hebrew practice of constructing sentences in a binary fashion: "*A* is true, and *B* is also." The second line generally reinforces or expands upon the first line.[49] There are three basic types of bicolon patterns: *parallelism, progression*, and *proverbial merismus*. True parallelism, traditionally called "synonymous parallelism,"[50] is a twofold statement of a single idea or concept that

---

[45]The following analysis builds upon K. A. Kitchen, "The Basic Literary Forms and Formulations of Ancient Instructional Writings in Egypt and Western Asia," in *Studien zu altagyptischen Lebenslehren*, ed. E. Hornung and O. Keel, *Orbis Biblicus et Orientalis* 28 (Göttingen: Vandenhoeck und Ruprecht, 1979), 278-80. I have, however, changed some of the terminology and classification. In particular, the traditional terms "synonymous, antithetic, and synthetic parallelism" should be abandoned in light of the analysis of J. L. Kugel, *The Idea of Biblical Poetry: Parallelism and Its History* (New Haven: Yale University, 1981).

[46]This form is most common in the late, Demotic wisdom. See Lichtheim, *Late Egyptian Wisdom*, 1-6.

[47]Kitchen, "Basic Literary Forms," 278.

[48]AEL 2:151.

[49]See Kugel, *Idea of Biblical Poetry*, 1-95. Kugel prefers to speak of the method as one line in binary structure. He also describes many other uses of the binary structure, including "mere comma," citation, sequence, etc.

[50]"Synonymous parallelism" is both misleading and somewhat redundant. It is redundant because "parallelism" already implies that the two lines have similar grammatical structures and use vocabulary that is more or less synonymous. It is an inaccurate designation, however, since the two lines are rarely *fully* synonymous; usually a slightly different emphasis is added in the second line.

employs near-synonymous or related vocabulary in a symmetrical fashion. The function of the bicolon is to emphasize or expand a teaching through slightly varied redundancy. Both proverbs and commands may be couched in this pattern. Often a slightly new concept is added in the second line. Proverbs 19:5 is an example of the proverb form:

> A false witness will not go unpunished
> and he who pours out lies will not go free.

Examples of the admonition form occur in 20:18 and 23:12:

> Make plans by seeking advice;
> if you wage war, obtain guidance.

> Apply your heart to instruction
> and your ears to words of knowledge.

The term preferred here for what is traditionally called "synthetic parallelism"[51] is *progression*. This is a structure in which the second line supplements the first. This pattern is used with a number of forms, such as the proverb; but it is very often found in the command or prohibition, in which the second line gives the reason for the admonition (sometimes this order is reversed). The second line of Prov 17:8 explains a figure used in the first line:

> A bribe is a charm to the one who gives it,
> wherever he turns, he succeeds.

Examples of admonition sayings occur in 14:7; 22:6:

> Stay away from the foolish man,
> for you will not find knowledge on his lips.

> Train a child in the way he should go,
> and when he is old he will not turn from it.

There are also examples in Egyptian literature:

> Set your mind on writing supremely,
> high office comes to whoever does so[52]
> (Hori).

> Do not raise your voice in the house of god;
> he abhors shouting[53]
> (The Instruction of Aniy).

---

[51]"Synthetic parallelism" is misleading as a designation since it implies there is something wrong or artificial in the structure.

[52]Kitchen, "Basic Literary Forms," 279.

[53]AEL 2:137.

Many proverbs employ a mixture of parallelism and progression. That is, the second line partially parallels and partially moves beyond the first line.

The traditional term for *proverbial merismus* is "antithetical parallelism," but this term is misleading since it implies that the two lines somehow contradict each other, which they do not. The term also misses the inner dynamic behind this pattern. Hebrew frequently employs expressions such as "old and young," "heaven and earth," or "day and night" to mean, respectively, "all people," "the universe," or "at all times." That is, two words that are more or less antonyms are combined to refer to a single, unified whole. This is called "merismus." Similarly, proverbial language can use apparent opposites to provide a global view of a particular issue. An Egyptian example of the use of merismus in a nonethical proverb is found in Ankhsheshonqy Col. 20:10-11:

> One who has run finds sitting down pleasant,/One who has sat finds standing up pleasant.[54]

In this example the two "antithetical" conditions come together to make a common, single statement. On the surface the two lines describe two separate phenomena, but on a deep level they reveal a single truth. In this case the deep-level meaning of the proverb is that people enjoy changing their routines.

The Book of Proverbs often uses proverbial merismus in moral categories (e.g., wise/fool; loves/hates). The function of the whole bicolon is to state a single concept as approached from two perspectives. On a deep level these proverbs assert that in a given area of life a single moral principle functions consistently. Proverbs 15:9 is an example:

> The Lord detests the way of the wicked
> but he loves those who pursue righteousness.

In other words, God's attitude toward an individual is determined by the presence or absence of virtue in that person's life. No true antithesis is present since the two lines actually complement each other. God does not favor the righteous and react with indifference toward the wicked, nor does he punish the evil and fail to notice those who love what is good. A global view of the attitude of God toward humans emerges with emphasis on the consistency of God's response to the individual's manner of life.

> Love maintains a family; hate destroys a family[55]
> (Shuruppak, Sumerian version).

---

[54]Kitchen, "Basic Literary Forms," 279.

[55]Ibid.

In this Sumerian proverb the phrases "love maintains" and "hate destroys" provide a global view of the importance of close relationships within the family. The two are complementary perspectives on a single, deep meaning: the attitudes that family members bring into family relationships will determine whether the family unit lives or dies.

TRICOLON (TRIPLET, TRISTICH). In simplest form, as Kitchen comments, the tricolon shows "synonymous or synthetic parallelism in all three lines. . . . But in instructional wisdom-literature, other and more complex configurations predominate."[56] These normally take a 2+1 or 1+2 pattern, in which two lines parallel each other in some fashion and the third line is distinct but complementary to the other two. Sometimes a 1/1/1 pattern is found, in which each line functions differently but together they present a single idea.

1+2
Do you see a man skilled in his work?
He will serve before kings;
he will not serve before obscure men (Prov 22:29).

2+1
Accept that death is humiliating for us,
Accept that life is exalting for us,
the house of death is for life[57]
(Djedefhor).

1+1+1
Like the coolness of snow at harvest time
is a trustworthy messenger to those who send him;
he refreshes the spirit of his masters (Prov 25:13).

Albright notes that the 2+1 tricolon is a characteristic Ugaritic pattern, and he considers the presence of his pattern in Proverbs to be evidence for the antiquity of much of its material. He compares Prov 10:26 ("As vinegar to the teeth/ And as smoke to the eyes,/ So is the sluggard to them that send him") to the Ugaritic I Aqhat i, 113 ("Like the feeling of a wild cow for her calf,/ Like the feeling of a wild ewe for her lamb,/ So [was] the feeling of Anat for Baal").[58]

QUATRAIN. Quatrains can be quite complex in structure and often occur in both admonition and proverb forms. One pattern, for example, is *a b a b*, in which the *a* lines to some degree parallel one another, as do the *b* lines. Nonparallel lines may also be found.

---

[56]Ibid., 255.

[57]Ibid., 280.

[58]W. F. Albright, "Some Canaanite-Phoenician Sources of Hebrew Wisdom," *VTSup* 3 (1969): 5.

a b a b
Do not control your wife in her house,
When you know she is efficient;
Don't say to her: "Where is it? Get it!"
When she has put it in the right place[59]
(The Instruction of Aniy).

a a b b
A wise man has great power,
and a man of knowledge increases strength;
for waging war you need guidance,
and for victory many advisors (Prov 24:5-6).

Do not fret because of evil men
or be envious of the wicked,
for the evil man has no future hope,
and the lamp of the wicked will be snuffed out (Prov 24:19-20).

a b a c
The sluggard's craving will be the death of him,
because his hands refuse to work.
All day long he craves for more,
but the righteous give without sparing (Prov 21:25-26).

PENTAD. Pentads are rare in the biblical text. The following example has a complex $a\ b\ c\ c^a\ c^b$ pattern:

There are three things that are never satisfied,
four that never say, 'enough!':
the grave, the barren womb,
land, which is never satisfied with water,
and fire, which never says, 'Enough!' (Prov 30:15-16).

The following example is a five-line "progressive" chain in a 1+2+2 pattern:

Insult not a nobleman—
When insult occurs, fighting follows;
When fighting occurs, killing follows.
No killing happens without God knowing;
Nothing happens except what God ordains[60]
(Ankhsheshonqy Col. 22:21-25).

HEXAD. The hexad pattern occurs in several numerical saying forms, as well as in extended proverb forms:

There are three things that are stately in their stride,
four that move with stately bearing:

[59]AEL 2:143.
[60]Kitchen, "Basic Literary Forms," 280.

a lion, mighty among beasts,
who retreats before nothing;
a strutting rooster, a he-goat,
and a king with his army around him (Prov 30:29-30).

Better is a bushel given you by the god,
Than five thousand through wrongdoing.
They stay a day in bin and barn,
They make no food for the beer jar;
A moment is their stay in the granary,
Comes morning and they have vanished[61]
(Amenemope chap. 6; 18:19-19:4).

LARGER UNITS. Larger units also occur and typically are found in extended proverb or admonition sections, wisdom poems, example stories, confessions, or the like. The internal structure of these patterns can be quite complex.

(3) Rhetorical Devices of Proverbs

An important aspect of the proverb is that it is easily remembered and readily popularized. For this reason proverbs contain wit, humor, and turns of phrases that are easy to speak or hear. J. M. Thompson notes that among the rhetorical devices that popularize proverbs are repetition, alliteration, assonance, simile, and metaphor.[62] "Look before you leap," for example, contains alliteration (repeated initial consonants), whereas "A stitch in time saves nine" is memorable for its assonance (repeated vowel sounds).

The biblical proverbs contain many of the same devices. Assonance is found in the Hebrew of Prov 10:9a; 13:20b; alliteration, in 15:27a, paronomasia (play on words), in 22:24; and even rhyme, in 11:2.[63] Humor and irony occur in such texts as 11:22 and 19:24.

Other rhetorical aspects of proverbs have been explored by R. B. Y. Scott,[64] who notes that proverbs frequently turn upon some comparison or contrast. Often identity or invariable association of two ideas or things is stressed, as in "A penny saved is a penny earned." A biblical example is "Without subjects a prince is ruined" (Prov 14:28). On the other hand, contrast or paradox may be present. Examples are "All is not gold that glitters" and "A gentle tongue can break a bone" (Prov 25:15). Often the

[61]AEL 2:152.

[62]J. M. Thompson, *The Form and Function of Proverbs in Ancient Israel* (The Hague: Mouton, 1974), 21-23.

[63]Thompson, *Form and Function of Proverbs*, 64-65.

[64]R. B. Y. Scott, "Folk Proverbs of the Ancient Near East," *Transactions of the Royal Society of Canada* 15 (1961): 47-56, reprinted in Crenshaw, *Studies*, 417-26.

comparison is a similarity set as a simile: "Like cold water to a weary soul/is good news from a distant land" (Prov 25:25).

Scott also observes that often proverbs turn upon that which is futile or absurd. Other proverbs deal with relative value but often with an unexpected reversal. That is, the item of apparently inferior value is actually superior. "Out of the frying pan into the fire" and the Latin proverb "Friendship is better than relationship" are examples. The biblical "Better a meal of vegetables where there is love/than a fattened calf with hatred" (Prov 15:17) is of this type.

5. The Structure of the Book of Proverbs

It is generally agreed that Proverbs is made up of a number of sections, each of which is headed by a superscription: chaps. 1–9; 10:1–22:16; 22:17–24:22; 24:23-34; chaps. 25–29; 30:1-33; 31:1-9; 31:10-31.[65] Proverbs 1:1 is often regarded as the title of the whole book[66] and is generally assumed to be a late addition.

The differences between Prov 1–9 and 10–29 have attracted much attention. The former is a presentation of lengthy, well-crafted discourses, whereas the latter is a collection of pithy sayings seemingly without editorial arrangement.[67] Many scholars regard Prov 1–9 as reflecting a later, more advanced development of Israelite wisdom from the postexilic period. The theological reflection here, as well as the personification of wisdom, seems to represent an advance over the secular and empirical approach of the maxims of Prov 10:1ff., which are thought to be earlier. The present redactional structure of the book is often dated ca. 450–350 B.C.[68]

The present debate over the structure and date of Proverbs entered an entirely new phase, however, with K. A. Kitchen's publication of his research on the formal structure of ancient Near Eastern wisdom literature.[69] As mentioned above, scholars have long recognized the importance of the titles at Prov 10:1; 25:1; 30:1; and 31:1, but the significance of these headings has long been a matter of dispute, largely because of a lack of adequate comparative analysis. It is just such analysis that Kitchen has provided. He forces us to look at Proverbs in its historical context and to interpret the structure and date of the texts accordingly.

Preliminary to his study, Kitchen distinguishes between the practical, instructional literature and the reflective works of wisdom, which tend to be

---

[65]Cf. Childs, *Old Testament*, 547; Gottwald, *Hebrew Bible*, 571.

[66]Childs, *Old Testament*, 551.

[67]But see "On Order and Disorder in Proverbs 10:1–24:23" on p. 46.

[68]E.g., Gottwald, *Hebrew Bible*, 572.

[69]K. A. Kitchen, "Proverbs and Wisdom Books of the Ancient Near East," *TB* 28 (1977): 69-114, and "Basic Literary Forms," 236-81.

more concerned with social issues than the instructional literature. He notes that in Egypt the instructional wisdom is the older of the two, having begun in the reigns of the Old Kingdom pharaohs Imhotep, Djedefhor, and Ptahhotep. In the breakdown of society during the First Intermediate, however, more reflective and pessimistic or socially oriented wisdom literature began to emerge. Chief among these were the Eloquent Peasant, Ipuwer, the Anthology of Words, and the programmatic Neferty.[70]

Kitchen devotes the bulk of his formal analysis to instructional wisdom of which Proverbs is an example. Within this genre he observes that two overall groups exist, which he calls Types A and B. Works of Type A have a formal title but then immediately move to the subject matter of the text, whereas works of Type B have both a title and a prologue and then the main text. They may also have subtitles and epilogues at the end.[71]

It is critical to recognize that neither Type A nor B is particularly early or late, that there is no literary development from Type A to B, and that both are equally popular throughout the ancient Near Eastern world. Examples of both types are found throughout the region, and both occur from the third millennium B.C. to the first.[72]

The titles of instructional works generally contain a word on the nature of the work and the name of the author or compiler set in the third person.

> The beginning of the instruction which the King of Upper and Lower Egypt . . . made for his son, King Meri-ka-Re[73] (Merikare, Egypt, third mill.).

In Egypt the title formulations generally have substantival keywords (e.g., "The instruction of [proper name]"), but in Mesopotamia the key words are verbs (e.g., "[proper name] gave instruction").[74] The titles are of varying length, and both long and short titles are equally popular in all periods.[75]

In addition to the titles of entire narratives, Type B wisdom literature also has what Kitchen calls "Subtitles," "Titular interjections," and "Recurrent Cross-headings." Subtitles occur within the body of a work and name the author of the work and, like the titles, have key words that are either substantival (Egypt, Levant) or verbal (Mesopotamia).

> Beginning of the formulations of excellent discourse spoken by the Prince, Count, God's Father, God's beloved, Eldest Son of the King, of his body, Mayor of the city and Vizier, Ptahhotep, in instructing the ignorant in knowledge and in the standard of excellent discourse, as profit for him who

---

[70]Kitchen, "Basic Literary Forms," 237-40.

[71]Ibid., 241-42.

[72]Ibid., 241-43. Type A occurs in both third millennium and first millennium texts, but as of yet no second millennium texts occur. As Kitchen notes, this is probably an accident of the survival of texts.

[73]ANET, 414-15.

[74]Kitchen, "Proverbs," 76.

[75]Kitchen, "Basic Literary Forms," 243-45.

will hear, as woe to him who would neglect them. He spoke to his son"[76] (Ptahhotep, Egypt, early second mill.).

A curious note is that elaborate subtitle schemes are found in the earliest Mesopotamian texts (e.g., the old Sumerian Shuruppak) but not in later texts (e.g., the Akkadian version). This is the reverse of what an evolutionary approach to the texts would predict.[77]

Titular interjections are breaks in the narrative in which the author directly addresses the reader.

Let me tell thee also of the builder of walls . . . Let me tell thee also of other matters"[78] (A Satire on the Trades, Egypt, second mill.).

They are less formal than subtitles but nevertheless serve to delineate subsections. They may be in either the indicative or imperative mood.

Recurrent cross-headings are regular, perhaps numbered headings that are analogous to chapter headings:[79]

Beginning of the teaching for life . . . Chapter 1 . . . Chapter 2 . . . Chapter 30. . . . That is its end"[80] (Amenemope, Egypt, New Kingdom).

The Prologue is the distinctive feature of the Type B didactic texts. The prologues tend to be of short to medium length in texts of the third and second millennia but longer in the first millennium. The trend toward longer prologues began around 1000 B.C. In content, third and second millennia prologues are exhortatory.

Risen as a god, hear what I tell you, that you may rule the land, govern the shores, increase well-being!"[81] (Amenemhet I, Egypt, early second mill.).

Late first millennium prologues, on the other hand, are exclusively narrative and biographical.[82] The best example of a first millennium prologue is the lengthy biographical prologue of the Mesopotamian work Ahiqar.

The main body of the ancient didactic texts, whether Type A or B, contained the teachings and could be either a unitary text or a multisegmented text. The unitary text has no subsections and is common in all periods.

Do not set out to stand around in this assembly. . . . Do good things, be kind all your days. . . . Do not marry a prostitute[83] (Counsels of Wisdom, Mesopotamia, late second mill.).

---

[76]AEL 1:63.

[77]Kitchen, "Proverbs," 79-80.

[78]Kitchen, "Basic Literary Forms," 245-47.

[79]ANET, 433-34.

[80]AEL 2:148-62.

[81]AEL 1:136.

[82]Kitchen, "Basic Literary Forms," 247-49.

[83]ANET, 595. The Egyptian Ptahhotep (early second mill.) and Ankhsheshonqy are also examples of this type. See Kitchen, "Basic Literary Forms," 275.

In this type the author moves from topic to topic without transitions. Some texts divided into two or three subsections are found in Egypt in the third and second millennia. The multisegmented text is divided into chapter-like divisions and is found in the late second and early first millennia in Egypt.[84]

A number of works, especially in the third and second millennia, have epilogues such as the following:

> Behold, I have set thee on the way of a god. The Renenut of a scribe is on his shoulder on the day of his birth"[85] (A Satire on Trades, Egypt, early second mill.).

No set form for the epilogue is apparent, and content also varies considerably. The use of the epilogue tended to disappear in the first millennium.[86]

In addition, the smaller formal elements of wisdom literature, such as one-line units, bicola with parallelism and merismus, and longer units of three or more cola, occur throughout the ancient Near Eastern texts in all periods. The bicolon is by far the most common, but no evolutionary development is apparent. Simple units of one or two lines occur in the latest texts, and complex discourses of many lines occur in the earliest texts.

Similarly, the grouping of material according to topic cannot be said to be a later development. In some ancient wisdom texts, individual teachings are topically grouped, but in others they are simply collected in an atomistic fashion without regard for whether one proverb or teaching has any relationship to the text. Neither method is earlier or later than the other.[87]

No longer can scholars analyze Proverbs according to *a priori* evolutionary standards that are unsupported by any real data from control documents from the ancient world. The idea that documents composed of short, pithy, proverbial statements must antedate texts with longer and more complex discourse has no validity. Alleged differences in theological sophistication are equally misleading as guides to historical development.[88] No such evolutionary progression emerges from the texts.[89]

---

[84]Kitchen, "Basic Literary Forms," 248-49. Examples of the two- or three-sectioned text include the Mesopotamian Shuruppak in the classical Sumerian version, the Egyptian Satire on Trades (early second mill.), and Aniy (late second mill.). Multisegmented texts include the Egyptian Amenemope.

[85]ANET, 434. The Renenut was a fortune goddess. The meaning is that the good fortune of a scribe was fixed at birth.

[86]Kitchen, "Basic Literary Forms," 251-52.

[87]Ibid., 256-57.

[88]The tendency to stratify Israelite wisdom literature according to evolutionary presuppositions of theological development appears, for example, in G. von Rad, *Wisdom in Israel*, 53-73.

[89]The failure of the evolutionary approach was actually evident before Kitchen's work. See B. Gemser, "The Instructions of Onchsheshonqy and Biblical Wisdom Literature," *VT* 7

Similarly, the texts of Proverbs cannot be divided according to arbitrary Western standards. Only real analogies from the ancient texts provide an adequate basis for structural analysis. In this light one may analyze the structure of the book as follows:

PROVERBS 1–24: SOLOMON. First, the whole of Proverbs 1–24 (hereinafter called Solomon[90]) is a Type B instructional text, which is divided as follows:

Title	1:1
Prologue	1:2-7
Main Text, Discourse Form	1:8–9:18
Subtitle	10:1
Main Text, Proverb Form	10:2–22:16
Titular Interjection	22:17
Main Text, Thirty Sayings	22:18–24:22
Titular Interjection	24:23
Main Text, Short Discourses	24:24-34[91]

The prologue marks Solomon as a Type B wisdom text. It contains no autobiography at all. This suggests that it comes from the early first millennium at the latest since most first millennium prologues are autobiographical.

The main text of Solomon is in four segments (called "Main Text" in the outline), but it is similar to the two/three-segmented type. This structuring is more a characteristic of earlier literature than of first millennium texts.[92] The references to "the wise" in the two "titular interjections" (22:17; 24:23) do not function as attributions of authorship but are rather conventional assertions that the teaching that follows is in accord with

(1960): 102-28, reprinted in J. Crenshaw, *Studies in Israelite Wisdom* (New York: KTAV, 1976), 134-60. Gemser concluded that "more developed forms and thought are not necessarily younger and later than the more simple ones" (Crenshaw, *Studies*, 160) and cautioned against evolutionary presuppositions. His warnings went unheeded, however, and a number of highly evolutionary redaction-critical studies followed. Even if one does not follow Gemser in viewing Ankhsheshonqy as a retrograde to a more primitive stage of wisdom (cf. Lichtheim, *Late Egyptian Wisdom*, 5), it is clear that a simple, evolutionary model will not work.

[90]Kitchen's term for this section is "Solomon I."

[91]My analysis differs at several points from Kitchen, "Proverbs," 70, 80, 84-86. The most significant difference is that Kitchen regards 1:1-6 as the title to Solomon and 1:7–9:18 as the prologue. Two factors force me to an alternative position. First, I cannot be persuaded that 1:8–9:16 can be called a "prologue." In my view we are here in the main body of the text. Second, I am impressed by the remarkable similarity of 1:2-7 to the prologue of Amenemope, a late second millennium text that certainly influenced Prov 22:17–24:22 and thus possibly 1:2-7 also.

[92]Kitchen, "Proverbs," 98.

received wisdom. While there can be little doubt that many of the individual proverbs were passed down from earlier generations, the subtitles do not assert the text as a literary work to be a product of "the wise." The convention of drawing on earlier wisdom is as early as Ptahhotep.[93]

Subtitles and titular interjections occur frequently in ancient Near Eastern wisdom texts and are by no means indications that the sections they head were once independent "documents" from different sources. The similarity between the titular interjection in Solomon to one in Aniy, for example, is striking:

> Pay attention and listen to the sayings of the wise; apply to your heart what I teach (Prov 22:17).
>
> See, I tell you these excellent things, which should you weigh them; do them, it will go well with you, and all evil shall be far from you" (Aniy V, 4-5).[94]

No Egyptologist would assert Aniy to be a collection of independent texts on the basis of the titular interjections, and the same standards should be applied to Proverbs.[95]

The predominance of bicola in the majority of ancient Near Eastern wisdom literature is mirrored in the heavy usage of that form in the main body (and prologue) of Solomon. The heavy usage of parallel couplets is a phenomenon generally found in earlier works.[96]

Finally, the absence of an epilogue to Solomon is of little significance since epilogues were never requisite and had no fixed form. Also, as mentioned above, the use of epilogues tends to antedate King Solomon (third mill., early second mill.).

HEZEKIAH, AGUR, AND LEMUEL. The remainder of Proverbs is a collection of three originally independent works, here called "Hezekiah" (Prov 25–29), "Agur" (chap. 30), and "Lemuel" (chap. 31). The final wisdom poem in the Lemuel text is often treated as an independent work, but this is unlikely for the following reasons:

Hezekiah is a Type A instructional text. The structure is simple:

Title	25:1
Main Text	25:2–29:27

As a Type A text, it has no prologue. Also there are no subtitles or titular interjection, the main text being a collection of proverbs, and neither is there an epilogue.

---

[93]Ibid., 93.

[94]Ibid., 110.

[95]The Instructions of Aniy, it should be noted, contains an epilogue in the form of a dialogue between father and son. If Proverbs had such an epilogue, many biblical scholars would certainly regard it as an obvious secondary addition.

[96]Kitchen, "Proverbs," 98.

The title states that the main text is composed of Solomonic proverbs that the men of Hezekiah "copied." The verb normally means "to move (something) forward," "to depart," or "to remove,"[97] but here alone it is generally translated "to transcribe." The implication is that Hezekiah's men moved Solomonic proverbs from other sources and collated them into a single work. The verb need not be taken to mean that they simply copied a single, already extant document verbatim.

In addition, the phrase "these are more" implies that the collection that follows was purposefully compiled as a supplement to the former text, Solomon (Prov 1–24). In other words, although the proverbs that make up chaps. 25–29 are old (i.e., Solomonic), the text here called "Hezekiah" did not exist as a collection until Hezekiah's men compiled it.

The Agur text (Prov 30) is also Type A undifferentiated didactic material. It has the following structure:

Title	30:1[98]
Main Text	30:2-33

Agur is distinguished by the presence of seven numerical sayings (vv. 7-9,15a,15b-16,18-19,21-23,24-28,29-31). Numerical sayings are found in second millennium ancient Near Eastern literature and continue well into the first millennium.[99] Compare the following lines from Ugaritic poetry to the text from Proverbs:

> For two kinds of banquets Baal hates,
> Three the Rider of the Clouds:
> A banquet of shamefulness,
> A banquet of baseness,
> And a banquet of handmaids' lewdness[100] (II AB iii).

> There are three things that are too amazing for me,
> four that I do not understand:
> the way of an eagle in the sky,
> the way of a snake on a rock,
> the way of a ship on the high seas,
> and the way of a man with a maiden (Prov 30:18-19).

The Lemuel text is also Type A didactic material. Kitchen has argued that the wisdom poem in vv. 10-31 is part of the Lemuel text on the grounds that, without the poem, the text is absurdly short. In addition, an isolated poem with no title is anomalous in wisdom literature, but a two-section wisdom piece is quite ordinary.[101] It is probably best to follow Kitchen's conclusions here. The structure of the Lemuel text is as follows:

---

[97]הֶעְתִּיקוּ; cf. Gen 12:8; 26:22; Job 9:5; 32:15.

[98]The meaning of 30:1b is discussed in the commentary.

[99]Kitchen, "Proverbs," 100.

[100]ANET, 132.

[101]Kitchen, "Proverbs," 100-101.

Title: 31:1	First Section (royal duties): 2–9
Main Text: 31:2-31	Second Section (the good wife): 10:31

Unlike the Hezekiah text, Agur and Lemuel appear to have existed independently prior to their inclusion in the canonical text of Proverbs. No evidence is available for determining when these two texts were written or added.

6. On Order and Disorder in Proverbs 10:1–24:23

Perhaps the most arresting feature of Prov 10:1–24:23 is what seems a complete lack of structure of arrangement in the collection of proverbs. They appear to have been assembled altogether at random. This feature seems odd in light of the Hebrew passion for parallel, chiasmus, merismus, and other such modes of structuring the written word. Thus Whybray has commented that to claim the proverbs have no context but occur in random order "amounts to no more than an admission that modern scholars have so far not been able satisfactorily to discover what such a 'context,' whether literary or theological, might be."[102] In unraveling this problem, several factors must be taken into account.

First, each proverb is an independent unit that can stand alone and still have meaning. Textual context is not essential for interpretation.[103] Also the very disorder of a collection of proverbs can serve a didactic purpose; it demonstrates that while reality and truth are not irrational, neither are they fully subject to human attempts at systemization.[104] The proverbs are presented in the seemingly haphazard way we encounter the issues with which they deal.[105]

Context, however, sometimes qualifies or gives a more precise meaning to a given proverb. Perhaps the best known example of this is Prov 26:4-5, where the reader is advised both against and in favor of answering a fool according to his folly. The two proverbs qualify each other, and the whole indicates that there are times when responding to a fool is appropriate and other times when it is not.

On close examination, in fact, many proverbs are found to have been grouped into small collections that provide context for the individual maxims. Proverbs 10–24, therefore, are characterized by both order and disorder. Each proverb has its own meaning, but it may also have a more

[102]Whybray, *Wealth and Poverty*, 65.

[103]Studies include H.-J. Hermission, *Studien zur israelitischen Spruchsweisheit*, WMANT 28 (Neukirchen-Vluyn, 1968), 171-83, and O. Ploger, "Zur Auslegung der Sentenzensammlungen des Proverbienbuches," in *Probleme biblischer Theologie* (Munich, 1971), 402-16.

[104]For a good study of the meaning of aphoristic thinking, see J. G. Williams, *Those Who Ponder Proverbs* (Sheffield: Almond, 1981).

[105]R. L. Alden, *Proverbs: A Commentary on an Ancient Book of Timeless Advice* (Grand Rapids: Baker, 1983), 10.

specific meaning in the context of a small collection of proverbs. Individual proverbs, collections of proverbs, and the random repetition of proverbial themes all serve to reinforce the lessons of the book. Identifying the small collections of proverbs is essential for the use of Proverbs in the church. By observing the context of individual proverbs in small collections and noting how the message of each collection coheres, the preacher or Bible teacher can actually take a congregation through a series of chapters of Proverbs without resorting to rearranging verses topically.[106]

Other examples of proverbs being grouped into related collections may be found in the ancient Near East. Collections one and two of the Sumerian proverbs link sayings into groups either by the initial sign of the saying or by a common topic.[107] The sayings of the Babylonian "Counsels of Wisdom" are also grouped by subject matter.[108]

Many Egyptian texts also have some kind of order. In Ptahhotep (Old Kingdom) the main body of teaching is divided into thirty-seven strophes, each of which begins with a condition (frequently but not always introduced by "if") and then gives instructions appropriate to that condition.[109] The strophes of Aniy are distinguished by an opening imperative followed by explanation and exposition.[110] In Ankhsheshonqy sayings are linked in a chainlike structure by verbal association.[111]

Several types of collections (with many variations and combinations of types) may be observed in the biblical Proverbs:

1. *Parallel collection*: proverbs grouped in an *A-B-A-B* pattern. The elements of the pattern may be individual cola (two-proverb collection; 11:16-17) or whole proverbs (four-proverb collection; 10:27-30).
2. *Chiastic collection*: proverbs grouped in an *A-B-B-A* pattern. Again, the elements of the pattern may be individual cola (two-proverb collection; 18:6-7) or whole proverbs (four-proverb collection; 12:19-22).
3. *Catchword collection*: a group of proverbs that contain a common catchword (15:15-17). Some specific word or phrase is repeated that signals that the verses are related to one another.
4. *Thematic collection*: a group of proverbs that maintain a common theme (10:31-32). That is, they deal with the same subject matter.
5. *Inclusio collection*: a group of proverbs between an inclusio, in which the first and last proverbs are similar or contain common catchwords. For example, 11:23-27 is set off by the catchword "good" as an inclusio

[106]See D. A. Garrett, "Preaching Wisdom," in *Reclaiming the Prophetic Mantle: Preaching the Old Testament Faithfully*, ed. G. Klein (Nashville: Broadman, 1992).

[107]Gordon, *Sumerian Proverbs*, 26, 154-55.

[108]Lambert, *Babylonian Wisdom*, 96.

[109]E.g., strophe 10: "If you are poor, serve a man of worth" (AEL 1:66).

[110]E.g., "Double the food your mother gave you,/ support her as she supported you" (AEL 2:141). Sometimes there is slight variation in this pattern.

[111]Lichtheim, *Late Egyptian Wisdom*, 64.

in vv. 23,27, and vv. 24-26 within that inclusio deal with the theme of generosity and its rewards. A variation on the inclusio is the *A-B* envelope series, which consists of two juxtaposed collections with similar proverbs at the beginnings and ends (as in 15:1–16:8).

In addition, certain sections of Proverbs employ what may be called "random repetition" for didactic purposes. Proverbs 17, for example, randomly returns to the theme of avoiding quarrelsome behavior in vv. 1,9, 14,19,27-28. For the reader the unexpected way in which teachings on a particular theme repeatedly appear more emphatically drives home the intended lesson. If related proverbs always stood together in a single cluster, much of the effect would be lost.

7. The Origin of the Book of Proverbs

(1) History of the Redaction of Proverbs

Despite the book's claims of essentially Solomonic origin (1:1; 10:1; 25:1) and of its collection during the reign of Hezekiah (25:1) in 729–686 B.C., critical scholars generally consider Proverbs to have had a long and complex history of development not completed until after the exile. Three major redaction-critical reconstructions of significance are those of P. W. Skehan, R. N. Whybray, and W. McKane. If either of the latter two analyses is correct, Proverbs does not have a single or even a major "author" at all in the traditional sense of the term but is instead the product of a long process of compilation, redaction, and theological revision.

Skehan, however, argues that a single editor stands behind the whole Book of Proverbs. He constructs his theory around an elaborate numerical theory in which he argues that the total number of lines is nearly equal to the numeric value of the names Solomon, David, and Israel from Prov 1:1. He also argues that Proverbs is constructed as the "house of wisdom" (Prov 9:1) such that the book is arranged in a numeric pattern that corresponds to the Solomonic temple.[112]

Skehan's theory is intriguing, but most scholars remain unconvinced of its validity. Its very complexity and the peculiar way some passages are combined[113] give the theory a contrived look. There is no compelling reason to suppose that Proverbs was written in the way Skehan proposes.[114]

[112]See P. W. Skehan, "The Seven Columns of Wisdom's House in Proverbs 1–9," *CBQ* 9 (1947): 190-98; "A Single Editor for the Whole Book of Proverbs," *CBQ* 10 (1948): 115-30; "Wisdom's House," *CBQ* 29 (1967): 162-80. All three are reprinted with revisions in P. W. Skehan, *Studies in Israelite Poetry and Wisdom, CBQ* Monograph Series I (Washington: Catholic Biblical Association of America, 1971), 9-45.

[113]E.g., "column 7" of the "porch" is said to be made up of Prov 4:1-9; 3:13-24,35 (Skehan, *Studies*, 33).

[114]Cf. D. Kidner, *The Wisdom of Proverbs, Job, and Ecclesiastes* (Downers Grove: Inter-Varsity, 1985), 49-50.

Whybray presents an evolutionary redaction history in a monograph on Prov 1–9. He attempts, on form-critical grounds, to separate an earlier "Book of Ten Discourses" within Prov 1–9 from later accretions to the text.[115] In particular he argues that the original ten discourses were relatively short admonitions, each begun with the vocative "My son" and containing admonitions to lay hold of wisdom, avoid the adulterous woman, and so forth.[116] This basic core, he believes, was constructed on analogy with the thirty chapters of the Egyptian Amenemope. Two major theological supplements were added to this, he says, in addition to a number of glosses. The personification of wisdom in Prov 8, for example, is a theological addition from a later period.

Whybray's method is suspect in that he extracts a single motif from the text ("My son" plus admonition) and elevates it to the status of the dominant form in the hypothetical original text. In addition his grounds for including some verses in the original ten discourses and excluding others are arbitrary.[117] Most significantly, however, Whybray's reconstruction attempts to force Proverbs into the grid of Amenemope. While comparisons among pieces of ancient Near Eastern wisdom literature are helpful, one text cannot be used as the procrustean bed of another.

W. McKane has proposed a redaction history of Proverbs that involves a major revision of early, secular, wisdom material by later scribes of a more religious bent. He argues that the wisdom sentences are divided into three classes: Class A, the older, nonreligious material that deals primarily with individual success; Class B, which deals with antisocial behavior in the community; and Class C, which is a Yahwistic reinterpretation of the older material in Class A. In short, the older, mundane wisdom was given a theological reinterpretation later in the redaction history.[118]

McKane argues that in the older wisdom the reader is exhorted to pursue wisdom as a secular enterprise but that in the later material a pious fear of the Lord and a negative appraisal of human wisdom has become the rule. An earlier optimism about learning has given way to a religious anti-intellectualism. Proverbs 13:14 and 14:27 are identical, he notes, except that instead of the "teaching of the wise" being a fountain of life (13:14), "the fear of the Lord" (14:27) has become the wise rule. The latter can be taken as a Yahwistic revision of the former.[119] From this and

[115]Whybray, *Wisdom in Proverbs*, 33-52.

[116]Examples included "Discourse I" (1:8-19), "Discourse II" (2:1,9,16-19), and "Discourse III" (3:1-2,3b,c-10).

[117]See F. M. Wilson, "Sacred and Profane? The Yahwistic Redaction of Proverbs Reconsidered," in *The Listening Heart*, ed. K. Hoglund et al., JSOTSup 58 (Sheffield: Sheffield Academic Press, 1987), 319-20.

[118]W. McKane, *Proverbs*, OTL (Philadelphia: Westminster, 1970), 17.

[119]Ibid., 18.

similar arguments McKane concludes that the older, humanistic, intellectually optimistic wisdom was superseded by a later religious revision.

F. Wilson, however, has shown that the evidence does not support this broad hypothesis.[120] He notes that Prov 14:27 can easily be taken as a variation on 13:14; it need not be regarded as a substitution.[121] He observes that the attacks on those who are "wise in their own eyes" in McKane's Class C material are not attacks on wisdom as such. McKane's Class A wisdom is itself marked by intellectual modesty and a shunning of pedantic arrogance (12:15; 26:5,12; 28:11).[122]

In addition, J. Priest observes that even Sirach contains a number of "secular" proverbs. These would have been assigned to the earliest stratum had they been in the biblical Book of Proverbs. And he notes that even if an evolutionary development had occurred in the Egyptian and Babylonian material (which, as we have seen, was not the case), this does not mean that the Israelites, who learned from them, would have repeated the whole process.[123] M. Lichtheim, similarly, observes that McKane got "lost in the proverbial woods" when trying to detect folk proverbs in the Egyptian material,[124] and the same can be said of his hypothesis for Hebrew wisdom.

Perhaps a most significant weakness of redaction histories that propose a movement from an early humanistic to a later religious wisdom is the supposition that it is possible to separate theology from ethics. The study of ethics is in fact a theological enterprise. Certainly the ancients did not attempt to develop secular ethics apart from religious presuppositions, and in the ancient world no nation was more dominated by its theological vision than Israel. The modern attempts to separate right behavior from duty to God are inadequate for us and unthinkable for those of the ancient Near East.

When the weight of the evidence of Kitchen's structural analysis of didactic wisdom is added to the objections to these proposed redaction histories, the case against them becomes overwhelming. The wisdom texts of the other nations are often complex bodies of literature, and some growth and development did occur. But no one imagines that any of them went through the massive theological supplementation and revision proposed for Proverbs. Inasmuch as Proverbs is structurally much like the other ancient Near Eastern material, it begs the question to assert that it had an altogether unique history.

---

[120]Wilson, "Sacred and Profane?" 320-27. Space does not permit us to deal with all of McKane's arguments here, particularly with his conclusions based on lexical studies. Wilson's article, however, provides a thorough analysis.

[121]Ibid., 323.

[122]Ibid., 325.

[123]J. F. Priest, "Where Is Wisdom to Be Placed?" in Crenshaw, *Studies*, 284.

[124]Lichtheim, *Late Egyptian Wisdom*, 5-6.

(2) Date

Earlier critical scholars regarded it as a matter beyond question that not only the present form of the book but much of the material of Proverbs was very late. C. Toy believed that the redaction of Proverbs took place in several stages from ca. 350 B.C. to the second century, although he allowed that some material was earlier. He believed that the assumed monotheism, the lack of covenant theology, the social conditions reflected in the book, and the lexical data all supported a later date. In addition, he thought the philosophical conceptions in Proverbs were derived from Greece and therefore after Alexander's conquest.[125] Other scholars shared his view that the work was fairly late.[126]

Kitchen's structural analysis indicates that the Book of Solomon (Prov 1–24) was written as a unified text at the beginning of the first millennium B.C. Even apart from that work, however, the older criteria for dating the sections of Proverbs are inappropriate. The lengthy wisdom discourses and the personification of wisdom in Prov 1–9, once regarded as proofs of the late origin of those chapters, are now acknowledged to be paralleled in early Egyptian literature.[127]

Linguistic evidence is inconclusive. The opinion that the word "covenant" is evidence that Prov 2:17 is relatively recent must be abandoned. The word appears as early as the fourteenth/thirteenth century in the Levant.[128] The value of "Aramaisms" as a tool for dating biblical texts has been greatly exaggerated,[129] and this is equally true in respect to Proverbs. The vocabulary of Proverbs by no means requires a late date.[130]

It is in fact difficult to find concrete support for a late date for Proverbs. The absence of references to Israel's covenant history, if anything, moves us in the opposite direction. Assertions about the nature of the social conditions behind Proverbs should be tentative at best, and Toy's efforts here are quite weak. His pronouncement that "malicious gossip, going security, greed of money, nocturnal robbery, murder, and unchastity" were "specially prominent in the postexilian cities"[131] is, as Kitchen characterizes it, "quaint and fanciful."[132] In addition, scholars have rightly abandoned the

---

[125]C. H. Toy, *A Critical and Exegetical Commentary on the Book of Proverbs*, ICC (Edinburgh: T & T Clark, 1977), xix-xxxi.

[126]Cf. R. H. Pfeiffer, *Introduction to the Old Testament* (New York: Harper and Row, 1941), 659. He asserts that "it is improbable that any collection of maxims was made before 600 B.C."

[127]Cf. Gottwald, *Hebrew Bible*, 571.

[128]Kitchen, "Proverbs," 104.

[129]Cf. L. Walker, "Notes on Higher Criticism and the Dating of Biblical Hebrew," in *A Tribute to Gleason Archer*, ed. W. C. Kaiser and R. Youngblood (Chicago: Moody, 1986), 40-42.

[130]For a good discussion of loan words and alleged loan words in Proverbs, see Kitchen, "Proverbs," 104-6.

[131]Toy, *Proverbs*, xxii.

[132]Kitchen, "Proverbs," 108-9.

position that biblical wisdom shows influence from Greek philosophy.[133] By contrast, for example, the late Egyptian work Ankhsheshonqy clearly reflects Hellenistic themes.[134]

The majority of Proverbs, particularly the Book of Solomon (chapters 1–24), may be confidently ascribed to the early monarchy on the basis of the evidence of the text itself and structural considerations. The other collections—Hezekiah, Agur, and Lemuel—are later but probably preexilic. No hard evidence supports the common assertion that Prov 1–9 is late.

(3) Authorship

R. B. Y. Scott, primarily on the basis of a historical-critical and lexical analysis of 1 Kgs 5; 10, argues that much of the attribution of great wisdom to Solomon is late, legendary, and of little historical value. He also contends, primarily from Prov 25:1, that the real dawn of literary wisdom in Israel was in the reign of Hezekiah.[135] Against Scott, however, there is no reason to maintain that Solomon could not have been the gifted student of the arts and sciences the Bible portrays (1 Kgs 4:29-34; Pss 72:1; 127:1; Prov 1:1; 10:1; 25:1; Song 1:1; Matt 12:24).[136] Scott exaggerates the importance of Hezekiah; his reign appears to have been more of a literary Indian Summer than an Augustine age or Renaissance, at least where wisdom literature is concerned. In addition, lexical and literary arguments that 1 Kgs 5; 10 are late and legendary are unconvincing.[137]

Kitchen's structural analysis supports an early first millennium date for the work, and linguistic and theological analysis does not overturn this conclusion. A prolonged and complex history of theological redaction is neither necessary nor probable. The biblical assertion that the Solomonic monarchy witnessed a great literary renaissance and that Solomon himself was the fountainhead is reasonable.

8. The Theology of Wisdom

The theological problems in Proverbs can be divided into five major questions.[138]

---

[133]See Crenshaw, "Prolegomenon," *Studies*, 8-9.

[134]See Lichtheim, *Late Egyptian Wisdom*, 65.

[135]R. B. Y. Scott, "Solomon and the Beginnings of Wisdom in Israel," *VTSup* 3 (1969): 362-79.

[136]See J. Ruffle, "The Teaching of Amenemope and Its Connection with the Book of Proverbs," *TB* (1977): 29-68 (esp. 34-5).

[137]Scott, "Solomon" 268-72. For example, "beyond the river" in 5:4 (Eng. 4:24) may indicate that the final redaction of Kings took place in Babylon, but this is scarcely evidence that the historical data are also late or are legendary. In addition, Scott's contention that words like the plural "trees" in 5:13 (Eng. 4:33) are evidence of a postexilic date (Scott, "Solomon," 269) is strange. The plural can mean "trees" in preexilic texts (e.g., Isa 7:2) or "wood" in a postexilic text.

[138]Cf. Childs, *Old Testament*, 550, from which I have taken the first three questions.

1. Is the search for a divine order a basic element of the old wisdom of Proverbs?

Many scholars assume that the search for order in creation is the essence of wisdom, and they assert that the task of the Israelite wise man was to integrate the individual's life into that order. Wisdom, according to this reconstruction, does not look for revealed truth. Instead, it seeks for clues to the divine order in nature, history, social order, and daily work. Gottwald, for example, can define wisdom as "a nonrevelatory mode of thought that focuses on individual consciousness of truth and right conduct, displaying a humanistic orientation and a didactic drive to pass on its understandings to others."[139]

This takes us to the question of whether Proverbs simply embodies an Israelite version of the Egyptian idea of *Maat. Maat*, often translated "justice," refers to the Egyptian concept of the natural order that is built into the world. To be in harmony with *Maat* is to live in peace and prosperity; to oppose it is to destroy oneself.[140] The task of the wise man, it is thought, is to unravel the mystery of *Maat* and comprehend this order and thus live in accordance with it.

Many people believe that the world has a certain order to it and that harmony with that order is essential to peace and fulfillment.[141] Indeed, the idea is fairly self-evident to all but the most radically existential. The question here is whether Israelite wisdom reckoned that this order or *Maat* is discovered by inquiry and reflection or by revelation. That is, is it a "secular" or a "revelatory" enterprise?

Israel's doctrine of creation is crucial to its wisdom. Genesis 1:1 stands behind all biblical wisdom literature. The created order is good, but humans fight against the divine order in their perversity and obstinacy (Eccl 7:29). Proverbs strives to explain that order not as an independent entity but as the pattern of God's creation (Prov 8:22-31).

But creation reveals the truth that stands behind it only partially at best, and human knowledge is not sufficient to divine what is hidden (Deut 29:29; Prov 30:2-4; Eccl 8:16-17; 1 Cor 2:7; Col 2:3; Heb 4:13). Even if we were to dig into the heart of the earth, our search would ultimately be futile (Job 28).[142] "God understands the way to it/and he alone knows where it dwells" (Job 28:23).

Therefore the determinative biblical proposition, as R. Murphy points out, is Israel's insistence that the "fear of Yahweh is the beginning of

[139]Gottwald, *The Hebrew Bible*, 567.

[140]Cf. E. Wurthwein, "Die Weisheit Agyptens und das Alte Testament," in *Wort und Existenz, Studien zum Alten Testament*, trans. B. Kovacs (Göttingen: Vandenhoeck und Ruprecht, 1970), 197-216 and reprinted in Crenshaw, *Studies*, 113-33.

[141]Cf. C. S. Lewis, *The Abolition of Man* (New York: Macmillan, 1947), where he discusses the "Tao" that is common to most cultures.

[142]Cf. the discussion in von Rad, *Wisdom in Israel*, 144-49.

wisdom" (Job 28:28; Prov 1:7). The meaning is not that the fear of the Lord is one aspect of wisdom, even the best, but that it is the place from which the search for wisdom must begin. The "fear of Yahweh" is a major theme of wisdom literature and is functionally the same as the "fear of God" (e.g., Job 1:1; Eccl 12:13). Reverence for God determines progress in wisdom, and this reverence includes the moral dimension of obedience and the spiritual dimension of worship.[143]

The Book of Proverbs does not simply attach the caboose of Yahwism to the train of secular, international wisdom. Murphy rightly comments that there is no "Yahwehizing" of wisdom in the Bible.[144] On the contrary, the Lord and the precepts of Israelite faith dominate biblical wisdom as the explicit fount of true understanding and the rule by which all is judged. As Waltke argues, the fundamental theological presuppositions of biblical wisdom do not differ from those of Law and Prophecy.[145]

The biblical texts are very much a part of the collection of instructional literature from the ancient Near East, and Solomon and the other biblical sages were full participants in the wider intellectual journey of their day. They were different, however, in bringing their faith in Yahweh to the task, and that not as some minor personal idiosyncrasy but as the ruling presupposition of their thought. Did they see themselves as part of a larger investigation of plan and order of the world? Of course they did, but only from the belief that the quest must begin in submission to the Maker of heaven and earth.

2. Does Israelite wisdom include a concept of divine retribution, or is it simply an act-consequence philosophy?

This question, closely related to the previous, brings us back to the issue of the relationship between Deuteronomy and Proverbs. As noted earlier, Deuteronomy does tend to stress more the concept of punishment or reward being direct acts of God whereas Proverbs tends to speak more of each action containing within itself a link to reward or punishment.

One must distinguish, however, between participation in a literary genre and full acceptance of the religious and philosophical presuppositions that underlie other representatives of that genre. In other words, Proverbs was written according to the formal conventions of ancient Near Eastern wisdom literature. Like other wisdom literature, it stresses the act-consequence relationship. But the theological perspective of the book

---

[143]R. Murphy, "Religious Dimensions of Israelite Wisdom," in *Ancient Israelite Wisdom* ed. P. D. Miller, Jr. et al. (Philadelphia: Fortress, 1987), 452-56.

[144]Murphy, "Religious Dimensions," 452. He comments that the word רֵאשִׁית in 1:7 is properly rendered "beginning" and not "best part."

[145]B. K. Waltke, "The Book of Proverbs and Old Testament Theology," *BSac* 136 (1979): 302-17.

is uniquely Israelite and is in agreement with the theology of the Torah. Proverbs must be interpreted in the context of the whole biblical canon.

3. How do Proverbs and the other biblical wisdom literature relate to the rest of the Old Testament and its theological outlook?

Old Testament theologians have stumbled at the point of integrating wisdom literature into the rest of the Old Testament. Theological themes that seem promising as unifying threads for the rest of the Old Testament are found to be cut short where Proverbs and Ecclesiastes are concerned.[146] No single "center" proposed for the Old Testament has shown itself to be able to incorporate all the texts, genres, and motifs of the Old Testament.[147]

Perhaps the literary distinction between covenant texts and wisdom texts is helpful here. A great deal of the Old Testament is primarily concerned with aspects of the covenant between God and Israel. The history, stipulations, rituals, and kerygma of the covenant dominate the Old Testament, as they should.[148] The primary purpose of the Old Testament is to bring people into fellowship with God.

Wisdom, however, tells its followers how to live in this world. Its teachings allow the willing heart to acquire "a disciplined and prudent life" (Prov 1:3). Submission to the Lord is not excluded; to the contrary, it stands at the very center. Nevertheless, the question of salvation is more a matter for covenantal texts, not wisdom literature.

This does not mean that wisdom is inferior to covenant theology or that wisdom only becomes genuinely biblical when it has been subordinated to the Torah and related to salvation history.[149] This approach to wisdom is found as early as Sirach and as recently as W. Eichrodt[150] and G. E. Wright.[151] Von Rad also, though in a different way, subordinated wisdom to covenant; he

[146]Cf. J. F. Priest, "Where Is Wisdom to Be Placed?" in Crenshaw, *Studies* 281-88. See also B. K. Waltke, "The Book of Proverbs and Old Testament Theology," *BSac* 136 (1979): 302-3. Waltke rightly notes that even Kaiser's evangelical approach (W. Kaiser, Jr., *Toward an Old Testament Theology* [Grand Rapids: Zondervan, 1978]) fails here.

[147]See G. Hasel, *Old Testament Theology: Basic Issues in the Current Debate*, rev. ed. (Grand Rapids: Eerdmans, 1972), 77-103.

[148]Each of these aspects of covenant literature is represented, respectively, by Genesis, Deuteronomy, Leviticus, and the Prophets.

[149]The notion that wisdom is nonhistorical and therefore problematic disappears if it is recognized that not all wisdom is academic (e.g., Proverbs) and that some is narrative (e.g., Ruth).

[150]W. Eichrodt, *Theology of the Old Testament* (Philadelphia: Westminster, 1967), 2:83-91. Eichrodt argues that Sirach and the Wisdom of Solomon are at the end of a process of Israel's assimilation of pagan wisdom to its faith.

[151]G. E. Wright, *God Who Acts* (Chicago: Alec R. Allenson, 1952), 103-5. Wright states that "Proverbs has the important function of supplying an explanation of the meaning of the law for individual life" (p. 104). Cf. F. M. Wilson, "Sacred and Profane? The Yahwistic Redaction of Proverbs Reconsidered," *Listening Heart*, 315. Wilson notes that Wright believes that wisdom "dehistoricizes" Israelite faith.

described wisdom as Israel's "response."[152] But it is a false approach that makes one part of the Bible the grid for another part. A true Old Testament theology must take wisdom into account from the very beginning.[153]

Covenant and wisdom stand together as the two pillars of Old Testament theology. They are the twin guides to life. To be sure, a great deal of overlap is present.[154] Many wisdom precepts are also to be found in covenantal texts, and many wisdom texts relate to salvation history. Deuteronomy calls the reader to the love of God but along the way gives him or her a great deal of practical guidance. Proverbs teaches the reader about the world but begins with the premise that the fear of God is the highest wisdom. To put it another way, the one is God coming to humankind with covenant love and divine authority, but the other is the sage counseling the disciple to begin the quest for discernment by submitting to God.[155]

Covenant and wisdom share the same essential beliefs. Proverbs 1–9 presents the theological framework in which the student is urged to pursue wisdom's benefits.[156] The fear of God, the rejection of temptations to easy gratification, and the acknowledgment that the world is God's creation are the foundations. The theological presuppositions in wisdom are the same as those of the covenantal texts.[157] Covenant and wisdom are therefore in theological agreement but belong to different genres and have distinct purposes. The distinction is primarily literary, but even a literary difference can cause significant differences in content.

4. Does Proverbs teach or endorse a theology that asserts that the rich are righteous and favored by God but the poor are evil, lazy, and only getting what they deserve?

Gottwald has noted that, "generously reckoned," no more than one third of the proverbs on wealth and poverty support the teaching that the poor have received what they deserve. He observes that a large number of proverbs, however, deal with social and economic oppression and in effect teach that the rich have stolen from the poor.[158]

---

[152]G. von Rad, *Old Testament Theology* (New York: Harper, 1962), 418-53.

[153]Cf. Wilson, "Sacred and Profane?" 314-17.

[154]Cf. B. Childs, *Old Testament Theology in a Canonical Context* (Philadelphia: Fortress, 1985), 210-12.

[155]See W. Zimmerli, "Zur Struktur der alttestamentlichen Weisheit," *ZAW* 10 (1933): 177-204, trans. B. Kovacs and reprinted in Crenshaw, *Studies*, 175-99. Zimmerli rightly notes that the divine commands in Deuteronomy are to be distinguished from the counsels of Proverbs. He is incorrect, however, in his assertion that "counsel" here is regarded as open to debate and modification. On that point see B. Gemser, "The Spiritual Structure of Biblical Aphoristic Wisdom," in *Adhuc Loquitur* (Leiden: Brill, 1968), 138-49, reprinted in Crenshaw, *Studies*, 208-19 (note especially pp. 214-16).

[156]Childs, *Old Testament*, 557-58.

[157]See Waltke, "Proverbs and Old Testament Theology," 304-17.

[158]Gottwald, *Hebrew Bible*, 573.

On the other hand, it is not correct to say, as Gottwald has, that the wisdom teachers were caught in a "class contradiction" that gave them the divided loyalty of both giving philosophic support to the system that sustained them and observing honestly the oppression and injustice around them.[159] The warnings that laziness precedes poverty are not meant to justify the position of the rich but to inspire the reader to diligence and economic prudence.

Proverbs does not support the often alleged maxim that the Israelites believed that the rich are righteous and favored by God but the poor are sinners and under his punishment. This assessment is a poor caricature of biblical wisdom.

The problem here is not with the Bible but with our failure to grasp the hermeneutics of wisdom literature. By its very nature and purpose, wisdom emphasizes the general truth over some specific cases and, being a work of instruction, frames its teachings in short, pithy statements without excessive qualification. It is not that the wisdom writers did not know that life was complex and full of exceptions, but dwelling on those cases would have distracted attention from their didactic purposes. It is general truth that those who fear God and live with diligence and integrity will have lives that are prosperous and peaceful but that those who are lazy and untrustworthy ultimately destroy themselves. And general truths are the stock in trade of Proverbs.

5. What is the message of Proverbs concerning education and learning?

In the final analysis Proverbs is a book of education. It is the textbook of Israelite *paideia* (Greek, "education").[160] What is the Hebrew ideal of education? This is a large question indeed, but a few points can be noted.

First, Proverbs does not subordinate the education of the individual to the needs of the state. This is remarkably different from the later Greek *paideia.* For the Greeks devotion to the *polis* ("state") was a fundamental element of education. Young Athenians were taught to love and defend their city, participate in their democracy, and exult in their culture. Plato, in the *Republic*, carried this concept to the extreme, but it was not unique to him; it was at the heart of his civilization. In Proverbs, however, such notions scarcely surface at all. Patriotism is not regarded as evil, but no attempt is made to glorify Israelite culture. Instead, everything is subordinate to the Israelite God. If God is honored, all will be well with the state; if he is not, things will not go well. "Righteousness exalts a nation,/ but sin is a disgrace to any people" (Prov 14:34).

---

[159]Ibid., 574.

[160]Heb. מוּסָר. Though little is known about education in ancient Israel, see J. Crenshaw, "Education in Ancient Israel," *JBL* 104,4 (1985): 601-15, and the entry by A. Lemaire, "Education," in ABD, vol. 2, ed. D. N. Freedman (New York: Doubleday, 1992): 301-12.

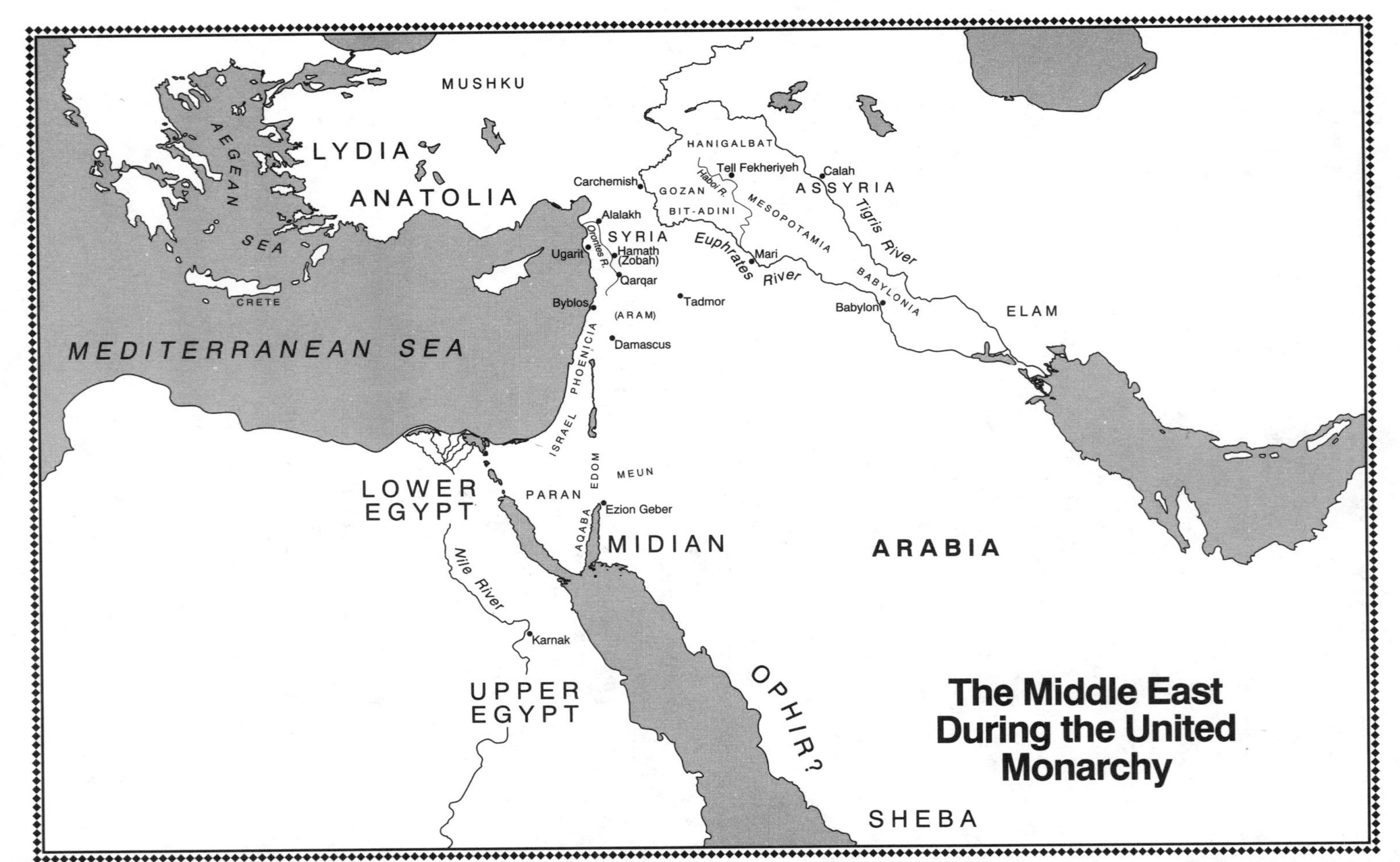
The Middle East During the United Monarchy
MUSHKU
AEGEAN SEA
LYDIA
ANATOLIA
CRETE
MEDITERRANEAN SEA
Carchemish
Alalakh
SYRIA
Ugarit
Orontes R.
Hamath (Zobah)
Qarqar
Byblos
(ARAM)
Damascus
Tadmor
PHOENICIA
ISRAEL
EDOM
MEUN
PARAN
Ezion Geber
AQABA
MIDIAN
LOWER EGYPT
Nile River
Karnak
UPPER EGYPT
OPHIR?
SHEBA
ARABIA
HANIGALBAT
Tell Fekheriyeh
Habor R.
GOZAN
BIT-ADINI
MESOPOTAMIA
Euphrates River
Mari
Calah
ASSYRIA
Tigris River
BABYLONIA
Babylon
ELAM

Second, Israelite wisdom does not promote any particular occupation or trade. This contrasts with Egyptian instructional literature, particularly the *Satire on the Trades* (which endorses the scribal trade). Proverbs is directed more toward aristocratic youth, but no hierarchy of trades is implied and no licit occupation is regarded as degrading. Agriculture (10:5), government (11:14), and business (31:18-24) are all esteemed. Only laziness is condemned (24:30-34).

Third, education is primarily the task of the parents. The family is the first and best school (Deut 6:4-9). The son is exhorted to heed his mother and father (23:22-25), and the parents are commanded to invest time and attention in their children (29:15,17).

Finally, biblical wisdom stresses the limitations of human knowledge. The gulf between human perception and divine reality is never really closed. The sage is commanded to go about his task with humility and reverence for God. The learned must never forget their limitations (30:2-4) and that they are prone to error and conceit. Above all, they must subordinate their quest to the Word of God. For "every word of God is flawless" (30:5).

OUTLINE OF PROVERBS

I. The Book of Solomon (1:1–24:34)
   1. Title (1:1)
   2. Prologue (1:2-7)
   3. Main Text, Discourse Form (1:8–9:18)
      (1) The First Exhortation (1:8-19)
      (2) The First Appeal of Wisdom (1:20-33)
      (3) The Second Exhortation (2:1-22)
      (4) The Third Exhortation (3:1-35)
      (5) The Fourth Exhortation: A Father's Plea (4:1-27)
      (6) The Fifth Exhortation (5:1-23)
      (7) The Four Teachings (6:1-19)
      (8) The Sixth Exhortation (6:20-35)
      (9) The Seventh Exhortation (7:1-27)
      (10) The Second Appeal of Wisdom (8:1-36)
      (11) The Two Appeals (9:1-18)
   4. Main Text, Proverb Form (10:1–24:22)
      (1) Subheading (10:1a)
      (2) A Diligent Son and a Lazy Son (10:1b-5)
      (3) The Mouth of the Wicked (10:6-11)

(4) Seven-Proverb Collection (10:12-18)
(5) On the Tongue, Personal Security, and Laziness (10:19-32)
(6) What the Lord Abhors (11:1-21)
(7) Beauty without Discretion (11:22)
(8) Generosity and Selfishness (11:23-27)
(9) The Source of Life (11:28–12:4)
(10) Plans and Schemes (12:5-7)
(11) Earned Respect (12:8)
(12) On Providing for One's Needs (12:9-11)
(13) On Fruit and Snares (12:12-14)
(14) Able to Take Advice (12:15)
(15) The Use and Abuse of Words (12:16-22)
(16) A Wholesome Life (12:23-28)
(17) The Use of the Mouth (13:1-4)
(18) Action and Reaction (13:5-6)
(19) The Ambiguity of Riches (13:7-11)
(20) A Hope Fulfilled (13:12-19)
(21) Choice Companions (13:20-21)
(22) Provision for the Family (13:22-25)
(23) Self-protective and Self-destructive Behavior (14:1-3)
(24) A Worthwhile Investment (14:4)
(25) Look Who's Talking (14:5-7)
(26) Appearance and Reality (14:8-15)
(27) A Patient Spirit (14:16-17)
(28) A Crown of Wisdom, A Wreath of Folly (14:18-24)
(29) An Honest Witness (14:25)
(30) The Fear of the Lord (14:26-27)
(31) National Security (14:28-35)
(32) Two Collections (15:1–16:8)
(33) Three Collections (16:9–17:1)
(34) Remarks on Behavior (17:2-8)
(35) Four Conjoined Collections (17:9-26)
(36) Appropriate Use of Words (17:27–18:4)
(37) Further Comments on Listening to Evil Talk (18:5-8)
(38) Security (18:9-12)
(39) Two Proverbs (18:13-14)
(40) Justice and the Courts (18:15-19)
(41) The Power of Words (18:20-21)
(42) Diverse Teachings (18:22–20:4)
(43) Various Proverbs (20:5–21:8)
(44) Under One Roof (21:9-19)
(45) Rewards for Doing Right (21:20-22)
(46) A Mouth in and out of Control (21:23-24)

(47) The Sluggard's Craving (21:25-26)
(48) Trying to Fool God (21:27)
(49) The False Witness (21:28-29)
(50) Counterwisdom (21:30-31)
(51) A Good Name (22:1)
(52) Wealth, Poverty, and a Prudent Life (22:2-5)
(53) Various Proverbs (22:6-16)
(54) The Thirty Sayings (22:17–24:22)
(55) On the Courts and on Laziness (24:23-33)

II. "Hezekiah" (25:1–29:27)
1. "Hezekiah" (25:1)
2. On Dealing with Kings (25:2-7)
3. Settling Disputes without Litigation (25:8-10)
4. Fine Jewelry and the Counsel (25:11-12)
5. Reliable and Unreliable People (25:13-14)
6. Be Patient with the Authorities (25:15)
7. Exercising Caution with People (25:16-27)
    (1) Enough Is Enough (25:16-17)
    (2) Beware of These People (25:18-20)
    (3) Strange but True (25:21-22)
    (4) Cold Rain and Cold Looks (25:23)
    (5) A Nagging Wife (25:24)
    (6) Good Water and Bad Water (25:25-26)
    (7) Sweets for the Body and Sweets for the Mind (25:27)
8. Portrait of a Fool (25:28–26:12)
9. Portrait of a Sluggard (26:13-16)
10. Portrait of a Busybody (26:17-22)
11. Portrait of a Liar (26:23-28)
12. Boasting and Praise (27:1-2)
13. Unbearable Personalities (27:3-4)
14. Honest Friendship (27:5-6)
15. Real Friends, Close at Hand (27:7-10)
16. Fatherly Advice (27:11-27)
17. A Life of Fear (28:1)
18. The Distortions Evil Causes (28:2)
19. Oppression, Keeping in the Right Way, and the Law (28:3-11)
20. Various Proverbs (28:12–29:27)
    (1) Good Government and Bad Government I (28:12)
    (2) Turning from Sin (28:13-14)
    (3) Tyranny (28:15-16)
    (4) Guilt and Innocence (28:17-18)
    (5) Prosperity by Fair Means and Foul (28:19-27)
    (6) Good Government and Bad Government II (28:28–29:2)

(7) Squandering Wealth and Squandering a Nation (29:3-4)
(8) Beware of the Traps (29:5-6)
(9) Concern for Justice (29:7)
(10) Order in the Court and in Society (29:8-11)
(11) The Throne Secured by Righteousness (29:12-14)
(12) Discipline at Home and in the Nation (29:15-18)
(13) Controlling the Servant and Controlling the Self (29:19-22)
(14) The First Shall Be Last (29:23)
(15) A Poor Choice for a Friend (29:24)
(16) Seek Deliverance from God (29:25-26)
(17) The Sum of It All (29:27)

III. The Sayings of Agur (30:1-33)
1. Title (30:1a)
2. The Limits of Human Understanding (30:1b-6)
3. Main Body (30:7-33)
(1) A Prayer of Humility (30:7-9)
(2) Respect for the Menial Worker (30:10)
(3) The Lowest Forms of Life (30:11-14)
(4) Two Sayings on Insatiable Things (30:15-16)
(5) The Fate of the Parent-Hater (30:17)
(6) A Riddle and a Clue (30:18-20)
(7) Unbearable People (30:21-23)
(8) Learn from the Animals (30:24-28)
(9) Royal Animals (30:29-31)
(10) Troublemakers Beware (30:32-33)

IV. The Sayings of Lemuel (31:1-31)
1. Title (31:1)
2. Main Body (31:2-31)
(1) Three Lessons for a King (31:2-9)
(2) The Good Wife (31:10-31)

SECTION OUTLINE

I. THE BOOK OF SOLOMON (1:1–24:34)
   1. Title (1:1)
   2. Prologue (1:2-7)
   3. Main Text, Discourse Form (1:8–9:18)
      (1) First Exhortation (1:8-19)
      (2) First Appeal of Wisdom (1:20-33)
      (3) Second Exhortation (2:1-22)
         The Protasis (2:1-4)
         The Apodosis (2:5-11)
         The Two Tempters (2:12-19)
         Concluding Summation (2:20-22)
      (4) The Third Exhortation (3:1-35)
         Opening Parental Appeal (3:1-4)
         True Piety (3:5-12)
         A Hymn to Wisdom (3:13-18)
         Wisdom and Creation (3:19-20)
         A Second Parental Appeal (3:21-26)
         Four Prohibitions against Infidelity (3:27-30)
         A Prohibition against Criminal Behavior (3:31-35)
      (5) The Fourth Exhortation: A Father's Plea (4:1-27)
         First Appeal (4:1-9)
         Second Appeal (4:10-19)
         Third Appeal (4:20-27)
      (6) The Fifth Exhortation (5:1-23)
         First Strophe (5:1-6)
         Second Strophe (5:7-14)
         Third Strophe (5:15-19)
         Fourth Strophe (5:20-23)
      (7) Four Teachings (6:1-19)
         Legal Entanglements (6:1-5)
         Laziness (6:6-11)
         The Conspirator (6:12-15)
         Israel's Seven Deadly Sins (6:16-19)
      (8) The Sixth Exhortation (6:20-35)
      (9) The Seventh Exhortation (7:1-27)
         The Paternal Appeal (7:1-5)
         A Sad Example (7:6-23)
         A Concluding Appeal (7:24-27)

(10) Second Appeal of Wisdom (8:1-36)
First Strophe (8:1-3)
Second Strophe (8:4-11)
Third Strophe (8:12-16)
Fourth Strophe (8:17-21)
Fifth Strophe (8:22-31)
Sixth Strophe (8:32-36)
Excursus: The Person of Wisdom in Proverbs 8
(11) The Two Appeals (9:1-18)
Woman Wisdom's Appeal (9:1-12)
Woman Folly's Appeal (9:13-18)
4. Main Text, Proverb Form (10:1–24:22)
(1) Subheading (10:1a)
(2) A Diligent Son and a Lazy Son (10:1b-5)
(3) The Mouth of the Wicked (10:6-11)
(4) Seven-Proverb Collection (10:12-18)
(5) On the Tongue, Personal Security, and Laziness (10:19-32)
Three-Proverb Collection (10:19-21)
Four-Proverb Collection (10:22-25)
Single Proverb (10:26)
Four-Proverb Collection (10:27-30)
Two-Proverb Collection (10:31-32)
(6) What the Lord Abhors (11:1-21)
Moral Integrity and God's Judgment (11:1-4)
Salvation for the Righteous (11:5-6)
Death of a Sinner (11:7-8)
Destructive Lips (11:9-13)
National and Personal Prudence (11:14-15)
Kindness and Cruelty (11:16-17)
The Wages of Sin and Righteousness (11:18-19)
Divine Judgment (11:20-21)
(7) Beauty without Discretion (11:22)
(8) Generosity and Selfishness (11:23-27)
(9) The Source of Life (11:28–12:4)
(10) Plans and Schemes (12:5-7)
(11) Earned Respect (12:8)
(12) On Providing for One's Needs (12:9-11)
(13) On Fruit and Snares (12:12-14)
(14) Able to Take Advice (12:15)
(15) The Use and Abuse of Words (12:16-22)
(16) A Wholesome Life (12:23-28)
(17) The Use of the Mouth (13:1-4)
(18) Action and Reaction (13:5-6)
(19) The Ambiguity of Riches (13:7-11)

(20) A Hope Fulfilled (13:12-19)
(21) Choice Companions (13:20-21)
(22) Provision for the Family (13:22-25)
(23) Self-protective and Self-destructive Behavior (14:1-3)
(24) A Worthwhile Investment (14:4)
(25) Look Who's Talking (14:5-7)
(26) Appearance and Reality (14:8-15)
(27) A Patient Spirit (14:16-17)
(28) A Crown of Wisdom, A Wreath of Folly (14:18-24)
(29) An Honest Witness (14:25)
(30) The Fear of the Lord (14:26-27)
(31) National Security (14:28-35)
(32) Two Collections (15:1–16:8)
(33) Three Collections (16:9–17:1)
(34) Remarks on Behavior (17:2-8)
(35) Four Conjoined Collections (17:9-26)
The Social and Antisocial (17:9-13)
Quick to Quarrel (17:14-19)
Heart and Family (17:20-22)
Justice and Family (17:23-26)
(36) Appropriate Use of Words (17:27–18:4)
(37) Further Comments on Listening to Evil Talk (18:5-8)
(38) Security (18:9-12)
(39) Two Proverbs (18:13-14)
(40) Justice and the Courts (18:15-19)
(41) The Power of Words (18:20-21)
(42) Diverse Teachings (18:22–20:4)
(43) Various Proverbs (20:5–21:8)
Discernment and Integrity (20:5-12)
Various Proverbs (20:13-21)
Dealing with the King and with the Lord (20:22–21:3)
The Devices and the Decline of the Wicked (21:4-8)
(44) Under One Roof (21:9-19)
(45) Rewards for Doing Right (21:20-22)
(46) A Mouth in and out of Control (21:23-24)
(47) The Sluggard's Craving (21:25-26)
(48) Trying to Fool God (21:27)
(49) The False Witness (21:28-29)
(50) Counterwisdom (21:30-31)
(51) A Good Name (22:1)
(52) Wealth, Poverty, and a Prudent Life (22:2-5)
(53) Various Proverbs (22:6-16)
(54) The Thirty Sayings (22:17–24:22)
Introduction (22:17-21)

Saying One (22:22-23)
Saying Two (22:24-25)
Saying Three (22:26-27)
Saying Four (22:28)
Saying Five (22:29)
Saying Six (23:1-3)
Saying Seven (23:4-5)
Saying Eight (23:6-8)
Saying Nine (23:9)
Saying Ten (23:10-11)
Saying Eleven (23:12)
Saying Twelve (23:13-14)
Saying Thirteen (23:15-16)
Saying Fourteen (23:17-18)
Saying Fifteen (23:19-21)
Saying Sixteen (23:22-25)
Saying Seventeen (23:26-28)
Saying Eighteen (23:29-35)
Saying Nineteen (24:1-2)
Saying Twenty (24:3-4)
Saying Twenty-one (24:5-6)
Saying Twenty-two (24:7)
Saying Twenty-three (24:8-9)
Saying Twenty-four (24:10)
Saying Twenty-five (24:11-12)
Saying Twenty-six (24:13-14)
Saying Twenty-seven (24:15-16)
Saying Twenty-eight (24:17-18)
Saying Twenty-nine (24:19-20)
Saying Thirty (24:21-22)

(55) On the Courts and on Laziness (24:23-34)

I. THE BOOK OF SOLOMON (1:1–24:34)

1. Title (1:1)

[1]The proverbs of Solomon son of David, king of Israel:

1:1 See the Introduction for remarks on the historical reliability of the title. The book is said to consist of "proverbs." The Hebrew term[1] has

[1]מָשָׁל can mean "comparison," "taunt," "proverb," or "ethical teaching." A. R. Johnson, "*mashal,*" *VTSup* 3 (1969): 162-69. See also *BDB*, 605, and *TWOT*, s.v. מָשָׁל, 1:533-34.

a wider meaning than the English, but the title does not mean that everything in the book would be called a "proverb."

2. Prologue (1:2-7)

2For attaining wisdom and discipline;
for understanding words of insight;
3for acquiring a disciplined and prudent life,
doing what is right and just and fair;
4for giving prudence to the simple,
knowledge and discretion to the young—
5let the wise listen and add to their learning,
and let the discerning get guidance—
6for understanding proverbs and parables,
the sayings and riddles of the wise.

7The fear of the LORD is the beginning of knowledge,
but fools despise wisdom and discipline.

1:2-7 The prologue challenges the reader to commit himself to the mastery of this book. It offers the significant benefit of acquiring the key to attaining capability in life. By this book, one can learn the principles that determine success or failure in the major arenas of human activity, including business, personal relationships, family life, and community life. Verses 2-6 describe the purpose of the book, that is, to teach wisdom to the reader. The primary purpose of Proverbs is the instruction of young people and those who have yet to learn wisdom (v. 4),[2] but it is not only for children. Those who are already mature and learned (v. 5) also have a great deal to learn from this book, and they should not shun it as unworthy of their time.

The vocabulary of this section indicates four characteristics of biblical wisdom. First, it is *practical.* "Wisdom"[3] includes the idea of "common sense" and the ability to cope with daily problems and can also refer to occupational skills (Exod 28:3; Ps 107:27). Second, it is *intellectual.* This is implied in words like "understanding" and "knowledge."[4] Solomon's own fascination with natural history illustrates this (1 Kgs 4:33).[5] Third,

---

[2]The book gives every indication of having been composed with boys and young men in mind. Besides the constant reference to the reader as "my son," the warning not to join gangs (1:10-19) and the admonition to avoid prostitutes (7:1-27) indicate the identity of the intended audience. The principles involved, however, apply to girls and young women as well. The selfish pursuit of gain or gratification is always wrong and self-destructive. The penalties of folly and the rewards of wisdom are the same for women and men.

[3]For a good survey of the meanings of חָכְמָה, see *TWOT*, s.v. חָכַם (1.282-84).

[4]While it is true that neither בִּינָה nor דַּעַת is exclusively intellectual in the Western sense, such a nuance is appropriate to this context.

[5]This is not to say that "knowledge" here refers to science as we understand it. Rather, the wise man of the Bible seeks to understand the principles that govern the world, and no rigid boundary between natural science and ethical categories is maintained. Cf. Prov 30:24-31.

it is *moral* and involves *self-control.* This is indicated in words like "right and fair"[6] and "discipline."[7]

Fourth, Proverbs draws the reader into the *mysteries of life.* This is implied in terms like "parables"[8] and "riddles." The ancients were intrigued at riddles (Judg 14:12-19), but more is involved here than casual entertainment. Biblical wisdom seeks to resolve or at least adjust to the ambiguities of life. It seeks the reality behind the appearances."[9] Not only that, it affirms that the believer can understand mysteries that outsiders cannot and so may couch its teaching in enigma (Matt 13:10-17).

Verse 7 ties the fundamental principle of biblical wisdom ("The fear[10] of the Lord is the beginning of knowledge") to recognition that many will reject wisdom and God ("fools despise wisdom"). A principle that believers must teach their children is that in their pursuit of wisdom they will be surrounded by others going the opposite direction who will be encouraging them to do likewise. In this fashion the polarity of the entire Book of Proverbs—the way of the wise and the way of the fool—is introduced. The reader faces the alternatives and is challenged to attain wisdom through the fear of God.

3. Main Text, Discourse Form (1:8–9:18)

(1) First Exhortation (1:8-19)

8Listen, my son, to your father's instruction
and do not forsake your mother's teaching.
9They will be a garland to grace your head
and a chain to adorn your neck.

10My son, if sinners entice you,
do not give in to them.
11If they say, "Come along with us;
let's lie in wait for someone's blood,
let's waylay some harmless soul;
12let's swallow them alive, like the grave,

---

[6]צֶדֶק וּמִשְׁפָּט here serve as a hendiadys to indicate the whole world of moral concerns.

[7]מוּסָר occurs thirty-six times in Proverbs and is thus a key concept in the "education" the book advocates. See *TWOT*, s.v. יָסַר (1.386-87).

[8]מְלִיצָה is appropriately rendered "parable" or "allusive saying" rather than "taunt." Cf. W. Holladay, *A Concise Hebrew and Aramaic Lexicon of the Old Testament* (Grand Rapids: Eerdmans, 1971), 198, and F. Delitzsch, *A Biblical Commentary on the Proverbs of Solomon* (Edinburgh: T & T Clark, 1875), 1:57-58.

[9]חִידָה is used of Samson's riddle in Judg 14:12-19, but a more appropriate comparison to the usage here is Ps 49:5, where the wealth and power of the ungodly is a חִידָה.

[10]The rabbis distinguish two types of "fear" of God: reverence and fear of retribution. Curiously, they consider the second to be meant here. See A. Cohen, "Proverbs," rev., A. J. Rosenberg, *The Soncino Bible* (London: Soncino Press, 1985), 3.

and whole, like those who go down to the pit;
[13]we will get all sorts of valuable things
and fill our houses with plunder;
[14]throw in your lot with us,
and we will share a common purse"—
[15]my son, do not go along with them,
do not set foot on their paths;
[16]for their feet rush into sin,
they are swift to shed blood.
[17]How useless to spread a net
in full view of all the birds!
[18]These men lie in wait for their own blood;
they waylay only themselves!
[19]Such is the end of all who go after ill-gotten gain;
it takes away the lives of those who get it.

1:8-19 Proverbs does not begin its instruction with lofty or abstract analysis but with a simple and straightforward appeal for the reader to reject association with criminals. From the very outset, therefore, this book is grounded in the lives and problems of real people. Apparently in ancient Israel, no less than in the modern world, the comradeship, easy money, and feeling of empowerment offered by gangs was a strong temptation to the young man who felt overwhelmed by the difficulties of the life he confronted every day. The lesson for the modern church, that it should clearly and directly address real life and real temptations, is evident.

Verses 8-9 are an introductory appeal to the young man to stay on the right path. Verse 8 is an admonition, and v. 9 a promise of reward[11] if the admonition is heeded. Verse 10 is a summary prohibition in two parts: v. 10a is the protasis (if a gang appeals for you to join them), and v. 10b is the prohibition (do not do it). Verses 11-14 expound upon the protasis; the gang appeals to the young man to join them with a promise of easy money. Verses 15-18 expound upon the prohibition with the warning that the gang members are all headed for an early grave. Verse 19 is a concluding warning about a life of crime.

The structure of the exhortation strengthens its message. The text presents the position of the young person between the alternative appeals of the gang and warnings of the teacher in vv. 11-18, a section marked off by an inclusio.[12] The steady repetition of "we" and "us" in the gang's

[11]The garland and chain are the adornments of wisdom and symbolize health and prosperity. Some read "and a golden chain" on the basis of the LXX, the Arabic, and a Palestinian lectionary. See D. W. Thomas, "Notes on Some Passages in the Book of Proverbs," *VT* 15 (1965): 271.

[12]Note נֶאֶרְבָה ("let's lie in wait") and נִצְפְּנָה ("let's waylay") in v. 11 and יֶאֱרֹבוּ ("they lie in wait") and יִצְפְּנוּ ("they waylay") in v. 18.

appeal graphically portrays the peer pressure to which a young person is susceptible. At the same time, the ironic language of the teacher persuasively shows that the gang is on a suicidal path.

The heart of the warning is that crime is self-destructive. This first appears in the irony of v. 12, in which the gang wants to be "like the grave" and swallow their victims "whole, like those who go down to the pit." The intended meaning is that *the gang* would be "like the grave"[13] and that *the victims* would be like those who descend to it. "Like those who go down to the pit," however, is in parallel to "like the grave" and would normally be taken to have the same referent. This throws an ambiguity into the text as the reader senses that in fact the gang members have unwittingly put themselves in the position of "those who go down to the pit." The ambiguity continues in v. 16. The feet of the gang members "rush into sin," but the Hebrew could be translated "rush into trouble," meaning they get themselves into trouble.[14]

Verse 17 is confusing as translated in the NIV and most versions. Even if one is willing to admit that a bird is intelligent enough to recognize the purpose of a trap when it sees it (which is doubtful), the proverb has no point in context. In addition, the Hebrew cannot sustain the translation "spread a net."[15] The line is best rendered, "In the eyes of a bird, the net is strewn [with grain] for no reason." In other words, the bird does not see any connection between the net and what is scattered on it; he just sees food that is free for the taking. In the process he is trapped and killed. In the same way, the gang cannot see the connection between their acts of robbery and the fate that entraps them.

In vv. 18-19 the teacher brings his point home: the gang members are really ambushing themselves. The very reverse of their proposal in v. 11 has come about. Also, v. 19 concludes, it will ever be that way.

(2) First Appeal of Wisdom (1:20-33)

20Wisdom calls aloud in the street,
she raises her voice in the public squares;
21at the head of the noisy streets she cries out,
in the gateways of the city she makes her speech:

---

[13]See Hab 2:5 for comparable imagery.

[14]The word רַע essentially means "bad," but it can mean anything from "evil" to "personal disaster."

[15]זרה means to "spread," but not in the sense "to stretch out a net." G. R. Driver ("Problems in the Hebrew Text of Proverbs," *Bib* 32 [1951]: 173-74) argues that this is from a root מזר, "to compress or draw tight," cognate with *zwr* or *zrr* from other Semitic languages. He emends the form here to מְזֻטוּרָה and translates, "In vain is the net drawn tight in the sight of any winged fowl." More plausibly, D. W. Thomas ("Textual and Philological Notes on Some Passages in the Book of Proverbs," in *Wisdom in Israel and the Ancient Near East, VTSup* III [1969]: 281-82) argues the זרה here means "winnow," "scatter," or "sow."

22"How long will you simple ones love your simple ways?
How long will mockers delight in mockery
and fools hate knowledge?
23If you had responded to my rebuke,
I would have poured out my heart to you
and made my thoughts known to you.
24But since you rejected me when I called
and no one gave heed when I stretched out my hand,
25since you ignored all my advice
and would not accept my rebuke,
26I in turn will laugh at your disaster;
I will mock when calamity overtakes you—
27when calamity overtakes you like a storm,
when disaster sweeps over you like a whirlwind,
when distress and trouble overwhelm you.

28"Then they will call to me but I will not answer;
they will look for me but will not find me.
29Since they hated knowledge
and did not choose to fear the LORD,
30since they would not accept my advice
and spurned my rebuke,
31they will eat the fruit of their ways
and be filled with the fruit of their schemes.
32For the waywardness of the simple will kill them,
and the complacency of fools will destroy them;
33but whoever listens to me will live in safety
and be at ease, without fear of harm."

1:20-33 This section, the first direct appeal by personified Wisdom, has a chiastic structure.[16]

A Introduction: an appeal for listeners (vv. 20-21)
B Address to the untutored, scoffers, and fools (v. 22)
C Declaration of disclosure (v. 23)
D Reason for the announcement (vv. 24-25)
E Announcement of derisive judgment (vv. 26-28)
D′ Reason for the announcement (vv. 29-30)
C′ Declaration of retribution (v. 31)
B′ Fate of the untutored and fools (v. 32)
A′ Conclusion: an appeal for a hearer (v. 33)

[16]See P. Trible, "Wisdom Builds a Poem: The Architecture of Proverbs 1:20-33," *JBL* 94 (1975): 509-18. I have followed Trible's analysis with a few minor changes, the most significant is that I have placed v. 28 with section *E*. Trible places it in section *D*.

Perhaps the easiest and most common excuse for doing wrong and falling into trouble is ignorance, that one just did not know any better. That excuse is implicitly rejected here. Wisdom is not some hidden treasure that has to be dug from the depths of the earth (compare Job 28) or the sole possession of the lonely sage sitting atop a mountain. To the contrary, Wisdom roams the streets looking for someone to instruct. The ways of right and wrong, as presented in this word of God, are open for all to read and follow. At the same time, this section is a true appeal from the Spirit for whoever has ears to turn and listen. Wisdom's appeal in the streets (vv. 20-21) is matched by a promise in v. 33 to whoever will listen. Wisdom reproaches "simple ones" and "fools" for their love of folly and hatred of wisdom in v. 22 and warns in v. 32 that death awaits them.[17] The promise that fools would receive instruction if they turned to her (v. 23) is matched by the reality that they will suffer the consequences of ignoring her (v. 31). Wisdom repeats the cause[18] of the demise of the fools in vv. 24-25 and vv. 29-30: they rejected her.

Verses 26-28, an announcement of judgment upon those who reject Wisdom, is the center and climax of the text. Verses 26 and 28 present Wisdom as laughing when disaster strikes the fools and as turning away when they call to her, and v. 27 gives a threefold assurance that disaster will indeed come.[19]

The passage personifies Wisdom in especially vivid terms. Wisdom cries out to people in the streets, from the tops of walls,[20] and at the gates. She appeals to the foolish but then mocks them when the promised calamity falls upon them. They call upon her, as if praying to God, but like God she laughs and refuses to answer.[21] Wisdom is not abstract, secular, or academic but personal and theological. To reject wisdom is to reject God.

---

[17]Note פְּתָיִם ("simple ones") and כְּסִילִים ("fools") in vv. 22,32. Only לֵצִים ("mockers") in v. 22 has no parallel in v. 32. J. A. Emerton ("A Note on the Hebrew Text of Proverbs i. 22-3," *JTS* 19 [1968]: 609-14) emends vv. 22-23 to read, "How long, ye simple ones, will ye love simplicity?/ When will you turn to my reproof?" with v. 22b,c regarded as a separate proverb. But his arguments are not strong enough to sustain such an emendation, and his conclusion is invalidated by the parallel to v. 22 in v. 32.

[18]Observe that vv. 24-25 and vv. 29-30, respectively, begin with יַעַן ("because") and כִּי תַּחַת ("since") and contain common vocabulary (קרא ["call"], v. 24 and v. 29; עֲצָתִי ["my advice"], vv. 25,30; אבה ["accept"], vv. 25,30; and תּוֹכַחְתִּי ["my rebuke"], vv. 25,30).

[19]This, the only tricolon in the chapter, is emphatic. Cola *a* and *b* are in perfect chiasmus except that בְּבֹא, an infinitive construct, is matched by a finite verb (יֶאֱתֶה). Colon *c*, however, repeats בְּבֹא from colon *a* to complete the symmetry of the verse. Therefore, contrary to *BHS* note *c*, the third colon need not be deleted.

[20]Verse 21a should read "from the tops of the walls (חֹמוֹת instead of הֹמִיּוֹת, "murmuring [feminine plural participle]) she cries out" with the LXX and in parallel to v. 21b. See also M. Dahood, *Proverbs and Northwest Semitic Philology* (Rome: Pontifical Biblical Institute, 1963), 4-5.

[21]Compare Pss 2:4; 37:13; Mic 3:4.

On the other hand, Wisdom is a personification and not a person or a goddess. The statement that fools call on her when they get into trouble is not a reference to literal prayer but a dramatic picture of fools trying to find a way out of the trouble they are in. They "call on" her in the sense that they are at last ready to listen to advice, but it is too late. Their indifference[22] to Wisdom has already destroyed them (v. 32).

The security and freedom from fear that the wise enjoy (v. 33a) contrasts with the idle indifference of the foolish (vv. 32, 33b). The wise are at ease because they have genuine security; the foolish are at ease out of carelessness.

(3) Second Exhortation (2:1-22)

1My son, if you accept my words
and store up my commands within you,
2turning your ear to wisdom
and applying your heart to understanding,
3and if you call out for insight
and cry aloud for understanding,
4and if you look for it as for silver
and search for it as for hidden treasure,
5then you will understand the fear of the Lord
and find the knowledge of God.
6For the Lord gives wisdom,
and from his mouth come knowledge and understanding.
7He holds victory in store for the upright,
he is a shield to those whose walk is blameless,
8for he guards the course of the just
and protects the way of his faithful ones.

9Then you will understand what is right and just
and fair—every good path.
10For wisdom will enter your heart,
and knowledge will be pleasant to your soul.
11Discretion will protect you,
and understanding will guard you.

12Wisdom will save you from the ways of wicked men,
from men whose words are perverse,

[22]Dahood (*Proverbs*, 6-7) argues that instead of deriving מְשׁוּבַת from שׁוּב ("turn") and understanding it to mean "apostasy," it is better to treat it as a derivative of ישׁב ("sit") with the meaning "idleness," notwithstanding the fact that one would not expect an original first ו root to form a noun with this form. The context does not indicate that the persons are apostates—they had never embraced Wisdom at all. Note also the parallel שַׁלְוָה ("complacency"). If here, as elsewhere, this is a derivation of שׁוּב, it should not be taken to mean "apostasy" but the status of being perpetually turned away from wisdom, perhaps "contrary" or "indifferent."

[13]who leave the straight paths
to walk in dark ways,
[14]who delight in doing wrong
and rejoice in the perverseness of evil,
[15]whose paths are crooked
and who are devious in their ways.

[16]It will save you also from the adulteress,
from the wayward wife with her seductive words,
[17]who has left the partner of her youth
and ignored the covenant she made before God.
[18]For her house leads down to death
and her paths to the spirits of the dead.
[19]None who go to her return
or attain the paths of life.

[20]Thus you will walk in the ways of good men
and keep to the paths of the righteous.
[21]For the upright will live in the land,
and the blameless will remain in it;
[22]but the wicked will be cut off from the land,
and the unfaithful will be torn from it.

The young man faces two major temptations. The first is the temptation to violence and crime and to the feelings of power and easy money that way offers, and the second is to easy and apparently uncomplicated sexual pleasures offered by the prostitute. Both ways, however, have complications the young man cannot see, complications that will drag him to his death.

This whole text hinges on an enormous "if" clause (vv. 1-4). The "if" represents a decision that every young man must make. He can either go in the way of Wisdom and find life, true love, and most importantly God, or he can turn his back on her and find only bitterness, isolation, and death. One cannot opt out of making this decision or choose a little of one and a little of the other. If the church, however, fails to present this stark decision to young people, many will go in the wrong way and never even know they had a choice.

This exhortation is made up of a lengthy protasis (condition) marked by the repetition of the word for "if"[23] (vv. 1-4), a twofold apodosis (the result) marked by the repetition of the word for "then"[24] (vv. 5-11), and promises of protection from the two tempters (vv. 12-15,16-19), each begun in the Hebrew text with words meaning "save you."[25] Verses 20-22, introduced by the word for "thus,"[26] serve as a concluding summation.

[23]אִם, vv. 1,3-4.
[24]אָז, vv. 5,9.
[25]One word in Heb., לְהַצִּילְךָ, vv. 12,16.
[26]לְמַעַן.

THE PROTASIS (2:1-4). **2:1-4** The protasis (i.e., the subordinate section of a sentence), in three conditional clauses, describes the attitudes the reader ought to bring to the quest for Wisdom. First, the student should listen attentively to the teacher (vv. 1-2). That is, he must accept the teachings as valid, commit them to memory, and focus all his attention on them.[27] Second, he must yearn for Wisdom in a way analogous to that of the supplicant pleading to God or the king for deliverance from trouble (v. 3).[28] Third, he must seek it as one seeks for lost money or hidden treasure (v. 4; Job 28; cf. Luke 15:8-10).

THE APODOSIS (2:5-11). **2:5-11** The apodosis is in two parts (vv. 5-8, 9-11), each of which begins with the word translated "then."[29] Both parts describe the greater insight that comes from Wisdom, but the first emphasizes understanding of God and his ways, while the second focuses on proper and careful behavior in life.

The theological discernment of vv. 5-8 is specifically the ability to see God's care for his people. The fool sees no evidence of this, but the one who is wise understands that God gives success[30] and protection to the pious. An alternative translation of vv. 7-8 is possible: "He will treasure up[31] success for the upright. He will be a shield for those who walk in integrity, for the one who keeps[32] the paths of justice. And the way of his pious ones[33] he will guard."

Verses 9-11 describe the moral discernment by which the wise both escape immoral behavior and gain competence. In v. 9 Wisdom gives a strong sense of personal ethics to her followers; they will know "what is right and just and fair."[34] These terms describe both integrity and an even-handed way of dealing with other people. Verses 10-11 assert that

---

[27]The word for "heart" (לֵב) here, parallel to "ear," refers to faculties of perception. Cf. C. Toy, *A Critical and Exegetical Commentary on the Book of Proverbs*, ICC (Edinburgh: T & T Clark, 1977), 33.

[28]Cf. the use of קָרָא ("call") in Ps 4:2 (Eng. 4:1) and Prov 21:13.

[29]אָז.

[30]In v. 7 "success" is perhaps a better translation of תּוּשִׁיָּה than "victory."

[31]Reading יִצְפֹּן with the *qere*, the LXX, and the Vg. Note the parallel to יִשְׁמֹר in v. 8b.

[32]Reading the participle לְנֹצֵר, parallel to the participle לְהֹלְכֵי ("for the ones walking") in v. 7b instead of the infinitive construct of the MT. The MT of v. 8a literally reads "to keep the paths of justice [מִשְׁפָּט]." The basis for the NIV rendition is unclear. It is not necessary to take the ל as an "emphatic ל," contra Dahood, *Proverbs*, 7.

[33]Reading the *qere* חֲסִידָיו.

[34]Verse 9 should either be emended or the cantillation repointed. וּמֵישָׁרִים ("and fairness") appears awkward before כָּל. Many read וְתִשְׁמֹר ("and you shall keep"). G. R. Driver emends to וּמְשַׁמֵּר, "and [you are] regarding" ("Problems," 174), on the grounds that it maintains the consonantal text, but a participle is awkward here. A better emendation, after the LXX κατορθώσεις (see BHS note *a*), is to וּתְיַשֵּׁר ("and you shall go straight"). An alternative is to read the three nouns (צֶדֶק וּמִשְׁפָּט וּמֵישָׁרִים) without emendation as a single phrase with the colon division properly belonging between וּמֵישָׁרִים and כָּל (contrary to the MT), as the NIV does.

Wisdom gives both pleasure and surefootedness in life. The more wisdom one learns, the more one desires and enjoys it. The protection wisdom gives, moreover, is that it keeps its follower from making decisions that will later bring only regret (v. 11).[35]

THE TWO TEMPTERS (2:12-19). **2:12-19** Two tempters face the young man as he enters adulthood and must make decisions about the course of life he will follow. The first is the evil man, the criminal, who holds out the promise of easy money (vv. 12-15; cf. 1:10-19), and the second is the evil woman, the prostitute, who holds out the promise of easy sex (vv. 16-19; cf. 5:1-23).

The tempters are distinct but in some ways similar. The corrupt man speaks words that are "perverse" (v. 12).[36] That is, he justifies his way of life with a distorted set of values in order to persuade others to join him. The immoral woman speaks words of "seduction" (v. 16)[37] to inflate the ego of her victim and draw him in. The immoral man abandons the straight paths (v. 13) whereas the immoral woman abandons her lawful husband[38] and the promises[39] she made before God (v. 17).[40] The evil man goes in paths that are dark, crooked, and devious (vv. 13,15); he leads those who follow him into a wilderness of confusion. Rather than lead her victims along *paths*, the evil woman draws them into her *house*, and the house is in fact the gateway to death itself (vv. 18-19).[41]

---

[35]This is implied in the noun מְזִמָּה (v. 11). This noun is often used of evil plots and schemes (Gen 11:6; Deut 19:19; Ps 31:14 [Eng. v. 13]). Here, however, it means the ability to think through a situation or decision and thus is rendered "discretion."

[36]תַּהְפֻּכוֹת. Except for Deut 32:20, this word is found only in Proverbs. It is used especially of twisted words.

[37]חֶלְקָה ("to make smooth," i.e., "to flatter") implies that seduction is achieved by appeal to the ego and not by sexuality alone.

[38]אַלּוּף ("tame, gentle") is a term of endearment and refers to the woman's husband and not, as W. McKane (*Proverbs*, OTL [Philadelphia: Westminster, 1970] 286-88) argues, her teacher.

[39]This is the only occurrence of בְּרִית in Proverbs. It does not refer to the Deuteronomic code or any other aspect of Israel's covenant history but to the marriage vow. It is a "covenant of her God" in that God is witness to the covenant between her and her husband. Contrary to G. Bostrom, *Proverbia Studien* (Lunds University Arsskrift, N.F., Avd. I, Bd. 30, Nr. 3, 1935), 103-4. אֱלֹהֶיהָ, "her God," does not imply that a god other than YHWH is meant (cf. McKane, *Proverbs*, 286-87).

[40]Participial forms of עזב ("abandon") begin both vv. 13 and 17.

[41]The Hebrew reads, "She sinks to death, her house." This is peculiar; it is hard to imagine death called the house of a single person. The NIV rendition smooths out the difficulty with a paraphrase. Various emendations have been proposed, but most require considerable changes in the text or questionable grammar (cf. Delitzsch, *Proverbs* 1:82-83). A likely proposal is that instead of שָׁחָה we should read שׁוּחָה, *pit*, a term that is applied to the prostitute in Prov 22:14; 23:17. שׁוּחָה could thus be regarded as governing both phrases. The verse would then mean, "Her house is a pit [leading] to death/her paths are a pit [leading] to the ghosts." The parallel structure of the proverb supports this. See J. A. Emerton, "A Note on Proverbs 2:18," *JTS* 30 (1979): 153-58.

Finally, both of the tempters lead their victims to destruction. The evil man draws his followers into moral decay, the corruption of taking pleasure in perverse evils (v. 14). Those who enter the house of the immoral woman, on the other hand, find only the ghosts of those who preceded them and discover too late that there is no exit (vv. 18-19).[42] This is a powerful image accurately and graphically describing the situation of those who have followed the allurement of sexual sin.

Concluding Summation (2:20-22). **2:20-22** Once again Proverbs appeals to the doctrine of the two ways. The way of the righteous (v. 20) contrasts with the twisted path of the wicked just as the promise of life (v. 21) contrasts with the certainty of death in the home of the adulteress. The promise of remaining "in the land" immediately recalls the Deuteronomic perspective, as McKane has noted. Israel itself is two nations, the righteous and the wicked, instead of one (cf. Rom 2:28-29).[43]

(4) The Third Exhortation (3:1-35)

1My son, do not forget my teaching,
but keep my commands in your heart,
2for they will prolong your life many years
and bring you prosperity.

3Let love and faithfulness never leave you;
bind them around your neck,
write them on the tablet of your heart.

4Then you will win favor and a good name
in the sight of God and man.
5Trust in the Lord with all your heart
and lean not on your own understanding;
6in all your ways acknowledge him,
and he will make your paths straight.

7Do not be wise in your own eyes;
fear the Lord and shun evil.
8This will bring health to your body
and nourishment to your bones.

9Honor the Lord with your wealth,
with the firstfruits of all your crops;
10then your barns will be filled to overflowing,
and your vats will brim over with new wine.

11My son, do not despise the Lord's discipline
and do not resent his rebuke,

[42]Another verbal parallel is evident here. The immoral woman diverts her victims from the paths (אָרְחוֹת) of life, v. 19, whereas the אָרְחוֹת of violent men are crooked (v. 15). See also the comments on 5:6.

[43]McKane, *Proverbs*, 288.

12because the LORD disciplines those he loves,
as a father the son he delights in.

13Blessed is the man who finds wisdom,
the man who gains understanding,
14for she is more profitable than silver
and yields better returns than gold.
15She is more precious than rubies;
nothing you desire can compare with her.
16Long life is in her right hand;
in her left hand are riches and honor.
17Her ways are pleasant ways,
and all her paths are peace.
18She is a tree of life to those who embrace her;
those who lay hold of her will be blessed.

19By wisdom the LORD laid the earth's foundations,
by understanding he set the heavens in place;
20by his knowledge the deeps were divided,
and the clouds let drop the dew.

21My son, preserve sound judgment and discernment,
do not let them out of your sight;
22they will be life for you,
an ornament to grace your neck.
23Then you will go on your way in safety,
and your foot will not stumble;
24when you lie down, you will not be afraid;
when you lie down, your sleep will be sweet.
25Have no fear of sudden disaster
or of the ruin that overtakes the wicked,
26for the LORD will be your confidence
and will keep your foot from being snared.

27Do not withhold good from those who deserve it,
when it is in your power to act.
28Do not say to your neighbor,
"Come back later; I'll give it tomorrow"—
when you now have it with you.

29Do not plot harm against your neighbor,
who lives trustfully near you.
30Do not accuse a man for no reason—
when he has done you no harm.

31Do not envy a violent man
or choose any of his ways,
32for the LORD detests a perverse man
but takes the upright into his confidence.

33The LORD's curse is on the house of the wicked,
but he blesses the home of the righteous.

[34]He mocks proud mockers
but gives grace to the humble.
[35]The wise inherit honor,
but fools he holds up to shame.

Devotion to God and devotion to Wisdom are inseparable. For the scholar, who may be tempted to seek knowledge without having first submitted to God, this means that the search will be futile and the wisdom gained will be distorted if one has not first oriented oneself to the Creator in faith, humility, and obedience. For the religious person, this means that one's alleged piety is hollow if it does not embrace the simple and indeed very earthy precepts of wisdom. Basic axioms of moral integrity, matters as ordinary as being a decent neighbor (vv. 28-29), must adorn the life of anyone who would claim to possess the fear of the Lord. In this time, when there are far too many examples of Christians and especially of ministers who seem to have forgotten that right living is essential for those who would claim to know God, this lesson cannot be proclaimed loudly enough.

This chapter engages in a kind of evangelism, but it is an evangelism of a most profound nature. It is neither formulaic nor facile. Instead, it calls the reader to the full richness of the life of faith. This includes the submission of the intellectual life and of material things to God, respect for other persons, and above all an eagerness to embrace the right way of living (i.e., wisdom) in this, God's world. It offers the promise of personal wholesomeness and of confidence in the face of an uncertain future.

This is the most lengthy and the most complex of the exhortation discourses. It includes a parental appeal (vv. 1-4), an exhortation to piety before Yahweh (vv. 5-12), a hymn to Wisdom (vv. 13-18), a didactic quatrain on wisdom in creation (vv. 19-20), a second parental appeal (vv. 21-26), four prohibitions against infidelity (vv. 27-30), and a prohibition against criminal behavior (vv. 31-35).

Opening Parental Appeal (3:1-4). **3:1-4** As in all introductions to discourse exhortations in Proverbs, the passage opens with an appeal for the young man to heed parental teaching (v. 1). Furthermore, as is also common in Proverbs, long life and prosperity are held out as the rewards of obedience (v. 2). "Prosperity," however, should not be taken as a crude financial enticement to righteousness. "Wholesomeness" would in fact be a better translation of *šalom* here.[44] The person with wholesomeness is not necessarily rich but is healthy physically, fiscally, and in relationship with others.

Verse 3 actually shows how far removed Proverbs is from an ethic of external obedience and reward. The command to maintain love and faithfulness demonstrates that the internal character of the heart is in view

[44]שָׁלוֹם implies a life that is healthy in every way. See *The New International Dictionary of New Testament Theology*, s.v. "Peace," by H. Beck and C. Brown, 2:777-80.

here. The general nature of this command ought to be preserved as well—the verse does not speak specifically of fidelity to the covenant or in some other particular arena of life but looks for inner integrity that manifests itself in all interactions with God and people. In this respect, Proverbs is different from earlier non-Israelite wisdom.[45]

The command to "bind them around your neck, write them on the tablet of your heart" further indicates that the character of the student is in view rather than just his behavior. Some have suggested that the binding of love to the neck means that it is here a kind of necklace that beautifies the individual. But the parallel between "neck" and "heart" here implies that fidelity is more than an ornament to the neck. The neck houses the throat which, in Hebrew anthropology, is the very life of the person. Love and faithfulness are to become part of the student's heart and life.[46] The influence of Deuteronomy here is evident.[47]

The translation "a good name" (v. 4) is somewhat paraphrastic. The text actually reads, "Then you will win favor and good *understanding* in the sight of God and man."[48] This means that others will recognize the competence and intelligence of the wise individual.

TRUE PIETY (3:5-12). **3:5-12** This section emphasizes piety toward the Lord rather than devotion to the abstractions of wisdom or righteousness.[49] True piety manifests itself as intellectual humility (vv. 5-8), submission of material wealth to God's rule (vv. 9-10), and patient acceptance of divine discipline (vv. 11-12). Formally, each section is an admonition composed of commands or prohibitions followed by an explanation of the reasons for the commands (motive clause).

The first section is itself made up of two quatrains (vv. 5-6,7-8).[50] The command to trust God "with all your heart" means that the total personality is to be committed to God's care, although it emphasizes the mind and volition. The prohibitions against depending on one's own understanding

---

[45]Egyptian wisdom particularly exhorts the pupil to the behavior that is likely to give success in a career. High moral concepts are by no means absent, but emphasis is on politically sensitive behavior rather than on the character of the inner person.

[46]The verb קָשַׁר ("bind") here implies that this is not a true parallel to 1:9 (*contra* Toy, *Proverbs*, 58) since one does not "bind" a necklace. The neck houses the נֶפֶשׁ, which may mean alternatively either "life," "breath," or "throat." But it would be harsh to speak of binding something to the נֶפֶשׁ, and thus "neck" is used. But the point is that sound teaching and virtues must become part of one's very life and breath. See also 6:21.

[47]Compare Deut 6:8-9 to Prov 3:3b,c. McKane (*Proverbs*, 290-91) asserts that Proverbs has influenced Deuteronomy rather than vice versa, but his conclusion springs from, rather than supports, his peculiar redaction history of Proverbs.

[48]Contrary to Toy (*Proverbs*, 63) שֵׂכֶל need not be emended to שֵׁם here.

[49]Note that the name יהוה appears at least once in every quatrain.

[50]Verse 6b is a motive clause related to the commands in vv. 5-6a, and vv. 7-8 contain another command plus motive. Verses 5-6 and vv. 7-8 could be treated as two entirely separate admonitions. They are, however, bound by a common theme.

and against intellectual pride (vv. 5b,7a) implicitly reject a "secular" search for wisdom and look back to the thesis of the book (1:7).

Although this passage certainly condemns any academic arrogance, it does not indulge in anti-intellectualism. The commitment of the heart to God means that all the beliefs and decisions of life are to be submitted to Yahweh. Even very practical decisions are in view here, and not just matters of academic pursuit. But the text is no more opposed to academic research per se than to any normal activity of life. Also, "understanding" implies not just intellectual capacity but one's own moral standards. One's private vision of right and wrong must be submitted to God.

The motive clause of v. 8 promises physical health. Health naturally proceeds from the peaceful and well-ordered life that is submitted to God.[51]

The second section is a quatrain composed of a command (v. 9) followed by the motive (v. 10). Commentaries note that this is the only place where Proverbs alludes to the ceremonial worship.[52] Even so, the language here is not nearly so explicitly cultic as in Sirach 7:29-31. Proverbs is not so much concerning itself with ceremonial religion here as it is exhorting the reader to demonstrate gratitude toward and confidence in God (rather than in wealth).

The third section is formally like the second. It is cited in Heb 12:5-6. While the idea of punishment is certainly present (cf. Job 5:17-18 and 2 Sam 7:14), "discipline" primarily involves teaching or training rather than punishment for wrongdoing.[53] It is analogous to military training, in which, although the threat of punishment is present, even stern discipline is not necessarily retribution for offenses. Hardship and correction are involved, however, which are always hard to accept.

A Hymn to Wisdom (3:13-18). **3:13-18** This section is more a hymn than typical exhortation. It has none of the imperatives generally associated with exhortation. It personifies Wisdom,[54] and its beginning ("Blessed . . .") is elsewhere used in the instructional hymn.[55] On the other hand, nothing suggests that it does not belong with the present text. In context it supports the general exhortation to pursue Wisdom.[56]

---

[51]שֹׁר means "navel," or "umbilical cord," but see BHS note. G. R. Driver ("Problems," 175) says that שֹׁר can mean "health" on the basis of cognate developments (e.g., Akkadian *qu* and Hebrew *qaw* "cord" are from the same root as Arabic *qawiya*, "was strong"). Also, in Sirach 30:15, שֹׁר is equivalent to ὑγεία. Driver is supported by McKane, *Proverbs*, 293. If שֹׁר is thus taken to mean "strength" rather than "body," it probably implies overall soundness of body and mind rather than just physical health.

[52]Delitzsch, *Proverbs* 1:89; Toy, *Proverbs*, 62; McKane, *Proverbs*, 293-94.

[53]מוּסָר is similar to the Latin *disciplina* and the Greek παιδεία.

[54]See especially v. 16.

[55]Cf. אַשְׁרֵי in Pss 1:1; 119:1.

[56]Cf. McKane, *Proverbs*, 294: "Yet there is not a sharp discontinuity between this section [vv. 13-20] and the preceding verses, certainly not in respect of subject-matter, while even the formal characteristics of the Instruction are not obliterated."

The hymn is formally structured as an inclusio with "blessed" marking both its beginning and ending.[57] It includes an introductory beatitude (v. 13) and assertions of the high value of Wisdom (vv. 14-15), and it promises other benefits (vv. 16-18). In effect, vv. 14-18 are arguments to prove the validity of v. 13.

Verses 14-15 make two claims. First, Wisdom "yields better returns than" money (v. 14). That is, Wisdom is a better investment than silver or gold because she never fails to pay interest. Time spent in gaining her is never lost. Second, Wisdom is more precious than the most exquisite forms of wealth (v. 15).[58] People desire money in order to obtain rare and beautiful possessions, but the innate beauty of Wisdom surpasses all else.

The picture of Wisdom holding a bounty in both hands is particularly vivid (v. 16). Kayatz notes that *Maatt*, Egyptian goddess of justice, is often portrayed holding a symbol of life in one hand and a scepter, symbolizing wealth and power, in the other.[59] The personification intensifies the idea of Wisdom giving gifts to her followers.

Verse 17 promises that Wisdom can make life both joyful and wholesome and thus counters the image of dour sobriety that many have of following her. The metaphor of the "tree of life" in v. 18 reinforces this. Both the pleasure of eating fruit and its wholesomeness as a source of life are implied.

On the other hand, the eschatological implications of "tree of life" cannot be denied. Genesis 3:24 states that separation from the tree means that man and woman have lost their chance for immortality. The Babylonian Epic of Gilgamesh speaks also of a plant of immortality (which Gilgamesh lost to a serpent).[60] With such an image not only as part of the biblical text but also as part of the common inheritance of ancient Near Eastern literature, it is unlikely that the highly literate court of Solomon would conceive of the tree of life merely as a metaphor of happiness. The words hold the promise of escape from the curse of death.[61]

WISDOM AND CREATION (3:19-20). **3:19-20** In a carefully crafted quatrain,[62] vv. 19-20 assert Wisdom's role in creation. It is a fitting appendix to

---

[57]אַשְׁרֵי in v. 13 and מְאֻשָּׁר in v. 18.

[58]It is unclear whether פְּנִינִים (*kethiv* פְּנִיִּים) means "rubies" or "corals." Cf. Toy, *Proverbs*, 68. Regardless, the word implies something that is not merely expensive but rare and beautiful as well.

[59]C. Kayatz, *Studien zu Proverbien 1-9*, WMANT 22 (1966): 105.

[60]ANET, 96.

[61]McKane (*Proverbs*, 296) speaks of the image as "moribund" and "just a pretty figure of speech." But it is doubtful that such a primary symbol could be so drained of its original larger implications in the minds of the ancient readers.

[62]יהוה stands outside of the chiastic structure of v. 19 (prepositional phrase with ב + verb [verb + object]/[verb + object] + prepositional phrase with ב); v. 20a, like v. 19a, begins with

the previous hymn. This section anticipates 8:22-31. The main point there and here is that whoever abandons wisdom runs against the very structure by which the world was made.

Verse 20, however, goes beyond this. The phrase "the deeps were divided" alludes to the bursting forth of the flood of Noah (Gen 7:11).[63] It is a picture of the destructive power of nature. But the image of clouds dropping dew on the crops of the land shows the gentle, beneficent side of creation. The world is both nurturing and dangerous. Yet creation itself is under the hand of God, and he governs according to wisdom. Wisdom is therefore essential for survival.

A SECOND PARENTAL APPEAL: ON PERSONAL SECURITY (3:21-26). **3:21-26** The affectionate appeal, "my son," which marks a new subsection, is appropriate to the subject matter at hand.[64] Every parent naturally desires his or her child to be safe, and the primary benefit of wisdom promised here is personal security and freedom from anxiety.

The essence of this section is given in v. 22: wisdom will preserve your life.[65] For this reason, the righteous can be free of the anxiety that plagues the wicked (vv. 23-25). Verse 23 is a general promise; it is not an absolute guarantee that the wise will never have occasion to stumble. Compared to the unwise, however, they will experience tranquility.

The climax of the text is the promise that God will be beside the follower of wisdom (v. 26).[66] Proverbs never implies that people can be safe through their own wisdom. "Common sense" and personal competence are soon exhausted if God's protection is missing.

FOUR PROHIBITIONS AGAINST INFIDELITY (3:27-30). **3:27-30** These four prohibitions against malevolent behavior have the positive effect of calling the reader to a life of goodwill and helpfulness. Verses 27-28 command the reader not to fail to do good whereas vv. 29-30 prohibit malicious activity.

---

a prepositional phrase with ב, but v. 20b, which has no prepositional phrase with ב, breaks the pattern and concludes the quatrain.

[63]Cf. תְּהוֹמוֹת נִבְקָעוּ to Gen 7:11, נִבְקְעוּ כָּל־מַעְיְנֹת תְּהוֹם ("and all the springs of the deep were burst open").

[64]The NIV, following most scholars, transposes v. 21a and v. 21b. Cf. BHS note *a* and Toy, *Proverbs*, 74.

[65]Rather than "an ornament to grace your neck," v. 22b should read "and grace for your neck." Although חֵן can mean "fair" or "beautiful" when used adjectivally with a substantive (e.g., לִוְיַת חֵן; Prov 1:9; 4:9), it is not used substantively as "ornament." Here, with חֵן in parallel with חַיִּים ("life") and גַּרְגְּרוֹת ("neck") in parallel with נֶפֶשׁ ("life, throat"), the meaning cannot be in doubt. It is that God will preserve your life. The notion of giving חֵן to a part of the anatomy may seem odd, but cf. Ps 45:3 (Eng. v. 2).

[66]The word כֶּסֶל can mean "confidence," but the preposition ב calls into question whether this is the meaning here. With Dahood (*Proverbs,* 10) one could take בְּכִסְלֶךָ as "at your side" after the Ugaritic parallel *ksl* ("back"). Cf. Vg, *Dominus enim erit in latere tuo*.

These verses have special significance for the conduct of the rich and of government officials, but they are of a general nature and need not be limited to a particular application.[67] "Those who deserve good"[68] may be laborers who have earned their pay, the poor who rightly plead for help, or suppliants at the city gates who call for justice. On the other hand, they could be those who have loaned money and deserve to be repaid.

Verse 29, which deals with unprovoked schemes[69] against others, is best illustrated in the Bible by Jezebel's conspiracy against Naboth (1 Kgs 21) and Haman's designs on Mordecai in Esther. Verse 30 prohibits frivolous litigation. It does not absolutely forbid bringing a suit in court, but abuse of the legal system by habitual or malicious use is condemned.

A Prohibition against Criminal Behavior (3:31-35). **3:31-35** Like the proverbs of the previous section, this section begins with a prohibition (v. 31). But instead of following the prohibition with a circumstantial clause, as vv. 27-30 do, it moves to a motive clause (v. 32). The motive clause is then expanded (vv. 33-34) and the section concludes with a relevant proverb (v. 35).[70]

The violent man is one of the two archetypical tempters (see 2:12-19 above). He represents the allure of easy prosperity by violence and crime. His destruction is assured, however, because God himself opposes him (vv. 32-34).

The text forcefully presents Yahweh's personal opposition or favor in the motive clauses (v. 32)—the benefits of wisdom are not confined to conformity to an impersonal order. Even the concluding proverb, which does not mention Yahweh, is not wholly "secular." The wise do not simply earn the respect of other people (as the NIV "honor" implies), but in a more profound sense they partake of God's "glory."[71] Wisdom, right behavior, and devotion to God are inseparably bound in Proverbs.

---

[67]McKane (*Proverbs*, 299) rightly notes that these verses are not "set in the framework of vocational instruction" of the Egyptian texts.

[68]Toy (*Proverbs*, 79) considers בַּעַל טוֹב linguistically questionable and emends בְּעָלָיו to רֵעֶיךָ ("your neighbors"), but the NIV translation should be retained. See Delitzsch, *Proverbs* 1:99.

[69]חרשׁ, which means "to plow or engrave," is often used in Proverbs with the meaning "to scheme." Hosea 10:13 artfully draws the two meanings "plow" and "scheme" together: "But you have planted (חרשׁ) wickedness/ you have reaped evil." Cf. *TDOT*, s.v. חָרַשׁ, 5:220-23.

[70]Observe that vv. 32-34 each take the form of a bicolon in which God's opposition to the evil (first line) contrasts with his favors toward the righteous (second line). Verse 35, however, is marked as the conclusion by a reversal of the order.

[71]Although כָּבוֹד frequently means "honor" as a human attribute, both כָּבוֹד and נחל ("inherit") are laden with theological and eschatological meaning, and their juxtaposition is significant. כָּבוֹד is ultimately a property of God, and נחל is closely associated with the fulfillment of the patriarchal promises related to the land. The phrase has implied eschatological significance.

(5) The Fourth Exhortation: A Father's Plea (4:1-27)

**1Listen, my sons, to a father's instruction;
pay attention and gain understanding.
2I give you sound learning,
so do not forsake my teaching.
3When I was a boy in my father's house,
still tender, and an only child of my mother,
4he taught me and said,
"Lay hold of my words with all your heart;
keep my commands and you will live.
5Get wisdom, get understanding;
do not forget my words or swerve from them.
6Do not forsake wisdom, and she will protect you;
love her, and she will watch over you.
7Wisdom is supreme; therefore get wisdom.
Though it cost all you have, get understanding.
8Esteem her, and she will exalt you;
embrace her, and she will honor you.
9She will set a garland of grace on your head
and present you with a crown of splendor."**

**10Listen, my son, accept what I say,
and the years of your life will be many.
11I guide you in the way of wisdom
and lead you along straight paths.
12When you walk, your steps will not be hampered;
when you run, you will not stumble.
13Hold on to instruction, do not let it go;
guard it well, for it is your life.
14Do not set foot on the path of the wicked
or walk in the way of evil men.
15Avoid it, do not travel on it;
turn from it and go on your way.
16For they cannot sleep till they do evil;
they are robbed of slumber till they make someone fall.
17They eat the bread of wickedness
and drink the wine of violence.**

**18The path of the righteous is like the first gleam of dawn,
shining ever brighter till the full light of day.
19But the way of the wicked is like deep darkness;
they do not know what makes them stumble.**

**20My son, pay attention to what I say;
listen closely to my words.
21Do not let them out of your sight,
keep them within your heart;**

[22]for they are life to those who find them
and health to a man's whole body.
[23]Above all else, guard your heart,
for it is the wellspring of life.
[24]Put away perversity from your mouth;
keep corrupt talk far from your lips.
[25]Let your eyes look straight ahead,
fix your gaze directly before you.
[26]Make level paths for your feet
and take only ways that are firm.
[27]Do not swerve to the right or the left;
keep your foot from evil.

The father (and mother), not the professional teacher or the pastor or government official, has the most profound responsibility and opportunity to lead a young man in the right way. Only a parent can implore the young man to do what is right with the depth of love and concern displayed here. This text more than any other brings out this urgency of parental love. In addition, this passage illustrates how wisdom is an inheritance that may be passed from generation to generation. It can preserve a whole family line through the passing of years. It is, however, an inheritance that each generation must choose to receive. If the chain is broken and the way of wisdom is rejected, the results will be disastrous for the family.

Each of the major exhortations of Prov 1–9 begins with an appeal for the son to heed his father's instruction. Here, however, the paternal entreaty is much more emphatic. The opening appeal covers a full nine verses (vv. 1-9) and includes within it a lengthy quote from the teacher's own father (vv. 4-9).[72] Direct appeal from the teacher to his son is resumed in vv. 10-13, and a second paternal appeal appears in vv. 20-22.[73] By recalling his own upbringing and citing his father, the teacher both identifies with the present struggles in his son's life and reinforces the paternal dignity of his words. These teachings have stood the test of time. Although several major themes of Proverbs are mentioned in this chapter,[74] the emphasis here is on the love that causes a father to plead with his son to stay in the right way.

[72]Hebrew does not contain quotation marks, but the resumption of paternal appeal at v. 10 implies that the quotation goes through v. 9.

[73]It is possible to regard vv. 10-19 and vv. 20-27 as two separate exhortations rather than as subsections of the fourth exhortation, but it is better to treat the whole chapter as one exhortation dominated by the paternal appeal. The shift from the plural "sons" (v. 1) to the singular (v. 10) is not significant; chap. 5, which is clearly a single exhortation on adultery, contains such a shift (5:1,7).

[74]E.g., the importance of Wisdom (vv. 5-9) and the folly of criminal life (vv. 14-19).

First Appeal (4:1-9). **4:1-9** The home is the primary place of education, especially moral education. "Still tender, and an only child of my mother" (v. 3) shows that references to father and son are literal and not meant to be taken metaphorically as the teacher in the place of the parent.[75] In addition, the affectionate and pleading tone of these verses shows why parents make the best teachers: they love their children.

Verse 5 appeals to the son to attain wisdom above everything else; he should not allow himself to become weary of the quest for understanding.[76] Also, the father does not hesitate to identify his own words with wisdom. He can in one breath say, "Keep *my* commands and you will live"[77] and in the next say, "Get wisdom, get understanding."[78] He knows that his words are right.

The short discourse in praise of wisdom (vv. 5-9) maintains the personification of Wisdom as a lady who rewards those who embrace her.[79] It is not clear that the Hebrew of v. 7a can bear the meaning, "Wisdom is supreme."[80] The alternative translation, "The beginning of wisdom is 'Get wisdom,'" is difficult in that it is both redundant and uses an imperative phrase as a predicate. But this can be a deliberate anacoluthon (violation of syntax) meant to drive home the idea that the first step in the pursuit of wisdom is to determine to obtain her.[81] Still, the sense of the text is clear: Wisdom is the greatest possession anyone can have, and the young man should make winning her the primary goal of his life.

---

[75]Cf. McKane, *Proverbs*, 303.

[76]Several scholars have been perplexed by the presence of אַל תִּשְׁכַּח ("do not forget") in v. 5b without any direct object (cf. Delitzsch, *Proverbs* 1:107, and Toy, *Proverbs*, 87). Dahood (*Proverbs*, 11-12) argues that שכח is not "to forget" but is from a second root, "to flag, slacken, be weary" (cf. Pss 102:5; 137:5b). A root *ṯkḥ* is found in the Ugaritic Text 67:I:4, which Dahood translates "wilt." Gordon, however, gives this occurrence the meaning "to shine" (UT, 502). If Dahood's suggestion is accepted, v. 5 could be translated: "Acquire wisdom, acquire understanding,/ do not slacken, do not turn away from the words of my mouth." Otherwise, if שכח means "forget," the object is implied in what follows.

[77]Emphasis added.

[78]We should note that the precise order of phrases here is somewhat uncertain, as indicated in the various readings of the major LXX codices. Cf. McKane, *Proverbs*, 304, and Toy, *Proverbs*, 90.

[79]It is possible, though doubtful, that סַלְסְלֶהָ (v. 8) could be translated "caress her" in parallel to תְחַבְּקֶנָּה ("embrace her"). At any rate, the notion of embracing is certainly present. Some have seen indications of a wedding feast in v. 9, with Wisdom playing the part of a bride placing a wreath on her groom's head. This interpretation cannot be sustained, however, since a bride does not protect or exalt her groom in the way Wisdom does. Cf. McKane, *Proverbs*, 306.

[80]רֵאשִׁית חָכְמָה. Cf. Toy, *Proverbs*, 88, and Delitzsch, *Proverbs* 1:107-8. Note that the LXX omits v. 7 altogether.

[81]See Kidner, *Proverbs*, 67.

SECOND APPEAL (4:10-19). **4:10-19** The second appeal has the normal structure of a paternal exhortation: an opening appeal to listen (vv. 10-13) followed by an exhortation in a specific area (vv. 14-19). In this case the exhortation warns the reader to avoid one of the two tempters, the criminal. But the relative length of the appeal to listen implies that the family bond is a major concern of this text. If the young man should go wrong, he not only hurts himself but also his parents.

The doctrine of the two ways dominates this section; the language of taking a journey appears throughout. The father guides the son in "the way of wisdom" and "along straight paths." The boy's "steps will not be hampered," and he "will not stumble" when he walks and runs. He must not "set foot on the path of the wicked" or "walk" or "travel" in their way. The righteous walk in the safe light of day,[82] but "the way of the wicked is like deep darkness;/they do not know what makes them stumble."

The passage also presents in vivid colors the depravity of the wicked. They live for crime. It is their food and drink and sleep (vv. 16-17). They do not commit crimes in order to live but live to commit crimes. Even so, their punishment will be appropriate. Their greatest satisfaction is in making others fall, but they too shall fall and not know how or why.[83]

THIRD APPEAL (4:20-27). **4:20-27** In the closing appeal the father scarcely concerns himself with specific moral issues. He simply urges the son to stay true to Wisdom.

Metaphoric use of body parts permeates this text. The eyes are to stay fixed on right teaching (vv. 21,25) as the feet are to stay in the right path (vv. 26-27). The mouth and lips must shun using twisted words (v. 24). Above all, the heart must be guarded by sound doctrine (vv. 21,23).[84] If the son listens to his father, the whole body will be healthy (v. 22).

The heart, v. 23 says, is "the wellspring of life." "Heart," here as always, refers not to the physical organ but to the mind and even the whole personality of the individual.[85] It is "the wellspring of life" in that the capacity to live with joy and vigor ultimately comes from within and not from circumstances. The corrupt heart draws one down to the grave, but Wisdom protects the heart from that corruption. This verse, perhaps

---

[82]Verse 18, הוֹלֵךְ וָאוֹר עַד־נְכוֹן הַיּוֹם. נְכוֹן, the niphal participle construct of כּוֹן, means "durable" or, as an adverb, "safely." It should be rendered "growing brighter and brighter until the safe light of day."

[83]Note the play on the two stems of כשל in v. 16 ("they make someone stumble," hiphil stem) and v. 19 ("they stumble over themselves," niphal stem).

[84]It is possible to read בְּכָל for מִכָּל in v. 23. The MT is supported by the Targum as well as A and Θ, whereas the Syr, the LXX, and the Vg support the alternative reading. If בְּכָל is read, the meaning is, "Guard your heart with all diligence" instead of "Above all else, guard your heart."

[85]Cf. Toy, *Proverbs*, 97-98, and McKane, *Proverbs*, 310-11.

in conjunction with Ezekiel's vision of the River of Life (Ezek 47:1-12), apparently was the source of Jesus' perplexing citation in John 7:38.

The fourth exhortation closes with a return to the image of the path (vv. 25-27). Of particular interest is v. 27, the warning to swerve neither to the right nor to the left.[86] Deuteronomy 5:32; 17:11; 28:14; and Josh 23:6 are similar.[87] The idea is that one should not be distracted from the way of wisdom (v. 25). Temptation to allegorize "right" and "left" in light of modern usage should be resisted. At the same time, the text can be taken to urge the reader to maintain the simplicity of biblical teaching. Modern theological schools of any and of all persuasions are not always careful to do this.

(6) The Fifth Exhortation (5:1-23)

1My son, pay attention to my wisdom,
listen well to my words of insight,
2that you may maintain discretion
and your lips may preserve knowledge.
3For the lips of an adulteress drip honey,
and her speech is smoother than oil;
4but in the end she is bitter as gall,
sharp as a double-edged sword.
5Her feet go down to death;
her steps lead straight to the grave.
6She gives no thought to the way of life;
her paths are crooked, but she knows it not.

7Now then, my sons, listen to me;
do not turn aside from what I say.
8Keep to a path far from her,
do not go near the door of her house,
9lest you give your best strength to others
and your years to one who is cruel,
10lest strangers feast on your wealth
and your toil enrich another man's house.
11At the end of your life you will groan,
when your flesh and body are spent.
12You will say, "How I hated discipline!
How my heart spurned correction!
13I would not obey my teachers
or listen to my instructors.

---

[86]The LXX adds, "For God knows the ways on the right,/ but the ways on the left are twisted./ He will make your paths straight/ and guide your journey in peace." This is evidently a Hellenistic addition, and it should not be used to interpret "left" and "right" in this passage. Cf. Toy, *Proverbs*, 99-100.

[87]McKane (*Proverbs*, 311) notes that in these texts the verb is סור, not נטה, and he correctly observes that there is no evidence of borrowing in either direction.

[14]I have come to the brink of utter ruin
in the midst of the whole assembly."

[15]Drink water from your own cistern,
running water from your own well.
[16]Should your springs overflow in the streets,
your streams of water in the public squares?
[17]Let them be yours alone,
never to be shared with strangers.
[18]May your fountain be blessed,
and may you rejoice in the wife of your youth.
[19]A loving doe, a graceful deer—
may her breasts satisfy you always,
may you ever be captivated by her love.
[20]Why be captivated, my son, by an adulteress?
Why embrace the bosom of another man's wife?

[21]For a man's ways are in full view of the LORD,
and he examines all his paths.
[22]The evil deeds of a wicked man ensnare him;
the cords of his sin hold him fast.
[23]He will die for lack of discipline,
led astray by his own great folly.

FIRST STROPHE (5:1-6). **5:1-6** The Bible does not hide from or obscure the power of the temptation to illicit sex. In language that is refreshingly clear and direct without itself indulging in titillation, the text warns the reader of the debacle that awaits him should he succumb in this area and at the same time promises profound sexual joy to those whose hearts are chaste and loving. If the church is to do its duty, it must be no less clear in its teachings. To assume that nice, Christian young people do not struggle in these areas or to speak only in whispers and innuendo on the grounds that they are inappropriate for the Christian pulpit is no less than gross neglect of duty on the church's part. Whether one is dealing with the ritual prostitution of a fertility cult, the ordinary prostitute on the street (or in a magazine), or the simple lure of extramarital sex, the temptations and dangers are the same.

The passage begins with a typical appeal to the young man to hold to his father's teaching (vv. 1-2). Verse 3 seems abrupt after v. 2 in that there is no transition. One expects before v. 3 a verse commanding the young man to avoid the prostitute. J. Goldingay argues that v. 20 originally stood between v. 2 and v. 3 and had this function.[88] But this is insufficient evi-

[88]He argues that it has been dislocated by an editor who noticed the occurrence of שׁגה in vv. 19,23 and moved what is now v. 20 to its present location to bring out the various uses of this verb. J. Goldingay, "Proverbs V and IX," *RB* 84 (1977): 80-87.

dence for emending the text, and vv. 21-23 are very harsh after vv. 15-19 without v. 20 between the two sections. The solution makes for a worse problem than the one now observed in the text.[89] Also a movement from a general introductory appeal (vv. 1-2) to a specific warning (v. 3) is not unusual (cf. 1:8-10).[90]

The "adulteress" of v. 3 is literally the "other woman,"[91] that is, someone other than the man's wife. The verse does not deny that the other woman is indeed tempting, but the temptation is not all sexual. The honey lips and smooth mouth of the other woman refer more to her flattery than her sexual availability. The man is drawn to her because she inflates his ego with hollow praise in ways his own wife will not.

Verses 4-6 describe the bitter outcome of the adulterous relationship. Anguish and disillusionment and emotional and even physical death all come from this illicit pleasure.

The Hebrew of v. 6 is difficult. The text is literally, "The path of life, lest she/you pay attention,[92] her ways wander, she/you will not know." An ambiguity is that the subjects of the verbs "pay attention" and "know" may be either third feminine singular or second masculine singular. Most commentaries and versions (including the NIV) emend the text by changing "lest" to "not"[93] and understand the woman to be the subject of the verbs. In favor of this, one may note that since it is the woman whose ways wander (v. 6b), one might presume that she is the subject of the verb "know."

On the other hand, the verse can be translated without changing the Hebrew as, "In order that you not pay attention to the path of life; her ways wander (from it), but you will not know it."[94] Taken in this way, the point of v. 6 is not that the woman is a lost and wayward soul (however true that might be). In other words, she is not made an object of pity. To the contrary, she is an agent of temptation who deliberately contrives to draw her prey off the path of life (cf. 2:19) and down to destruction. The whole point of 5:1-6 is that the young man should heed wisdom and be preserved; one would therefore expect the text to warn of how the prostitute draws him away from the path of life. This is the perspective

---

[89]For other possible emendations of v. 2, cf. the LXX and *BHS* note *a*, as well as Toy, *Proverbs*, 106.

[90]Note also that שְׂפָתַיִם ("lips") serves as a catchword between v. 2 and v. 3.

[91]זָרָה = "stranger" (feminine).

[92]On the meaning of תְּפַלֵּס, "to pay attention" or "scrutinize," see McKane, *Proverbs*, 311.

[93]פֶּן is emended to לֹא or בַּל. Cf. Toy, *Proverbs*, 107, and McKane, *Proverbs*, 314. This would seem to be an unusual scribal error. The strongest objection to reading פֶּן here is that it normally begins a clause, but אֹרַח חַיִּים may stand first to emphasize its contrast to v. 5, where the path of the adulteress leads to death.

[94]Reading תְּפַלֵּס and תֵּדַע as second masculine singular rather than third feminine singular.

Proverbs always takes with regard to the adulteress (cf. 6:26; 7:6-26; 9:17-18). She is the hunter, not the victim.[95]

SECOND STROPHE (5:7-14). **5:7-14** The teacher warns the young men[96] of the ruin and disgrace that accompany adultery. A difficulty here is the identity of "others," "cruel one," "strangers," and "another man" in vv. 9-10. All four are masculine and do not refer to the adulteress herself.[97]

Several interpretations are possible. (1) The woman is a prostitute, and the other man is her agent. He thus feeds upon the prostitute's victims. (2) The woman is a mistress, and the strangers are those who profit from her access to easy money. The mistress carelessly spends her lover's wealth. (3) The adulteress is married, and the other man is her outraged husband. He extracts a heavy fine, if not a death penalty, from the adulterer (see 6:31-35). (4) The adulteress is a foreign woman, thus implying a covenant breach.[98] The adulterer is therefore giving his virility and his wealth to non-Israelites. There is an implicit analogy between adultery in marriage with infidelity toward God. (5) The woman is a cult prostitute. The strangers are priests and cult officials who prey upon Israelite men who are seduced by the cult.[99]

Each of these possibilities has merit, and none can be proven to be the sole explanation. The passage uses general language to make the point that adultery leads to personal degeneration and financial depletion. The man who indulges himself will pay the price a hundred times over.

Verse 14 could refer to legal proceedings against the adulterer (see Deut 22:22), but the text is not explicit on this point; it probably refers to the adulterer's public disgrace and humiliation.[100]

THIRD STROPHE (5:15-19). **5:15-19** Verse 15 obviously means that a man should have sexual relations only with his wife, but the metaphors of

---

[95]Again, however, we should note that this is because the book is written primarily for boys and young men and has the purpose of dissuading them from pursuing the other woman. This does not mean that the Bible takes the position that the woman is always at fault.

[96]The Hebrew only has "sons," and not "my sons." Dahood (*Proverbs*, 12) argues that v. 7 should not read בָּנִים, "sons," but בְּנִים, the vocative "my son" with the *enclitic mem.* This would bring it into agreement with v. 1. This, however, would require the emendation of the verbs שִׁמְעוּ ("listen") and תָּסוּרוּ ("turn away") to the singular. Variation between the singular and plural is not surprising.

[97]It is possible to read אַכְזָרִי ("cruel one," v. 9) as a feminine since this adjective always takes this form, but in context there is no reason to do so.

[98]Numbers 25 and Ezra 10:2-4 are clear indications of the attraction foreign women could hold over the Israelite men. At the same time, נָכְרִיָּה ("foreign woman") in Proverbs does not mean a non-Israelite but simply another man's wife. That is, she is "foreign" in respect to the marriage bond. Cf. K. Van Der Toorn, "Female Prostitution in Payment of Vows in Ancient Israel," *JBL* 108.2 (1989): 199.

[99]Some have suggested that אַכְזָרִי is here related to a class of the Ishtar prostitutes, the *kizritu*, and that the "cruel one" is Ishtar herself. See McKane, *Proverbs*, 316.

[100]See McKane, *Proverbs*, 317.

v. 16 and the injunction of v. 17 are more difficult. If the "cistern" and "well" are the wife, what are the "springs" and "streams" of v. 16, and what is meant by not "sharing them with strangers"?

Several interpretations are possible but unlikely. The streams of water in the street could refer to the adulterer's wife, who is no longer confined to the home ("cistern") but is herself having sexual liaisons with other men in retaliation for her husband's faithlessness. This interpretation would appear to be supported by implication in v. 17, but it has no explicit support in the text. The injunctions of vv. 16-17 concern something that the man has control over; but whether or not he is faithful, he cannot exercise control over his wife's fidelity. The claim that vv. 16-17 deal with the behavior of the man's wife is at crosscurrents with the purpose of the passage.

A second interpretation is that a man should not waste his semen and father children for other households.[101] This is most implausible. Even in a prescientific age the Israelites knew from polygamy and concubinage that a man could father many children by many women. Also, as Toy notes, water here is a metaphor for sexual pleasure and not reproductive power.[102]

A third possibility is that the streams in the street (v. 16) are the prostitutes, and the man is commanded not to go to them.[103] This is ruled out, however, by the reference to "*your* springs," meaning that the streams belong to the man. The prostitute, of course, does not.

The best interpretation is that "springs" and "streams of water" refer to the husband's sexual affections as the "cistern" refers to the affections of his wife. The man should not take his love and desire to anyone else by going out into the street. The analogy implies that husband and wife fill and refresh each other, the one like a flowing stream and the other like a peaceful well. Sexual anarchy results when people cross over the bounds of fidelity. Verse 17 means that a man should never be willing to share a woman with another man. This naturally excludes visiting prostitutes and immoral women, since they belong to many men.

The blessing in v. 18 might appear to be a promise of many children,[104] but again the passage emphasizes the sexual pleasure of marriage and not having offspring (v. 19). The command to "take pleasure[105] in your first wife"[106] implies negatively that a man should never have sexual relations

[101]Cf. McKane, *Proverbs*, 318-19.

[102]Toy, *Proverbs*, 113.

[103]Thus Toy, *Proverbs*, 113.

[104]Thus McKane, *Proverbs*, 319.

[105]In context this is a better translation of שמח than "rejoice."

[106]This is the most reasonable interpretation of "wife of your youth," אֵשֶׁת נְעוּרֶךָ. The point is that he should not look for a second wife, concubine, or prostitute.

with another woman (whether in adultery or by divorce on contrived grounds) and positively that marriage should include sexual joy and fulfillment.

Verse 19 brings out both the tender affection and the exuberant pleasure of love. She is a loving doe, and he will be drunken with satisfaction[107] in the pleasure she gives.

FOURTH STROPHE (5:20-23). **5:20-23** Verse 20 is linked chiastically to v. 19b,c. The man should not "stagger"[108] from the affection of another woman, nor should he embrace her "bosom."[109] The use of the catchword "stagger" also ties together the conclusion of the exhortation. A man will stagger in the pleasure his wife gives (v. 19). He can embrace the bosom of another woman and stagger (v. 20), but the terms of sensual pleasure are absent here; with the adulteress it is the staggering of confusion and weakness. Finally, the man who indulges in adultery will stagger to his own destruction (v. 23).[110]

(7) Four Teachings (6:1-19)

1My son, if you have put up security for your neighbor,
if you have struck hands in pledge for another,
2if you have been trapped by what you said,
ensnared by the words of your mouth,
3then do this, my son, to free yourself,
since you have fallen into your neighbor's hands:
Go and humble yourself;
press your plea with your neighbor!
4Allow no sleep to your eyes,
no slumber to your eyelids.
5Free yourself, like a gazelle from the hand of the hunter,
like a bird from the snare of the fowler.

6Go to the ant, you sluggard;
consider its ways and be wise!
7It has no commander,
no overseer or ruler,
8yet it stores its provisions in summer
and gathers its food at harvest.

9How long will you lie there, you sluggard?
When will you get up from your sleep?

---

[107]The piel of רוה means "to give a full drink," and שׁגה means "to stagger" (as from drunkenness; Isa 28:7). The NIV translation "be captivated" is unusual.

[108]שׁגה in v. 20a corresponds to שׁגה in v. 19c.

[109]חֵק, "bosom," in v. 20b corresponds to דַּדֶּיהָ, "her breasts," in v. 19b.

[110]"Led astray" is a possible translation of שׁגה, but it obscures the tie between vv. 19-20,23.

10A little sleep, a little slumber,
a little folding of the hands to rest—
11and poverty will come on you like a bandit
and scarcity like an armed man.

12A scoundrel and villain,
who goes about with a corrupt mouth,
13who winks with his eye,
signals with his feet
and motions with his fingers,
14who plots evil with deceit in his heart—
he always stirs up dissension.
15Therefore disaster will overtake him in an instant;
he will suddenly be destroyed—without remedy.

16There are six things the LORD hates,
seven that are detestable to him:
17haughty eyes,
a lying tongue,
hands that shed innocent blood,
18a heart that devises wicked schemes,
feet that are quick to rush into evil,
19a false witness who pours out lies
and a man who stirs up dissension among brothers.

No one is prepared for life who has not learned some basic lessons on financial prudence, a meaningful work ethic, and moral precepts for dealing with society. In this text, Proverbs steps away from its larger exhortations and gives teachings in regard to four specific areas of behavior.

The four teachings (vv. 1-5,6-11,12-15,16-19) that make up this section are neither a Wisdom appeal nor a paternal exhortation. The first teaching has one similarity to the paternal exhortation in that it uses the vocative "my son" as a division marker (v. 1), but it lacks a distinctive characteristic of the paternal appeal, the plea for the son to heed the father's words. Also, unlike the paternal exhortation, this section has no thematic unity. Each of the four teachings is discrete.

We should note, however, that the four teachings are joined to one another by catchwords and common ideas. In the first teaching, the man who is entrapped by contractual obligations should allow himself neither sleep nor slumber until he has freed himself (v. 4), whereas the sluggard of the second teaching is caught by "a little sleep, a little slumber" (v. 10).[111] The second teaching ends with poverty coming upon the sluggard like a vagrant or beggar (v. 11),[112] and the third teaching begins

[111]שֵׁנָה ("sleep") and וּתְנוּמָה ("slumber") in v. 4, מְעַט תְּנוּמוֹת ("a little sleep and a little slumber") in v. 10.

[112]See comments on the meaning of v. 11 on pp. 96-97.

with a condemnation of the "scoundrel and villain" (v. 12).[113] Finally, the mark of the villain is that "he always stirs up dissension" (v. 14), a sin that occupies the significant place of the seventh thing the Lord hates in the fourth teaching (v. 19).[114] Therefore, although the four teachings are individual and distinct, they are not joined to one another in a haphazard fashion.

Legal Entanglements (6:1-5). **6:1-5** At first glance this passage would seem to say no more than that one should not cosign a note or, if one has already made that mistake, should get out of the arrangement as quickly as possible.[115] While the text does say at least this much, it also implies that no one should get into legal entanglements and indebtedness in which circumstances are out of one's control. This is certainly the case where giving security for another is concerned.

Note that the Bible does not absolutely forbid taking on legal responsibilities for another person (Phlm 18). It does, however, here state that risking home and liberty in an enterprise over which one does not have direct control is consummate folly. Although we have no information on Israelite laws of surety,[116] seizure of assets and home and even the selling of the debtor into slavery were common penalties for failure to make payment,[117] and the cosigner could well have met the same fate.

Laziness (6:6-11). **6:6-11** The ants are models of diligence in that they work tirelessly in spite of having no taskmaster to goad them on, and they prepare for the winter[118] in spite of having no administration to lay out economic plans. Wisdom literature often examines the natural world for moral lessons.[119] Laziness leads to inescapable poverty and ruin. Instead of poverty coming "like a bandit" and an "armed man," it is better to translate v. 11 to say that poverty will come like a "vagabond" and a "beggar."[120]

---

[113]The verbal similarity between v. 11b and v. 12a is in the Hebrew but not the English. The term אִישׁ מָגֵן ("beggar," v. 11) rhymes with אִישׁ אָוֶן ("man of iniquity," v. 12). Also compare הוֹלֵךְ ("walking," v. 12) to מְהַלֵּךְ ("walking," i.e., "loiterer," v. 11).

[114]מְדָנִים יְשַׁלֵּחַ ("he stirs up dissension") in v. 14, וּמְשַׁלֵּחַ מְדָנִים ("stirring up dissension") in v. 19.

[115]The meaning of the Hebrew of v. 1 is disputed on three points. First, does עָרַבְתָּ לְרֵעֶךָ mean "you have put up security *for* your neighbor" or "*to* your neighbor"? Second, is רֵעֶךָ here equal to זָר ("stranger"), or is the former the friend for whom security is given and the latter the creditor? Finally, does זָר have some special nuance here such as "outcast" or "enemy"? Because of the parallel structure of the verse, it is best to follow the NIV in answering these questions. Cf. Toy, *Proverbs*, 120, and Delitzsch, *Proverbs* 1:135-36. See McKane, *Proverbs*, 321-22, on the various theories that have been built around this verse.

[116]Cf. Toy, *Proverbs*, 121-22.

[117]See 1 Sam 22:2; Amos 2:6-8; Neh 5:1-5. Cf. *ISBE*, rev. ed., s.v. "Debt."

[118]Several species of Palestinian ants store grain for winter. See *ISBE*, rev. ed., s.v. "Ant."

[119]Note that the LXX adds moral observations on the diligence of bees here.

[120]Thus Albright, "Canaanite-Phoenician Sources," 9-10. Although precise evidence for the meaning of מְהַלֵּךְ is lacking, it is not clear how the piel of הלך could mean "bandit." The

The point is not that it will attack suddenly, like armed robbers in ambush. Rather, poverty and indebtedness cling to the slothful like incorrigible beggars who always linger about the house and always want more. Laziness will siphon off resources until the indolent have nothing left.

THE CONSPIRATOR (6:12-15). **6:12-15** The behavior of the scoundrel—winking his eyes, shuffling his feet, and pointing with his fingers—would be obscure to us were it not for the act that context indicates he is planning malice against someone and stirring up dissension (v. 14). Therefore, although it is possible to regard these gestures as part of casting curses on someone in black magic,[121] it is better to take them as simple nonverbal communication with fellow conspirators.

The "scoundrel" is someone who works to undermine social and personal relationships for his own benefit. In particular he attempts to corrupt the judicial system or subvert the government's authority, as this text implies.[122] The man of *bĕliyya^{c}al* is someone who openly rejects the rules of society and thus undermines normal social relations. Examples are the depraved men of Gibeah who thought themselves beyond the reach of the law (Judg 20:13), those who mock justice (Prov 19:28), and especially those who undermine the king's authority (1 Sam 10:27; 2 Sam 20:1; 2 Chr 13:7). But his own destruction is certain (v. 15).

ISRAEL'S SEVEN DEADLY SINS (6:16-19). **6:16-19** The medieval church had its list of "seven deadly sins" (pride, anger, envy, impurity, gluttony, slothfulness, and avarice). Here, Proverbs provides us with a list that may be considered the Israelite version of the seven deadly sins. This teaching, a numerical saying, is arranged for easy memorization. The first five things the Lord hates are body parts set in a sequence that moves generally from the head to the feet (eyes, tongue, hands, heart, feet), and the last two are specific types of persons (the false witness and the troublemaker). Also, note that the first five items concern general moral characteristics (pride, deceitfulness, a violent or conniving character, etc.), whereas the last two (v. 19) specifically belong to a judicial or governmental setting.

In each of the first five members of the list, some body part is associated with a particular type of sin. More specifically, the body parts that

---

association of the word with the English "highwayman" in the older commentaries (Toy, *Proverbs*, 125; *BDB*, 235) is far-fetched. One who "walks about" should more naturally be taken as a loiterer or vagrant. אִישׁ מָגֵן is also difficult, but the verb *mgn*, "to beg," in Ugaritic indicates that "beggar" is meant here. The interpretation that it means "man of a shield" and thus "armed man" is, as Albright says, meaningless.

[121]Cf. McKane, *Proverbs*, 325.

[122]"Scoundrel" here is אָדָם בְּלִיַּעַל. The etymology of בְּלִיַּעַל is uncertain, but its meaning is clear from the texts in which it occurs. See *TDOT*, s.v. בְּלִיַּעַל (2:131-36).

act out certain sins (e.g., hands that shed blood) represent the distorted personalities behind such actions. Thus it is that the verse uses such strong language in v. 16, saying that God "hates" or "detests" these things. The person whose eyes, hands, or feet carry out such deeds has a twisted soul and thus grossly corrupts the image of God that should be recognizable in every human.

"Haughty eyes" are eyes that are lifted up[123] in arrogance. The position of the eyes describes the attitude of the heart. The arrogant spirit may vaunt itself against any and all people, but fundamentally this reflects haughtiness before God and refusal to reckon with one's finitude and creatureliness.

A "lying tongue" is metonymy for a person who has no regard for truth. To lie is to distort reality for one's own purposes and bespeaks a refusal to submit to norms of right and wrong; by lying, one seeks to rearrange not just individual facts but one's just place in the world and so avoid having to live by the normal rules of life. Habitual lying thus leads to the psychological distortions described as "psychopathic personality."

The phrase "hands that shed innocent blood" describes the violent personality and as such is one who would be prone to murder if circumstances were conducive. A lack of control over anger is implied, as is a profound lack of regard for the value of human life. This is the personality that will beat or even kill another person out of anger over a presumed insult.

The "heart that devises wicked schemes" might be in modern parlance a sociopathic personality. Such a person has no regard for anything but that which might work to his or her advantage. Rules and values are used when it is beneficial to do so, but they are disregarded when they are inconvenient. Such a one is always looking for an edge over everyone else.

"Feet that rush to do evil" bespeak a terrible enthusiasm for opportunities to do wrong. Such an individual regards the occasion to sin, when it appears, as a stroke of good luck and a terrific chance to get away with breaking a rule and perhaps get something for nothing. But the benefit that may come is secondary; like the vandal who destroys property that he cannot steal, the real object is the simple joy of wrongdoing.

The "false witness" seeks to subvert justice in the courts, while the "one who stirs up dissension," like the "scoundrel" in the previous section, attempts to break apart the bonds that hold a society together.[124] These two figures are fundametnally antisocial in that they break bonds of friendship, promote the decay of public justice, and ultimately bring a community into chaos.

---

[123]The word רָמוֹת ("raised up"), used of the eyes, describes the opposite of turning one's eyes downward out of humility and respect.

[124]"Brothers" here does not necessarily refer to members of one family. Israelite men commonly called each other "brothers" (e.g., 2 Sam 19:41).

(8) The Sixth Exhortation (6:20-35)

[20]My son, keep your father's commands
and do not forsake your mother's teaching.
[21]Bind them upon your heart forever;
fasten them around your neck.
[22]When you walk, they will guide you;
when you sleep, they will watch over you;
when you awake, they will speak to you.
[23]For these commands are a lamp,
this teaching is a light,
and the corrections of discipline
are the way to life,
[24]keeping you from the immoral woman,
from the smooth tongue of the wayward wife.
[25]Do not lust in your heart after her beauty
or let her captivate you with her eyes,
[26]for the prostitute reduces you to a loaf of bread,
and the adulteress preys upon your very life.
[27]Can a man scoop fire into his lap
without his clothes being burned?
[28]Can a man walk on hot coals
without his feet being scorched?
[29]So is he who sleeps with another man's wife;
no one who touches her will go unpunished.

[30]Men do not despise a thief if he steals
to satisfy his hunger when he is starving.
[31]Yet if he is caught, he must pay sevenfold,
though it costs him all the wealth of his house.
[32]But a man who commits adultery lacks judgment;
whoever does so destroys himself.
[33]Blows and disgrace are his lot,
and his shame will never be wiped away;
[34]for jealousy arouses a husband's fury,
and he will show no mercy when he takes revenge.
[35]He will not accept any compensation;
he will refuse the bribe, however great it is.

In ancient as in modern societies, both father and mother fear for the sexual future of their child. Their deepest desire is that the child have a fulfilling and joyful married life. Against them stands the lure of illicit sex personified in the prostitute or other woman. Parents know that the aftermath of such behavior is disgrace at best and personal destruction at worst.

6:20-35 The sixth exhortation begins typically with an appeal for the son to heed his father's words (vv. 20-24). As in 3:3, the command to bind the teachings to the neck means that they are vital to the young man's survival.[125] The father's teachings are personified as guide, guardian, and companion[126] (v. 22) and objectified as a lamp and a way (v. 23). The last verse of the paternal appeal (v. 24) indicates that what follows will be a warning to avoid the adulteress.

If there is uncertainty regarding the identity of the strange woman in chap. 5, there is none here. She is the wife of another man.[127] This does not mean that in every case where Proverbs discusses the immoral woman it means the adulterous wife (as opposed to the common prostitute), nor does the fact that the woman is another man's wife exclude that she may also be a foreigner or a cult prostitute.[128] The descriptions of the immoral woman of Proverbs are too diverse to allow her to be identified with a single category.[129] The text does not conceal the fact that she is alluring and even beautiful to the young man (v. 25), but she is deadly. To embrace her is to embrace fire.

The Hebrew of v. 26 is most difficult. Although support can be found for the NIV rendition in scholarly literature,[130] it is a conjectural and quite questionable translation. The verse is best rendered, "Although the price of a prostitute may be as much as a loaf of bread,/ [another] man's wife hunts the precious life."[131] The man's life, which the wayward woman hunts, is called "precious" (i.e., valuable) in contrast to meager payment the prostitute demands. This obviously is not meant to endorse going to a prostitute as opposed to having an affair with another man's wife but to show the complete folly of getting involved with another man's wife. Indeed, "prostitute," in parallel here with the "[other] man's wife," may well be one and the same person. She takes a small payment as prostitute from her victim but as adulteress steals away his very life. The price also indicates the degradation of this act to both man and woman; it is cheap. Going to the immoral woman is the quintessential self-destructive act.

---

[125]See the comments on 3:3.

[126]Specifically a female companion (הִיא). The portrait of the young man awakening with Wisdom at his side prepares the way for the counterpart to Wisdom, the adulteress.

[127]Some scholars separate vv. 20-26 from vv. 27-35 and thus contend that the "immoral woman" of v. 24 is not the married woman of vv. 27-35. But this interpretation is forced. See McKane, *Proverbs*, 328-31.

[128]Note that the Babylonian *Counsels of Wisdom*, lines 72-79 (*ANET*, 595) warn against marrying a cult prostitute. The two categories of adulteress wife and cult prostitute are not mutually exclusive. See also the comments on 7:19-20.

[129]McKane (*Proverbs*, 337) points out the "unwisdom of trying to make her conform to an exact pattern."

[130]E.g., Delitzsch, *Proverbs* 1:151-52.

[131]Reading בְּעַד as "price" (LXX τιμή) and עַד as "as much as." Thomas ("Textual and Philological Notes," 283-84) takes נֶפֶשׁ יְקָרָה to mean "person of weight [i.e., significance]" instead of "precious life," but this is doubtful. See Toy, *Proverbs*, 136-37, and McKane, *Proverbs*, 329, for other possible interpretations.

The outraged husband will bring all his fury down upon the adulterer, who will be at least humiliated and beaten if not executed (implied in v. 35).[132] Even if the adulterer is wealthy, that will do him no good. The comparison to the thief in vv. 30-31 is meant to bring home the point that there can be no escape for the adulterer once he is finally found out. People have compassion for a thief who steals out of hunger, but even so they require that he repay his victim seven times over. How much more will society bring down a harsh verdict on an adulterer, a man for whom they feel only contempt?

(9) The Seventh Exhortation (7:1-27)

[1]My son, keep my words
and store up my commands within you.
[2]Keep my commands and you will live;
guard my teachings as the apple of your eye.
[3]Bind them on your fingers;
write them on the tablet of your heart.
[4]Say to wisdom, "You are my sister,"
and call understanding your kinsman;
[5]they will keep you from the adulteress,
from the wayward wife with her seductive words.

[6]At the window of my house
I looked out through the lattice.
[7]I saw among the simple,
I noticed among the young men,
a youth who lacked judgment.
[8]He was going down the street near her corner,
walking along in the direction of her house
[9]at twilight, as the day was fading,
as the dark of night set in.

[10]Then out came a woman to meet him,
dressed like a prostitute and with crafty intent.
[11](She is loud and defiant,
her feet never stay at home;
[12]now in the street, now in the squares,
at every corner she lurks.)
[13]She took hold of him and kissed him
and with a brazen face she said:

[14]"I have fellowship offerings at home;
today I fulfilled my vows.
[15]So I came out to meet you;
I looked for you and have found you!

[132]Leviticus 20:10 stipulates the death penalty for adultery, but it is not known how consistently this was carried out in Israelite society.

[16]I have covered my bed
with colored linens from Egypt.
[17]I have perfumed my bed
with myrrh, aloes and cinnamon.
[18]Come, let's drink deep of love till morning;
let's enjoy ourselves with love!
[19]My husband is not at home;
he has gone on a long journey.
[20]He took his purse filled with money
and will not be home till full moon."

[21]With persuasive words she led him astray;
she seduced him with her smooth talk.
[22]All at once he followed her
like an ox going to the slaughter,
like a deer stepping into a noose
[23]till an arrow pierces his liver,
like a bird darting into a snare,
little knowing it will cost him his life.

[24]Now then, my sons, listen to me;
pay attention to what I say.
[25]Do not let your heart turn to her ways
or stray into her paths.
[26]Many are the victims she has brought down;
her slain are a mighty throng.
[27]Her house is a highway to the grave,
leading down to the chambers of death.

The paternal appeal that opens this exhortation includes vv. 1-5, and v. 5 introduces the subject at hand, the immoral woman. The body of the exhortation (vv. 6-23) takes the form of an example story. The exhortation concludes with an appeal from the father to avoid the adulteress (vv. 24-27). This gives the whole chapter an *A-B-A* pattern (see comment on 8:32-36).

THE PATERNAL APPEAL (7:1-5). **7:1-5** In the appeal the father urges the son to keep his "commands" (vv. 1-2), the same word that is often used of God's commands. The authority of God in the covenant and the authority of the parent as a teacher of wisdom are joined. In addition, the son should write the instruction on his heart, much as God will write the new covenant on the hearts of his people (v. 3; see Jer 31:33). The teaching should be internal, part of the son's character and personality, rather than an external requirement.

Calling Wisdom "my sister" anticipates the warning against the adulteress in v. 5. "Sister" is a term of endearment for a girlfriend or wife.[133]

[133]E.g., Song 5:1. Perhaps מֹדָע should be rendered "an intimate" (i.e., one who is well known, from ידע; cf. the LXX, γνώριμον) rather than "a kinsman." The word appears elsewhere as "kinsman" only in the *qere* of Ruth 2:1.

The young man is to love Wisdom rather than the immoral woman.

A SAD EXAMPLE (7:6-23). **7:6-23** The father tells of an occasion when he actually observed a young man being seduced by an adulteress. He saw it all as he looked out his window, and he had no doubt about what was transpiring.[134] The young man walked toward her house at twilight.[135] It is not certain whether he was deliberately going there or just passing by (v. 8). The woman's loud, seductive behavior[136] and open kissing of the man (vv. 10-13; cf. Song 8:1) show her immodesty.

Verse 14 is especially curious. Most interpreters argue that the woman is saying that she has just completed a sacrifice of peace offerings and therefore has a banquet of freshly roasted meat at home. She is trying to attract the man with the prospect of a feast.[137] The sacred significance of the sacrifice is said to be lost on the woman. For her it has degenerated to a secular feast, much as Christmas has for many in modern Christendom.[138]

This interpretation has problems, however, in that she nowhere offers the man a festal meal.[139] The NIV translation, "I have fellowship offerings at home" is doubtful; a better rendition is "Peace offerings [were] due from me."[140] In addition, she makes no attempt to conceal that she is taking him home for a sexual encounter (vv. 16-18), not a meal.

This leads to an alternative interpretation, that the woman is claiming she has vows yet to fulfill and needs money to pay for the peace offerings that are part of the vows. "Today I fulfilled my vows" can be rendered, "Today I am fulfilling my vows."[141] The idea is that her vows are already due and she needs the money now. Also her claim in v. 20 that her husband has gone off with the moneybag may not be just an assurance that he will not be back soon but also a further claim that she has no money and needs it for the vow.

---

[134]Following the LXX, some scholars contend that it was actually the adulteress who was looking out the window as she waited for her prey. But the MT makes excellent sense and does not stand in need of alteration. See McKane, *Proverbs*, 334-35.

[135]אִישׁוֹן לַיְלָה, "pupil of the night," with the meaning "in the middle of the night" seems unusual. Dahood, *Proverbs*, 14–15, says it is derived from the root ישׁן, "sleep," and here means "in the quiet time" or "in the time of night when people go to sleep." But McKane (*Proverbs*, 336) considers this farfetched. One might conjecture that the "pupil of the night" was the evening star, and thus twilight.

[136]לֶקַח ("persuasiveness," v. 21) may be alluring mannerisms and not just verbal persuasion. See Thomas, "Textual and Philological Notes," 284.

[137]Thus Cohen, *Proverbs*, 41. Only a portion of the "peace offering" was devoted to Yahweh and consumed on the fire. Another portion was given to the priests, and the rest went to the one who brought the sacrifice. A votive peace offering had to be consumed within one day of the sacrifice (Lev 7:16-17); the woman's assertion that she had just fulfilled her vow that day could mean that she was within the time frame in which the meat was to be eaten.

[138]Cf. Delitzsch, *Proverbs* 1:163-64, and Kidner, *Proverbs*, 75, n 1.

[139]Contrast the explicit invitation in 9:2-5.

[140]The preposition עַל is not generally used of possession. Here it refers to a duty imposed upon a person; cf. *BDB*, 753, and McKane, *Proverbs*, 221.

[141]See Van Der Toorn, "Female Prostitution," 198.

The prohibition in Deut 23:17-18 against using money earned by prostitution for paying vows implies that such did in fact occur. Otherwise the reference to her vows is strange because in v. 14 she is not so much offering something to the man as describing her own religious duties.

Her claim to need money for a vow, however, is a lie.[142] She uses the pretext of religious devotion in order to assuage the young man's conscience about going to her.[143] Having dealt with his moral qualms, she devotes the rest of her seduction to a promise of a night of luxurious lovemaking (vv. 15-20). At last the man yields. He is both docile, like the ox going to slaughter, and stupid, like a deer[144] or bird going into a trap (vv. 21-23). He is about to pay the full fee for her services—his life.[145]

A CONCLUDING APPEAL (7:24-27). **7:24-27** As a final appeal the father unmasks the adulteress to reveal the monster beneath the beautiful exterior. People should not be assumed to be good or evil based on external appearances, for real *good* and real *evil* are in one's soul (Matt 23:25-28; Mark 7:23). The language of v. 26 is military in tone.[146] The lady who was so desirable has slain whole armies.

There is some resemblance between this description of the adulteress and the picture of Anat/Astarte in Ugaritic literature. The following description of Anat from *V AB* is illustrative: "For she plunges knee-deep in knights' blood/ Hip deep in the gore of heroes."[147] The goddess is at the same time the patroness of sensuality and a bloodthirsty devil. The same can be said for the adulteress.[148]

---

[142]"With a brazen face" (v. 13) indicates she is lying. The phrase is found only here and in Prov 21:29, where it refers to a straight-faced lie. This is the telling weakness of the interpretation in that she is a member of a fertility cult and that the sexual encounter with the young man is actually part of a vow to Astarte, goddess of love (Von Rad, *Wisdom in Israel*, 167; see also McKane, *Proverbs*, 339). In the fertility cult interpretation, her words are not an expression of a hypocritical Yahwism but actually part of her duty to her goddess. But if she is lying about the vow, as v. 13 implies, there is no reason to assume that her encounter with the young man has anything to do with a fertility ritual. See also D. A. Garrett, "Votive Prostitution Again: A Comparison of Proverbs 7:13-14 and 21:28-29," *JBL* (1990): 681-82.

[143]Van Der Toorn ("Female Prostitution," 193-205) has developed this interpretation. He also argues that fertility cult ritual prostitution never existed but that prostitution to pay for vows may have been fairly common. But one cannot eliminate fertility prostitution from the ancient Near East. It is doubtful that the devotees of Astarte and Baal would have cognitively separated the prostitution in their temples from the worship of fertility gods. The former naturally would have been a ritual celebration of the latter.

[144]The NIV, "like a deer stepping into a noose," is the best alternative for the unintelligible MT, "like an anklet to the correction of a fool" (v. 22c). Cf. McKane, *Proverbs*, 340-41.

[145]בְּנַפְשׁוֹ = "at the price of his life" (v. 23).

[146]חֲלָלִים ("victims") can mean "casualties," and v. 26b is drawn from a battlefield scene.

[147]ANET, 136.

[148]One could argue that this implies that the woman is in fact a devotee of Astarte, as Von Rad contends.

(10) Second Appeal of Wisdom (8:1-36)

[1]Does not wisdom call out?
Does not understanding raise her voice?
[2]On the heights along the way,
where the paths meet, she takes her stand;
[3]beside the gates leading into the city,
at the entrances, she cries aloud:
[4]"To you, O men, I call out;
I raise my voice to all mankind.
[5]You who are simple, gain prudence;
you who are foolish, gain understanding.
[6]Listen, for I have worthy things to say;
I open my lips to speak what is right.
[7]My mouth speaks what is true,
for my lips detest wickedness.
[8]All the words of my mouth are just;
none of them is crooked or perverse.
[9]To the discerning all of them are right;
they are faultless to those who have knowledge.
[10]Choose my instruction instead of silver,
knowledge rather than choice gold,
[11]for wisdom is more precious than rubies,
and nothing you desire can compare with her.
[12]"I, wisdom, dwell together with prudence;
I possess knowledge and discretion.
[13]To fear the LORD is to hate evil;
I hate pride and arrogance,
evil behavior and perverse speech.
[14]Counsel and sound judgment are mine;
I have understanding and power.
[15]By me kings reign
and rulers make laws that are just;
[16]by me princes govern,
and all nobles who rule on earth.
[17]I love those who love me,
and those who seek me find me.
[18]With me are riches and honor,
enduring wealth and prosperity.
[19]My fruit is better than fine gold;
what I yield surpasses choice silver.
[20]I walk in the way of righteousness,
along the paths of justice,
[21]bestowing wealth on those who love me
and making their treasuries full.
[22]"The LORD brought me forth as the first of his works,
before his deeds of old;

[23]I was appointed from eternity,
from the beginning, before the world began.
[24]When there were no oceans, I was given birth,
when there were no springs abounding with water;
[25]before the mountains were settled in place,
before the hills, I was given birth,
[26]before he made the earth or its fields
or any of the dust of the world.
[27]I was there when he set the heavens in place,
when he marked out the horizon on the face of the deep,
[28]when he established the clouds above
and fixed securely the fountains of the deep,
[29]when he gave the sea its boundary
so the waters would not overstep his command,
and when he marked out the foundations of the earth.
[30]Then I was the craftsman at his side.
I was filled with delight day after day,
rejoicing always in his presence,
[31]rejoicing in his whole world
and delighting in mankind.
[32]"Now then, my sons, listen to me;
blessed are those who keep my ways.
[33]Listen to my instruction and be wise;
do not ignore it.
[34]Blessed is the man who listens to me,
watching daily at my doors,
waiting at my doorway.
[35]For whoever finds me finds life
and receives favor from the LORD.
[36]But whoever fails to find me harms himself;
all who hate me love death."

FIRST STROPHE (8:1-3). **8:1-3** This is Wisdom's second appeal, after 1:20-33. Wisdom calls for an audience at the places where she is most likely to find one: from the heights by the road, at crossroads,[149] and at entrances to the city. She is like a merchant hawking her wares. This would not seem to be a dignified posture for one so exalted as she, but the important point is that wisdom is for ordinary people—she is not confined to the academic classroom or to sacred precincts of the temple.[150] Nor is she high atop some mountain where only the hardiest and most determined will find her. To the contrary, she wants to attract all and be accessible to all.[151] The attainment of Wisdom is not a quest but a response.[152]

[149]On the phrase בֵּית נְתִיבוֹת ("at the crossroads," v. 2), see Delitzsch, *Proverbs* 1:173.

[150]See McKane, *Proverbs*, 344-45.

[151]נִצָּבָה ("she takes a stand") implies that she has permanently planted herself at the crossroads (v. 2; cf. Delitzsch, *Proverbs* 1:173). She is not there for just a short time.

[152]Thus Kidner, *Proverbs*, 77.

SECOND STROPHE (8:4-11). **8:4-11** Wisdom begins by asserting that her words are instructive for all humanity, are right, and are more valuable than gold and jewels. While claiming that her gifts are for everyone (v. 4), Wisdom especially offers understanding[153] to the foolish (v. 5). Attainment of biblical wisdom is not so much a matter of intellect as it is faith and obedience.

Wisdom claims that her words are right[154] and proper (v. 6). She also claims to speak them "in righteousness" and without anything twisted or perverse (v. 8). In other words, there is nothing crafty or calculating in her teaching. She has nothing to hide. Also her words are vindicated in the lives of those who know her (v. 9; see Luke 7:35).

The availability of Wisdom to all does not mean that she is cheap or common. To the contrary, she is better than silver, gold, or corals.[155] The superior value of Wisdom over money lives in her ability both to deliver true happiness and protect the life of her possessor.

THIRD STROPHE (8:12-16). **8:12** The third strophe[156] is governed by Wisdom's claim to "dwell together with prudence" and possess "knowledge and discretion" (v. 12). The word translated "prudence"[157] can be used in a bad sense ("craftiness"—Exod 21:14; Josh 9:4), but in Proverbs it is used in a good sense for "sensible behavior" (1:4; 8:5). The word rendered "discretion"[158] can also mean "evil plans," but in Proverbs it often refers to careful behavior that arises from clear thinking.[159] Wisdom teaches how to live a discreet and careful life as opposed to a reckless one.

8:13-16 The prudence of Wisdom implies three things. First, evil behavior, pride, and cunning speech are all rejected (v. 13). Those who practice such imprudent behavior, however intelligent they may be, are fools in the fullest sense that they are without wisdom. Second, wisdom gives direction to life and strength to meet its challenges (v. 14). Decisions made apart from prudence and discretion are bound to fail. Third, wisdom is essential in the all-important arena of government (vv. 15-16). Rulers may not possess Wisdom, but they should,[160] and apart from her

---

[153]On the meaning of הֲבִינוּ לֵב, see McKane, *Proverbs*, 345. לֵב here means "acumen," "mental capacity," or, as the NIV has it, "understanding."

[154]NIV properly emends text. For the MT נְגִידִים ("princes") read נְכֹחִים ("right"). Cf. v. 9.

[155]פְּנִינִים, rendered "rubies" in the NIV, might be translated "corals." See *BDB*, 819, and Holladay, 294.

[156]Both strophes 3 (v. 12) and 4 (v. 17) begin with the noun אֲנִי, whereas strophe 5 (v. 22) begins with the noun יהוה. Strophe 6 uses the adverb וְעַתָּה to begin the conclusion to the discourse.

[157]עָרְמָה.

[158]מְזִמָּה.

[159]Used in parallel to דַּעַת or תְּבוּנָה.

[160]יִמְלֹכוּ ("they should rule") and יְחֹקְקוּ ("they should legislate," v. 15) should be taken as jussives rather than imperfects. The text does not assert that all rulers are wise.

they have no legitimacy.[161] The prudence she bestows allows them to make correct decisions.

FOURTH STROPHE (8:17-21). **8:17-21** Following the theme of v. 17, this strophe emphasizes the material benefits of Wisdom. She has riches and wealth (v. 18) and bestows her treasures on those who love her (v. 21). These claims should be taken in a literal rather than a metaphorical sense; through wise behavior one can attain material prosperity. At the same time, not all her benefits are material in nature. She also possesses "righteousness"[162] (vv. 18,20), a quality that is far better than gold or silver.

The point of the strophe is that Wisdom offers the way to prosperity, but it is a way completely devoid of any cynical manipulation of the world. It is based on principles that are woven into the fabric of creation (vv. 22-31), and thus those who follow her avoid self-destructive patterns. Refraining from both self-indulgence and schemes for quick money gradually but surely leads to a life that is healthy in every way.

FIFTH STROPHE (8:22-31). This, the heart of the chapter, describes Wisdom's role in creation. It is divided into three subsections: the birth of Wisdom (vv. 22-26), Wisdom present at the creation (vv. 27-29), and the laughter of Wisdom (vv. 30-31).

8:22-25 Verse 22 begins with an allusion to the creation narrative of Gen 1 in the word "beginning."[163] In saying that the Lord fathered[164] her at (or "as"[165]) the beginning of his ways, Wisdom is claiming to be the first principle of the world and the pattern by which it was created. References to the oceans, waters, mountains, and fields (or "rivers"[166]) also point back to the creation account[167] and emphasize the antiquity of Wisdom.

---

[161] כָּל־שֹׁפְטֵי צֶדֶק is emended in the NIV rendition, but צֶדֶק can mean "legitimacy," as attested in Ugaritic and Phoenician. See Dahood, *Proverbs*, 15. One can thus translate, "By me rulers should rule, and [by me] princes are all legitimate judges."

[162] צְדָקָה in v. 18 as in v. 20 means "righteousness" rather than "prosperity." Cf. McKane, *Proverbs*, 350.

[163] The parallel of רֵאשִׁית to בְּרֵאשִׁית of Gen 1:1 is surely no accident. Versional evidence supports including the prefix ב in this verse, which makes for a more obvious parallel; see BHS note *a*.

[164] The meaning of קָנָנִי here is debated. It could mean "acquired"; but, as McKane (*Proverbs*, 352) points out, this meaning is not appropriate here. Other possible meanings are "create" and "procreate"; Ugaritic usage and the present context (vv. 24-25) support the latter. Even if "procreate" is the meaning, however, this does not establish that a real hypostasis of Wisdom is meant. The "birth" of Wisdom is metaphorical and part of a poetic personification. Cf. also R. Murphy, "Wisdom and Creation," *JBL* 104 (1985): 3-11.

[165] The absence of the ב before רֵאשִׁית, if that be the correct text, may imply that Wisdom herself is the "beginning" of creation.

[166] The Peshitta, Targum, and Vg all render this as "rivers." Thomas ("Notes," 271-72) states that an Arabic cognate supports this and therefore argues that the versions do not represent a variant text but the correct translation. If this is correct, it may allude to the rivers of Gen 2:10-14.

[167] See Gen 1:6-10; 2:10-12.

8:26 An intriguing point is Wisdom's claim to be older than the "dust of the world" (v. 26). Although this could be taken simply at face value, allusions to the creation story in context imply that this is a veiled reference to the formation of Adam from the dust (Gen 2:7). The Hebrew of v. 26 literally reads, "Before he made . . . the head of the dusts of the world."[168] In Gen 1–2 "dust" is associated only with the creation of humanity; there is no account of the creation of dust itself. The "dusts of the world" is humanity, formed of the dust; and its head is Adam.[169]

The term "dust" also indicates our fragility and mortality and implies that the decision to accept or reject Wisdom is a life-or-death choice. When God cursed Adam, he told him that he was but dust and would return to the dust (Gen 3:19). This concept frequently reappears in biblical wisdom, where "dust" represents human mortality.[170] The frailty that comes of being human only increases our need for Wisdom.

Wisdom was here before us or our world. Humans, as dust, are part of the created world and cannot live contrary to the order by which the world was created. By Wisdom the formless, chaotic dust became Adam, the human race. People who reject Wisdom, therefore, are certain to return to their prior state.

8:27-29 Wisdom claims to have been present at the creation in vv. 27-29. She specifically points to two of the most spectacular aspects of creation, namely, the making of the heavens and the placing of restraints over the power of the sea (Gen 1:1-10). This carries two implications. First, if Wisdom had a part in these two most awesome works of God, surely she should be present if human endeavors are to succeed. Second, if the very universe is made in accordance with the principles of Wisdom, it is folly for anyone to live contrary to those principles.

8:30-31 The laughter of Wisdom (vv. 30-31) poses the question, Why is she laughing? The key is in the word that the NIV renders "craftsman."[171] An alternative translation for the word here is "child"[172]

---

[168]וְרֹאשׁ עָפְרוֹת תֵּבֵל. The noun תֵּבֵל never has the definite article but is translated like a proper noun and hence definite. The use of the plural of עָפָר is found only here and in Job 28:6, where it refers to nuggets and flakes of gold hidden in the rocks. The phrase certainly does not mean "the sum of the dust of the earth" (Delitzsch, *Proverbs* 1:185-87), which, though linguistically possible, makes no sense here. Nor is it to be rendered "the mass of the earth's soil" (McKane, *Proverbs*, 355), a speculative rendition of ראשׁ. The phrase may be rendered "the first of the dusts of the earth" (cf. Toy, *Proverbs*, 175; NIV "any" is similar), but even so the association between dust and humanity is strong.

[169]Note בְּנֵי־אָדָם in v. 31.

[170]See Job 4:19; 10:9; 21:26; 30:19; 34:15; Eccl 3:20; 12:7. Cf. J. G. Janzen, *Job*, INT (Atlanta: John Knox, 1985), 255-58, on Job 42:6.

[171]Cf. the LXX ἁρμόζουσα, "joiner." On אָמוֹן cf. Jer 52:15. It is possible to emend to אָמָּן, which has a similar meaning (Song 7:2).

[172]Cf. הָאֱמֻנִים, "those who were reared," in Lam 4:5.

or "ward,"[173] and other renditions have been proposed as well.[174] While the notion of Wisdom as a laughing child makes sense in context, evidence favors the interpretation "craftsman" or "artisan."

If Wisdom is here an artisan, the message again is that principles of wisdom are woven into the fabric of the created order. The laughter of Wisdom then looks back again to Gen 1, where God's creation is repeatedly called "good." This is not the laughter of child's play or of scorn (contrast 1:26) but satisfaction in the beauty of creation. The joy extends even to the human race, another good work of God (Gen 1:31). Her laughter is an invitation to people to enjoy creation by participation in its goodness. And the path to that goodness is found in Wisdom.

SIXTH STROPHE (8:32-36). **8:32-34** The final strophe is composed of two sections. The first (vv. 32-34) is fashioned in parallel as follows:

A	*Admonition*	"Now . . . listen to me" (v. 32a)
B	*Beatitude*	"Blessed . . . ways" (v. 32b)
A′	*Admonition*	"Listen . . . it" (v. 33)
B′	*Beatitude*	"Blessed . . . doorway" (v. 34)

8:35-36 The second section (vv. 35-36) is a two-proverb collection with elements of both parallelism and inclusio in which the proverbs together form an ethical merismus. "Finds me" (v. 35) is paralleled by "fails to find me" in v. 36, and "life" in v. 35 is answered by "death" in v. 36. Obtaining the Lord's favor contrasts embracing death.

The conclusion strongly emphasizes the doctrine of the two ways, a concept developed most completely in Proverbs and Deuteronomy.[175] The choice is laid down in the most stark terms. The reader will either be so devoted to her that he will hang onto her every word ("watching daily at my doors," v. 34), or he will hate her (v. 36). No one can remain neutral, and it is a matter of life and death.

EXCURSUS: THE PERSON OF WISDOM IN PROVERBS 8. What is the meaning of the "hypostatization" of Wisdom in Prov 8? This is perhaps the most discussed and debated issue in Proverbs. The text has been interpreted in various ways and used in support of diverse theories and practices.

Some scholars have argued that the figure of Woman Wisdom is originally mythological and derived from an Israelite or pagan goddess. Recently, Prov 8 has been drafted into the service of feminist theology

---

[173]Cf. Aquila, τιθηνουμένη.

[174]McKane (*Proverbs*, 357-58) renders it as "confidant," but his evidence is tenuous.

[175]This should not obscure the difference between wisdom and Deuteronomic theology. While here, as elsewhere in Proverbs, the pursuit of wisdom is tied to devotion to Yahweh, the link between Yahwism and wisdom is the doctrine of "creation." In Deuteronomy the "covenant" is the critical point of decision.

and goddess worship.[176] Whybray, however, has correctly noted that mythological figures are generally absent from Egyptian and Babylonian wisdom literature, which calls into question how Israelite wisdom literature would be exceptional. He cites Ringren, moreover, to point out that it is strange that a goddess would have the abstract noun "Wisdom" substituted for her name.[177]

A number of motifs are often alleged to indicate the mythological background of Wisdom. These are (a) Wisdom as an object of incomparable value (3:13-15), (b) Wisdom as directing the rule of kings (8:15-16), (c) Wisdom as woman and bride (4:8-9), and (d) Wisdom as building a house of seven pillars (9:1).[178] None of these concepts, however, is distinctively mythological. Of concept *a*, for example, Whybray comments: "The simple observation of the advantages which have accrued to men who possessed wisdom, rather than a mythological figure, probably lies behind these passages."[179]

Another alleged mythological motif in this passage concerns v. 24, which, according to Albright, reflects a Canaanite myth of conflict between El and the primordial dragon Tehom. He argues that Prov 8 draws on this imagery to depict God as bringing forth Wisdom even before subduing Tehom. In addition, the "mountains" of v. 25 recall the Canaanite myths, he contends.[180]

Albright's analysis has been answered in detail by McKane, who points out that neither Gen 1 nor Prov 8 imply a precreation watery chaos and that Prov 8:25 only states that Wisdom existed before the hills—nothing in the verse relates to Mount Zaphon of the Canaanite myths. He also rightly observes that Albright's theories have no clear exegetical application to the text.[181] Also, Tsumura has demonstrated that Gen 1 has no

---

[176]Cf. C. V. Camp, *Wisdom and the Feminine in the Book of Proverbs* (Sheffield: Almond, 1985), and B. Lang, *Wisdom and the Book of Proverbs: An Israelite Goddess Redefined* (New York: Pilgrim, 1986).

[177]Whybray, *Wisdom in Proverbs*, 82-83.

[178]Ibid., 87-92.

[179]Ibid., 88. Whybray also rejects a mythological source to *b* and *d* as well, although he does allow that the cult of Astarte is behind *c*, wisdom as bride, in that wisdom is portrayed as the better alternative to the fertility cult of the goddess. This too, however, seems unnecessary. Proverbs is attempting to portray Wisdom as the proper object of the yearning of young men and at the same time dissuade them from pursuing the easy pleasures of the adulteress. With this background it is entirely appropriate that Wisdom should be personified as a woman. The sexual temptations described in Proverbs, moreover, do not appear to be related to the Canaanite cults, and the book contains no polemic against idolatry.

[180]Albright, "Canaanite-Phoenician Sources," 8. See also W. F. Albright, *From Stone Age to Christianity*, 2d. ed. (New York: Doubleday, 1957), 367-70, and cf. Whybray, *Wisdom in Proverbs*, 83-87.

[181]McKane, *Proverbs*, 354-56.

myth of combat with a primordial dragon.[182]

The hypostatization of Wisdom is, as it appears to be, a powerful personification. But it is no more than that. Similar personifications are found in Pss 85:10-13 and 89:14, and Israel and Judah are personified in Ezek 23. It is true that Prov 8 is a considerably more developed, extended personification than found in some of the above texts,[183] but that does not mean that Prov 8 is fundamentally different.

If Woman Wisdom is a personification, however, what does she personify? Does she represent an attribute of God, as is sometimes argued? To this the answer must be an emphatic no. While wisdom is certainly an attribute of God, this text does not deal with it in that sense. To the contrary, since Prov 8 is an invitation to the reader to partake of wisdom, it cannot mean that access to a divine attribute is open to humans when they desire to acquire it, but rather it is a gift given by God.

In the same way, Wisdom is not the Second Person of the Trinity. Perhaps the strongest argument for taking Prov 8 to be an Old Testament portrait of Christ is 1 Cor 1:24, where Paul calls Christ "the wisdom of God." Close examination of the text, however, reveals that Paul's description of Christ is not an allusion to Prov 8 and that it provides no basis for interpreting Proverbs in this way.

First, Paul's purpose in 1 Cor 1:24 is not to point to Old Testament texts that relate to Christ but to address the scandal of the cross. In particular he faces the issue of the offense created when he proclaims that the crucified Jesus is the Son of God and Savior of the world. To the Greeks this is sheer folly. When he says that Christ is the wisdom of God, he means it functionally[184] in the sense that the crucified Christ is God's profound way of salvation despite whatever human reason may think of the idea. He also calls Christ the power of God in the same verse in response to Jews who expect the Messiah to come in overwhelming power.

Second, it is not appropriate to take Paul's comment and make it the interpretive grid for an Old Testament text to which Paul made no allusion whatsoever. Similarly, one should not take a text that describes the power of God (e.g., Ps 78:4ff.) and claim that it is really a description of

---

[182]D. T. Tsumura, *The Earth and the Waters in Genesis 1 and 2: A Linguistic Investigation*, JSOTSS 83 (Sheffield: JSOT Press, 1989).

[183]Whybray, *Wisdom in Proverbs*, 81-82. Whybray argues that the personifications in the Psalms and Ezekiel are "embryonic" and therefore asserts that the figure of wisdom is more than a simple personification. But it is hard to see in what sense the other texts are less than personifications or how the figure of wisdom in Proverbs is more than a personification.

[184]Cf. H. Conzelmann, *1 Corinthians*, Her (Philadelphia: Fortress, 1975) 48: "The conjunction of δύναμις, 'power,' and σοφία, 'wisdom,' shows that here 'wisdom' is not a hypostasis but a conceptual term. This is confirmed by the variant of v 30 (ἡμῖν—ἀπὸ θεοῦ, 'our—by God'). The seemingly personifying mode of expression is stylistically typical."

Christ on the basis of 1 Cor 1:24. It would be as if one were to take 1 John 4:8 ("God is love") and on that basis claim that 1 Cor 13 is really intended to be read as a description of God.

Finally, Woman Wisdom of Prov 8 does not personify an attribute of God but personifies an attribute of *creation*. She is personification of the structure, plan, or rationality that God built into the world. She is created by God and fundamentally an attribute of God's universe.[185] To quote von Rad's analysis:

> What is objectified here, then, is not an attribute of God but an attribute of the world, namely that mysterious attribute, by virtue of which she turns to men to give order to their lives. Thus, Israel was faced with the same phenomenon which more or less fascinated all ancient religions, namely that of the religious provocation of man by the world. But Israel did not agree to the mythicization and deification of the first principle of the world. Her interpretation was quite a different one, because she held fast to this phenomenon within the sphere of her faith in Yahweh as creator.[186]

Israel, like Egypt, sought the moral structure behind the visible world. But unlike Egypt, Israel saw this structure as the plan of the one true God and subordinated its search to him.

(11) The Two Appeals (9:1-18)

1 Wisdom has built her house;
she has hewn out its seven pillars.
2 She has prepared her meat and mixed her wine;
she has also set her table.
3 She has sent out her maids, and she calls
from the highest point of the city.
4 "Let all who are simple come in here!"
she says to those who lack judgment.
5 "Come, eat my food
and drink the wine I have mixed.
6 Leave your simple ways and you will live;
walk in the way of understanding.

7 "Whoever corrects a mocker invites insult;
whoever rebukes a wicked man incurs abuse.

---

[185] H. Ridderbos (*Paul: An Outline of His Theology* [Grand Rapids: Eerdmans, 1975] 79) similarly comments that Col 1:15 cannot be based on Prov 8: "[Wisdom in Prov 8] is and remains a creature of God, pertaining to that which is created; while Christ, precisely distinguished from all that is created, stands on the side of God (Col 1:15) . . . [N]o connection between Wisdom on the one hand and the Messiah on the other can be shown in the Jews or in Paul."

[186] G. von Rad, *Wisdom in Israel* (Nashville: Abingdon, 1972), 156.

8Do not rebuke a mocker or he will hate you;
rebuke a wise man and he will love you.
9Instruct a wise man and he will be wiser still;
teach a righteous man and he will add to his learning.

10"The fear of the LORD is the beginning of wisdom,
and knowledge of the Holy One is understanding.
11For through me your days will be many,
and years will be added to your life.
12If you are wise, your wisdom will reward you;
if you are a mocker, you alone will suffer."

13The woman Folly is loud;
she is undisciplined and without knowledge.
14She sits at the door of her house,
on a seat at the highest point of the city,
15calling out to those who pass by,
who go straight on their way.
16"Let all who are simple come in here!"
she says to those who lack judgment.
17"Stolen water is sweet;
food eaten in secret is delicious!"
18But little do they know that the dead are there,
that her guests are in the depths of the grave.

The first major section of the Book of Solomon closes with a wisdom appeal. But in a remarkable twist, the appeal of Woman Wisdom (vv. 1-12) is set against an appeal by Woman Folly (vv. 13-18).[187] This follows upon the more detailed seduction by the prostitute in 7:14-20 and the larger wisdom appeal in chap. 8.

Several scholars regard vv. 7-12 as a later intrusion into the text.[188] It is true that vv. 9-10 are missing from one Hebrew manuscript, vv. 10-12, from another,[189] and that the LXX *adds* several verses to the chapter. But the teachings here show an unmistakable similarity to Wisdom's appeals in 1:20-33 and 8:1-36. Note especially the incorrigible nature of the "mock-

[187]R. J. Clifford ("Proverbs IX: A Suggested Parallel," *VT* 25 [1975]: 298-306) suggests that this chapter parallels the Aqht legend of the Ugaritic texts. The hero Aqht was slain by the goddess Anat, but the pious Dan'el obtained his request for children from the more benevolent god El. Both the Ugaritic text and the biblical text contain banquet scenes, and the two use similar terminology. Clifford draws two conclusions from this. First, because of the antiquity of the Aqht legend, an early, preexilic date for Prov 9 is also implied. Second, Prov 9 may be deliberately set in a framework similar to the Canaanite legend in order to serve as an alternative to Canaanite religion.

[188]E.g., Toy, *Proverbs*, 192-93; McKane, *Proverbs*, 359-60; see also Kidner, *Proverbs*, 82. Goldingay ("Proverbs V and IX," 87-93) argues 9:1-6,11 is the original core of Prov 9. He contends that the parallel to 9:1-6,13ff. is secondary.

[189]See BHS notes.

ers" (1:22; 9:7-8) and the certainty of retribution for rejecting Wisdom (1:23-32; 8:36; 9:12). A promise of life in a wisdom appeal (9:11) is found also in 1:33; 3:35; and 9:6. Also compare 9:10 to 1:29 and 8:13.

This chapter draws together major themes of chaps. 1–8. Beyond the similarities mentioned earlier, note how the opening appeal of Wisdom (vv. 1-6) compares to 1:20-21 and 8:1-6. Verse 17 alludes to the two tempters (2:12-19; see the comments below). The final destruction of the fool (v. 18) looks back to 1:28-32; 2:18-19; 5:21-23; and 7:26-27. The major ideas of chaps. 1–8 are thus set before the reader in the context of a choice between the two ways, that of Woman Wisdom and that of Woman Folly.

WOMAN WISDOM'S APPEAL (9:1-2). **9:1-12** The general meaning of this passage is quite clear, but a few mysteries remain. The nature of Wisdom's house of seven pillars is uncertain. Is it a simple house or a temple? Solomon's temple had two pillars at the vestibule (1 Kgs 7:15), but shrines with seven pillars have been found.[190] The significance of "seven" here is also not elucidated. Some have connected it to the seven planets,[191] but a more reasonable explanation is that it refers to the seven days of creation (note Wisdom's role in creation in 8:22-31).

Another question is whether Wisdom dismisses her servant girls prior to the banquet as a matter of decorum[192] or whether she sends them out to invite in the guests. The latter interpretation probably is to be preferred as a contrast to the description of Woman Folly sitting in ambush to waylay passers-by (v. 14). The picture of servants sent out to bring guests to a feast may have contributed to the parable of the great banquet (Luke 14:15-24); note also that v. 5 may be behind Jesus' words in John 6:51-56.

The feast Wisdom provides is emblematic of life, health, and celebration. It contrasts with the banquet of the dead (v. 18) behind Woman Folly's door.

The warning against trying to instruct mockers (vv. 7-9) is characteristic of Proverbs. Even as it urges the young man to faithfulness and prudence, it always recognizes that there are some who will never listen. This reality appears even in 1:7, the theme verse of Proverbs.

Verse 10, which also relates to 1:7, reasserts the teaching that Wisdom apart from the covenant God is impossible.[193] The verse implicitly rejects secular or atheistic ethics.

---

[190]Albright, "Canaanite-Phoenician Sources," 8-9. The most noteworthy is a shrine to Aphrodite on Cyprus that dates from the Roman period.

[191]See McKane, *Proverbs*, 362.

[192]Dahood (*Proverbs*, 16-17) argues that a woman would not send maidservants to invite male guests to a banquet. He cites a Ugaritic parallel that implies that servant girls would be dismissed prior to a banquet.

[193]The use of קְדֹשִׁים, "holy ones," for God as the Holy One is unusual. It most often refers to the saints or angels. It is perhaps here formed on the analogy of אלהים, as in Josh 24:19: כִּי אֱלֹהִים קְדֹשִׁים הוּא.

The promise of life (v. 11) and statement of individual responsibility (v. 12) are a fitting conclusion to Wisdom's final appeal. The joy she offers is for the taking, but everyone must bear responsibility for his or her own decisions.

WOMAN FOLLY'S APPEAL (9:13-18). **9:13-16** Like the prostitute (7:11), Woman Folly is a loud and careless temptress.[194] The parallel of vv. 14-16 to vv. 3-4 is obvious, but Woman Folly sits and waylays those who pass by like a prostitute (Gen 38:14) or like a criminal ambush (Prov 1:11).

9:17 Woman Folly's promise of "stolen water" and "food eaten in secret" (v. 17) is especially significant. Some have suggested that bread and water contrast with the sumptuous feast of Woman Wisdom, but more is implied than that. "Stolen water" looks back to 5:15-18, where sexual relations are described as the drinking of water, and is thus another man's wife. "Food eaten in secret" is literally "bread of secrecy." It refers to the criminal conspiracies that tempt the young man to easy money, as in 1:11-14; 4:14-17 (see esp. v. 17); and 6:12-15.

9:18 This verse therefore looks back to the two tempters—the man who draws the youth into a life of crime and the woman who draws him into promiscuity. Both are in the house of Woman Folly, and both draw more victims to the banquet of the dead in Sheol.

4. Main Text, Proverb Form (10:1–24:22)

(1) Subheading (10:1a)

¹The proverbs of Solomon:

10:1a As indicated in the introduction, 10:1a is a subheading that separates the discourse portion of the main text from the proverb portion. It does not mark the beginning of a separate book.

(2) A Diligent Son and a Lazy Son (10:1b-5)

A wise son brings joy to his father,
but a foolish son grief to his mother.

²Ill-gotten treasures are of no value,
but righteousness delivers from death.

³The LORD does not let the righteous go hungry
but he thwarts the craving of the wicked.

---

[194]The translation of 9:13 is difficult. Instead of the obscure פְּתַיּוּת, it is best to read וּמְפַתָּה, "and seductive." See BHS note as well as Toy, *Proverbs*, 191, and McKane, *Proverbs*, 366-67. G. R. Driver ("Problems," 179) translates וּבַל יָדְעָה מָּה as "cares nought." D. W. Thomas ("Note on בַּל־יָדְעָה in Proverbs 9:13," *JTS* 4 [1953]: 23-24) takes ידע to mean "at rest" on the basis of an Arabic *wd*ᶜ, "to be still." He sees in this verse an assertion of folly's restlessness and debauchery. Perhaps one may translate, "The Woman Folly is loud and seductive and cares for nothing."

[4]Lazy hands make a man poor,
but diligent hands bring wealth.

[5]He who gathers crops in summer is a wise son,
but he who sleeps during harvest is a disgraceful son.

TYPE: THEMATIC, INCLUSIO (10:1b-5). Verses 1b-5 form a collection marked off by the inclusio of "wise son/foolish son" (v. 1) and "wise son/disgraceful son" (v. 5).[195] The theme of the collection is that a family will thrive if the children are diligent in their work but collapse if they are lazy or resort to crime.

10:1b,c Verse 1b,c forms a complete merismus, that is, all the parts interrelate. "Father" and "mother" are of course the parents of the household, and the proverb points out how much their happiness as a family depends on the child's behavior. The collection emphasizes the economic aspect since sons were responsible for the care of parents in old age. They could either squander the family estate or build it up. This section forces the young man to face the economic responsibility he bears for the family.

10:2,4 Verse 4 makes the point that diligence leads to wealth as laziness to poverty,[196] but the collection goes beyond secular aphorisms. "Righteousness delivers from death" (v. 2) has an eschatological sense. More is indicated in the promise than a long life (although the life and security of the family must be the primary meaning). Verse 2a implies in context that God will be the enemy of the family if the son tries to enrich it by crime or corruption.

10:3 Significantly, the text does not attribute the security of the wise strictly to their work habits. Even the most diligent are subject to powers beyond their control. It is the Lord who protects them from the pangs of starvation (v. 3a).[197] Verse 3, standing in the middle of this collection, is crucial. Nothing else the son might ever do can have as positive an impact on his family as a life of faithfulness to God.

10:5 Verse 5 is obviously drawn from agricultural life, but it has implications in other areas as well. As McKane notes, "It is also a representative saying about any son who displays acumen and mettle when his father most needs him, or, contrariwise, who fails when he is put to the test and by his weakness and uselessness brings his father into contempt."[198]

---

[195]Note that in v. 1 the two בֵּן noun phrases each begin a colon, whereas in v. 5 they each end a colon. Verse 1 gives the effect on parents of having a wise or foolish son, whereas v. 5 points out how one may discern whether the son is wise or foolish. This is a tightly bound unit.

[196]Reading רֵאשׁ, "poverty," instead of רָאשׁ, "poor man." Cf. Toy, *Proverbs*, 201-2.

[197]Note that נֶפֶשׁ here means "appetite," a meaning well attested in Ugaritic. See Dahood, *Proverbs*, 18.

[198]McKane, *Proverbs*, 415.

(3) The Mouth of the Wicked (10:6-11)

6 Blessings crown the head of the righteous,
but violence overwhelms the mouth of the wicked.

7 The memory of the righteous will be a blessing,
but the name of the wicked will rot.

8 The wise in heart accept commands,
but a chattering fool comes to ruin.

9 The man of integrity walks securely,
but he who takes crooked paths will be found out.

10 He who winks maliciously causes grief,
and a chattering fool comes to ruin.

11 The mouth of the righteous is a fountain of life,
but violence overwhelms the mouth of the wicked.

TYPE: INCLUSIO, PARALLEL (10:6-11). **10:6-11** Verses 6 and 11 form an inclusio as indicated by the repetition of the line, "But the mouth of the wicked conceals violence."[199] Within this inclusio vv. 7-10 are arranged in parallel (*A B A B*); v. 7 and v. 9 parallel each other (the fate of the righteous versus the fate of the wicked), and v. 8 and v. 10 parallel each other (both contain the line "a chattering fool comes to ruin"). The repetition of two lines in this section, both of which concern the mouth of the wicked, points to the major emphasis of the collection.

Deceitfulness is the mark of the wicked, but the godly are known by the evidence of God's favor upon them and the salutary effects of their words (vv. 6,11). Thus the righteous secure their place in the world, whereas a life of deception holds only the promise of detection and disgrace (vv. 7,9). One would be well advised, therefore, to listen with discernment and "consider the source" when weighing someone's words (vv. 8,10).

(4) Seven-Proverb Collection (10:12-18)

12 Hatred stirs up dissension,
but love covers over all wrongs.

13 Wisdom is found on the lips of the discerning,
but a rod is for the back of him who lacks judgment.

---

[199] This rendition of וּפִי רְשָׁעִים יְכַסֶּה חָמָס is preferable to the NIV, which follows Delitzsch (*Proverbs* 1:212-13) in taking פִּי as the object rather than subject. While it is true that כסה can mean "overwhelm" in a context such as Exod 14:28, where the sea covers the Egyptians, the actual meaning "cover" is never out of sight. In Prov 10:6, however, "overwhelm" is forced and is not a reasonable interpretation of כסה. The idea is that the wicked use their mouths (i.e., their words) to conceal their violence. See REB, NRSV.

[14]Wise men store up knowledge,
but the mouth of a fool invites ruin.

[15]The wealth of the rich is their fortified city,
but poverty is the ruin of the poor.

[16]The wages of the righteous bring them life,
but the income of the wicked brings them punishment.

[17]He who heeds discipline shows the way to life,
but whoever ignores correction leads others astray.

[18]He who conceals his hatred has lying lips,
and whoever spreads slander is a fool.

TYPE: INCLUSIO WITH TWO-PROVERB PAIRS (10:12-18). Verses 12 and 18 form an inclusio (see the discussion of v. 18 below), and vv. 13-14 and 15-16 are proverbial pairs; catchwords also are used.[200] Themes include wealth and poverty, wisdom and folly, and contentiousness.

10:12 This verse, which teaches forbearance and a forgiving spirit, is cited in 1 Pet 4:8 and Jas 5:20.

10:13-14 Verse 13 seems an odd bicolon since the two parts have little to do with each other.[201] Yet v. 14, the other half of the pair, has the same conceptual outline: the wise use their tongues carefully,[202] but fools bring suffering on themselves by their words. The two proverbs together reinforce this idea. In the context of vv. 12 and 18, the wise avoid trouble by not engaging in verbal retaliation and slander against others.

10:15-16 By itself v. 15 states the obvious if not somewhat cynical truth that it is better to be rich than poor. But this verse is qualified by the moral outlook of v. 16. While money may provide a measure of protection, money wrongfully gained carries the sentence of death with it.[203]

10:17 Verse 17 is a warning to follow the example of the wise rather than the wicked.[204] By itself the proverb is a general maxim of the kind

[200]The catchwords are vv. 14-15, מְחִתָּה ("terror"), and vv. 16-17, לְחַיִּים ("to life").

[201]Although of course נָבוֹן ("an intelligent man") contrasts with חֲסַר־לֵב ("a man lacking sense"), and there may be a wordplay on שִׂפְתֵי ("lips") and שֵׁבֶט ("rod").

[202]The use of the tongue is explicit in vv. 13a and 14b. In v. 14a צפן may mean "conceal" in the sense "the wise do not blurt out what they know." Cf. Toy, *Proverbs*, 208.

[203]The Hebrew could mean that the righteous use their wages for good purposes; but the wicked, for evil. On the other hand, the notion that the righteous spend their wages "for life" is odd. Dahood (*Proverbs*, 19-20) convincingly argues that the ל is *lamed emphaticum* and takes חַטָּאת as either "punishment" (1 Kgs 13:34) or "death" (in contrast to "life" in v. 16a). He translates, "The reward of the virtuous is truly life,/The fruit of the wicked is truly punishment" and sees here a doctrine of afterlife. See also D. W. Thomas, "The Meaning of חַטָּאת in Proverbs X.16," *JTS* 14:1 (1963): 295-96, who takes חַטָּאת as "penury" on the basis of the ancient versions.

[204]Contrary to Delitzsch (*Proverbs* 1:220), מַתְעֶה should be taken in a causative sense ("lead astray"). See McKane, *Proverbs*, 419.

frequently found in Proverbs. In context it implies one should avoid quarrelsome and greedy people.

10:18 Verse 18a should be emended following the LXX.[205] In this collection "conceal" is not used in the bad sense of maliciously hiding something (unlike 10:6,11) but in a good sense of forgiving or not finding fault (11:13; 12:16,23; 17:9; 28:13; note especially 10:12).[206] In addition, all the other proverbs of this collection make use of ethical merismus, whereas this verse only, as usually translated, is in parallel. Following the LXX, however, it reads, "He who forgives hatred has righteous lips,/ but he who spreads defamation is a fool."

As emended v. 18 clearly echoes v. 12. Two key words are repeated,[207] and the main idea of each verse is the same. The wise overlook offenses and seek to put an end to, rather than inflame, a quarrel.

(5) On the Tongue, Personal Security, and Laziness (10:19-32)

19 When words are many, sin is not absent,
but he who holds his tongue is wise.

20 The tongue of the righteous is choice silver,
but the heart of the wicked is of little value.

21 The lips of the righteous nourish many,
but fools die for lack of judgment.

22 The blessing of the LORD brings wealth,
and he adds no trouble to it.

23 A fool finds pleasure in evil conduct,
but a man of understanding delights in wisdom.

24 What the wicked dreads will overtake him;
what the righteous desire will be granted.

25 When the storm has swept by, the wicked are gone,
but the righteous stand firm forever.

26 As vinegar to the teeth and smoke to the eyes,
so is a sluggard to those who send him.

27 The fear of the LORD adds length to life,
but the years of the wicked are cut short.

28 The prospect of the righteous is joy,
but the hopes of the wicked come to nothing.

29 The way of the LORD is a refuge for the righteous,
but it is the ruin of those who do evil.

30 The righteous will never be uprooted,
but the wicked will not remain in the land.

---

205 καλύπτουσιν ἔχθραν χείλη δίκαια.
206 See also Toy, *Proverbs*, 210. מְכַסֶּה is best translated "forgive" here.
207 שִׂנְאָה ("hatred") and כסה ("cover").

31The mouth of the righteous brings forth wisdom,
but a perverse tongue will be cut out.

32The lips of the righteous know what is fitting,
but the mouth of the wicked only what is perverse.

This section is a chiasmus made up of four separate collections with a single proverb standing at the center as a somewhat humorous "bridge." The structure is:

A: On the tongue (vv. 19-21)
B: On personal security (vv. 22-25)
C: On laziness (v. 26)
B′: On personal security (vv. 27-30)
A′: On the tongue (vv. 31-32)[208]

THREE-PROVERB COLLECTION. *Type: Thematic, with One-Proverb Pair (10:19-21).* **10:19-21** The use of the tongue is the theme of this collection, and each verse is merismatic. Verses 20-21 closely parallel each other and can be regarded as a proverb pair. Verse 19 then is an ironic heading to vv. 20-21: Although the wise person gives sound advice, wisdom is found more in those who are silent than in those who are verbose! The message here is that you should be careful about who you listen to and that when a person talks too much, that is a good sign that his words are not worth hearing.

FOUR-PROVERB COLLECTION. *Type: Thematic, Parallel (10:22-25).* **10:22-25** Only through righteousness and wisdom can one attain real security in life. The righteous can have wealth without the trouble that often goes with it (sycophants, legal problems), whereas the wicked will ultimately be brought down by the disaster they fear (vv. 22,24).[209] And while the wicked find great amusement in their crimes, they will not withstand a real calamity when it comes (vv. 23,25).[210] Verse 25 may be behind Matt 7:24-27. Jesus has been described as acting at times like a sage who used the proverb formula in his teaching (e.g., Mark 2:17; 4:21-25). That some of the sayings in Proverbs would be the source for Jesus' teaching is no surprise.

SINGLE PROVERB. *Type: Tricolon (10:26).* **10:26** The humor of this proverb well compares the irritation of an unreliable person with that of vinegar in the mouth and smoke in the eyes. Whereas the smoke and vinegar are irritable to the physical person, the sluggard is irritable to the

[208]Note that the parallel couplet of vv. 20-21 closely parallels that of vv. 31-32 and that both "B" sections are four-proverb collections set in parallel.

[209]Note the parallel structure of vv. 22a,24a: noun phrase + הִיא + feminine imperfect verb.

[210]Note that both vv. 23 and 25 begin with the preposition כְּ.

emotion of the individual and to the fabric of society. The double simile in a structure of three cola gives greater force to the proverb.[211]

FOUR-PROVERB COLLECTION. *Type: Thematic, Parallel (10:27-30).* The four proverbs of this collection all deal with the theme of long life for the righteous and destruction for the wicked. In addition, the proverbs are in an *A-B-A-B* pattern.[212] This pattern is found in vv. 27 and 29, which are parallel with each other linked by the motif of *the Lord*, while vv. 28 and 30 are linked by the motif of the *righteous*. All four verses are linked by the motif of the fate of the *wicked* (*rešāᶜîm*, vv. 27-28,30) and those who do *evil* (*ʾāwen*).

10:27 Verse 27 makes the general statement that those who fear God will live longer than the impious. This is not a fixed law with no exception but a maxim that the prudent will heed.

10:28 It is perhaps better to render v. 28a as, "The expectation of the righteous flourishes" in contrast to v. 28b.[213] But whether or not the NIV interpretation is retained, the point is that the righteous will not see life as a bitter disappointment but will have their fondest hopes fulfilled.

10:29 A number of scholars emend v. 29a to read, "The Lord is a fortress for those whose way is upright."[214] This emendation is somewhat smoother than the MT. On the other hand, the "way of the Lord," as the MT has it, parallels the "fear of the Lord" of v. 27 and makes good sense. It ought to be retained as the correct reading.[215] God's moral governance of the world is security for the righteous and a (an unknown) terror for sinners.

10:30 To have a place in the land is to have security and refuge, in contrast to the homelessness of the alien (v. 30). The promise implies long life, a sense of belonging, and a family heritage.

TWO-PROVERB COLLECTION. *Type: Thematic, Parallel (10:31-32)* **10:31-32** The theme of this pair is the use of the tongue. The cola are in an *A-B-A-B* pattern, but note the inclusio using "mouth"[216] in v. 31a and v. 32b.

---

[211]Albright ("Canaanite-Phoenician Sources," 5-6) cites this proverb with I Aqht 1, 113 ("Like the feeling of a wild cow for her calf,/Like the feeling of a wild ewe for her lamb,/ So [was] the feeling of Anath for Baal"). He notes that the tricolon, though common in the older Canaanite material, had disappeared by about the seventh century B.C. It is not found, for example, in Ahiqar.

[212]Note that v. 27 corresponds to v. 29 (both refer to יהוה), and v. 28 (צַדִּיקִים) corresponds to v. 30 (צַדִּיק).

[213]The noun שִׂמְחָה seems odd in context; the parallel תֹּאבֵד is a verb. BHS note *a*, צָמְחָה, "sprouts," may be correct. On the other hand, G. R. Driver ("Problems," 179) suggests the meaning "spring up" for שׂמחה on the basis of Akkadian and Arabic forms. Either way, the meaning would be that the hope of the righteous flourishes.

[214]Cf. BHS note *a*, McKane, *Proverbs*, 427, and Toy, *Proverbs*, 219. לְתַם is read for לַתֹּם and is connected to דֶּרֶךְ (rather than דֶּרֶךְ with יהוה).

[215]See also the arguments in Delitzsch, *Proverbs* 1:227-28. Cf. also the Vg *via Domini* and the LXX φόβος κυρίου.

[216]פִּי.

In parallel with v. 31a, v. 32a can be translated, "The lips of the righteous pour forth what is fitting."[217] The two cola assert that the morally upright speak what is wise and pleasing. By contrast, perverse words only invite punishment, and the morally depraved speak nothing but perversity. The emphasis on perversity in v. 31b and v. 32b is striking; perverse words are those that play the devil's advocate and confound and twist sound moral judgment.[218]

The penalty of having the tongue cut out (v. 31) is metaphoric.[219] It describes either the community's rejection of the perverse speaker or divine punishment.

(6) What the Lord Abhors (11:1-21)

[1]The Lord abhors dishonest scales,
but accurate weights are his delight.

[2]When pride comes, then comes disgrace,
but with humility comes wisdom.

[3]The integrity of the upright guides them,
but the unfaithful are destroyed by their duplicity.

[4]Wealth is worthless in the day of wrath,
but righteousness delivers from death.

[5]The righteousness of the blameless makes a straight way for them,
but the wicked are brought down by their own wickedness.

[6]The righteousness of the upright delivers them,
but the unfaithful are trapped by evil desires.

[7]When a wicked man dies, his hope perishes;
all he expected from his power comes to nothing.

[8]The righteous man is rescued from trouble,
and it comes on the wicked instead.

---

[217]The form יֵדְעוּן means "know," but the idea of lips "knowing" is odd, although of course the lips may stand for the whole person by metonymy. A few Hebrew MSS have ירעון, "to feed" (cf. v. 21). The LXX has ἀποσάζει, "to let fall drop by drop," here and in v. 31 for יָנוּב, but Theod., Aq., and Quinta support the LXX (γνώσονται). Thomas ("Textual," 285) suggests that a root דעה meaning "seek" may be indicated and translates, "The lips of the righteous seek goodwill." But apart from the validity of a Hebrew root דעה being uncertain, the idea of lips "seeking" is as odd as lips "knowing," and reference to the lips implies that sound instruction comes from a righteous person, not that he seeks it. Perhaps the best analysis is from Dahood (*Proverbs*, 20-21), who argues cogently that both יָנוּב and יֵדְעוּן mean "to flow" (the latter being dialectical for יֵזְעוּן). This finds support in the LXX and makes good sense in context.

[218]Thus McKane, *Proverbs*, 424.

[219]Old Testament law does not impose this penalty; instead, a false witness was to receive the punishment he intended for his victim (Deut 19:15-21).

[9]With his mouth the godless destroys his neighbor,
but through knowledge the righteous escape.

[10]When the righteous prosper, the city rejoices;
when the wicked perish, there are shouts of joy.

[11]Through the blessing of the upright a city is exalted,
but by the mouth of the wicked it is destroyed.

[12]A man who lacks judgment derides his neighbor,
but a man of understanding holds his tongue.

[13]A gossip betrays a confidence,
but a trustworthy man keeps a secret.

[14]For lack of guidance a nation falls,
but many advisers make victory sure.

[15]He who puts up security for another will surely suffer,
but whoever refuses to strike hands in pledge is safe.

[16]A kindhearted woman gains respect,
but ruthless men gain only wealth.

[17]A kind man benefits himself,
but a cruel man brings trouble on himself.

[18]The wicked man earns deceptive wages,
but he who sows righteousness reaps a sure reward.

[19]The truly righteous man attains life,
but he who pursues evil goes to his death.

[20]The Lord detests men of perverse heart
but he delights in those whose ways are blameless.

[21]Be sure of this: The wicked will not go unpunished,
but those who are righteous will go free.

In 11:1-21 a group of proverb collections are held together by the inclusio formed by "the Lord abhors"[220] and "he delights"[221] in vv. 1,20.[222] Two major themes of this section are ill-gotten gain and the sin of slander.

Moral Integrity and God's Judgment. *Type: Chiastic (11:1-4).* **11:1-4** Verse 1 describes God's abhorrence of fraud, and v. 4 answers it with the promise that the wrongfully gained wealth of the wicked will do them no good in the day of judgment. Between these verses vv. 2-3 assert that humility[223] and integrity, rather than their opposites, are the best guides in life.

[220]תּוֹעֲבַת יהוה.
[221]רְצוֹנוֹ.
[222]Verses 20-21 stand together as a proverb pair.
[223]צְנוּעִים suggests not timidity but "intellectual reticence." See McKane, *Proverbs*, 428.

An implied pun links vv. 1b,2a. God delights in "accurate weights" (weights that are as heavy as they should be and not lightened for purposes of fraud); the arrogant, however, have no dignity at all but only disgrace (literally "lightness").[224] Both false weights and arrogant people claim to be "heavier" than they really are. This series of proverbs implicitly links arrogance to fraud and deceit while linking humility to moral integrity. Sins do not come in isolation but in clusters. Someone who thinks only of self and has no regard for others can easily resort to cheating in business affairs.

SALVATION FOR THE RIGHTEOUS. *Type: Thematic, Parallel Proverb Pair (11:5-6).* **11:5-6** These two proverbs parallel each other and describe the respective fates of the righteous and the wicked. In both verses the punishment fits the crime. God's justice is not only appropriate but is also slightly ironic.

DEATH OF A SINNER. *Type: Inclusio, Proverb Pair (11:7-8).* **11:7-8** As the text stands, these two proverbs are bound by the inclusio of the word "wicked"[225] in v. 7a and v. 8b. Some suggest that v. 7 be emended to read, "When the *righteous* man dies, his hope does *not* perish/but the expectation *of fools* perishes."[226] But the text makes sense as it stands. In addition, these verses assert that God brings utter destruction to the wicked and imply a promise of eternal life to the righteous.

DESTRUCTIVE LIPS. *Type: Chiastic, with an Afterword (11:9-13).* **11:9-12** Verses 10-11 are an obvious pair in parallel, whereas vv. 9,12 are bound by the theme of the slanderous gossip of the wicked against the restrained silence of the righteous. The four proverbs together thus form a chiasmus.[227] In v. 9 the righteous escape verbal attacks unharmed by following the teachings of wisdom, and that, according to v. 12, without resorting to a counterattack in kind. But the wicked can only spread vicious gossip. In this context the joy of the city at the death of the wicked has concrete meaning: its people will finally be free of their wagging tongues.

11:13 This verse is an afterword on the subject of the tongue: The wicked are not only malevolent with their words, but they also are indiscreet and cannot be trusted. The wise not only refrain from lies and slander, but they also know how to keep a matter private.

NATIONAL AND PERSONAL PRUDENCE. *Type: Parallel (11:14-15).* **11:14-15** Both proverbs here follow the pattern "imprudent action brings

---

[224] קָלוֹן ("lightness," "disgrace," v. 2) contrasts with כָּבוֹד ("weight, dignity," implied but not used in this text), a quality that is present in accurate weights but absent in proud people.

[225] רָשָׁע.

[226] See BHS notes; cf. the LXX.

[227] Note also that בְּפֶה (perhaps read בְּפִי) in v. 9 is a catchword to וּבְפִי in v. 11 and that vv. 9-12 all begin with ב.

disaster/prudent action gives security," but the first involves national matters where the second concerns personal business. Seeking advice from many counselors can avert disaster.[228] A ruler or governor can squander the resources of a nation or city as easily as an individual can waste personal assets. The individual, however, often needs to keep to his own counsel since friends and acquaintances may drag him into a foolish business venture.

KINDNESS AND CRUELTY. *Type: Parallel (11:16-17).* **11:16-17** The pattern of these two proverbs is "kind woman/cruel man//kind man/ruthless man." By itself v. 16 could be read cynically ("A kind woman gets respect, but a cruel man gets rich" [the word "only" is not in the text]) to justify unscrupulous behavior. In conjunction with v. 17, however, the self-destructive nature of the "hard-nosed" approach to life is apparent.[229] Note also that v. 17 is almost medical in tone: A kind heart is full of health and well-being, but a ruthless spirit makes a man sick.[230] Setting a "kindhearted woman" against a "ruthless man" is significant. Many men seek to establish themselves and learn respect through their accomplishments; the kindhearted woman personifies the somewhat more feminine trait of placing relationships above career and achievements.

THE WAGES OF SIN AND RIGHTEOUSNESS. *Type: Chiasmus (11:18-19).* **11:18-19** This pair has the chiastic pattern "wicked man/he who sows righteousness/righteousness[231]/he who pursues evil." The wages of sin are deceptive in that they are fleeting and illusory, whereas the wages of righteousness are permanent. "Life" in v. 19 therefore implies eternal life. Both patterns of behavior have their own outcome and reward. Righteousness leads to life (which would include long life, emotional health, and posterity) while evil leads to death (the demise of one's estate, family, and self). Both "life" and "death" have eschatological implications as well.

Note that this pair has links to vv. 16-17. The wealth of the cruel man corresponds to deceptive wages as the honor given a kind woman is genuine. Also the health/self-inflicted pain of v. 17 corresponds to the life and death of v. 19.

DIVINE JUDGMENT. *Type: Parallel (11:20-21).* **11:20-21** God's attitude toward individuals (disgust/pleasure) in v. 20 corresponds to the out-

---

[228]The ancient versions read "counsel" (LXX: βουλῇ) instead of "counselor." But note that the qal active participle singular יוֹעֵץ at the end of v. 14 is paralleled by another qal active participle singular, בּוֹטֵחַ, at the end of v. 15.

[229]The expanded reading of v. 16 in the LXX should not be followed. See McKane, *Proverbs*, 430-31.

[230]גֹּמֵל נַפְשׁוֹ ("benefits his life") and עֹכֵר שְׁאֵרוֹ ("troubling his flesh") speak respectively of healthy and unhealthy behavior.

[231]The NIV "righteous man" apparently reads בֵּן צְדָקָה here (cf. BHS note). The MT כֵּן ("thus") is preferable; if it is read, v. 19 is the conclusion drawn from v. 18.

come of their lives (inescapable trouble/deliverance) in v. 21. The language in v. 21 is also somewhat forensic in that the evil are convicted ("not go unpunished") but the righteous acquitted ("go free"). God's judgment follows his evaluation of people. On the other hand, the NIV may well be wrong to emend the text of v. 21b, as it has. The MT reads, "But the offspring of [the] righteous are delivered."[232] The implication is that one's behavior effects not just oneself but one's children as well.

(7) Beauty without Discretion (11:22)

[22]Like a gold ring in a pig's snout
is a beautiful woman who shows no discretion.

TYPE: INDIVIDUAL PROVERB (11:22). **11:22** The humor of this proverb is obvious. The point of the comparison is that in both cases beauty is in an inappropriate place. Note that the woman has actually *abandoned*[233] discretion; an immoral way of life is implied.

(8) Generosity and Selfishness (11:23-27)

[23]The desire of the righteous ends only in good,
but the hope of the wicked only in wrath.

[24]One man gives freely, yet gains even more;
another withholds unduly, but comes to poverty.

[25]A generous man will prosper;
he who refreshes others will himself be refreshed.

[26]People curse the man who hoards grain,
but blessing crowns him who is willing to sell.

[27]He who seeks good finds goodwill,
but evil comes to him who searches for it.

TYPE: INCLUSIO (11:23-27). **11:23-27** It is axiomatic that greedy and selfish people, epitomized in Western literature as Mr. Scrooge, are hated by the populace at large while generous people gain love and respect. What the hoarder fails to realize, however, is that in the economy of God the greedy ultimately lose even the material things they try so hard to keep while the benevolent only prosper more and more. Verses 23,27 closely parallel each other[234] and form an inclusio around vv. 24-26, all of which

---

[232]The MT literally reads, "The offspring of the righteous," which is somewhat unexpected. See BHS notes for possible emendations.

[233]סוּר means "turn away from."

[234]Note that תַּאֲוַת ("desire") and תִּקְוַת ("hope") in v. 23 are answered by שֹׁחֵר ("seeking") and וְדֹרֵשׁ ("looking for") in v. 27. Note also that the reward of the righteous, "good" (טוֹב), in v. 23a contrasts with "evil" (רָעָה) in v. 27b as עֶבְרָה ("[divine] wrath") in v. 23b contrasts with רָצוֹן ("[divine] favor") in v. 27a.

center on the theme of generosity and selfishness. The inclusio states the general truth that one receives back according to one's own behavior while vv. 24-26 deal with the concrete issue of hoarding. Those who hoard by refusal either to give (v. 24)[235] or to sell (v. 26) finally face not only widespread hatred (v. 26) but the poverty they dread as well (v. 24). The generous only have greater and greater prosperity (v. 25).[236]

(9) The Source of Life (11:28–12:4)

28Whoever trusts in his riches will fall,
but the righteous will thrive like a green leaf.

29He who brings trouble on his family will inherit only wind,
and the fool will be servant to the wise.

30The fruit of the righteous is a tree of life,
and he who wins souls is wise.

31If the righteous receive their due on earth,
how much more the ungodly and the sinner!

1Whoever loves discipline loves knowledge,
but he who hates correction is stupid.

2A good man obtains favor from the Lord,
but the Lord condemns a crafty man.

3A man cannot be established through wickedness,
but the righteous cannot be uprooted.

4A wife of noble character is her husband's crown,
but a disgraceful wife is like decay in his bones.

Type: Inclusio (11:28–12:4). **11:28–12:4** The structure of this collection is complex. Proverbs 11:28 has a close parallel in 12:3; both concern the flourishing of the righteous and the failure of the wicked to establish themselves through wealth and cunning.[237] Proverbs 11:29, which concerns a son's behavior in the family (see 17:2), is answered by 12:4, which deals with the wife's contribution to the family. Proverbs 11:28-29 and 12:3-4 thus form an inclusio around 11:30–12:2.

Proverbs 11:28-29 and 12:3-4 teach that a man cannot provide for the security of his family through any means that violate basic principles of

---

[235]Charitable giving is the primary focus of v. 24, but refusal to give fair pay to workers may be implied in מִיֹּשֶׁר (cf. Jas 5:1-4).

[236]Dahood (*Proverbs*, 23-24) vocalizes the difficult form יוֹרֶא as יוּרָא and takes it as either a pual or hophal of ורא, "to be fat." The parallel תְדֻשָּׁן ("be fat prosperous") supports this.

[237]Note that יִפֹּל (he will fall, 11:28a) corresponds to לֹא־יִכּוֹן (he will not be established) in 12:3a and that 11:28b (וְכֶעָלֶה צַדִּיקִים יִפְרָחוּ, and like a leaf the righteous will thrive) and 12:3b (וְשֹׁרֶשׁ צַדִּיקִים בַּל־יִמּוֹט, but the righteous cannot be uprooted) closely parallel each other in following the analogy of a tree.

right and wrong. Rather than focus his attention on making as much money as possible, a man should give thought to the choice of a good wife and then to the spiritual nurture of his children. Above all else, he must conduct his own life with integrity if he expects the same from his family.

The two pairs—11:30-31 and 12:1-2—each deal with behavior (11:30; 12:1) and its reward or punishment (11:31; 12:2). The collection is thus structured as follows:

Aa The true source of life (11:28)
  Ab Family life (11:29)
    Ba Behavior of righteous and wicked (11:30)
      Bb Divine judgment (11:31)
    Ba′ Behavior of righteous and wicked (12:1)
      Bb′ Divine judgment (12:2)
Aa′ The true source of life (12:3)
  Ab′ Family life (12:4)

Proverbs 11:30 is often taken as commending the evangelizing or enriching of others morally or spiritually. While this is a valid and laudable conviction, the Hebrew probably does not have this meaning. The phrase translated "win souls" is actually a Hebrew idiom that means to "kill," and the interpretation "win souls" is without analogy and therefore suspect. Also, as the NIV has it, the verse deals exclusively with positive behavior, contrary to the pattern of righteous/wicked (or vice versa) found in all the other verses in 11:30–12:2. The pattern is maintained, however, if 11:30b is translated, "But violence takes away lives,"[238] as the evidence suggests it should, rather than, "He who wins souls is wise."[239]

In 11:30–12:2 a violent, undisciplined life is contrasted with a virtuous life carried out in submission to God's ways. This text, moreover, indicates that God is directly involved in the matter of punishing the evil and rewarding the good. Proverbs does not always maintain an impersonal "cause and effect" outlook on rewards and punishment but teaches divine

[238]Reading וְלֹקֵחַ נְפָשׁוֹת חָמָס. Alternatively, one could render the line, "But a violent man is a murderer" with the vocalization חֹמֵס. Several factors weigh against the traditional "he who wins souls is wise." First and foremost, לָקַח נֶפֶשׁ elsewhere always means to "kill" and never to "win souls" in a positive sense of influencing a person for good (Ps 31:14 [Eng. v. 15]; 1 Sam 24:12 [Eng. v. 11]; 1 Kgs 19:14; Prov 1:19). Second, the emendation from חָכָם to חָמָס involves a minor and common type of scribal error. Third, the emendation is supported by the LXX rendition παρανόμων. Fourth, the reading "violent" here is echoed by "brutish" (בָּעַר) in 12:1.

[239]Most modern translations emend the text in a way similar to the proposal here. See the RSV, REB, NRSV, and JB. The Tanakh, a Jewish translation that explicitly eschews emendation, has the rendition, "A wise man captivates people" (NJB is similar), but this has no more to recommend it as a translation of לֹקֵחַ נְפָשׁוֹת than does "win souls."

intervention as well. The metaphor of the fruit of the righteous being a tree of life (11:30a) is striking. As the seed of one fruit can give rise to a tree and thus much more fruit, so also the beneficial repercussions of a righteous life are far reaching. In the context of 11:28–12:2, one might presume that the family of a righteous man is the immediate beneficiary of the good he generates.

This section teaches that life and health for both individual and family is obtained by virtue and submission to God. Violent or selfish activity is sure to be punished, however, and even wealth affords no security. Heavy emphasis here is upon the favor or disfavor of God.

(10) Plans and Schemes (12:5-7)

5The plans of the righteous are just,
but the advice of the wicked is deceitful.

6The words of the wicked lie in wait for blood,
but the speech of the upright rescues them.

7Wicked men are overthrown and are no more,
but the house of the righteous stands firm.

TYPE: THEMATIC (12:5-7). **12:5-7** The unity of this collection is indicated in the Hebrew structure.[240] These three proverbs follow a logical progression: the righteous make plans that are just, but the wicked scheme with deceitful counsel (v. 5); the wicked attempt to ambush the righteous with their lies, but the righteous are delivered by their integrity (v. 6); the wicked are totally destroyed, but the righteous stand secure (v. 7).

(11) Earned Respect (12:8)

8A man is praised according to his wisdom,
but men with warped minds are despised.

TYPE: INDIVIDUAL PROVERB (12:8). **12:8** Respect is gained by wisdom. The term here implies integrity and capacity to deal with problems in life.

(12) On Providing for One's Needs (12:9-11)

9Better to be a nobody and yet have a servant
than pretend to be somebody and have no food.

10A righteous man cares for the needs of his animal,
but the kindest acts of the wicked are cruel.

---

[240]Note the following pattern in vv. 5-7:
v. 5: X רְשָׁעִים X / X צַדִּיקִים X
v. 6: X יְשָׁרִים X / X רְשָׁעִים X
v. 7: X צַדִּיקִים X / X רְשָׁעִים X.

[11]He who works his land will have abundant food,
but he who chases fantasies lacks judgment.

Type: Inclusio (12:9-11). **12:9-11** Verse 9, a "better saying," asserts that even modest prosperity is more important than status. Verse 10 teaches that a good man cares for those who provide for him, even if they are only animals. The wicked only exploit. Verse 11 teaches that prosperity comes by hard work rather than by chasing fantasies and schemes. The well-earned prosperity of the righteous contrasts with the feigned wealth, the acts of exploitation, and the idle plans of the foolish and wicked.[241]

(13) On Fruit and Snares (12:12-14)

[12]The wicked desire the plunder of evil men,
but the root of the righteous flourishes.

[13]An evil man is trapped by his sinful talk,
but a righteous man escapes trouble.

[14]From the fruit of his lips a man is filled with good things
as surely as the work of his hands rewards him.

Type: Thematic (12:12-14). **12:12-14** This collection employs two metaphors of gathering food: hunting with snares[242] (symbolizing the wicked) and laboring to raise crops[243] (symbolizing the righteous).[244] The wicked are always looking for ways to defraud people (v. 12a)[245] but are trapped by their own machinations (v. 13a). The righteous, however, allow their prosperity to grow gradually from deep, strong roots (v. 12b), escape the traps set for them (v. 13b), and see their way of life ("fruit of his lips") yield a bountiful harvest (v. 14).

(14) Able to Take Advice (12:15)

[15]The way of a fool seems right to him,
but a wise man listens to advice.

Type: Single Bicolon Proverb (12:15). **12:15** Fools are so sure of themselves that they never seek advice, but the wise readily seek it

[241]חֲסַר־לֶחֶם ("without food," v. 9) and חֲסַר־לֵב ("without sense," v. 11) together form an inclusio. לֶחֶם in v. 11a also provides a link to v. 9, and "servant" in v. 9 and "animal" in v. 10 are conceptually linked as the man's laborers.

[242]מְצוֹד רָעִים (v. 12; it should be rendered "net" rather than the NIV "plunder"; thus, "a wicked man takes pleasure in a net of evils") corresponds to מוֹקֵשׁ רָע (v. 13; "evil snare").

[243]Implied in the metaphors "root" (v. 12) and "fruit" (v. 14) and in the line "the work of his hands" in v. 15.

[244]Compare the concern with food in the previous collection.

[245]The Hebrew of v. 12 is difficult, but the NIV gives a reasonable solution. None of the proposed emendations are convincing. See McKane, *Proverbs*, 449-50, and Toy, *Proverbs*, 249-50.

out.[246] Those who think they know it all are foolish, but those who look for guidance and knowledge are wise (cf. Ps 1:1-6).

(15) The Use and Abuse of Words (12:16-22)

16A fool shows his annoyance at once,
but a prudent man overlooks an insult.

17A truthful witness gives honest testimony,
but a false witness tells lies.

18Reckless words pierce like a sword,
but the tongue of the wise brings healing.

19Truthful lips endure forever,
but a lying tongue lasts only a moment.

20There is deceit in the hearts of those who plot evil,
but joy for those who promote peace.

21No harm befalls the righteous,
but the wicked have their fill of trouble.

22The LORD detests lying lips,
but he delights in men who are truthful.

TYPE: LINKED PARALLELISM AND CHIASMUS (12:16-22). **12:16-22** These seven verses are made up of four verses arranged in parallel (vv. 16-19) conjoined by a common verse to a four-verse chiasmus (vv. 19-22). The structure is as follows:

A: Thoughtless reactions (v. 16)
  B: Honesty and lying (v. 17)
A′: Reckless words (v. 18)
  B′: Honesty and lying (v. 19)
    C: Plotting evil and promoting peace (v. 20)
    C′: Trouble to the wicked, not the righteous (v. 21)
  B″: Honesty and lying (v. 22)

The characteristics of fools described in this text are that (a) they react thoughtlessly to real or imagined insults and hurt others with careless words (vv. 16-18), (b) they are liars but will last only a short time and incur the wrath of God (vv. 17,[247] 19,[248] 22), and (c) they scheme and deceive but

[246] חָכָם here after פְּרִי (v. 14) may account for the apparent scribal error in 11:30, where חָכָם was written for חָמָס.

[247] Gordon (UT, 412) argues that Ugaritic *yph* ("witness") = Hebrew יָפִיחַ. If so, this would indicate that יָפִיחַ here is a noun (parallel to עֵד, "witness") and not the hiphil imperfect of פּוּחַ. Cf. McKane, *Proverbs*, 445.

[248] The NIV "only for a moment" generalizes and so obscures a quaint Hebrew expression. וְעַד־אַרְגִּיעָה means "until I wink [my eye]." Cf. Delitzsch, *Proverbs*, 262-63.

only bring trouble on their own heads (vv. 20[249]-21). The wise, however, (a) react with patience in the face of insults and heal others with their words (vv. 16,18), (b) are honest and gain long life and divine favor (vv. 17,19,22), and (c) seek the well-being of others and obtain the same for themselves (vv. 20-21). The text stresses the importance of the right use of the power of words (i.e., the benefit of all concerned).

(16) A Wholesome Life (12:23-28)

23 A prudent man keeps his knowledge to himself,
but the heart of fools blurts out folly.

24 Diligent hands will rule,
but laziness ends in slave labor.

25 An anxious heart weighs a man down,
but a kind word cheers him up.

26 A righteous man is cautious in friendship,
but the way of the wicked leads them astray.

27 The lazy man does not roast his game,
but the diligent man prizes his possessions.

28 In the way of righteousness there is life;
along that path is immortality.

TYPE: PARALLEL (12:23-28). **12:23-28** This text is structured as a six-verse parallel as follows:

A: Caution and incaution (v. 23)
B: Diligence and laziness (v. 24)
C: Anxiety and joy (v. 25)
A′: Caution and incaution (v. 26)
B′: Laziness and diligence (v. 27)
C′: Life and immortality (v. 28)

The six proverbs of this section do not have a single theme but describe types of activity that may promote or undermine a wholesome life. One should be cautious in both speech and the choosing of friends[250] (vv. 23,26), hard-working (vv. 24,27[251]), and able to control stress

---

[249]Note the wordplay on the assonance of מִרְמָה at the beginning of v. 20 and שִׂמְחָה at the end.

[250]This interpretation of v. 26 follows the NIV rendition, but v. 26a is admittedly extremely difficult. Cf. McKane, *Proverbs*, 447-48, and Delitzsch, *Proverbs*, 265-67. J. A. Emerton ("A Note on Proverbs xii.26," *ZAW* 76:2 [1964]: 191-93) wants to emend v. 26a to read, "The righteous is delivered from harm," but this is not persuasive.

[251]Transpose אָדָם יָקָר to read "but the precious wealth of a man is [his] diligence"; cf. BHS note *c*. G. A. Driver ("Problems," 180) emends to וְהוֹן אָדָם חָרוּץ יָקָר, "but the wealth of the diligent man is much."

(v. 25[252]). The culmination of such behavior is joy in life. From these general principles on the relationship between integrity and life, the text goes on to assert that the outcome of righteousness is in fact immortality (v. 28).

Careful people show their caution both in the words they speak and the friends they choose (vv. 23,26). Someone who is careful in what he says will be equally careful about whom he confides in. In vv. 24 and 27 the very serious matter of one's diligence determining whether one will be a master or a slave is linked to a humorous proverb that shows a lazy man to be foolish enough to go to the trouble of hunting game but then be too slack to get around to roasting it (and thus lets it go to waste). Verses 25 and 28 exploit the richness of the biblical usage of the word "life," which includes both joy and fulfillment as well as immortality.

(17) The Use of the Mouth (13:1-4)

1 A wise son heeds his father's instruction,
but a mocker does not listen to rebuke.

2 From the fruit of his lips a man enjoys good things,
but the unfaithful have a craving for violence.

3 He who guards his lips guards his life,
but he who speaks rashly will come to ruin.

4 The sluggard craves and gets nothing,
but the desires of the diligent are fully satisfied.

TYPE: CATCHWORD (13:1-4). **13:1-4** Those who receive parental instruction (v. 1a[253]) and know when to be silent[254] (v. 3a) will enjoy many benefits (vv. 2a,4b), but those who shut their ears and open their mouths (vv. 1b,3b) become violent and lazy (vv. 2b,4a[255]). A number of words and concepts bind this text together. The "mocker" corresponds to the one who "speaks rashly," while shutting one's mouth corresponds to receiving instruction (vv. 1,3). Verses 2-3 refer to the mouth, and the *nepeš* is mentioned in vv. 2-4 with a range of meanings.[256]

---

[252] יַשְׁחֶנָּה appears to be a hapax hiphil stem from שחה with the meaning "to force [someone] down." Dahood (*Proverbs*, 27) proposes a meaning "to be feverish" from the root שחן on the basis of Ugaritic parallels and the Hebrew noun שְׁחִין, "inflammation."

[253] This line is highly elliptical: בֵּן חָכָם מוּסַר אָב ("a wise son, a father's instruction"). Nevertheless, it need not be emended (e.g., McKane, *Proverbs*, 453). Proverbs are often elliptical. The point here is that whenever one finds a wise son, one can be sure that a father has made an effort to instruct him. Line *b* introduces the counterthought that a mocker will reject instruction.

[254] Verse 3 primarily concerns silence versus speech, not restraint of appetite versus gluttony. See McKane, *Proverbs*, 457.

[255] On the syntax of this line, see Delitzsch, *Proverbs*, 272.

[256] In v. 2 נֶפֶשׁ is *appetite* used metaphorically; in v. 3 it is *life*; in v. 4 it is *appetite* both literally and metaphorically.

The text uses the idea of "eating" in striking ways. Verses 2a and 4b are at the same time literal and metaphoric. By the fruit of his mouth a man "eats well" (v. 2a),[257] that is, his apt words benefit him in every way; moreover, the life (*nepeš*) of the diligent "grows fat" (v. 4b),[258] that is, his life is full and his physical needs are met. The treacherous man, however, has an appetite (*nepeš*) for violence (v. 2b), but the *nepeš* of the sluggard remains unsatisfied (v. 4a), that is, he has nothing to eat.

Verse 1, at the head of this collection, describes respect for fatherly advice as the key to attaining the satisfaction in life described in vv. 2-4. Those who reject wisdom, on the other hand, are apt to become violent (due to their lack of self-control) and finally achieve only an empty life.

(18) Action and Reaction (13:5-6)

5The righteous hate what is false,
but the wicked bring shame and disgrace.

6Righteousness guards the man of integrity,
but wickedness overthrows the sinner.

TYPE: PARALLEL, CATCHWORD (13:5-6). **13:5-6** These two proverbs are set in parallel on the basis of "righteous" and "wicked" in v. 5 and "righteousness" and "wickedness" in v. 6. The NIV translation of v. 5b is flat; it ought to be rendered, "But a wicked man makes a stench[259] and causes shame." The tie between the two cola of v. 5 is that whereas the righteous are concerned for the truth (over against malicious gossip), the wicked promote scandal. By itself v. 6[260] is a rather colorless proverb. In context with v. 5, however, it implies that disregard for truth and the spreading of scandal is ultimately self-destructive. Those who care about the truth, however, are preserved by their integrity.

(19) The Ambiguity of Riches (13:7-11)

7One man pretends to be rich, yet has nothing;
another pretends to be poor, yet has great wealth.

8A man's riches may ransom his life,
but a poor man hears no threat.

9The light of the righteous shines brightly,
but the lamp of the wicked is snuffed out.

---

[257] יֹאכַל טוֹב ("enjoy good things"). For further discussion of this verse, see J. A. Emerton, "The Meaning of Proverbs XIII.2," *JTS* 35 (1984): 91-95.

[258] תְּדֻשָּׁן ("are fully satisfied").

[259] יַבְאִישׁ (root = באשׁ), "he causes a stench." NIV apparently reads יָבִישׁ (root = בושׁ), he causes shame, with BHS note. Cf. McKane, *Proverbs*, 460.

[260] תָּם־דָּרֶךְ ("integrity of way") and חַטָּאת ("sin") are abstract for concrete (i.e., persons who practice such things). Hence there is no need to emend. See Delitzsch, *Proverbs*, 273-74.

[10]Pride only breeds quarrels,
but wisdom is found in those who take advice.

[11]Dishonest money dwindles away,
but he who gathers money little by little makes it grow.

TYPE: THEMATIC (13:7-8). **13:7-8** The acquisition, possession, and use of money dominate vv. 7-8,11. Verses 9-10 do not refer to money, but the overall context throws new meaning on these proverbs as well.

There is more to v. 7 than that some people deceitfully pretend to be rich or poor. More profoundly, things are not always what they seem.[261] One person may appear rich (and may or may not have money) and yet on a more fundamental level have nothing,[262] and the reverse is true as well. This is illustrated in v. 8, in which the point is made that although the rich have some protection from their money, the poor have little need for such protection since they have nothing worth stealing.[263] Wealth is thus a prison, and the one who appears rich has nothing enviable. Similarly, if one has not acquired wealth properly,[264] that wealth will soon disappear (v. 11). The apparent wealth of those who acquired money without learning the lessons of financial prudence is fleeting.

13:9-11 Verse 9, which means that the life and joy[265] of the righteous flourishes while the hope of the evil fades, and v. 10, which means that contentiousness is borne of arrogance,[266] of themselves have nothing to do with money. They may have been placed in this context, however, to draw the reader to reflect that true wealth consists of a pure life and a patient spirit. By implication the arrogant rich only appear to be wealthy; their lives are filled with strife, and their light is quickly extinguished.

(20) A Hope Fulfilled (13:12-19)

[12]Hope deferred makes the heart sick,
but a longing fulfilled is a tree of life.

---

[261]Although the translation "pretend" is possible, it is probable that מִתְעַשֵּׁר and מִתְרוֹשֵׁשׁ are more neutral in meaning and should be rendered "appear to be rich" and "appear to be poor." Such persons may or may not be deliberately feigning wealth or poverty.

[262]וְאֵין כֹּל is elliptical for וְאֵין כֹּל לוֹ, "and he has nothing."

[263]Taking גְּעָרָה to mean "threat" (with NIV). Cf. Delitzsch, *Proverbs*, 274-75; McKane, *Proverbs*, 458.

[264]Verse 11a is literally, "Wealth from nothing [מֵהֶבֶל] shrinks away." Such wealth is not necessarily "dishonest," although it may be. It is wealth that has not been acquired through prudence and diligence. A modern example might be "lottery" winnings.

[265]The metaphor of אוֹר־צַדִּיקִים יִשְׂמָח, "[the] light of [the] righteous rejoices," is leveled out in the NIV, which may be emending to יִזְרָח, "shines." The metaphoric link between "light" and "rejoice" ought to be preserved in translation. Dahood (*Proverbs*, 28-29) sees here reference to immortality.

[266]רַק־בְּזָדוֹן יִתֵּן מַצָּה should be rendered, "It is only from arrogance that one makes strife." The meaning is that those who claim to be fighting for a just cause often are only being contentious for pride's sake.

[13]He who scorns instruction will pay for it,
but he who respects a command is rewarded.

[14]The teaching of the wise is a fountain of life,
turning a man from the snares of death.

[15]Good understanding wins favor,
but the way of the unfaithful is hard.

[16]Every prudent man acts out of knowledge,
but a fool exposes his folly.

[17]A wicked messenger falls into trouble,
but a trustworthy envoy brings healing.

[18]He who ignores discipline comes to poverty and shame,
but whoever heeds correction is honored.

[19]A longing fulfilled is sweet to the soul,
but fools detest turning from evil.

TYPE: INCLUSIO (13:12-19). **13:12-19** Every person desires to see his or her longings fulfilled. In the wisdom of the world, the way to sucess is through diligent effort. There is truth in this, and this text also extols the worth of a trustworthy person (v. 17). Yet the Bible goes beyond the secular wisdom of relating success to hard work and more fundamentally ties it to the development of a mature, virtuous soul by submission to wise teachers. Diligence is thus a fruit of a soul that has cultivated goodness, and success follows naturally.

This text has a general inclusio pattern, but there are many cross-connections.

A: "Hope deferred" (v. 12)
  B: "He who scorns instruction" (v. 13)
    C: "Teaching of the wise" (v. 14)
    C′: "Good understanding" (v. 15)
      D: "Prudent man/fool" (v. 16)
      D′: "Wicked messenger/trustworthy envoy" (v. 17)
  B′: "He who ignores discipline" (v. 18)
A′: "Longing fulfilled" (v. 19)

Other cross-connections include "tree of life" (v. 12) and "fountain of life" (v. 14) as well as "healing" (v. 15). Also "rewarded" (v. 13), "wins favor" (v. 15), and "honored" (v. 18) indicate that the concrete benefits of wisdom are in view. The peculiar bicolon of v. 19 is also significant. By itself v. 19b has nothing to do with v. 19a, but in the context of vv. 13,18 it summarizes the attitude of the obstinate. Surrounding the whole text is the idea of having one's desires fulfilled (vv. 12,19); the point is that the deepest longings of the soul are filled only by integrity and wisdom, not by treachery.

The structure of the text produces a coherent message. Verse 12 gives the premise that everyone rejoices to see their hopes and aspirations fulfilled. This sentiment is restated in the companion verse, v. 19a; but the second colon, v. 19b, asserts that fools will not turn from evil. The implication is that fools will not see their desires fulfilled. The intervening verses develop the thesis that life and happiness can only be obtained by wisdom.

Verses 13[267] and 18 both assert that submission to instruction[268] is essential for success in life. Verses 14-15 closely parallel each other and both teach that prudence saves one from death and destruction. Verse 15b should be translated, "But the way of the treacherous leads to their calamity."[269] The parallel is thus "teaching . . . life" (v. 14a) // "understanding . . . favor" (v. 15a) and "turning . . . death" (v. 14b) // "way . . . calamity" (v. 15b).

Verses 16-17 chiastically parallel each other, and the parallel is strengthened by rendering v. 17b as, "For the faithful envoy *there is health*,"[270] similar to "acts out of knowledge" in v. 16a. The messenger is an example of a person charged with a serious responsibility. Those who are reliable are appropriately rewarded, but those who are not soon find themselves in serious trouble. The whole text thus teaches that by learning from the wise, one can enjoy a life of fulfilled aspirations.

(21) Choice Companions (13:20-21)

20He who walks with the wise grows wise,
but a companion of fools suffers harm.

21Misfortune pursues the sinner,
but prosperity is the reward of the righteous.

TYPE: CHIASTIC (13:20-21). **13:20-21** Verse 20 speaks of choosing human companions wisely, and v. 21 answers that "misfortune" and "prosperity" will follow, respectively, the sinners and the righteous and in that sense be their "companions." The comparison is made stronger if,

---

[267]Authorities are divided over whether יְחֻבָּל is from חבל I, "be pledged," or חבל II, "be destroyed" (cf. BDB, 286-87). The parallel יְשֻׁלָּם, "be repaid," indicates that the former is meant. Cf. Delitzsch, *Proverbs*, 278-79.

[268]Note the rich vocabulary of instruction in these two verses: דָּבָר ("word"), מִצְוָה ("command"), מוּסָר ("instruction), and תּוֹכַחַת ("reprimand"). The parallelism of the two verses is reinforced by ending both with a pual imperfect verb.

[269]The view that אֵיתָן ("lasting, perennial") can here mean "hard" is unpersuasive. The LXX has ἐν ἀπωλείᾳ, "in destruction," which suggests the emendation אֵידָם, "their calamity" (BHS). Alternatively, G. R. Driver ("Problems," 181) proposes that the particle אִי ("not") has fallen out before אֵיתָן due to haplography and reads, "But the way of treachery is not lasting." Either way, there is a parallel to מָוֶת ("death") in v. 14.

[270]Since v. 17a teaches that the wicked messenger "falls into trouble" (יִפֹּל בְּרָע), i.e., hurts himself, it is reasonable to suppose that מַרְפֵּא ("health") is a benefit to himself rather than to others.

with the LXX, one translates v. 21b as "and prosperity overtakes the righteous"[271] instead of "is the reward of the righteous." Note also the chiastic structure of "wise" (v. 20a), "fools" (v. 20b), "sinner" (v. 21a), and "righteous" (v. 21b).

(22) Provision for the Family (13:22-25)

[22]A good man leaves an inheritance for his children's children,
but a sinner's wealth is stored up for the righteous.

[23]A poor man's field may produce abundant food,
but injustice sweeps it away.

[24]He who spares the rod hates his son,
but he who loves him is careful to discipline him.

[25]The righteous eat to their hearts' content,
but the stomach of the wicked goes hungry.

TYPE: PARALLEL (13:22-25). **13:22-25** This text deals with providing for the needs of one's family and is structured as a parallel text.

A: A material inheritance (v. 22)
  B: Hunger because of injustice (v. 23)
A′: A moral heritage (v. 24)[272]
  B′: Hunger because of divine displeasure (v. 25)[273]

All people desire to leave a good heritage for their children, and vv. 22,24 speak, respectively, of providing for the material and moral needs of one's descendants. Proverbs regularly keeps these two in balance. It emphasizes the need for moral training without deprecating the physical needs of family life.

Verse 23[274] and v. 25[275] describe two reasons a family may be impoverished and hungry. On the one hand, it may be injustice in society (i.e., it is not the family's fault, and their hunger points to a need for changes in the system). On the other hand, poverty may be a result of sin in the family. Addiction to alcohol, indolence, and financial irresponsibility are all potential causes of poverty, although the terms "righteous" and "wicked"

---

[271]LXX: τοὺς δὲ δικαίους καταλήψεται ἀγαθά. The Hebrew equivalent to καταλήψεται would be יַשִּׂיג. As a parallel to תְּרַדֵּף ("pursues") it is much stronger than יְשַׁלֶּם ("rewards").

[272]Observe that v. 22a ends with בְּנֵי־בָנִים ("children's children") where v. 24a ends with בְּנוֹ ("his son").

[273]Verse 23a begins רָב־אֹכֶל ("much food") whereas v. 25a begins צַדִּיק אֹכֵל ("a righteous man eats").

[274]רָאשִׁים here means "poor" (= רוּשׁ); it should not be translated as "heads" or "leaders" (Vg = *patrum*) or emended to יְשָׁרִים ("righteous"; LXX = δίκαιοι).

[275]Scott (*Proverbs*, 95) is incorrect in rendering v. 25a as, "A good man eats only to satisfy his hunger." Neither the meaning of שֹׂבַע ("plenty," "satiation") nor v. 25b supports this rendition.

imply divine favor or disfavor as well. Proverbs takes a balanced position; it neither dehumanizes the poor on the grounds that they are to blame for all their troubles nor absolves the individual of personal responsibility.

(23) Self-protective and Self-destructive Behavior (14:1-3)

[1]The wise woman builds her house,
but with her own hands the foolish one tears hers down.

[2]He whose walk is upright fears the LORD,
but he whose ways are devious despises him.

[3]A fool's talk brings a rod to his back,
but the lips of the wise protect them.

TYPE: INCLUSIO (14:1-3). **14:1-3** Verse 1 speaks of how wise women[276] build their homes and the foolish one[277] destroys hers; v. 3[278] describes how the foolish man brings punishment on himself by his words and wise men by the same means increase their security.[279] Between these two proverbs is an assertion that one can recognize genuine piety in the behavior of those who possess it (v. 2). This inserted proverb adds a theological dimension to aphorisms on the self-destructiveness of folly. Simply stated, good people benefit themselves and bad people bring trouble on their own heads, but one's attitude toward God fundamentally determines whether one is good or bad. On the other hand, v. 2 also implies that an unethical life gives the lie to one's pretense of piety.

(24) A Worthwhile Investment (14:4)

[4]Where there are no oxen, the manger is empty,
but from the strength of an ox comes an abundant harvest.

---

[276]The plural subject with the singular verb seems odd, and numerous emendations are proposed. Cf. the notes to the BHS text and McKane, *Proverbs*, 472. Probably the singular בָּנְתָה ("she builds") refers to individual members of the class of חַכְמוֹת נָשִׁים ("wise women"). A literal translation would be, "As for wise women, she builds." Dahood (*Proverbs*, 30) argues that חַכְמוֹת נָשִׁים is superlative, "the wisest of women," on the basis of 2 Aqht:VI:45.

[277]אִוֶּלֶת is a feminine noun normally meaning "folly," but here it is used concretely of the foolish woman. A feminine form of אֱוִיל ("foolish," "fool") does not occur in the Hebrew Bible.

[278]חֹטֶר גַּאֲוָה = "stick of pride." Emend to גֵּוֹו, "his back," as the NIV apparently does. Thus his mouth is a "rod [for beating] his own back." Similarly, תִּשְׁמוּרֵם is often emended to תִּשְׁמְרוּם (= תִּשְׁמֹרְנָה אֹתָם, "protects them"). As an alternative one might conjecture that תשמור is a noun hapax legomenon meaning "protection" analogous to תַּגְמוּל (Ps 116:12, root = גמל), "benefit." Perhaps repointing to תַּשְׁמוּרָם, one would then have "their protection," a noun phrase balancing the noun phrase in the first colon.

[279]Hence the pattern חַכְמוֹת, אִוֶּלֶת, אֱוִיל, חֲכָמִים in vv. 1,3.

TYPE: SINGLE BICOLON PROVERB (14:4). **14:4** The structure of the verse implies that in some way having oxen is superior to not having oxen. The NIV rendition of this verse could be taken to have one of two meanings. (1) In the absence of oxen the feed-trough is clean (a minor advantage); but where there are oxen, despite the messy feed-trough, there is a greater harvest (a major advantage). (2) In the absence of oxen one does not need to put grain in the feed-trough (i.e., make an investment, a minor advantage), but oxen provide for an even greater harvest (a return on investment, a major advantage). A problem here, however, is that the word rendered "empty" does not appear elsewhere with that meaning.[280] The word can describe moral purity[281] and thus perhaps could mean "clean," but it is doubtful that anyone would really consider a clean feed-trough to be a distinct advantage. Indeed, if cleanliness were the concern, attention would be directed to the stable floor rather than to the feed-trough.

An altogether different rendition is called for. A preferable translation is, "In the absence of oxen there is a feed-trough [full] of grain,[282] but in the strength of the bull there is abundant harvest." If there are no oxen, one need not refill the feed-trough so often (the smaller livestock do not eat as much), but it is the ox that enables the farmer to bring in a good harvest. The point is that one must make an investment (obtain and feed the oxen) to get a large return.[283]

(25) Look Who's Talking (14:5-7)

5A truthful witness does not deceive,
but a false witness pours out lies.

6The mocker seeks wisdom and finds none,
but knowledge comes easily to the discerning.

7Stay away from a foolish man,
for you will not find knowledge on his lips.

TYPE: THEMATIC (14:5-7). **14:5-7** One should evaluate what a person says on the basis of his or her overall credibility (v. 5). Similarly, one should not expect to get sound advice from a person who shows no respect for the precepts of wisdom (vv. 6-7[284]). In short, the character of the speaker serves as a warning about whether his or her words are true or wise.

---

[280]The Hebrew word for "empty" is רֵק.

[281]The adjective בָּר elsewhere means "clean" in the sense of moral purity rather than physical cleanliness (Job 11:4; Pss 2:12; 19:9; 24:4; 73:1; in Song 6:9-10 the word is used for the high value and radiance of the beloved woman). But it never means "empty," and given its positive usage elsewhere, it is doubtful that it ever could.

[282]The noun בָּר regularly means "grain" (Gen 41:35,49; Amos 5:11, etc.).

[283]Cf. McKane, *Proverbs*, 470-71. Note also the pun בָּר וְרָב.

[284]The MT וּבַל יָדַעְתָּ, "and you have not known," is peculiar, but proposed emendations are unconvincing. The point apparently is that in the fool one has not come to know a wise teacher and therefore one should look for another.

(26) Appearance and Reality (14:8-15)

[8]The wisdom of the prudent is to give thought to their ways,
but the folly of fools is deception.

[9]Fools mock at making amends for sin,
but goodwill is found among the upright.

[10]Each heart knows its own bitterness,
and no one else can share its joy.

[11]The house of the wicked will be destroyed,
but the tent of the upright will flourish.

[12]There is a way that seems right to a man,
but in the end it leads to death.

[13]Even in laughter the heart may ache,
and joy may end in grief.

[14]The faithless will be fully repaid for their ways,
and the good man rewarded for his.

[15]A simple man believes anything,
but a prudent man gives thought to his steps.

TYPE: CHIASMUS (14:8-15). **14:8-15** Life is often deceptive, and the text here implicitly exhorts readers not to be taken in by appearances. One should not be too quick to ascribe happiness to others since no one can be sure of the true condition of another's heart, regardless of appearances. Above all, one should not be taken in by the apparent freedom from grief that one sometimes sees in those who do not concern themselves with God or his ways. In the end the righteous will be vindicated. Fools, however, are quickly taken in by what they see and thus think they can sin without penalty.

This series of proverbs is a carefully balanced chiasmus.

A: The prudent and the fools (v. 8)
  B: Making amends for sin (v. 9)
    C: Secrets of the heart (v. 10)
      D: Destruction of the wicked (v. 11)
      D′: The way to death (v. 12)
    C′: Secrets of the heart (v. 13)
  B′: Being repaid for sin (v. 14)
A′: The simple and the prudent (v. 15)

The meaning of "the folly of fools is deception" (v. 8) is not immediately evident, but the parallel in v. 15[285] implies that the naivete of fools

[285]Note the parallel of עָרוּם הָבִין דַּרְכּוֹ ("a prudent man understands his way," v. 8) and עָרוּם יָבִין לַאֲשֻׁרוֹ ("a prudent man understands his step," v. 15).

is in view. Fools are easily deceived, but the prudent[286] look beneath surface appearances. Verses 10,13 likewise observe that no one knows the inner life of another's heart and that the appearance of happiness can be deceptive. Verse 9 states that the wicked believe they can avoid making restitution, but v. 14 gives assurance of divine retribution.[287] In other words, the appearance of getting away with crime is belied by a justice that is not obvious or quick but is certain. In vv. 11-12, at the heart of the chiasmus, the apparent success of the wicked is short-lived. Their prosperity would seem to be permanent ("house of the wicked" versus "tent of the upright"), but their easy road leads to death. The message of the whole is to avoid a superficial analysis of the lessons of life.

(27) A Patient Spirit (14:16-17)

16 A wise man fears the Lord and shuns evil,
but a fool is hotheaded and reckless.

17 A quick-tempered man does foolish things,
and a crafty man is hated.

Type: Chiasmus, Thematic (14:16-17). **14:16-17** These verses should be translated, "A wise man is cautious[288] and stays out of trouble,/but a fool is hotheaded and reckless.//A quick-tempered man does foolish things,/but a thinking man[289] endures provocation."[290] Patient consideration before acting or speaking, even in the face of provocation, averts disaster.

(28) A Crown of Wisdom, A Wreath of Folly (14:18-24)

18 The simple inherit folly,
but the prudent are crowned with knowledge.

19 Evil men will bow down in the presence of the good,
and the wicked at the gates of the righteous.

20 The poor are shunned even by their neighbors,
but the rich have many friends.

21 He who despises his neighbor sins,
but blessed is he who is kind to the needy.

---

[286] עָרוּם often means "cunning"; penetrating insight is implied.

[287] For the unintelligible מֵעָלָיו ("from him") in v. 14, McKane (*Proverbs*, 474) suggests either מִמַּעֲלָלָיו ("from his deeds") or מִמַּעְגָּלָיו ("from his tracks"). The parallel suggests that the latter is to be preferred.

[288] יָרֵא ("fears"); the NIV inserts "the Lord," but that is not the point here.

[289] אִישׁ מְזִמּוֹת need not be taken in a negative sense. Here it should be regarded as the equivalent to חָכָם ("wise men," v. 16).

[290] Reading יִשָּׂא ("endures" ["provocation"]) for the MT יִשָּׂנֵא ("is hated"). The LXX has πολλὰ ὑποφέρει ("endures many things").

[22]Do not those who plot evil go astray?
But those who plan what is good find love and faithfulness.

[23]All hard work brings a profit,
but mere talk leads only to poverty.

[24]The wealth of the wise is their crown,
but the folly of fools yields folly.

TYPE: INCLUSIO (14:18-24). **14:18-24** As was the case with Joseph, who saw his jealous and scheming brothers bow before him, this text promises that the righteous will be crowned with wisdom and see fools bow before them. The passage also gives a few specific guidelines for right behavior, including compassion and personal diligence.

Verse 18 should be translated, "The simple are adorned[291] in folly,/but the prudent are crowned with knowledge." Similar to the notion of being crowned with knowledge is v. 19, in which the evil bow down before the good as to kings. A more direct parallel to v. 18 is v. 24, which should be rendered, "The crown of the wise is their wealth,/but the wreath[292] of fools is folly." Verses 18 and 24 thus form an inclusio, and v. 19 further amplifies the teaching of v. 18.

Verses 20-23 fall between these verses and are themselves bound together in a complex manner. Verses 20 and 23 both deal with wealth and poverty, and vv. 21-22 both contrast those who are kind with those who plot evil.[293] Viewed in this manner, vv. 20-23 are in a chiastic pattern. On the other hand, vv. 20-21 both describe the different ways a "neighbor" is treated,[294] and vv. 22-23 both concern the respective gain or loss that comes to the good/diligent as opposed to the evil/lazy. Viewed in this manner, vv. 20-23 are two sets of parallel proverbs.

Both the chiasmus and the parallel pattern may be viewed as follows:

A1: The crowns of wisdom and folly (v. 18)
A2: The evil bow to the wise (v. 19)
B1: The poor and rich (treatment of a neighbor) (v. 20)

---

[291]Rather than "they inherit," it is better to read the verb as נֶחְלוּ, "they are adorned with," from חלה (cf. חֲלִי, "necklace." See G. R. Driver, "Problems," 181. McKane (*Proverbs*, 467) correctly notes that the simple do not inherit folly but are already in that condition.

[292]וְאִוֶּלֶת כְּסִילִים אִוֶּלֶת, "but the folly of fools is folly," appears hopelessly redundant; the NIV adds "yields" to make better sense of the text. A preferable solution is to emend וְאִוֶּלֶת to לִוְיַת ("wreath") in parallel with עֲטֶרֶת ("crown"). Another proposal is that of Dahood (*Proverbs*, 31-32) that the first אִוֶּלֶת be regarded as the Ugaritic ʾ*alt* ("throne").

[293]חטא ("miss the mark," "sin," "make a mistake," v. 21) and תעה ("to err," "go astray," v. 22) are conceptually parallel, as are מְחוֹנֵן ("he who shows mercy," v. 21) and חֹרְשֵׁי טוֹב ("those who devise good," v. 22).

[294]An obvious parallel is גַּם־לְרֵעֵהוּ ("even to his friend," v. 20) and בָּז־לְרֵעֵהוּ ("he who despises his friend," v. 21). Also the poor man being hated (v. 20) contrasts with showing mercy to the impoverished (v. 21).

C1: Scheming and benevolence (treatment of a neighbor) (v. 21)
C2: Scheming and benevolence (reward for kindness) (v. 22)
B′2: Wealth and poverty (reward for diligence) (v. 23)
A′: The crowns of wisdom and folly (v. 24)

The full text deals with the recompense that accompanies wisdom or folly. Ethical issues here include concern for the poor, diligence in work, and integrity in dealing with others. The promised reward for correct behavior is esteem in the eyes of others and personal prosperity.

(29) An Honest Witness (14:25)

**25 A truthful witness saves lives,
but a false witness is deceitful.**

TYPE: SINGLE BICOLON PROVERB (14:25). **14:25** This proverb appears to have legal proceedings in view. Honesty in court is not a mere fine point of law; people's lives depend upon it.

(30) The Fear of the Lord (14:26-27)

**26 He who fears the LORD has a secure fortress,
and for his children it will be a refuge.**

**27 The fear of the LORD is a fountain of life,
turning a man from the snares of death.**

TYPE: THEMATIC (14:26-27). **14:26-27** The fear of the Lord is the theme of this pair of proverbs. True piety is both security from the storms of life (v. 26) and a kind of early warning system against the moral traps that confront us (v. 27).

(31) National Security (14:28-35)

**28 A large population is a king's glory,
but without subjects a prince is ruined.**

**29 A patient man has great understanding,
but a quick-tempered man displays folly.**

**30 A heart at peace gives life to the body,
but envy rots the bones.**

**31 He who oppresses the poor shows contempt for their Maker,
but whoever is kind to the needy honors God.**

**32 When calamity comes, the wicked are brought down,
but even in death the righteous have a refuge.**

**33 Wisdom reposes in the heart of the discerning
and even among fools she lets herself be known.**

**34 Righteousness exalts a nation,
but sin is a disgrace to any people.**

**[35]A king delights in a wise servant,
but a shameful servant incurs his wrath.**

TYPE: INCLUSIO (14:28-35). **14:28-35** The health and well-being of a nation depends upon both the ruler and the governed. A ruler must be fair and above all must respect the rights of his people. The people, on the other hand, must have virtue in their lives or they will bring society into chaos. No government can succeed without the people, and no people can thrive if corruption and evil abound.

The inclusio here is formed by v. 28, which describes a king's need for a sizable populace, and v. 35, which obliquely asserts a king's need for capable servants.

Verse 29 stresses the importance of patience. In this context an impatient king may lose his following (v. 28), and a headstrong courtier may lose his place before the king (v. 35), although the proverb naturally applies equally well to nonpolitical situations. Verse 30 looks at patience from a different perspective: it is essential for a healthy life. Verse 31 stands in the ancient Near Eastern tradition of warning rulers not to trample upon the rights of the poor; the king who ignores this advice will soon find himself without a nation.

Verse 32b may appear to describe the hope of eternal life, but one should use it in this way with caution. The MT literally reads, "But a righteous man seeks refuge in his death." The NIV smooths over this by translating it more neutrally that "even[295] in death the righteous have a refuge." In other words, the MT as it stands speaks of the righteous actively running to death for refuge;[296] it does not speak simply of a consolation offered by the hope of afterlife. If the MT is to be followed, it should be followed fully.

The notion of seeking refuge in death, however, is incompatible with the rest of Proverbs and indeed with biblical theology. Elsewhere in Proverbs, death is the result of evil behavior and is often associated with the prostitute (2:18; 5:5,23; 7:27; 8:36; 10:2,21; 11:19; 14:12; 16:25; 19:16, 18; 21:6,25; 24:11). Conversely, righteousness saves from death (11:4; 12:28; 13:14; 14:27; 16:14). For the New Testament Christian, death is an enemy overcome by the resurrection of Christ (1 Cor 15). Even though Paul faced death courageously and yearned to be with Christ, he chose life over death (Phil 1:21-26) and did not speak of death as a refuge toward which he would flee. To do so approximates the theological justification of suicide that Augustine warned against (*City of God* 1.20).

---

[295]The word "even" is not in the original. The conjunction on וְחֹסֶה cannot have that function here, and at any rate the NIV has attached the word "even" to the noun "death."

[296]The verb חָסָה (in the participle form in this verse) speaks of actively seeking refuge in something (Judg 9:15) or someone (usually God: Pss 2:12; 5:12 [Eng. v. 11]; 7:2 [Eng. v. 1]; 11:1; 71:1; Prov 30:5, etc.).

Following the LXX, an alternative translation of v. 32 is, "When trouble comes, a wicked man is cast down,/but a righteous man seeks refuge in integrity."[297] This suits the context better. While some may advance themselves through scheming opportunism, their lack of integrity will one day be their undoing. Conversely, those who have behaved fairly will be vindicated when under examination (v. 35).

A similar problem occurs in v. 33, where it is entirely out of character with the rest of Proverbs to assert that wisdom may be found among fools.[298] It is better to follow the LXX and Syriac and translate v. 33 as, "Wisdom reposes in the heart of the discerning,/but among fools she is unknown."[299] In the political context this means that the ruler should choose counselors carefully.

Verse 34 is a general statement that a nation's political health depends to a great degree on the moral integrity of its people,[300] and v. 35 closes the inclusio by contrasting the inept and the capable public servants.[301]

(32) Two Collections (15:1–16:8)

1A gentle answer turns away wrath,
but a harsh word stirs up anger.

2The tongue of the wise commends knowledge,
but the mouth of the fool gushes folly.

3The eyes of the LORD are everywhere,
keeping watch on the wicked and the good.

4The tongue that brings healing is a tree of life,
but a deceitful tongue crushes the spirit.

5A fool spurns his father's discipline,
but whoever heeds correction shows prudence.

6The house of the righteous contains great treasure,
but the income of the wicked brings them trouble.

7The lips of the wise spread knowledge;
not so the hearts of fools.

---

[297]See BHS note. The LXX has τῇ ἑαυτοῦ ὁσιότητι ("in his own integrity"), for which the Hebrew equivalent would be בְּתוּמּוֹ. This involves only a transposition of the letters מ and ת from the MT בְמוֹתוֹ ("in his death"). If בְמוֹתוֹ is intended, one might expect it to be in the initial position of colon *b* (parallel to בְּרָעָתוֹ, "in his trouble").

[298]Once again the NIV is somewhat gratuitous in its addition of the word "even"; it is doubtful that the conjunction can bear that meaning in this construction. The MT literally reads, "And in the midst of fools she is known." One might object that this is a case where the "more difficult reading is to be preferred." That canon is not inviolable, however. It is one thing to choose a harder reading, but it is another to choose a reading that directly contradicts the whole message of Proverbs regarding the exclusive nature of wisdom and folly.

[299]The LXX has οὐ διαγινώσκεται.

[300]The word חֶסֶד here means "shame" and not the familiar "grace" or "faithfulness."

[301]See the rendition of this verse in McKane, *Proverbs*, 233.

8The LORD detests the sacrifice of the wicked,
but the prayer of the upright pleases him.

9The LORD detests the way of the wicked
but he loves those who pursue righteousness.

10Stern discipline awaits him who leaves the path;
he who hates correction will die.

11Death and Destruction lie open before the LORD—
how much more the hearts of men!

12A mocker resents correction;
he will not consult the wise.

13A happy heart makes the face cheerful,
but heartache crushes the spirit.

14The discerning heart seeks knowledge,
but the mouth of a fool feeds on folly.

15All the days of the oppressed are wretched,
but the cheerful heart has a continual feast.

16Better a little with the fear of the LORD
than great wealth with turmoil.

17Better a meal of vegetables where there is love
than a fattened calf with hatred.

18A hot-tempered man stirs up dissension,
but a patient man calms a quarrel.

19The way of the sluggard is blocked with thorns,
but the path of the upright is a highway.

20A wise son brings joy to his father,
but a foolish man despises his mother.

21Folly delights a man who lacks judgment,
but a man of understanding keeps a straight course.

22Plans fail for lack of counsel,
but with many advisers they succeed.

23A man finds joy in giving an apt reply—
and how good is a timely word!

24The path of life leads upward for the wise
to keep him from going down to the grave.

25The LORD tears down the proud man's house
but he keeps the widow's boundaries intact.

26The LORD detests the thoughts of the wicked,
but those of the pure are pleasing to him.

27A greedy man brings trouble to his family,
but he who hates bribes will live.

28The heart of the righteous weighs its answers,
but the mouth of the wicked gushes evil.

29The LORD is far from the wicked
but he hears the prayer of the righteous.

30A cheerful look brings joy to the heart,
and good news gives health to the bones.

31He who listens to a life-giving rebuke
will be at home among the wise.

32He who ignores discipline despises himself,
but whoever heeds correction gains understanding.

33The fear of the LORD teaches a man wisdom,
and humility comes before honor.

1To man belong the plans of the heart,
but from the LORD comes the reply of the tongue.

2All a man's ways seem innocent to him,
but motives are weighed by the LORD.

3Commit to the LORD whatever you do,
and your plans will succeed.

4The LORD works out everything for his own ends—
even the wicked for a day of disaster.

5The LORD detests all the proud of heart.
Be sure of this: They will not go unpunished.

6Through love and faithfulness sin is atoned for;
through the fear of the LORD a man avoids evil.

7When a man's ways are pleasing to the LORD,
he makes even his enemies live at peace with him.

8Better a little with righteousness
than much gain with injustice.

TYPE: A-B ENVELOPE SERIES (15:1–16:8). **15:1–16:8**[302] This text is, in effect, random repetition (see introduction) but with recognizable clusters of proverbs. It is composed of two collections, 15:1-17 and 15:18–16:8, which parallel each other not structurally so much as in content. Each major collection begins with a word on patience versus the provocation of wrath (15:1,18), and each ends with "better sayings" on apparent

[302]I distinguish what I here call an "A-B Envelope" from simple inclusio in that the inclusio has the same or similar material at both the beginning and end of a text to mark off its limits, whereas the A-B envelope figure repeats a series of proverbs to mark text boundaries. The pattern is: Proverb A [first group of miscellaneous proverbs] Proverb B / Proverb A′ [second group of miscellaneous proverbs] Proverb B′/etc., in which all the proverbs marked "A" are in some way similar, and all the proverbs marked "B" are in some way similar.

versus real prosperity (15:16-17; 16:8). Between these markers the two collections (here referred to as "I" and "II") contain teachings that correspond to one another in remarkable detail. In the following chart, collection I is set forth in its normal order, while units in collection II are set out in an order that corresponds to those in collection I. This does not imply that verses in collection II need to be transposed; it is done merely to make the comparison clearer and facilitate exegesis. Similarly, this analysis does not dispute that there are other parallels and ties among these verses other than those mentioned here.

COLLECTION I	COLLECTION II
1. **15:1** gentle versus harsh answer; calming versus provoking anger	**15:18** hot-tempered versus patient man; calming versus provking anger
2. **15:2-4** chiasmus: use of the tongue (2,4) and divine retribution (3)	**15:24-27** chiasmus: life and death (24,27) and divine retribution (25-26)
3. **15:5** foolish son; heeding admonishment	**15:20-22** wise/foolish son; need for advisers
4. **15:6** income of righteous/wicked	**15:19** way of sluggard/upright
5. **15:7** speech of the wise/fools	**15:28** speech of the righteous/wicked
6. **15:8-9** Lord rejects sacrifices of wicked	**15:29** Lord rejects prayers of wicked
7. **15:10-11** severity of the Lord's dealing with people	**15:30-32** cheerful look and heart correction (30); accepting/rejecting correction (31-32)
8. **15:12-15** accepting/rejecting 12,14); cheerful face and heart (13,15)	**15:33–16:7** the Lord's ways of judgments
9. **15:16-17** better sayings on true prosperity	**16:8** better saying on true prosperity

Collection II (twenty-four verses) is not only longer than collection I (seventeen verses) but it also contains one verse that has no parallel in collection I (15:23). On the other hand, 15:23 concerns the ability to give an appropriate answer and thus obliquely relates to the lead verses, 15:1,18.

Section 1 (15:1,18[303]*).* The ability to avert needless quarreling and to live in harmony with others is a virtue of wisdom. Many conflicts arise not because the issues separating the parties are so great but because of the temperaments people bring to a confrontation. Verse 18 also implies that a calm person avoids litigation if possible.[304]

---

[303]Note the verbal links between the two verses: חֵמָה ("wrath") and אַף ("anger") in v. 1 and חֵמָה and אַפַּיִם in v. 18.

[304]As indicated by רִיב ("quarrel," "lawsuit"). Cf. McKane, *Proverbs*, 482.

Section 2 (15:2-4,24-27). In the first series (vv. 2-4) a single proverb on God's administration of justice (v. 3) falls between two proverbs on the use of the tongue (vv. 2,4). In the second series (vv. 24-27) two proverbs on divine justice (vv. 25-26) fall between two proverbs on behavior that leads either to life and prosperity or to the grave (vv. 24,27[305]). In both sections the middle proverbs reveal that the moral principles that govern the world are not mere abstractions but are actively maintained by God's intervention.

Verse 2 deals with the influence for good or evil one's words have on others,[306] whereas v. 4 asserts that one can either sustain or break another's spirit with words. In v. 4b the disappointment of having been deceived is in view. Both verses stress the power of words for good or evil.

In v. 24 it is unclear whether "upward" and "down" express a doctrine of immortality. In v. 27, however, the issue is obviously this-worldly life and prosperity and not the afterlife. The "widow" (v. 25) represents the weak and impoverished, whose few possessions are the objects of wicked men's greed (v. 27) but who are also the objects of God's special concern.

Verse 26 draws on the Levitical law for its metaphor. It should be translated, "The thoughts of the wicked are an abomination to Yahweh,/ but kind words are clean." "Abomination"[307] and "clean"[308] are terms used of sacrifices and other religious objects or activities that are either repugnant or acceptable to God. The words and thoughts of people may be either a pleasing sacrifice or a blasphemous sacrilege.

Section 3 (15:5; 20:22). These texts both draw together two concepts, namely, the wise/foolish son who pleases/disgraces his parents and the importance of heeding wise counsel. One's attitude toward parental teaching (v. 5) will determine one's lifelong attitude toward authority and instruction (vv. 21-22). To "keep a straight course" (v. 21) is to avoid the moral pitfalls of life; it does not refer to headstrong determination. Verse 22 does not describe making decisions by committee but advocates an internal attitude of willingness to hear and heed advice.[309]

---

[305]A thematic link exists between אֹרַח חַיִּים ("path of life") and מִשְּׁאוֹל ("from the grave") in v. 24 and יִחְיֶה ("he will live") in v. 27.

[306]G. R. Driver ("Problems," 181) suggests a root *טבב, with the meaning "announce," for the MT תֵּיטִיב. Dahood (*Proverbs*, 32-33) argues that this is a dialectical form of יטף, cognate to נטף, meaning "drop" or "distill." Dahood's suggestion is preferable; the text contrasts the slow, steady dripping of wisdom from the wise with the flood of folly from the mouths of fools.

[307]תּוֹעֲבָה.

[308]וּטְהֹרִים.

[309]The feminine singular תָּקוּם ("she will arise," "be established") with no feminine singular subject seems odd; one would expect another infinitive absolute on the analogy of הָפֵר ("to fail"). The LXX is quite different, which may imply a textual problem, but the Vg is close to the MT (it translates תָּקוּם with the plural *confirmantur*).

Section 4 (15:6,19). In Proverbs lasting prosperity is attained by high moral character and diligence. Using the "house" symbolically as the storehouse of one's possessions (v. 6) and the "way" metaphorically for the success of one's life (v. 19), Proverbs links righteousness to wealth (v. 6) and contrasts laziness with uprightness (and not simply with diligence, as we might expect from v. 19[310]).

Section 5 (15:7,28). The "lips of the wise" or "heart of the righteous" contrasts with the "heart of fools" or "mouth of the wicked." Verse 7 establishes the simple fact that knowledge is found with the wise and not with fools. Verse 28 goes beyond this and describes a practical means for distinguishing the two: the wise/righteous speak only after careful consideration,[311] while the fools/wicked spew forth whatever mischief or perversity is on their minds.

Section 6 (15:8-9,29[312]). These verses are near prophetic in their theological concern (compare Amos 5:21-24; Mic 6:6-8). Religious zeal is no substitute for integrity.

Section 7 (15:10-11; 15:33–16:7). These verses, which are linked by their focus on how Yahweh deals with people, make for an intriguing collection. Proverbs 15:10-11 describes the punishment of death that awaits the wicked,[313] while 15:33–16:7 describes in detail the divine administration of justice. Included here are the general warning to fear God (15:33), general statements on divine providence and judgment (16:1-5), and a teaching on how to receive God's favor and a promise of the benefits thereby gained.

Righteousness is here defined primarily as the fear of the Lord and humility (15:33[314]); it is more a matter of motives[315] than deeds and thus excludes self-justification (16:2). Biblical righteousness is fundamentally

---

[310]Contrary to the BHS note, there is no need to emend יְשָׁרִים ("upright") to חָרוּצִים ("determined"), which is anyway not equivalent to the LXX ἀνδρείων ("manly").

[311]הגה, "to mumble," comes to mean "to meditate deeply," as in Ps 1:2.

[312]Both vv. 8-9 and 29 explicitly mention יהוה in their first cola, and the phrase וּתְפִלַּת יְשָׁרִים ("and the prayer of the upright") in v. 8 closely parallels וּתְפִלַּת צַדִּיקִים ("and the prayer of the righteous") in v. 29. Note also that vv. 8-9 are linked together by the phrase תּוֹעֲבַת יהוה ("an abomination to the Lord").

[313]There is more to v. 11 than a mere comparison (i.e., as Yahweh can see into Sheol, so he can also penetrate the human heart). The examination of the heart is an act of judgment, and the reference to death and Sheol implicitly warns of the fate of the condemned.

[314]Verse 33 literally reads, "The fear of the Lord is wisdom's correction (יִרְאַת יהוה מוּסַר חָכְמָה), and humility is before honor." Contrary to the BHS, there is no need to emend מוּסַר to מוּסָד ("foundation"); see McKane, *Proverbs*, 487. The point is not so much that the fear of the Lord teaches wisdom as that the wise are governed by the fear of the Lord.

[315]רוּחוֹת in 16:2 is rightly translated "motives" and not "spirits." This verse is not related to the Egyptian conception of final judgment, at which Thoth weighs the hearts of the dead. Cf. McKane, *Proverbs*, 496.

an attitude of trust in God, an attitude implicitly and explicitly demanded in 16:1,3. Wickedness, too, is more than simple disobedience to the commandments; it is above all manifest in an attitude of pride (16:5). Reading these verses, one cannot but reflect on the gospel proclaimed by the apostle Paul. Righteousness is committed trust in the Lord (16:3[316]) and acknowledgment that no one can conceal from God the evil of his or her heart (15:11; 16:2). Thus all efforts at righteousness "by the works of the Law," whereby, in the words of Prov 16:2, "a man's ways seem innocent to him," are abandoned. The supreme qualities of the righteous life are "love and faithfulness" (16:6), and it is by these that one attains to the forgiveness of sin.[317] Similarly, the fate of the wicked (death, 15:10) and the benefit of righteousness (a peaceful life, 16:7) are also amplified in the New Testament. While the emphasis in Proverbs is again this-worldly, deeper theological significance is implicit.

Section 8 (15:12-15[318]; 15:30-32). Both texts combine the ideas of a cheerful look (15:13,30a) and the importance of heeding correction (15:12,14,31-32). Verse 13, however, speaks of a happy heart producing a cheerful face (i.e., for the one who has the happy heart) whereas v. 30a speaks of a cheerful look giving joy to the heart (i.e., of someone else).[319] By placing vv. 13,15 in the context of a warning to heed correction (vv. 12,14), the text implies that mental and emotional wholeness proceed from submission to sound teaching. Similarly, by placing v. 30 at the head of warnings to submit to instruction (vv. 31-32), the passage draws the reader to reflect on the importance of influencing others by an affirming attitude and positive reports rather than exclusively by the negative way of correcting faults. The text also teaches that circumstances can negatively or positively affect one's mental health (oppression in v. 15a, good news in v. 30b).

Section 9 (15:16-17; 16:8). In three better sayings[320] true prosperity is described. Contrary to the common understanding, it is not to be found

---

[316]גלל ("to roll") is here a colorful metaphor for trust in Yahweh, a usage established in Ps 22:9.

[317]The use of the Levitical term כפר ("to atone") is significant here. It implies that atonement is not merely a matter of ceremonial repentance and sacrifice but is contingent upon the attitude of the heart.

[318]These four verses are arranged in parallel fashion: *A*: rejecting or accepting correction/*B*: happy heart or heartache/*A'*: rejecting or accepting correction/*B'*: oppressed or happy heart.

[319]The phrase מְאוֹר־עֵינַיִם ("lamp/light of the eyes") is difficult. The LXX appears to be offering speculative paraphrase in rendering it θεωρῶν ὀφθαλμὸς καλὰ ("an eye observing beautiful things"); the Vg *lux oculorum* ("light of the eyes") is more literal. It would appear that the absolute עֵינַיִם is adjectival (thus, "eye-light") and that the NIV interpretation is correct.

[320]All begin with טוֹב ("good").

in wealth, possessions, and rich food. The greatest possessions are a pious life, a loving home, and personal integrity.

15:23 The ability to give an apt reply is skill highly valued in wisdom literature. This proverb may be placed here because of the stress on the value of good counsel in v. 22.

(33) Three Collections (16:9–17:1)

9In his heart a man plans his course,
but the LORD determines his steps.

10The lips of a king speak as an oracle,
and his mouth should not betray justice.

11Honest scales and balances are from the LORD;
all the weights in the bag are of his making.

12Kings detest wrongdoing,
for a throne is established through righteousness.

13Kings take pleasure in honest lips;
they value a man who speaks the truth.

14A king's wrath is a messenger of death,
but a wise man will appease it.

15When a king's face brightens, it means life;
his favor is like a rain cloud in spring.

16How much better to get wisdom than gold,
to choose understanding rather than silver!

17The highway of the upright avoids evil;
he who guards his way guards his life.

18Pride goes before destruction,
a haughty spirit before a fall.

19Better to be lowly in spirit and among the oppressed
than to share plunder with the proud.

20Whoever gives heed to instruction prospers,
and blessed is he who trusts in the LORD.

21The wise in heart are called discerning,
and pleasant words promote instruction.

22Understanding is a fountain of life to those who have it,
but folly brings punishment to fools.

23A wise man's heart guides his mouth,
and his lips promote instruction.

24Pleasant words are a honeycomb,
sweet to the soul and healing to the bones.

25There is a way that seems right to a man,
but in the end it leads to death.

26 The laborer's appetite works for him;
his hunger drives him on.

27 A scoundrel plots evil,
and his speech is like a scorching fire.

28 A perverse man stirs up dissension,
and a gossip separates close friends.

29 A violent man entices his neighbor
and leads him down a path that is not good.

30 He who winks with his eye is plotting perversity;
he who purses his lips is bent on evil.

31 Gray hair is a crown of splendor;
it is attained by a righteous life.

32 Better a patient man than a warrior,
a man who controls his temper than one who takes a city.

33 The lot is cast into the lap,
but its every decision is from the LORD.

1 Better a dry crust with peace and quiet
than a house full of feasting, with strife.

TYPE: A-B ENVELOPE SERIES (16:9–17:1). **16:9–17:1** The above proverbs are in a threefold A-B envelope series, as follows:

COLLECTION I
A: Human plans and divine providence (16:9)
  Nine proverbs (16:10-18)
  B: Better saying on humble circumstances (16:19)
COLLECTION II
A′: Prosperity through careful decision making and faith in God (16:20)
  Eleven proverbs (16:21-31)
  B′: Better saying on patience (16:32)
COLLECTION III
A″: Casting lots and divine providence (16:33)
  B″: Better saying on humble circumstances (17:1)

The verses marked "A" (16:9,20,33) all concern divine providence over human affairs. The issue in these verses is wisdom in the decision-making process. Whether one makes detailed plans or resorts to casting lots, events and circumstances are all in God's control. As such the wise are cautious but above all put their faith in God and not human plans. Verse 20 should be translated, "He who carefully considers a matter[321]

[321] So translating מַשְׂכִּיל עַל־דָּבָר. מַשְׂכִּיל means more than to "give heed" in the sense of "listen" or "obey." It is rather to consider a matter carefully and come to the point of full comprehension so that one can deal with the matter effectively.

will prosper, and blessed is he who trusts in the Lord." The point of this verse is not that one should heed instruction but that one should carefully consider the facts before making a decision; even so, trusting in Yahweh is more important than prudence. In all three verses human planning and perceptiveness is linked to and perhaps also contrasted with trust in God.

The verses marked "B" (16:19,32; 17:1) all imply that a peaceable attitude makes the position that is apparently lower or less aggressive preferable to one of power. All are "better" sayings. Set in context with the "A" sayings, these texts imply that success is not necessarily to be measured by the size of one's bank account.

The intervening verses in texts I and II do not correspond to one another (unlike 15:1–16:8), but several discrete groups, as described below, are apparent in these collections. Collection III has no intervening verses at all.

16:10-15 These verses concern righteousness in government and are organized as a thematic collection. Also the catchword "king"[322] occurs in every verse except 11, which nevertheless plainly deals with justice in government. The royal government is described in highly favorable terms here; indeed, the king appears to be a flawless minister of justice in vv. 10 and 12. These pronouncements, however, should be understood as ideal rather than actual. They represent what a king *should* be.[323] Devotion to justice and truth are preconditions for good government. Verse 10 is striking for describing a king's words as an "oracle." Normally used of divination by pagans and false prophets, the word here[324] metaphorically describes the king as having a deep, mysterious wisdom (cf. 2 Sam 14:17,20).

Verse 11 does not mention the king and is theologically important in that, using the concrete image of scales and measures, it teaches that the principle of justice is derived from God. Equity is not a human invention, and thus kings do not have the authority to suspend or violate the laws of fairness.

Verse 13 implicitly counsels the young court official to be honest in all dealings with the king, and vv. 14-15 speak of the need for reverential respect for monarchs but also imply that they can be arbitrary if not irrational. Closing this section with these two verses reinforces the importance of learning how to deal with political power.

16:16-17 This pair of verses concerns choices in life and employs the metaphor of wealth (v. 16) and the metaphor of the way (v. 17). The meaning of both proverbs is transparent, but together they link the ideas of choosing wisdom, shunning evil, and avoiding destruction.

---

[322] מֶלֶךְ in vv. 10,14-15; מְלָכִים in vv. 12-13.

[323] The imperfect in v. 10 (יִמְעַל) is rightly taken in a jussive sense.

[324] קֶסֶם.

16:18-19 Verse 18 is linked to v. 19, the closure of this A-B envelope, in that both concern humility and the consequences of pride. Proverbs here links pride to robbery. In doing so, it alludes either to the arrogant certainty of the criminal that he will not be caught or to the act of robbery itself as an expression of self-centeredness and indifference to the rights of others. At any rate, v. 18 teaches that the apparent prosperity of the proud is short-lived.

16:20-24 Verses 21-24 concern the value of wise words and constitute a thematic unity. Verse 20, the opening of the second A-B envelope, also serves to introduce this particular section. In what follows, the value of sound speech is extolled. Verse 20a thus alerts the reader to the need to weigh words and matters accurately, and v. 20b draws attention to the fact that wise behavior is impossible without fear of God. The meanings of the individual proverbs that follow are self-evident. The overall thrust of this text is that wise teachers choose their words carefully and in so doing enhance the learning experience for their students. The wisdom of the true sage not only benefits the disciples morally but is a joy to receive as well.

16:25 This is an individual proverb, but perhaps it is set here as a contrast to vv. 18-19 and 21-24. In the Hebrew text the metaphor is more vividly expressed: "There is a way that seems right *before*[325] a man, but at its end are ways of death." A man stands at the beginning of a road and it looks fine to him; but when he comes to the end, he discovers death lies before him no matter which way he turns.

16:26 This proverb speaks of the importance of incentive. It is a good example of a proverb that easily could be twisted for evil purposes; that is, to justify giving meager pay to laborers. Contrast Jas 5:1-6.

16:27-30 Verses 27-30 describe the man who has evil schemes and are another thematic unity. Verses 27-29 concern the evil machinations of the scoundrel, the perverse man, and the violent man,[326] and v. 30 is a conclusion or commentary on those three descriptions. The winking eye and pursed lips of v. 30 may be taken either as signals among conspirators or as a general statement of shiftiness in the facial mannerisms of scheming people.[327] The point may be that the reader should learn to read the faces of others in order to spot the three kinds of evil men described in vv. 27-29.

16:31 Verse 31 is an individual proverb,[328] but its position before v. 32 perhaps makes the implicit link between old age and patience, namely, that one attains the former by means of the latter.

---

[325]The word לִפְנֵי means more than "seems" here; it establishes a metaphor of a person standing at the beginning of a road.

[326]Note that vv. 27-29 each begin with אִישׁ.

[327]The latter interpretation is advocated in McKane, *Proverbs*, 495.

[328]Note the assonance in עֲטֶרֶת תִּפְאֶרֶת . . . בְּדֶרֶךְ.

17:1 This better saying is related to 16:19,32 (both better sayings) in that all insist that "better" does not imply "more," "bigger," or "richer"; rather "better" simply means "spiritual integrity" (16:19), "temperance" (16:32), and "a life of peace" (17:1). This is part of the message of Jesus in the Sermon on the Mount (Matt 5:3-12).

(34) Remarks on Behavior (17:2-8)

2A wise servant will rule over a disgraceful son,
and will share the inheritance as one of the brothers.

3The crucible for silver and the furnace for gold,
but the LORD tests the heart.

4A wicked man listens to evil lips;
a liar pays attention to a malicious tongue.

5He who mocks the poor shows contempt for their Maker;
whoever gloats over disaster will not go unpunished.

6Children's children are a crown to the aged,
and parents are the pride of their children.

7Arrogant lips are unsuited to a fool—
how much worse lying lips to a ruler!

8A bribe is a charm to the one who gives it;
wherever he turns, he succeeds.

TYPE: RANDOM PROVERBS (17:2-8). Although these verses contain the hint of an inclusio[329] and repeat certain themes and terms,[330] no specific pattern is apparent.

17:2 Ability and character can overcome the disadvantages of birth. At the same time, those born to advantage can forfeit their birthright through immorality and incompetence.

17:3 The metaphor of the refining furnace perhaps implies that the Lord's testing of hearts is by adversity.

17:4 Taking gossip seriously is itself a form of malice practiced by those who have no respect for the truth.[331]

17:5 To make light of those who are suffering misfortune is to invite God's punishment.[332]

---

[329]מַשְׂכִּיל, v. 2, and יַשְׂכִּיל, v. 8.

[330]Family matters, vv. 2,6; divine judgment, vv. 3,5; the lips, vv. 4,7.

[331]The Hebrew of v. 4b is difficult. Dahood (*Proverbs*, 38) repoints שֶׁקֶר, "lie," to שֹׁקֵר, "liar," a hypothetical qal participle. He also argues that the root of מֵזִין is not אזן but *וזן, "to *weigh*," after the Ugaritic form *mznm*, "scales." This makes for a smoother text than the MT, but the meaning would be essentially the same.

[332]It is possible that לְאֵיד ("over"), "disaster," should be emended to לְאֹבֵד ("over"), "one who is perishing," on the basis of the LXX ἀπολλυμένῳ; cf. BHS note. The text as it stands, however, makes sense.

17:6 Behind this apparently innocuous proverb is a profound assertion of the psychological interdependence of the generations. Elders derive a sense of pride from their descendants, and children get their self-worth from parents. On the other hand, one generation can cause shame and a sense of worthlessness in another.

17:7 Emphasis here is on the noble; the fool is simply a foil to provide contrast. Persons of honor and responsibility should make no space for lying in their lives.[333]

17:8 This is an observational proverb; it merely points out that those who give gifts often receive special favors. It does not moralize or attempt to set out guidelines to distinguish a legitimate gift from a bribe. Contrast v. 23. McKane aptly paraphrases the verse as, "A bribe works like magic."[334]

(35) Four Conjoined Collections (17:9-26)

9He who covers over an offense promotes love,
but whoever repeats the matter separates close friends.

10A rebuke impresses a man of discernment
more than a hundred lashes a fool.

11An evil man is bent only on rebellion;
a merciless official will be sent against him.

12Better to meet a bear robbed of her cubs
than a fool in his folly.

13If a man pays back evil for good,
evil will never leave his house.

14Starting a quarrel is like breaching a dam;
so drop the matter before a dispute breaks out.

15Acquitting the guilty and condemning the innocent—
the LORD detests them both.

16Of what use is money in the hand of a fool,
since he has no desire to get wisdom?

17A friend loves at all times,
and a brother is born for adversity.

18A man lacking in judgment strikes hands in pledge
and puts up security for his neighbor.

19He who loves a quarrel loves sin;
he who builds a high gate invites destruction.

---

[333]The contrast is perhaps more complete if one emends יֶתֶר, "excess" (here = "arrogant"), to יֹשֶׁר, "uprightness," with the LXX πιστά. But in either case the point is clear.

[334]McKane, *Proverbs*, 502. אֶבֶן־חֵן, literally "stone of favor," is a magical charm.

20A man of perverse heart does not prosper;
he whose tongue is deceitful falls into trouble.

21To have a fool for a son brings grief;
there is no joy for the father of a fool.

22A cheerful heart is good medicine,
but a crushed spirit dries up the bones.
23A wicked man accepts a bribe in secret
to pervert the course of justice.

24A discerning man keeps wisdom in view,
but a fool's eyes wander to the ends of the earth.

25A foolish son brings grief to his father
and bitterness to the one who bore him.

26It is not good to punish an innocent man,
or to flog officials for their integrity.

The proverbs of vv. 9-16 have many interconnections, but it is difficult to tell if any specific pattern is intended. It appears, however, that these verses divide into four inclusio or chiasmus collections (vv. 9-13, vv. 14-19, vv. 20-22, and vv. 23-26) on the basis of thematic parallels or catchwords. The connections among the proverbs are as follows:

COLLECTION I
A: Gracious forgiveness (v. 9)
  B: The irrationality of a fool (v. 10)
    C: Just punishment carried out (v. 11)
  B: The behavior of a fool (v. 12)
A: Irrational retaliation (v. 13)

COLLECTION II
A: Quarrels (v. 14)
    C: Perversion of justice (v. 15)
      D: Poor use of money (v. 16)
      D: A friend in adversity (v. 17)
      D: Poor use of money (v. 18)
A: Quarrels (v. 19)

COLLECTION III
        E: Heart and tongue (v. 20)
  B: Foolish son (v. 21)
        E: Heart and spirit (v. 22)

COLLECTION IV
    C: Perversion of justice (v. 23)
  B: The eyes of a fool (v. 24)
  B: A foolish son (v. 25)
    C: Perversion of justice (v. 26)

THE SOCIAL AND ANTISOCIAL. *Type: Chiasmus (17:9-13).* This section describes those who are or are not sociable and easy to live with. The implied warning is that one should beware of antisocial, incorrigible, or vindictive behavior in oneself or others.

17:9,13 The ability to practice forgiveness and discretion is essential for the survival of an atmosphere of friendship. Probably a whole community and not just a single friendship is in view in v. 9. The covering of an offense would thus include forgiveness but would go beyond it. The "offense" may be against oneself or against a third party. Either way, if a discreet silence is not practiced where appropriate, the atmosphere of trust and mutual love quickly breaks down. The opposite extreme of a forgiving spirit is to take offense and retaliate against those who are only doing good (v. 13). Such a person will not only be friendless but will bring all manner of troubles on his or her head.

17:10,12 These verses focus on the stubbornness of a fool who is willfully wrong-headed, no matter how much it hurts (v. 10). This obstinate spirit makes the fool dangerous to be near (v. 12). Folly does not make for socially acceptable behavior. A person who can accept criticism has an approachable personality and can function well in social interaction. People who cannot accept a rebuke, however, cause chaos in the public arena. It would be better to try to deal with an angry bear in search of her cubs!

17:11 This verse is wholly concerned with relations with the community at large. Those who cannot submit themselves to governmental authority will soon come to regret it. They are more than socially outcast by the community; they receive judicial punishment from the community.

QUICK TO QUARREL. *Type: Inclusio (17:14-19).* The boundaries of this text are set by the inclusio on quarreling in vv. 14,19.[335]

17:14,19 A small breach in a dam soon grows until the dam is destroyed and the area is flooded. Even so, a conflict can take on a life of its own and devastate a long friendship and lead to litigation.[336] Those who love to quarrel and bring suits, however, build a "high gate"; that is, they become isolated. Such persons are alone in the world and bring disaster upon themselves.

17:15 To acquit the guilty and punish the innocent is the judicial equivalent of individuals retaliating against those who seek to do them good. Such a society undermines its own structure and invites divine wrath as well.[337] The context (vv. 14,19) implies that the injustice here

---

[335]There is also a link between 17:14-19 and 17:9-13 in the contrast between the forgiving person who מְבַקֵּשׁ אַהֲבָה ("seeks love," v. 9) and the quarrelsome person who מְבַקֵּשׁ שָׁבֶר ("seeks a breakup," v. 19).

[336]רִיב, "dispute," "litigation," implies that a personal quarrel can lead to a court fight.

[337]Also a society characterized as under תּוֹעֲבַת יהוה, "the abomination of the Lord," is one that is fundamentally perverted and in which normal human relationships cannot function.

may involve showing favor to those who are quick to bring lawsuits.

17:16,18 Verse 16 would seem to be out of place in this context, but its function here is clarified by v. 18. A common source of conflict among friends is tension over money, as is brought about when one friend loans money to or cosigns for another (v. 18). A fool does not understand the use of money, including how to avoid complicating a relationship with financial entanglements.[338]

17:17 This verse is the other side of vv. 14,19 and vv. 16,18. Far from being quarrelsome, the true friend is supportive. Also, while the wise man knows that lending money can ruin friendships, he does not close his heart to his friend in time of crisis. Prudence is balanced by a generous and caring spirit.

Heart and Family. *Type: Inclusio (17:20-22).* **17:20-22** Verses 20 and 22 describe various mental states (heart, spirit) and how they affect one's life. This text, when read as a series, asserts first that the twisted, scheming man will have a life of trouble (v. 20). Second, it teaches that a bad son (perhaps one who embodies the description in v. 20) is an affliction for his parents (v. 21). Third, a happy heart is the key to a full, healthy life (v. 22). Following v. 21, the implication is that the greatest source of a crushed spirit is trouble in the family.[339]

Justice and Family. *Type: Chiasmus (17:23-26).* **17:23-26** Verses 23 and 26 describe the perversion of justice through bribery and its results, that the innocent are wrongly punished. These proverbs are thus linked to v. 15. The interpretation of v. 24 is difficult. In what sense do the fool's eyes "wander to the ends of the earth"? The clue may be provided by v. 23: the wise man heads straight on in the path of wisdom while the fool is attracted by temptations of every kind and wanders off the right path. The bribe of v. 23 would be such a temptation.[340] The wandering eyes of the fool therefore represent his greed,[341] as epitomized by Lot's yearning gaze after the pros-

---

[338]Against Scott (*Proverbs*, 111) and McKane (*Proverbs*, 504-5), I do not believe v. 16 has anything to do with paying fees to a professional teacher. It is merely an assertion that fools cannot handle money well and is here brought into a context of relationships. Cf. Toy, *Proverbs*, 346.

[339]A number of verbal links appear among these three verses. The perverse heart (עִקֶּשׁ־לֵב) of v. 20 contrasts with the cheerful heart (לֵב שָׂמֵחַ) of v. 22. The perverse man of v. 20 does not prosper (לֹא יִמְצָא־טוֹב); the evil son of v. 21 does not give joy to his father (וְלֹא־יִשְׂמַח). The lack of joy in v. 21 (וְלֹא־יִשְׂמַח) contrasts with the joyful heart of v. 22 (לֵב שָׂמֵחַ).

[340]The case for linking the interpretation of v. 24 to v. 23 is strengthened by noting that the end of v. 23, לְהַטּוֹת אָרְחוֹת מִשְׁפָּט ("to twist paths of justice"), is followed immediately by אֶת פְּנֵי מֵבִין חָכְמָה ("before the man of insight is wisdom"). The sense from reading the verses in sequence is that to keep wisdom before one's face is to stay in the path of justice.

[341]Scott (*Proverbs*, 109) seems to take it to mean that the wise can see the proper course of action right in front of them while the fools look far afield for answers. This is most unlikely. Toy (*Proverbs*, 350-51) takes it to mean that the fool has a poor attention span and

perity of the cities of the plain (Gen 13:10). Verse 25 would appear to have nothing to do with bribery and the miscarriage of justice, but with v. 21 it provides a link to the previous text. The "foolish son grieves his father" verses in the contexts of vv. 20-22 and vv. 23-26 thus serve a didactic purpose; they urge the reader (the implied "son") not to become the evil man described in these verses and thus not to grieve either his real father or the implied father behind the Book of Proverbs.

(36) Appropriate Use of Words (17:27–18:4)

27 A man of knowledge uses words with restraint,
and a man of understanding is even-tempered.

28 Even a fool is thought wise if he keeps silent,
and discerning if he holds his tongue.

1 An unfriendly man pursues selfish ends;
he defies all sound judgment.

2 A fool finds no pleasure in understanding
but delights in airing his own opinions.

3 When wickedness comes, so does contempt,
and with shame comes disgrace.

4 The words of a man's mouth are deep waters,
but the fountain of wisdom is a bubbling brook.

TYPE: INCLUSION AND PARALLEL (17:27–18:4). **17:27–18:4** Sometimes the Book of Proverbs seems to value nothing so much as appropriate words. This is because it views words as the index to the soul. By paying attention to what a person says (and indeed to how much he or she says), one can determine whether a person is wise or a fool. Words are the fruit that show the quality of the heart. A parallel structure (17:28–18:3) is embedded in an inclusio (17:27; 18:4). The structure of the whole is as follows:

A: The wise person's restrained use of words (17:27)
  B: A silent fool appears wise (17:28)
    C: A schismatic person is irrational (18:1)
  B′: A fool cannot remain silent (18:2)
    C′: A base person is shameful (18:3)
A′: The wise person's words are profound (18:4)

Profundity, not verbosity, is the mark of wisdom (17:27; 18:4). The metaphor of water in 18:4 describes the opinions of the sage as deep (i.e.,

---

quickly loses interest in wisdom. So also McKane, *Proverbs*, 504, and Delitzsch, *Proverbs*, 369-70. This is an overly intellectual interpretation. Looking to the ends of the earth is more likely to refer to an ambitious or greedy mind rather than one that is easily distracted.

rich with meaning) and refreshing, like a flowing wadi in the desert. Even an imbecile can appear intelligent if he can avoid putting his foot in his mouth, but this is all but impossible for a fool (17:28; 18:2).

An alternative translation of 18:1 is: "A schismatic person[342] seeks an opportunity for a quarrel[343]; / he rails against all sound policy." Such a one objects just for the sake of objecting, even in a situation where silent acquiescence would be a mark of wisdom. Instead of "wickedness"[344] in 18:3, one should translate "a base person." The point of the verse is concrete and not abstract. In context this is not any kind of vice generally but specifically obnoxious and vociferous behavior. When a base person enters a discussion, the atmosphere soon turns sour.

(37) Further Comments on Listening to Evil Talk (18:5-8)

5It is not good to be partial to the wicked
or to deprive the innocent of justice.

6A fool's lips bring him strife,
and his mouth invites a beating.

7A fool's mouth is his undoing,
and his lips are a snare to his soul.

8The words of a gossip are like choice morsels;
they go down to a man's inmost parts.

TYPE: CHIASTIC (18:5-8). **18:5-8** The chiasmus in vv. 6-7 is obvious (lips, mouth, mouth, lips). Somewhat less conspicuously, v. 5 refers to heeding evil talk at the gate, and v. 8 describes the pleasures that malicious slander can give. This section appears to be further commentary on 17:27–18:4. In official proceedings, whether they be court cases or community decisions, one obviously should not take the side of[345] an evil person (v. 5).[346] The odds of such happening are reduced by the fact that caustic and selfish people[347] expose themselves by their words (vv. 6-7). On the other hand, many have a perverse attraction to malicious gossip (v. 8). This points to the need to be a judicious and thoughtful listener.

(38) Security (18:9-12)

9One who is slack in his work
is brother to one who destroys.

---

[342]The word נִפְרָד, from פרד, "to separate," is not a "selfish man" but a "divisive man."

[343]Reading לְתֹאֲנָה, "pretext" ("for a fight"), as in Judg 14:4, instead of the MT לְתַאֲוָה, "desire." The LXX has προφάσεις ("pretexts"), and the Vg has *occasiones*.

[344]The MT רָשָׁע, "an evil man," is preferable to the emendation to רֶשַׁע, "wickedness," apparently followed by the NIV.

[345]"Take the side of" is perhaps a better translation of שְׂאֵת than "be partial to."

[346]The רָשָׁע, "base man," reappears here from v. 3.

[347]One needs to bear in mind that the "fool" of Proverbs is not a buffoon or simpleton. He or she is rather an obstinate, selfish, and obnoxious individual.

[10]The name of the LORD is a strong tower;
the righteous run to it and are safe.

[11]The wealth of the rich is their fortified city;
they imagine it an unscalable wall.

[12]Before his downfall a man's heart is proud,
but humility comes before honor.

TYPE: THEMATIC (18:9-12). **18:9-12** Several proverbs on personal security here stand together. First, it is axiomatic in Proverbs that laziness leads to personal calamity (v. 9). Second, Yahweh is the only real source of security (v. 10). Third, wealth does afford a measure of protection, but the danger of wealth is precisely that it gives its possessor the illusion of greater security than it can provide (v. 11).[348] Fourth, the very time when one feels most secure (and thus is most arrogant) is when disaster is likely to occur (v. 12). There is something of a first-shall-be-last quality to this teaching.

(39) Two Proverbs (18:13-14)

[13]He who answers before listening—
that is his folly and his shame.

[14]A man's spirit sustains him in sickness,
but a crushed spirit who can bear?

TYPE: INDIVIDUAL PROVERB (18:13-14). **18:13-14** These two proverbs have no direct relationship to each other. Interestingly, however, v. 13 looks back to 17:27–18:4 while v. 14 repeats the sentiment of 17:22. It is possible that they serve some macrostructural function, but such would be difficult to establish. To "answer before listening" (v. 13) implies an arrogant (and indeed rude) spirit. It indicates that one is unwilling to be instructed or, in the case of interpersonal dealings, that one is prejudiced and unwilling to hear contrary opinions. Verse 14 points out that one's attitude, for good or ill, is the single most important factor in confronting adversity.

(40) Justice and the Courts (18:15-19)

[15]The heart of the discerning acquires knowledge;
the ears of the wise seek it out.

[16]A gift opens the way for the giver
and ushers him into the presence of the great.

[17]The first to present his case seems right,
till another comes forward and questions him.

---

[348]Note that וְנִשְׂגָּב and נִשְׂגָּבָה ("high") serve as catchwords for vv. 10-11. Also v. 10 uses the metaphor of the מִגְדָּל ("tower") while v. 11 uses קִרְיָה ("fortified city"). It is best not to read anything into the difference here; they are simply alternative metaphors.

[18]Casting the lot settles disputes
and keeps strong opponents apart.

[19]An offended brother is more unyielding than a fortified city,
and disputes are like the barred gates of a citadel.

TYPE: THEMATIC (18:15-19). **18:15-19** Verse 15 is somewhat insipid taken by itself; it is almost redundant to say that the wise possess or seek wisdom. As the head of vv. 16-19, however, it is programmatic. The text tells the readers what rules astute leaders follow when sorting out public and judicial matters. In short, v. 15 says, "Be wise," and vv. 16-19 are the wise man's précis of guidelines for evaluating public matters.

Like 17:8, 18:16 merely makes an observation without making moral judgment. Gifts to public officials may or may not have been acceptable for a given set of circumstances, but the intelligent juror would have need at least to know of the practice. Verse 17 warns against a too hasty decision; one must listen to both sides.[349] Verse 18 speaks of a practice that was widely practiced and highly regarded in ancient Israel, the casting of lots to settle disputed matters. The intent is to give the controversy over to God. Finally, v. 19 warns that controversies must be justly and equitably settled if the life of the community is to continue to function smoothly. The wise jurist will not leave a dispute unresolved, lest greater troubles follow.

(41) The Power of Words (18:20-21)

[20]From the fruit of his mouth a man's stomach is filled;
with the harvest from his lips he is satisfied.

[21]The tongue has the power of life and death,
and those who love it will eat its fruit.

TYPE: THEMATIC, CATCHWORD (18:20-21). **18:20-21** There is little doubt that these two verses go together;[350] what is much more in question is the meaning of the verses. Some scholars take "fruit" to refer to consequences, good or evil, that follow upon one's words. The point would be that one must bear the consequences of one's words.[351] An alternative view is that "fruit" here is good fruit as opposed to barrenness. The meaning would be that speech is powerful and the wise use it economically in order to achieve the intended result. Through the careful choice of words, their language is fruitful.[352]

---

[349]The first to speak would be the plaintiff, and the last would be the defendant. See G. R. Driver, "Problems," 183.

[350]Besides the common theme of the two, note that v. 20 begins with מִפְּרִי ("from the fruit of"), and v. 21 ends with פִּרְיָהּ ("its fruit").

[351]Thus Toy, *Proverbs*, 365; Scott, *Proverbs*, 113-14; and Delitzsch, *Proverbs*, 2, 14.

[352]McKane, *Proverbs*, 514-15.

In my view neither is satisfactory. On the one hand, the statement that people are satisfied with the fruit (v. 20) excludes the view that good or bad consequences are in view. No one is satisfied with something that does not have its intended effect. On the other hand, not all fruit is good, as the text implies in speaking of tongues' having the power of death, a destructive force (v. 21).

Rather, v. 20 asserts that people have a sense of self-satisfaction about their own words. To put it another way, they delight in airing their own opinions. And yet the tongue can be highly dangerous. The purpose of these verses is to warn against being too much in love with one's own words. One should recognize the power of words and use them with restraint. Voicing one's own views, here ironically described as eating the fruit of the tongue, can be an addictive habit with dangerous results.

(42) Diverse Teachings (18:22–20:4)

22He who finds a wife finds what is good
and receives favor from the LORD.

23A poor man pleads for mercy,
but a rich man answers harshly.

24A man of many companions may come to ruin,
but there is a friend who sticks closer than a brother.

1Better a poor man whose walk is blameless
than a fool whose lips are perverse.

2It is not good to have zeal without knowledge,
nor to be hasty and miss the way.

3A man's own folly ruins his life,
yet his heart rages against the LORD.

4Wealth brings many friends,
but a poor man's friend deserts him.

5A false witness will not go unpunished,
and he who pours out lies will not go free.

6Many curry favor with a ruler,
and everyone is the friend of a man who gives gifts.

7A poor man is shunned by all his relatives—
how much more do his friends avoid him!
Though he pursues them with pleading,
they are nowhere to be found.

8He who gets wisdom loves his own soul;
he who cherishes understanding prospers.

9A false witness will not go unpunished,
and he who pours out lies will perish.

10 It is not fitting for a fool to live in luxury—
how much worse for a slave to rule over princes!

11 A man's wisdom gives him patience;
it is to his glory to overlook an offense.

12 A king's rage is like the roar of a lion,
but his favor is like dew on the grass.

13 A foolish son is his father's ruin,
and a quarrelsome wife is like a constant dripping.

14 Houses and wealth are inherited from parents,
but a prudent wife is from the LORD.

15 Laziness brings on deep sleep,
and the shiftless man goes hungry.

16 He who obeys instructions guards his life,
but he who is contemptuous of his ways will die.

17 He who is kind to the poor lends to the LORD,
and he will reward him for what he has done.

18 Discipline your son, for in that there is hope;
do not be a willing party to his death.

19 A hot-tempered man must pay the penalty;
if you rescue him, you will have to do it again.

20 Listen to advice and accept instruction,
and in the end you will be wise.

21 Many are the plans in a man's heart,
but it is the LORD's purpose that prevails.

22 What a man desires is unfailing love;
better to be poor than a liar.

23 The fear of the LORD leads to life:
Then one rests content, untouched by trouble.

24 The sluggard buries his hand in the dish;
he will not even bring it back to his mouth!

25 Flog a mocker, and the simple will learn prudence;
rebuke a discerning man, and he will gain knowledge.

26 He who robs his father and drives out his mother
is a son who brings shame and disgrace.

27 Stop listening to instruction, my son,
and you will stray from the words of knowledge.

28 A corrupt witness mocks at justice,
and the mouth of the wicked gulps down evil.

29 Penalties are prepared for mockers,
and beatings for the backs of fools.

[1]Wine is a mocker and beer a brawler;
whoever is led astray by them is not wise.

[2]A king's wrath is like the roar of a lion;
he who angers him forfeits his life.

[3]It is to a man's honor to avoid strife,
but every fool is quick to quarrel.

[4]A sluggard does not plow in season;
so at harvest time he looks but finds nothing.

TYPE: THEMATIC, RANDOM REPETITION, INCLUSIO SERIES (18:22–20:4). The verses of this text do not readily organize into small, discrete units. At the same time, this is not simply a jumbled collection of unrelated proverbs. Within this section are many parallel or similar verses, and some of these serve as structural markers. Also, a number of proverbs are collected into groups that follow distinct themes, although the borders of these groups may not be clearly marked.

First, 18:22 and 19:13-14, describing family life and repeating the assertion that a good wife is from the Lord, are an inclusio that marks off a section of verses. This does not mean that all intervening verses concern wife and family, but the opening and closing assertions that a good wife is a gift of Yahweh are significant, as explained below. Second, proverbs on laziness (19:15,24; 20:4) demarcate two further sections. Once again, this does not mean that the intervening proverbs concern laziness. In addition, two pairs of similar proverbs in chiastic order on forbearance and a king's wrath (19:11-12; 20:2-3) close off the major sections.

Three sections that for the most part adhere to common themes occur within these three divisions. There are (1) the inequities and abandonment suffered by the poor (18:23–19:10), (2) the disciplined life (19:16-23), and (3) the mocker (19:25–20:1). Thus the structure of the whole is illustrated below.

Section A (18:22–19:14)
- A good wife (18:22)
  1. The poor (18:23–19:10)
- (Patience and royal anger [19:11-12])
- A bad family/a good wife (19:13-14)

Section B (19:15–20:4)
- Laziness (19:15)
  2. Personal discipline (19:16-23)
- Laziness (19:24)
  3. The mocker (19:25–20:1)
- (Royal anger and patience [20:2-3])
- Laziness (20:4)

In addition, many verses closely parallel each other either within or between the sections. Close parallels include 19:1 and 19:22; 19:4 and 19:7a,b; 19:5 and 19:9; 19:8 and 19:16. Also 19:17, on kindness to the poor, appears to be a response to 18:23–19:10. These interrelationships among the verses have two functions. First, they help to tie the whole text together; and second, by randomly repeating certain points, they reinforce the lessons in the reader's mind.

18:22; 19:13-14 Happiness is impossible without domestic tranquility, and the wife is the anchor of that tranquility. Proverbs 31:10-31 is a description of the biblical ideal of the good wife, whom 18:22 declares to be from the Lord. She is "from the Lord" in that even the wisest of men can choose a particular woman for the wrong reasons. It is only by divine providence that one's choice will turn out to have been a good one.

Proverbs 19:13 requires special attention. It is often taken to mean only that a nagging wife is like an incessant dripping. First of all, the modern reader should beware of making an anachronistic transfer of imagery. This is not the "leaky faucet" that is irritating and may deprive one of sleep but is only a minor household problem and is easily repaired. In a similar context in Prov 27:15 and in the verb form in Eccl 10:18, the word describes a leaking roof.[353] A leaking roof is an irritation, but it is more than that. It can cause severe damage to a house, be expensive to repair, and can render a building unfit to live in. Second, a "quarrelsome wife" is more than a nagging wife. The Hebrew word implies antisocial behavior that stirs up discord and even prompts lawsuits.[354] Such a woman no doubt does nag her husband (21:9; 25:24), but she is equally apt to create quarrels with those outside of the home (neighbors, people in the market, etc.). Third, 19:14, which parallels 19:13, states that the antithesis to the quarrelsome wife is not strictly the submissive wife but the "prudent"[355] wife, implying someone who is adept in all kinds of circumstances and knows how to deal with people. In short, she is the highly capable woman of Prov 31 who is an asset rather than a loss to her husband. The quarrelsome woman destroys her house.

This is significant since so much of 18:23–19:10 in some ways relates to poverty. One's family may either enhance or destroy one's personal financial status. A foolish son is the ruin of his father, and a quarrelsome wife causes much damage in the home.[356]

18:23–19:10 Since a poor person is not in a position to demand fair treatment, he or she seldom gets it. These verses primarily concern the poor man before the courts, especially where he has found himself unable

[353]The word is דֶּלֶף. Proverbs 27:15 specifies that it leaks during a rain, so a roof is implied. In Eccl 10:18 (יִדְלֹף) it is explicitly a leaking house.

[354]Cf. the use of מָדוֹן in 18:18-19.

[355]The word מַשְׂכָּלֶת implies both capable and successful.

[356]For further discussion on how the prudent wife relates to attaining wisdom, see the comments on 31:10ff.

to pay debts to a wealthy creditor. His pleas for mercy—perhaps for an extension on his loan—go unheeded (18:23[357]). Even if the poor man's case is just and the rich man has abused the legal system to get an advantage over him, the poor man is still at a loss. His friends abandon him (19:4,7a,b[358]); in this context this may especially refer to friends who are unwilling to stand up for him at the gate and risk antagonizing the rich. Even so, there are some faithful friends who remain supportive in times of crisis (18:24[359]), and poverty with moral dignity is preferable to wealth without character (19:1). The rich man has considerable influence over people (19:6) and can also bribe false witnesses, although punishment for perjury, whether it be divine or human punishment, is certain (19:5,9). The whole situation is all the more irksome in that some are altogether unworthy of the power and influence they control (19:10).

Three proverbs in this section are more general encouragements to seek instruction and avoid a bullheaded determination that only falls into trouble (19:2-3,8). Simply to "do something" without instruction is to invite disaster, and people often blame the consequences of such actions on God (19:2-3). Better to learn how to handle problems well (19:8). Of themselves these verses have nothing to do with the plight of the poor, but they may be here to encourage the poor to recognize that the inequities described here are part of life and that they must be wise and cautious in dealing with such circumstances. Also in this context 19:3 is an implied warning that the poor should not blame God for their circumstances.

19:15; 19:24; 20:4 Laziness[360] is assaulted on three fronts: it brings one to ruin (19:15[361]), it is laughably absurd (19:24), and it is irrational

[357]The תַּחֲנוּנִים ("supplications") are not strictly calls for charity. Still less are they the "wheedling tones" the poor may use to extract a gift from the wealthy (McKane, *Proverbs*, 239, 518). For that, a term such as מַחֲלִיק לָשׁוֹן ("a flattering tongue") would have been better suited. תַּחֲנוּנִים is generally used of calls for divine help or mercy in a quasijudicial setting such as divine judgment or conflict with adversaries (cf. [Heb. text] Pss 28:2,6; 31:23; 86:6; 130:2; 140:7; 143:1). Hence they are appeals for help or mercy.

[358]Proverbs 19:7c, מְרַדֵּף אֲמָרִים לֹא הֵמָּה ("a pursuer of words not they"), is unintelligible and ought to be untranslated. The NIV rendition is doubtful. The LXX is radically different and attests to a different *Vorlage*. With present evidence no convincing reconstruction of the original is available.

[359]The text of v. 24a is difficult, and various interpretations and emendations are proposed. One could emend אִישׁ ("a man") to יֵשׁ ("there are") with some support from the versions (see BHS note *a*). It is also possible to emend לְהִתְרֹעֵעַ ("to be broken apart") to לְהִתְרָעוֹת ("to make companions") with versional support (see BHS note *b*). Scott (*Proverbs*, 113) takes the latter and translates, "A man has companions for company." In my view the NIV rendition is reasonable.

[360]It is intriguing that a section dominated by the inequities suffered by the poor is followed by warnings against laziness.

[361]It is somewhat difficult to see how תַּרְדֵּמָה, "deep sleep," is equivalent to going hungry. Dahood (*Proverbs*, 40) proposes that the word here means "bedroom" and that the point is that because of laziness the sleeping quarters collapse. Cf. Eccl 10:18.

(20:4[362]). One cannot expect prosperity or success without putting forth effort.

19:16-23 These verses all revolve around the theme of the disciplined and prudent life. At the beginning and end of the section[363] is the teaching that a good life is founded on keeping God's commandments (19:16[364]) and on living in reverence for him (19:23[365]). Two further proverbs relate to poverty (19:17,22). To be compassionate to the poor is figuratively to put God in your debt, which is always a good place to be (19:17). On the other hand, poverty is preferable to loss of integrity (19:22[366]). Proverbs 19:18-19 concerns dealing with those who have fallen into trouble, be it a son or someone else. In both cases the transgressor should suffer the consequences of his actions. This not only does the wrongdoer some good, but it also makes life easier for the parent or friend. Finally, a humble spirit, ready to submit to sound advice and to acknowledge divine providence, should govern one's life (19:20-21). A presumptuous spirit does neither.

19:25–20:1 The structure of 19:25–20:1 is an inclusio (19:25 and 19:29, on the beatings mockers receive) between which are three characteristics of the mocker (fails to honor parents [v. 26], rejects instruction [v. 27], and has no respect for truth [v. 28]). Proverbs 20:1 is an afterword

---

[362]The word מֵחֹרֶף ("in season") should be rendered "at the onset of winter" or perhaps "at the end of harvest." Either way, it is the clearing of the fields done after the harvest is over. The point is that as soon as harvest is over one must begin preparation for the next year's crop. The sluggard fails to do this and thus is disappointed the following year.

[363]This section has been structured as follows:

A: Adherence to God's ways is life (19:16)
- B: Give to the poor (19:17)
  - C: Discipline your son (19:18; נשׂא)
  - C′: Allow the intemperate to pay the price (19:19; נשׂא)
    - D: Submit to instruction (19:20; עצה)
    - D′: Acknowledge providence (19:21; עצה)
- B′: Better poor but honest (19:22)

A′: Fear of Yahweh (19:23)

[364]The word מִצְוָה ("commandment") is better taken as a divine command than a wisdom instruction. Also דְּרָכָיו ("his ways") refers to God's ways.

[365]Dahood (*Proverbs*, 41), taking the ל in לְחַיִּים as an emphatic *lamed* and בַּל ("not," "without") as an asseverative, translates v. 23 as, "Reverence for the Lord is truly life,/ But he who sleeps to satiety will surely be visited by calamity." This is possible, but the MT is intelligible as traditionally understood.

[366]The translation of v. 22a, תַּאֲוַת אָדָם חַסְדּוֹ, is difficult, but the NIV is most unlikely. חֶסֶד does mean "faithful love," "piety," and the like, but it is unreasonable to take this word with the suffix וֹ ("his") to mean that people want to be loved. Rather, "his חֶסֶד" is one's own faithfulness or integrity. The LXX reads καρπός ("fruit") for תַּאֲוַת ("desire"), which prompts the suggestion that the Hebrew should be emended to תְּבוּאַת ("produce," "fruit"). The translation would thus be, "A man's fruit is [i.e., comes from] his integrity," meaning that what a person produces is tied to his or her character. If the MT is retained, the meaning is, "A man's desire is his integrity." Either is possible.

that employs the catchword "mocker."[367] It does not describe the human mocker but calls wine a mocker. The point here is probably that mockers are prone to consume this mocking beverage in excess and that drinking in excess in turn degrades one's respect for authority and propriety.

The mocker is one who has no regard for authority or moral integrity. As such, mockers receive many beatings and serve as negative examples for others (v. 25).[368] In fact, it was for such people that beatings were invented (v. 29).[369]

To mistreat parents is the quintessential act of the mocker because it is a rejection of the most basic form of respect for authority (v. 26). "Shame and disgrace" is a hendiadys for "absolutely disgraceful."

Verse 27 is ironic. It should not be understood as a conditional sentence ("If you stop listening") but as an imperative ("Stop listening to instruction, my son, so that you may wander from knowledgeable words").[370] The sarcasm is a reflection on the fact that it is addressed to a mocker, who has no respect for traditional teaching.

As the mocker has no respect for parents, even so he has no regard for truth or the law (v. 28).

19:11-12; 20:2-3 These verses do not have a direct relationship to the discussions on the poor, personal discipline, or the mocker; but they do function as structural markers. Taken together, they are in chiastic order (patience, the king's wrath, the king's wrath, patience). The point of the whole is that the patient person knows how to avoid quarrels and quarrelsome people and stays out of trouble with the government as well.

(43) Various Proverbs (20:5–21:8)

5The purposes of a man's heart are deep waters,
but a man of understanding draws them out.

6Many a man claims to have unfailing love,
but a faithful man who can find?

7The righteous man leads a blameless life;
blessed are his children after him.

8When a king sits on his throne to judge,
he winnows out all evil with his eyes.

9Who can say, "I have kept my heart pure;
I am clean and without sin"?

---

[367]The word לֵץ is also found in 19:25,29 and as a verb in 19:28.

[368]In v. 25 it is a mocker (לֵץ) who receives a beating but the simpleton (פֶּתִי, not the obstinate wrongdoer but the uninstructed) who learns a lesson.

[369]For the MT שְׁפָטִים ("judgments"), read either שׁוֹטִים ("whips") or שְׁבָטִים ("rods"). The LXX has μάστιγες.

[370]See McKane, *Proverbs*, 525.

**10Differing weights and differing measures—
the LORD detests them both.**

**11Even a child is known by his actions,
by whether his conduct is pure and right.**

**12Ears that hear and eyes that see—
the LORD has made them both.**

**13Do not love sleep or you will grow poor;
stay awake and you will have food to spare.**

**14"It's no good, it's no good!" says the buyer;
then off he goes and boasts about his purchase.**

**15Gold there is, and rubies in abundance,
but lips that speak knowledge are a rare jewel.**

**16Take the garment of one who puts up security for a stranger;
hold it in pledge if he does it for a wayward woman.**

**17Food gained by fraud tastes sweet to a man,
but he ends up with a mouth full of gravel.**

**18Make plans by seeking advice;
if you wage war, obtain guidance.**

**19A gossip betrays a confidence;
so avoid a man who talks too much.**

**20If a man curses his father or mother,
his lamp will be snuffed out in pitch darkness.**

**21An inheritance quickly gained at the beginning
will not be blessed at the end.**

**22Do not say, "I'll pay you back for this wrong!"
Wait for the LORD, and he will deliver you.**

**23The LORD detests differing weights,
and dishonest scales do not please him.**

**24A man's steps are directed by the LORD.
How then can anyone understand his own way?**

**25It is a trap for a man to dedicate something rashly
and only later to consider his vows.**

**26A wise king winnows out the wicked;
he drives the threshing wheel over them.**

**27The lamp of the LORD searches the spirit of a man;
it searches out his inmost being.**

**28Love and faithfulness keep a king safe;
through love his throne is made secure.**

**29The glory of young men is their strength,
gray hair the splendor of the old.**

**30Blows and wounds cleanse away evil,
and beatings purge the inmost being.**

[1]The king's heart is in the hand of the LORD;
he directs it like a watercourse wherever he pleases.
[2]All a man's ways seem right to him,
but the LORD weighs the heart.
[3]To do what is right and just
is more acceptable to the LORD than sacrifice.
[4]Haughty eyes and a proud heart,
the lamp of the wicked, are sin!
[5]The plans of the diligent lead to profit
as surely as haste leads to poverty.
[6]A fortune made by a lying tongue
is a fleeting vapor and a deadly snare.
[7]The violence of the wicked will drag them away,
for they refuse to do what is right.
[8]The way of the guilty is devious,
but the conduct of the innocent is upright.

The proverbs of this section for the most part focus on the theme of discriminating between people of good character and people of evil character. Some proverbs speak of the elusiveness of virtue (20:6,9,15), others describe how the king must sort out the good from the bad (20:8,26, 28), while others speak of God as the ultimate judge of character (20:10, 12,23-24,27; 21:2-3).

Verses 20:5 and 21:8 can be read as an envelope. The former articulates the importance of discernment in dealing with people: a person is not always what he or she seems. The latter gives the simplest, most basic guideline in character discernment: the evil are twisted, but the good are upright. By itself 21:8 seems like a pointless tautology; but when read as the conclusion to the series of proverbs begun in 20:5, it is an apt closure to the whole. Like Jesus' teaching that a tree is judged by its fruit, this text ends by saying that people can be evaluated by their conduct (Matt 7:17-19; 12:33; Luke 6:43-44).

Several smaller collections are found in this larger unit. These are (1) 20:5-12: proverbs on discernment and integrity, (2) 20:13-23: various proverbs on moral character, (3) 20:22–21:3: proverbs that concern the judgmental authority of the king and of Yahweh, and (4) 21:4-8: proverbs on the fate of the wicked.

DISCERNMENT AND INTEGRITY. *Type: A-B Envelope, Thematic (20:5-12).* This section begins by telling how difficult it is to discern a person's inner motives and ends by asserting that the ears and eyes, the means of discernment, are made by God. Thus God alone has perfect insight into human character, and he cannot be deceived.

20:5 To say that a person's purposes are "deep" (v. 5) does not mean that they are necessarily profound, as in the English expression "still waters run deep." The metaphor is of a well whose waters are far beneath the surface of the ground so that one must use a bucket with a long rope to draw water to the surface.[371] Thus a person's real motives are "deep" in that they are difficult to extract; one must be wary of the pretenses of others.[372]

20:6-7,9 Verses 6 and 9 should not be regarded as cynical. They simply make the point that true loyalty and character are rare commodities. Also v. 9 is doubled-edged. While it warns the reader that all are sinful and thus explodes naive trust, it also forces the reader to reckon with his or her own sin and thus not to be harshly judgmental. Verse 7, moreover, is considerably more optimistic: some people do conduct themselves with integrity and leave behind a solid family heritage. In short, no one is sinless, and finding someone to trust is difficult. On the other hand, this text provides reason to hope for good in future generations, something the cynic never has.

20:8 Verse 8 calls attention to the importance of moral insight in government. The first line should not be translated as a dependent clause, as the English versions have done ("When a king sits"). It should be rendered more literally as, "A king sits on a throne of justice."[373] This is an idealized vision of royal authority. It represents the standard to which a king should aspire and the perception ordinary people should have of the throne as the seat of justice. Should a king fail to maintain justice, his people will lose respect for the crown's moral authority, and the government will collapse.

20:10 A crafty merchant could use weights that were lighter or heavier than their stated amounts as it worked to their advantage. Verse 10, a fairly common proverb on Yahweh's hatred of corrupt practices, takes on new meaning in this context. False weights and measures are not what they seem. Hence the proverb here goes beyond an isolated type of fraud and bespeaks God's ability to recognize and his hatred of all pretense.

20:11 The translation of v. 11 is not altogether clear,[374] but the thrust of the verse is conspicuous. Conduct is the best proof of character in a child. Certainly no child who says, "I am well behaved" will find his or her words taken at face value. People will evaluate the child by how he or she behaves. The implication is that appearances and words can be deceiving; behavior is a better criterion of judgment.

20:12 Various interpretations of v. 12 are suggested, but in this context at least two points stand out. First, people ought to use the senses

---

[371]The root דלה, "to draw up," implies the image of the well.

[372]Against McKane (*Proverbs*, 536-37), who interprets the verse according to Platonic educational theory. Cf. Toy, *Proverbs*, 384.

[373]Thus translating מֶלֶךְ יוֹשֵׁב עַל־כִּסֵּא־דִין.

[374]The position of גַּם ("also, even") before בְּמַעֲלָלָיו ("by his deeds") is at issue. Delitzsch (*Proverbs* 2:46) says it is acceptable to treat נַעַר ("youth") as the referent for גַּם (thus, "Even a child," as in the NIV), but McKane (*Proverbs*, 545-46) denies this. He treats the גַּם as emphasizing the deeds and not the child ("It is for what he does"). The latter is preferable.

God gave them. They should look deeply rather than make superficial evaluations. Second, since God made the eyes and ears, he is the infallible judge. No one can deceive him with appearances.[375]

Various Proverbs. *Type: Individual Proverbs (20:13-21).* Individual proverbs are various moral proverbs that of themselves do not tie to any particular topic. In this context, however, they may describe aspects of character for which one should be on the alert. On the positive side this includes diligence (v. 13), ability to give sound advice (v. 15), sound judgment (v. 16), and honor for parents (v. 20). On the negative side one must be aware that deception, from the most petty kind (v. 14) to outright fraud (v. 17), is common. Awareness of these and other criteria enable the reader to determine where someone's character, be it his or her own or someone else's, will lead.

20:13 The number of hours one sleeps per day is not the point here. Love of sleep refers to laziness, but one can be lazy although sleeping very little.

20:14 People will say what is to their advantage at the moment. Their words should not always be taken at face value. Here again the text draws on the distinction between appearances and reality.

20:15 The rarest and finest treasure is a person who has sound judgment and can give good advice.

20:16 The Israelites were not to hold the cloak of a debtor as collateral on a loan (Exod 22:26-27). In an ironic tone this verse says one should go ahead and take the garment of someone who has fallen into financial trouble by putting up security for a stranger—especially if he did it for an alluring woman.[376] The message is that one should be wary of dealing with people who lack sound judgment.

20:17 The text strongly contrasts the initial sweetness of the con artist's gain and his final mouth full of gravel.[377] Charlatans may not be easily uncovered, but they ultimately come to ruin.

20:18 The importance of seeking sound advice is reiterated (v. 15). To enter into so serious an undertaking as a war without carefully considering the matter is the ultimate in superficial judgments. In light of the number of teachings that deal with the king in the larger context, the making of war need not be regarded as metaphor.

20:19 This is to some extent the counterpart to v. 18. The former advises the king to make war only after seeking wise counsel, and the latter advises the reader not to share plans and ideas with those who talk too much. One must discern whether another is worthy of trust.

---

[375]For further discussion see Delitzsch, *Proverbs* 2:47-48.

[376]Reading the *qere* נָכְרִיָּה ("strange woman") instead of the *kethiv* נָכְרִים ("strangers") on the basis of the parallel in 27:13.

[377]The word עָרֵב ("sweet") is in the initial position, and חָצָץ ("gravel") is in the final position. This accentuates the sense of contrast.

20:20 The law provides for the execution of those who curse parents (Exod 21:17; Lev 20:9), although one may doubt how frequently this was carried out. The present text is not legal but is a curse, and it expresses complete disdain for those who so speak of parents. Such a one is to be regarded as contemptible.

20:21 Easy money does not foster financial responsibility. The easily gained money is here not necessarily dishonestly gained, but even so, those who have amassed wealth slowly know better how to keep it.

DEALING WITH THE KING AND WITH THE LORD. *Type: Thematic (20:22–21:3).* These verses concern dealings with the two arbiters of justice, namely, the king and Yahweh. Proverbs 20:22-25,27 and 21:2-3 concern Yahweh, while 20:26,28,30 concerns the king. Proverbs 21:1 draws the two together and asserts the superior power of Yahweh over the king; only 20:29 does not clearly fit in this context.

20:22 The first principle of justice is not to seek vengeance for oneself but to commit the grievance to God. Significantly, it is not the government but God to whom one turns for redress when wronged by another. While governments (the king, in this context) are rightly charged with the task of upholding the law, vindication is found in God.

20:23 Compare 20:10. After v. 22 this verse may be meant to assure the reader that God does see those occasions when someone has cheated another person. This verse is thus an assurance that the reader can trust God to punish; one need not extract personal revenge.

20:24 Human discernment is severely limited. In the final analysis we do not understand all that is going on around us or happening to us, and we are guided through life in ways we do not recognize. Trusting in divine providence therefore is best.

20:25 Compare Eccl 5:4-6. To make a vow and then seek to retract it is to invite divine judgment. It is remarkable that the text here calls a foolish vow a "trap" in a context that devotes so much attention to the discernment of reality behind appearances. A vow is called a trap because it can be only a pretentious piety. This is a sham that does not deceive God (Matt 6:16-18).

20:26 Compare 20:8. It is neither in the king's interest nor that of his country to treat criminals gently.

20:27 The NIV rendition is difficult to justify from Hebrew.[378] This verse could be rendered, "The human breath is Yahweh's lamp; it searches the rooms of the belly" (i.e., inmost being).[379] The "breath" is not really

[378]The NIV apparently regards חֹפֵשׂ ("searching out") as doing double duty and so translates it twice.

[379]Thus Toy, *Proverbs*, 396; Scott, *Proverbs*, 120; McKane, *Proverbs*, 242; Delitzsch, *Proverbs* 2:57-59.

the mind or spirit[380] but the life force that, according to Gen 2:7, God breathed into man. If this proverb deliberately looks back to Genesis,[381] the point is that the life that men and women have from God shines within them like a burning lamp before his eyes. People are, as it were, illuminated from within before his eyes. That being the case, they cannot hide their plans, attitudes, and thoughts from God.

20:28 The translation "love" to some degree misrepresents the Hebrew here. The word[382] connotes loyalty, fidelity, and kindness. The king is urged to promote a positive atmosphere of mutual loyalty and respect in order to insure the stability of his kingdom. Political power cannot long rest on brute force.

20:29 On the surface there is no connection between the topic of this verse and its context, which discusses the power of Yahweh and the king. An implied connection, however, may exist between this and the preceding verse. Young men tend to rely upon the sheer exercise of power (as did Rehoboam). Older men have learned the importance of wisdom and restraint, as depicted by their gray hair.

20:30 In context this is not parental discipline but beatings administered by the king's officers as punishment for crime. Yahweh can peer directly into a person's innermost being (v. 27), but the king can touch the criminal's soul by harsh retribution.[383]

21:1 While Yahweh and the king are the two administrators of justice, there can be no doubt about who is the dominant power. Yahweh is over every king. This verse does not teach that everything the king does is wise or good, and still less does it teach that the king has no need of counselors.[384] Rather, it asserts that the king is simply another of Yahweh's tools for dispensing justice as he sees fit.

21:2 Most people feel that their actions and patterns of life are perfectly acceptable. God, however, looks into the heart and judges thoughts and motives. Yahweh's power of discernment goes beyond unmasking those who fool others; he even finds out those who have fooled themselves.

21:3 One puts on an external form of piety through observation of religious ceremony. While such ceremonies are not of themselves evil, they matter little to God in comparison with the true devotion of an obedient heart. This proverb once again subtly alludes to God's ability to discern the intentions of the heart.

THE DEVICES AND THE DECLINE OF THE WICKED. *Type: Thematic (21:4-8).* These five verses focus upon the losses incurred by those who live wrongfully.

---

[380]One would expect רוּחַ or לֵב if that had been the meaning here.

[381]The likelihood that this is the case is increased by the use of אָדָם here.

[382]חֶסֶד.

[383]Both verses refer to the חַדְרֵי־בָטֶן ("chambers of the belly").

[384]Contrary to McKane, *Proverbs*, 559-60.

21:4 The metaphor of the lamp implies that which gives guidance or direction. In describing the "haughty eyes" and "proud heart" as the "lamp of the wicked" (v. 4), the text is saying that the devious are sure of themselves and think that their cunning can guide them through life. Their treachery is a "lamp unto their feet."

21:5-7 The "haste" of v. 5 is the desire to gain wealth without the sacrifice of honest labor and frugality. Two specific means to easy money, fraud and violence, are mentioned in v. 6[385] and v. 7.

21:8 Verse 8 aptly summarizes all that has been said on recognizing honest and dishonest people. It is the simple difference between those who are open and honest and those who try to hide what they are really up to.

(44) Under One Roof (21:9-19)

9Better to live on a corner of the roof
than share a house with a quarrelsome wife.

10The wicked man craves evil;
his neighbor gets no mercy from him.

11When a mocker is punished, the simple gain wisdom;
when a wise man is instructed, he gets knowledge.

12The Righteous One takes note of the house of the wicked
and brings the wicked to ruin.

13If a man shuts his ears to the cry of the poor,
he too will cry out and not be answered.

14A gift given in secret soothes anger,
and a bribe concealed in the cloak pacifies great wrath.

15When justice is done, it brings joy to the righteous
but terror to evildoers.

16A man who strays from the path of understanding
comes to rest in the company of the dead.

17He who loves pleasure will become poor;
whoever loves wine and oil will never be rich.

18The wicked become a ransom for the righteous,
and the unfaithful for the upright.

19Better to live in a desert
than with a quarrelsome and ill-tempered wife.

TYPE: INCLUSIO (21:9-19). **21:9** The better saying that any living conditions (in the corner of a roof, in the desert, 21:9,19) are preferable to

---

[385]The translation of v. 6 is difficult, but the NIV rendition is reasonable. It follows the majority of scholars in reading וּמוֹקְשֵׁי־מָוֶת ("traps of death") instead of the MT מְבַקְשֵׁי־מָוֶת ("pursuers of death").

living with a quarrelsome woman form the inclusio for this series of proverbs. The proverbs between the inclusio do not themselves examine domestic harmony but concern a variety of topics.

Lessons from the Merciless (21:10-13). **21:10,13** These verses concern merciless behavior, and vv. 11-12 describe how one can learn a lesson by observing the punishment that befalls the evil. These four verses thus form a chiasmus. The point of the whole is that the merciless and insolent will themselves receive no mercy, and one should learn a lesson from their fate.

21:11-12 In this verse a mocker is punished and learns nothing from it, but a simpleton looks on and gains instruction. The mocker, in contrast to the simpleton, is incorrigibly evil. The simpleton is uninstructed but can at least learn a few vividly demonstrated lessons. I would suggest that v. 12 should be translated in a similar vein: "A righteous man observes the house of the wicked, how wickedness brings [it] to ruin."[386] Not only the simpleton but the righteous and wise also take it to heart when they see a deserved punishment applied to one who scorns virtue.

Reconciliation and Justice (21:14-15). **21:14-15** Verse 14 is an observational proverb; that is, it does not necessarily approve of every case of giving a gift or bribe. The text is subject to two interpretations, one of which regards gift giving as an appropriate, positive thing to do, and the other of which treats it as a perversion of justice. If someone has offended another and is subject to being a defendant in litigation, a gift to the offended party may resolve the problem. It is, in effect, settling out of court. Even in modern society the terms of out-of-court settlements are often kept secret, and the reference to secrecy need not imply bribery.[387] At the same time, the practice of giving bribes to thwart justice cannot be excluded from this verse. As such v. 14 should be read in context with v. 15, which in effect asserts that justice is essential if society is to function and evildoers are to be held in check. Taken together the verses state that one should avoid litigation if possible and that a gift may be the means of doing so; on the other hand, one should beware of bribery lest criminals be free to scorn the justice system.

---

[386]Reading מְסַלֶּפֶת רִשְׁעָה ("wickedness ruins") instead of the MT מְסַלֵּף רְשָׁעִים ("ruining the wicked"). Cf. Prov 13:6, רִשְׁעָה תְּסַלֵּף. I doubt that צַדִּיק means "The Righteous One" (i.e., God) in this context; as is elsewhere always the case in Proverbs, צַדִּיק is most likely simply "a righteous one" (cf. Prov 10:3,6-7,11,16,20-21,30-32; 11:8,30-31; 12:10,13,26; 13:5,25; 14:19,32; 15:6,28; 17:15; 18:5,10,17; 20:7; 23:24; 24:15-16,24; 25:26; 29:7). See the discussion in Toy, *Proverbs*, 402-3. This necessitates a reinterpretation of v. 12b. Also the use of the hiphil stem of שׂכל ("look upon," "perceive") in v. 12 probably is parallel to the use of the same word in v. 11. The point is that a righteous man thoughtfully observes the downfall of the wicked man's house, not that he personally brings it about.

[387]On the other hand, the reference to secrecy would seem to preclude drawing purely personal conflicts, such as those between a husband and wife, into the interpretation of this verse.

Rewards for Doing Wrong (21:16-18). **21:16** These three proverbs all follow the theme of the ultimate fate of those who do wrong. Verse 16 uses the word for "wander"[388] for a poetic image of someone who has gone off the right path, is lost, and wanders wearily in search of a resting place. He or she can only find rest among the ghosts; that is, he or she comes to an untimely death.

21:17-18 These verses each have a paradoxical quality. In v. 17 those who most love good times[389] and consumable goods associated with wealth will not be able to afford them. Those who show restraint in the amount of time and money they invest in pleasure will have the means to attain them. In v. 18 the wicked are the atonement[390] for the upright. This seems odd since presumably the upright would not need a ransom.[391] If, however, "upright" and "righteous" are defined not by sinless perfection but by the overall orientation of one's life toward God and wisdom, the point is that God extracts penalty from those who despise the right way as a ransom payment for the sins of the just.[392] In short, the wicked are perpetually under divine wrath for the sins in the world.

(45) Rewards for Doing Right (21:20-22)

20In the house of the wise are stores of choice food and oil,
but a foolish man devours all he has.

21He who pursues righteousness and love
finds life, prosperity and honor.

22A wise man attacks the city of the mighty
and pulls down the stronghold in which they trust.

TYPE: THEMATIC (21:20-22). These verses closely correspond to vv. 16-18. It is significant that the intervening verse (v. 19) concerns the quarrelsome wife. The implication is that the poverty and trouble of vv. 16-18 follow whoever has a quarrelsome wife, whereas the wealth and benefits of vv. 20-22 attend the man who has a prudent wife.[393]

21:20 Verse 20 should not be read as a facile "Be good and God will make you rich" sentiment. Rather, when read as a contrast to v. 17, it

---

[388]תעה is used for wandering in the sense of being lost or in search of a place of rest in Gen 21:14; Exod 23:4; Isa 53:6; etc.

[389]"A lover of good times" is perhaps the best translation of אֹהֵב שִׂמְחָה here. It is not only the epicure but anyone who is excessively devoted to having fun who is in view here.

[390]The כֹּפֶר is the payment made to atone for guilt (e.g., Exod 21:30).

[391]McKane (*Proverbs*, 561) thus objects that this verse cannot be pressed, but his interpretation, that "the righteous man's meat is the wicked man's poison," hardly fits the text.

[392]It is out of place to object that this verse somehow contradicts the NT doctrine of atonement through Christ. Proverbs 21:18 is a proverbial adage; it is not technical soteriology.

[393]See the discussion of 31:10ff.

maintains that the diligence and restraint that characterize the wise naturally allow them to accumulate possessions.[394] Lack of restraint, however, brings about incessant consumption on the part of the fools.

21:21 In v. 21, however, the rewards of goodness are not material but spiritual. "Righteousness and love" are here faithfulness to God and a compassionate life. Instead of "prosperity" v. 21 should read "righteousness."[395] The point is that those who seek virtue not only find that but also find life (be it long life, eternal life, or the inner life of emotional heath) and honor in the community as well.

21:22 This verse is often taken to mean simply that "brains is better than brawn,"[396] but context implies more than that. Both vv. 20 and 22 speak of a "wise man."[397] In v. 20 he has treasures in his home (which presumably is not a fortress); but in v. 22 he can assault an armed, fortified city. In the ancient world an army assaulted a city in order to plunder it. The picture of a wise man besieging and plundering a fortified city may seem inappropriate, but the meaning is more metaphorical than literal or military. The wise man is secure and prosperous without an army to surround him, but against him even the greatest human opposition is insecure. The fruit of wisdom is a life of victory.

(46) A Mouth in and out of Control (21:23-24)

23He who guards his mouth and his tongue
keeps himself from calamity.

24The proud and arrogant man—"Mocker" is his name;
he behaves with overweening pride.

TYPE: THEMATIC (21:23-24). **21:23-24** Verse 23 simply states that one can avoid trouble by controlling one's mouth, and v. 24 is a functional definition of the scorner as full of arrogant pride. Each is clear enough on its own, but side by side they throw light on each other. The "mocker" is recognized precisely for his obnoxious mouth,[398] and thus the refusal to control the tongue (v. 23) springs directly from arrogance

---

[394]It is not clear to me why the NIV translates אוֹצָר נֶחְמָד ("precious treasure") as "choice food." One can "devour" wealth in a metaphorical sense.

[395]The NIV translators perhaps felt it was redundant to say that those who seek righteousness find righteousness and so translated the second occurrence of צְדָקָה as "prosperity" instead. A number of commentaries, following the LXX, simply drop the second צְדָקָה altogether (thus Toy, *Proverbs*, 407; McKane, *Proverbs*, 556-57). This misses the intended meaning; the second צְדָקָה stands for צְדָקָה וָחָסֶד from v. 21a and makes the point that those who desire these virtues find both the virtues they seek and other benefits as well.

[396]E.g., Scott (*Proverbs*, 126), who compares Eccl 9:13-16.

[397]The חָכָם; vv. 20-22 seem to have an *A-B-A* inclusio pattern on the basis of this catchword.

[398]The "mocker" (לֵץ, the qal participle of לִיץ, ["to scorn, mock, or belittle"]) is by definition one who is verbally offensive.

(v. 24). On the other hand, just as those who show humility in their language avoid trouble, one can presume that the mocker gets into trouble with his scornful words and attitudes.

(47) The Sluggard's Craving (21:25-26)

25The sluggard's craving will be the death of him,
because his hands refuse to work.
26All day long he craves for more,
but the righteous give without sparing.

TYPE: CATCHWORD,[399] THEMATIC (21:25-26). **21:25-26** The text here revisits the theme of the prosperity of the wise/righteous over against the poverty of the lazy/wicked. As in 20:21, where one must seek righteousness and compassion, here too prosperity is linked to an attitude that not only is diligent but generous. One might think that those who work hard would want to hoard what they struggled to obtain, but in God's economy the two virtues of self-reliance and compassion for others must be linked. Also looking back to 21:17, the lazy man's life is portrayed as one of unabated wanting.[400]

(48) Trying to Fool God (21:27)

27The sacrifice of the wicked is detestable—
how much more so when brought with evil intent!

TYPE: INDIVIDUAL PROVERB (21:27). **21:27** The text does not make clear what is the "evil intent" of the sacrifice. It could be to assuage one's conscience without making true repentance, or it could be for the sake of hypocritical display, or it could be because the individual sincerely believes that a sacrifice can bribe God to help cause some nefarious plans come to pass. Probably the proverb is deliberately vague in order to cover a multitude of twisted motivations.

(49) The False Witness (21:28-29)

28A false witness will perish,
and whoever listens to him will be destroyed forever.

29A wicked man puts up a bold front,
but an upright man gives thought to his ways.

---

[399]The word תַּאֲוָה ("craving") is repeated in these verses.

[400]Contrary to Scott (*Proverbs*, 125) and Toy (*Proverbs*, 412), the phrase הִתְאַוָּה תַאֲוָה need not be emended; the word תַּאֲוָה ("desire") is simply a cognate accusative, as in Num 11:4, הִתְאַוּוּ תַּאֲוָה ("they greedily desired"). The LXX ἀσεβὴς ("impious") is a moralizing addition (as in LXX 21:22) and is not a basis for emendation.

TYPE: THEMATIC (21:28-29). **21:28-29** These two verses should be read together as follows:

A false witness will perish,
and whoever listens to him will be driven out[401] forever.
A wicked man puts up a bold front,
but the just man understands[402] his [the wicked man's][403] ways.

Verse 28 promises destruction for false witnesses and social disgrace (or exile) for those who side with them. The setting is the law court at the gate, and the warning to jurors is that they will be held accountable should they allow false testimony to stand. Verse 29 then states that the wicked can lie with a brazen face, much as English says that one can be a "bald-faced" liar.[404] The just man, however, can see through the charade. The exhortation of the whole text is to be both perceptive and diligent about disallowing perjury in court.

(50) Counterwisdom (21:30-31)

30 There is no wisdom, no insight, no plan
that can succeed against the LORD.

31 The horse is made ready for the day of battle,
but victory rests with the LORD.

TYPE: THEMATIC (21:30-31). **21:30-31** In Proverbs "wisdom" almost always includes true piety (that is, the fear of Yahweh). It seldom recognizes or deals with the phenomenon of intellectual antipathy to devotion to God. Here, however, it speaks of a kind of human "wisdom" that seeks understanding without first submitting to Yahweh and declares that such efforts are futile. Verse 31 gives a concrete example, from a military setting, of what v. 30 describes abstractly. Readying a horse for battle is the application of technical skills in pursuit of a goal (in this case, military victory). Just as a trained, prepared army can be defeated if God wills it, so also all efforts at success in life (the goal of wisdom) without God are vain. The text does not demean practical skills (e.g., horsemanship), for that also is part of wisdom; but it says that all knowledge is hollow without God.

---

[401]The MT has the unintelligible וְאִישׁ שׁוֹמֵעַ לָנֶצַח יְדַבֵּר ("but a man who listens will speak forever"). Dahood (*Proverbs*, 45) repoints יְדַבֵּר to יְדֻבָּר ("he will be pursued, driven out") on the basis of *duppuru* ("to drive out") in the Amarna texts. Other solutions are unsatisfactory. See D. A. Garrett, "Votive Prostitution Again: A Comparison of Proverbs 7:13-14 and 21:28-29, *JBL* 109 (1990): 681-82. The NIV rendition "destroyed" is perhaps on the basis of the parallel in v. 28a.

[402]The *kethiv* here reads יָכִין ("he makes firm"), but the *qere* has יָבִין ("he understands"). The *qere* should be followed here.

[403]Contrary to the NIV and most versions, there is no grammatical reason to suppose that "his" refers to the righteous man.

[404]See Garrett, "Votive Prostitution," 681-82.

(51) A Good Name (22:1)

[1]A good name is more desirable than great riches;
to be esteemed is better than silver or gold.

TYPE: INDIVIDUAL PROVERB (22:1). **22:1** This proverb does not oppose wealth but implies that it must be rightly obtained. One who has obtained riches at the cost of a notorious reputation has paid too high a price. This text could be read as a prologue to vv. 2-5, which follow.

(52) Wealth, Poverty, and a Prudent Life (22:2-5)

[2]Rich and poor have this in common:
The LORD is the Maker of them all.

[3]A prudent man sees danger and takes refuge,
but the simple keep going and suffer for it.

[4]Humility and the fear of the LORD
bring wealth and honor and life.

[5]In the paths of the wicked lie thorns and snares,
but he who guards his soul stays far from them.

22:2-5 TYPE: PARALLEL The structure of this text is as follows:

A: Rich and poor are equal before Yahweh (v. 2)
B: Prudence and folly in the face of danger (v. 3)
A′: Riches come from fear for Yahweh (v. 4)
B′: Prudence and folly in the face of danger (v. 5)

Although the Hebrew of v. 2 is difficult,[405] the main point is transparent: rich and poor have equal standing before Yahweh. While this might have humanitarian implications (e.g., that the rich should respect and help the poor), that is not the main point in this context (contrast 29:13 in a different context). Rather, the central idea is that those who are well off must never forget that they, no less than the impoverished, are contingent beings who wholly depend on God for life and livelihood. In short, one must live with humility before God. This naturally feeds into v. 4, which asserts that all the good things of life proceed from humility before God.

On the surface vv. 3,5 both simply state that the wise see and avoid trouble but the ignorant or headstrong plunge into it. In the context of vv. 2,4, however, this text asserts that the failure to spot danger arises precisely from the arrogance of refusal to submit to God. Notably, although v. 3 describes such people as "simple" (perhaps even "stupid"[406]), in v. 5

[405]The verb פגשׁ properly means to "meet" or to "encounter." More is implied than that they coexist (thus McKane, *Proverbs*, 569-70). The NIV is perhaps paraphrastic but captures the main idea.

[406]While וּפְתָיִים could refer to those who are ignorant but open to learning, that is not the sense here.

they are described in moral terms as "wicked."[407] Also "thorns" and "snares" may not be just economic or personal danger but moral danger as well. To be humble in the sight of God is to be aware of one's limitation and contingency; thus the humble are more secure, more aware of dangers, and more financially stable than the proud.

(53) Various Proverbs (22:6-16)

6 Train a child in the way he should go,
and when he is old he will not turn from it.

7 The rich rule over the poor,
and the borrower is servant to the lender.

8 He who sows wickedness reaps trouble,
and the rod of his fury will be destroyed.

9 A generous man will himself be blessed,
for he shares his food with the poor.

10 Drive out the mocker, and out goes strife;
quarrels and insults are ended.

11 He who loves a pure heart and whose speech is gracious
will have the king for his friend.

12 The eyes of the LORD keep watch over knowledge,
but he frustrates the words of the unfaithful.

13 The sluggard says, "There is a lion outside!"
or, "I will be murdered in the streets!"

14 The mouth of an adulteress is a deep pit;
he who is under the LORD's wrath will fall into it.

15 Folly is bound up in the heart of a child,
but the rod of discipline will drive it far from him.

16 He who oppresses the poor to increase his wealth
and he who gives gifts to the rich—both come to poverty.

TYPE: INCLUSIO (22:6-16). Verse 6 and 15 (on disciplining children) in parallel with vv. 7 and 16 (on wealth and poverty) form an inclusio for this text of various proverbs.

Discipline for Children (22:6,15). **22:6,15** This verse is popularly debated on two fronts. Some take v. 6a to mean, "Train a child in accordance with his nature," meaning that the teacher must take into account the idiosyncrasies of the child and customize the method of training accordingly. Others, including the NIV, take it to mean simply that one should train a child in the way he should go.[408] A better interpretation is,

---

[407]The word עִקֵּשׁ is perhaps more accurately "twisted."
[408]E.g., McKane, *Proverbs*, 564.

loosely rendered, "Train a child in a manner befitting a child."[409] In other words, one should train a child using vocabulary, concepts, and illustrations a child can understand. It does not mean that instruction should be tailor-made for each individual child (however valid that concept may be) but that one should begin instructing a child in elementary principles of right and wrong as soon as possible.

Another contention is whether "and when he is old" implies he will come back to the right way in later years after a period of straying or whether it simply means that he will faithfully persevere in the right way. "Old" here does not mean after he is "elderly," however; the point, after v. 6a, is that he will build on the fundamental principles as he grows up and persevere in the right way. The whole could be translated, "Train a child in a manner befitting a child, and even as he grows old he will not turn from it."

Verse 15 is fairly clear. In conjunction with v. 6, it implies that if one gets the folly out of a child in the beginning, the child will continue in the right way.

Creditor and Debtor (22:7,16). Verse 7 is an observational proverb and makes the point that debt is a form of slavery (this was all the more clear in ancient Israel, where the debtors were apt to find themselves enslaved; see 2 Kgs 4:1). The Hebrew of v. 16 is extraordinarily difficult; Toy notes that there are "a great number of forced translations."[410] At a risk of adding yet another, I would suggest the meaning is, "One oppresses the weak to enrich himself; another gives to the rich only for poverty [i.e., with no future in sight but deeper poverty for himself]." This should be read in the context of v. 7. The "giving" to the rich is not giving presents to wealthy people but the pitiful attempts of the poor to meet the exorbitant demands of the wealthy creditor. In sum v. 16 represents not two separate activities but the two sides of the one coin in the ancient creditor-debtor relationship, one in which the former gets richer while the latter is ground deeper into poverty. The point of these two verses together is that one must regard indebtedness only as a last resort (wary of those who offer to lend money) and endeavor to get out of debt as rapidly as possible. Debt is debilitating and demoralizing. No one can live the happy, prosperous life Proverbs recommends in that condition.

---

[409]The phrase עַל־פִּי דַרְכּוֹ is literally "in accordance with his way," and it is difficult to see how this could mean "in the way he should go." But as Delitzsch (*Proverbs* 2:86-87) points out, the "way" is not the child's individual nature but the way of children as such.

[410]Toy, *Proverbs*, 420. See the various versions and commentaries for a wide variety of interpretations. The NIV (and other versions) can be sustained. It reads the phrase עֹשֵׁק דָּל לְהַרְבּוֹת לוֹ ("one oppressing the poor to make much for himself") and נֹתֵן לְעָשִׁיר ("one giving to a rich man") as a compound subject with אַךְ־לְמַחְסוֹר ("only for poverty") as the predicate, but this is most unlikely since לְמַחְסוֹר plainly parallels לְהַרְבּוֹת. Also it is odd to read אַךְ as "both."

Reaping What You Sow (22:8-9). **22:8-9** The metaphor of reaping what one sows is familiar in the Bible, but v. 8 is more than a stock expression. While the wicked sow injustice, the righteous share the end product of their literal sowing and harvesting, their bread, with the poor. In light of v. 8 (also vv. 7,15), the crop the wicked sows is oppression of the poor. The industry and generosity of the righteous is implicitly contrasted with the "industry" of the oppressor.

Words and What Comes of Them (22:10-14). Proverbs, like the rest of wisdom literature warns regarding the significance of words. Specifically, Proverbs teaches that one's words betray one's character. Five character types here represent five ways speech can be used. The mocker engenders quarrels (v. 10), the pure impresses even a king (v. 11), the liar is undone by God (v. 12), the shiftless produces only a stream of improbable excuses (v. 13), and the prostitute uses language for seduction and entrapment (v. 14).

22:10-11 In v. 10 the speaker is an obnoxious (and possibly litigious) troublemaker. One can restore harmony to a situation by removing such people.[411] By contrast, those whose minds and words are peaceable find themselves welcomed on the highest level (v. 11) rather than being driven away.

22:12 In v. 12 the "knowledge" Yahweh guards is functionally the same as "wisdom," and the "unfaithful" are those who use their words to oppose the right way. God causes their distortions of the truth to be shown for what they are.[412]

22:13 In v. 13 the speaker is the sluggard. Once again he is the butt of proverbial humor. Here the point is that any excuse, however far-fetched, is enough to keep him inside and away from work.[413]

22:14 In v. 14 the speaker (implied by the word "mouth") is the seductive woman. Her enticing words draw men into a trap. At the same time, she is also the means God uses to punish those whom he has cursed.

(54) The Thirty Sayings (22:17–24:22)

17Pay attention and listen to the sayings of the wise;
apply your heart to what I teach,

---

[411]The LXX of v. 10b reads ὅταν γὰρ καθίσῃ ἐν συνεδρίῳ, πάντας ἀτιμάζει ("when he sits in council"; "he dishonors all"). On this basis G. R. Driver ("Problems," 186) emends to וְיֵשֵׁב בֵּית דִּין וְיַקְלֶנּוּ ("and when he sits in the courthouse he dishonors it"). The MT is clear as it stands, however; Driver's reconstruction may tell us more about how the LXX translators read that text than about what the *Urtext* really was.

[412]On the other hand, the verbal image of God "watching over knowledge" is rather harsh; and one could understand v. 12a to mean, "The eyes of the Lord watch over a claim [in court]," meaning that God frustrates the machinations of those who bring false charges and lawsuits. See D. W. Thomas, "A Note on דַּעַת in Proverbs XXII.12," *JTS* 14:1 (1963): 93-94. Cf. Prov 29:7, where דַּעַת refers to a legal claim.

[413]The verb רצח is generally used of murder at the hands of people, but here it may mean, "I shall be mauled [by a lion]." See McKane, *Proverbs*, 569.

18 for it is pleasing when you keep them in your heart
and have all of them ready on your lips.
19 So that your trust may be in the LORD,
I teach you today, even you.
20 Have I not written thirty sayings for you,
sayings of counsel and knowledge,
21 teaching you true and reliable words,
so that you can give sound answers
to him who sent you?

22 Do not exploit the poor because they are poor
and do not crush the needy in court,
23 for the LORD will take up their case
and will plunder those who plunder them.

24 Do not make friends with a hot-tempered man,
do not associate with one easily angered,
25 or you may learn his ways
and get yourself ensnared.

26 Do not be a man who strikes hands in pledge
or puts up security for debts;
27 if you lack the means to pay,
your very bed will be snatched from under you.

28 Do not move an ancient boundary stone
set up by your forefathers.

29 Do you see a man skilled in his work?
He will serve before kings;
he will not serve before obscure men.

1 When you sit to dine with a ruler,
note well what is before you,
2 and put a knife to your throat
if you are given to gluttony.
3 Do not crave his delicacies,
for that food is deceptive.

4 Do not wear yourself out to get rich;
have the wisdom to show restraint.
5 Cast but a glance at riches, and they are gone,
for they will surely sprout wings
and fly off to the sky like an eagle.

6 Do not eat the food of a stingy man,
do not crave his delicacies;
7 for he is the kind of man
who is always thinking about the cost.
"Eat and drink," he says to you,
but his heart is not with you.
8 You will vomit up the little you have eaten
and will have wasted your compliments.

9Do not speak to a fool,
for he will scorn the wisdom of your words.

10Do not move an ancient boundary stone
or encroach on the fields of the fatherless,
11for their Defender is strong;
he will take up their case against you.

12Apply your heart to instruction
and your ears to words of knowledge.

13Do not withhold discipline from a child;
if you punish him with the rod, he will not die.
14Punish him with the rod
and save his soul from death.

15My son, if your heart is wise,
then my heart will be glad;
16my inmost being will rejoice
when your lips speak what is right.

17Do not let your heart envy sinners,
but always be zealous for the fear of the LORD.
18There is surely a future hope for you,
and your hope will not be cut off.

19Listen, my son, and be wise,
and keep your heart on the right path.
20Do not join those who drink too much wine
or gorge themselves on meat,
21for drunkards and gluttons become poor,
and drowsiness clothes them in rags.

22Listen to your father, who gave you life,
and do not despise your mother when she is old.
23Buy the truth and do not sell it;
get wisdom, discipline and understanding.
24The father of a righteous man has great joy;
he who has a wise son delights in him.
25May your father and mother be glad;
may she who gave you birth rejoice!

26My son, give me your heart
and let your eyes keep to my ways,
27for a prostitute is a deep pit
and a wayward wife is a narrow well.
28Like a bandit she lies in wait,
and multiplies the unfaithful among men.

29Who has woe? Who has sorrow?
Who has strife? Who has complaints?
Who has needless bruises? Who has bloodshot eyes?
30Those who linger over wine,
who go to sample bowls of mixed wine.

31Do not gaze at wine when it is red,
when it sparkles in the cup,
when it goes down smoothly!
32In the end it bites like a snake
and poisons like a viper.
33Your eyes will see strange sights
and your mind imagine confusing things.
34You will be like one sleeping on the high seas,
lying on top of the rigging.
35"They hit me," you will say, "but I'm not hurt!
They beat me, but I don't feel it!
When will I wake up
so I can find another drink?"

1Do not envy wicked men,
do not desire their company;
2for their hearts plot violence,
and their lips talk about making trouble.

3By wisdom a house is built,
and through understanding it is established;
4through knowledge its rooms are filled
with rare and beautiful treasures.

5A wise man has great power,
and a man of knowledge increases strength;
6for waging war you need guidance,
and for victory many advisers.

7Wisdom is too high for a fool;
in the assembly at the gate he has nothing to say.

8He who plots evil
will be known as a schemer.
9The schemes of folly are sin,
and men detest a mocker.

10If you falter in times of trouble,
how small is your strength!

11Rescue those being led away to death;
hold back those staggering toward slaughter.
12If you say, "But we knew nothing about this,"
does not he who weighs the heart perceive it?
Does not he who guards your life know it?
Will he not repay each person according to what he has done?

13Eat honey, my son, for it is good;
honey from the comb is sweet to your taste.
14Know also that wisdom is sweet to your soul;
if you find it, there is a future hope for you,
and your hope will not be cut off.

15Do not lie in wait like an outlaw against a righteous man's house,
do not raid his dwelling place;
16for though a righteous man falls seven times, he rises again,
but the wicked are brought down by calamity.

17Do not gloat when your enemy falls;
when he stumbles, do not let your heart rejoice,
18or the LORD will see and disapprove
and turn his wrath away from him.

19Do not fret because of evil men
or be envious of the wicked,
20for the evil man has no future hope,
and the lamp of the wicked will be snuffed out.

21Fear the LORD and the king, my son,
and do not join with the rebellious,
22for those two will send sudden destruction upon them,
and who knows what calamities they can bring?

This section (type: titular interjection and multisegmented text), while being an original work by the inspired author, is modeled on the Egyptian teachings of Amenemope, a text that is also divided into thirty sayings.[414] It is beyond the scope of this commentary to attempt a detailed presentation of similarities and differences between the two works. A considerable number of both exist. One should not be surprised that the biblical writers knew of, drew upon, and used many patterns found in other ancient authors. The humanity of Scripture and its locus in a historical and cultural setting is no less a part of our doctrine of inspiration than that it is the Word of God.

Sayings one to ten generally concern the desire for wealth through various means, sayings eleven to seventeen follow the theme of parental instruction, while sayings eighteen to thirty are more miscellaneous in nature.

INTRODUCTION (22:17-21). The "Thirty Sayings" that follow are here for two reasons. The first is to draw the reader into a deeper trust in God, and the second is to develop integrity. Craving for wealth and the favors of the wealthy, drunkenness, gluttony, disobedience to parents, going to prostitutes, and other such behavior are certain to lead one away from God and into personal dissolution.

[414]Despite a few dissenting opinions, it is best to follow the majority of scholarship in the belief that Proverbs is modeled on Amenemope rather than vice versa (the latter being the position of R. O. Kevin, "The Wisdom of Amen-em-apt and Its Possible Dependence on the Hebrew Book of Proverbs," *JROR* 14 [1930]: 115-57). Nor is it necessary to postulate that both go back to another source (W. O. E. Oesterly, "The Teaching of Amenemope," *ZAW* 45 [1927]: 9-24; see also R. J. Williams, "The Alleged Semitic Original of the Wisdom of Amenemope," *JEA* 47 [1961]: 100-6) or that there is simply no relationship between the two. The first scholar to propose that this text of Proverbs made use of Amenemope was A. Erman, "Eine agyptische Quelle der Spruche Salomos," in *Sitzungsberichte der preussischen Akademie der Wissenschaften zu Berlin, Phil. Hist. Klasse*, XV (1924): 86-93.

22:17-21 An exhortation to listen (v. 17) is followed by two reasons (vv. 18-19) and a description of what follows (vv. 20-21). Verse 17a serves the role of a title. Its direct address to the reader is analogous to the discourse literature of Prov 1–9, but its employment of thirty distinct teachings is unlike the discourse material.

Verse 18 is a motive clause[415] and stresses the pleasantness of wisdom. Verse 18b is sometimes emended to read, "[When] they are fixed [like] a tent peg on your lips,"[416] on the basis of Amenemope. The emendation gives a harsh simile, however, and the text cited in Amenemope is not fully analogous here.[417] The emendation is unnecessary.

Verse 19, a final clause, stresses the result of wisdom's work: the reader is drawn closer to Yahweh.[418] The material that follows is described in v. 20 as thirty sayings.[419] According to v. 21, they are meant to instruct the reader in the truth[420] and in so doing mold him into a reliable person.[421]

SAYING ONE (22:22-23). **22:22-23** Concern for the poor is common in both biblical and pagan wisdom literature. The distinctive Israelite perspective, however, is that Yahweh is viewed as protector of the oppressed.[422] Here the text warns the powerful not to use legal devices to exploit the poor, lest they find themselves arraigned before a much higher judge. The warning is punctuated with an image of God doing to the rich exactly what they do to the poor (v. 23).

SAYING TWO (22:24-25). **22:24-25** This could be taken to mean simply that if one associates with quarrelsome people, one will become like them and get into trouble. On the other hand, as in 1:10-19 it may be that the reader is warned to stay clear of criminal enticements.[423] The word translated "ensnared" also can mean "bait," and the "bait" of the criminal is the enticement of easy money. Either way, the point is that one should be

---

[415]Introduced by כִּי.

[416]Reading (כ)יתד ("like"), "a tent peg," for the MT יַחְדָּו ("together"). See BHS note *a*.

[417]For further detail see the discussion in McKane, *Proverbs*, 375.

[418]It is possible that, following the LXX Alexandrinus and Sinaiticus codices, אַף־אַתָּה ("even you") should be emended to אָרְחֹתָיו ("his ways").

[419]As in the NIV and the BHS note *b*, one should here read שְׁלֹשִׁים, "thirty," and neither the *kethiv* שִׁלְשׁוֹם, "the day before yesterday," nor the qere שָׁלִישִׁים, "third/adjutant."

[420]On the somewhat unusual phrase אֲמָרִים אֱמֶת, "words truth," Dahood (*Proverbs*, 47) argues that אמרים is not an absolute but a construct with enclitic *mem*, thus "words of truth." The NIV translates it as "sound answers."

[421]A. Cody ("Notes on Proverbs 22,21 and 22,23b," *Bib* 61 [1980]: 418-24) shows that efforts at emending v. 21 are futile. He explains that קֹשְׁטְ here means "probity" or "integrity" and corresponds to Egyptian *ma'at*.

[422]See A. Cody, "Notes," 425-26, on the meaning of קבע with נֶפֶשׁ here.

[423]The בַּעַל אַף ("lord of rage") and אִישׁ חֵמוֹת ("man of anger") mean more than just a person who tends to lose his temper, since such a person does not entice others with a מוֹקֵשׁ ("bait, snare") to follow in his way. Cf. 1:10-11.

careful about choosing friends because they inevitably affect one's character. Something of the nature of Proverbs comes out here as well. Few things can cause parents as much anxiety as their child's choice of companions.

SAYING THREE (22:26-27). **22:26-27** As in 6:1-5, the text warns the reader against entanglements in debts. The bed, as the place of rest, is metonymy for all that is home.

SAYING FOUR (22:28). **22:28** To move a boundary stone was to attempt to seize land furtively. More is involved here, however, than real property. The boundary stone represented the ancient constitution of Israel, and to violate that heritage was to undermine the distinctive character of the land in Israelite society.

SAYING FIVE (22:29). **22:29** Quality work deserves recognition. This is a verse for those unwilling to stop at what seems good enough in job performance and push on to doing it right.

SAYING SIX (23:1-3). **23:1-3** Beware when feasted by someone rich and powerful.[424] To put a knife to the throat is to take extraordinary measures to avoid overindulging. The rich do not give away their favors for free. They want something in return,[425] and it is generally much more than what they have invested. One can lose one's own soul in the exchange.

SAYING SEVEN (23:4-5). **23:4-5** Wealth is a mirage. This saying is similar to the much longer seventh saying of Amenemope. The phrase "have the wisdom to show restraint" might better be rendered, "Desist from your purpose [of getting rich]."[426] To "cast a glance" at wealth is literally to let one's eye fly toward it. But the wealth itself can fly like the eagle and thus can outstrip all attempts to capture it.[427]

SAYING EIGHT (23:6-8). **23:6-8** Cultivating the friendship of the wealthy is a waste of effort. The NIV rendition of v. 7 ("for he is the kind of man who is always thinking about the cost") is improbable.[428] On a

---

[424]The emphatic phrase בִּין תָּבִין אֶת־אֲשֶׁר לְפָנֶיךָ (v. 1) could be rendered, "Make sure you understand what is really going on in front of you." The NIV seems to imply that one should take an inventory of the evening's menu.

[425]The phrase לֶחֶם כְּזָבִים ("bread of lies") here means that the food offered is itself a snare or a trap. It does not mean that the food is of poor quality.

[426]In the phrase מִבִּינָתְךָ חֲדָל ("from your understanding desist") the word בִּינָה could be taken to mean "plan" or "purpose," or perhaps it is one's (faulty) understanding of how the world works that one should abandon. See Toy, *Proverbs*, 429.

[427]McKane (*Proverbs*, 383) proposes that v. 5a means, "If you take your eyes off it for an instant." While such a translation is possible, it is not the most natural rendering of הֲתָעִיף עֵינֶיךָ בּוֹ. Also such a condition might indicate that one should pursue wealth with unswerving diligence, not that one should abandon the search for wealth, as context demands.

[428]While שָׁעַר means "a measure of grain" in Gen 26:12 and a verb שׁער in the piel stem can mean to set the price of goods in postbiblical Hebrew, no other use of שׁער as a verb (here in the qal stem) exists in the Bible. Also one would expect a participle after כְּמוֹ and not a finite verb as is found here.

Ugaritic analogy Dahood suggests the translation, "For like one serving his own appetite, such he is."[429] A simpler solution is to follow the LXX and translate, "For like a hair in the throat, so he is."[430] Just as getting a hair in the throat while eating causes a gag reflex and sometimes vomiting (v. 8), even so the wealthy man's hospitality will leave one feeling disgusted. These proverbs contradict the common notion that Proverbs regards the rich as righteous and thus favored by God. To the contrary, wealthy people often are viewed with a marked suspicion, and their company is not always valued.

SAYING NINE (23:9). **23:9** As in Jesus' warning not to throw pearls before pigs (Matt 7:6), the point here is that one should not waste sound teaching on the stubbornly unresponsive.

SAYING TEN (23:10-11). **23:10-11** This text envisages a court battle in which one party has wrongfully seized the property of another party, and God himself takes on the role of attorney for the wronged, weaker party.[431] The party that attempted to defraud cannot possibly win.

SAYING ELEVEN (23:12). **23:12** The acquisition of instruction is not to be taken lightly. The verse is in the imperative and suggests that education is vital to one's whole life.

SAYING TWELVE (23:13-14). **23:13-14** This text focuses on the parents' desire to preserve the life of their child. Disciplining with the rod may save a child from an early grave (the result of an undisciplined life). This text does not justify brutalizing children. Parents who find it only too easy to apply the rod, and especially those who lose their tempers when doing so, should consider Eph 6:4.

SAYING THIRTEEN (23:15-16). **23:15-16** The joy of giving one's parents or teachers a sense of pride and satisfaction should serve as a motivation to pursue the right path.

SAYING FOURTEEN (23:17-18). **23:17-18** What parents fear most is that their teaching will be undermined by the child's peers or by adults who are bad role models. It probably is best to translate v. 18 as, "For if you maintain [the fear of Yahweh], you will have a future,/and your hope will not be cut off."[432]

SAYING FIFTEEN (23:19-21). **23:19-21** Those who live like Shakespeare's Falstaff soon exhaust their resources. Christians should note that both drunkenness and gluttony are condemned. We often eschew the former and practice the latter.

---

[429]Dahood, *Proverbs*, 47. He repoints as a participle and takes the meaning "to serve [food]" from the Ugaritic verb $t^{c}r$.

[430]Reading שֵׂעָר ("hair") for the MT שָׁעַר (the LXX has τρίχα). Cf. BHS note *a* and see McKane, *Proverbs*, 383-85, for a full discussion.

[431]Note the use of the legal terms גֹּאֵל, "redeemer" (an important term in Israelite property law), and רִיב, "lawsuit."

[432]Inserting תִּשְׁמְרֶנָּה, "you will keep it," with BHS note *a*. The LXX has τηρήσῃς αὐτά.

SAYING SIXTEEN (23:22-25). **23:22-25** The child is encouraged to make his parents proud, as in saying thirteen. Since both father and mother are mentioned, it is clear that these are actual parents and not the teacher in place of parents.[433] The warning not to despise the mother (and by metonomy the father also) because she is old (v. 22) does not mean that the parents are well advanced in years, merely that the son perceives them in that way.

SAYING SEVENTEEN (23:26-28). **23:26-28** Access to prostitutes brings on moral decline in society. A number of scholars prefer the *kethiv* (what is written in the Heb.) of v. 26b, which reads, "Let your eyes approve[434] of my ways." The *qere* (what is to be read in the Heb. according to the Masoretes), followed by the NIV as well as the ancient versions, says the eyes should "keep"[435] to the teacher's paths. The *qere* is preferable; it leads into the metaphor of the prostitute as an attractive distraction that pulls the young man's eyes off the path. The two metaphors of the pit and the highwayman both emphasize that the prostitute sets a trap, or rather is herself a trap. The charge in v. 28b that she "multiples the unfaithful among men" is unusual. The word for "the unfaithful" could be taken abstractly to mean "faithlessness."[436] If, however, the text is read in its normal sense (as in the NIV), the meaning is that prostitution brings about a general decline in the moral values of the community with the result that lawlessness increases.

SAYING EIGHTEEN (23:29-35). **23:29-35** This poem is a small masterpiece; it is surely the most effective combination lampoon and lament over the sorry state of the drunkard. Although the precise meaning of a few phrases is uncertain,[437] the text describes with profound accuracy and bite the pathetic physical and emotional decline of those addicted to alcohol. Wine (and in modern society, illicit drugs) brings physical pain and debilitation, exhausts one's resources, takes away mental acuity, and yet leaves one craving for more of the same. "Lingering over" alcohol (vv. 30-31) describes those who derive comfort and security in knowing that a glass of wine is at hand, ready to deaden the senses. In the end, however, it only leaves people more confused and in deeper pain than ever before (vv. 32-35a).

---

[433]It is pointless to contend that the mother here is actually Lady Wisdom.

[434]The kethiv is תִּרְצֶנָה from the root רצה.

[435]The qere is תִּצֹּרְנָה from the root נצר.

[436]Thus McKane (*Proverbs*, 392; Toy, *Proverbs*, 438) similarly emends to בֶּגֶד ("treachery") and takes it to mean that she works much treachery among men.

[437]In v. 29 חַכְלִלוּת עֵינָיִם could be translated as "bloodshot eyes," as "blackened eyes" (from beatings), or as "dull eyes" (blurred vision). In v. 32 the bite of the serpent could simply be a metaphor for the effect of alcohol, or it could allude to the frightening hallucinations some alcoholics have (the latter is implied in v. 33). In v. 34 חִבֵּל could mean the "top of the mast" of a ship or the "rigging" (the former makes for a more dramatic metaphor of unsteadiness, while the implication of the latter is somewhat unclear).

Saying Nineteen (24:1-2). **24:1-2** In this saying the reader is warned against joining with evildoers not on the grounds that some disaster will overtake them or even on the grounds that God will judge them but simply because what they do is wrong. A benefit of moral instruction is that one comes to hate evil simply because it is evil.

Saying Twenty (24:3-4). **24:3-4** Is the promised wealth literal or metaphorical? While either is possible, and perhaps both are meant, in light of 23:4-5 the primary focus must be on the metaphorical meaning. The precious jewels that fill the house are a harmonious, loving family and a sense of security and stability.

Saying Twenty-one (24:5-6). **24:5-6** It probably is best to emend v. 5a to read, "A wise man excels a strong one."[438] Whether or not one emends, however, this teaching urges the reader not to rely on raw force in dealing with enemies. Intelligence and stratagem are better. The saying would seem to have application to kings only, since only they are likely to initiate wars and have counselors, but the majority of the thirty sayings are clearly addressed to someone who is not in high office. A metaphorical sense that one should engage life with discernment rather than by exercise of force is therefore likely.

Saying Twenty-two (24:7). **24:7** A slightly different translation is possible: "Wisdom is too high[439] for a fool; let his mouth stay shut at the gate."[440] The meaning is that the matters discussed at the gate are too important to waste time listening to the perverse arguments of the intellectually and morally inept. This is a piece of ideal legislation; it is of course impossible to enforce, but it sets up a theoretical model on how business ought to be conducted.

Saying Twenty-three (24:8-9). **24:8-9** Those who connive soon have a reputation for being connivers. The loss of a good name is no small penalty, since it is not easily regained. Verse 9a should be emended to "the scheme of an unprincipled person is sin."[441]

---

[438]The MT literally reads, "The wise man is in the strength," which, though perhaps possible, seems odd. Emend גֶּבֶר ("man") to גָּבַר ("excels") on the basis of the LXX κρείσσων and בַּעוֹז ("in the strength") to מֵעָז ("than a strong man") on the basis of the LXX ἰσχυροῦ. Cf. BHS notes *a* and *b*.

[439]Reading רָמוֹת ("high") for רָאמוֹת ("coral").

[440]Taking לֹא יִפְתַּח־פִּיהוּ as a negated jussive ("let his mouth not open") rather than a negated indicative ("his mouth will not open"). Other proverbs teach that the fool's mouth is wide open in court proceedings—if anything, that is his trademark. The NIV gives the phrase the paraphrastic translation, "He has nothing to say." Apparently it avoids the jussive translation on the grounds that jussives are usually negated by אַל and not לֹא. Perhaps לֹא is used with the jussive here in order to give a permanent prohibition on the analogy of the negatives used in the Decalogue (Exod 20:13ff.). At any rate, jussives negated by לֹא are found in the OT (e.g., 1 Kgs 2:6).

[441]Reading אֱוִיל ("fool," "unprincipled person") for the MT אִוֶּלֶת ("folly"). Cf. versional and manuscript evidence cited in BHS note *a*.

SAYING TWENTY-FOUR (24:10). **24:10** This text calls the reader to summon courage to face whatever challenges lie ahead. Difficult times can manifest one's lack of mettle, but this proverb is meant to encourage the reader *not* to falter in the face of adversity.

SAYING TWENTY-FIVE (24:11-12). **24:11-12** Who are the ones staggering toward death whom the reader is charged to rescue?[442] Two possibilities are evident. These could be literal prisoners who have been (presumably wrongfully) condemned to die. The reader is to take extraordinary measures to secure their release (a dramatic modern example would be the extermination of the Jews in Europe during the Second World War). Alternatively, these are people stumbling toward death because of their moral and spiritual blindness. The reader should therefore sway them into the right path by moral persuasion. In light of the graphic language, the former interpretation appears more likely.

SAYING TWENTY-SIX (24:13-14). **24:13-14** The offer of honey serves as an opening to encourage the son to gain wisdom. The text associates wisdom with delightful pleasure. In other words, right behavior is not recommended solely on the grounds of austere morality but also because it is the best route to sheer pleasure and the fulfillment of dreams.

SAYING TWENTY-SEVEN (24:15-16). **24:15-16** This saying is a warning addressed to the evildoer to leave the righteous alone. Instead of, "Do not lie in wait like an outlaw," v. 15 should read, "Do not lie in wait, outlaw, against a righteous man's estate!"[443] The resilience of the good man (expressed in his getting back up seven times) is such that the evil cannot win.

SAYING TWENTY-EIGHT (24:17-18). **24:17-18** The motive for not gloating over an enemy's downfall is curious: one's gloating may cause Yahweh to relent and stop afflicting the enemy. It seems perverse to refrain from gloating in order that Yahweh may further injure an enemy. Behind this proverb, however, stands a profound sense of the fear of God, which has the effect of *humanizing* the reader. It is impossible to refrain from gloating and at the same time be malevolent. The reader should place justice in the hands of God and stand back in silent dread of God's power.

SAYING TWENTY-NINE (24:19-20). **24:19-20** The translation "Do not fret" (v. 19) is too mild. "Do not get yourself infuriated[444] over evildoers" is more accurate. Those who love the truth are naturally enraged by the effrontery of those who promote or practice godless behavior—anyone who has ever watched the evening news broadcasts has surely experienced something of this. Impotent raging is pointless and unnecessary. Faith in a

---

[442]G. R. Driver ("Problems," 188-89) points out that אִם need not be emended in v. 11. Cf. Ps 81:9.

[443]The word רָשָׁע ("outlaw") is vocative here. The NIV apparently considers a כְּ ("like") to be implied.

[444]The hithpael of חרה ("to burn") is literally, "Do not get burnt up!" So also in Ps 37:1,7-8.

just God is the only remedy for such misapplied righteous indignation. The phrase "no future hope" is pregnant with meaning. While the earthly destruction of the wicked may be foremost, a doctrine of eternal life cannot be excluded.

SAYING THIRTY (24:21-22). **24:21-22** This text contains a lexical difficulty,[445] but the overall meaning is clear. God and the king are the sustainers of justice. In this the king is God's earthly representative (Rom 13:1-7). Submission to moral governance is the best way to live a life of peace and security.

(55) On the Law Courts and on Laziness (24:23-34)

23 These also are sayings of the wise:

To show partiality in judging is not good:
24 Whoever says to the guilty, "You are innocent"—
peoples will curse him and nations denounce him.
25 But it will go well with those who convict the guilty,
and rich blessing will come upon them.

26 An honest answer
is like a kiss on the lips.

27 Finish your outdoor work
and get your fields ready;
after that, build your house.

28 Do not testify against your neighbor without cause,
or use your lips to deceive.
29 Do not say, "I'll do to him as he has done to me;
I'll pay that man back for what he did."

30 I went past the field of the sluggard,
past the vineyard of the man who lacks judgment;
31 thorns had come up everywhere,
the ground was covered with weeds,
and the stone wall was in ruins.
32 I applied my heart to what I observed
and learned a lesson from what I saw:
33 A little sleep, a little slumber,
a little folding of the hands to rest—

---

[445] The meaning of שׁוֹנִים is uncertain. It is difficult to see how a qal participle of שׁנה ("to be different," "to change"; in a different root, "to repeat") could mean "the rebellious," although Toy (*Proverbs*, 450) argues that it means "those who are given to change," and thus, "revolutionists." This is plainly stretching things, since שׁוֹנִים properly ought to mean "those who change" rather than "those who advocate change." A number of scholars (e.g., McKane, *Proverbs*, 249) take it to mean "noblemen" (but McKane's rendition "do not get involved with noblemen" implies that nobles are innately opposed to the king and God). This can hardly be the point of the proverb. It is better to emend to עִם שְׁנֵיהֶם אַל הִתְעַבֵּר ("do not rebel against either of the two"). Cf. the LXX καὶ μηθετέρῳ αὐτῶν ἀπειθήσῃς ("do not disobey either of them").

**34 and poverty will come on you like a bandit
and scarcity like an armed man.**

TYPE: PARALLEL (24:23-34). Verse 23a serves as the titular interjection to introduce the new text, simply called the "Sayings of the Wise." The structure of this text is as follows:

A: On the law courts (vv. 23-26)
B: On economic priorities (v. 27)
A′: On the law courts (vv. 28-29)
B′: On laziness (vv. 30-34)

There is no intrinsic link between these two concepts; the parallel structure exists simply for organizational purposes.

24:23-26 These verses introduce the principle of jurisprudence that there should be no prejudice or favoritism. Verse 26, at least in this context, is not a general proverb that one should not deceive when answering a question. The text here could more accurately be rendered, "He who gives a proper verdict[446] silences [hostile] lips."[447] All attempts to deceive the court and pervert justice fail when the upright man stands and gives a straight analysis of the case before the other elders.

24:27 This verse does not address laziness in the direct terms that vv. 30-34 do, but it relates to the principle that one should not provide for personal comfort until a means of income is established here. As such, it emphasizes the practical rule of producing before consuming, a rule the slothful do not accept. It is possible that "building a house" refers not just to the building in which one lives but to the establishment of a family.[448] If so, the guideline is even more appropriate: one should be able to provide for a family before starting one.

24:28-29 These verses, returning to the courts, move from the role of the judge to the role of the witness. In particular the witness is urged not to commit perjury[449] or use the courts as a tool for settling a personal score against another person.

---

[446]The word נְכֹחִים refers to that which is "opposite, "fair," or "right." It is particularly well suited to a judicial setting. Cf. 2 Sam 15:3; Isa 59:14.

[447]The phrase שְׂפָתַיִם יִשָּׁק here does not mean "kiss the lips" but "seal the lips." This usage is attested in Gen 41:40, in which all the people would not kiss Joseph's mouth but sealed their own mouths at his, meaning they would be silent when he spoke. See especially Job 31:27, וַתִּשַּׁק יָדִי לְפִי ("[and if] my hand has sealed my mouth"). Here Job clearly was not saying that his hand had not kissed his mouth but that his hand had not covered his mouth as a sign of reverence toward the sun and moon. See J. M. Cohen, "An Unrecognized Connotation of NSQ PEH with Special Reference to Three Biblical Occurrences," *VT* 32 (1982): 416-24.

[448]See McKane, *Proverbs*, 575-76, Toy, *Proverbs*, 453-54.

[449]The word וַהֲפִתִּיתָ is difficult, but the simplest solution is that of McKane, (*Proverbs*, 574), who deletes the initial ו. This leaves a piel perfect of פתה with ה interrogative, with the resulting transition, "Will you deceive with your lips?"

24:30-34 These verses are an example story in which the poet quotes a traditional proverb (vv. 33-34) that summarizes the lesson of the example story. By joining the evidence of observation to a customary saying, the text is all the more powerful and credible. Also the anecdote invites the reader to recall similar observations of homes in disrepair and to draw the same conclusions even while participating in the poet's disgust over the shameful condition of the lackadaisical man's home.

SECTION OUTLINE

II. "HEZEKIAH" (25:1–29:27)
   1. "Hezekiah" (25:1)
   2. On Dealing with Kings (25:2-7)
   3. Settling Disputes without Litigation (25:8-10)
   4. Fine Jewelry and the Counsel (25:11-12)
   5. Reliable and Unreliable People (25:13-14)
   6. Be Patient with the Authorities (25:15)
   7. Exercising Caution with People (25:16-27)
      (1) Enough Is Enough (25:16-17)
      (2) Beware of These People (25:18-20)
      (3) Strange but True (25:21-22)
      (4) Cold Rain and Cold Looks (25:23)
      (5) A Nagging Wife (25:24)
      (6) Good Water and Bad Water (25:25-26)
      (7) Sweets for the Body and Sweets for the Mind (25:27)
   8. Portrait of a Fool (25:28–26:12)
   9. Portrait of a Sluggard (26:13-16)
   10. Portrait of a Busybody (26:17-22)
   11. Portrait of a Liar (26:23-28)
   12. Boasting and Praise (27:1-2)
   13. Unbearable Personalities (27:3-4)
   14. Honest Friendship (27:5-6)
   15. Real Friends, Close at Hand (27:7-10)
   16. Fatherly Advice (27:11-27)
   17. A Life of Fear (28:1)
   18. The Distortions Evil Causes (28:2)
   19. Oppression, Keeping in the Right Way, and the Law (28:3-11)
   20. Various Proverbs (28:12–29:27)
      (1) Good Government and Bad Government I (28:12)
      (2) Turning from Sin (28:13-14)
      (3) Tyranny (28:15-16)
      (4) Guilt and Innocence (28:17-18)
      (5) Prosperity by Fair Means and Foul (28:19-27)
      (6) Good Government and Bad Government II (28:28–29:2)
      (7) Squandering Wealth and Squandering a Nation (29:3-4)
      (8) Beware of the Traps (29:5-6)
      (9) Concern for Justice (29:7)
      (10) Order in the Court and in Society (29:8-11)

(11) The Throne Secured by Righteousness (29:12-14)
(12) Discipline at Home and in the Nation (29:15-18)
(13) Controlling the Servant and Controlling the Self (29:19-22)
(14) The First Shall Be Last (29:23)
(15) A Poor Choice for a Friend (29:24)
(16) Seek Deliverance from God (29:25-26)
(17) The Sum of It All (29:27)

II. "HEZEKIAH" (25:1–29:27)

1. "Hezekiah" (25:1)

1These are more proverbs of Solomon, copied by the men of Hezekiah king of Judah:

As described in the Introduction to Proverbs, Prov 25–29 constitutes a separate book within Proverbs, which is here called "Hezekiah" in accordance with Prov 25:1. Here, as in Prov 10–19, individual proverbs are organized into small collections. The introduction, 25:1, indicates that the following ancient proverbs were compiled and edited by the scribes of Hezekiah. See the commentary introduction for further remarks on the type and characteristics of this collection.

2. On Dealing with Kings (25:2-7)

2It is the glory of God to conceal a matter;
to search out a matter is the glory of kings.

3As the heavens are high and the earth is deep,
so the hearts of kings are unsearchable.

4Remove the dross from the silver,
and out comes material for the silversmith;
5remove the wicked from the king's presence,
and his throne will be established through righteousness.

6Do not exalt yourself in the king's presence,
and do not claim a place among great men;
7it is better for him to say to you, "Come up here,"
than for him to humiliate you before a nobleman.
What you have seen with your eyes

Type: Thematic, Parallel (24:2-7). Verses 2-27 form a major division of Hezekiah, and v. 16 further divides this section into two parts (see the discussion on v. 27).

The proverbs of vv. 2-7 are all bound by the subject of dealing with royalty. They may have been placed at the beginning of the Hezekiah collection as a gesture of respect for the two great patrons of Israelite wisdom, Solomon and Hezekiah. The tone here is highly deferential to the royalty. In addition these proverbs are set up as three parallel pairs (vv. 2-3,4-5,6-7).[1]

25:2 Verse 2 appears to be an intentional tribute to Solomon and Hezekiah as scholar-kings. This proverb comes from a time when academic inquiry and governmental power were closely linked; in the modern world they are more separated. God is glorious in concealing matters in that a certain level of mystery about the divine increases the sense of wonder and awe. Those who assume they have full comprehension of theological truth, however "religious" they may be, lose true piety. On the other hand, people do honor those who uncover truth, be it theological or scientific.

25:3 While v. 3 appears to be outlandish praise of the height and depth[2] of royal wisdom, it is in effect more prescriptive than descriptive. This is how a leader must appear. Predictability and lack of imagination are fatal for a ruler, since he no longer will be taken seriously.

25:4-5 Although aspects of the Hebrew of v. 4 are disputed,[3] the general sense of vv. 4-5 is clear. As the silversmith must remove impurities from silver in order to create a thing of beauty, so the king must remove evil from his kingdom and especially his court if the kingdom is to be secure.

25:6-7 Verses 6-7 go together, but in accordance with the Hebrew text and against the NIV's division of the lines, the end of v. 7 should be read as part of that verse and not as the beginning of v. 8. Verse 7 should thus be translated, "It is good that he say to you, 'Come up here!' rather than that you be demoted in the presence of a noble whom your eyes see." The point is that no one wants to have to look his peers in the face while being publicly humiliated by a superior. Jesus may have had this text in mind in Luke 14:7-11.

3. Settling Disputes without Litigation (25:8-10)

8do not bring hastily to court,
for what will you do in the end

---

[1]Note that the word מֶלֶךְ appears four times in this text (vv. 2,3,5,6), at least once in each pair of verses.

[2]Ugaritic evidence indicates the אֶרֶץ can mean "underworld," and this could be the sense here. See M. Dahood, *Proverbs and Northwest Semitic Philology* (Rome: Biblical Institute Press, 1963), 52.

[3]Instead of the NIV "material," כֶּלִי is here a vessel or some artistic creation. On the basis of the LXX καθαρὸν ἅπαν ("all clean"), BHS note *b* recommends נִצְרָף כֻּלּוֹ ("all of it refined") instead of לַצֹּרֵף כֶּלִי ("a vessel for the refiner"). This destroys the parallel between "king" and "refiner." Dahood (*Proverbs*, 52) argues that יצא here means "shine" on the basis of UT 125:52-53 and Job 23:10. One could thus render the line, "And the vessel will shine for the refiner." I find this solution most appealing, but the MT is not impossible. See McKane, *Proverbs*, 590-91.

if your neighbor puts you to shame?

9 If you argue your case with a neighbor,
do not betray another man's confidence,
10 or he who hears it may shame you
and you will never lose your bad reputation.

TYPE: THEMATIC (25:8-10). **25:8-10** Although the idea of public shame links this text to the preceding verses, the subject matter is entirely different. Verses 6-7 concern the status of a courtier before the king, and vv. 8-10 concern civil litigation. The translation of this text, particularly v. 8, is difficult. A reasonable alternative to the NIV[4] is as follows: "Do not take a matter to litigation quickly, lest[5]—what will you do afterwards, when your adversary[6] humiliates you? Make your case to your adversary and do not reveal it to another arbitrator,[7] lest when he hears it he finds against you and there be no end to your disgrace." Jesus gave a similar teaching in Luke 12:57-59.

4. Fine Jewelry and Fine Counsel (25:11-12)

11 A word aptly spoken
is like apples of gold in settings of silver.

12 Like an earring of gold or an ornament of fine gold
is a wise man's rebuke to a listening ear.

TYPE: THEMATIC, CATCHWORD (25:11-12). **25:11-12** The metaphor of jewelry dominates these two proverbs, and both concern the importance of good counsel.[8] The "apples of gold" are not golden colored fruit but are some kind of jewelry or artwork. An intriguing alternative reading of

---

[4]The NIV follows C. Toy (*A Critical and Exegetical Commentary on the Book of Proverbs* [Edinburgh: T & T Clark, 1899], 460-61), W. McKane (*Proverbs*, OTL [Philadelphia: Westminster, 1970], 580-81), and R. B. Y. Scott (*Proverbs and Ecclesiastes*, AB [Garden City: Doubleday, 1965], 155) in linking v. 7c to v. 8. One wonders, moreover, what this reading really implies. Is it an injunction against gossip? If so, it is oddly worded. Is it a warning not to be too quick to report a crime you witness? That hardly fits the context of Proverbs.

[5]This פֶּן has been the subject of much discussion. A number of scholars would emend it to כִּי ("for") or simply omit it (e.g., Toy, *Proverbs*, 461, and Scott, *Proverbs*, 53, who suggests that it is a conjunction *pa* meaning "and" with a suffixed *nun*). The simplest explanation is that it is simply anacoluthon, or, more precisely, that the פֶּן clause is interrupted here and resumed in v. 10, פֶּן־יְחַסֶּדְךָ.

[6]A רֵעַ is not necessarily a "friend" but may be a "peer" with whom one is in an adversarial relationship.

[7]The word סוֹד means "counsel" or "council"; here, in conjunction with שֹׁמֵעַ (v. 10), it refers to the arbitrator (be it one man or a council) who adjudicates the case.

[8]Note also the catchword זָהָב ("gold") in both proverbs.

"a word aptly spoken" is that it is "a word spoken in its two lines," that is, that it refers to the two lines of a proverb.[9]

5. Reliable and Unreliable People (25:13-14)

13Like the coolness of snow at harvest time
is a trustworthy messenger to those who send him;
he refreshes the spirit of his masters.

14Like clouds and wind without rain
is a man who boasts of gifts he does not give.

TYPE: THEMATIC, PARALLEL (25:13-14). **25:13-14** Both of these proverbs begin with some aspect of weather and its affects on an agrarian society; from that analogy they move on to the importance of personal reliability. Verse 13 does not mean that it snows at harvest time—that would be an unmitigated disaster. It refers to bringing down snow from the mountains during the heat of harvest and the refreshment that gives to workers. Verse 14 speaks of clouds that hold the promise of rain for parched crops but pass by without leaving a drop. The proverbs speak of the joy or bitter disappointment that comes from reliable or unreliable employees.

6. Be Patient with the Authorities (25:15)

15Through patience a ruler can be persuaded,
and a gentle tongue can break a bone.

TYPE: INDIVIDUAL PROVERB (25:15). **25:15** This proverb, describing the importance of patience in dealing with an authority,[10] answers 25:2-7 (with its high regard for royal authority) in inclusio fashion and so serves to mark off 25:2-15 as the first major section of Hezekiah. The bones are the most rigid body parts inside of a person, and fracturing the bones here refers to breaking down the deepest, most hardened resistance to an idea a person may possess.

7. Exercising Caution with People (25:16-27)

These proverbs are bound by the inclusio of proverbs on eating honey in excess (25:16,27). They generally concern dealing with friends, family,

---

[9]The word אָפְנָיו is usually taken to mean "its circumstances" or the like, but אֹפֶן is a hapax legomenon, and we cannot be sure of its meaning. McKane (*Proverbs*, 584), following a suggestion in *KB*2, argues that אֹפֶן means "wheel," is here a dual form, and is metaphorical for the two lines of a proverb. He also notes that an obscure line in Sir 50:27 could be read as referring to a proverb of two wheels.

[10]Contrary to Toy (*Proverbs*, 464-65), there is no need to emend.

and others; several focus on actions that are either inappropriate or paradoxically appropriate.

(1) Enough Is Enough (25:16-17)

[16]If you find honey, eat just enough—
too much of it, and you will vomit.
[17]Seldom set foot in your neighbor's house—
too much of you, and he will hate you.

TYPE: PARALLEL (25:16-17). **25:16-17** Verse 17 is obviously the social response to the dietary exhortation of v. 16: just as you get sick of honey when you eat too much, so your friends get tired of you when you are around too much.[11]

(2) Beware of These People (25:18-20)

[18]Like a club or a sword or a sharp arrow
is the man who gives false testimony against his neighbor.

[19]Like a bad tooth or a lame foot
is reliance on the unfaithful in times of trouble.

[20]Like one who takes away a garment on a cold day,
or like vinegar poured on soda,
is one who sings songs to a heavy heart.

TYPE: THEMATIC. **25:18-20** All three of these proverbs are similes (although the word for "like" is not in the Hebrew text), and all concern people one should avoid (the perjurer, the undependable, and the tactless). The point of each is evident. The perjurer is a dangerous weapon,[12] to rely on unreliable people on a day of trouble is futile and excruciatingly painful, and being ebullient to the depressed only jolts them and makes matters worse. A sensitive person knows how to sorrow with the sorrowing.

(3) Strange but True (25:21-22)

[21]If your enemy is hungry, give him food to eat;
if he is thirsty, give him water to drink.
[22]In doing this, you will heap burning coals on his head,
and the LORD will reward you.

TYPE: THEMATIC (25:21-22). **25:21-22** These proverbs state the paradoxical truth that one can get back at one's enemy with kindness. Feeding

---

[11]The parallel of פֶּן־תִּשְׂבָּעֶנּוּ וַהֲקֵאתוֹ ("lest you have your fill of it and spew it out") to פֶּן־יִשְׂבָּעֲךָ וּשְׂנֵאֶךָ ("lest he have his fill of you and hate you") is obvious, as the NIV translation indicates.

[12]The NIV is correct to render מֵפִיץ ("one scattering") as מַפֵּץ ("war club"), as in Jer 51:20.

an enemy will "heap burning coals on his head" in the sense that he or she will be humiliated at having to take bread from a hated rival. The metaphor of burning coals implies intense pain; the proverb does not foresee the possibility of reconciliation with one's foe, however true and noble that may be.[13] Still, the implication that one should refrain from extracting vengeance is obvious. Paul quoted this proverb in his discussion of "love" in Rom 12:9-21. It must also be noted that Jesus' instruction on the love of enemies (Matt 5:43-47) be read in light of this proverb and that the love of enemy is originally an Old Testament idea that was both enacted and commanded by Jesus.

(4) Cold Rain and Cold Looks (25:23)

23 As a north wind brings rain,
so a sly tongue brings angry looks.

TYPE: INDIVIDUAL PROVERB (25:23). **25:23** This little proverb is extraordinarily beset with problems.[14] The first is that the north wind does not bring rain in Israel; the second is that the phrase "brings rain" is literally "has the birth pangs of rain" (which is subject to various interpretations),[15] and the third is that the Hebrew does not make clear whether the "sly tongue brings angry looks" or whether it is the other way around. Yet one could interpret it, with paraphrase, as follows: "As a cold wind gives birth to rains, so cold looks[16] give birth to a storm of slander." The point of the north wind is not meteorological accuracy for Israel. The proverb may have arisen in Egypt, where the rains could be from the north and are as unwelcome as they are usually welcomed in Israel. Rather, the north wind is cold, and it corresponds to cold looks on the faces of people in a hostile environment. The downpour of water in the rains corresponds to a flood of secret defamation that occurs where people do not communicate with one another.

(5) A Nagging Wife (25:24)

24 Better to live on a corner of the roof
than share a house with a quarrelsome wife.

TYPE: INDIVIDUAL PROVERB (25:24). **25:24** This proverb is almost a verbatim repetition of 21:9. The meaning is self-evident.

---

[13]Contrary to F. Delitzsch, *The Proverbs of Solomon* (Edinburgh: T & T Clark, 1884), 2:168.

[14]For a good survey of problems and proposed solutions for this verse, see McKane, *Proverbs*, 582-83.

[15]The phrase is תְּחוֹלֵל גָּשֶׁם. This could be taken to mean that the north wind is frightful to rain and thus inhibits it, but I consider this implausible.

[16]Taking וּפָנִים נִזְעָמִים ("indignant face[s]") as the subject rather than the object.

(6) Good Water and Bad Water (25:25-26)

25Like cold water to a weary soul
is good news from a distant land.

26Like a muddied spring or a polluted well
is a righteous man who gives way to the wicked.

TYPE: THEMATIC (25:25-26). **25:25-26** These two proverbs are linked by the implied idea of drinking water. As nothing is more refreshing than good news from afar, so few things are more disappointing than for a righteous person to yield to pressures to do or assent to evil. The precise significance of "a distant land" is unclear. It may refer to good news "out of the blue," or it may describe a positive report on a consignment of goods shipped off for trade. For a thirsty traveler expecting relief, the effect of coming upon a polluted well is disbelief and disappointment, and it serves as an apt metaphor for the profound disillusionment one feels when the righteous yield to evil.

(7) Sweets for the Body and Sweets for the Mind (25:27)

27It is not good to eat too much honey,
nor is it honorable to seek one's own honor.

TYPE: INDIVIDUAL PROVERB (25:27). **25:27** Verse 27 closes off the first major division. The Hebrew of v. 27b is difficult: "The seeking of their glory is glory."[17] With minor emending, however, it can be translated, "But seeking out difficult things is glorious."[18] While this creates a surprising response to line *a*, it looks back to v. 2 in the same way that line *a* looks back to v. 16. The chiastic structure of the whole is as follows: glory (v. 2)/ honey (v. 16)/honey (v. 27a)/glory (v. 27b).[19] While an excess of sweets does no one good, the wise never can get enough of unraveling the riddles of the sages.

8. Portrait of a Fool (25:28–26:12)

28Like a city whose walls are broken down
is a man who lacks self-control.

---

[17]The text is וְחֵקֶר כְּבֹדָם כָּבוֹד. It is not clear to me how the NIV arrived at its reading. A. A. Macintosh ("A Note on Proverbs XXV 27," *VT* 20 [1970]: 112-14) suggests the words כבדם כבוד be read כבד מכבד, with מכבד read as a hophal participle, "weighed down." Thus, "He who seeks glory will be distressed."

[18]Reading וְחֵקֶר כְּבֵדִים כָּבוֹד. See G. E. Bryce, "Another Wisdom 'Book' in Proverbs," *JBL* 91 (1972): 145-57. The word כְּבֵדִים is here short for דְּבָרִים כְּבֵדִים ("difficult things").

[19]Ibid., 153. More precisely the Hebrew chiasmus shows the following word pairs:

כבד ″ חקר (v. 2) and חקר ″ כבד (v. 27b)
דבש ″ אכל (v. 16a) and אכל ″ דבש (v. 27a).

1Like snow in summer or rain in harvest,
honor is not fitting for a fool.
2Like a fluttering sparrow or a darting swallow,
an undeserved curse does not come to rest.
3A whip for the horse, a halter for the donkey,
and a rod for the backs of fools!
4Do not answer a fool according to his folly,
or you will be like him yourself.
5Answer a fool according to his folly,
or he will be wise in his own eyes.
6Like cutting off one's feet or drinking violence
is the sending of a message by the hand of a fool.
7Like a lame man's legs that hang limp
is a proverb in the mouth of a fool.
8Like tying a stone in a sling
is the giving of honor to a fool.
9Like a thornbush in a drunkard's hand
is a proverb in the mouth of a fool.
10Like an archer who wounds at random
is he who hires a fool or any passer-by.
11As a dog returns to its vomit,
so a fool repeats his folly.
12Do you see a man wise in his own eyes?
There is more hope for a fool than for him.

TYPE: THEMATIC, CATCHWORD (25:28–26:12). These verses describe the fool in all his destructiveness. The word for "fool" is something of a catchword here as well, as indicated by its frequent repetition.[20]

25:28–26:2 The collection begins with three similes (25:28–26:2)[21] on foolish actions. Lack of self-control makes one vulnerable (25:28); the one who cannot maintain such control will always be outmaneuvered by an adversary who keeps emotions in check. Giving honor to a fool is not only inappropriate (snow in summer) but destructive (rain in harvest), as the similes imply (26:1), since he may think of himself as competent and actually try to take charge. Reproaches and curses from a fool are ineffective[22] since people are aware of the source (26:2).

---

[20]The word כְּסִיל is used in 26:1,3,4,5,6,7,8,9,10,11,12. Also note that the description אִישׁ אֲשֶׁר עֵין מַעְצָר לְרוּחוֹ ("a man without control in his spirit," 25:28) is echoed by the phrase אִישׁ חָכָם בְּעֵינָיו ("a man wise in his own eyes") in 26:12.

[21]Only 26:1-2 actually begins with כְּ ("like"), but 25:28 is also a comparison.

[22]One should read the *kethiv* לֹא ("not") rather than the *qere* לוֹ ("to him") since the negative is required by the metaphor.

26:3-5 These verses tell how one should speak to a fool. Verse 3 implies that all speech is ineffective; fools are not amenable to wise counsel. Like brute animals, force is the only language they understand. Verses 4-5 obviously belong together; they illustrate the principle that aphorisms are by nature generalizations that do not give the exhaustive truth on a given subject and that each proverb must be read in the context of the whole corpus of wisdom. To "answer a fool according to his folly" is to engage in the same emotional invective that the fool uses. On the one hand, one should not deal with a fool on his own terms lest the imitation of folly become habitual. On the other hand, one *must* sometimes answer fools in the words they understand in order to reprimand them effectively.

26:6-10 The similes in vv. 6-10 all concern how one should deal with a fool. They are arranged in chiastic fashion as follows:

A: Committing important business to a fool (v. 6)
  B: A proverb in a fool's mouth (v. 7)
    C. Honoring a fool (v. 8)
  B′: A proverb in a fool's mouth (v. 9[23])
A′: Committing important business to a fool (v. 10)

To cut off one's legs (v. 6) is to make it impossible to move; in the same way, to send a message by a fool is to insure that it will not get through. The metaphor of "drinking violence" is harsh though intelligible. A suggested alternative is that the Hebrew text originally meant "baring his bottom."[24] To do such a thing would be to humiliate oneself (see 2 Sam 10:4). Thus, one who sends an important message by a fool both guarantees that his message will not get through (cutting off the feet) and exposes himself to public mockery as well for having made such a poor choice for an agent (exposing the bottom).

Verses 7 and 9 imply that no one will (or should) take a fool's words seriously. Even if the proverb he speaks is true, he invalidates its effects by his own character. Limp, paralyzed legs[25] imply ineffectiveness; and a thorn in a drunkard's[26] hand implies lack of response on the hearer's part.

---

[23]Note repetition of וּמָשָׁל בְּפִי כְסִילִים ("a proverb in a fool's mouth") with v. 7.

[24]Reading חָמֵס שֵׁתוֹ. Note that חמס means "to be stripped" (niphal stem) in Jer 13:22 in accordance with the parallel. This suggestion was first made by N. H. Tur Sinai, *The Book of Job* (Jerusalem: Kiryat-Seper, 1957), 259-60. McKane considers this emendation "far-fetched," but he fails to see that it could be taken as a metaphor of humiliation separately from the prior metaphor of cutting off the feet. Instead, McKane sees the baring of the bottom as a consequence of cutting off of feet, which is indeed impossible. If the emendation is valid, this may be a case of deliberate scribal alteration of the text.

[25]It is not clear whether the peculiar form דַּלְיוּ is from דלה or דלל, but in either case it means "dangle." There may be a conceptual link between this and the cutting off of the feet in v. 6.

[26]Note the wordplay between שִׁכּוֹר ("drunkard") here and שֹׂכֵר ("hiring") in v. 10.

Alternatively, the drunkard may refer to the fool himself; he seizes a proverb to make use of it without realizing that it applies directly to him.

Verse 8, like v. 1, reveals that honoring a fool is absurd and dangerous. The stone tied in the sling may swing back around and hit the slinger (i.e., the one who honored the fool).

The Hebrew of v. 10 is almost unintelligible and thus subject to numerous interpretations, all of which are hypothetical.[27] As the NIV has it, the verse reaffirms that one should not commit important tasks to fools (as in v. 6). Notwithstanding all the difficulties of the text, that does seem to be the main point.

26:11-12 The meaning of v. 11 is self-evident: fools do not learn from their mistakes. Verse 12 is an apt closure to this section. The quintessential fool is the one who is so sure he has all the facts of life straight that he refuses to submit to wisdom for instruction and is far worse off than the run-of-the-mill fool.

9. Portrait of a Sluggard (26:13-16)

[13]The sluggard says, "There is a lion in the road,
a fierce lion roaming the streets!"

[14]As a door turns on its hinges,
so a sluggard turns on his bed.

[15]The sluggard buries his hand in the dish;
he is too lazy to bring it back to his mouth.

[16]The sluggard is wiser in his own eyes
than seven men who answer discreetly.

TYPE: THEMATIC (26:13-16). **26:13-16** Like 22:13, 26:13 teaches that lazy people can come up with outrageous excuses to avoid work. Verse 14 implies that the sluggard's only movement is confined to his bed, which he never leaves. Verse 15, like 19:24, portrays laziness as taken to ludicrous lengths. Verse 16 points out the slothful person's conceit; he thinks that avoiding work is the surest proof of his wisdom.[28]

10. Portrait of a Busybody (26:17-22)

[17]Like one who seizes a dog by the ears
is a passer-by who meddles in a quarrel not his own.

[18]Like a madman shooting
firebrands or deadly arrows

---

[27]Several emendations are possible, but there are too many variables for any one to be convincing. See, for example, the various suggestions cataloged in Toy, *Proverbs*, 476; Delitzsch, *Proverbs* 2:184-87; and the suggestion of Scott, *Proverbs*, 157.

[28]"Seven" is a general number and has no special significance here.

[19]is a man who deceives his neighbor
and says, "I was only joking!"

[20]Without wood a fire goes out;
without gossip a quarrel dies down.

[21]As charcoal to embers and as wood to fire,
so is a quarrelsome man for kindling strife.

[22]The words of a gossip are like choice morsels;
they go down to a man's inmost parts.

TYPE: THEMATIC (26:17-22). These proverbs discuss anyone who involves himself or herself in the affairs of others, who spreads gossip, or is a general source of mischief. Metaphors of violence and destruction dominate this text since these qualities characterize the aftereffects of the busybody.

26:17 Verse 17 could be translated, "Like one who seizes the ears of a passing dog is the one who meddles."[29] Busybodies cannot resist the temptation to inject themselves into private disputes, and they have no excuse for being surprised at the violent outbursts that are sure to follow.

26:18-19 Verses 18-19 could be taken to condemn any kind of antics (such as modern practical jokes played on a groom on his wedding day). While practical jokes can be destructive and hurtful, the larger context here implies that such may not be precisely the nature of the deceit implied here. Rather, this is a person who enjoys gossiping about or tampering with the affairs of other people. Such a person will purposefully confuse others and engage in a kind of social disinformation. When called to account, he or she will treat the whole thing as a game and be oblivious to all the hurt such actions created.

26:20-22 Verses 20-21 describe the slanderer as the fuel that maintains quarrels. In the absence of such a person,[30] old hurts can be set aside, and discord can die a natural death. Even so, we often find a juicy tidbit of defamation irresistible. Verse 22 is a direct warning to the reader. Gossip makes its way to the innermost being of the hearer; that is, it corrupts the soul.

11. Portrait of a Liar (26:23-28)

[23]Like a coating of glaze over earthenware
are fervent lips with an evil heart.

[24]A malicious man disguises himself with his lips,
but in his heart he harbors deceit.

---

[29]Moving the *athnach* to עֹבֵר.

[30]The word נִרְגָּן describes the individual slanderer and not "gossip" as an abstract concept, contrary to the NIV.

[25]Though his speech is charming, do not believe him,
for seven abominations fill his heart.
[26]His malice may be concealed by deception,
but his wickedness will be exposed in the assembly.
[27]If a man digs a pit, he will fall into it;
if a man rolls a stone, it will roll back on him.
[28]A lying tongue hates those it hurts,
and a flattering mouth works ruin.

TYPE: THEMATIC (26:23-28). This final "portrait" rounds off the larger collection of 25:28–26:28. The fool, the meddler, and the liar are the three agents of social discord.

26:23 The simile of v. 23 introduces the reader to the liar. The text here is difficult, but the NIV probably is right to emend it to read, "Like a coating of glaze" instead of the Hebrew "silver of dross."[31] On the other hand, one probably should read "smooth lips" instead of "fervent lips."[32] The point is that the congenial lips of the liar are but a pretty coating on a cheap interior. The smoothness of the liar's lips corresponds to the smoothness of a glaze on pottery.

26:24-26 Verses 24-26 appear to be an expansion and explanation of the simile in v. 23. The words are phony, so do not believe them. The "assembly" in v. 26 probably is not a judicial proceeding but society at large. Sooner or later everyone will know the fool is a liar.

26:27 Verse 27 is a common Old Testament proverb that those who lay traps for others will themselves be caught in their snares (see Pss 7:15; 9:15; Eccl 10:8). Here, however, it has special application to the liar whose ways and character are laid bare before the whole community.

26:28 Verse 28 develops an idea already begun in v. 26, that lying is an act of hatred. In one way or another, lies destroy those whom they deceive.[33] Therefore the liar despises not only the truth but his victims as well.

12. Boasting and Praise (27:1-2)

[1]Do not boast about tomorrow,
for you do not know what a day may bring forth.
[2]Let another praise you, and not your own mouth;
someone else, and not your own lips.

---

[31]Reading כספסגים ("like glazes") instead of the Masoretic כֶּסֶף סִיגִים ("silver of dross") with BHS note *a*. The words *spsg* (Ugaritic) and *zapzagya* (Hittite) are attested to mean "glaze." See G. R. Driver, "Problems in the Hebrew Text of Proverbs," *Bib* 32 (1951): 191.

[32]Reading חֲלָקִים ("smooth") instead of דֹּלְקִים ("flaming"). The LXX has λεῖα ("smooth").

[33]The word דַּכָּיו ("his oppressed ones") appears awkward and has provoked a great deal of discussion (cf. McKane, *Proverbs*, 605-6, and Toy, *Proverbs*, 481), but no proposals are convincing. Perhaps "his victims" would be a valid translation here.

TYPE: CATCHWORD (27:1-2). **27:1-2** These two proverbs both begin with the same verbal root.[34] Behind both is the contrast between arrogance and humility. One should neither be too certain of the future or of one's own gifts. The two verses together espouse an attitude of humility before the sovereignty of God and the judgment of the community.

13. Unbearable Personalities (27:3-4)

3Stone is heavy and sand a burden,
but provocation by a fool is heavier than both.

4Anger is cruel and fury overwhelming,
but who can stand before jealousy?

TYPE: THEMATIC, GRAMMATICAL PARALLEL (27:3-4). **27:3-4** These two proverbs strongly parallel each other in the Hebrew.[35] Both concern behavior that cannot be endured. The provocation of the fool is not precisely defined; it could be, for example, obnoxious behavior or incompetence on the job. In v. 4 jealousy is portrayed as a kind of intensification of anger. Dealing with ordinary ire is hard enough, but a fury that stems from jealousy is not open to reason or moderation.

14. Honest Friendship (27:5-6)

5Better is open rebuke
than hidden love.

6Wounds from a friend can be trusted,
but an enemy multiplies kisses.

TYPE: THEMATIC CATCHWORD (27:5-6). **27:5-6** A true friend gives time and attention (v. 5) but is not always flattering (v. 6). In addition to a common catchword,[36] both verses concern the nature of genuine friendship. Verse 5 especially points to the need for communication and interaction among people; few things are worse than being ignored, and the studied avoidance of honest contact destroys any relationship.

Verse 6 is somewhat different.[37] Whereas v. 5 concerns stifled or hidden emotions, v. 6 contrasts genuine and phony expressions of friendship.

---

[34]The words are אַל־תִּתְהַלֵּל ("do not boast") and יְהַלֶּלְךָ ("let him praise you"), both from the root הלל.

[35]The order of both is: first comparison (predicate + subject) + וְ + second comparison (predicate + subject) + lesson (subject + verb + prepositional phrase).

[36]Both contain the root אהב ("love").

[37]The NIV translation is valid here. Despite lengthy discussions of alternative interpretations or an emendation for נַעְתָּרוֹת, the traditional understanding of it as "abundant" is still the most persuasive (see Delitzsch, *Proverbs* 2:201-2, and McKane, *Proverbs*, 610-11). Also in context with v. 5, the NIV is right to read v. 6 as a kind of implied better saying, although the text literally only says, "The wounds of a friend are faithful, and the kisses of an enemy are abundant."

One must distinguish between salutary rebukes that spring from honest love and hollow displays of affection where no true love exists. The two verses together advise that in any relationship, an open exchange of honest and caring communication is essential.

15. Real Friends, Close at Hand (27:7-10)

7He who is full loathes honey,
but to the hungry even what is bitter tastes sweet.

8Like a bird that strays from its nest
is a man who strays from his home.

9Perfume and incense bring joy to the heart,
and the pleasantness of one's friend springs from his earnest counsel.

10Do not forsake your friend and the friend of your father,
and do not go to your brother's house when disaster strikes you—
better a neighbor nearby than a brother far away.

TYPE: PARALLEL (27:7-10). The four verses are arranged in parallel (*A B A B*) and generally concern forming significant friendships. Verses 7 and 9 both deal with pleasant substances (honey, incense, oil)[38] and the paradox that what may seem bitter (bitter food or direct advice) can actually be sweet. Verse 8 decries the man who wanders far from home while v. 10 urges the reader to cultivate neighbors as friends to whom one can go in time of crisis.

27:7 On the surface v. 7 only says that any food tastes good if you are hungry enough. As in the English "One man's meat is another man's poison," however, an aphorism about food can be applied to a whole range of situations. Verse 9 asserts that parties[39] are fun for a while, but everyone needs an earnest friend.[40] It may be that the "honey" of v. 7 is in context a casual friend who is fun but of no help in a crisis, whereas the "bitter" is the more staid decorum of the wise; they are not great party animals but offer solid support in hard times, when one is "hungry."

27:8,10 Verse 8 to some degree contrasts with v. 10; the former counsels the reader to stay close to home, which presumably refers to family and not to a house, while the latter addresses someone who is far from family support. The "brother" in v. 10 is a close relative, one to whom people naturally turn in difficult times. Normally the close family

---

[38]Note also מָתוֹק ("sweet") in v. 7 and מֶתֶק ("sweetness") in v. 9, as well as the repetition of נֶפֶשׁ ("soul," "appetite") in these two verses.

[39]Understanding "perfume and incense," luxurious toiletries likely to be used on festive occasions, by metonomy to refer to the occasions themselves. Also יְשַׂמַּח־לֵב ("rejoices the heart") can describe an attitude of mirth or celebration (e.g., Eccl 2:10).

[40]No emendation of וּמֶתֶק רֵעֵהוּ מֵעֲצַת־נָפֶשׁ (lit., "and the sweetness of his friend is from counsel of soul") is persuasive; the NIV should be followed.

identity of the Israelites would dictate that one go to a relative for help, and this verse is surprising for appearing to go against custom here. Line *c* helps to clarify the matter: the brother may be too distant (either geographically or emotionally) to be of help. The four verses together teach that one should seek solid, meaningful relationships among one's neighbors and family, but not focus on people who are fun but lack substance and not turn exclusively to relatives, however distant they may be.

16. Fatherly Advice (27:11-27)

11Be wise, my son, and bring joy to my heart;
then I can answer anyone who treats me with contempt.

12The prudent see danger and take refuge,
but the simple keep going and suffer for it.

13Take the garment of one who puts up security for a stranger;
hold it in pledge if he does it for a wayward woman.

14If a man loudly blesses his neighbor early in the morning,
it will be taken as a curse.

15A quarrelsome wife is like
a constant dripping on a rainy day;
16restraining her is like restraining the wind
or grasping oil with the hand.

17As iron sharpens iron,
so one man sharpens another.

18He who tends a fig tree will eat its fruit,
and he who looks after his master will be honored.

19As water reflects a face,
so a man's heart reflects the man.

20Death and Destruction are never satisfied,
and neither are the eyes of man.

21The crucible for silver and the furnace for gold,
but man is tested by the praise he receives.

22Though you grind a fool in a mortar,
grinding him like grain with a pestle,
you will not remove his folly from him.

23Be sure you know the condition of your flocks,
give careful attention to your herds;
24for riches do not endure forever,
and a crown is not secure for all generations.
25When the hay is removed and new growth appears
and the grass from the hills is gathered in,
26the lambs will provide you with clothing,
and the goats with the price of a field.

[27]You will have plenty of goats' milk
to feed you and your family
and to nourish your servant girls.

TYPE: THEMATIC (27:11-27). Verse 11 is a fatherly plea for the son to heed wisdom similar to those that begin lengthy exhortations in Prov 1–9. If v. 11 does form a heading to a series of paternal teachings here (and is not just an interjection with no following material), one may ask how much of what follows may be placed under this heading. It is perhaps significant that vv. 12-27 for the most part concern matters about which a father might naturally teach his son: sound business practices and skills in dealing with men in the community.

27:11 In v. 11 the father wants to be able to "answer anyone who treats me with contempt." In other words, his son will either publicly disgrace the father or enable him to stand proudly before even his enemies.

27:12-13 Verses 12-13 are the first of a series of teachings on business and fiscal well-being (vv. 12-13,15-16,18,20,23-27). Verse 12 is similar to 22:3; here the danger may be especially economic. The wise avoid impulsive and unsound business ventures. Verse 13 is almost identical to 20:16. A young man should not risk his wealth for the sake of his irresponsible companions.

27:14 Verse 14 is the first of several proverbs on dealing with men in the community (vv. 14,17,19,21-22). The meaning of v. 14 is obvious; beneath the surface is a warning that it is possible to be well-meaning but regarded as obnoxious if social sensitivity is lacking.

27:15-16 Verse 15, like 19:13b, compares a contentious woman to the aggravation of a steady drip. I have argued that the woman in 19:13 is not just a nagging woman but a woman who quarrels with people generally and is the negative counterpart to the prudent wife of 19:14.[41] She destroys the social and financial well-being of the home. The same interpretation applies here as well, but v. 16 is extremely difficult in the Hebrew.[42] The NIV rendition, although supported by other modern translations, is impossible. First, v. 16a seems to state that her husband cannot "restrain" her from her nagging, but the verb here does not mean that.[43] Second, v. 16b cannot possibly mean "or grasping oil with the hand."[44]

---

[41]See commentary above.

[42]The text simply may be corrupt. The LXX apparently reads צָפוֹן ("north wind") here and שֵׁם ("name") instead of שֶׁמֶן and thus has a radically different interpretation: "The north wind is a hard wind, but by name it is called 'of the right hand' [lucky]."

[43]The word צפן means to "treasure" or "hide" something, not to "restrain" it. D. Kidner (*Proverbs*, [Downers Grove: InterVarsity, 1964], 167) contends that it can mean "restrain," but the text he cites as a comparison (Hos 13:12) has nothing to do with holding back something that wants to get away.

[44]The "right hand" cannot be the subject of יִקְרָא ("he will call," "meet") since יְמִינוֹ is feminine; anyway, יִקְרָא does not mean "to grasp." Some take it to mean, "Oil meets the right

A better rendering of v. 16 might be, "He who keeps her[45] keeps wind, and he will call [her][46] the perfume[47] of his right hand."[48] The man does not try to "restrain" her in the sense of trying to get her to stop nagging him. Rather, he tries to treasure someone who can do him no good or, alternatively, he tries to keep her in the house and outside of society so that he will not suffer further embarrassment from her behavior. The phrase "the perfume of the right hand" is apparently an idiom, and its meaning can only be a matter of speculation. I suspect, however, that it means "high-priced perfume" on the analogy of Benjamin's name ("son of the right hand"), meaning that he was precious to Jacob or had been acquired at a high price (Rachel's death). Calling the wife "high-priced perfume" would mean that she serves little useful purpose, perhaps loves luxury, but costs her husband a great deal. Simply put, a woman who is "high-priced perfume" is the antithesis of the productive wife of Prov 31.

27:17 Verse 17 explains that people must not shy away from interaction with their peers since it is an education in itself. The "sharpening" can occur in any area in which people are engaged, be it business, intellectual, or physical competition.

27:18 In v. 18 tending a tree and eating its fruit is the analogy, and honor gained by being faithful about one's superior's business is the main lesson. This proverb straddles both areas of economic prosperity and learning to deal with others. It need not be taken as a proverb just for slaves since free people routinely spoke to and of their superiors as "my lord."

27:19 Verse 19 is subject to a wide range of interpretations. The Hebrew could be more literally rendered, "Like the water, the face to the face, so the heart of the man to the man." Some take it to mean that one sees one's inner self reflected in the face of a companion;[49] and others, that one comes to self-understanding by introspection.[50] Rather, the point is that as there is an exact correspondence between the original and its reflection in still water, even so the heart of the man (his mind, inner self,

---

hand," and thus, "The right hand grasps oil." If anything, this is grasping at straws. Also the NIV treats the perfect צָפַן as having the same syntactical function as the imperfect יִקְרָא; it is more likely that some shift in the discourse is implied. If so, we do not have in line *b* another metaphor for trying to "hide" the quarrelsome woman but a new line of thought entirely. Finally, one might note that while it is impossible to hide the wind, it is in fact possible to hold oil in the hand (see Lev 14:15-16).

[45]It is perhaps possible to have a plural participle (צֹפְנֶיהָ) as subject of a singular predicate (צָפַן) (cf. 3:18). But this does seem odd and may indicate that the text is corrupt.

[46]With שְׁמָהּ ("her name") understood as implied. It is possible that the word was actually in the text but fell out due to similarity to שֶׁמֶן.

[47]Or "oil." שֶׁמֶן can have either meaning.

[48]Cf. Vg, *et oleum dexterae suae vocabit.*

[49]E.g., Delitzsch, *Proverbs* 2:214-15.

[50]McKane, *Proverbs*, 616.

character) corresponds to the man himself (i.e., the whole person). In other words, people have a basic consistency to them. Those who have integrity will maintain it in their inner and outer lives, and those who are perverse will be thoroughly perverted. The point is that one should learn how to read people and thus learn whom to trust.

27:20 As in v. 18 the voracious appetite of death in v. 20 is the analogy and not the main point. Eyes that are not satisfied are eyes that are covetous, and the implied warning is to beware of such greed in self and others.

27:21 Verse 21 should be interpreted, "A crucible is for silver and a smelter is for gold, but as for a man, go by his reputation."[51] This, like v. 19, warns the "son" of v. 11 to evaluate men carefully. One of the quickest and safest means of assessing someone's character is his reputation with those who already know him.

27:22 Verse 22 follows here because of the similarity of the imagery (the crucible [v. 21] and the mortar and pestle [v. 22]). The message of this proverb is self-evident: fools and their folly are inseparable. The implication is that one should choose companions wisely.

27:23-27 Verses 23-27 give the most basic of economic lessons: take care of your business, and it will take care of you. The language is highly poetic in the tradition of ancient poets who celebrated the pastoral life (e.g., Virgil). Verse 27 need not be taken to imply that goat's milk will be the staple of everyone's diet; after v. 26b the intent is rather that one can sell surplus milk or barter it for other kinds of food. It might be loosely rendered, "The milk of your goats [alone] will be enough [to provide] your food and food for your household and sustenance for your serving girls." In other words, you will have more than enough to meet all of your family's needs.

17. A Life of Fear (28:1)

[1]The wicked man flees though no one pursues,
but the righteous are as bold as a lion.

TYPE: INDIVIDUAL PROVERB (28:1). **28:1** A guilty conscience and awareness that many enemies have been made leaves the wicked person perpetually anxious and paranoid.

18. The Distortions Evil Causes (28:2)

[2]When a country is rebellious, it has many rulers,
but a man of understanding and knowledge maintains order.

---

[51]This may be the intent of the NIV, "but man is tested by the praise he receives." The phrase, לְפִי מַהֲלָלוֹ means, "according to his praise," and refers to the means of evaluating a person. Notwithstanding the fact that מַהֲלָל is a hapax legomenon, it evidently refers to praise and by extension reputation.

TYPE: INDIVIDUAL PROVERB (28:2). **28:2** This verse contrasts the stability of governance under a capable person with the frequent changes of government observed in unstable societies.[52]

19. Oppression, Keeping in the Right Way, and the Law (28:3-11)

3A ruler who oppresses the poor
is like a driving rain that leaves no crops.
4Those who forsake the law praise the wicked,
but those who keep the law resist them.
5Evil men do not understand justice,
but those who seek the LORD understand it fully.
6Better a poor man whose walk is blameless
than a rich man whose ways are perverse.
7He who keeps the law is a discerning son,
but a companion of gluttons disgraces his father.
8He who increases his wealth by exorbitant interest
amasses it for another, who will be kind to the poor.
9If anyone turns a deaf ear to the law,
even his prayers are detestable.
10He who leads the upright along an evil path
will fall into his own trap,
but the blameless will receive a good inheritance.
11A rich man may be wise in his own eyes,
but a poor man who has discernment sees through him.

TYPE: PARALLEL (28:3-11). These verses set up a parallel with an extra verse on the law in the middle of the parallel, as follows:

A: Oppression of the poor (v. 3)
  B: The law (v. 4)
    C: Understanding or not understanding justice (v. 5)
      D: Poor can be better than rich (v. 6)
  B: The law (v. 7)
A: Oppression of the poor (v. 8)
  B: The law (v. 9)
    C: The right path (v. 10)
      D: Poor can be smarter than rich (v. 11)

[52]Although asyndeton (omission of conjunctions that ordinarily connect words or clauses) is possible, the phrase מֵבִין יֹדֵעַ is difficult. Also the preposition ב in וּבְאָדָם ("and in a man") is hard to reckon with (it is apparently deleted by the NIV). The LXX is quite different: δί ἁμαρτίας ἀσεβῶν κρίσεις ἐγείρονται, ἀνὴρ δὲ πανοῦργος κατασβέσει αὐτάς ("through the sins of the impious quarrels break out, but a capable man quenches them"). On this basis BHS notes *a* and *c*, as well as Driver ("Problems," 191-92), suggest emending the text in various ways. The changes are fairly radical, however, and this diminishes the probability of their validity.

28:3,8 Translated, the Hebrew of v. 3 actually says, "A poor man who oppresses," but the NIV probably is correct to emend it to "a ruler."[53] The analogy to a driving rain that destroys crops is apt; a ruler ought to nurture the rights of the poor as rain should nurture a garden, but instead he only beats them down. Verse 8 stipulates the principal means of oppression of the poor[54] by the wealthy—making loans and charging interest. It adds that those guilty of such abuses will lose all their money to generous people. Together these verses describe the effects of oppressing the poor (v. 3), the means (v. 8a), and the resulting divine judgment (v. 8b).

28:4,7,9 Verses 4,7,9 are somewhat unusual in Proverbs in that they directly speak of the law (*Torah*). In v. 4 one's attitude toward the law will determine one's evaluation of people and thus one's choice of companions. This naturally leads to the sentiment of v. 7, which by itself looks like an unusual bicolon: keeping the law is contrasted with being a companion of gluttons (one might expect something about forsaking the law in line *b*). Following the teaching of v. 4, however, the son who does not keep *tōrâ* naturally picks bad friends. In doing so, he also disgraces his father and thereby breaks down family cohesion. Verse 9 adds yet another twist: those who spurn the law will lose the companionship of God, as indicated by his rejection of their prayers. Taken together these verses teach that the law is a guide to choosing friends and maintaining sound relations with family and God.

28:5,10 Verse 5 deals with understanding or not understanding justice while v. 10 describes people who lead others into error. Verse 5b is in agreement with the central teaching of Proverbs that the fear of Yahweh is the beginning of knowledge (1:7). The profound comprehension of issues of right and wrong on the part of the just contrasts with the abysmal ignorance of the wicked. It would not be so bad, however, if the evil were merely ignorant. Unfortunately, they actively draw others into their folly (v. 10). The text promises a just resolution, however, and encourages the reader to persevere in the right.

28:6,11 Verse 6 implies that it is possible to have integrity and be poor; biblical wisdom does not assume that virtue is always monetarily rewarded. Verse 6b could be translated, "Than he who perverts [the] two ways,[55] although he be rich." If this alludes to the doctrine of the two ways, the point is that the evil call the good way bad and the bad way good. Verse 11 turns the haughty rich man into the laughingstock of the discerning poor. In this context the idea probably is that the wealthy think that their money proves they are smarter and morally superior, but the poor see that they are just more ruthless.

---

[53]Read רֹאשׁ ("head") for the MT רָשׁ ("poor"). Cf. McKane, *Proverbs*, 628-29.

[54]Both verses use the term דַּלִּים ("weak" or "poor") as the objects of oppression or help.

[55]The word דְּרָכַיִם ("two ways") is dual, not plural.

It is significant that Hebrew catchwords also link v. 5 to v. 11 and v. 6 to v. 10.[56] The passage as a whole stresses that seeking the Lord and keeping the law has its rewards despite appearances to the contrary.

20. Various Proverbs (28:12–29:27)

The remainder of the verses of "Hezekiah" are for the most part concerned with the general health of society. The text emphasizes the need for moral leadership, decries all attempts at easy money, and stresses the need to maintain the fundamental institutions of society.

(1) Good Government and Bad Government I (28:12)

12When the righteous triumph, there is great elation;
but when the wicked rise to power, men go into hiding.

TYPE: INDIVIDUAL PROVERB (28:12). **28:12** This verse appears to mean no more than that good people make themselves scarce[57] when a bad government is in power. It is intriguing, however, that the text in fact does not say a "good man"[58] hides himself but uses the word *ʾādām.* I would suggest that the meaning here and in 28:28a is not just that good people are afraid (although that is true) but that humanity itself is hard to find in the sense that institutions are dehumanized. Man as he came from the hand of God, *ʾādām* is no longer in evidence as society sinks to the level of bestiality. The proverbs that follow therefore generally contrast the operation of a degenerate society with a healthy one. When the righteous triumph,[59] similarly, more happens than open celebration. The community is glorified;[60] that is, it is closer to the creation ideal.

(2) Turning from Sin (28:13-14)

13He who conceals his sins does not prosper,
but whoever confesses and renounces them finds mercy.

14Blessed is the man who always fears the LORD,
but he who hardens his heart falls into trouble.

---

[56]In v. 5 the understanding of the seekers of Yahweh contrasts with the ignorance of the impious, and in v. 11 the poor see through the rich. Both verses emphasize the verb בין ("understand"). In v. 6 the poor maintains integrity (תֹם) while the rich perverts the two ways (דֶּרֶךְ), and in v. 10 the wicked lead others into the wrong way (דֶּרֶךְ); but those with integrity (וּתְמִימִים) are promised rewards.

[57]This is apparently the meaning of יְחֻפַּשׂ ("to be sought for") in parallel with יִסָּתֵר ("to be hidden") in 28:28. The search for an alternative meaning for יְחֻפַּשׂ, as in Driver "Problems," 191-92, is pointless.

[58]E.g., using a phrase like אִישׁ טוֹב.

[59]On the word עלץ ("to exult," "triumph over"), see A. R. Millard, "עלץ 'to Exult,'" *JTS* 26 (1975): 87-89.

[60]The word תִּפְאֶרֶת means "beauty" or "glory" and implies more than a simple celebration.

TYPE: THEMATIC (28:13-14). **28:13-14** These verses have obvious theological meaning despite the fact that "the Lord" is not found in the Hebrew of v. 14. The text almost reads like 1 John 1:9. It is perhaps noteworthy, however, that the Hebrew is not explicitly theological. Most of the verses of 28:12–29:2 relate to how good versus evil relates to the social fabric of society. A nontheological meaning may also be present. Thus those who confess their crimes and are remorseful are more likely to get the mercy of the court than those who try to the end to conceal their guilt, and the hardened criminal will be more severely treated than someone who shows fear[61] of the power of the state.

(3) Tyranny (28:15-16)

**15 Like a roaring lion or a charging bear
is a wicked man ruling over a helpless people.**

**16 A tyrannical ruler lacks judgment,
but he who hates ill-gotten gain will enjoy a long life.**

TYPE: THEMATIC (28:15-16). **28:15-16** The tyrant is compared to the lion and the bear as being both vicious and subhuman (v. 15). This judgment is reinforced in v. 16,[62] in which he is said to "lack judgment," or perhaps more specifically to be without the insights of wisdom.[63] Understanding is a fundamental human trait; to lack it is to be reduced to the animal level. The ruler who rejects such practices and thus does not degrade himself will enjoy a long life.

(4) Guilt and Innocence (28:17-18)

**17 A man tormented by the guilt of murder
will be a fugitive till death;
let no one support him.**

**18 He whose walk is blameless is kept safe,
but he whose ways are perverse will suddenly fall.**

TYPE: THEMATIC (28:17-18). **28:17-18** Verses 17-18, like vv. 13-14, may be read in a theological or social sense. Theologically, the murderer is oppressed by guilt in his conscience, and no one should seek to make him feel better about what he has done (v. 17), whereas someone with a clear conscience is free of such torments (v. 18a). Socially, the courts should punish murderers to the utmost (v. 17), but the innocent have no fear of

[61]The word מְפַחֵד ("in dread") is not a phrase normally used of the fear of Yahweh.

[62]The phrase נָגִיד חֲסַר תְּבוּנוֹת וְרַב מַעֲשַׁקּוֹת ("a ruler without insights and [having] much oppressions") is odd for having a compound subject but no predicate. Probably the simplest solution is to read יַרְבֶּה ("he increases" [hiphil of רבה]) for וְרַב. The NIV apparently follows a similar emendation.

[63]Taking חֲסַר תְּבוּנוֹת in this sense.

such retribution (v. 18a). Whether by the hand of God or of men, the wicked[64] will fall (v. 18b).[65]

(5) Prosperity by Fair Means and Foul (28:19-27)

[19]He who works his land will have abundant food,
but the one who chases fantasies will have his fill of poverty.

[20]A faithful man will be richly blessed,
but one eager to get rich will not go unpunished.

[21]To show partiality is not good—
yet a man will do wrong for a piece of bread.

[22]A stingy man is eager to get rich
and is unaware that poverty awaits him.

[23]He who rebukes a man will in the end gain more favor
than he who has a flattering tongue.

[24]He who robs his father or mother
and says, "It's not wrong"—
he is partner to him who destroys.

[25]A greedy man stirs up dissension,
but he who trusts in the LORD will prosper.

[26]He who trusts in himself is a fool,
but he who walks in wisdom is kept safe.

[27]He who gives to the poor will lack nothing,
but he who closes his eyes to them receives many curses.

TYPE: THEMATIC (28:19-27). **28:19** While not condemning possessions in themselves, Proverbs always rejects greed. It contrasts financial prudence, diligence, and generosity with the desire for quick and easy money. Greed can be manifested in unrealistic business enterprises (v. 19), accepting bribes (v. 21), ingratiating oneself with powerful people (v. 23), taking from one's parents (v. 24), and general greediness (vv. 22,25). "Fantasies" is perhaps too specific a translation in v. 19. The Hebrew only describes someone who follows "empty pursuits."[66] It could refer to idle fantasies, but it also could be unprofitable occupations or business speculations. The point of the verse is that hard work is the only way to prosperity; anything else is a waste of time. McKane observes that in this verse agri-

[64]As in v. 6, the evil man here is said to be perverted in regards to the two ways (נֶעְקַשׁ דְּרָכַיִם).

[65]It is doubtful that בְּאֶחָת ("in one") can mean "at once" or "suddenly." BHS note *b* emends to בְּשָׁחַת ("in a pit") with the Syriac. This has the value of paralleling עַד־בּוֹר ("as far as a cistern") in v. 17.

[66]The word רֵקִים applies to anything that is worthless.

culture is viewed as making "a basic contribution to the stability and health of the community."[67]

28:20 Verse 20 is like v. 19, but instead of the concrete images of working in agriculture and having food to eat, this verse contrasts the moral abstractions of "faithfulness" (devotion to duty, etc.) and being eager for wealth. Any society is in trouble when people think they can find a quick route to riches by taking shortcuts.

28:21-22 One quick route to a little easy money is by accepting a bribe to render a wrong judgment in a court case, the setting of v. 21. And yet people can be bought very cheaply indeed.[68] The full irony of those who will sell their integrity in any way for money is brought home in v. 22. They end up in poverty.

28:23 This verse speaks of another way of gaining position and thus wealth—by flattery. This contrasts with the one who speaks without regard to personal benefit, who will in the end prosper. This does not endorse tactless speech.

28:24 Defrauding parents (v. 24) is perhaps the utmost in antisocial behavior for the sake of money since no institution is more fundamental or honored in wisdom than parenthood. The language is strong. The word for "robs"[69] could be rendered "plunders." "Him who destroys" is someone who causes havoc in society.

28:25-26 Verse 25 is a general proverb that summarizes much of what has gone before. A greedy person upsets the equilibrium in society. The Hebrew here is picturesque; a greedy man is one who has a "wide throat."[70] By contrast, those who trust in Yahweh can wait for their appetites to be satisfied, cause no discord, and in fact will be satisfied. Verse 26 extends the theology of trust to one of submission to God's teaching. Those who trust in God do not lean on their own devices to keep them safe. The teaching here recalls the wise and foolish builders of Matt 7:24-27.

28:27 Verse 27 poses the apparent paradox that those who give more have more. The curses hurled down on the selfish are both theological, in that they are calls for God to avenge, and social, in that they reveal class discord in society.

(6) Good Government and Bad Government II (28:28–29:2)

28 When the wicked rise to power, people go into hiding;
but when the wicked perish, the righteous thrive.

---

[67]McKane, *Proverbs*, 631.

[68]Verse 19 states that the hard worker can have his fill of לֶחֶם ("bread"), but v. 21 states a man will sell his integrity for a mere פַּת־לֶחֶם ("piece of bread"). The implication is that integrity is valuable but selling out is always cheap.

[69]The word גּוֹזֵל is used of the violent or cruel seizure of possessions, as in Mic 2:2.

[70]רְחַב־נֶפֶשׁ.

[1]A man who remains stiff-necked after many rebukes
will suddenly be destroyed—without remedy.

[2]When the righteous thrive, the people rejoice;
when the wicked rule, the people groan.

TYPE: THEMATIC, INCLUSIO (28:28–29:2). **28:28–29:2** The verses echo 28:12.[71] When the wicked leaders of society fall, people are more likely to follow sound moral principles. By contrast, if the highest leaders in government and business are corrupt, that corruption will filter down to the lowest segment of society. Proverbs 29:1 promises that one day, by some means, the wicked in fact will fall. The implicit warning here is that one should heed rebukes when they are given. Verse 2 summarizes the whole. When society is good, society is happy; when evil rules, society is miserable.

(7) Squandering Wealth and Squandering a Nation (29:3-4)

[3]A man who loves wisdom brings joy to his father,
but a companion of prostitutes squanders his wealth.

[4]By justice a king gives a country stability,
but one who is greedy for bribes tears it down.

TYPE: PARALLEL (29:3-4). **29:3-4** This pair of proverbs creates a parallel between the son who squanders his family estate and a ruler who squanders the wealth of his nation through corruption.[72] In both cases lust or greed destroys a heritage.

(8) Beware of the Traps (29:5-6)

[5]Whoever flatters his neighbor
is spreading a net for his feet.

[6]An evil man is snared by his own sin,
but a righteous one can sing and be glad.

TYPE: THEMATIC (29:5-6). **29:5-6** The idea of the trap or snare links these proverbs together.[73] Verse 6 should be translated, "There is a snare

[71]Verse 28a, בְּקוּם רְשָׁעִים יִסָּתֵר אָדָם, is an almost verbatim repetition of v. 12b, בְּקוּם רְשָׁעִים יְחֻפַּשׂ אָדָם; and the meaning is the same.

[72]The two verses have several grammatical parallels; both have the following pattern: colon 1 (good side) = subject + modifier + imperfect verb + object // colon 2 (bad side) = conjunction + construct chain subject (composed of person + the object of his temptation) + imperfect verb + object. In both verses the temptation of the second colon is a feminine plural noun (זוֹנוֹת ["prostitutes"] and תְּרוּמוֹת ["bribes"]).

[73]Although the words are not identical, רֶשֶׁת ("net") and מוֹקֵשׁ ("snare") are semantically close.

in an evil man's iniquity,[74] but a righteous man runs on[75] and rejoices." Flattery is a trap, but it is one the righteous can see and avoid.

(9) Concern for Justice (29:7)

[7]The righteous care about justice for the poor,
but the wicked have no such concern.

TYPE: INDIVIDUAL PROVERB (29:7). **29:7** The righteous recognize the rights of the poor. Instead of "have no such concern" read "do not understand knowledge," a more literal rendition of the Hebrew of v. 7b.[76] McKane rightly compares Jer 22:15-16 and comments that the Hebrew can be understood as is.[77] To "understand knowledge" is to know right from wrong, especially in the treatment of the poor, and to know Yahweh's ways. The setting for this proverb, in conjunction with the following verses, probably is the court.

(10) Order in the Court and in Society (29:8-11)

[8]Mockers stir up a city,
but wise men turn away anger.

[9]If a wise man goes to court with a fool,
the fool rages and scoffs, and there is no peace.

[10]Bloodthirsty men hate a man of integrity
and seek to kill the upright.

[11]A fool gives full vent to his anger,
but a wise man keeps himself under control.

TYPE: PARALLEL, CATCHWORD (29:8-11). **29:8-11** Verse 7, since it concerns justice for the weak, may serve as a heading to this set of proverbs. The proverbs of this collection parallel each other as follows:

A Mockers create havoc; the wise restore order (v. 8).
  B′ The wise have decorum at court; fools do not (v. 9).
A′ Violent men hate the good; the just seek justice for them (v. 10).
  B′ The wise have self-control; fools do not (v. 11).

---

[74]The justification for the NIV, "An evil man is snared by his own sin" is unclear to me, although this is the interpretation of the Syriac. The NIV appears to translate מוֹקֵשׁ ("snare") as a hophal participle (unattested elsewhere), but the usage of the word as a noun is well known; and there is no need to resort to the Syriac.

[75]Reading יָרוּץ ("he runs"). Taking the form יָרוּן as a qal imperfect of רנן ("sing") is unusual for a geminate pattern. Cf. *BDB* s.v. רנן.

[76]The NIV rendition of לֹא־יָבִין דָּעַת is paraphrastic.

[77]McKane, *Proverbs*, 641-42.

The unity of this text is indicated by the presence of catchwords arranged in a chiastic sequence.[78]

Verses 8,10 describe how principled people try to turn society upside down. They inflame others (v. 8a) and are not averse to resorting to violence (v. 10a). The wise, however, restore order to the streets and the justice system (vv. 8b,10b). Verse 10b should be translated, "But the upright avenge him [the man of integrity who is abused]."[79] The point here, as in v. 8b, is that the just set things right.

The setting of v. 9 is the court, in which the recklessness of the fool is given full vent. In v. 11 the wise man controls himself in any confrontation with a fool. If the context is still that of v. 9, one can assume he also restores order to the courtroom and brings a case to its proper conclusion.

(11) The Throne Secured by Righteousness (29:12-14)

**12If a ruler listens to lies,
all his officials become wicked.**

**13The poor man and the oppressor have this in common:
The Lord gives sight to the eyes of both.**

**14If a king judges the poor with fairness,
his throne will always be secure.**

Type: Thematic, Inclusio (29:12-14). **29:12-14** Two proverbs on integrity in royal government sandwich a proverb on the poor and their oppressors here. In turn there is a kind of progression. A proverb that mentions wicked officials is followed by one that refers to the oppressors of the poor, which in turn is followed by a third on the need of the king to protect the poor from oppression.

A king, a president, or any chief executive officer must set a high standard and rigorously maintain it or face the consequences of corruption running rampant in his administration (v. 12). Verse 12 is much the same as 22:2. In this context the proverb should be read with an emphasis on the duty of the powerful to respect and protect the rights of the weak

---

[78]Compare חָכָם and אֱוִיל (v. 9) to חָכָם and כְּסִיל (v. 11) and אַנְשֵׁי לָצוֹן (v. 8) to אַנְשֵׁי דָמִים (v. 10). Also vv. 8,10 are fully parallel in structure: evil subject + imperfect verb + object + conjunction + good subject + imperfect verb + object, as is readily apparent when the two are set against each other.

אַנְשֵׁי לָצוֹן יָפִיחוּ קִרְיָה וַחֲכָמִים יָשִׁיבוּ אָף׃
אַנְשֵׁי דָמִים יִשְׂנְאוּ־תָם וִישָׁרִים יְבַקְשׁוּ נַפְשׁוֹ׃

[79]The NIV reads וִישָׁרִים יְבַקְשׁוּ נַפְשׁוֹ in a most unnatural sense as "and seek to kill the upright." It literally is "but the upright seek his soul." This could be translated "but the upright seek to kill him," i.e., kill the wicked, following established usage for the idiom בַּקֵּשׁ נֶפֶשׁ. It probably is better, however, to take "seek his soul" here to mean to avenge someone who has suffered injustice. Cf. the Hebrew text of Eccl 3:15 and the notes to that verse in this commentary. McKane (*Proverbs*, 637) comes to a similar conclusion.

(contrast the context of 22:2). The poor are no less created in the image of God than the rich, and they have God as their avenger should the rich fail in their duty. For this reason the security of a king's reign depends on equitably dispensing justice (v. 14).

(12) Discipline at Home and in the Nation (29:15-18)

15The rod of correction imparts wisdom,
but a child left to himself disgraces his mother.

16When the wicked thrive, so does sin,
but the righteous will see their downfall.

17Discipline your son, and he will give you peace;
he will bring delight to your soul.

18Where there is no revelation, the people cast off restraint;
but blessed is he who keeps the law.

TYPE: PARALLEL (29:15-18). **29:15-17** Discipline must be maintained at home and in society at large. In this parallel text vv. 15,17 concern the former, and vv. 16,18 concern the latter. Verses 15,17 set up a simple contrast: those who do not discipline their children suffer grievous embarrassment; those who do will be at ease[80] (able to trust their children) and delighted with the children's growth and accomplishments.[81]

Verse 16a, literally, "When the wicked increase, rebellion increases," repeats the notion that as ruthless people come to the forefront, society begins to experience widespread moral decay. Verse 16b, however, gives the assurance that those who stay in the right way will yet see the fall of evildoers. A contrast between immoral society and the moral individual is more pronounced in v. 18, which establishes the need for people to submit to the word of God. It implies that people at large may cast off restraint when free of prophetic sermons, but one can still follow the law.

29:18 Verse 18 is remarkable for being a wisdom verse that alludes to both the prophetic movement and the law. The word for "revelation" is commonly associated with the visions of the prophets[82] and stands for the importance of prophetic exhortation to the community here. Verse 18b, however, pronounces a blessing on whoever keeps the law. The teachers of wisdom did not oppose either prophecy or the law. Social harmony and restraint cannot be achieved without the exhortations of the prophets and the teaching of the law.

---

[80]The hiphil of נוח implies that the parent will be able to relax and not worry about what the child is going to do next.

[81]"Dainties for your soul" (מַעֲדַנִּים לְנַפְשֶׁךָ) is metaphoric for the joyful, legitimate pride a parent has when a child does well in life.

[82]The word חָזוֹן is used for the prophetic vision, as in Dan 8:13; Nah 1:1; Ezek 12:27; etc.

(13) Controlling the Servant and Controlling the Self (29:19-22)

[19]A servant cannot be corrected by mere words;
though he understands, he will not respond.

[20]Do you see a man who speaks in haste?
There is more hope for a fool than for him.

[21]If a man pampers his servant from youth,
he will bring grief in the end.

[22]An angry man stirs up dissension,
and a hot-tempered one commits many sins.

TYPE: PARALLEL (29:19-22). **29:19-22** Verses 19,21, on controlling one's servant, seem to have nothing to do with vv. 20,22, on self-control. The link is the issue of control and discipline with the implication being that one must give as much attention to governing one's own passions as to governing one's servants.

Verse 21b is obscure in the Hebrew;[83] the NIV appears to be following the LXX here.[84] Even so, v. 21a indicates that this proverb has something to do with failing to exercise strict control over slaves, as v. 19 obviously does. In this democratic age the idea that one should have this kind of authority over someone is perhaps offensive, but in any age workers can become undisciplined and unreliable if some kind of authority and discipline procedure is not established.

People who are quick to speak and lose their tempers are all but hopeless cases. They also cause problems wherever they go (vv. 20,22).

(14) The First Shall Be Last (29:23)

[23]A man's pride brings him low,
but a man of lowly spirit gains honor.

TYPE: INDIVIDUAL PROVERB (29:23). **29:23** The arrogant will be brought down, and the humble will be lifted up. The reversal of fortunes here recalls Jesus' saying that the first shall be last and the last first (Matt 19:30; and see Prov 30:21-23[85]).

(15) A Poor Choice for a Friend (29:24)

[24]The accomplice of a thief is his own enemy;
he is put under oath and dare not testify.

TYPE: INDIVIDUAL PROVERB (29:24). **29:24** According Lev 5:1, if someone has direct knowledge of the circumstances of a crime, hears a

---

[83]The meaning of מָנוֹן is lost.

[84]Reading ὀδυνηθήσεται ("he shall be grieved").

[85]See R. C. Van Leeuwen, "Proverbs 30:21-23," *JBL* 105 (1986): 599-610.

public call to come and give testimony about that crime, but fails to do so, then the silent witness will himself be culpable (at least before God even if his deed is unknown to the people). The call to testify is actually a curse pronounced on anyone who will not testify. This proverb, using the same word for oath or curse,[86] describes someone who has befriended a thief, becomes aware of his wrongdoing, but remains silent when he hears a call to come forward and give evidence. He has brought a curse down on his own head.

(16) Seek Deliverance from God (29:25-26)

25Fear of man will prove to be a snare,
but whoever trusts in the LORD is kept safe.

26Many seek an audience with a ruler,
but it is from the LORD that man gets justice.

TYPE: THEMATIC (29:25-26). **29:25-26** The "fear of man" (v. 25) describes any situation in which one is anxious about not offending another person. For example, someone might be afraid to oppose the unethical actions of a superior out of fear of losing a job. This verse tells the reader to do what is right and trust the outcome to Yahweh.

Verse 26 does not forbid seeking relief from injustice through the legal system, but it does state that one should place more faith in Yahweh than in human institutions. These two verses, coming near the end of so many proverbs on corruption and injustice in society, call the reader back to the reality that the Bible after all is not a book about social reform but calls for committed faith in Yahweh.

(17) The Sum of It All (29:27)

27The righteous detest the dishonest;
the wicked detest the upright.

TYPE: INDIVIDUAL PROVERB (29:27). **29:27** This proverb, a moral merismus bicolon, serves as an apt summation of the whole Hezekiah text. Righteousness and immorality are mutually exclusive. One must follow one path or the other (Jer 6:16).

---

[86] The word אָלָה has both senses because to break an oath is to come under a curse. Compare also the use of נַפְשׁוֹ with נֶפֶשׁ in Lev 5:1. The NIV rendition appears to assume that the elders already had called the witness individually before the court and put him under oath, but that is not necessarily the case. More likely, they simply issued a public call for a witness to testify with a curse pronounced on any knowledgeable witness who did not come forward.

SECTION OUTLINE

III. THE SAYINGS OF AGUR (30:1-33)
1. Title (30:1a)
2. The Limits of Human Understanding (30:1b-6)
3. Main Body (30:7-33)
(1) A Prayer of Humility (30:7-9)
(2) Respect for the Menial Worker (30:10)
(3) The Lowest Forms of Life (30:11-14)
(4) Two Sayings on Insatiable Things (30:15-16)
(5) The Fate of the Parent-Hater (30:17)
(6) A Riddle and a Clue (30:18-20)
(7) Unbearable People (30:21-23)
(8) Learn from the Animals (30:24-28)
(9) Royal Animals (30:29-31)
(10) Troublemakers Beware (30:32-33)

III. THE SAYINGS OF AGUR (30:1-33)

1. Title (30:1a)

[1]The sayings of Agur son of Jakeh—an oracle:

30:1a The words "an oracle" belong with the next section. Nothing is known of Agur son of Jakeh, but there is no reason to take this as a pseudonym (see Introduction).

2. The Limits of Human Understanding (30:1b-6)

This man declared to Ithiel,
to Ithiel and to Ucal:

[2]"I am the most ignorant of men;
I do not have a man's understanding.
[3]I have not learned wisdom,
nor have I knowledge of the Holy One.
[4]Who has gone up to heaven and come down?
Who has gathered up the wind in the hollow of his hands?
Who has wrapped up the waters in his cloak?
Who has established all the ends of the earth?
What is his name, and the name of his son?
Tell me if you know!

5“Every word of God is flawless;
he is a shield to those who take refuge in him.
6Do not add to his words,
or he will rebuke you and prove you a liar.

TYPE: WISDOM TEXT PROLOGUE (30:1b-6). **30:1b** This sections begins with two technical terms for prophetic utterances.[1] This fits well with the message of vv. 1b-6 that wisdom comes only by divine revelation. Verse 1b is, however, fraught with obscurity. The NIV rendering “to Ithiel and to Ucal” reads the MT as is.[2] It is possible that this is the intended meaning, but the LXX and Vulgate are very different, which may imply a corrupt text. Numerous emendations have been proposed. Dahood sees a different proper name behind the text and renders the line as, “The word of the man Lithiel, Lithiel and Ucal.”[3] Another alternative is, “I am weary, O God;[4] I am weary and exhausted.”[5] An even more negative translation is that of Scott: “There is no God! There is no God, and I can [not know anything].”[6] In context, “I am weary, O God; I am weary and exhausted” looks most likely since it fits well with what follows.

30:2-3 The author declares ignorance in v. 2. With the suggested reading for v. 1b above, the meaning is that he has struggled to come to an understanding of the truth, and he must confess that he has reached his limit. His self-confessed lack of wisdom (v. 3) should not be taken too literally (else this section should not be included in Proverbs), nor should it be regarded as bleak epistemological pessimism. It is rather both an acknowledgment of the limits of human understanding and a humble confession that only God is truly wise.

30:4 In a series of rhetorical questions (v. 4), he first challenges the reader to admit that no one has achieved direct understanding of the world and the truth behind the world. To “go up to heaven and come back down” is to attain and bring back direct knowledge of eternal truth. Then, with three questions that allude to the creative power of God (and human lack of that power), he implies that no one can explain the metaphysical powers

---

[1]The words are הַמַּשָּׂא (“oracle”) and נְאֻם (“a saying of”), reading the text without emendation.

[2]But the NIV’s “This man declared” is a little loose; נְאֻם הַגֶּבֶר would be more accurately rendered as “The statement of the man.”

[3]M. Dahood, *Proverbs and Northwest Semitic Philology* (Rome: Biblical Institute Press, 1963), 57. The name would mean “I, El, prevail,” or “I am strong, O El.” Dahood observes that the root *lʾy* is common in proper names in Northwest Semitic, as in the Ugaritic *aliyn* Baal (“I, Baal, prevail”).

[4]Reading לָאִיתִי אֵל.

[5]Reading the וָאֵכֶל from the root כלה, “to be finished,” “exhausted,” “dying,” for the word וְאֻכָל. The LXX has παύομαι (“I desist”). Cf. P. Franklyn, “The Sayings of Agur in Proverbs 30: Piety or Scepticism,” *ZAW* 95 (1983): 238-52.

[6]R. B. Y. Scott, *Proverbs and Ecclesiastes*, AB (Garden City: Doubleday, 1965), 175-76. He emends to *laʾ ʾitay ʾel*, an Aramaic phrase.

behind the visible creation.[7] This language recalls both Qoheleth's confessions (Eccl 7:24) and God's confrontation of Job (Job 38:8-11). Finally, he ironically demands that the reader produce such a sage if he can.

Strictly interpreted, the line "What is his name, and the name of his son?" is no more than a request for identification. The Christian interpreter, however, cannot but think of the Son of God here and recall that he came down from above to reveal the truth to his people (John 3:31-33). Also, since "God" is the only possible answer to the questions here,[8] it is striking that the text speaks of his "son."

30:5 The word of God, in contrast to human wisdom, is a reliable source of truth (v. 5). Instead of "flawless" here, one should translate with McKane that it has "stood the test."[9] In the real world of experience, people have found that God's revelation stands true. Thus God is a shield to those who flee to him. The knowledge offered here is not mere abstraction but is practical for dealing with day-to-day life.

30:6 Verse 6 is an injunction against adding to God's words similar to the injunctions found in Deut 12:32 and Rev 22:18. It is noteworthy that this text does not warn the reader not to reject or take away from divine revelation; it is more concerned that no one supplement it. This is therefore not a warning to the unbelieving interpreter but to the believer. The temptation is to improve on the text if not by actually adding new material then by interpreting it in ways that make more of a passage's teaching than is really there. It is what Paul called "going beyond what is written" (1 Cor 4:6). Such a practice is apt to make one a popular Bible teacher since people think that the teacher has profound insight into the text and can find hidden truths.[10] Sooner or later, however, such superinterpreters will be shown to be wrong (v. 6b).

3. Main Body (30:7-33)

(1) A Prayer of Humility (30:7-9)

7"Two things I ask of you, O LORD;
do not refuse me before I die:

[7]Following a Ugaritic cognate, it is possible that מִי אָסַף־רוּחַ בְּחָפְנָיו should be translated, "Who has collected the wind in his garments?" (parallel to שִׂמְלָה, "mantle") rather than "the hollow of his hands." See K. J. Cathcart, "Proverbs 30,4 and Ugaritic HPN 'Garment,'" *CBQ* 32 (1970): 418-20. Cf. the LXX.

[8]See Franklyn, "Agur," 248.

[9]W. McKane, *Proverbs*, OTL (Philadelphia: Westminster, 1970), 258. The word צְרוּפָה means "refined" (as in a smelter).

[10]In 1 Cor 4 Paul attempts to dissuade the Corinthians from setting his ministry against that of Apollos and professes that he and Apollos are examples of not going beyond what was written. The implication seems to be that those who do go beyond the simple message of the text seek to appeal to those with "itching ears" and so aggrandize themselves (cf. 1 Cor 4:6b).

[8]Keep falsehood and lies far from me;
give me neither poverty nor riches,
but give me only my daily bread.
[9]Otherwise, I may have too much and disown you
and say, 'Who is the LORD?'
Or I may become poor and steal,
and so dishonor the name of my God.

TYPE: NUMERICAL SAYING, PRAYER (30:7-9). **30:7-9** As the first numerical saying ("Two things"), this verse begins the main body of Agur. The humility of the author of this prayer is evident from its self-awareness. The author recognizes his weaknesses, both in his tendency to forget God when life is too easy and to turn in desperation away from God when life is too hard. "Before I die" apparently means "As long as I live." The "two requests" are not (1) keep lies away from me and (2) do not let me be rich or poor. Instead, "keep falsehood and lies far from me" is introductory; the two requests are (1) do not give me poverty and (2) do not give me wealth. The explanatory clauses (v. 9) are exclusively concerned with wealth and poverty and disclose the real concerns of this passage. The "falsehood and lies" of v. 8 are the deceptiveness of both wealth and poverty. The former convinces one that God is not necessary; and the latter, that either he is of no help or that his laws are impossible to keep. Verse 9 also reveals a marked fixation on the glory of God (rather than personal needs) as the prime motivation for the requests.

(2) Respect for the Menial Worker (30:10)

[10]"Do not slander a servant to his master,
or he will curse you, and you will pay for it.

TYPE: INDIVIDUAL PROVERB (30:10). **30:10** One should be hesitant to impugn a laborer to his master (or, in modern terms, to his employer). Otherwise one will be subject to verbal retaliation and be guilty of being a meddler.[11] Behind this injunction is a demand that one respect the person of the menial worker. His work relationship with his master is between the two of them; one should no more interfere here than one would interfere in a matter involving a superior or an equal.

(3) The Lowest Forms of Life (30:11-14)

[11]"There are those who curse their fathers
and do not bless their mothers;

[11]It is not clear that וְאָשָׁמְתָּ by itself can bear the meaning of the NIV "you will pay for it" (in the sense of making restitution) as opposed to meaning simply "you will be guilty." Cf. McKane, *Proverbs*, 650.

12those who are pure in their own eyes
and yet are not cleansed of their filth;
13those whose eyes are ever so haughty,
whose glances are so disdainful;
14those whose teeth are swords
and whose jaws are set with knives
to devour the poor from the earth,
the needy from among mankind.

TYPE: THEMATIC, CATCHWORD (30:11-14). **30:11-14** It is difficult to imagine persons more onerous to wisdom than those described here. This is characterization of four types of sinners: those who dishonor parents (v. 11), those who reek with moral filthiness[12] but do not have enough sense of decency to know it (v. 12), the arrogant (v. 13), and those who plunder the poor (v. 14[13]).

(4) Two Sayings on Insatiable Things (30:15-16)

15"The leech has two daughters.
'Give! Give!' they cry.

"There are three things that are never satisfied,
four that never say, 'Enough!':
16the grave, the barren womb,
land, which is never satisfied with water,
and fire, which never says, 'Enough!'

TYPE: NUMERICAL SAYING, RIDDLE (30:15-16). **30:15-16** Verse 15a, although actually a separate numerical saying from vv. 15b-16, is linked to it by the common theme of insatiability. Also the numerical pattern of the two sayings together is 2-3-4, and this also serves to hold the whole unit together. As it stands, v. 15a is simply an observational proverb in the realm of natural history: the leech has two "daughters" (the two suckers at either end of the leech's body) that always want more. It probably was used as a taunt; anyone who gained a reputation as a parasite may have heard this proverb echoing in his or her ears. Instead of adding "they cry" (not found in the Hebrew text), "Give! Give!" should be regarded as the proper names of the two "daughters."[14]

---

[12]The word צֹאָה is used of vomit (Isa 28:8) and human excrement (Isa 36:12). The metaphor is of gross iniquity.

[13]It is possible that אָדָם ("man") should be emended to אֲדָמָה ("land") in parallel with אֶרֶץ ("earth"). Dahood (*Proverbs*, 57-58) suggests that אָדָם is here a masculine form of אֲדָמָה with the same meaning.

[14]Normally one would not expect to see two imperatives (הַב הַב) used as proper names; but in the ironic setting of a proverb that probably was a taunt, this grammatical twist adds to the impact of the verse.

Verses 15b-16 comprise a riddle. Although it is fairly easy to establish in what sense each of the four things is insatiable, the real question is what might be the reason this list is here at all. What message is behind this apparently transparent text? One could take it to be a simple observation with no message or moral whatsoever,[15] but it is difficult to believe that this intriguing series of insatiable things in fact has no point to it. The most reasonable solution is that all serve as metaphors for the insatiably greedy or parasitic people. Kidner points out that the images of the grave and fire portray such persons as menacing, and the barren womb[16] and parched land[17] make them look pathetic.[18]

(5) The Fate of the Parent-Hater (30:17)

17"The eye that mocks a father,
that scorns obedience to a mother,
will be pecked out by the ravens of the valley,
will be eaten by the vultures.

TYPE: INDIVIDUAL SAYING (30:17). **30:17** This verse conspicuously looks back to v. 11 (as perhaps vv. 15-16 look back to v. 14). Following the LXX, one could read "scorns an aged mother" rather than "scorns obedience to a mother."[19] The image is especially graphic; Toy observes that birds picking out the eyes implies that the corpses lie unburied.[20] To shun parental discipline is to embark on a life characterized by lack of discipline and excessive violence, and such persons are naturally prone to die a violent death.

(6) A Riddle and a Clue (30:18-20)

18"There are three things that are too amazing for me,
four that I do not understand:
19the way of an eagle in the sky,
the way of a snake on a rock,
the way of a ship on the high seas,
and the way of a man with a maiden.

20"This is the way of an adulteress:
She eats and wipes her mouth
and says, 'I've done nothing wrong.'

15Thus C. Toy, *A Critical and Exegetical Commentary on the Book of Proverbs* (Edinburgh: T & T Clark, 1899), 529.

16It is the barrenness of the womb (עֹ֫צֶר רָ֫חַם) and not the barren woman that is portrayed as insatiable. The phrase does not imply that barren women are hysterical or impossible to satisfy.

17This image is drawn from the desert regions around Canaan that quickly soaked up whatever little rain fell on them. Obviously land can be sated with water if it is flooded.

18D. Kidner, *Proverbs* (Downers Grove: InterVarsity, 1964), 180.

19The LXX has γῆρας μητρός. Cf. BHS note *a* and McKane, *Proverbs*, 657.

20Toy, *Proverbs*, 530.

TYPE: NUMERICAL SAYING, RIDDLE (30:18-20). **30:18-20** What is there about an eagle in the sky, a snake on a rock, a ship on the sea, and a man with a young woman[21] that mystifies the author? What do these four have in common? Once again the reader is confronted with a riddle. Kidner argues that the common element of the four items of v. 19 is "easy mastery."[22] It is difficult to see, however, how a ship can be said to "master" the sea, and it is especially doubtful that this text means that a man will master a young woman (as if she were a horse or a dog). McKane argues that the "marvel and grace" of these four tie them together, but he has a problem linking the fourth to the other three.[23] More fundamentally, one does not solve the problem by saying that the four are wonderful because they are marvelous.

A better solution is that the eagle, the snake, and the ship can cross the sky, a rock, or the sea and leave no tracks. No trace of their passing through remains.[24] The link between these three and the way of a man with a young woman is in v. 20, which serves as a clue.[25] Wiping her mouth after eating means that the adulteress treats sexual liaisons the same way she does eating: she just finishes up and goes home without a care and certainly without a sense of guilt.

The marvel of the way of a man with a young woman is therefore that they can have a sexual encounter and walk away from it without a pang of conscience and perhaps even without another thought for each other. For them the encounter was no more significant than a meal, and it no more leaves an impression on their psyches than an eagle leaves a trail in the sky. It is important to recognize that this text is not saying that there are no repercussions to illicit sex, nor is it saying that the immoral couple believe that they can keep their encounter secret from God or other people. If anything, the woman of v. 20 does not care if anyone else knows about her sexual liaisons. Therefore matters of pregnancy, detection in society, and modern concerns such as venereal disease do not enter this discussion. It is the attitude of the couple, their moral indifference, that astounds the writer. How can two people involve themselves in something as intimate as sexual union and then think nothing of it.

(7) Unbearable People (30:21-23)

[21]"Under three things the earth trembles,
under four it cannot bear up:

---

[21]The word translated "maiden" is עַלְמָה, a young woman who may or may not be married and may or may not be a virgin. The ambiguity of the word is significant for Isa 7:14, but here עַלְמָה is simply "young woman."

[22]Kidner, *Proverbs*, 180.

[23]McKane, *Proverbs*, 657-58.

[24]Cf. Wisdom of Solomon 5:10-11.

[25]It is bound to the previous section by the catchword דֶּרֶךְ ("way").

22 a servant who becomes king,
a fool who is full of food,
23 an unloved woman who is married,
and a maidservant who displaces her mistress.

TYPE: NUMERICAL SAYING (30:21-23). **30:21-23** Here we are confronted with no mystery, only with four types of people we could well do without. The structure of vv. 22-23 contains both chiasmus and parallelism:

A: *Male* servant becomes king.
B: *Male* fool is sated with food.
B′: *Female* is deprived of love.
A′: *Female* servant becomes mistress.

A servant who gains authority over others has neither the training nor disposition to rule well. A well-fed fool is insufferable; and a woman desperate for love, however sad her plight may be, is a torment to all around her.

(8) Learn from the Animals (30:24-28)

24 "Four things on earth are small,
yet they are extremely wise:
25 Ants are creatures of little strength,
yet they store up their food in the summer;
26 coneys are creatures of little power,
yet they make their home in the crags;
27 locusts have no king,
yet they advance together in ranks;
28 a lizard can be caught with the hand,
yet it is found in kings' palaces.

TYPE: NUMERICAL SAYING (30:24-28). **30:24-28** The text describes the four animals as small, weak, lacking in authority structure, or easily caught in order to emphasize their frailty relative to humans. Despite their weaknesses, however, they survive and provide four distinct lessons in survival. The lesson of the ant is to provide for bad times during good times; the lesson of the coney is to provide for personal security; the lesson of the locust is to cooperate.[26] The lesson of the lizard, which is slightly more difficult to extract, is that one can succeed despite disadvantages. The lizard is relatively defenseless; lacking in significant claws or teeth as it is, even a child can grab it without fear. Even so, it can attain residence in a palace. This, to be sure, has no meaning to a lizard; but in the literary (not scientific) context of the proverb, living in a royal palace implies having made it to the highest circles of society.

---

[26]The phrase חֹצֵץ כֻּלּוֹ is difficult, but the NIV rendition "they advance together in ranks" is appropriate. The LXX has εὐτάκτως ("in good order"). BHS note *a* emends to חָלֻץ ("ready for battle"), but this is not necessary since the Hebrew can be taken in the sense of the LXX. Cf. D. W. Thomas, "Notes on Some Passages in the Book of Proverbs," *VTS iii* (1955): 276.

(9) Royal Animals (30:29-31)

29"There are three things that are stately in their stride,
four that move with stately bearing:
30a lion, mighty among beasts,
who retreats before nothing;
31a strutting rooster, a he-goat,
and a king with his army around him.

TYPE: NUMERICAL SAYING (30:29-31). **30:29-31** Insomuch as Proverbs is concerned with human affairs rather than natural history, the focus of this text is on the king, and the three animals serve as analogies. Verse 31 is difficult in the Hebrew.[27] Unless some irony is intended (which, considering the difficulty of the text, is impossible to demonstrate), the message is that there is a grandeur to a king as he exercises his authority, and that grandeur ought to be respected.

(10) Troublemakers Beware (30:32-33)

32"If you have played the fool and exalted yourself,
or if you have planned evil,
clap your hand over your mouth!
33For as churning the milk produces butter,
and as twisting the nose produces blood,
so stirring up anger produces strife."

TYPE: ADMONITION (30:32-33). **30:32-33** Those who make trouble get into trouble. In v. 33 the author uses a neat device to get this point across. On the surface we have two similes for inevitability—churning milk makes butter, and twisting the nose produces blood. Hidden in the second simile, however, is the warning that those who make trouble are liable to get punched in the nose! Also the "strife" that follows trouble-making may not just be discord but also lawsuits.[28]

---

[27]The translation "rooster" follows the LXX ἀλέκτωρ ἐμπεριπατῶν θηλείαις εὔψυχος ("a rooster walking about bravely among the females [hens]"). The Hebrew זַרְזִיר מָתְנַיִם seems to mean "girt of loins" (זַרְזִיר is a hapax legomenon), however; the Vg combines the two ideas as *gallus succinctus lumbos*, "a rooster with girded loins." Aside from rooster, alternative interpretations include greyhound, war horse, and starling. Cf. F. Delitzsch, *The Proverbs of Solomon* (Edinburgh: T & T Clark, 1884), 2:306-9, and McKane, *Proverbs*, 662-63. Also the word אַלְקוּם ("band of soldiers" according to *BDB*) is a hapax legomenon and has been interpreted and emended in various ways. The LXX has βασιλεὺς δημηγορῶν ἐν ἔθνει ("a king making an address among a people"). G. R. Driver ("Problems in the Hebrew Text of Proverbs," *Bib* 32 [1951]: 173-97) emends to עָמוֹ לֹא־קָם ("against whom there is none rising up"). I would suggest that the text is correct as it is but that we cannot be certain about the meanings of the phrases in question. Probably זַרְזִיר מָתְנַיִם was the common name of some animal, and I am inclined to Delitzsch's solution that it is a kind of hunting dog; also, in the absence of other evidence, the *BDB* analysis of אַלְקוּם probably is the best definition available.

[28]The word רִיב ("strife") often implies legal action.

SECTION OUTLINE

IV. THE SAYINGS OF LEMUEL (31:1-31)

1. Title (31:1)

[1]The sayings of King Lemuel—an oracle his mother taught him:

31:1 Lemuel, like Agur, is unknown. With a minor punctuation change, however, one may translate v. 1a as, "The sayings of Lemuel, king of Massa," instead of "The sayings of King Lemuel—an oracle."[1] McKane notes that Massa may have been a north Arabian tribe (Gen 25:14; 1 Chr 1:30) and that several Aramaisms appear in the text.[2]

2. Main Body (31:2-31)

(1) Three Lessons for a King (31:2-9)

[2]"O my son, O son of my womb,
O son of my vows,
[3]do not spend your strength on women,
your vigor on those who ruin kings.

[4]"It is not for kings, O Lemuel—
not for kings to drink wine,
not for rulers to crave beer,
[5]lest they drink and forget what the law decrees,
and deprive all the oppressed of their rights.
[6]Give beer to those who are perishing,
wine to those who are in anguish;
[7]let them drink and forget their poverty
and remember their misery no more.

[8]"Speak up for those who cannot speak for themselves,
for the rights of all who are destitute.

---

[1]Reading מֶלֶךְ מַשָּׂא as a construct chain. Otherwise, מֶלֶךְ should have the article in apposition to the proper name Lemuel.

[2]W. McKane, *Proverbs*, OTL (Philadelphia: Westminster, 1970), 407. Aramaisms include בַּר ("son," v. 2) and מְלָכִין ("kings," v. 3).

[9]Speak up and judge fairly;
defend the rights of the poor and needy."

Type: Admonition (31:2-9). With remarkable conciseness the mother of Lemuel describes the moral requirements of good government. These lessons are, simply put: do not use your authority as a means to debauchery (v. 3), keep your head clear from the stupefying effects of alcohol (vv. 4-7), and use your power to help the powerless (vv. 8-9).

31:2 The threefold "O" (Heb. *mah/mah*, lit. "what") appears to be short for, "What should I tell you?" or "What will you do as king?" She addresses him with terms of endearment; "O son of my womb, O son of my vows" means "My own son, the answer to my prayers."

31:3 The keeping of a harem of wives and concubines was not only a large expense but was also a distortion of the purpose of royal power. The king should use his authority for his people and not to serve himself (v. 3).

31:4-7 Verses 4-7 advise the king to maintain sobriety in order to carry out the work of establishing justice in the kingdom.[3] The queen-mother does not recommend a free beer program for the poor or justify its use as an opiate for the masses; her point is simply that the king must avoid drunkenness in order to reign properly. The comparison to the suffering poor and to their use of alcohol is meant to awaken Lemuel to the duties that go with his class and status rather than to describe some kind of permissible drunkenness.

31:8-9 The plea to "speak up for those who cannot speak for themselves" is as eloquent a statement of the royal duty of doing justice as one can find anywhere. It is noteworthy that this is her sole political concern; she does not say anything about building up the treasury, creating monuments to his reign, or establishing a dominant military power. For her the king's throne is truly founded on righteousness.

(2) The Good Wife (31:10-31)

[10]A wife of noble character who can find?
She is worth far more than rubies.
[11]Her husband has full confidence in her
and lacks nothing of value.
[12]She brings him good, not harm,
all the days of her life.
[13]She selects wool and flax
and works with eager hands.
[14]She is like the merchant ships,
bringing her food from afar.

---

[3]Read אַו ("desire," following *BDB*) for אוֹ ("or," *qere* has אֵי, "where") in v. 4.

15 She gets up while it is still dark;
she provides food for her family
and portions for her servant girls.
16 She considers a field and buys it;
out of her earnings she plants a vineyard.
17 She sets about her work vigorously;
her arms are strong for her tasks.
18 She sees that her trading is profitable,
and her lamp does not go out at night.
19 In her hand she holds the distaff
and grasps the spindle with her fingers.
20 She opens her arms to the poor
and extends her hands to the needy.
21 When it snows, she has no fear for her household;
for all of them are clothed in scarlet.
22 She makes coverings for her bed;
she is clothed in fine linen and purple.
23 Her husband is respected at the city gate,
where he takes his seat among the elders of the land.
24 She makes linen garments and sells them,
and supplies the merchants with sashes.
25 She is clothed with strength and dignity;
she can laugh at the days to come.
26 She speaks with wisdom,
and faithful instruction is on her tongue.
27 She watches over the affairs of her household
and does not eat the bread of idleness.
28 Her children arise and call her blessed;
her husband also, and he praises her:
29 "Many women do noble things,
but you surpass them all."
30 Charm is deceptive, and beauty is fleeting;
but a woman who fears the LORD is to be praised.
31 Give her the reward she has earned,
and let her works bring her praise at the city gate.

TYPE: WISDOM POEM, ACROSTIC, CHIASMUS (31:10-31). While this poem apparently does not describe the wife of a king and is not addressed to Lemuel, we cannot say that it is not part of the Lemuel text. Ancient wisdom texts could combine material in a way that seems incongruous to the modern reader, and the poem could come from Lemuel or his mother. If it is not part of the Lemuel text, it is an anonymous poem perhaps added as an epilogue to the canonical text. If that is the case, it is probably fairly late since epilogues are a late phenomenon. Either way, however, the interpretation of the text is not affected, and the significance that the canonical Book of Proverbs ends in this manner remains.

The poem is skillfully crafted. It is both acrostic (each verse begins with a successive letter of the Hebrew alphabet) and chiastic in structure. Either one of these is sufficient evidence of the poet's skill; the integration of the two is astounding. The chiasmus is as follows:

A: High value of a good wife (v. 10)
  B: Husband benefited by wife (vv. 11-12)
    C: Wife works hard (vv. 13-19)
      D: Wife gives to poor (v. 20)
        E: No fear of snow (v. 21a)
          F: Children clothed in scarlet (v. 21b)
            G: Coverings for bed, wife wears linen (v. 22)
              H: Public respect for husband (v. 23)
            G′: Sells garments and sashes (v. 24)
          F′: Wife clothed in dignity (v. 25a)
        E′: No fear of future (v. 25b)
      D′: Wife speaks wisdom (v. 26)
    C′: Wife works hard (v. 27)
  B′: Husband and children praise wife (vv. 28-29)
A′: High value of a good wife (vv. 30-31)

The center point of the chiasmus is v. 23, the declaration that the husband is highly regarded at the gate. The verse has been read as almost an intrusion on the poem; all the other verses praise the wife, but this verse alone focuses on the esteem the husband commands. Far from being an intrusion, however, v. 23 actually establishes the central message of the poem: this woman is the kind of wife a man needs in order to be successful in life.

In short, the original intended audience was not young women ("this is what kind of wife you should be") but young men ("this is what kind of wife you should get"). This does not mean that the poem cannot be used to instruct women, but the interpreter must recognize its primary objective. Although it may seem strange that a wisdom poem on the virtues of a good wife should be directed at young men, it is in keeping with the whole thrust of Proverbs. The book everywhere addresses the young man ("my son") and not the young woman. It expounds in great detail on evils of the prostitute and how she is a snare for a young man; it says nothing about lusty boys and the threats they pose for young women. It is a false reading, however, to suppose that biblical wisdom despises women or views them as fundamentally corrupt (this poem alone contradicts that notion). There is no double standard; the gender slant in Proverbs is a matter of audience orientation rather than ideological bias. Proverbs directs the reader away from the prostitute and toward the good wife because its implied reader is a young man.[4] For the same reason, Wisdom is personified as a woman and not as a man.[5]

31:10 In v. 10, "Who can find?" does not mean that no one can find such a wife but that she is of surpassing value to those who do find her. The precise meaning of the word translated "rubies" is unknown; other suggested translations are "pearls" and "corals." The reference is to some kind of precious stone.

31:11-12 The husband has "full confidence" (v. 11) in her in every area of life; he trusts in her good sense, her fidelity, and her industry.[6] Verse 11b emphasizes the latter: his house is full of the "booty"[7] she brings in. Verse 12 similarly states that she is a continual source of benefits.

31:13 The large number of verses devoted to the industrious spirit of the woman establishes this as a major theme of the poem (vv. 13-19). In an age long before the industrial revolution, women had to work at spinning wool and making clothes in every spare moment; fidelity in this labor was a mark of feminine virtue. Rather than "with eager hands," v. 13b might be translated somewhat more literally "at the pleasure of her hands."[8] The hands are semipersonified as taking pleasure in their creation and going about their work with a set purpose.[9]

31:14 She adds variety to the lives of her family by trading goods produced at home for food and merchandise the household cannot itself produce (v. 14). She has moved her household from a subsistence economy to a mercantile economy, and all enjoy the fruit of her enterprising spirit.

---

[4]For further discussion, see D. A. Garrett, "Ecclesiastes 7:25-29 and the Feminist Hermeneutic," *CTR* 2 (1988): 309-21.

[5]On the other side, I believe that Ruth, Esther, and possibly Song of Songs are wisdom texts that have young women as their intended primary audience.

[6]The phrase בָּטַח בָּהּ לֵב בַּעְלָהּ ("his heart trusts in her") is of a general nature and need not be confined to a specific area of life.

[7]The word שָׁלָל describes the rich plunder of a victorious army. It is metaphoric for the abundance of good things she brings into the home. Contrary to D. W. Thomas ("Textual and Philological Notes on Some Passages in the Book of Proverbs," in *Wisdom in Israel and the Ancient Near East*, ed. M. Noth and D. W. Thomas, *VTSup* 3 [Leiden: E. J. Brill, 1969], 291-92, and "Notes on Some Passages in Proverbs," *VT* 15 [1965]: 277-78) the word שָׁלָל here has its normal meaning of "plunder" and not "wool" (following an Arabic cognate). Apart from the fact that it is dangerous to redefine a Hebrew word (the normal meaning of which is well established and which is intelligible in context) on the basis of Arabic, the context of v. 11 does not support the change. This verse describes the benefits the man receives from her and not the woman herself. For a shift of topic in v. 11b to be recognizable, something like לָהּ would be needed (thus "wool is not lacking *to her*").

[8]So interpreting בְּחֵפֶץ כַּפֶּיהָ. The Vg has *consilio manuum suarum*, "by the counsel of her hands." The suggestion by M. Dahood (*Proverbs and Northwest Semitic Philology* [Rome: Biblical Institute Press, 1963], 60-61) that it be rendered "which her hands turn into a thing of beauty" does not bear up. Cf. McKane, *Proverbs*, 667.

[9]The word חֵפֶץ also implies a purpose or plan, as in Judg 13:23 and Isa 44:28.

31:15 Arising before dawn obviously implies that she has none of the vices of the sluggard. Verse 15c could be translated "and instructions for her serving girls" on the grounds that it is not likely that the lady of the house would provide breakfast for the servant girls. The translation "portions" is permissible,[10] however, and need not be taken to mean that she personally makes breakfast for the slaves; instead, she supervises preparation of the morning meal and sees to it that all have a fair share. This implies first that she cares even for the serving girls and second that she is diligent about overseeing them.

31:16-17 Qualities that some may regard as masculine are not to be despised in a woman. Verse 16 implies that she has both a good head for business and personal initiative. Verse 17 reads, "She girds her loins with strength."[11] The NIV takes this to be an idiom for setting about one's work energetically ("She sets about her work vigorously"). With the parallel in v. 17b, however, it probably means that she is physically capable of doing hard work. An English analogy would be, "She has a strong back."

31:18-19 Encouraged by previous business success, she continues her work into the night (v. 18).[12] Verse 19 asserts again that she is steadfast about the womanly work of spinning and weaving (cf. v. 13). It has the structural purpose of closing off this section of the poem (vv. 13-19).

31:20 Verse 20 describes her generous spirit.[13] Concern for the poor is a fundamental virtue of wisdom literature; in being generous, therefore, she is doing wisdom. This provides the link to the parallel in v. 26, in which she teaches wisdom.

31:21 It seems odd that she should regard scarlet clothing as a reason to be confident against winter weather, and thus many emend to read "double" instead (v. 21). The ancient versions support this emendation,[14] but the MT "scarlet" is preferable. McKane correctly observes that this prudent matron would not keep her family warm by sending them out

---

[10]The word חק is used for a portion of food in Gen 47:22; cf. also Prov 30:8. The parallel in v. 15b also implies that food is meant here.

[11]Thus rendering חָגְרָה בְעוֹז מָתְנֶיהָ.

[12]C. Toy (*A Critical and Exegetical Commentary on the Book of Proverbs* [Edinburgh: T & T Clark, 1899], 545) takes "her lamp does not go out at night" to mean that the house is prosperous (because it has plenty of oil) rather than that she works into the night. This misses the implied contrast with v. 15, however; the point is that she gets up early and does not quit work until well after dark.

[13]Verse 20 is tied to v. 19 by the catchwords יָדֶיהָ ("her hands") and כַּף ("palm of hand") arranged in chiastic fashion. The reason for this arrangement is to imply that her hands work hard, but they are also open and giving.

[14]Reading δισσὰς χλαίνας ("double cloaks") from the LXX v. 22 with v. 21. The Vg has *vestiti duplicibus* ("clothed with double [layers]"). The emendation is from שָׁנִים ("scarlet") to שְׁנָיִם.

wearing "two of everything" and that scarlet means that they have clothing of the highest quality.[15]

31:22 For all her strength and business acumen, she is still elegant (v. 22). Dressing well and decorating the home with pride is not here regarded as frivolous. "Linen" implies imports from Egypt, and "purple" describes the dyed fabric from Phoenicia.

31:23 A man with a wife like this will be well respected by his peers (v. 23). As described earlier, the presence of this verse in the structural center of the poem implies that the message is for the young man.

31:24 She not only has fine clothing and furnishings for herself and her home (from v. 22), but she also has manufactured enough to sell the excess for a profit (v. 24).

31:25 In v. 21 she had no worry for the cold because her children were in scarlet; in v. 25 she laughs at whatever troubles the future may bring because she is metaphorically clothed in "strength and dignity." Being a woman of character and strength, she is prepared for whatever may come.

31:26 She is a capable teacher and well acquainted with wisdom (v. 26). Her children are perhaps her primary pupils, but the text is not specific here. One cannot exclude the possibility that she also sets her husband right from time to time.

31:27 Verse 27 is a brief, summarizing counterpart to the lengthy description of the wife's diligence in vv. 13-19. Here the text explicitly states that she avoids laziness; eating the "bread of idleness" is idiomatic for indulging in laziness.

31:28-29 Her family gratefully acknowledges all the benefits they have had from her. As far as they are concerned, she is the greatest wife and mother in the world.

31:30-31 As the NIV indicates with quotation marks, vv. 30-31 are separate from vv. 28-29 and do not constitute part of the husband's praise. Otherwise, he would be implying that she lacks charm and beauty. This is something that no woman, however virtuous she may be, would care to hear. Rather, in keeping with the chiastic structure of the poem, these two verses are a summary and conclusion. Charm and beauty are not bad; they simply are inadequate reasons to marry a girl. The young man should first seek a woman who fears the Lord. And whoever finds such a woman should make sure that her gifts and accomplishments do not go unappreciated (v. 31).

The closure of Proverbs with this poem is not accidental. Near the beginning of the book stands a personification, Woman Wisdom, calling out for young men to come to her (1:20-33; also 8:1-36; 9:1-6). At the end an actual (albeit idealized) woman serves as the model for the young

---

[15]McKane, *Proverbs*, 668-69.

man seeking a wife. As the prostitute or quarrelsome wife is the actual counterpart to Woman Folly (9:13-18), so the good wife corresponds to Woman Wisdom.

The good wife described here has every virtue wisdom can offer. She is diligent, has a keen sense for business matters, is compassionate, is prepared for the future, is a good teacher, is dedicated to her family, and above all else possesses the primary characteristic of biblical wisdom, the fear of the Lord (looking back to Prov 1:7, the theme of the book). She is no less than Woman Wisdom made real. The riches Woman Wisdom offers (8:18) are brought home by the hard work of the good wife (31:11). Proverbs has, in effect, come full circle. It began by saying that the young man must embrace the imaginary ideal of Woman Wisdom in order to have a fulfilling life, and it ends by saying that one needs a good wife to achieve this goal.

The young man has no choice but to follow one woman or the other. He will either pursue Woman Wisdom or Woman Folly, and with them he will take their counterparts, the good wife or the prostitute/quarrelsome wife. He cannot attain wisdom without the good wife because she creates the environment in which he can flourish. If he chooses an evil woman, he has little hope of transcending the context she will make for him. Wisdom is not simply a matter of learning rules and precepts but is a matter of socialization, and a man is socialized first by his parents and then by his wife.

Here too wisdom is founded in creation theology. The woman is the "fitting helper" (Gen 2:18). She will either exalt or destroy her husband, and for better or for worse he will turn from his parents and cling to her (Gen 2:24[16]). That is, he will go from the world created by his parents to the world made by his wife. The man is her "lord"[17] and yet is dependent on her if he is to attain the status of sage elder who commands respect in the gate (Prov 31:23).

In Proverbs wisdom is not merely or even primarily intellectual; it is first of all relational. The young person finds wisdom through three specific relationships. A man must fear Yahweh, heed parents, and find the good wife. Moreover, one will gain the fear of Yahweh and the good wife in the same way: both are gifts from God (Eph 2:8-9; Prov 19:14).

---

[16]The Hebrew of Gen 2:24 clearly states that the man will cling to the woman (וְדָבַק בְּאִשְׁתּוֹ). The NIV's rendition "be united" obscures this.

[17]He is her בַּעַל (cf. vv. 11,23,28).

Ecclesiastes

INTRODUCTION OUTLINE

INTRODUCTION

Ecclesiastes is often looked upon as the Bible's resident alien. Other books may be considered perplexing (Job) or as superseded by New Testament revelation (Leviticus). Many read Ecclesiastes, however, with the distinct feeling that this book does not belong in the Bible. What other book immediately meets the reader with such pessimism and despair: "Everything is meaningless" (1:2)? What other book challenges the idea of afterlife (3:19-21)? The poetic power of 3:1-8 is evident to all, but the meaning of the words is far less clear. Furthermore, it is not helpful that almost every aspect of the book's origin and background is hotly debated. The authorship, date of composition, purpose, message, and even the original language of the book have all been disputed. In what sense can Ecclesiastes be called a word of God?

1. Authorship and Date of Composition

On the basis of Eccl 1:1, Christians and Jews have traditionally believed Solomon to have been the author of Ecclesiastes. This belief prevailed until the rise of historical criticism in the eighteenth and nineteenth centuries when the notion of Solomonic authorship was widely challenged. By the beginning of the twentieth century, G. A. Barton could call the notion of Solomonic authorship "unthinkable,"[1] and the situation has changed little since. Today the belief that Ecclesiastes cannot be Solomonic, and indeed probably is a postexilic work, prevails among biblical scholars. What is the reason for this dramatic change?[2]

(1) Arguments for Non-Solomonic Authorship

LINGUISTIC EVIDENCE. The most important issue is the linguistic evidence. The language of Ecclesiastes is unusual. In fact, D. S. Margoliouth and F. C. Burkitt considered the Hebrew of Ecclesiastes to be so strange as to be foreign. F. Zimmermann proposed in 1945 that the book was originally written in Aramaic and then translated into Hebrew, and this proposal was supported by C. C. Torrey and H. L. Ginsberg.[3] The belief that Ecclesiastes was originally written in very late Hebrew or even in Aramaic arose partly because scholars found an unusually high number of apparent Aramaisms in the text.

---

[1]G. A. Barton, *Ecclesiastes*, ICC (Edinburgh: T & T Clark, 1912), 58-59.

[2]In his recent commentary J. L. Crenshaw (*Ecclesiastes* [Philadelphia: Westminster, 1987]) hardly considers the notion of Solomonic authorship worth mentioning. Crenshaw dates the book to 250–225 B.C.

[3]See the discussion in M. A. Eaton, *Ecclesiastes*, TOTC (Downers Grove: InterVarsity, 1983), 17-18. A full presentation of F. Zimmermann's arguments is found in *The Inner World of Qohelet* (New York: KTAV, 1973), 98-122.

Indeed, no scholar was more zealous in discovering Aramaisms in the text than the relatively conservative F. Delitzsch, who produced a list of ninety-six words he considered to be Aramaisms or of late origin.[4] In addition, he noted four linguistic peculiarities of the Hebrew of Ecclesiastes.[5] So convinced was he that the Aramaisms rendered Solomonic authorship impossible that he issued the famous judgment, "If the book of Koheleth were of old Solomonic origin, then there is no history of the Hebrew language."[6]

The language of Ecclesiastes has several other unusual features. C. Whitley notes that the article is often omitted but that there is a preponderance of particles.[7] Also many scholars note the frequent appearance of a less common and allegedly later form of the relative particle in Ecclesiastes.[8]

In addition to the Aramaisms, the presence of two apparently Persian words, *pardes* and *pitgam*, seems to make the case for a late date of Ecclesiastes beyond doubt.[9] To many it proves that the book was written in or after the rise of the Persian Empire.[10]

INTERNAL EVIDENCE. *Hints of Non-Solomonic Authorship.* Evidence in the text itself seems to indicate that it was not written by Solomon. Ecclesiastes 1:12 says, "I, the Teacher [Qoheleth], was king over Israel in Jerusalem." But Solomon remained king until the day he died. The use of the perfect tense is therefore odd.

Similarly, Delitzsch argues that Ecclesiastes is written as if by the spirit of the dead Solomon. He argues that the name *Qoheleth* [the Teacher], from the Hebrew root *qhl*, looks back to 1 Kgs 8:55-61, where it is said that Solomon spoke to the assembled[11] people of Israel.[12] Thus the actual author, aware of the description of Solomon as the one who assembled the congregation in 1 Kgs 8, gave his implied Solomonic author the name "the Teacher."

---

[4]F. Delitzsch, *Ecclesiastes* (Grand Rapids: Eerdmans, n.d.), 190-96.

[5]Ibid., 197-98. First, third א verbs are inflected like third ה verbs. Second, only three instances of the imperfect waw-consecutive occur. Third, the personal pronoun is often used with finite verbs. Finally, Delitzsch asserted that the use of the pronoun זֹה is similar to that found in the *Mishna*.

[6]Ibid., 190.

[7]C. F. Whitley, *Koheleth* (Berlin: Walter de Gruyter, 1979), 1. Especially frequent are גַּם, כִּי, and כַּאֲשֶׁר.

[8]The pronoun שֶׁ is generally used rather than אֲשֶׁר, which is more common elsewhere in the OT.

[9]The word פַּרְדֵּס ("park" or "garden") is found in 2:5, and פִּתְגָם ("decree") is found in 8:11.

[10]Cf. the conservative Eaton, *Ecclesiastes*, 19.

[11]קהל, "to assemble."

[12]Delitzsch, *Ecclesiastes*, 20-34.

A number of scholars contend that Ecclesiastes only maintains the so-called Solomon fiction through the first two chapters and then abandons all reference to him.[13] Childs asserts that the fiction of Solomonic authorship is discarded at 8:2-4; 10:16-17; 12:9-14 He claims that the Solomonic guise was taken on in the early part of the book to assure the reader that the thrust of Ecclesiastes was not to attack wisdom but to serve as an official corrective to its excesses.[14]

The Frame-Narrator. Eaton argues that Eccl 1:2; 7:27; 12:8 indicate that one man is reporting the wisdom material of another man. Eaton believes that the recurring phrase "says 'the Teacher'" reveals that the actual author is one who presents himself as an editor for the Teacher. Now it happens, Eaton contends, that the editor's reworking of the material is so thorough that the entire book is in his style, making him more of an author than an editor. Even so, the author-editor and the Teacher are two separate people. "Thus one style pervades the book; but two people, Qoheleth [i.e., the Teacher], the originator of the material, and an unnamed author-editor, lay behind it."[15] The author-editor makes his presence known by framing the work with brief narration that describes something of the life of the Teacher (1:1-2; 12:9-10); he is often called the "frame-narrator."[16]

HISTORICAL AND LITERARY ARGUMENTS. Scholars also present historical and theological lines of argument in favor of a post-Solomonic date for the book. Some urge that Ecclesiastes shows a dependence on Greek thought and literature. A common assertion is that Ecclesiastes betrays an awareness of Hesiod's *Works and Days*, an earthy, pessimistic work of Boeotian poetry written in the late eighth century B.C. Others compare Ecclesiastes to the cynic and stoic traditions in Greek philosophy. Whitley compares the Teacher's apparent skepticism (3:19-21) about an afterlife to Epicurean annihilationism and says that the Teacher's analogy to death as the breaking of the "golden bowl" (12:6) is like Lucretius's speaking of death as the shattering of a vessel.[17]

Some scholars have tried to pinpoint historical allusions in the Persian or Greek periods of Jewish history. Barton, for example, says that the "wise youth" of Eccl 4:13 probably was Ptolemy V, who came to the throne in 205 B.C.[18] If so, then Ecclesiastes was certainly written after

[13]See R. B. Y. Scott, *Proverbs and Ecclesiastes*, AB (Garden City: Doubleday, 1965), 200, and R. N. Whybray, *Ecclesiastes*, NCB (Grand Rapids: Eerdmans, 1989), 4.

[14]B. Childs, *Introduction to the Old Testament as Scripture* (Philadelphia: Fortress, 1979), 584.

[15]Eaton, *Ecclesiastes*, 22; see pp. 21-24.

[16]See especially the discussion in M. V. Fox, *Qohelet and His Contradictions*, JSOTSup 71 (Sheffield: Almond, 1989), 311-21.

[17]Whitley, *Koheleth*, 167-68.

[18]Barton, *Ecclesiastes*, 120.

that date. Delitzsch, similarly, contends that Eccl 6:3 alludes to Artaxerxes II, Mnemon, and Artaxerxes III, Ochus. He also contends that 4:13-16 refers to the career of Cyrus and that 9:14-16 may allude to Themistocles of Athens.[19] More recently Whybray has argued that the general sense of security and prosperity in the book, together with its use of commercial terms like "profit," argue for the Ptolemaic period in Palestine as the setting of the book.[20]

QUESTIONS OF CANONICITY. The issue of the book's canonicity also enters here. The Mishnaic tractate *Yadayim* 3:5 mentions that there was some dispute in the early rabbinic circles about the canonical status of the book. Barton argues that the New Testament makes no clear reference to Ecclesiastes as Scripture since Rom 8:20 and Jas 4:14 are not ambiguous allusions.[21] He supports his argument by comparing Ecclesiastes to the Wisdom of Solomon and Ben Sira. Barton asserts that the Teacher was among the ungodly men whom the author of the Wisdom of Solomon set about to correct (Wis 2:1-9).[22] He further argues that Ben Sira knew and used a copy of Ecclesiastes that had not yet received its Hasidic (Jewish purists who fought Greek influence; the pious of Judah) glosses. Ben Sira was written ca. 180 B.C.; the latest date for Ecclesiastes can therefore be placed about twenty years before that, or about 200–195 B.C.[23] Barton also asserts that references to Ecclesiastes in the *Talmud* are inconclusive since the *Talmud* itself was written in the third to fifth centuries A.D. Stories in the *Talmud*, therefore, only prove that the rabbis of that period accepted the book.[24] The evidence that the book was late in being accorded canonical status, therefore, attests to its late date of composition.

Most scholars consider the late date for Ecclesiastes to be beyond dispute. Scott, for example, speaks for most in asserting the linguistic and historical evidence to indicate that Ecclesiastes was written in the late Persian or early Greek period. He bluntly states that claiming Solomon wrote Ecclesiastes is "like claiming that a book about Marxism in modern English idiom and spelling was written by Henry VIII."[25]

(2) Arguments for Solomonic Authorship

Conservatives have felt the weight of these arguments. The conservative Lutheran H. C. Leupold dated Ecclesiastes in the early postexilic

[19]Delitzsch, *Ecclesiastes*, 214-15.
[20]Whybray, *Ecclesiastes*, 9-11.
[21]Barton, *Ecclesiastes*, 4-5.
[22]Ibid., 2.
[23]Ibid., 59-60.
[24]Ibid., 3-4.
[25]Scott, *Proverbs and Ecclesiastes*, 196.

period.[26] R. K. Harrison, an evangelical scholar, also considers the book to be post-Solomonic.[27] As Childs has written, "There is almost universal consensus, shared by extremely conservative scholars, that Solomon was not the author of the book."[28] But the critical arguments have not gone unchallenged.

Linguistic Evidence. The question of the language of Ecclesiastes has naturally received the most attention. In answer to Delitzsch's oft-quoted remark regarding Ecclesiastes and the history of the Hebrew language, one might note that our knowledge of the particulars of the history of Hebrew is quite limited. For Greek the history of the dialectical, orthographic, and lexical development of the language is well documented. Indisputable evidence concerning the history of the Hebrew language, however, is relatively scarce. Eaton remarks that "[t]he difficulty is that the linguistic data show that Ecclesiastes does not fit into any known section of the history of the Hebrew language."[29]

Nevertheless, linguistic evidence is sufficient at least to challenge the late date for the composition of Ecclesiastes. In a major study D. Fredericks argues that Ecclesiastes cannot come from the postexilic period.[30] His work, together with other recent studies, calls for a major reassessment of the date of the book.

Fredericks's study is too lengthy and detailed for more than a cursory summary here. He examines the language of Ecclesiastes from the standpoints of both grammar and lexicology in comparison to established features of early biblical Hebrew, late biblical Hebrew, Second Temple Hebrew, and Mishnaic Hebrew. Insofar as evidence permits, he also takes into account factors that tend to complicate such studies (differences due to genre, archaizing in late texts, dialectical differences, etc.).

Following this methodology, Fredericks contends, for example, that no grounds exist for asserting Mishnaic Hebrew influence. Fredericks found forty-six points in which the language of Ecclesiastes agrees exclusively or primarily with biblical Hebrew over against Mishnaic Hebrew. He found only two points at which Ecclesiastes was more like Mishnaic Hebrew (these two can be explained satisfactorily by genre or dialectical considerations).[31] In addition, Fredericks found six grammatical features

[26] H. C. Leupold, *Exposition of Ecclesiastes* (Grand Rapids: Baker, 1952), 8-17.

[27] R. K. Harrison, *Introduction to the Old Testament* (Grand Rapids: Eerdmans, 1969), 107-28.

[28] Childs, *Introduction to Old Testament*, 582.

[29] Eaton, *Ecclesiastes*, 19.

[30] D. C. Fredericks, *Qoheleth's Language* (Lewiston, N.Y.: Edwin Mellen, 1988).

[31] Ibid., 51-109. For example, Ecclesiastes uses ִים rather than ִין for the masculine plural ending of the participle (like biblical Hebrew, unlike Mishnaic Hebrew). The two exceptional traits are the infrequency of the waw consecutive imperfect and the use of זָה as the feminine demonstrative.

of Ecclesiastes that appear to be dependent on early biblical Hebrew and none that are dependent on late biblical Hebrew.[32] He concludes that the language of Ecclesiastes is "fully in the realm of the preexilic language."[33] Although further work into this area needs to be done,[34] no longer can one confidently claim that the language of Ecclesiastes proves it to be late.

Certainly no convincing evidence has emerged that the book was first written in Aramaic. Whitley has shown that Zimmermann's argument for an Aramaic original behind the Hebrew text of Ecclesiastes is weak. More than that, he demonstrates that Zimmermann's retranslations are often inferior to the Hebrew source.[35] In addition, Gordis notes that certain wordplays that exist in the Hebrew of Ecclesiastes would be nonexistent in the Aramaic "original" that has been proposed. The pun in 7:1 ("a good name is better than good oil")[36] would not appear in Aramaic. The Hebrew of Ecclesiastes is also rhythmic and sometimes parallels other biblical passages. Ben Sira shows dependence on the Hebrew text of Ecclesiastes. Finally, the Hebrew of Ecclesiastes sometimes reflects authentic Canaanite vocabulary. All this makes the idea of an Aramaic *Urtext* (base text) unlikely.[37]

Delitzsch greatly exaggerated the amount of Aramaic influence detectable in the book. He asserted many words to be Aramaisms on the basis of the noun endings *ut*, *on*, and *an*, a basis Archer has shown to be inadequate.[38] E. Kautzsch contended that there are twenty-nine Aramaisms in the book,[39] but this figure also should be regarded as excessive. Fredericks examines forty-eight alleged Aramaisms and concludes that only seven terms are of Aramaic origin, of which four are attested elsewhere in early biblical Hebrew.[40] What Aramaisms do exist, however, by no

---

[32]Ibid., 125-59. For example, the linking of singular and plural forms of the same noun (שִׁדָּה וְשִׁדּוֹת; Eccl 2:8) is characteristically early. Fredericks does isolate one feature that is characteristic of late biblical Hebrew (the absence of the infinitive absolute plus cognate finite verb to emphasize the verb), but other considerations nullify the significance of this feature.

[33]Ibid., 267.

[34]Aspects of Fredericks's work have been criticized in a review by A. Hurvitz in *Hebrew Studies* 31 (1990): 144-54. These criticisms, while providing a corrective, do not invalidate Fredericks's thesis; but they do point to the need for further study.

[35]Whitley, *Koheleth*, 106-10.

[36]Hebrew: טוֹב שֵׁם מִשֶּׁמֶן טוֹב.

[37]R. Gordis, *Koheleth: The Man and His World* (New York: Schocken, 1968), 413-14.

[38]G. Archer, *A Survey of Old Testament Introduction* (Chicago: Moody, 1964), 139.

[39]E. Kautzsch, *Die Aramaismen im Alten Testament* (1902), 102, cited in Whitley, *Koheleth*, 1, n. 4.

[40]These are אִלּוּ (*if*), מְדִינָה (*province*), רְאוּת (*aspiration*), רַעְיוֹן (*striving*), חוּץ מִן (*without*), כְּאֶחָד (*alike*), and תָּקַף (*to overpower*). The first four are found in early biblical Hebrew or Phoenician.

means prove that Ecclesiastes is a late work. Aramaic itself existed from early times; and in the Bible, Aramaisms are especially likely to occur in wisdom and poetic texts.[41] Eaton remarks that "[The Aramaisms] are of comparatively little significance for dating."[42]

The presence of the two Persian words seems to be irrefutable proof of a late date for the book, but here too the matter is not as settled as it appears. Archer says the words could be of Sanskrit origin and that they may have entered the language during Solomon's period of extensive foreign trade.[43] That hypothesis is open to question, but it is noteworthy that Pope also expresses doubt about whether *pardes* and the related Greek word *paradeisos* are of Persian origin.[44] The word *pitgam* alone is slender evidence since we in fact have no idea when it entered the language. Fredericks notes that Persian influence and vocabulary spread through the ancient Near East long before the establishment of the Persian Empire and that the words need not have entered Hebrew via Aramaic, as is commonly assumed.[45]

The peculiar Hebrew of Ecclesiastes cannot be evidence for a late date since it does not fit anywhere in the known history of the language. In no way, for example, does it specifically resemble the Hebrew of Malachi, Esther, or of the Chronicler.[46]

A related question is whether or not Phoenician or Canaanite linguistic forms appear in the book. This approach was championed by M. Dahood, who argued extensively that the linguistic peculiarities of Ecclesiastes are best explained by assuming that the author, although a Hebrew, was immersed in a Phoenician-Canaanite linguistic environment and thus produced a work with many affinities to Phoenician.[47] The theory of a Phoe-

---

[41]See Fredericks, *Qoheleth*, 208-41, for the full discussion of the evidence.

[42]Eaton, *Ecclesiastes*, 17.

[43]Archer, *Survey*, 470.

[44]M. Pope, *Song of Songs*, AB (Garden City: Doubleday, 1977), 31. "The other alleged Persianism, פִּתְגָם, is slender evidence for establishing a date for the text since we have no idea when it entered the language."

[45]Fredericks, *Qoheleth's Language*, 245.

[46]The frequently used relative שֶׁ is found in only one other book, Song of Songs, which also claims Solomonic authorship.

[47]M. J. Dahood, "Canaanite-Phoenician Influence in Qoheleth," *Bib* 33 (1952): 30-52, 191-221. Dahood continues his argument in "Qoheleth and Recent Discoveries," *Bib* 39 (1958): 302-18; "Qoheleth and Northwest Semitic Philology," *Bib* 43 (1962): 349-65; "Canaanite Words in Qoheleth 10,20," *Bib* 46 (1965): 210-12; and "The Phoenician Background of Qoheleth," *Bib* 47 (1966): 264-82. He contends for Phoenician influence on the grounds that many problems are best explained by assuming that Qoheleth was originally written without the *matres lectionis* (i.e., consonants used for indicating vowels). He further contends on the basis of grammatical and lexical features of Ecclesiastes such as the use of the third masculine plural pronoun suffix for a feminine antecedent, the feminine pronoun זה, the emphatic ל (9:4), the use of interrogatives as indefinites and of the infinitive absolute as a finite verb, and the enclitic מ.

nician provenance for Ecclesiastes has been rejected by scholars who argue that the peculiar linguistic features of the text are best explained in the context of biblical Hebrew.[48] Although Dahood's thesis and a number of his arguments must be set aside, in individual cases his insights indicate that the difficulties of the Teacher's language can be explained as ancient tendencies in the languages of the Levant, that is, the eastern Mediterranean, rather than as late developments in Hebrew.

INTERNAL EVIDENCE. *Hints of Non-Solomonic Authorship.* Internal evidence cannot be said to demand non-Solomonic authorship of the book. The use of the perfect tense in 1:12 proves nothing; certainly it does not establish that we here have a later author writing in behalf of the now-dead Solomon. It may indicate that Ecclesiastes was written by an aged Solomon near the end of his life.[49] Throughout the book, in fact, the perspective seems to be that of an older man, as in the description of old age in 12:1-5. Nor is it clear that texts like 8:2-8; 10:16-17; 12:9-14 abandon Solomonic authorship. Certainly we cannot say that a king could not have reflected critically on a king's role and on appropriate behavior in the royal presence.

More than that, these reflections pose a special problem for those who support a postexilic date for the book. After the exile the Jewish people no longer were under their own local kings but were ruled by the distant emperors of Persia and the subsequent Seleucid and Ptolemaic monarchs. A few Jewish officials (e.g., Nehemiah) had personal dealings with these distant rulers, but these were the rare exceptions. Even the wealthy Jew of the postexilic period probably never saw a king in his life. Why then so much concern, in a book of Jewish wisdom, with how to deal with the king? The book must have been written for an audience that lived relatively near the seat of central government and could be expected, at least on occasion, to have to face the monarch. Nor can we say, simply because no further clear allusions to Solomon appear, that the idea of Solomonic authorship is dropped after chap. 2. With the exception of autobiography, very few books repeatedly refer to or mention their author from beginning to end.

No clear relationship has been established between Ecclesiastes and 1 Kgs 8 on the basis of the root *qhl*. The two passages do not resemble each other in either structure or content, and no literary link between the texts exists. It is doubtful that the author of Ecclesiastes was drawing on the portrait of Solomon in Kings.

[48]See R. Gordis, "Was Koheleth a Phoenician?" *JBL* 74 (1955): 103-14; Whitley, *Koheleth*, 111-18; and Fredericks, *Qoheleth*, 18-23. See also Gordis, *Koheleth*, 416-17.

[49]אֲנִי קֹהֶלֶת הָיִיתִי מֶלֶךְ might better be translated, "I have been king" rather than "*was* king." The former can indicate an ongoing situation, as in "I have been in this job a long time." The latter would more likely be taken to imply a former, terminated status. The perfect can even be translated as a present. See P. Joüon, *A Grammar of Biblical Hebrew*, rev., T. Muraoka, ed. (Rome: Pontifical Biblical Institute, 1991), III.i.

The Question of a "Frame-Narrator" and the Three Levels of Discourse. The argument that references to the Teacher in the third person prove the author/editor to be someone other than the Teacher is inconclusive. The text of Ecclesiastes calls for a more sensitive approach than a mere redaction-historical separation between the Teacher and the one who edited his words, even if that editor is thought to have been so thorough as to produce an essentially original work.

Third person frame narratives are known from the ancient world, especially from Egypt.[50] Most of these simply serve to identify the name and circumstances of the author (whether actual or fictional), and none achieve the literary sophistication of Ecclesiastes. Most "frame narratives" simply introduce or conclude a wisdom work with a few remarks about the apparent author (contrast Eccl 7:27).[51]

In Ecclesiastes, moreover, we have not just the two discourse levels of the frame narrator and the Teacher but *three* levels of discourse. The first level, that of the frame-narrator, is found where the Teacher is referred to in the third person (e.g., 1:1-2; 12:8-10). At this level the reader learns something about the character and background of the Teacher. More importantly, the biographical details of this level place the Teacher in the realm of history and set a degree of objectivity and distance between the reader and the Teacher, a distance that would not exist if the entire book were written in the first person. The frame-narrator thus lifts the book above the level of personal reflection and presents the Teacher as an authority whose words ought to be heard.

The second level of discourse is the wisdom level, at which we are not in the realm of biography and history (level one), but neither are we in

[50]Fox (*Qohelet*, 312-14) lists a number of works with a "frame narrative."

[51]A more ambitious attempt to tie Ecclesiastes to an ancient genre is T. Longman III, "Comparative Methods in Old Testament Studies: Ecclesiastes Reconsidered," *TSF Bulletin* 7 (1984): 5-9. He argues that Ecclesiastes is of the genre of (fictional) didactic autobiography and compares it to the Cuthean Legend of Naram-Sin, an Akkadian text that in its oldest form goes back to about 1800 B.C. Longman's analysis is not persuasive. His assertion that in 1:13–6:12 Qoheleth "recounts his experiences" while 7:1–12:7 "is composed mostly of advice" (p. 7) is patently untrue. Ecclesiastes (including the latter half of the book) contains many examples of what may be called "observations" but little that could be accurately described as "experiences." Even 2:4-11 does not describe "experiences"; it merely asserts that Qoheleth was fabulously wealthy but found his wealth unsatisfying. Certainly there is nothing comparable to the detailed quasihistorical war account found in the Naram-Sin legend. Autobiography should (as the Naram-Sin account does) tell some kind of story and involve more characters than the author alone. Merely to assert that one is in a position to speak intelligently on issues of wealth and wisdom and to recall ethical observations is not to write an autobiography, fictional or otherwise. Similarly, "advice" is found throughout the book (not only in the latter half). The comparison to the Naram-Sin material is forced. In particular it maintains the impossible division of the text between the skeptic Qoheleth and the pious author of the epilogue.

the realm of the Teacher's personal musings. Rather, the nature of reality is described in terms that are universal and didactic. Wisdom is speaking. Here the text frequently employs a poetic or aphoristic style associated with the Book of Proverbs in order either to describe the nature of the world (1:3-11; 3:1-8) or to give direction or insight (2:14a; 4:5-6,9,12; 5:3,10-12,15; 6:7-9; 7:1-12,19-21; 9:17–10:4; 10:8–12:7; 12:11-14).[52] At this level the book speaks with authority, and the reader is to accept its teachings as corresponding to reality. Second level discourse sometimes forms the basis for the Teacher's personal reflections.

The third level of discourse is first person recollections and meditations (1:12-14,16-17; 2:1-13,14b-26; 3:9-14; 3:16–4:4; 4:7-8; 5:13-14; 5:16–6:6; 7:15-18,23-29; 8:9-10; 8:14–9:1; 10:5-7). Here the Teacher invites the reader both to learn from the Teacher's experiences and to join him in confronting life's lessons, however brutal they may be at times. The first level thus gives us something of the external world and person of the Teacher, the second level gives us the wisdom teachings that make up the framework of his intellectual world, and the third level gives us his personal meditations.

These three are seamlessly joined. A number of texts, particularly those that give direct advice to the reader, mix second level and third level discourse or could be assigned to either (e.g., 5:1-6; 8:2-8; 9:7-16). The first and third levels can be juxtaposed (1:12; 7:27); proverbial teaching (second level) can be inserted into third level discourse (1:15; 9:4b); first person comments can flow out of what begins as a second level discourse (4:13-16, which begins with a proverb). The "better saying," a characteristic of wisdom literature, is also used in the context of third level discourse.[53] What is important to grasp here, however, is that *all the levels of narration are a matter of literary technique and are not indications of redaction history.* The reason they all flow together so well is that they are all part of the single perspective of a single author. The frame-narrator, wisdom, and the Teacher are all masks behind which we hear the one voice of the author.[54]

The Teacher (Qoheleth) is obviously a pseudonym; there is no reason to suppose that the author who writes "the Teacher says" (the frame-narrator) and the author who gives us the bulk of the book (the Teacher) are two different people. Otherwise we would expect the frame-narrator

[52]Cf. Fox, *Qohelet*, 312.

[53]Cf. S. Ogden, "The 'Better' Proverb (Tob-Spruch), Rhetorical Criticism, and Qoheleth," *JBL* 96 (1977): 489-505. "For Qoheleth the T-S [*Tob-Spruch*] has become a literary device in the presentation of a highly individual viewpoint" (p. 496).

[54]The use of several levels of discourse within a single work is found elsewhere in literature. A recent example is R. M. Pirsig's *Zen and the Art of Motorcycle Maintenance* (New York: Bantam, 1975).

to have given us the Teacher's actual name. When he says, "I, the Teacher" (1:12), any notion that the Teacher and the frame-narrator (or "author/editor") are actually two separate individuals must be abandoned as a fancy of biblical criticism.

Can such an understanding of the nature of the text coexist with the idea of Solomonic authorship? I believe it can. The use of the name "the Teacher" indicates that the author is distancing himself from his role as absolute monarch and taking on the mantle of the sage. Both the name "the Teacher" and the use of third person (frame-narrator) allow him to do this. The device is certainly a literary success. What emerges from Ecclesiastes is not a royal pronouncement but the reflection of a wise man who "has been" king. As we read the book, we are more and more absorbed in the words not of "King Solomon" but of "Solomon-become-'the-Teacher.'"

LITERARY AND HISTORICAL EVIDENCE. Evidence fails to support the view that Ecclesiastes reflects Greek influence. Many scholars have abandoned the search for Greek philosophy in Ecclesiastes, though some have continued to maintain that a Greek spirit is evident. Some recent scholars hesitate to isolate specific cases of allusion to Greek philosophic texts. Nevertheless, they urge that Ecclesiastes betrays a knowledge of the general tenets of Greek thinking (such as any third-century Jerusalemite would have possessed[55]), or they claim that Ecclesiastes reflects the "Greek cult of the individual."[56]

The pessimism found in Ecclesiastes, however, is evident in the ancient Near East from the third millennium onward; there is no need to suppose it is Hellenistic.[57] Even many scholars who hold to a late date concur here.[58] While similarities naturally exist among various examples of pessimistic literature, no certain case of literary dependence has been demonstrated. It is pointless to try to make a case for Greek influence with nebulous concepts like a Hellenistic "spirit" or Greek "individualism."

No one has shown convincingly that Ecclesiastes alludes to any historical event. Although earlier scholars, such as Barton and Delitzsch, felt great freedom to assert that certain passages referred to various kings and events of the Hellenistic age, that practice has been rightly discontinued. Although Crenshaw adopts a third-century date for the book, he comments that the "so-called historical references in 4:13-16; 8:2-4; 9:13-15; and 10:16-17 invited use because of their typicality. Therefore they offer no real assistance in dating the book or in locating its cultural setting."[59]

---

[55]Crenshaw, *Ecclesiastes*, 51.

[56]Whybray, *Ecclesiastes*, 6.

[57]Cf. Eaton, *Ecclesiastes*, 20-21.

[58]Scott, *Proverbs and Ecclesiastes*, 197, and Childs, *Introduction to the Old Testament*, 582.

[59]Crenshaw, *Ecclesiastes*, 49.

Even Whybray's more general effort to relate Ecclesiastes to the Ptolemaic era in Palestine[60] has little concrete evidence to support it.

By contrast, strong evidence supports linking Ecclesiastes to the literary and intellectual world of the ancient Near East. Ecclesiastes is in many ways conceptually and structurally similar to examples from ancient Egyptian literature. Egyptian words comparable to Ecclesiastes include *Instruction of Ptahhotep*, which describes how to deal with inferiors and superiors; *Instruction of Duauf*, which praises the occupation of government official; *Instruction of King Amenemhet*, which recalls Eccl 12; *Instruction for King Merikare*, which combines political, moral, and religious advice; and the *Teaching of Amenemope*, which strongly resembles Prov 22:17–23:14. Parallels to Ecclesiastes also are found in several pessimistic works, including *The Man Tired of Life*, *The Admonitions of a Prophet*, and *The Song of the Harper* (fourteenth cent. B.C.).

The Song of the Harper contains conspicuous parallels to Ecclesiastes. Compare the following excerpt to Eccl 3:22 and 9:7-9:

Follow thy desire, as long as thou shalt live
Put Myrrh upon thy head and clothing of fine linen upon thee,
Being anointed with the genuine marvels of the god's property.
Set an increase to thy good things;
Let not thy heart flag.
Follow thy desire and thy good.
Fulfill thy needs upon earth, after the command of thy heart,
Until there come for thee that day of mourning.[61]

Babylonian literature also contains several examples of literature of the same type as Ecclesiastes. *The Pessimistic Dialogue of a Master and Slave* and the *Complaint of a Sage over the Injustice of the World* are comparable to Ecclesiastes. The latter has been called the "Babylonian Koheleth."[62]

Perhaps the most striking parallel of all is with the *Epic of Gilgamesh*. Compare Eccl 9:7-9 to this section from *Gilgamesh* in the old Babylonian version:

Gilgamesh, whither rovest thou?
The life thou pursuest thou shalt not find.
When the gods created mankind,
Death for mankind they set aside,
Life in their own hands retaining.
Thou, Gilgamesh, let full be thy belly,
Make thou merry by day and by night,

[60]Whybray, *Ecclesiastes*, 6-12.
[61]ANET, 467.
[62]Gordis, *Koheleth*, 12.

Of each day make thou a feast of rejoicing,
Day and night dance thou and play!
Let thy garments be sparkling fresh,
Thy head be washed; bathe thou in water.
Pay heed to the little one that holds on to thy hand,
Let thy spouse delight in thy bosom!
For this is the task of [humankind]!"[63]

The Teacher likely knew the story of Gilgamesh. The importance of this evidence should not be underestimated since it provides invaluable information regarding both the date of composition and setting of Ecclesiastes. Tradition ascribes Ecclesiastes to Solomon, and this evidence supports the reasonableness of that view. Furthermore, Scripture presents Solomon as one who had access to the wealth of Egyptian and Babylonian literature and who was renowned for wide literary and intellectual interests. It is much less likely that someone in the postexilic period would have had acquaintance with these texts.

More than that, these passages indicate that Ecclesiastes may have been written primarily for the intellectual elite of ancient Jerusalem. The court of Solomon, like the king himself, certainly knew of the reflective literature of the great centers of civilization. The Teacher spoke to that audience about issues with which they were familiar.

CANONICITY. Matters concerning the book's canonicity (the book's status as Scripture) are equally indecisive for determining the date of its composition. Certainly it was generally regarded as canonical by the first century A.D. Josephus[64] mentions that the book "contains hymns to God" along with Psalms, Proverbs, and Canticles. Fragments of Ecclesiastes were found at Qumran. Although neither Josephus nor Qumran proves its canonicity, Ecclesiastes was accepted as being canonical in the mishnaic tractate *Baba Bathra* (14b-15a).

The council of Jamnia (A.D. 90), often regarded as the council that closed the Hebrew canon, did not admit new books to the canon but only examined those that were already in it, with the result that some books in the "canon" of Alexandrian Judaism (LXX) and apocalyptic works cherished at Qumran were excluded. Even Ezekiel, a book that must have been canonized long before A.D. 90, was debated there.[65] Ancient rabbinical debate no more invalidates the canonicity of the book than does modern scholarly debate.

Among Christians, Melito of Sardis, Epiphanium, Origen, and Jerome explicitly call it canonical. The argument is groundless that the failure of

[63]Tablet 10, section 3. ANET, 90.
[64]*Against Apion* 1.37-43.
[65]Harrison, *Introduction*, 278.

the New Testament writers to mention Ecclesiastes proves that they did not accept it. The subject matter of Ecclesiastes makes it unlikely that the New Testament authors would have had occasion to mention it. The New Testament viewpoint would be significant only if it rejected Ecclesiastes.

Finally, Barton's argument is highly doubtful that Ben Sira used an early edition of Ecclesiastes that had not yet been revised by the hypothetical "Hasid" glossator[66] (see discussion under "Unity of the Text"). Even if such interpolations to the text of Ecclesiastes are allowed, the data in the two books are not complete enough to allow for such a precise redaction history.

2. Text, Structure, and Style

(1) Text-Critical Problems

The text of Ecclesiastes is generally well preserved, and disputed passages are rare. Four pieces of an Ecclesiastes manuscript were found at Qumran in 1954. These contained portions of Eccl 5–7. Besides orthographic differences, variants from the MT were few and insignificant.[67]

(2) Unity of the Text

The unity of the book and its freedom from interpolations can be maintained with a high degree of confidence. At the beginning of the twentieth century, A. H. McNeile in England, G. A. Barton in America, and E. Podechard in France claimed to find many interpolations in Ecclesiastes. They believed that various passages were added by a "wise man" and other editors and especially that a pious "Hasid" added pious sentiments to bring the text into agreement with orthodoxy.[68]

Recent scholars have turned away from this position, and most scholars believe that most, if not all, of the book is from a single author. Childs, for example, says that the work is basically a unified composition, although the prologue and epilogue may be additions.[69] M. Fox observes that material scholars omit as late is stylistically identical to alleged original material, that the alleged additions do not remove the sting of the Teacher's "skeptical" outlook, that it would have been easier to suppress Ecclesiastes outright, and that no consistent original Ecclesiastes can be produced by eliminating parts of the text.[70] Eaton, too, has observed that

---

[66]Barton, *Ecclesiastes*, 59-60.

[67]Eaton, *Ecclesiastes*, 15.

[68]Ibid., 38-39. For a defense of the idea of the pious glossator, see Barton, *Ecclesiastes*, 43-46.

[69]Childs, *Introduction to the Old Testament*, 582.

[70]Fox, *Qohelet*, 23-25.

it is odd that a pious editor would issue a work with which he extensively disagrees: "No wisdom document exists in two recensions with opposite theologies; it is doubtful if one ever did."[71] He notes that it is strange that the editor adds contradictory ideas to the original text without removing lines he considered offensive.[72]

The case for the overall unity of Ecclesiastes is strong. The matter of the "Epilogue" and its relation to the rest of the book will be taken up in the exegetical section.

(3) Structure

The question of the structure of Ecclesiastes has received considerable attention in recent years. Following F. Delitzsch, scholars have considered it to have virtually no structure whatsoever;[73] but later studies have attempted to demonstrate various kinds of elaborate, complex patterns in the book.[74] Perhaps the most complicated venture of this kind was made by A. D. G. Wright, whose analysis attempts to provide intricate numerical patterns within the book.[75] Fox has correctly observed that the content of individual units, both in phrases used and in topics of discussion, does not correspond well to the boundaries Wright attempts to mark off.[76]

Another attempt to demonstrate logical structure within Ecclesiastes was made by H. L. Ginsberg, who divides the text into four parts.

A: the vanity of life mitigated only by the use of one's goods (1:2–2:26)
    B: all is foreordained but not foreseeable (3:1–4:3)
A′: a pendant to A (4:4–6:9)
    B′: a pendant to B (6:10–12:8)[77]

This outline has not been widely accepted either,[78] and it is but one example of many attempts to structure the book according to a chiastic or parallel framework.[79]

---

[71]Eaton, *Ecclesiastes*, 41.

[72]Ibid.

[73]Cf. Delitzsch, *Ecclesiastes*, 185-88.

[74]For a good survey and critique of recent positions and alternatives, see Crenshaw, *Ecclesiastes*, 34-49. Crenshaw's own conclusion is that all the elaborate efforts to discover the structure of the book have "failed to resolve a single issue" (p. 47).

[75]See A. D. G. Wright, "The Riddle of the Sphinx: The Structure of the Book of Qoheleth," *CBQ* 30 (1968): 313-34, and "The Riddle of the Sphinx Revisited: Numerical Patterns in the Book of Qoheleth," *CBQ* 42 (1980): 35-51.

[76]Fox, *Qohelet*, 156-57. See also Crenshaw, *Ecclesiastes*, 41-42.

[77]H. L. Ginsberg, "The Structure and Contents of the Book of Koheleth," in *Wisdom in Israel and the Ancient Near East*, ed. Noth and Thomas, *VTS* 3M (Leiden: Brill, 1969), 138-49. The chart above is a simplified summary of Ginsberg's chart on p. 138.

[78]Cf. J. A. Loader, *Polar Structures in the Book of Qohelet, BZAW* 152 (Berlin: Walter de Gruyter, 1979), 7-8.

[79]Cf. Crenshaw, *Ecclesiastes*, 38-47.

The debate between those who see Ecclesiastes as unstructured verbal meanderings and those who maintain that a logical structure is present thus continues.[80] A more moderate position is that of Childs. He accepts that the book is a collection of wisdom sayings, with the qualification that "the present form of the book reflects far more inner coherence than the advocates of the collection theory admit."[81] It may be, however, that a more precise explanation is available.

THE STRUCTURE OF ECCLESIASTES IN LIGHT OF ANCIENT PARALLELS. The conspicuous parallels between Ecclesiastes and other ancient Near Eastern wisdom texts, described above, have implications regarding the structure of the text. Based on this evidence, it is possible that Ecclesiastes was modeled after Egyptian instructional literature (with a fair amount of influence also coming from Babylonian and other sources).

In this literature the authors give advice on a whole range of subjects. For example, one author tells his reader how to deal with superiors, subordinates, wife, and friends (*Ptahhotep*, 120ff., 280ff., 325ff.). The importance of justice and the evil of oppression receive a great deal of attention (e.g., *Merikare* 45ff.). In addition, an author may give advice regarding religion and service to the gods (*Aniy* 7.12) or warn his reader on the use of the tongue and the use of wealth (*Amenemhet* 3.2). An author, moreover, can move back and forth among several topics in an apparently random fashion. The hierarchical outline employed in modern essays is not employed. Nevertheless, as the book moves to and fro among its several topics, it moves steadily toward its final conclusion.

The *Instructions of Aniy* are a particularly good example. It moves about among the topics of family matters (e.g., the choice of a good wife, avoidance of harlots, duties to one's parents), religious duty (e.g., the observation of feasts, propriety in worship), social graces (e.g., behavior in another's home, avoidance of public drunkenness, respect for superiors, dealing with brawlers), choosing good companions, personal discretion, and financial advice. It concludes this with a dialogue between father and son that challenges the reader to consider seeking the way of wisdom. Like Ecclesiastes, *Aniy* does not follow any hierarchical outline, but it has structure nevertheless.

An outline of Ecclesiastes, as seen in this historical and literary context, may be set forth in the following form:

OUTLINE OF THE BOOK

1. Introduction (1:1-2)
2. On Time and the World (1:3-11)

---

[80]See Loader, *Polar Structures*, 4-9.

[81]Childs, *Introduction to the Old Testament*, 582-83.

3. On Wisdom (1:12-18)
4. On Wealth (2:1-11)
5. On Wisdom (2:12-17)
6. On Wealth (2:18-26)
7. On Time and the World (3:1-15b)
8. On Politics (3:15c-17)
9. On Death (3:18-22)
10. On Politics (4:1-3)
11. On Wealth (4:4-8)
12. On Friendship (4:9-12)
13. On Politics (4:13-16)
14. On Religion (5:1-7)
15. On Politics (5:8-9)
16. On Wealth (5:10–6:6)
17. Transition (6:7-9)
18. On Wisdom and Death (6:10–7:4)
19. Transition (7:5-6)
20. On Wisdom and Politics (7:7-9)
21. Transition (7:10)
22. On Wisdom and Wealth (7:11-14)
23. On Wisdom and Religion (7:15-29)
24. Transition (8:1)
25. On Politics (8:2-6)
26. Transition (8:7-8)
27. On Theodicy (8:9–9:1)
28. Transition (9:2)
29. On Death and Contentment (9:3-10)
30. Transition (9:11-12)
31. On Politics (9:13–10:17)
32. Transition (10:18-20)
33. On Wealth (11:1-6)
34. On Death and Contentment (11:7–12:7)
35. Conclusion (12:8-14)

The structure of Ecclesiastes is thus not a hierarchical outline but a kind of wandering among several topics.[82] Contrary to some, therefore, it is not utterly without structure; but contrary to others, it follows no elaborate or symmetrical scheme. Even so its "wandering" is not purposeless but moves steadily toward a final destination.

[82]Fox, *Qohelet*, 157-58, notes that Wittgenstein had a somewhat random, criss-cross approach to writing his *Philosophical Investigations* as well.

(4) Stylistic and Literary Devices

Perhaps due to a testimony to the stylistic complexity of Ecclesiastes, scholars are not even able to agree on whether the book is predominately prose or poetry. Loader surveys recent opinions and argues that the book is poetry by trying to demonstrate scansion in some of the most prosaic passages.[83] It is perhaps better to say that, like Proverbs, Ecclesiastes is poetic but is not a poem. A few passages, however, properly might be called poems (e.g., 3:2-8).

Ecclesiastes employs many of the devices employed by other wisdom writings (as discussed in the Introduction to Proverbs). These include the "better saying" (4:3,6,9), the metaphor (7:26), the example story (9:14-15), the comparison (11:5), the rhetorical question (2:19,25), the autobiographical narrative (2:1-11), the woe-saying and benediction (10:16-17), and the admonition (7:9).[84] Loader has also pointed out that the book uses a number of minor rhetorical devices, including *figura etymologica* (a wordplay turning on the repetition of a root, 8:17[85]), anaphora (deliberate repetition of a word or phrase at the beginning of a verse, 3:1-8), hyperbole (6:3,6), and rhyme (10:11[86]).[87]

3. Theology and Purpose

Ecclesiastes has been subjected to a bewildering array of interpretations.[88] Conservative Christians have generally assumed that the purpose of Ecclesiastes is to show the futility of the world over against eternity;[89] that is, the book is evangelistic. This was the view of the Reformers and Puritans (Whitaker, Pemble, Cocceius, Matthew Poole, Matthew Henry), and John Wesley. In like manner, Ralph Wardlaw used Ecclesiastes to point to the cross.[90] Today, however, the interpretation of this book is anything but unified.

---

[83]Loader, *Polar Structures*, 16-18.

[84]Ibid., 19-27, and Crenshaw, *Ecclesiastes*, 29-31.

[85]The phrase is אֶת־הַמַּעֲשֶׂה אֲשֶׁר נַעֲשָׂה.

[86]Rhyme occurs in הַנָּחָשׁ בְּלוֹא־לָחַשׁ and יִתְרוֹן לְבַעַל הַלָּשׁוֹן.

[87]Loader, *Polar Structures*, 14-15.

[88]One recent interpretation of Ecclesiastes is exceedingly strange. Zimmermann (*Inner World of Qohelet*, 1-97) argues that Qoheleth was a highly neurotic, impotent bureaucrat with homosexual tendencies. His reading is, to say the least, arbitrary.

[89]For a brief survey of interpretations from G. Thaumaturgus to Luther, see R. E. Murphy, "Qohelet Interpreted: The Bearing of the Past on the Present," *VT* 32 (1982): 331-37, which has been expanded in his commentary (*Ecclesiastes*, xlviii-lvi). For a survey of early interpretation in the LXX, the Syr, and Jerome, see S. Holm-Nielsen, "On the Interpretation of Qoheleth in Early Christianity," *VT* 24 (1974): 168-87.

[90]R. Wardlaw, *Exposition of Ecclesiastes* (1868; reprint, Minneapolis: Klock & Klock, 1982).

(1) A Pessimistic Skeptic?

In recent years scholars have emphasized the pessimism and apparent skepticism of the book. Scott describes the message of Ecclesiastes under the following points: (1) The endless motion that we see brings about no real change and no real profit. (2) Everything that happens seems to be predetermined, but no one can comprehend what will happen to him. Hence life is an enigma and a waiting on fate. (3) The theory that retribution always overtakes wickedness is contradicted by experience. (4) Death is the universal negation of all values. In the same way, misfortune can overcome every kind of virtue.[91] Crenshaw, too, argues that the Teacher rejects the ways of the traditional sages as futile; that he regards God as distant, inscrutable, and capricious; and that, since death cancels every gain in life, one should at least enjoy a woman, wine, and food while health allows.[92]

Delitzsch also adopted a negative view of Ecclesiastes. He urged that Ecclesiastes on the whole shows that the Old Testament was inadequate and incomplete. The book is in many ways dark and pessimistic and points out the need for a New Testament. Delitzsch explained that the fear of death evident in the book is a result of its outlook being pre-Christ and asserted that its notion of the fear of God is not balanced by understanding of the love of God.[93] He implied that Ecclesiastes is the low point of the Bible: "In the Book of Koheleth the Old Covenant digs for itself its own grave."[94]

Although all of the points made by the above scholars could be supported with ample citations from the text, they do not tell the full story and in fact misconstrue its message. The Teacher's faith in the justice of God and the goodness of his commands runs far deeper than these analyses imply (e.g., 8:12-13; 11:9).[95] Even where the Teacher does not know and cannot explain, his response is a response of faith (e.g., 3:16-17 [see commentary]). His recommendations that the reader enjoy life, moreover, arise not from a skeptic's despair but from a profound understanding of human mortality.

Finally, Ecclesiastes is not the inferior piece of theology that Delitzsch asserts it to be. It should not be looked upon as dark and inferior just because it is pre-Christ and therefore does not reflect the fullness of the revelation of God. The entire Old Testament would suffer from such an evaluation.

---

[91] Scott, *Proverbs and Ecclesiastes*, 202-3.

[92] Crenshaw, *Ecclesiastes*, 23-28.

[93] Delitzsch, *Ecclesiastes*, 182-84.

[94] Ibid., 182.

[95] Cf. Whybray, *Ecclesiastes*, 27.

(2) The Preacher of Joy?

R. N. Whybray contends that seven pessimistic sections within Ecclesiastes each have, usually toward the end, an exhortation to rejoice. His division of the text is described in the following chart:

Text	Problem Described	Exhortation to Rejoice
1:12–2:26	Pleasure does not satisfy	2:24-26
3:1-15	Ignorance of the future	3:12
3:16-22	Injustice	3:22
5:9-19	Wealth does not satisfy	5:17
8:10-15	Injustice	8:15
9:1-10	God inscrutable; death certain	9:7-9
11:7–12:7	Old age and death	11:9-10; 12:1

Thus the text would seem to be saying that the best thing one can do is to rejoice in the face of life's unresolved problems. For Whybray, therefore, the Teacher is not the teacher of dour pessimism but the preacher of joy.[96] To this Fox replies that true joy (i.e., "intense happiness") is not so much an option for the Teacher as mere pleasure and that even pleasure is not wholeheartedly endorsed.[97] Indeed, it seems excessive to call the Teacher a "preacher of joy"; his distress is too great for that. Also the term implies that the goal of Ecclesiastes is to drive the reader toward joy, and this emphasis obscures the theological dimension of the book.[98] Its aim is to drive the reader to God. Whybray has, however, provided a good counterbalance to those who emphasize the negative in Ecclesiastes.

(3) A Thinker Caught in the Tensions of Life?

Loader attempts to demonstrate that the Teacher everywhere draws together opposing realities in life (wisdom and folly, power and powerlessness, talk and silence, etc.). These "polar opposites" bring about tensions that the book openly acknowledges but does not always resolve. Or, to put it more precisely, the only resolution is that life is devoid of security or

---

[96]R. N. Whybray, "Qoheleth, Preacher of Joy," *JSOT* 23 (1982): 87-98. The above chart does not appear within Whybray's article. It is my summation of his argument. Whybray also argues that texts that look very pessimistic (e.g., 4:2-3) need to be read in context. However, compare his more recent commentary (*Ecclesiastes*, NCB [Grand Rapids: Eerdmans, 1989], 17-31).

[97]Fox, *Qohelet*, 70; cf. p. 62.

[98]Whybray himself appears to shy away from calling the Teacher a "preacher of joy" in his later (1989) commentary on Ecclesiastes. He instead speaks of him as a realist and also gives a good deal of attention to the Teacher's theological emphasis (*Ecclesiastes*, 24-28). At the same time, Whybray's general approach is unchanged. For example, on 3:12 he comments that "Qoheleth's intention here is to lay emphasis on man's possibility of happiness" (*Ecclesiastes*, 74).

meaning. Following this method, Loader argues that every passage in the book except the prologue and 7:8-10 has the polar pattern.

Thus, for example, in the tension between wisdom and folly, wisdom is found to be relatively superior. But in the tension between wisdom and the realities of life, wisdom is found to be worthless since life often contradicts the teachings of wisdom, and the wise share the fate of fools anyway.[99] Loader describes the tensions in a simple diagram.

Thought:	Generally accepted wisdom
Counterthought:	Folly
Tension:	*Relative* priority of wisdom
and	
Thought:	Generally accepted wisdom
Counterthought:	Life's happenstances
Tension:	Worthlessness of wisdom[100]

Loader's analysis here is illuminating.[101] Even so, his approach has a number of problems, not the least of which is that his presentation is often quite confusing.[102] It is significant that he begins his analysis with 3:1-9, which does contain a list of polar opposites,[103] and then goes on to find polar opposites everywhere. In short, 3:1-9 has been made programmatic for the entire book. He often forces the notion of polar opposites on passages where it does not belong.

For example, he examines 11:1-6 under the heading "risk and assurance" and argues that the tension of the passage is that there is no security in life.[104] While it is true that these concepts play a part in this text, it is artificial to claim that Ecclesiastes is concerned with maintaining a polar opposition here. Instead, it is simply telling the reader how to obtain a measure of financial security by minimizing risk (see commentary). Loader's analysis is questionable in other areas as well; he wrongly concludes, for example, that the Teacher rejects the notion of retribution altogether.[105]

---

[99]Loader, *Polar Structures*, 35-66.

[100]J. A. Loader, *Ecclesiastes: A Practical Commentary*, trans. J. Vriend, TI (Grand Rapids: Eerdmans, 1986), 33. I have here cited the simpler form of the diagram as it appears in his commentary rather than the more technical form found in the monograph.

[101]But cf. Fox, *Qohelet*, 32-33.

[102]Ibid., 115, n. 38.

[103]Even here, however, the text does not establish the kind of polar tension Loader claims to see, that humanity is trapped between forces of life and death and is in a state of insecurity (*Polar Structures*, 29-33). Rather it teaches the reader what it means to be mortal and urges acceptance of the fact of mortality.

[104]Ibid., 66-69. Loader is able to maintain his polar opposite only by some peculiar exegesis of vv. 1-2. His analysis makes the Teacher in effect a champion of antiwisdom in which prudence and imprudence in the final analysis are equals.

[105]Ibid., 96-105. Loader's conclusion is strange since he also contends that the tension posed by the problem of retribution is maintained. But if the doctrine is simply rejected, in what sense does a tension exist?

Ecclesiastes contains a great deal of tension, and many ambiguities are left unresolved; however, to say that the book is preoccupied with the idea of polar opposites or even uses the concept as a primary method of analysis is a considerable exaggeration. At the same time, Loader has forced us to reckon with the tension of unresolved contradiction in Ecclesiastes. Life, in short, has many unanswered questions.

(4) An Apologetic Work?

Eaton attempts to interpret Ecclesiastes as essentially an apologetic work. He observes that much of the book does not take God into account and is characterized by gloom and pessimism. He argues that when God is introduced, however, the "under-the-sun" terminology drops out and the Teacher speaks of the joy of man (2:25; 3:12; 5:18,20; 9:7; 11:7-9) and the generosity of God (2:26; 3:13; 5:19).[106] Like earlier Protestant scholars, he asserts the book to be evangelistic and apologetic: "What, then, is the purpose of Ecclesiastes? It is an essay in apologetics. It defends the life of faith in a generous God by pointing to the grimness of the alternative."[107]

On the other hand, if Ecclesiastes is an apologetic work, it is surely unlike any other defense of the faith we know. It raises more questions than it answers. It is also doubtful whether we can legitimately separate two viewpoints within Ecclesiastes—the one being the worldly, under-the-sun perspective and the other being the true, evangelistic heart of the Teacher. As noted earlier, those who read Ecclesiastes as pessimism and skepticism do not do so without substantial support from the text. Also, one would not expect in an apology such a frank *carpe diem* ("seize the day," a statement of the brevity of life) as in 11:10. While Eaton has correctly observed that the Teacher believes both in God and in his goodness and generosity, we cannot say that Ecclesiastes is evangelizing *in the conventional sense.* The Teacher's words are unlike those of the prophets and apostles. Nevertheless, he does drive the reader to God (see below).

(5) The Original Existentialist?

Scholars have long noted the similarities—at times superficial and at times profound—between Ecclesiastes and existentialist philosophy.[108] M. Fox has recently exploited these similarities to the full. Drawing heavily upon *The Myth of Sisyphus* by A. Camus, he paints a picture of the Teacher as a man wrestling with the absurdity of the world.

---

[106]Eaton, *Ecclesiastes*, 45.

[107]Ibid., 44.

[108]Cf. Gordis, *Koheleth*, 112-21.

He argues that the Teacher's main concern is the "*rationality of existence.* This rationality [the Teacher] denies, calling everything *hebel*" although rationality itself remains an "irreducible value."[109] Fox further contends that the Teacher does not so much challenge wisdom as bemoan the fact that wisdom is not rewarded. Fox concludes that the Teacher, having faced the absurdity of life, "affirms the grasping of *inner experience*, emotional and intellectual, as the one domain of human freedom."[110]

Although acutely aware of the negative side of wisdom, the Teacher is himself committed to it. He has a "compulsion for knowledge." He is a Sisyphus whose triumph comes at the moment when he has pushed the rock of inquiry up to the very peak, to the point of lucidity, even though the knowledge gained by that struggle may be painful and the rock inevitably rolls back down the hill before full illumination is attained.[111]

Fox is correct that the rationality of existence is for the Teacher a more fundamental problem than mere matters of material wealth and pleasure. Nevertheless, these too are a part of his quest to understand what makes life worth living. He does not deal in abstractions. Similarly, the Teacher's challenge to the intellectual quest is far more fundamental than grief over the wise not being adequately compensated. More significantly, he doubts whether it is possible for the wise to find the answers to their questions at all (7:23-24).

Fox has correctly observed that other sages were also aware of the limitations of wisdom,[112] and he is also correct in noting that the Teacher does not attack traditional wisdom but rather grieves over the "inevitability of ignorance."[113] Nevertheless, the Teacher looks upon the intellectual quest—what Fox calls the "wisdom imperative"—as a road with no destination. He will not play the part of the scholar who walks the road simply for the sake of being on the journey. If there is no goal, if "truth" can never be attained, what is the point? He will not (and here is Fox's fundamental error) play the part of Sisyphus and forever be pushing the rock up the hill just to see it roll down again. He abandons the intellectual quest not because of a collapse of nerve but out of conviction that it was a manifest failure. It had been for him what the quest for righteousness had been for Saul of Tarsus. In Ecclesiastes he turns away resolutely from the search for truth through reason although rejecting neither the validity of reason itself nor the moral insight of traditional wisdom.

---

[109]Fox, *Qohelet*, 10. It is here possible to give only a brief summary of Fox's conclusions (far too brief to do his work justice).

[110]Ibid., 11. Cf. p. 77, "By exploiting our limited possibilities we become most fully human."

[111]Ibid., 117-20.

[112]For example, Agur (Prov 30:3-4); Fox, *Qohelet*, 109.

[113]Ibid., 111-12.

His solution to the dilemma of absurdity is thus not what Fox perceives it to be. He does not celebrate emotional and intellectual experiences as the givers of human value. To be sure, he does counsel that his readers enjoy the fleeting pleasures of life and assures them that these pleasures can be appreciated as long as their transitory nature and limited value are understood.

Nevertheless, the Teacher's arguments drive the readers not to the self but *to God* as the only giver of permanent worth—not simply to doctrines about God or to the teachings of the wise but to the very person of God. Thus he does not deny but rather emphasizes that much about God is beyond our ability to know. Even if, however, he does as Paul in Athens and preaches the unknown God, it is nevertheless *God* he preaches and not *humanity*. The Teacher anticipates the existentialists in perceiving the absurdities they see, but his response is quite different.

(6) Reflection for the Wise

If Ecclesiastes is to be understood as having an evangelistic purpose, it can only be interpreted as such within its genre and context. The work is written for the educated elite in the ancient Near Eastern setting. It is addressed, in short, to the "wise."

Childs rightly notes that "Koheleth's (the Teacher's) sayings do not have an independent status but function as a critical corrective (to conventional wisdom), much as the book of James serves in the New Testament as an essential corrective to misunderstanding the Pauline letters."[114] The book is unintelligible if it is not assumed that it is primarily addressed to an aristocratic audience. The implied readers were people who were likely to have access to the king and to the circles of power. They were people for whom the pursuit of wealth was a real possibility and not just a fantasy and who had the leisure time for intellectual pursuits.

Some of his audience were adherents of traditional, conventional wisdom. He warns these readers of the limits of wisdom. Many were wealthy bureaucrats or were at least comfortable in their situations. For these the Teacher is trying to strip away the illusion of having achieved permanence and value in life. Still others knew the Babylonian and Egyptian skeptical philosophy and already were familiar with pessimistic literature. To these he asserts that although life is often arbitrary, despair and cynicism are not appropriate responses. The wise reader will enjoy the good things life offers and yet maintain reverence for God.

Ecclesiastes could be accurately described as a report on the failed quest for eternal life. In this it stands well in the tradition of ancient Near Eastern literature, especially the *Epic of Gilgamesh*. "Eternal life" is not

[114]Childs, *Introduction to the Old Testament*, 588.

merely perpetual existence. It includes this, but it is especially the sense that one's life and work are fundamentally meaningful rather than of no lasting value. A writer seeks "immortality" through the masterpiece of literature, an athlete wishes to be "immortalized in the record books," and an actor desires to live forever through fame (all of which the Teacher would pronounce futile).[115] The search for value also includes the hedonist's attempt to make life worth living through pleasure, the politician's effort to control life through power, and the intellectual's attempt to master life through knowledge. Ecclesiastes therefore examines not only the specific question of life after death but also the vain attempts to gain genuine personal worth through wealth and pleasure, through accomplishments and power, and through knowledge.

The Teacher tells his readers how to live in the world as it really is instead of living in a world of false hope. In short, *Ecclesiastes urges its readers to recognize that they are mortal.* They must abandon all illusions of self-importance, face death and life squarely, and accept with fear and trembling their dependence on God.

Recognition of personal mortality leads necessarily to three conclusions. First, all pretense of pride in oneself must be abandoned. For the ruling elite this means a humble acceptance of the limitations on both their political power and on their ability to achieve intellectual comprehension of life.[116]

Second, life should be enjoyed for what it is—a gift of God. The book counsels that while avoiding the temptation to consider pleasure to the point of being the goal of life, one should not miss the fleeting joys life affords. This too is an act of humility, for it is an admission that one's work is not as important is one might wish and that it has no eternal validity. It is also, ironically, an antidote to the madness of the quest for wealth. Although money is ostensively sought for the pleasure it can provide, personal happiness and the enjoyment of life's pleasures are often the price paid for wealth.

Third, and most important for us and for the book, one must revere God. To refuse to do so is to deny one's dependency on God.

(7) Reflections on Creation and the Fall

One other aspect of the theology of Ecclesiastes that deserves mention is its theological and literary dependence on the early chapters of Gene-

---

[115]See 9:1; 12:12.

[116]Loader, *Ecclesiastes*, 15: "For all those who have been disillusioned by the discovery that the all-embracing systems on which they relied were not in fact reliable, how thrilling and astonishing it is to discover that in Scripture itself a similarly disillusioned and desperate voice may be heard." He notes that Ecclesiastes "cries out" for "a deliverance from the misery of meaninglessness."

sis. In these chapters humanity is subjected to a life of toil and condemned to death. The presentation of God in Ecclesiastes as absent and hidden arises directly from Gen 3 (where humanity loses access to God). The frequent refrain that all is "meaningless" may be a play on the name of Abel, the murdered son of Adam.[117] More to the point, the Teacher ponders what has become of *ʾādām* ("humanity, Adam") as a result of sin. Ecclesiastes can also be called a collection of reflections on creation and the fall, or even reflections on the continuing significance of creation and the fall. The reasons for this are not difficult to imagine. Genesis tells the story of how humans—originally in a state of life, paradise, and innocence—fell into guilt, toil, and mortality. Ecclesiastes tells how persons now made weak and mortal should live.

[117]In Hebrew both are written הבל. C. C. Forman, "Koheleth's Use of Genesis," *JSS* 5 (1960): 256-63.

OUTLINE OF THE BOOK

1. Introduction (1:1-2)
2. On Time and the World (1:3-11)
3. On Wisdom (1:12-18)
4. On Wealth (2:1-11)
5. On Wisdom (2:12-17)
6. On Wealth (2:18-26)
7. On Time and the World (3:1-15b)
8. On Politics (3:15c-17)
9. On Death (3:18-22)
10. On Politics (4:1-3)
11. On Wealth (4:4-8)
12. On Friendship (4:9-12)
13. On Politics (4:13-16)
14. On Religion (5:1-7)
15. On Politics (5:8-9)
16. On Wealth (5:10–6:6)
17. Transition (6:7-9)
18. On Wisdom and Death (6:10–7:4)
19. Transition (7:5-6)
20. On Wisdom and Politics (7:7-9)
21. Transition (7:10)
22. On Wisdom and Wealth (7:11-14)
23. On Religion, Wisdom, and Evil (7:15-29)
24. Transition (8:1)
25. On Politics (8:2-6)
26. Transition (8:7-8)
27. On Theodicy (8:9–9:1)
28. Transition (9:2)
29. On Death and Contentment (9:3-10)
30. Transition (9:11-12)
31. On Politics (9:13–10:17)
32. Transition (10:18-20)
33. On Wealth (11:1-6)
34. On Death and Contentment (11:7–12:7)
35. Conclusion (12:8-14)

1. Introduction (1:1-2)

[1]The words of the Teacher, son of David, king in Jerusalem:
[2]"Meaningless! Meaningless!"
says the Teacher.
"Utterly meaningless!
Everything is meaningless."

These verses form the introduction to the book. Verse 1 is historical in that it gives the author of the book, and v. 2 is thematic in that it describes the dominant theme or idea of the book. This text is first level discourse, where the Teacher is referred to in the third person.

1:1 The author is called "the Teacher [*Qoheleth*], son of David, king in Jerusalem." This verse, in conjunction with v. 12, implies Solomonic authorship. The precise meaning of *Qoheleth* (here rendered "the Teacher") is uncertain.[1] The word may mean a "speaker in the assembly." The verse indicates that although the author of the work is Solomon, he writes under the role-name "the Teacher." He is not speaking in the capacity of a king but as a teacher. The book contains advice and reflection rather than decrees.

1:2 He now starkly sets forth the theme of his book in a manner befitting the theme itself: "Everything is meaningless." Indeed, the very meaning of this verse is itself a mystery. The word used here, *hebel*,[2] means "vapor" or "breath" and is used in Isa 57:13 parallel with "wind" and in Prov 21:6 for "a fleeting vapor."[3] The word can thus combine the notions of being insubstantial and transitory, as in Ps 144:4, "Man is like a breath." In this sense the English word that best approximates the meaning of this word is "vapid." The Hebrew word is also used in Zech 10:2 ("in vain"), which says that idols give vapid comfort; that is, the comfort is empty, fleeting, and therefore a lie.

On the other hand, "vapid" does not begin to capture the full range of meaning for *hebel*. The word can refer to that which is deceitful or ineffectual, especially as used of false gods (Jer 16:19). In addition, as M. Fox points out, *hebel* is often used in Ecclesiastes in ways for which translations like "fleeting" or "meaningless" are not appropriate. In 8:14, for example, the Teacher pronounces as *hebel* the injustice of the righteous receiving the recompense due to the wicked (and the converse). He does not here mean

---

[1]It is related to the root קהל, "to gather, congregate." In form קֹהֶלֶת is a Qal feminine participle and is grammatically comparable to סֹפֶרֶת, "scribe" (Ezra 2:55; Neh 7:57), and פֹּכֶרֶת, "binder [of gazelles]" (Ezra 2:57; Neh 7:59). This participle form appears to have a functional meaning. C. F. Whitley (*Koheleth: His Language and Thought* [Berlin: Walter de Gruyter, 1979], 4-6) argues that the word means "skeptic," but his interpretation is based on doubtful readings of Neh 5:7 and Job 11:10.

[2]הֶבֶל.

[3]R. Gordis, *Koheleth: The Man and His World* (New York: Schocken, 1968), 204.

"ephemeral" (which in this case would be a good thing) or "meaningless" (i.e., of no real significance) but "absurd." In other words, injustice is contrary to how the world should operate; it is an active violation of what ought to be the moral order. The dictates of wisdom and reason are no longer sure guides because the world itself is warped and capricious. Thus, for example, the man who works hard but sees all his profit go to one who has not shared in his labor is a victim of *hebel* (2:18-21). It is also an absurdity—an offense to reason—that the wise and the fool share the same fate (2:14-15).[4] People ought to get what they deserve. In fact, *hebel* has become a catchword for the negation of values.[5]

Even this does not exhaust the meaning of *hebel*. When the Teacher says that pleasure is a *hebel* and accomplishes nothing (2:1-2), he does not mean that pleasures are strictly absurd or even primarily that they are fleeting. Rather, he means that they are a waste of time in that they fail to satisfy. In this sense *hebel* might correctly be translated "meaningless" ("foolish"). Verbosity too is *hebel*: "The more the words, the less the meaning" (6:11; cf. 5:7). The multiplying of words is not strictly absurd, nor is it to be understood as ephemeral. It is simply an activity without real significance.

How then is *hebel* to be translated? The NIV consistently translates it as "meaningless," but in many passages this falls short of the mark. Fox attempts to justify "absurd" as the best single-word translation of the term, but his exposition is overly influenced by the existentialist philosophy of Camus; in some cases "absurd" is plainly inadequate.[6] Other single-word equivalents such as "vapid" or the older "vanity" are equally inadequate. It is doubtful, in fact, whether an ancient Israelite would have grasped the full range of meaning inherent in the Teacher's use of *hebel* prior to the writing of Ecclesiastes itself.

One option, of course, is to translate *hebel* with a number of different words in accordance with context. This is legitimate translation procedure; but, as Fox points out, the Teacher is building a case around the word *hebel*. A variety of translations obscure this.[7] It may be that the modern, Christian reader can do no better than to import *hebel* into his or her vocabulary, much as has been done with *agape* and to a lesser extent *koinonia*.

Everything is transitory and therefore of no lasting value. People are caught in the trap of the absurd and pursue empty pleasures. They build their lives on lies.

---

[4] See M. V. Fox, *Qohelet and His Contradictions*, JSOTSup 71 (Sheffield: Almond, 1989), 29-46.

[5] See K. Seybold, "הֶבֶל," in *TDOT* 3:313-20.

[6] For his indebtedness to Camus, see Fox, *Qohelet*, 13-16, 31-32. Contrary to pp. 42-43, כָּל־יְמֵי חַיֵּי הֶבְלֶךָ (9:9) clearly means "all the days of your fleeting life" and not "all the days of this meaningless life."

[7] Fox, *Qohelet*, 36.

2. On Time and the World (1:3-11)

3What does man gain from all his labor
at which he toils under the sun?
4Generations come and generations go,
but the earth remains forever.
5The sun rises and the sun sets,
and hurries back to where it rises.
6The wind blows to the south
and turns to the north;
round and round it goes,
ever returning on its course.
7All streams flow into the sea,
yet the sea is never full.
To the place the streams come from,
there they return again.
8All things are wearisome,
more than one can say.
The eye never has enough of seeing,
nor the ear its fill of hearing.
9What has been will be again,
what has been done will be done again;
there is nothing new under the sun.
10Is there anything of which one can say,
"Look! This is something new"?
It was here already, long ago;
it was here before our time.
11There is no remembrance of men of old,
and even those who are yet to come
will not be remembered
by those who follow.

A poetic picture of the structure of the world, this text depicts the human environment as a monotonous prison.

1:3 No one can show a net profit for a life of hard labor.[8] The phrase "under the sun" is comparable to "under heaven" in Exod 17:14; Deut 7:24; 9:14 and refers to this world. The phrase is also found in Elamite and Phoenician inscriptions.[9] After a life of hard labor, no one can show a net gain; everything one has is vapid.

1:4 The transitory nature of human generations contrasts with the permanence and apparent immutability of the physical world. No one has

---

[8]The word יִתְרוֹן is a commercial term and means "profit," and עָמָל refers to hard physical labor.

[9]Whitley, *Koheleth*, 8. The Phoenician occurrences date from the sixth and fifth centuries B.C.; and the Elamite, from the twelfth century B.C. Hence there is no need to regard this as a Grecism (ὑφ' ἡλίῳ).

changed the course of nature. Like ants on a rock, we leave no trace of having been here. The birth of one generation and the passing of another are just nature's cycles.[10]

1:5 The sun is on a monotonous cycle of rising, setting, and then racing back to the place from which it rises. The verb translated "hurries"[11] means "to pant." The sun is like a runner endlessly making his way around a racetrack.

1:6 As the movement of the sun implies an east-west course, now the wind is described as moving north and south.[12] The repetition in "going round and round"[13] heightens the sense of monotony and purposelessness.

1:7 The sense of accomplishing nothing is reinforced here. The rivers continually empty into the sea but cannot fill it. The last phrase does not refer to the cycle of evaporation and rainfall as implied in the NIV translation. Gordis correctly calls such an interpretation "linguistically forced."[14] It should read, "To the place where the rivers go, there they continually go."[15] The implication here is not cyclic motion but futile activity.

These verses profoundly impress certain sensations on the reader. First comes a sense of the indifference of the universe to our presence. It was here before we came, and it will be here, unchanged, after we have gone. Second, however, the universe, like us, is trapped in a cycle of monotonous and meaningless motion. It is forever moving, but it accomplishes nothing. Finally, a sense of loneliness and abandonment pervades the text. No one has described this better than Paul. The creation is "subjected to frustration," in "bondage to decay," and awaiting "freedom" (Rom 8:19-21).

Note also that the *form* of the text reinforces the *content*. As a wisdom discourse, the passage maintains a tone of authority and objectivity. Its poetic rhythm, moreover, increases the sense of monotony and futility.

1:8 The interpretation of this verse is notoriously difficult. A survey of modern translations reveals points of agreement and disagreement among them; many are similar to the NIV.[16]

Another approach is to translate v. 8c,d as negative rhetorical questions.[17] They would read, "Is not the eye satisfied with seeing and the ear filled with hearing?" A third approach is to translate v. 8c,d as an indirect

---

[10]Cf. G. S. Ogden, "The Interpretation of דור in Ecclesiastes 1.4," *JSOT* 34 (1986): 91-92. Ogden emphasizes the cyclic motion implicit in the text, but transitoriness is also present.

[11]שׁאף.

[12]Gordis, *Koheleth*, 206.

[13]סוֹבֵב סֹבֵב.

[14]Gordis, *Koheleth*, 207.

[15]שׁוּב with an infinitive can mean "to do something repeatedly."

[16]See the RSV, NASB, GNB, and Moffatt.

[17]As is done in the NEB: "Is not the eye surfeited with seeing and the ear sated with hearing?"

statement subordinate to v. 8b[18] as, "Nobody can say that the eyes have not been satisfied with seeing or that the ears have not been filled with hearing."

None of these three interpretations, however, is likely. The lines in v. 8b,c,d form a tristich consisting of three coordinate clauses that are structurally parallel. All three lines are of approximately the same length, and each is composed of a negative followed by a main verb, subject, and infinitive complement to the verb.[19] Since lines 8b,c,d are parallel, they should be translated as such.

Lines *a* and *b* present other difficulties. First is the problem of the meaning of "weary" in line *a*.[20] Although the LXX translates it "weary," BDB, like KB, gives "wearisome" as the meaning of the word in this verse. This suggestion is followed by the NIV and other modern translations. The word elsewhere occurs only in Deut 25:18 and 2 Sam 17:2. In these passages it clearly does not mean "wearisome" but "weary."[21] The proper translation of v. 8a is, "All things are weary."[22]

The Masoretes erred in punctuating the line as the beginning of v. 8 instead of as the end of v. 7. Lines *b, c*, and *d*, as the parallelism shows, comprise a distinct unit grammatically unrelated to line *a*. Line *a* is the summary and conclusion to the discourse of vv. 3-7. In this passage the world is described as being in constant, cyclic, but purposeless motion. Generations come and go, the sun rises and sets, the wind goes round and round, and the rivers ever rush to the sea. The sum of all this is, "All things are weary."

Line *b* translates easily enough: "A person cannot speak," or, "No one is able to speak."[23] Translators qualify it either by supplying an object such as "it" or by grammatically combining line *a* with *b* (NIV). All these translations assume that what the text means is that no one can adequately say how "wearisome" the world is.[24] As mentioned above, however, the parallel structure of *b, c*, and *d* separates line *a* from line *b*. Neither can one supply an

---

[18]Cf. the JB: "No man can say that eyes have not had enough of seeing, ears their fill of hearing."

[19]B: לֹא־יוּכַל אִישׁ לְדַבֵּר

C: לֹא־תִשְׂבַּע עַיִן לִרְאוֹת

D: וְלֹא־תִמָּלֵא אֹזֶן מִשְּׁמֹעַ

[20]יְגֵעִים.

[21]Another occurrence of the word, following the emendation suggested in BHS, is in Ps 88:16. Here it also means "weary" or "toiling." Indeed, the adjective יָגֵעַ is most naturally taken as the participle form of the Qal stative verb stem יגע, "to toil," "be weary," which renders the proposed meaning "wearisome" most unlikely.

[22]Thus F. Delitzsch (*Ecclesiastes* [Grand Rapids: Eerdmans, n.d.], 223-24), G. A. Barton (*Ecclesiastes*, ICC [Edinburgh: T & T Clark, 1912], 74-75), and M. A. Eaton (*Ecclesiastes*, TOTC [Downers Grove: InterVarsity, 1983], 59) all translate the word as "weary."

[23]לֹא־יוּכַל אִישׁ לְדַבֵּר.

[24]This interpretation is also followed by E. M. Good, "The Unfilled Sea: Style and Meaning in Ecclesiastes 1:2-11," in *Israelite Wisdom: Theological and Literary Essays in Honor of Samuel Terrien* (New York: Union Theological Seminary, 1978), 69.

object such as "it"; to do so misunderstands the function of the verb "speak" used here.[25] This line should be translated, "No one is able to speak."

This obviously does not mean that humans are physiologically or intellectually incapable of speech. Rather, the line must be interpreted as part of the tristich of v. 8b,c,d, a response to the situation described in vv. 3-8a. Humans, confronted by the monotony and aimlessness of the situation in which they have been placed, have nothing to say.

In Ecclesiastes the correct use of language is of crucial importance. The task of the wise is to know the explanation of things (8:1) and to put wisdom into exactly the right words (12:9-10). The wise individual can control his or her tongue (10:20). Therefore what the wise says is important and to be heeded (9:17). The fool, on the other hand, multiplies words but says nothing (10:12-14) and commits the supreme folly of babbling on before God (5:1-2; Eng., vv. 2-3). It is all the more significant, therefore, that no one, not even the wise, can say anything in the face of the purposeless enigma that is the world (1:8; cf. 8:16–9:1). No one can speak meaningfully to or about the world; that is, no one can explain, influence, or control it. Humanity, for all its intellectual investigations, must accept life and death and the coming and going of generations in this world as an unexplained and inexplicable given. Before this riddle humans are like the dumb animals. Language, the greatest power human beings have, is of no advantage.

Lines *c* and *d* carry this concept further. Part of the "vanity" of this world is that it does not satisfy. The eyes cannot be satisfied, not even by wealth (cf. 4:8). People keenly feel this sensation of deficiency (3:9-11). The ear also cannot be filled; no amount of learning can answer people's needs (8:17; 12:12). The resources of human reason leave humanity facing a blank wall.

An appropriate translation of Eccl 1:8 is as follows:

All things are weary.
No one is able to speak,
the eye is not satisfied by seeing,
and the ear is not filled by hearing.[26]

---

[25]The Piel stem דבר, in contrast to the Qal of אמר, can occur in the absolute, i.e., without an object (e.g., Gen 24:15, [NIV has "praying" rather than "speaking"]; Job 1:16; 16:4,6). One uses אמר when giving the content of what was said, but the Piel of דבר is used to describe the act of speaking itself. Generally "the content of the speech itself is not suggested by *dibber* (e.g., in Judg 14:7) but is presupposed on the basis of what precedes or follows (e.g., in Gen 27:5-6), or is only roughly indicated" (W. H. Schmidt, "דָּבָר *dabhar*," *TDOT* 3:84-125; the quote is from p. 99). The Piel of דבר is usually followed by some form of אמר if the content of the speech is given.

[26]The LXX supports the division of v. 8 into the cola proposed here: πάντες οἱ λόγοι ἔγκοποι / οὐ δυνήσεται ἀνὴρ τοῦ λαλεῖν / καὶ οὐκ ἐμπλησθήσεται ὀμθαλμός τοῦ ὁρᾶν / καὶ οὐ πληρωθήσεται οὖς ἀπὸ ἀκροάσεως.

There is a link between v. 8a and b,c,d: "things" serves as a catchword with "say."[27] Verse 8a is the summary of the world situation described in 1:3-7, and 1:8b,c,d is humanity's condition in that situation.

1:9-11 In vv. 9-11 the Teacher gives another implication of the description of the world in vv. 3-8a: "What[28] has been will be again." Nothing is new, and nothing gains eternal fame. The Teacher's words are not contradicted by technological advances or by the fact that we can remember the names of famous people such as Homer, Caesar, and Shakespeare. The fundamental events of life (birth, marriage, work, death, etc.) remain unchanged.[29] The desire for something new is the desire for something that alters the nature of life in the world. Cars, computers, and jet airplanes may have made some things easier and faster. For us, however, as for our ancient predecessors, the sun rises and sets; the rivers run their courses; and people continue their endless quest for fame, power, and happiness even as they move steadily toward death. The vast majority of people never achieve lasting fame, while those who do gain nothing by it.

This passage is not a contradiction to the gospel but a call for it. The world is in bondage; and humanity is unable to explain, find satisfaction in, or alter it. Only the Word, who came into the world from above, can open the way of understanding and escape (John 8:23,31-32). He has done a new thing: he has created a new covenant, given the new birth, new life, and a new commandment (Jer 31:31-34). He gives a new name that will last forever. Everything else is old and passing away.

3. On Wisdom (1:12-18)

[12]I, the Teacher, was king over Israel in Jerusalem. [13]I devoted myself to study and to explore by wisdom all that is done under heaven. What a heavy burden God has laid on men! [14]I have seen all the things that are done under the sun; all of them are meaningless, a chasing after the wind.

[15]What is twisted cannot be straightened;
what is lacking cannot be counted.

[16]I thought to myself, "Look, I have grown and increased in wisdom more than anyone who has ruled over Jerusalem before me; I have experienced much of wisdom and knowledge." [17]Then I applied myself to the understanding of wisdom, and also of madness and folly, but I learned that this, too, is a chasing after the wind.

---

[27]הַדְּבָרִים and לְדַבֵּר.

[28]On the use of מָה as an indefinite pronoun, see Whitley, *Koheleth*, 10-11. See also BDB, 552.

[29]These are the "archetypal events." Cf. Fox, *Qohelet*, 172-73.

**[18]For with much wisdom comes much sorrow;
the more knowledge, the more grief.**

1:12 The book reminds us that its author is Solomon (the Teacher). This personal reflection gives credibility to the discussion below. No one but Solomon could have pursued and attained wisdom to the degree described here. The perfect tense of the verb, "was,"[30] does not mean that the real Solomon is dead and the author is here speaking in his behalf but that Solomon, the author, is speaking to the reader not as king but as teacher, as is implied in his use of the name "the Teacher."

1:13 The Teacher gave himself wholly to the task of acquiring wisdom and knowledge, but he found it to be a miserable work with which to be busied[31] (cf. 1 Kgs 4:29-34). A universal theme in wisdom and philosophic writings is that the life of wisdom is the highest of all callings.[32] In Plato the task of the philosopher is the purest of all. Here, however, it is a grievous task (we could translate the phrase as a "lousy job"). Why is the Teacher's attitude so negative, and why does he say this job has been imposed on him by God? First, he is challenging the widely held notion that pursuit of knowledge fulfills life and gives a person permanent significance. Second, he finds it a hopeless task; the answers he seeks he cannot find. Third, the Teacher sees all of life as under the rule of a sovereign God. The intellectuals and their work are as much under his authority as anyone else (cf. 1 Cor 3:19).

1:14 The Teacher again asserts here that all work is doomed to disappear in the face of time and death and that none of it is of eternal value. In context he is specifically referring to intellectual labor. The implication of the phrase "a chasing[33] after the wind" may be described as follows: You never can catch it; but if you do catch it, you do not have anything anyway.[34]

1:15 The Teacher reinforces the idea of the hopelessness of intellectual pursuit with a proverb. That which is "twisted" refers to a problem that

---

[30]"Have been" is a better translation of הָיִיתִי here. Fox (*Qohelet*, 173) captures both the power and simplicity of this verse: "I am Qohelet. I have been king over Israel in Jerusalem." Also see J. Crenshaw, *Ecclesiastes*, OTL (Philadelphia: Westminster, 1987), 71; R. Murphy, *Ecclesiastes*, WBC (Dallas: Word, 1992), 13.

[31]The meaning of the infinitive לַעֲנוֹת has been disputed. Gordis notes that the evidence for a verb form of this root (ענה) meaning "to be busy" is weak since it only occurs in Ecclesiastes. He argues that this is a Qal form of the root to "to be afflicted" (Gordis, *Koheleth*, 210). His argument is plausible, but see the LXX and Vg and cf. Whitley, *Koheleth*, 12.

[32]The Egyptian *Satire on Trades* does not specifically address what we would call the "intellectual quest," but it too exalts what may be called loosely the life of scholarship.

[33]On רְעוּת see Whitley, *Koheleth*, 13.

[34]While this implies "vexation" on the part of the individual, it is the *task*, not the individual involved in the task, that is a "chasing after the wind." Fox (*Qohelet*, 48-51) sees this as a description of the psychological state of the pursuer.

cannot be solved, and that which is "lacking" refers to lack of information (i.e., missing data cannot be taken into account[35] and thus contribute toward finding an answer). Some problems cannot be solved, and some information we can never find. The intellectual more than anyone else should be aware of the futility of the human position. No matter how he or she searches, the intellectual cannot answer some fundamental questions of life. The implication behind this is that God's ways are inscrutable.

1:16-18 Having felt that he had mastered intellectual pursuits, the Teacher decided he would understand "foolishness" (i.e., pursuit of pleasure). This text anticipates 2:1-11, where the actual pursuit of physical pleasure is described, but here he means that he examined the idea of the life of pleasure from a philosophical standpoint. He finds what we might call epicureanism to be unsatisfactory. His turn to folly, however, is based on his prior disappointment with the intellectual quest; he had found that increased knowledge only meant increased grief (v. 18).[36]

4. On Wealth (2:1-11)

[1]I thought in my heart, "Come now, I will test you with pleasure to find out what is good." But that also proved to be meaningless. [2]"Laughter," I said, "is foolish. And what does pleasure accomplish?" [3]I tried cheering myself with wine, and embracing folly—my mind still guiding me with wisdom. I wanted to see what was worthwhile for men to do under heaven during the few days of their lives.

[4]I undertook great projects: I built houses for myself and planted vineyards. [5]I made gardens and parks and planted all kinds of fruit trees in them. [6]I made reservoirs to water groves of flourishing trees. [7]I bought male and female slaves and had other slaves who were born in my house. I also owned more herds and flocks than anyone in Jerusalem before me. [8]I amassed silver and gold for myself, and the treasure of kings and provinces. I acquired men and women singers, and a harem as well—the delights of the heart of man. [9]I became greater by far than anyone in Jerusalem before me. In all this my wisdom stayed with me.

[10]I denied myself nothing my eyes desired;
I refused my heart no pleasure.
My heart took delight in all my work,
and this was the reward for all my labor.

[35]Thus לְהִמָּנוֹת. Fox (*Qohelet*, 175-76) emends לְהִמָּנוֹת to לְהִמָּלוֹת (מלא, with Mishnaic-type spelling) and translates, "No deficiency can be made up for." His emendation does not improve the sense but rather misses the point altogether, and it is not clear that the Niphal stem of מלא can bear this meaning.

[36]Verse 18 is another level two (traditional wisdom) discourse assertion. Delitzsch (*Ecclesiastes*, 232) notes that יוֹסִיף is an imperfect tense functioning nominally. He is followed by Whitley, *Koheleth*, 17; Fox, *Qohelet*, 177; and Gordis, *Koheleth*, 214.

[11]**Yet when I surveyed all that my hands had done**
and what I had toiled to achieve,
everything was meaningless, a chasing after the wind;
nothing was gained under the sun.

In this passage the Teacher describes his grand experiment into pleasure and its total failure.

2:1 He introduces his experiment by a dialogue with his heart. He proposes a test,[37] the goal of which is to determine if pleasures provide an adequate justification for human existence. But he anticipates the results of his experiment—all the joys were fleeting.

2:2 This continues his proleptic explanation of his conclusions. Laughter was insanity, and fun accomplished nothing. He does not imply that all laughter is to be squelched as an evil; rather, as a solution for the basic problems of life (above all the problem of death), it is a total failure. Throughout the book the Teacher will recommend enjoying life, but here he warns that partaking of pleasure does not of itself give meaning to existence.

2:3 He experimented with alcohol as a means of alleviating the pain of life. His attempt to embrace "folly"[38] while still being guided[39] by "wisdom" was not an act of cognitive dissonance (a way of having his cake and eating it too) but an attempt to indulge in pleasure without being consumed by it. All will agree that a life of total dissipation and indulgence is reprehensible—we need no "Teacher" to show us that. Rather, he wanted to know if *rationally controlled* indulgence in pleasure gave meaning to life. He did not become a drunk. His experiment was an experiment in pleasure, not debauchery.

There is a veiled reference to impending death in the phrase "in the few days of their lives." He wanted to find out if drinking and drinking parties were the best solution to the emptiness of life in the face of death. He found that alcohol does not take away the pain.

2:4 "I undertook great projects" (cf. 1 Kgs 7; 9:1; 10:21; 2 Chr 8:3-6) could be rendered "I enlarged my spheres of activity." This general statement is followed by more specific lines. Notice how frequently "for myself" appears. This is the "gospel" of selfishness.

2:5 Great gardens were the pride of ancient kings, as indicated especially by the "Hanging Gardens of Babylon."

---

[37]The form אֲנַסְּכָה (Piel stem of נסה) is unusual for having a *plene* form of the second person masculine singular pronoun suffix. The Vg misreads it as *affluam* from the root נסך ("to pour out"). See Whitley, *Koheleth*, 18, for discussion.

[38]The BHS suggestion (followed by Fox, *Qohelet*, 180) to emend וְלֶאֱחֹז to וְלֹא אֹחֵז ("and not embracing [folly]") misses the point of the text.

[39]On נהג referring to the conduct of one's life, see Whitley, *Koheleth*, 19-20.

2:6 He even had technical feats of engineering, including aqueducts and other waterworks. The traditional pools of Solomon in the Valley of Artas southwest of Jerusalem may be part of that system. Three ancient stone pools are found there.

2:7 Solomon was the ultimate genteel landowner. His own slaves, herds, and flocks (the real measure of wealth to the average man) were greater than any in local history (cf. 1 Kgs 4:20-23).

2:8 Solomon (whose wealth is the subject of 1 Kgs 10:14-29) was a wealthy patron of the arts for his personal pleasure, as indicated by his personal choir. He also indulged in sexual pleasure.[40]

2:9 As in v. 3, his claim that he retained his wisdom is an assurance to the reader that he did not go berserk in his quest for luxury and pleasure. His problem was not lack of self-restraint; but any attempt to find a rationale for existence in pleasure and affluence is bound to fail, even if that attempt is sobered by self-control.

2:10-11 The Teacher felt he had earned the right to enjoy himself. He had worked hard for all of this. But the payoff did not match the effort expended.

5. On Wisdom (2:12-17)

12Then I turned my thoughts to consider wisdom,
and also madness and folly.
What more can the king's successor do
than what has already been done?
13I saw that wisdom is better than folly,
just as light is better than darkness.
14The wise man has eyes in his head,
while the fool walks in the darkness;
but I came to realize
that the same fate overtakes them both.
15Then I thought in my heart,
"The fate of the fool will overtake me also.
What then do I gain by being wise?"
I said in my heart,
"This too is meaningless."
16For the wise man, like the fool, will not be long remembered;
in days to come both will be forgotten.
Like the fool, the wise man too must die!

17So I hated life, because the work that is done under the sun was grievous to me. All of it is meaningless, a chasing after the wind.

---

[40]The words שִׁדָּה וְשִׁדּוֹת are somewhat obscure and may be related to the word שַׁד, "breast." This seems to be a colloquialism for a girl of pleasure or a concubine. Whitley (*Koheleth*, 22) comments that in an Amarna tablet the ideogram *salumun*, one meaning of which is *concubine*, has the Canaanite gloss *saditum*.

2:12 The beginning of this verse should not be translated, "I turned to see that wisdom was madness and folly," as Gordis has done.[41] The NIV rendition "and also madness" is best here.

Verse 12b, however, is extraordinarily difficult. The NIV ("What more . . . been done?") is quite paraphrastic and depends on emending the text.[42] Its apparent meaning is that no subsequent king could possibly do more to investigate wisdom and folly than Solomon. This reading is more or less followed by most modern interpreters.[43] This interpretation, however, is strangely out of place in this context and involves significant alterations or peculiar translations of the text.[44]

Fox emends to obtain a different interpretation: the "king" is concerned about whether his successor will be a fool who wastes all that was earned for him.[45] In light of 2:18-19 this solution to the text is reasonable, but it does involve considerable emendation of the text.

Ancient interpreters, however, saw the text quite differently. The Septuagint takes "king" to refer to wise counsel,[46] which no one adequately follows. The Vulgate understands the "king" to be God, while the Targum reads the verse to mean that no one need attempt to reverse a royal decree after it has been executed.[47]

If the Hebrew is to be interpreted as it stands, the line can be translated literally as, "What is the man who will come after the king whom they have already made?"[48] This would seem to make no sense. One could take "made" to mean "crowned," but this is not the idiom one would expect.[49]

The phrase, "What is the man?" however, is analogous to the familiar "What is man?" question in Pss 8:4; 144:3; Job 7:17. The word "man" (*ʾādām*), moreover, is a catchword in Ecclesiastes for the human as a child

---

[41]Gordis, *Koheleth*, 220. On the other hand, Gordis is correct that there is no need to emend the verse.

[42]The NIV apparently follows BHS note *a* in reading מַה־יַּעֲשֶׂה before הָאָדָם and takes הָאָדָם שֶׁיָּבוֹא אַחֲרֵי הַמֶּלֶךְ as periphrasis for "the king's successor." It takes אֵת אֲשֶׁר as a comparative ("more . . . can do"), although מִן is characteristically used in such an expression; cf. BDB, 582-83.

[43]Gordis, *Koheleth*, 219-21; Whitley, *Koheleth*, 23-24; Whybray, *Ecclesiastes* (Sheffield: JSOT, 1989), 56-57; Eaton, *Ecclesiastes*, 68-69.

[44]Cf. C. D. Ginsburg, *The Song of Songs and Coheleth* (1857; reprint, New York: KTAV, 1970), 289-90.

[45]Fox, *Qohelet*, 183. Fox is following H. L. Ginsberg, but he admits the interpretation is problematic. J. A. Loader (*Ecclesiastes: A Practical Commentary*, trans. J. Vriend, Text and Interpretation [Grand Rapids: Eerdmans, 1986], 29) follows a similar interpretation.

[46]τῆς βουλῆς.

[47]See C. D. Ginsburg, *Coheleth*, 289.

[48]Taking הַמֶּלֶךְ as antecedent to אֲשֶׁר. This implies that עָשׂוּהוּ means "made" rather than "did." Cf. Delitzsch, *Ecclesiastes*, 243-46.

[49]The Hiphil stem of מלך would more likely be used instead of עשׂה.

of Adam. It represents all the folly, mortality, futility, and evil that humanity has inherited. From this one may hypothesize that "the king" refers to none other than "Adam" of Gen 2–4. The term "king" may have been chosen because "What is the *ʾādām* who will come after *ʾādām*" was unsatisfactory. Also the *ʾādām* of Gen 2–3 is in reality the king of humanity.

The Hebrew phrase "whom they have already made" would then refer to the divine creation of Adam. The plural may seem troubling, but three interpretations are possible. The plural may be a corruption; a number of Hebrew manuscripts read a singular verb here. The general plural may represent a passive; the translations would then be, "Who has already been made."[50] More likely the plural is in direct imitation of the plural verb in Gen 1:26.[51] The meaning of the line can be paraphrased, "Is a human likely to come along who will be better than the king—Adam—whom God made long ago?"

In context this line states that there is little chance that humans will behave with greater wisdom than their first ancestor, Adam, who came directly from the hand of God. The apple does not fall far from the tree. The Teacher cannot confine his investigation to wisdom; he must also understand folly, for that is the stuff of human nature.

2:13 Wisdom is like light. The wise know where they are going, even if they only know they are heading for trouble. They therefore can avoid some disasters and be prepared for others. Fools, however, are always surprised by events that befall them.

2:14 The wise man can see death coming and contemplate it. This is better than the mindless tumble into death taken by the fool, but he can do nothing to stop it. Both the wise and the fools are equal heirs of human mortality described in Gen 3.

2:15 The awareness of his own mortality is sobering to the Teacher.[52]

2:16 The intellectual's real hope is that he will achieve lasting fame and be long remembered for his great contributions. The Teacher pronounces all this to be an illusion. Future generations will no more remember the scholar than they will the beggar on the street.

2:17 Here the Teacher reveals his bitter disappointment in life. It had, in effect, played a trick on him. All his life he had thought that he was pursuing a grand task in his quest for wisdom, but he had been trying to catch the wind. His efforts were destined for oblivion.

---

[50]See Delitzsch, *Ecclesiastes*, 245; Fox, *Qohelet*, 183.

[51]נַעֲשֶׂה אָדָם ("let us make man"). Note also the plural form בּוֹרְאֶיךָ ("your creator") in Eccl 12:1.

[52]Note the emphatic גַּם־אֲנִי ("even me"). Cf. Whitley, *Koheleth*, 24. Also, Whitley probably is correct that one should read אֵי for אָז in this verse.

6. On Wealth (2:18-26)

[18]I hated all the things I had toiled for under the sun, because I must leave them to the one who comes after me. [19]And who knows whether he will be a wise man or a fool? Yet he will have control over all the work into which I have poured my effort and skill under the sun. This too is meaningless. [20]So my heart began to despair over all my toilsome labor under the sun. [21]For a man may do his work with wisdom, knowledge and skill, and then he must leave all he owns to someone who has not worked for it. This too is meaningless and a great misfortune. [22]What does a man get for all the toil and anxious striving with which he labors under the sun? [23]All his days his work is pain and grief; even at night his mind does not rest. This too is meaningless.

[24]A man can do nothing better than to eat and drink and find satisfaction in his work. This too, I see, is from the hand of God, [25]for without him, who can eat or find enjoyment? [26]To the man who pleases him, God gives wisdom, knowledge and happiness, but to the sinner he gives the task of gathering and storing up wealth to hand it over to the one who pleases God. This too is meaningless, a chasing after the wind.

2:18 The word "toil"[53] here moves us out of the quest for wisdom and back into the quest for wealth and its rewards described in 2:1-11.

2:19 The Teacher rejects the view that life is made worthwhile by working to provide for one's children or, more generally, for "posterity." Who knows how long it will be before the family fortune is squandered? (For example, cf. 1 Kgs 12:16-19; 14:25-26.)

2:20 He does not "despair" but decides to disillusion himself.[54] He will no longer live by the myth that hard work and well-earned wealth validate one's life. Otherwise, obsession with fulfillment through work and accomplishments ultimately leads to the crisis point at which one's whole life is seen to have been lived for nothing.

2:21 Not only the man's possessions but even the skill and intelligence by which he acquired them are nullified by death. Hence the fact that he was a great businessman means very little.

2:22 The point here is not what happens to his wealth after he dies but what happens to the man himself[55] as he strives to achieve wealth.[56]

---

[53]עָמָל. This root reappears repeatedly in this text, and it seems to refer both to the wealth that is a result of toil and the toil itself. In v. 18, for example, it is not just the labor itself that disgusts the Teacher but the fact that he must leave his earnings to others. See Fox, *Qohelet*, 186-87.

[54]See Whitley, *Koheleth*, 27, on the meaning of לְיַאֵשׁ. He realizes that all his wisdom has given him no advantage over the fool, for he will soon be no less dead than the lowest alcoholic, thief, or prostitute.

[55]לָאָדָם.

[56]Note the rare participle of היה (this form found only here and in Neh 6:6), "to become." The progressive sense of the action should be understood.

2:23 The Teacher describes the plight of the man consumed with his job. He burns himself up for what has no real, lasting value.

2:24 The Teacher now counsels enjoyment of life. We should not understand "nothing is better than"[57] in a rigidly literal sense, as if the Teacher were saying that enjoyment of food and possessions is the goal of of life. In context he is talking about how one should view life with respect to labor and the fruit of labor. He is not, therefore, negating the worth of higher values. But he insists that people should learn how to enjoy the return they get on their labor. Indeed, the ability to enjoy and use the good things of life (i.e., material things) is itself a gift of God. Those who belong to God should above all others have a capacity to enjoy life.

2:25 Context implies that "him" in "for without him" refers to God (v. 24).[58] Life is empty without God.

2:26 Here again the Teacher notes how God uses those who are opposed to him.[59] The sovereignty of God is implicit in this concept. God uses the lives of the wicked to achieve his own purpose.[60] This verse is sometimes taken to mean that the Teacher views divine activity as hopelessly arbitrary[61] and little more than an equivalent for "fate." To the contrary, this verse does not present God as capricious but does relate to the biblical idea of the *grace* of God. To believe that one's life is ruled by impersonal fate is intolerable; to believe that life is controlled by a personal God is a comfort.

---

[57]The formula אֵין טוֹב is used here and in 3:12,22; 8:15. Each signals the reader to reckon with the importance of enjoying the fleeting moments of happiness life offers. For an analysis of the formula, see G. S. Ogden, "Qoheleth's Use of the 'Nothing Is Better' Form," *JBL* 98 (1979): 339-50. A comparative מִן should be inserted before שֶׁיֹּאכַל.

[58]The verb חוּשׁ normally means "to hasten"; the root used here is a hapax legomenon in the OT and carries a different sense. Gordis relates this form to an Arabic root meaning to "refrain" and so takes it as the opposite of indulging in eating (*Koheleth*, 226-27). The word is more likely related to the Akkadian *hss*, "to be happy," and so means "to enjoy." Yet another possibility is that it means to "reflect" or "consider"; see Whitley, *Koheleth*, 28-29, and Eaton, *Ecclesiastes*, 75, n. 1. Another problem is whether the final word of the verse is to be read מִמֶּנִּי or מִמֶּנּוּ. The former is supported by the MT, Targum, and Vg; and the latter is supported by some Hebrew manuscripts, the LXX, and the Syr. The former, however, is almost meaningless unless the idea is "Who could eat and enjoy life more than me?" (therefore I am an authority). But חוּץ מִמֶּנִּי ("outside of me") would be a strange way to say that. It is therefore best to take it as "outside of him" (i.e., God), with the idea that no one can really enjoy life apart from God. See also R. N. Whybray, *Ecclesiastes*, NCB (Grand Rapids: Eerdmans, 1989), 63-64, and Fox, *Qohelet*, 188.

[59]In 1:13b-14 he asserted that those dedicated to the task of acquiring knowledge have been given a futile and hopeless task (עִנְיָן) by God. The same word (עִנְיָן) is here used again of those who acquire material things.

[60]The last phrase here (גַּם־זֶה הֶבֶל וּרְעוּת רוּחַ) does not refer to God's use of the wicked to achieve his purpose but to the life of acquiring things.

[61]Cf. J. A. Loader, *Ecclesiastes*, 32.

7. On Time and the World (3:1-15b)

[1]There is a time for everything,
and a season for every activity under heaven:

[2]a time to be born and a time to die,
a time to plant and a time to uproot,
[3]a time to kill and a time to heal,
a time to tear down and a time to build,
[4]a time to weep and a time to laugh,
a time to mourn and a time to dance,
[5]a time to scatter stones and a time to gather them,
a time to embrace and a time to refrain,
[6]a time to search and a time to give up,
a time to keep and a time to throw away,
[7]a time to tear and a time to mend,
a time to be silent and a time to speak,
[8]a time to love and a time to hate,
a time for war and a time for peace.

[9]What does the worker gain from his toil? [10]I have seen the burden God has
laid on men. [11]He has made everything beautiful in its time. He has also set
eternity in the hearts of men; yet they cannot fathom what God has done from
beginning to end. [12]I know that there is nothing better for men than to be
happy and do good while they live. [13]That everyone may eat and drink, and
find satisfaction in all his toil—this is the gift of God. [14]I know that everything
God does will endure forever; nothing can be added to it and nothing taken
from it. God does it so that men will revere him.

[15]Whatever is has already been,
and what will be has been before;

This text is a masterpiece of wisdom poetry. J. A. Loader observes that the verses move back and forth among desirable and undesirable aspects of life,[62] and he correctly notes that the book is not telling the reader how to attain the former and avoid the latter. Nevertheless, he, like others, wrongly supposes that the point of this text is that an arbitrary deity manipulates human affairs and that the only appropriate response is resignation to fate.[63] Ecclesiastes is not concerned about questions of "cyclic" versus "linear" time. These verses concern not divine providence or abstract notions of time but human mortality.[64]

---

[62]For a presentation of chiastic structuring in this passage, see J. A. Loader, *Polar Structures in the Book of Qohelet, BZAW* 152 (Berlin: Walter de Gruyter, 1979), 11-13.

[63]Ibid.; see also Loader, *Ecclesiastes*, 33-38. Cf. J. L. Crenshaw, *Ecclesiastes* (Philadelphia: Westminster, 1987), 92.

[64]Contrary to Fox (*Qohelet*, 192) vv. 11,14 do not establish that divine activity is in view in vv. 1-8. Verse 14 stresses the eternal character of God's work, but vv. 1-8 stress the brevity and impermanence of human activity.

Life is composed of joy and sorrow, building and destroying, and living and dying. Each comes at the proper time. This reminds us that we are creatures of time and not yet able to partake of the joys of eternity. No one can be happy who has not come to grips with the reality that life is full of changes and sorrows as well as continuity and joy. We must accept that we are mortal and governed by time.

3:1 The poem concerns life "under heaven." It is not so much a theological statement as an observation on human life in the human world.

3:2 Instead of a time to "be born" the Hebrew term should be rendered "give birth."[65] Giving birth and planting are both ways of giving life.

3:3 Destruction and killing are part of life and cannot be avoided, although healing and building are certainly preferable. Ecclesiastes is not concerned here with ethical questions of what constitutes a just war or the like. The Teacher is merely asserting that in a world where death is a central fact of life, there will also be a time to kill.

3:4 There is a progression of intensity from line *a* to line *b*. Both sorrow and joy are part of life; without one the other is unrecognizable.

3:5 The meaning of line *a* is uncertain, but the *Midrash Rabbah* took it to refer to sexual union. This is possible in light of line *b*.[66] Other possibilities include casting stones to make a field unworkable (as in warfare), or clearing a field of stones to prepare the soil, or the use of stones as counters to record the number of sheep in a flock.[67] If a sexual meaning is present, the verse would be saying that this too is fleeting.

3:6 Nothing in this world is ours forever.

3:7 This may allude to mourning and funerals. Mourners tore their clothes, and their comforters kept silent during times of grief, but people were free to repair clothes and freely converse at other times.[68]

3:8 Perfect peace does not exist on earth. The verse is arranged chiastically: love: hate: war: peace. "Love" and "hate" represent personal feelings, while "war" and "peace" represent sociopolitical conditions.[69]

Verses 9-15a are not formally part of the wisdom poem of vv. 1-8 but are a reflection on and exposition of it. The logic of vv. 9-14 may be described as follows:

> First Conclusion: Our entrapment in time is another indication of our mortality (v. 9).

---

[65]Note the use of the Qal infinitive of ילד rather than the Niphal stem. Cf. Crenshaw, *Ecclesiastes*, 94-95.

[66]Cf. Loader, *Polar Structures*, 31.

[67]See Crenshaw, *Ecclesiastes*, 94-95.

[68]See Loader, *Polar Structures*, 32. Crenshaw (*Ecclesiastes*, 96) observes that Job's friends tore their clothes and sat in silence for seven days but comments that this verse need not be restricted to the idea of mourning.

[69]Murphy, *Ecclesiastes*, 34.

Second Conclusion: Our labor is thus a lifelong affliction with no eternal results (v. 10).

Qualification: Yet every aspect of life is appropriate in its time and should be accepted as such (v. 11a).

Counterqualification: But we long for eternity and cannot be content with time alone (v. 11b).

First Addendum: People prefer the joys of life to the sorrows (v. 12).

Correlative to First Addendum: But the ability to enjoy life is itself a gift of God and thus under his control (v. 13).

Second Addendum: Only God's work has the perfection and eternal worth for which people long (v. 14a,b).

Correlative to Second Addendum: God uses time and mortality to humble the human race (v. 14c).

3:9 Human mortality extends beyond the fact of physical death; it is the nullification of all that people do as well (cf. Gen 3:17-19).

3:10 This verse should be rendered, "I have seen all the business God has given to people to afflict them."[70] Work is not simply a part of nature but is an affliction from God (Gen 3:17-19).

3:11 "Beautiful" here means "appropriate."[71] If we can accept life as it is, even the hard parts will be bearable. Yet there is a catch. We feel like aliens in the world of time and yearn to be part of eternity.[72] We feel the need for ourselves and our work to be eternal and yet are grieved to be trapped in time. We also desire to understand our place in the universe against the backdrop of eternity. But we cannot find out what God has done from beginning to end. That is, we are not able to discern any plan or pattern to all of this. God's purposes are outside our realm of control or investigation. We thus have a sense of alienation and bewilderment in time.

3:12 This verse does not mean that we should just forget about our longing for eternity and try to have a good time. "I know" does not introduce a conclusion; rather, it begins a premise, an additional piece of information, or a concession.[73] The Teacher admits that we do not regard the alternatives of life and death, joy and sorrow, and love and hate as

---

[70]Or "to keep them busy." If "be busy" is the meaning of the word ענה here, it only carries that meaning elsewhere in the Bible in Eccl 1:13. Otherwise it must have the more common meaning, in the Piel, "to afflict." See BHS note.

[71]Fox, *Qohelet*, 193.

[72]עוֹלָם here means "eternity" and not "world" (which makes no sense in context) or "darkness" (an interpretation maintained by R. F. Youngblood, "Qoheleth's Dark House," in *A Tribute to Gleason Archer*, ed. W. C. Kaiser, Jr. and R. F. Youngblood [Chicago: Moody, 1986], 211-27; it is not supported by sufficient evidence). Nor should the text be emended to עָמָל (*labor*), as in Fox, *Qohelet*, 195.

[73]Cf. the use of יָדַעְתִּי כִּי in Gen 12:11; 20:6; Ps 140:13 (Eng. v. 12); Jonah 4:2. עַתָּה יָדַעְתִּי כִּי ("now I know") can introduce a statement of confidence or assurance (Judg 17:13). A statement of realization or a conclusion may be introduced by וָאֵדַע ("and I knew"; Jer 32:8; Ezek 10:20); Eccl 2:14 similarly uses וְיָדַעְתִּי.

indifferent matters. While he urges the reader to accept personal mortality for what it is, he recognizes that life and joy and love are preferred by all.

3:13 He further acknowledges that the ability to enjoy life—both moments of recreation and labor—is a gift of God. The paradox is that one cannot genuinely face personal mortality and finitude without first facing God's immortality and infinite power.

3:14 In a second addendum the Teacher observes that the eternal perfection of God's work overwhelms all human endeavors and mocks human aspirations to become eternally significant. No one can thwart or change God's will, and his ways are beyond our understanding. This verse may be compared to Gen 3:5,22. There the origin of human suffering and alienation is the desire to be like God. If we were able to know all, to master life, and be like God, we would feel no need for piety. But humanity is far from divine stature. We are altogether contingent beings, and our only appropriate response is reverence.

3:15a,b No one can alter the fundamental nature of the world. The idea of the changelessness of the world provides a transition between this section on time and the following on oppression. That too is an unchanging fact of human existence. Verse 15c, although formally part of this paragraph, proleptically prepares the reader for the subject of the next section, oppression. It should, therefore, be regarded as part of the following paragraph for purposes of interpretation.

8. On Politics (3:15c-17)

And God will call the past to account.
16And I saw something else under the sun:
In the place of judgment—wickedness was there,
in the place of justice—wickedness was there.
17I thought in my heart,

"God will bring to judgment
both the righteous and the wicked,
for there will be a time for every activity,
a time for every deed."

This passage looks awkward as it appears in most translations. The preceding passage, 3:9-15b, contrasts the transitory nature of human accomplishments with the eternal significance of God's works. A brief discourse on corruption and injustice suddenly follows (3:16-17). The apparent abruptness of this change of topic is reduced if one understands 3:15c to be transitional.

3:15c The meaning of this line[74] is much debated. The central problem is the meaning of *rdp* in the Niphal stem. In the Qal stem it always means

[74] וְהָאֱלֹהִים יְבַקֵּשׁ אֶת־נִרְדָּף.

"pursue" or "chase" and thus "to persecute."[75] It occurs in the Niphal only here and in Lam 5:5, where it describes persecution or oppression.

Translators assume that the natural meaning, "God seeks the persecuted," is out of place in the context of Eccl 3:9-15 and render it as "that which has passed by" or something similar. The NIV reading ("the past") also follows this approach. This and other such translations, however, neither accurately render the Hebrew nor make theological sense.[76] The line is best understood as meaning "God seeks [justice for] the persecuted."

The use of the word "seeks"[77] is particularly significant. Sometimes it simply means to seek objects, as in 1 Sam 9:3 and 1 Kgs 2:40; or it can be used with an auxiliary verb in a figurative sense, as in "to seek to kill" (1 Sam 19:10). But "seek" is also used in a legal sense.[78] For example, in 2 Sam 4:11 "should I not demand [Hebrew "seek"] his blood from your hand?" means "I will require from you justice for the shedding of his blood."[79] When Eccl 3:15c says that God seeks the persecuted, it means that he holds their persecutors accountable.

The translation "God seeks [justice for] the persecuted" appears strange in a discussion of the brevity of human life and the timelessness of God. This problem is solved by linking v. 15c to vv. 16-17, a discussion of corruption and oppression (vv. 16-17); but this solution looks impossible since the opening words of v. 16 ("And I saw something else") clearly begin a new paragraph.

The Teacher, however, often gives a short, proleptic summary of a topic he is about to discuss or of a conclusion he will reach before he actually begins a detailed discourse. Sometimes, as here, when he is about to move on to a new paragraph with a new topic, the Teacher introduces

---

[75]E.g., Amos 1:11; Ezek 35:6.

[76]Despite the best efforts by scholars, no real analogy or justification has been found for rendering נִרְדָּף as "the past." Barton (*Ecclesiastes*, 107) argues that the passive can mean "that which has been driven off," i.e., things in the past. But his evidence is not analogous, and the semantic shift from "that which is driven off" to "things in the past" is strained, as Whybray (*Ecclesiastes*, 75-76) all but admits. Eaton (*Ecclesiastes*, 83) says it can mean "hurry along" and thus argues that 3:15c means that God watches over the flurry of human activity. But "God seeks that which hurries along" is very peculiar. Delitzsch's translation, "God seeks that which is crowded out" (*Ecclesiastes*, 264), is also based on weak evidence and really does not make sense. Gordis (*Koheleth*, 234) and Crenshaw (*Ecclesiastes*, 100) interpret it to mean that God seeks to repeat the past. This is contrary to the natural sense of the Hebrew. The Teacher does not mean that God causes the repetition observed in the world or that he stamps out any innovation in order to maintain a safe level of repetition and monotony.

[77]בקשׁ, in the Piel.

[78]S. Wagner, בִּקֵּשׁ "*biqqes*," *TDOT* 2:233-35.

[79]See also Ezek 3:18,20; Gen 43:9, where the Hebrew phrase "seek him from my hand" means "consider me to be accountable for his life." Note that in this idiom it is the victim (or his blood) that is sought. Ecclesiastes 3:15c therefore speaks of God seeking justice for the persecuted, i.e., the victims at the hand of their oppressors.

the new topic at the end of the paragraph before the new one. The proleptic line serves as a transition.[80] This means that while the paragraph division of the present text is at the end of v. 15, we must treat v. 15c as part of the following paragraph, 3:16-17.

In addition, the transition from a discussion of time to a statement on oppression is not as abrupt as it may appear. The Teacher has just asserted that people are creatures of time and that the best they can do is find happiness and contentment in the gifts of God (vv. 1-14). He then turns the discussion on the line "and God seeks [justice for] the oppressed." Oppression and injustice fill the heart with bitterness and make it impossible for anyone to live according to the practice, recommended in v. 11a, of accepting one's lot in life with contentment. No one can pass through the cycles of life (3:1-8) with serenity while under the oppression of corrupt political power.

3:16 The "place of justice" is the law courts. The Teacher sees injustice and oppression where the rights of the poor ought to be protected.

3:17 The NIV translation "there will be a time" should be rendered "a time for everything and every deed is there." But what does he mean by "there"?[81] Barton emends the text to read, "He has set a time for every matter," but this proposal is not only without any textual support but is grammatically most unlikely.[82] Other, not quite persuasive interpretations of "there" have also been proposed.[83]

This usage is eschatological.[84] The word "there" is also used in Ps 14, another passage that deals with God's eschatological judgment on those

---

[80]Other examples of prolepsis are 1:2 (which proleptically gives the theme of the whole book), 2:1b-2 (which states in advance his conclusions, found in v. 11, regarding the life of sensuality), and 8:1 (a proleptic introduction to the matter of political prudence, discussed in 8:2-6). A major transitional passage appears in 10:18-20. Ecclesiastes 3:17 anticipates the conclusion of the work (12:13-14).

[81]שָׁם.

[82]Barton, *Ecclesiastes*, 111. Barton wants to emend שָׁם to שָׂם, but the word is at the end of the line, a most unusual place for a Hebrew verb. See Ginsburg, *Coheleth*, 315, and Gordis, *Koheleth*, 235.

[83]See Whybray, *Ecclesiastes*, 78. Delitzsch (*Ecclesiastes*, 266) says that שָׁם here means "with God" and compares Gen 49:24, but that text hardly proves that שָׁם has that meaning in Eccl 3:17. Eaton (*Ecclesiastes*, 85) compares Isa 48:16 and argues that it can mean "with reference to those events," but again the comparison is weak.

[84]Fox (*Qohelet*, 197-98) contends that there can be no eschatology here since the Teacher does not believe in an afterlife and that if he did believe in such a judgment, his problem would be solved. This analysis is superficial. The Teacher is caught in a tension between earthly realities (unpunished injustice and the apparent finality of death) and faith in the goodness of God. (The biblical conception of God's חֶסֶד ["faithfulness," "grace"] does not need to be expressly stated; it is a given.) His faith does not "solve" the problem in such a way that he can close the book on it. His integrity is such that he neither ignores injustice nor abandons faith.

who plunder his people. Psalm 14:5a reads, "There evildoers are overwhelmed with dread, for God is present in the company of the righteous." In context the line must refer to the day of judgment and vindication of Yahweh's people. "There" is either shorthand for the time and place of eschatological judgment[85] or refers to Sheol (Heb.; "grave"), in which case the ideas of the grave and the judgment have been merged.[86]

In both texts "there" is the place of God's judgment on the rapacious and oppressive. The time and place of this judgment are uncertain, but they are related to the idea of death and the grave. Beyond that, this "eschatological hope" is not clearly defined. It is only "there," with no clear indication of how or when this judgment will take place. The Teacher does not speculate about what type of punishment the wicked will receive.

The prophets often decried the plundering of the defenseless in the courts of ancient Israel. The Teacher, although he did not proclaim his indignity in the streets, was moved by what he saw. He too understood the hopelessness of the poor and awaited divine judgment (v. 17), but he was not a prophet. He neither warned of a day of wrath nor offered a clear vision of a day when the righteous will be gathered to Zion. His approach was more abstract than prophetic. Nevertheless, he did speak of a coming divine judgment. Ecclesiastes 3:15c-17 acknowledges that political oppression is a universal phenomenon but offers the hope, albeit an undefined one, of divine judgment and vindication.

9. On Death (3:18-22)

18I also thought, "As for men, God tests them so that they may see that they are like the animals. 19Man's fate is like that of the animals; the same fate awaits them both: As one dies, so dies the other. All have the same breath; man has no advantage over the animal. Everything is meaningless. 20All go to the same place; all come from dust, and to dust all return. 21Who knows if the spirit of man rises upward and if the spirit of the animal goes down into the earth?"

22So I saw that there is nothing better for a man than to enjoy his work, because that is his lot. For who can bring him to see what will happen after him?

These verses astonish many believing readers in that they appear to deny afterlife itself. The difficulty is not so keenly felt in the KJV, which translates v. 21, "Who knoweth the spirit of man that goeth upward, and the spirit of the beast that goeth downward to the earth?" Although

---

[85]Cf. also the use of "there" (שָׁם) in Zeph 1:14.

[86]A related usage is found in Job 3:17-19, where "there" refers to the grave, an impartial judge that treats the mighty and the weak alike. Cf. Gordis, *Koheleth*, 235.

defended by a number of conservative scholars,[87] the KJV rendition should not be accepted.[88] Even without v. 21, moreover, vv. 19-20 are powerful statements on their own.

The text makes four assertions: (1) God desires people to see that they are in some sense like "animals"; (2) people and animals share the same fate in that both return to the dust; (3) nobody knows[89] if the spirit of a human rises at death while that of an animal descends to the earth; and (4) we ought to enjoy the life we have. While these verses may appear to be a categorical denial of afterlife, such an interpretation would miss the mark.

Once again Ecclesiastes asserts that humans are mortal; it is in that sense that they are like the animals. If anything, these verses may be taken as a challenge to the idea that humans possess an innate immortality, but they are not an assertion that no form of afterlife whatsoever is possible for humans.[90] Plato gave classic expression to the idea of innate immortality, that is, that the soul is by nature immortal,[91] but the notion did not originate or end with him. Various conceptions of afterlife are common in pagan religion, yet the biblical idea of resurrection is absent. This is true not only of ancient Egyptian religions and of religions that include a doctrine of reincarnation but also of modern "New Age" reli-

---

[87]See W. C. Kaiser, Jr., *Ecclesiastes: Total Life* (Chicago: Moody, 1979), 71; H. C. Leupold, *Exposition of Ecclesiastes* (Grand Rapids: Baker, 1952), 99; and Eaton, *Ecclesiastes*, 88-89. The exegesis provided by these scholars is forced and hopelessly contrary to context.

[88]A debated issue is whether the ה prefix on הָעֹלָה and הַיֹּרֶדֶת is an interrogative or a definite article. As written they appear to be articles, which seems to support the KJV. But the LXX, Peshitta, Vg, and *Talmud* all read the letters ה as interrogatives, as do the modern versions. Some suggest that scribes deliberately altered the vocalization to make the sentiment a little more orthodox, but Gordis (*Koheleth*, 238) cites examples of the interrogative ה being pointed with full vowels before א and י. The whole debate is misguided, however. Taking the letters ה as articles (as is probably correct) does not vindicate the KJV translation. Delitzsch (*Ecclesiastes*, 270) points out that the particles הִיא show that הָעֹלָה and הַיֹּרֶדֶת are not modifiers of רוּחַ and וְרוּחַ but mark separate, interrogative phrases (cf. Jer 2:14). He thus translates, "Who knoweth with regard to the spirit of men, whether it mounteth upward; and with regard to the spirit of the beast, whether it goeth downward to the earth?" This is certainly the correct rendition.

[89]"Who knows" is equivalent to "nobody knows" (contrary to Leupold, *Ecclesiastes*, 99-100). Cf. J. L. Crenshaw, "The Expression *mî yôdēaᶜ* in the Hebrew Bible," *VT* 36.3 (1986): 274-88.

[90]For an excellent analysis, see R. Wardlaw, *Exposition of Ecclesiastes* (1868; reprint, Minneapolis: Klock & Klock, 1982), 103-6.

[91]For Plato the human is composed of two parts: the divine and preexistent mind or soul and the body, which is itself a shell or prison that drags the soul down through its carnal appetites. Immortality is thus the natural possession of the human soul and is not dependent on resurrection of the body (itself unthinkable in light of the corruption a body carries with it) or any specific act of God. To enjoy the full blessings of immortality, one must purge the soul of the carnal influences of the body through philosophy.

gions as well. Death is only a "door," and the body is not raised.[92] Today many believe that they are able to enter eternal bliss without any help from God, as it were.

In biblical Christianity, however, death is consistently described as a curse and an enemy (1 Cor 15:26,54-55; Rev 20:14). The resurrection of Christ, moreover, has conquered death and has opened the way for the resurrection. The whole person, body and soul, enters immortality. This immortality, however, is dependent on the power of God and the resurrection.[93]

Ecclesiastes does not deny afterlife but does force the reader to take death seriously. In this the book echoes the psalmist's prayer that he be taught to number his days (Ps 90:10-12). It is not the biblical believer who denies the power of death but the unbeliever.

Since humans are truly mortal, two conclusions follow. First, neither possessions nor accomplishments are eternal, and we should properly use and enjoy them while we still see the light of day. Second, because we are by nature dependent and contingent, our hope of eternal life must be founded in God and not ourselves (Eccl 12:7,13-14). For the Christian this means that immortality is in the risen Christ (1 Cor 15:12-19).

3:18 The Hebrew is quite convoluted here, but the NIV rendition is reasonable.[94]

3:19-22 Beyond the issues previously noted, the text here is fairly clear. It is not certain whether "after him" (which ought to be rendered "afterwards"[95]) in v. 22 refers to future events on earth or to the afterlife itself, but context favors the latter.[96]

10. On Politics (4:1-3)

[1]Again I looked and saw all the oppression that was taking place under the sun:

I saw the tears of the oppressed—
and they have no comforter;

---

[92]This does not by any means imply that these religions and philosophies are identical in their conception of the afterlife. For surveys of the Egyptian beliefs, see T. G. H. James, *An Introduction to Ancient Egypt* (New York: Harper & Row, 1979), 155-57, and J. E. M. White, *Ancient Egypt* (New York: Dover, 1970), 36-43.

[93]Cf. Matt 22:29-32, where Jesus declared the resurrection to be contingent upon the power and faithfulness of God. For a good study of related issues, see M. J. Harris, *Raised Immortal: Resurrection and Immortality in the New Testament* (Grand Rapids: Eerdmans, 1983), and C. Blomberg, *Matthew*, NAC, vol. 22 (Nashville: Broadman, 1992), 333-34.

[94]On לְבָרָם see V. Hamp, "בָּרַר (*bārar*)," *TDOT* 2:308-12, especially p. 309. On וְלִרְאוֹת see Whitley, *Koheleth*, 37. In view of the chiastic rhyming structure of שְׁהֶם בְּהֵמָה הֵמָּה לָהֶם, any temptation to emend should be resisted.

[95]אַחֲרָיו; see Eccl 9:3.

[96]See Fox, *Qohelet*, 199.

power was on the side of their oppressors—
and they have no comforter.
[2]And I declared that the dead,
who had already died,
are happier than the living,
who are still alive.
[3]But better than both
is he who has not yet been,
who has not seen the evil
that is done under the sun.

The Teacher grieves for the oppressed, but he offers no hope for a solution to oppression. To the contrary, he confesses that a person is better off dead or, better still, never having been born than to be alive and see this heartbreaking reality. The candor of his words should not be taken as the musings of a cynic or a suicide. He is describing, albeit in hyperbole, the pain this situation gives him (cf. Job 3; Jer 20:14-18).

4:1 "Power was on the side of their oppressors" is literally, "And from the hand of their oppressors is power."[97] The power from their hands is not only their acts of oppression but is also the unrestrained freedom they have to do as they please. Because of this power structure, the poor are thwarted in their efforts to enjoy the benefits life under the sun offers.[98]

4:2-3 The Teacher's outrage at the cruelty of the social structure is such that it makes him feel that death is preferable to life.[99] Death in fact permeates his reflections on injustice. In 3:15c-17 death appears as the area of hope for the oppressed; it is "there" that God judges the oppressor. Here death is simply the better alternative to life. It is not surprising that in 3:18-22, which comes between these two texts, the subject is death itself.

11. On Wealth (4:4-8)

[4]And I saw that all labor and all achievement spring from man's envy of his neighbor. This too is meaningless, a chasing after the wind.

---

[97]Gordis takes this to mean "in the hands of" rather than understand a verb such as "goes forth" to be implied (*Koheleth*, 238). See also Eaton, *Ecclesiastes*, 91.

[98]The repetition of the refrain "and they have no comforter" heightens the sense of pathos. Crenshaw (*Ecclesiastes*, 105) notes that repetition is also used in 3:16.

[99]Although the meaning of these verses is transparent, the Hebrew does have some unusual features. In v. 2 וְשַׁבֵּחַ appears to be an infinitive absolute (cf. Crenshaw, *Ecclesiastes*, 106) acting as a finite verb. Also אֵת אֲשֶׁר (v. 3), with no governing verb, is unusual; but it need not be taken as a nominative analogous to Mishnaic את שׁ (contra Gordis, *Koheleth*, 239; Whitley, *Koheleth*, 42). Probably וְשַׁבֵּחַ אֲנִי (v. 2) still functions as subject and verb. See C. Ginsburg, *Coheleth*, 322-23.

[5]The fool folds his hands
and ruins himself.
[6]Better one handful with tranquillity
than two handfuls with toil
and chasing after the wind.

[7]Again I saw something meaningless under the sun:

[8]There was a man all alone;
he had neither son nor brother.
There was no end to his toil,
yet his eyes were not content with his wealth.
"For whom am I toiling," he asked,
"and why am I depriving myself of enjoyment?"
This too is meaningless—
a miserable business!

4:4 Seeking happiness in wealth is folly because people desire money for the worst possible reasons—especially covetousness and envy. With that as a motivation, no amount of wealth will ever satisfy.

4:5-6 Two apparently contradictory proverbs are inserted in juxtaposition. The first (v. 5) is a traditional wisdom saying—the fool consumes himself by laziness. That is, laziness is sure to bring poverty.[100] The second (v. 6) states that it is better to have a few things (one handful) and yet be satisfied and happy than to have many things (two handfuls[101]) and yet be consumed with work and worries. The Teacher steers away from both idleness and slavery to work.

4:7-8 The Teacher gives one more example of the foolishness of slavery to work. People devote their lives to acquiring wealth but have no one to share it with. Money is their only kin.[102]

12. On Friendship (4:9-12)

[9]Two are better than one,
because they have a good return for their work:
[10]If one falls down,
his friend can help him up.
But pity the man who falls
and has no one to help him up!

---

[100]Crenshaw (*Ecclesiastes*, 107-9) takes the proverb to mean that the fool has adequate food in spite of his laziness. This is a most unlikely interpretation; cf. Whybray, *Ecclesiastes*, 84.

[101]חָפְנַיִם is a dual construct with enclitic *mem*. See Whitley, *Koheleth*, 42-43.

[102]Note that the words "he asked" (v. 8) are not in the original. The Targum and Vg insert "he does *not* ask." Neither approach is necessary. The Teacher vividly places himself in the position of the miser (with an autobiographical reflection?). See Ginsburg, *Coheleth*, 327; Fox, *Qohelet* 204; and Crenshaw, *Ecclesiastes*, 110.

11Also, if two lie down together, they will keep warm.
But how can one keep warm alone?
12Though one may be overpowered,
two can defend themselves.
A cord of three strands is not quickly broken.

The need for someone with whom to share the good things of life (vv. 7-8) prompts a discussion on friendship. Several benefits of friendship are enumerated (cf. Gen 2:18).

4:9 First, two can work better than one and so have a larger profit. Note the proverbial form.

4:10 Second, they can help each other in time of need.

4:11 Third, they give emotional comfort to each other. The warmth of lying beside each other does not refer to sexual activity, nor are the two necessarily husband and wife.[103] It is an image derived from that of travelers who must lie beside each other to stay warm on cold desert nights. But the usage is here metaphorical for emotional comfort against the coldness of the world.

4:12 Fourth, they give each other protection; for that, in fact, a third friend is even better![104] This verse also appears to be a proverb (note the numerical pattern).

13. On Politics (4:13-16)

13Better a poor but wise youth than an old but foolish king who no longer knows how to take warning. 14The youth may have come from prison to the kingship, or he may have been born in poverty within his kingdom. 15I saw that all who lived and walked under the sun followed the youth, the king's successor. 16There was no end to all the people who were before them. But those who came later were not pleased with the successor. This too is meaningless, a chasing after the wind.

By means of an example story,[105] the Teacher asserts that it is better to be politically weak but aware and active than to be powerful but inflexible and isolated from reality. The political world is unstable and therefore dangerous; the wise stay abreast of these changes. Even so, the fulfillment

---

[103]See Whybray, *Ecclesiastes*, 87; Crenshaw, *Ecclesiastes*, 111.

[104]It is noteworthy that this is one aspect of life that the Teacher does not class as הֶבֶל.

[105]By example story (*exemplum*), I mean a fictionalized narrative that is meant to typify some lesson the Teacher is setting forth. It is thus analogous to some of the parables of Jesus. Contrary to Fox (*Qohelet*, 206) there is no need of a specific historical incident to reinforce the point the Teacher is making. All efforts to isolate such an incident have failed. Perhaps the best such attempt is G. S. Ogden, "Historical Allusion in Qoheleth IV 13-16?" *VT* 30 (1980): 309-15, who argues that v. 14a refers to Joseph and that v. 14b refers to David. Ogden's arguments notwithstanding, Joseph did not become king, and 1 Sam 18:23 does not establish that the reader would connect רָשׁ ("poor") with David.

of political ambitions is transitory; and the motivation behind political ambition, fame, and the praise of the masses is vapid.

4:13 The youth is "better" than an old but foolish king in that he knows how to "take warning." He is aware of both danger and opportunity as he moves up the political ladder. The king, however, is entrenched, immobile, and out of touch with changing circumstances. He has become vulnerable despite his power and foolish despite his age. The irony here is that contrary to traditional thinking, neither age nor might insures wisdom and success.

4:14 Against many interpreters this verse does not refer to the poor youth of v. 13.[106] It should be translated, "Although he arose from prison[107] to become king, in spite of having been poor in his kingdom." The subject is the old king. Once young and powerless, he nevertheless was astute and able to seize opportunity. Now, however, he is cut off from political reality.

4:15 Verse 15 should be translated, "I saw that all the living, those who walked about under the sun, were with the latter youth[108] who would arise[109] after him."[110] Eventually a second youth moves in to take the old king's throne. The "latter youth" is none other than the one mentioned in v. 13; he is chronologically second since the now-aged king who rose from obscurity to power (v. 14) is the implied first youth. Like Absalom in David's old age, the latter youth uses his energy and political cunning to gain the hearts of a people who are weary of the now-aloof, inflexible, and aged monarch.

4:16 Nevertheless, the new king is no more significant than the old one. The two together are only points in history. Just as those who lived before them knew nothing of them, so those who come after will soon forget them.[111]

---

[106]The nearer substantive, מֶלֶךְ, is more likely to be the subject of v. 14 than יֶלֶד. Also the text has not yet stated that the youth of v. 13 became king. The only king yet mentioned is that of v. 13. Therefore v. 14 means that the old king too had once been in poverty and even in prison. See D. A. Garrett, "Qoheleth on the Use and Abuse of Political Power," *TJ* 8 NS (1987): 164-65.

[107]הָסוּרִים is short for הָאֲסוּרִים, "fetters"; see *GK*, 35d and Crenshaw, *Ecclesiastes*, 113.

[108]Gordis's argument that הַשֵּׁנִי here means "successor" (*Koheleth*, 245) is not convincing.

[109]The imperfect tense יַעֲמֹד does not imply that a third character is meant (contrary to Whybray, *Ecclesiastes*, 90; and Fox, *Qohelet*, 208). The sudden appearance of a third character needs more than a verb tense to signal it. The imperfect tense is used because the text is written from the perspective of the old king's still being on the throne and the latter youth's still being in process of climbing to the top (hence the translation "would arise" rather than "arose").

[110]W. A. Irwin ("Eccles 4:13-16," *JNES* 3 [1944]: 255-57) strangely takes תַּחְתָּיו to mean that the youth continued in his own station in life—i.e., remained poor.

[111]לִפְנֵיהֶם means "prior to," not "standing before them." See R. B. Y. Scott, *Proverbs and Ecclesiastes*, AB (New York: Doubleday, 1965), 225. As Gordis (*Koheleth*, 245) observes, the king stands before his people, not the people before the king.

14. On Religion (5:1-7)

**1Guard your steps when you go to the house of God. Go near to listen rather
than to offer the sacrifice of fools, who do not know that they do wrong.**

2Do not be quick with your mouth,
do not be hasty in your heart
to utter anything before God.
God is in heaven
and you are on earth,
so let your words be few.
3As a dream comes when there are many cares,
so the speech of a fool when there are many words.

**4When you make a vow to God, do not delay in fulfilling it. He has no plea-
sure in fools; fulfill your vow. 5It is better not to vow than to make a vow and
not fulfill it. 6Do not let your mouth lead you into sin. And do not protest to the
[temple] messenger, "My vow was a mistake." Why should God be angry at
what you say and destroy the work of your hands? 7Much dreaming and many
words are meaningless. Therefore stand in awe of God.**

This text is set up in two parallel segments as follows:

A: Positive: Go to the temple in humble silence; beware of the "sacrifice of fools" (v. 1).
- B: Negative: Do not be quick to speak before God, for he is awesome (v. 2).
  - C: Proverb: Big dreams are the mark of a fool (v. 3).

A′: Positive: If you make a vow, fulfill it (v. 4).
- B′: Negative: Make no vow that you are not certain to keep, lest God punish you (vv. 5-6).
  - C′: Proverb: Big dreams are the mark of a fool (v. 7a).

Conclusion: Fear God (v. 7b).

This text is similar to Deut 23:21-23, but the emphasis in Ecclesiastes is on the limitations of human knowledge and the contingency of human existence. We should be careful about making great promises to God because we do not know if our circumstances tomorrow will be what they are today. We may be unable to fulfill the vows we make. Thus our promises before God would be shown to be no more than idle boasts, and we will fall under judgment.

5:1 An alternative rendering of the verse is: "Watch your feet when you go to the house of God. It is more acceptable[112] to listen than when

---

[112]Taking קָרוֹב not as an infinitive absolute but as an adjective with comparative force; see Ginsburg, *Coheleth*, 335. Fox (*Qohelet*, 210) suggests that the idea here is "acceptable" to God.

fools give sacrifice.[113] [Those who merely listen] do not know how to do wrong."[114] "Guard your steps" means "to proceed with reverence" and may allude to God's admonition to Moses at the burning bush (Exod 3:5). Reference to sacrifice shows that the "house of God" is the temple, not the synagogue.[115] Those who draw near simply to listen (i.e., in reverence) do not give themselves any occasion for getting into trouble (as in vv. 2-6). It is in this sense that they do not know how to do wrong.

5:2 For the Teacher the supreme act of impiety is the presumption that one can be in a position of control when dealing with God. He does not reject or even criticize prayer,[116] but he does contend that we have nothing to offer God and thus are in no position to bargain with or impress him.

5:3-7 Verse 3, which is apparently a common proverb,[117] is difficult; the meaning of the parallel proverb in v. 7a is also debated. Nevertheless, the word "dreams" refers not to literal dreams, whether as revelations sought by sleeping in a holy place or as the disturbed sleep of one who has many anxieties.[118] Instead, the word is used metaphorically, as in the English, "He has big dreams."[119] Those who have many troubles may fantasize of performing great and noble acts, but their aspirations are meaningless. Similarly, many words (which proceed from the speaker's presumption that he is wise) mark a person as a fool. Verse 7a could be translated, "In excess dreaming there is an abundance of both vanities and words."[120] In context these proverbs mean that fools seek to advance themselves before God with great vows and promises.[121]

Many suggestions on the meaning of "messenger" (v. 6) have been proposed. These include (1) a reverential term for God, (2) an angel (possibly the angel of death), (3) a prophet, (4) a priest, and (5) a messenger

---

[113]מִתֵּת הַכְּסִילִים זָבַח means "than when fools give sacrifice" and not "than to give the sacrifice of fools."

[114]אֵינָם יוֹדְעִים לַעֲשׂוֹת רָע means, "They do not know how to do evil," yet some contend that this cannot be the idea here (thus NIV "do not know that they do wrong"). Cf. Eaton, *Ecclesiastes*, 98; and Whybray, *Ecclesiastes*, 93. Gordis (*Koheleth*, 247-48) boldly takes this as sarcasm on the Teacher's part: Fools are good only because they lack the brains to do evil! His interpretation makes it seem as though the Teacher is sneering at religious people, but this is not the point of this passage. It probably is better to assume that those who draw near to listen are the implied subject here. Cf. Ginsburg, *Coheleth*, 353-56.

[115]See Whybray, *Ecclesiastes*, 92.

[116]Ibid., 94.

[117]See Gordis, *Koheleth*, 248; and Whybray, *Ecclesiastes*, 93-94.

[118]Cf. Crenshaw, *Ecclesiastes*, 116; and Whybray, *Ecclesiastes*, 93-94.

[119]Admittedly, there is no other OT usage fully parallel to this (but see Ps 126:1). Even so, context demands that the meaning is that many have delusions of their competence before God and acceptability to him. Cf. Ginsburg, *Cohelet*, 337.

[120]Taking וַהֲבָלִים וּדְבָרִים as coordinate predicates.

[121]Contrary to Gordis (*Koheleth*, 248) the first half of v. 3 is also relevant to the discussion.

from the temple. The first solution is most unlikely; the Teacher nowhere else speaks so circumspectly. The third and fourth solutions are also doubtful. The fifth suggestion is probable and is indicated by the NIV, but the second must be regarded as a real possibility.[122]

15. On Politics (5:8-9)

[8]If you see the poor oppressed in a district, and justice and rights denied, do not be surprised at such things; for one official is eyed by a higher one, and over them both are others higher still. [9]The increase from the land is taken by all; the king himself profits from the fields.

This passage, as translated in the NIV (and in most other versions as well), makes little sense. In v. 8 the Teacher complains about the prevalence of corruption, but in v. 9 (in the NIV rendition) he suddenly speaks of the benefits of farming. Any meaningful interpretation must tie the two verses together.

5:8 The reader is warned not to be shocked if corruption in high places is discovered. The mere existence of many levels of government administered by many officials[123] makes at least some corruption inevitable. A certain justified cynicism is displayed here: if enough people have opportunity to enrich themselves by abuse of political power, some are bound to succumb to the temptation. Alternatively, the last line may mean that government officials have a network for protecting one another and thus it is impossible to root out corruption.[124]

5:9 This should be translated, "But in all, an advantage for a land is this: a king, for the sake of agriculture."[125] Although the Teacher recognizes the corruption and abuse inherent in any political system (v. 8), he is not an anarchist. The king, who by metonymy represents the entire government, is on balance[126] an advantage rather than a liability to the nation. The example that makes this point is agriculture. In an anarchic society no boundaries or property rights can be maintained, access to wells and other common resources cannot be fairly regulated, aqueducts and dikes will not be kept in good repair, and no organized resistance to ravaging armies can be offered. In short, the agricultural economy will collapse. Government may be evil, but it is a necessary evil.

---

[122]Cf. Crenshaw, *Ecclesiastes*, 117. He cites a parallel from *Aniy*.

[123]Neither שֹׁמֵר nor וּגְבֹהִים refers to God. See Gordis, *Koheleth*, 250.

[124]Cf. Fox, *Qohelet*, 213.

[125]מֶלֶךְ לְשָׂדֶה נֶעֱבָד is literally "a king for a cultivated field." See Garrett, "Qoheleth," 165-67. By metonymy, "cultivated field" refers to the whole enterprise of agriculture.

[126]בַּכֹּל here means "on the whole." See Barton, *Ecclesiastes*, 126. In other words, when all the advantages and disadvantages of government are taken into consideration, government is found to be a benefit.

16. On Wealth (5:10–6:6)

10Whoever loves money never has money enough;
whoever loves wealth is never satisfied with his income.
This too is meaningless.

11As goods increase,
so do those who consume them.
And what benefit are they to the owner
except to feast his eyes on them?

12The sleep of a laborer is sweet,
whether he eats little or much,
but the abundance of a rich man
permits him no sleep.

13I have seen a grievous evil under the sun:

wealth hoarded to the harm of its owner,
14or wealth lost through some misfortune,
so that when he has a son
there is nothing left for him.
15Naked a man comes from his mother's womb,
and as he comes, so he departs.
He takes nothing from his labor
that he can carry in his hand.

16This too is a grievous evil:

As a man comes, so he departs,
and what does he gain,
since he toils for the wind?
17All his days he eats in darkness,
with great frustration, affliction and anger.

18Then I realized that it is good and proper for a man to eat and drink, and
to find satisfaction in his toilsome labor under the sun during the few days of
life God has given him—for this is his lot. 19Moreover, when God gives any
man wealth and possessions, and enables him to enjoy them, to accept his lot
and be happy in his work—this is a gift of God. 20He seldom reflects on the
days of his life, because God keeps him occupied with gladness of heart.
1I have seen another evil under the sun, and it weighs heavily on men: 2God
gives a man wealth, possessions and honor, so that he lacks nothing his heart
desires, but God does not enable him to enjoy them, and a stranger enjoys them
instead. This is meaningless, a grievous evil.
3A man may have a hundred children and live many years; yet no matter
how long he lives, if he cannot enjoy his prosperity and does not receive proper
burial, I say that a stillborn child is better off than he. 4It comes without meaning, it departs in darkness, and in darkness its name is shrouded. 5Though it
never saw the sun or knew anything, it has more rest than does that man—
6even if he lives a thousand years twice over but fails to enjoy his prosperity.
Do not all go to the same place?

5:10-15 The Teacher gives a series of reasons for not falling into the trap of making the pursuit of wealth life's goal.[127] These include: (1) wealth is both addictive and unsatisfactory (v. 10);[128] (2) wealth attracts human leeches, who give the rich man no peace (v. 11a); (3) wealth accumulated and taken out of circulation no longer meets the owner's needs and now serves only as a miser's feast of staring at money (v. 11b); (4) wealth does not give peace or rest but only promotes insomnia because of worries over how the wealth is to be maintained (v. 12); (5) love of wealth often causes a person to hoard even to the point causing suffering to himself (v. 13);[129] (6) wealth is an insecure basis for happiness since it may be easily lost in a bad business venture (v. 14);[130] and (7) wealth is *certain* to disappear at death (v. 15).[131] The Teacher typically looks upon death as the final negation of misplaced human values.

5:16–6:6 The mention of death as the ultimate proof of the folly of a life spent trying to amass wealth (5:15) leads to another call for the reader to enjoy the few days he has under the sun. But the context is still a discussion on wealth.

The Teacher makes three main points here. (1) Life is wasted when it is spent in a quest for more money; worse than that, it is filled with anger and gloom (5:16-17).[132] The "darkness" in which the miser eats (v. 17) is

---

[127]Verses 10-12,15 are in proverb form (second level discourse), whereas vv. 13-14 are the Teacher's reflection (third level discourse).

[128]It probably is best to follow Gordis (*Koheleth*, 251) in revocalizing תְּבוּאָה as a verb תְּבוּאֶהָ (parallel to יִשְׂבָּע) instead of the noun "produce." Thus, "And as for him who loves wealth, it does not come," not meaning that greedy people never get rich (they often do) but that they never get rich enough to satisfy themselves. Alternatively, יִשְׂבַּע may serve double duty with תְּבוּאָה as a second direct object: *he will not be satisfied with income.* Cf. Ginsburg, *Coheleth*, 348.

[129]Against Gordis (*Koheleth*, 252) שָׁמוּר לִבְעָלָיו may be taken as "kept *by* the owner." See Crenshaw, *Ecclesiastes*, 122. The "harm" he experiences probably is failing to meet his own legitimate needs because he cannot bear to part with the money.

[130]The mention of the birth of a son indicates that financial disaster may strike at a particularly inappropriate time. Gordis's suggestion (*Koheleth*, 252-53) that בְּיָדוֹ is a phonetic misspelling for בַּעֲדוֹ, "for him," is attractive.

[131]As the NIV has it, the ב in בַּעֲמָלוֹ means "from," a usage well attested in Phoenician and Ugaritic. See Whitley, *Koheleth*, 52.

[132]The translation of v. 17 (Heb. v. 16) is difficult and has prompted a number of conjectural emendations. The MT יֹאכֵל ("he eats") probably is preferable as the more difficult reading to the LXX καί πένθει ("and in grief"). Also וְכָעַס ("and he is vexed") is often emended to וְכַעַס ("and frustration"—thus NIV). Crenshaw (*Ecclesiastes*, 120-24) takes this reading and then argues that the ב of בַּחֹשֶׁךְ then governs all the following nouns with the meaning "he eats in darkness and much vexation, sickness, and resentment" (following the versions, he excises the pronoun suffix of וְחָלְיוֹ as a dittograph). Gordis (*Koheleth*, 254-55), however, retains כָּעַס as a verb and argues that וְחָלְיוֹ is equivalent to וְחֳלִי לוֹ. Thus, "He is greatly vexed, and he has illness and anger." See Whitley, *Koheleth*, 54-55, for other views.

metaphorical for isolation and joylessness.[133] (2) To be able rightly and fully to enjoy the things of this world is a gift of God's grace;[134] those who receive this gift are free from preoccupation with the pain of mortality (5:18-20).[135] (3) Nothing is more pitiful than to be rich but unable to enjoy it; no amount of prosperity can make up for a life without joy (6:1-6). To have a hundred children (v. 3) or live two thousand years (v. 6) are oriental exaggerations; the three traditional conditions for happiness were wealth, long life, and many children. Verses 4-5 refer to the miscarried child who goes from the darkness of the womb to the darkness of Sheol but is superior to the rich man because he or she has not wasted a life pursuing that which is meaningless.

An apparent incongruity in the text is "he . . . does not receive a proper burial" in v. 3. Most rich people are given elaborate funerals. Even so, it is hard to see how the Teacher would regard a joyless life as vindicated by virtue of a good burial. Some have suggested that the hypothetical rich man did not receive a burial because he was despised[136] or had committed some crime.[137] Both ideas are far-fetched and alien to the text. Gordis emends the text to omit the negative and reads, "Even if he has an elaborate funeral."[138] A better solution is Crenshaw's, that the line is not predicated on the rich man but is a proleptic reference to the miscarriage, "Even if it does not have a proper burial, I say that the stillborn is better off than he."[139]

17. Transition (6:7-9)

7All man's efforts are for his mouth,
yet his appetite is never satisfied.
8What advantage has a wise man
over a fool?

---

[133]Against Gordis (*Koheleth*, 254) who argues that "darkness" is meant literally: the miser refuses to burn his fuel for light. But חֹשֶׁךְ is regularly a metaphor for sorrow and confusion in Ecclesiastes; see 2:13-14; 6:4; 11:8; 12:2-3.

[134]טוֹב אֲשֶׁר־יָפֶה (v. 18; Heb. 17) appears odd. Fox (*Qohelet*, 217) rightly notes that these words do not constitute a phrase and translates, "Here is what I have seen to be good: it is appropriate to eat."

[135]The NIV paraphrase "he seldom reflects" captures the intent of לֹא הַרְבֵּה יִזְכֹּר in v. 20 (Heb. v. 19). More difficult is מַעֲנֶה, which may be taken as "afflicts," "keeps occupied," "answers," or perhaps with Gordis (*Koheleth*, 256) "provides."

[136]Eaton, *Ecclesiastes*, 106.

[137]Whybray, *Ecclesiastes*, 105.

[138]Gordis, *Koheleth*, 258-59. The required emendation is very slight—from לֹא to לֻא.

[139]Crenshaw, *Ecclesiastes*, 120. No emendation is required, and the change of tense from imperfects (referring to the rich man) to perfect (הָיְתָה, referring to the fetus) enhances the plausibility of this reading.

What does a poor man gain
by knowing how to conduct himself before others?
9Better what the eye sees
than the roving of the appetite.
This too is meaningless,
a chasing after the wind.

6:7-9 This text moves the reader from a discussion of wealth (5:10–6:6) to a discussion of wisdom (6:7–7:5). It is a series of three proverbs bound together by two catchwords.[140]

The first proverb (v. 7) states that although the appetite is the real motive behind human efforts, no one is ever fully satisfied.[141] Wisdom, moreover, is no particular advantage here (v. 8). The point is not only that the wise do not necessarily get wealthy but that they no less than others are bound to the drives of the appetite.[142]

The reader might assume that the Teacher is still talking strictly about the insatiable appetite of the greedy; but there is an implicit, unexpected reversal: the aphorism of v. 7 is as true of the desire of the intellectual for knowledge as it is of the greedy for wealth (cf. 1:16-18). Verse 8 anticipates that the reader, by now convinced that the pursuit of wealth is folly, might conclude that a life devoted to the quest for knowledge is the better way. The Teacher argues that in fact the learned really have no significant advantage over the unlettered, and that sound judgment and social skills do not do a poor man all that much good.[143] The third proverb (v. 9) asserts that it is better to be satisfied with what one has (be it money or knowledge) than to be continually driven to obtain more.[144]

18. On Wisdom and Death (6:10–7:4)

10Whatever exists has already been named,
and what man is has been known;
no man can contend
with one who is stronger than he.

---

[140]The catchwords הַנֶּפֶשׁ in v. 7 and לַהֲלֹךְ in v. 8 link with מֵהֲלָךְ־נָפֶשׁ in v. 9.

[141]Sheol (v. 6) should not be regarded as the antecedent of לְפִיהוּ (v. 7). Cf. Whybray, *Ecclesiastes*, 107; Whitley, *Koheleth*, 58-59.

[142]One might argue that the notion of the power of the appetite reflects Platonic thought, but "the Teacher's" conclusion is the opposite of Platonism: wisdom does *not* release the mind from the power of the appetite.

[143]The translation of v. 8b is much debated, but the solution adopted by the NIV is to be preferred. See the discussion in Gordis, *Koheleth*, 260-61.

[144]Whybray (*Ecclesiastes*, 108-9) argues that מֵהֲלָךְ־נָפֶשׁ cannot mean "than the wandering of the appetite" but must refer to the departure of life—i.e., death. Thus, "Better is seeing with the eyes [being alive] than the departure of life." If so, this would anticipate the discussion of death and wisdom that follows.

11 The more the words,
the less the meaning,
and how does that profit anyone?

12 For who knows what is good for a man in life, during the few and mean-
ingless days he passes through like a shadow? Who can tell him what will hap-
pen under the sun after he is gone?

1 A good name is better than fine perfume,
and the day of death better than the day of birth.
2 It is better to go to a house of mourning
than to go to a house of feasting,
for death is the destiny of every man;
the living should take this to heart.
3 Sorrow is better than laughter,
because a sad face is good for the heart.
4 The heart of the wise is in the house of mourning,
but the heart of fools is in the house of pleasure.

This section is in two parts: (1) a reflection on the fall of humanity (6:10-12) and (2) aphorisms on the importance of confronting one's own mortality (7:1-4). The whole text invites the reader to learn wisdom by confronting the reality of death.[145]

6:10-12 This text is held together by the fourfold use of the catchword *ʾādām* ("man"), here used not merely as a generic for human beings but as a term that points back to Gen 2–3. Ecclesiastes 6:10 ("Whatever exists has already been named") does not refer to the divine naming of all things at creation;[146] it is a literary allusion to Adam's naming of all living things in Gen 2:19.[147] Verse 10b,c should be rendered, "And it is known that he is *ʾādām* [human] and that he is not able to contend against one stronger than he."[148] The noun *ʾādām* looks back to the substance from which humanity came, the *ʾādamâ* ("soil"), and so draws attention to human mortality.[149] The participle "known" alludes to the tree of knowledge of good and evil,[150]

[145]Note that this is not simply a discussion of death but a discussion of *how the wise confront death*. The vocabulary of wisdom is much in evidence.

[146]A number of scholars relate this line to the opening of *Enuma Elish* (e.g., Barton, *Ecclesiastes*, 136; Gordis, *Koheleth*, 262-63).

[147]נִקְרָא שְׁמוֹ (Eccl 6:10) clearly recalls Gen 2:19: מַה־יִּקְרָא לוֹ . . . שְׁמוֹ.

[148]Gordis (*Koheleth*, 263) notes that אֲשֶׁר after a verb of perception means "that," but he fails to see the significance of אֲשֶׁר הוּא אָדָם and so treats the whole line as equivalent to וְנוֹדָע אֲשֶׁר הָאָדָם לֹא יוּכַל. Other attempts at translation (e.g., Crenshaw, *Ecclesiastes*, 130; Fox, *Qohelet*, 223-24) are even less appealing.

[149]The full phrase in Gen 2:7, that God formed Adam as עָפָר מִן־הָאֲדָמָה ("dust from the ground"), attests to human mortality.

[150]It is difficult to see why the Teacher would bring in a form of the verb ידע here if he were not looking back to the fall, the fundamental issue of which is that humanity came to *know* good and evil (Gen 3:5,22).

the place at which Adam discovered that he could not contend with God and win.

Adam contended with one "stronger" than he[151] in an attempt to become "like God, knowing good and evil" (Gen 3:5). Adam was in effect the first "Teacher."[152] He sought an encyclopedic mastery of knowledge (cf. Eccl 1:13) and even experimented with firsthand experience in good and evil (cf. Eccl 1:17). What he discovered was his own mortality and weakness before God. That is, he discovered the real meaning of his own name.

No sage, however brilliant or daring, has substantially added to Adam's discovery. Indeed, more exhaustive attempts at explaining the human situation only confound the facts and are of no benefit to humanity (v. 11).[153] Adam has already shown us what we are. The following question ("For who knows what is good for *ʾādām*?" [v. 12]) plays on the situation of Adam prior to the fall. The trees had "good" fruit, and the land had "good" gold (Gen 2:9,12). It also plays on the name of the tree of his demise, the tree of knowledge of good and evil.[154] Adam's days, though they numbered 930 years (Gen 5:5), passed like a shadow, and no one could tell him what was to follow him. What is true of him is equally true of all who bear his name, *ʾādām*/humanity. We are but weak mortals before an omnipotent God.

7:1-4 In another series of proverbs, the Teacher now urges the reader to face death and take its lessons to heart. He begins with an apparently harmless and perhaps popular proverb, "A good name is better than fine perfume"[155] but adds to that a startling complement, "And the day of death is better than the day of birth." Links between the two halves of the verse are tenuous but suggestive: (1) A good name is not securely established until the day of death; someone who still lives may still ruin his reputation. (2) Fine perfume speaks of wealth and luxury (Isa 3:20), but it may also allude to funeral preparations (cf. John 19:39).[156] (3) The "day of birth" may contrast the birthday party with the sobriety of a funeral.[157]

Verses 2-4 are straightforward and make a simple point: there is much to be gained by sober reflection on death.[158] Those who do so realize that

---

[151]The "stronger" one is God and not simply a stronger person. Cf. Fox, *Qohelet*, 223-24.

[152]Or the first Faust.

[153]לָאָדָם in vv. 11-12 plays on the double meaning of "for Adam" and "for humanity."

[154]There may also be an ironic allusion to the tree of life, עֵץ הַחַיִּים (Gen 3:22), the symbol of lost immortality, in the phrase בַּחַיִּים מִסְפַּר יְמֵי־חַיֵּי הֶבְלוֹ ("in life—the few days of his fleeting life," v. 12).

[155]Note the chiastic wordplay: טוֹב שֵׁם מִשֶּׁמֶן טוֹב.

[156]Gordis (*Koheleth*, 267) also suggests that newborns may have been rubbed with oils.

[157]Thus Eaton, *Ecclesiastes*, 109.

[158]The sad face of v. 3, in context, is the sober and meditative heart of the one who considers the meaning of death. Contrary to Fox (*Qohelet*, 228) the verse does not envisage one

the same end awaits them, and their hearts are turned from folly. Herein the *carpe diem* of the Teacher differs from that of the libertine, for whom death is either a subject to be avoided or an incentive to party all the more furiously.

19. Transition (7:5-6)

5It is better to heed a wise man's rebuke
than to listen to the song of fools.
6Like the crackling of thorns under the pot,
so is the laughter of fools.
This too is meaningless.

7:5-6 These two proverbs relate equally to both the preceding and following texts. On the one hand, the rebuke of a wise man over against the mirth[159] of a fool corresponds to the superiority of a house of mourning to a feast. On the other hand, the smirking laughter of fools is their response to the advice of the wise as described in v. 7: they laugh because in their eyes the wise man's rebuke is empty—they think he has no idea what he is talking about.[160] The simile portrays the fool as both worthless (like thorns) and about to be destroyed (burning under a pot).[161]

20. On Wisdom and Politics (7:7-9)

7Extortion turns a wise man into a fool,
and a bribe corrupts the heart.

8The end of a matter is better than its beginning,
and patience is better than pride.
9Do not be quickly provoked in your spirit,
for anger resides in the lap of fools.

Once again we have a discussion of politics (extortion and bribery are political matters), but it is not simply a reflection on political matters in and of themselves but a reflection on how the wise man confronts political reality.[162]

---

person with a sad face rebuking and thus making wise another person. See C. Ginsburg, *Coheleth*, 370-71.

[159]The contrast to גַּעֲרַת חָכָם is more complete if שִׁיר כְּסִילִים is taken to mean "flattery of fools" instead of "song of fools" (see Gordis, *Koheleth*, 269), but Whybray (*Ecclesiastes*, 115) rejects this as a possible interpretation. But as Crenshaw (*Ecclesiastes*, 135) notes, the שִׁיר may have both meanings here.

[160]See commentary on v. 7.

[161]Note the wordplay on הַסִּירִים and הַסִּיר.

[162]The instructional form (second level discourse) continues.

7:7 Extortion makes a wise man into a fool precisely in that it shows that his advice is wrong.[163] Behind this text stand the admonitions not only of biblical texts but of all ancient Near Eastern wisdom (particularly Egyptian) that those who hold political power should shun all corrupt practices. Still, when people see how pervasive abuse of political power is, that it is indeed so common that it is impossible to function in politics without being tainted, they conclude that the words of the wise are hopelessly idealistic. Thus it is that they smirk and laugh at wisdom (v. 6).[164] Bribery also undoes the work of wisdom in that it corrupts the heart.

7:8-9 Nevertheless, the final verdict is not in, and people prematurely conclude that warnings to avoid corruption are naive. If one is patient, one will finally see that moral integrity is indeed the better way (v. 8). At the same time, to allow oneself to be vexed and grief stricken over corruption in the world is also foolish (v. 9). The wise man is neither naive nor cynical and embittered.

21. Transition (7:10)

10Do not say, "Why were the old days better than these?"
For it is not wise to ask such questions.

7:10 This verse picks up on the previous text: it is pointless to look back to the good old days when corruption was not so common. Such days never existed. At the same time, v. 10 anticipates the following passage, which deals with economic cycles. It is foolish to long for the days of prosperity. Apart from the fact that such longing does no one any good, every period has its hardships and opportunities.

22. On Wisdom and Wealth (7:11-14)

11Wisdom, like an inheritance, is a good thing
and benefits those who see the sun.
12Wisdom is a shelter
as money is a shelter,

---

[163]The verb יְהוֹלֵל ("to make a fool of") is found in Isa 44:25, where God makes fools of diviners by causing their predictions to fail, and Job 12:17, where God makes fools of judges in showing his wisdom to be higher than theirs. In other words, they are made to be fools in that their sage opinions are shown to be false. Cf. H. Cazelles, "הלל *hll* III," in *TDOT* 3:411-13. Cazelles notes that the word here has the sense of "deceive" and comments that it "was admirably suited to Ecclesiastes for describing the utter ineffectiveness of political wisdom" (pp. 412-13).

[164]כִּי ("because") in v. 7 establishes the link between this and v. 6. NIV incorrectly leaves the word untranslated. Nor is it correct to translate כִּי as "surely" or postulate that another verse has dropped out. See Garrett, "Qoheleth," 167-68.

but the advantage of knowledge is this:
that wisdom preserves the life of its possessor.

13 Consider what God has done:

Who can straighten
what he has made crooked?
14 When times are good, be happy;
but when times are bad, consider:
God has made the one
as well as the other.
Therefore, a man cannot discover
anything about his future.

The topic of wisdom is as much in evidence here as in 6:10–7:4 and 7:7-9. On the other hand, terms like "inheritance" and "money" have also returned us to a discussion of wealth. The wise man must know how to confront prosperity and deprivation, the cycles of boom and bust.

7:11-12 Verse 11a should be translated, "Wisdom, *with* an inheritance, is good."[165] Even the wise prefer prosperity to poverty. Those who possess both money and wisdom are under the protection of both.[166] The superiority of wisdom, however, is that it guides one through difficult times and thus preserves life. Money, to the contrary, often vanishes in hard times.

7:13-14 Verse 13 harkens back to the insoluble problem of 1:15. Here, however, the point is that God is in control of the times, and nothing can be done to resist his will. Verse 14 clarifies that this is to be understood in an economic context. God brings both prosperity and recession. When times are good, one should enjoy the prosperity; when times are bad, one should reflect on the fact that this too is from God's hand. God does not allow us to know whether tomorrow will bring unexpected wealth or sudden calamity,[167] but we can find peace if we accept all as from God (see Lam 3:38).

---

[165]The NIV, "*like* an inheritance," is incorrect. עִם־נַחֲלָה means *with an inheritance*, notwithstanding the attempts of many to render עִם "like" here. Whitley (*Koheleth*, 64) and Fox (*Qohelet*, 231) defend the translation "like" particularly on analogy to 2:16. There the wise man, *along with* the fool (עִם הַכְּסִיל), dies and is not long remembered. The two are "alike" in that they share the same fate; but this is not at all analogous to the usage in 7:11. Note also that the word is rendered *cum* in the Vg, μετά in the LXX, and עִם in the Targum.

[166]כִּי בְּצֵל הַחָכְמָה בְּצֵל הַכָּסֶף (v. 12), a highly abbreviated line (note asyndeton), has caused a great deal of speculation and discussion (cf. Delitzsch, *Ecclesiastes*, 321; Gordis, *Koheleth*, 273-74). The easiest solution is to take those who have both wisdom and an inheritance (v. 11) as the implied subject. Thus, "For [those who possess both are] in the shadow of wisdom, [they are] in the shadow of money."

[167]The strength of עַל־דִּבְרַת שֶׁ ("in order that") should not be weakened to "therefore" as the NIV has done. Our ignorance of the future is in the purpose and plan of God.

23. On Religion, Wisdom, and Evil (7:15-29)

15In this meaningless life of mine I have seen both of these:

a righteous man perishing in his righteousness,
and a wicked man living long in his wickedness.
16Do not be overrighteous,
neither be overwise—
why destroy yourself?
17Do not be overwicked,
and do not be a fool—
why die before your time?
18It is good to grasp the one
and not let go of the other.
The man who fears God will avoid all [extremes].

19Wisdom makes one wise man more powerful
than ten rulers in a city.

20There is not a righteous man on earth
who does what is right and never sins.

21Do not pay attention to every word people say,
or you may hear your servant cursing you—
22for you know in your heart
that many times you yourself have cursed others.

23All this I tested by wisdom and I said,
"I am determined to be wise"—
but this was beyond me.
24Whatever wisdom may be,
it is far off and most profound—
who can discover it?
25So I turned my mind to understand,
to investigate and to search out wisdom and the scheme of things
and to understand the stupidity of wickedness
and the madness of folly.

26I find more bitter than death
the woman who is a snare,
whose heart is a trap
and whose hands are chains.
The man who pleases God will escape her,
but the sinner she will ensnare.

27"Look," says the Teacher, "this is what I have discovered:

"Adding one thing to another to discover the scheme of things—
28while I was still searching
but not finding—
I found one [upright] man among a thousand,
but not one [upright] woman among them all.

[29]This only have I found:
God made mankind upright,
but men have gone in search of many schemes."

At first glance these verses are a disparate collection that embraces several distinct themes. On closer examination, however, the search for virtue in self and others is found to be at the core of the entire discussion. Behind this text and emerging from it is recognition that the universality of human sin undoes all attempts to find unsullied virtue in human life. The structure of this passage is (1) a warning against excessive zeal in religion (vv. 15-18), (2) two teachings on coping with the evil that pervades humanity (vv. 19-22), and (3) the search for a man or woman of virtue (vv. 23-29).

7:15-18 The simple equation that links prosperity and long life to religious zeal and wisdom, while associating suffering and an early death with sin, is only a generalization. There are many exceptions. Those who with pathological devotion embrace the precepts of religion and wisdom (the two are conceived together here) will be disappointed. Like Job's three friends, such people are convinced that the question of how a human is to relate to God and the world is easily answered: If you obey all the rules, you will be safe. The practical result of such a philosophy is asceticism (self-denial in spiritual discipline). For the Teacher such asceticism is futile (in that it is bound to fail), arrogant (in that it stems from a smug certainty about one's own righteousness), and miserable (in that ascetics have cut themselves off from the normal joys of life). The Teacher anticipates Paul's understanding of grace and the law (cf. Rom 7–8).[168]

The warning not to be "overrighteous" or "overwise" is not an exhortation to do a little sinning.[169] The Teacher is not dealing here with the issue of personal sins as such. Rather, he is concerned with a philosophy of life that seeks the benefits of long life, prosperity, and personal happiness through the strict observation of religious and wisdom principles. A modern way to put it would be, "Do not be a fanatic."

Also, as Crenshaw observes, v. 17 does not counsel that sin in moderation is acceptable.[170] Rather, it implies that while some sin in everyone's life is inevitable, those who embrace evil as a way of life are destroyed by it.

Verse 18b, a famous crux, should be rendered, "He who fears God comes forth with both of them."[171] But what are the two things the God-fearer

[168]Cf. D. A. Garrett, "Inerrancy as a Principle of Biblical Hermeneutics," in *Authority and Interpretation*, ed. D. A. Garrett and R. R. Melick, Jr. (Grand Rapids: Baker, 1987), 61-63.

[169]Cf. Loader, *Polar Structures*, 48.

[170]Crenshaw, *Ecclesiastes*, 140. He aptly observes that Deut 27:24 does not imply that public homicide is acceptable.

[171]יֵצֵא אֶת־כֻּלָּם, taking אֶת as "with" and יֵצֵא in its normal sense. The NIV translation "will avoid all extremes" is a doubtful paraphrase. A number of scholars compare the usage of יצא here to a Mishnaic idiom, "to do one's duty" and thus be released from an obligation

should hold to, and in what sense does he come forth with both? In this context the two things to be maintained are, on the one hand, devotion to God and the teachings of wisdom and, on the other hand, enjoyment of the good things of life. The God-fearer "comes forth" with them in that he maintains both through his life. While the ascetic looks upon every form of indulgence or mirth as sin (against religion) or folly (against wisdom) and the libertine looks upon any restraint as a threat to his pleasure-seeking, the Teacher counsels combining true religion—the fear of God—with true enjoyment of the good things of life.

7:19-22 This text is structured as two teachings (vv. 19,21), each of which has an attached explanation (vv. 20,22).[172] Verse 19[173] at first seems alien to this context, but v. 20 supplies the link:[174] wise men are necessary in human society because human sin is universal (cf. Rom 3:23).[175] Rulers can try to curb evil by brute force; but because of all the pettiness, weakness, and ambition people bring into society, only the wise can maintain an equilibrium among them. Verses 21-22 are self-explanatory. The teaching of the whole text is that the reader must accept that all are sinners and learn to deal with people as they are.

7:23-29 Verses 23-29 are in effect further reflections on the fall of humanity.[176] Verses 23-25[177] bespeak the Teacher's determination to understand human behavior and are comparable to 1:17-18. Verses 26-28, which appear outrageously antiwoman, are incomprehensible if two factors are not considered: (1) Ecclesiastes was originally written for a male audience, and (2) these verses look back to the early chapters of Genesis.

The portrait of woman as snare and trap does not refer to a prostitute or to Woman Folly of Prov 9:13-18. Instead, it refers to domestic conflict between husband and wife as *given from a man's perspective* and based upon Gen 3:16, "You will try to trap your husband, but he will dominate

---

(Delitzsch, *Ecclesiastes*, 326; Gordis, *Koheleth*, 277-78; Crenshaw, *Ecclesiastes*, 142); but it is difficult to see how fulfilling an obligation enters here. Rather, we have a continuation of the metaphor of v. 18a: the one who fears God is to hold fast to both the one and the other and come out with both.

[172]Note the use of כִּי at the beginning of vv. 20,22. In both cases the normal translation "because" applies. The NIV has left כִּי untranslated in v. 20 but rendered it "for" in v. 22. Also גַּם introduces v. 21 as a second teaching.

[173]The NIV translation of v. 19 is reasonable; תָּעֹז should be taken transitively (Whitley, *Koheleth*, 67) as in the NIV.

[174]The dislocation of v. 19 (Fox, *Qohelet*, 232) is thus unnecessary.

[175]אָדָם ("human") alludes to the fall and the discussion in 6:10-12. בָּאָרֶץ, "in the land," corresponds to בָּעִיר, "in the city" (v. 19). Both refer to society as a whole.

[176]Note the return to the Teacher's reflections (third level discourse).

[177]The syntax of v. 25b is difficult; the NIV emends to produce two construct chains. It probably is better to follow the LXX and read four separate objects after לָדַעַת: "to understand wickedness, stupidity, folly, and madness." See Fox, *Qohelet*, 240-41.

you."[178] In other words, because of sin, married life will be a war instead of a joy. Women will try to ensnare and control men; but most men, often through sheer brutality, will dominate their wives. Yet it will be miserable for all. The Teacher, a man writing for men, looks at it from the masculine perspective: many men are made wretched by their wives. The man who is righteous before God, however, escapes this fate (v. 26b). This does not mean that such men never marry (!) but that God gives them women who are loving and who are not human traps.

Verse 28 does not mean that men are slightly better than women. It describes the reality that although most men can find at least one man who is a true friend, they never find a woman with whom they can enjoy such companionship without competition.

It is important to note that it is equally possible and legitimate to reflect on Gen 3:16c from the woman's perspective. For many women a husband is a hard, cold taskmaster. Human history has no shortage of examples of emotional and physical brutality against women. Similarly, many women find at least one true female friend even though they can never find a loving man. The one who teaches this text must present it from both perspectives.[179]

The passage concludes with a final reflection on the fall (v. 29): "God made *ʾādām* upright, but people have gone in search of many schemes."[180] A more succinct yet complete statement of "total depravity" could not be given.

24. Transition (8:1)

[1]Who is like the wise man?
Who knows the explanation of things?
Wisdom brightens a man's face
and changes its hard appearance.

8:1 An alternative translation is possible: "Who is like the wise man? Who knows the explanation of a situation?[181] A man's wisdom causes

---

[178]Traditionally, "Your desire will be for your husband, and he will rule over you" (NIV). But the line has an exact parallel in Gen 4:7c, as follows:

3:16c: וְאֶל־אִישֵׁךְ תְּשׁוּקָתֵךְ וְהוּא יִמְשָׁל־בָּךְ

4:7c: וְאֵלֶיךָ תְּשׁוּקָתוֹ וְאַתָּה תִּמְשָׁל־בּוֹ.

In the latter context תְּשׁוּקָה ("desire") is a desire to entrap, and מָשַׁל ("rule") is domination over. The parallel being so profound, it is impossible to take 3:16c in a different sense. The "desire" of the woman is not a loving or sexual desire, and the "rule" of the man is not benevolent but selfish (this verse is a curse, not instruction).

[179]For further discussion, see D. A. Garrett, "Ecclesiastes 7:25-29 and the Feminist Hermeneutic," *CTR* 2 (1988): 309-21.

[180]הִשְּׁבֹנוֹת here means "devious," "irregular," or "questionable things." See Whitley, *Koheleth*, 70.

[181]דָּבָר here means "situation," not "word." Cf. Barton, *Ecclesiastes*, 151, and Delitzsch, *Ecclesiastes*, 336.

[the king[182]] to show him favor[183] so that the power of [the king's] face is redirected."[184] The verse looks back to the previous quest for wisdom/virtue, as the mention of an "explanation" looks back to 7:23-24.[185] In 8:1, however, the tone is more optimistic: some attainment of wisdom *is* possible and has real advantages. In particular it enables one to influence those who exercise power, the topic of the following discussion. Verse 1b is thus another proleptic marker of a topic change, the shift here being to the question of how to deal with absolute authority. This in turn draws the Teacher into further discussion of injustice, maladministration, and the problem of theodicy.

25. On Politics (8:2-6)

[2]Obey the king's command, I say, because you took an oath before God. [3]Do not be in a hurry to leave the king's presence. Do not stand up for a bad cause, for he will do whatever he pleases. [4]Since a king's word is supreme, who can say to him, "What are you doing?"

[5]Whoever obeys his command will come to no harm,
and the wise heart will know the proper time and procedure.
[6]For there is a proper time and procedure for every matter,
though a man's misery weighs heavily upon him.

8:2-6 In dealings with the king, the Teacher counsels patience and perseverance despite the arbitrary exercise of power one encounters. The reasons are (1) the courtier is bound by an oath (v. 2);[186] (2) to abandon one's

---

[182]Implied from the subsequent discussion, vv. 2-17.

[183]The parallel of תָּאִיר פָּנָיו to יָאֵר יהוה פָּנָיו אֵלֶיךָ ("May the Lord make his face to shine toward you," Num 6:25) and related passages (Heb.: Pss 31:17; 67:2; 119:135; Dan 9:17) is too strong to overlook. Commentaries and translations uniformly assume that the *wise man's* face is made to shine, but this disregards the fact that the shining of the face is the bestowal of favor from a more powerful figure (in the benediction, God) to a weaker figure. It is not, as Crenshaw (*Ecclesiastes*, 149) and Gordis (*Koheleth*, 286) assert, merely a manner of maintaining the *appearance* of a pleasant demeanor. Thus תָּאִיר פָּנָיו, lit. "makes his [i.e., the king's] face to shine," means that the holder of power will show favor to the wise man.

[184]וְעֹז פָּנָיו יְשֻׁנֶּא, often rendered "and his strong face is transformed" (i.e., the wise man's face becomes less aggressive). But "his strong face" would be פְּנֵי עֻזּוֹ on the analogy of זְרוֹעַ עֻזּוֹ ("his strong arm," Isa 62:8; cf. Ps 89:11) and קוֹל עֹז ("a strong voice," Ps 68:34). A better translation is "the power of his face," again referring to the face of the king from the following context. Since the subject here is עֹז ("power") and not the face, יְשֻׁנֶּא (byform of שׁנה, "to change") does not mean that the facial expression is transformed. Rather, it means the royal exercise of power is redirected (cf. Jer 2:36; Prov 31:5). The verse thus concerns not a facial expression but influencing the exercise of political power. Compare 10:4, where the counselor patiently holds to his post (as in 8:3) and in so doing turns aside the king's anger.

[185]Similarly, the reference to אָדָם in 8:1 may be retrospective to the reflections on אָדָם in 6:10–7:29.

[186]אֲנִי apparently means "I say," as in NIV. וְעַל דִּבְרַת introduces a special motive for obedience (Ginsburg, *Coheleth*, 392). This analysis is rejected by Fox (*Qohelet*, 246-47), but his interpretation is scarcely persuasive.

place before the king is to lose all influence (v. 3a); (3) the king is autocratic and one cannot simply correct him (v. 4); and (4) the one who continues to work patiently for good causes will be so recognized by the king (vv. 5-6a).[187] The wise man thus waits for the proper moment to make his case or take a stand and does not waste his influence on a lost cause (v. 3b).[188] He maintains his patience, moreover, in spite of the moral burdens he carries that might otherwise cause him to act impetuously (v. 6b; "for the trouble of humanity is heavy upon him").[189]

26. Transition (8:7-8)

7Since no man knows the future,
who can tell him what is to come?
8No man has power over the wind to contain it;
so no one has power over the day of his death.
As no one is discharged in time of war,
so wickedness will not release those who practice it.

8:7-8 The injustice and sorrows of life force us to come to terms with the powers that govern us. On the human level this is the king (8:2-6), but on the higher level this is God (8:9–9:1). These verses are thus transitional between the two. The future is an enigma (v. 7[190]), and the power that confronts us is irresistible (v. 8a,b,c: "wind" represents the power of God;[191] "discharged[192] in time of war" exemplifies the power of the king; "death" is ultimately in the power of God but is also in the king's hands). Verse 8d should be translated "but wickedness will not deliver[193] its master." That is, no amount of cunning can save one from control by the governing powers.[194]

187As the NIV has it, וְעֵת וּמִשְׁפָּט means "proper time and procedure"; see Gordis, *Koheleth*, 289. Contrary to Fox (*Qohelet*, 247-48), it does not mean "the time of [divine] judgment." This interpretation is contrary to context, and anyway the wise man certainly does not know the time of God's judgment (v. 5b).

188A "bad cause" (בְּדָבָר רָע, v. 3) is not a morally evil cause but a cause that is politically impossible, i.e., one that the king will never accept. Alternative interpretations (e.g., Scott, *Ecclesiastes*, 240; Delitzsch, *Ecclesiastes*, 340) are unlikely. אַל תַּעֲמֹד בְּדָבָר רָע could be paraphrased, "Do not champion an idea the king opposes." See Garrett, "Qoheleth," 169.

189כִּי־רָעַת הָאָדָם רַבָּה עָלָיו. רָעַת הָאָדָם is not, as in the NIV "a man's misery," i.e., a private problem. It is sorrow and vexation over the human condition, and it is because of his moral concern that he desires to influence royal decisions.

190On the political level this makes one's position before the king all the more tenuous. On the theological level this alludes to God's control over our destiny.

191Against Gordis (*Koheleth*, 290) this is not a reference to physical death. See Garrett, "Qoheleth," 170. Since רוּחַ can mean "Spirit," the wordplay implies that no one can resist God.

192On מִשְׁלַחַת see Whitley, *Koheleth*, 72-73.

193Giving יְמַלֵּט its more common meaning "deliver" rather than "release."

194Cf. Ginsburg, *Coheleth*, 397.

27. On Theodicy (8:9–9:1)

[9]All this I saw, as I applied my mind to everything done under the sun. There is a time when a man lords it over others to his own hurt. [10]Then too, I saw the wicked buried—those who used to come and go from the holy place and receive praise in the city where they did this. This too is meaningless.

[11]When the sentence for a crime is not quickly carried out, the hearts of the people are filled with schemes to do wrong. [12]Although a wicked man commits a hundred crimes and still lives a long time, I know that it will go better with God-fearing men, who are reverent before God. [13]Yet because the wicked do not fear God, it will not go well with them, and their days will not lengthen like a shadow.

[14]There is something else meaningless that occurs on earth: righteous men who get what the wicked deserve, and wicked men who get what the righteous deserve. This too, I say, is meaningless. [15]So I commend the enjoyment of life, because nothing is better for a man under the sun than to eat and drink and be glad. Then joy will accompany him in his work all the days of the life God has given him under the sun.

[16]When I applied my mind to know wisdom and to observe man's labor on earth—his eyes not seeing sleep day or night—[17]then I saw all that God has done. No one can comprehend what goes on under the sun. Despite all his efforts to search it out, man cannot discover its meaning. Even if a wise man claims he knows, he cannot really comprehend it.

[1]So I reflected on all this and concluded that the righteous and the wise and what they do are in God's hands, but no man knows whether love or hate awaits him.

The Teacher describes his indignation over how injustice in the world encourages people to choose evil over good. He deals with the apparent distortion of values in the world under three headings: (1) the prosperity of the wicked (vv. 9-11), (2) God's justice (vv. 12-13), (3) God's apparent participation in injustice in that wickedness often goes unpunished (v. 14).

8:9-11 An alternative translation of vv. 9-10 is as follows: "All this I have seen and have given attention to every deed done under the sun while[195] man rules men to their hurt.[196] And in such circumstances[197] I saw the wicked buried. And [people] came and attended[198] the funeral,[199]

---

[195]עֵת אֲשֶׁר; see Crenshaw, *Ecclesiastes*, 153.

[196]The NIV's "to his own hurt" is unlikely. The antecedent of the pronoun "his" (לוֹ) is certainly the nearer noun (בְּאָדָם) and not the more distant noun (הָאָדָם). Also, while ל can be reflexive, it is generally used thus only with a verb of motion. Finally, a reflexive translation contradicts this passage. If oppression harms the oppressor, then the problem of theodicy disappears. See Garrett, "Qoheleth," 171.

[197]וּבְכֵן; cf. Eaton, *Ecclesiastes*, 121, and see Esth 4:16.

[198]The Piel stem of הלך generally means to "walk about"; here it apparently means to "attend" a service.

[199]מְקוֹם קָדוֹשׁ, lit. "holy place." But Gordis (*Koheleth*, 295) has argued persuasively that the phrase here is a euphemism either for the burial site or a memorial service. Fox (*Qohelet*,

and [the wicked] were praised[200] in the city where they had behaved in this manner [i.e., wickedly].[201] This too is absurd."[202] With v. 11 this means that in spite of a notorious reputation, the wicked achieve prosperity and come to an end that is at least officially honorable. The fact that they achieved such success in life in spite of and indeed because of their oppression of others encourages people to follow in their path. Verse 9 also brings out the irony of oppression: *ʾādām* (a *person*) rules *ʾādām* (people). The use of *ʾādām* brings out both the unity and sinfulness of the race as well as the tragedy that they are under human rather than divine government.

8:12-13 This affirmation of faith in God's justice is remarkable in that it is made without presenting any supporting evidence; it is merely asserted that because of their impiety, the wicked will not enjoy a prolonged life.[203] It is a word of faith in the face of apparently contradictory evidence. An interpretation of this confession as a gloss[204] or as a quote of conventional theology[205] is superficial. As in 3:12,14 "I know" introduces something of a concession or addendum by the Teacher, yet it is as valid a part of his beliefs and teachings as are the challenging questions he raises. His refusal to rationalize the situation or to explain and defend his belief in divine justice all the more strikingly characterizes his affirmation as an act of faith.

8:14 Verse 14 is a blunt statement of the evidence. Virtue is not always rewarded. The Teacher's assessment of this is stated in personal terms (third level discourse).

From this consideration of injustice in the world, the Teacher now draws three conclusions: (1) people should enjoy the good things life offers and not waste themselves in vexation over the problem of evil (v. 15), (2) God has deliberately made life unpredictable in order to thwart human efforts to master and control it (vv. 16-17), and (3) God is showing us that all things are in his hands and not ours (9:1).

---

250) rejects the view that it is the cemetery on the grounds that was unclean and not holy, but even he allows that it may be a synagogue as a place where a eulogy was given. The words are best translated paraphrastically as "funeral."

[200]Reading וישתבחו ("and they were praised") instead of וְיִשְׁתַּכְּחוּ ("and they were forgotten"). Cf. BHS note.

[201]An alternative translation of the MT is quite possible, "But those who behaved justly were forgotten in the city." But cf. Gordis, *Koheleth*, 296. If this is the meaning of this line, however, the overall thrust of the text remains the same: the wealthy wicked are honored even in death, and the righteous are not.

[202]For other approaches see Crenshaw, *Ecclesiastes*, 154, and Fox, *Qohelet*, 250-51.

[203]It is possible that instead of translating כַּצֵּל as "like a shadow," the phrase should be read בְּצֵל אֲשֶׁר and rendered simply as "because." Cf. M. O. Wise, "A Calque from Aramaic in Qoheleth 6:12, 7:12, and 8:13," *JBL* 109.2 (1990): 249-57.

[204]Crenshaw, *Ecclesiastes*, 155.

[205]Gordis, *Koheleth*, 297. Dealing with "contradictions" in Ecclesiastes by claiming that one or the other of viewpoints expressed is a quotation of a view that the Teacher personally rejects is a hermeneutical act of desperation. See Fox, *Qohelet*, 25-28.

8:15 The Teacher is not here advocating hedonistic indifference to injustice and suffering, but he does counsel that we come to terms with the limits of our ability to explain (much less eliminate) unjust suffering. Unending vexation over this problem is pointless.

8:16-17 The Teacher's great discovery about the nature of God's activity ("then I saw all that God has done") is that he does not comprehend it. Every endeavor of wisdom to find the key by which one may master life is bound to fail. Our inability to know the future (8:7) is evidence of this. If we could know with certainty what actions bring prosperity, happiness, and long life, then we could control life and even God. But such knowledge and such powers are ever out of reach.

9:1 The Teacher finally takes the problem of theodicy in an astonishing direction: the apparent injustice in the world is proof of the sovereignty of God. No one by even righteous deeds can gain control over God and coerce blessing from him ("love" and "hate" refer respectively to divine favor or disfavor). One must acknowledge that all is in God's hands. The Teacher's understanding of divine sovereignty is much closer to Paul's teaching on grace and the law than is generally recognized.

28. Transition (9:2)

2All share a common destiny—the righteous and the wicked, the good and the bad, the clean and the unclean, those who offer sacrifices and those who do not.

As it is with the good man,
so with the sinner;
as it is with those who take oaths,
so with those who are afraid to take them.

Death is equally certain regardless of how righteously or wickedly one has lived. This both raises the question of whether or not righteousness is adequately rewarded and forces the Teacher again to reflect on the problem of death. This verse thus looks back to the problem of divine justice (8:9–9:1) and ahead to the problem of death (9:3-12).

29. On Death and Contentment (9:3-10)

3This is the evil in everything that happens under the sun: The same destiny overtakes all. The hearts of men, moreover, are full of evil and there is madness in their hearts while they live, and afterward they join the dead. 4Anyone who is among the living has hope—even a live dog is better off than a dead lion!

5For the living know that they will die,
but the dead know nothing;
they have no further reward,
and even the memory of them is forgotten.

[6]Their love, their hate
and their jealousy have long since vanished;
never again will they have a part
in anything that happens under the sun.

[7]Go, eat your food with gladness, and drink your wine with a joyful heart,
for it is now that God favors what you do. [8]Always be clothed in white, and
always anoint your head with oil. [9]Enjoy life with your wife, whom you love, all
the days of this meaningless life that God has given you under the sun— all
your meaningless days. For this is your lot in life and in your toilsome labor
under the sun. [10]Whatever your hand finds to do, do it with all your might, for
in the grave, where you are going, there is neither working nor planning nor
knowledge nor wisdom.

9:3-6 Death is "the evil" (v. 3), not simply a natural phenomenon. This too is a meditation on the fall; humanity has been cut off from the tree of life. The astonishing thing, however, is that instead of reckoning with the meaning of death, humans fill their lives with the distractions of a thousand passions and squander what little time they have to immediate but insignificant worries.

To be sure, the Teacher prefers life to death. Even a lowly dog is better off than a dead lion. But the reason[206] The Teacher puts forward for choosing life is another surprise: because the living know they will die! The explanation is that the living may yet reckon with the reality of death and in so doing embrace the joy life has to offer,[207] but no such possibility exists for those who have already died. Their time has passed.[208]

9:7-10 This section has parallels in ancient Near Eastern literature (see Introduction). Here, in another *carpe diem* ("seize the day"), the Teacher urges the reader not to let life go by without experiencing happiness. To rejoice is no sin; to the contrary, "God favors what you do" (v. 7). Wearing white clothes and anointing the hair (v. 8) symbolize joy and contrast with the familiar use of sackcloth and ashes as a sign of mourning or repentance. Three specific areas of joy recommended are feasting (v. 7), marital relations (v. 9), and occupation (v. 10). Verse 9 is further evidence that the Teacher is no woman hater.

---

[206]כִּי is explanatory and not, contrary to Gordis (*Koheleth*, 304), emphatic.

[207]Fox (*Qohelet*, 258) objects to translating בִּטָּחוֹן as "hope" on the grounds that "knowing that one will die is not a 'hope.'" The validity of that point notwithstanding, בִּטָּחוֹן and its cognates always have the positive sense of hope, security, or confidence about the future. See A. Jepsen, "בָּטַח (*batach*)," *TDOT* 2:88-94. Unless Ecclesiastes is being highly ironic, it is difficult to see how knowledge that one will someday die can be called a בִּטָּחוֹן. The hope or confidence of the living is not simply the awareness that they will die but that the possibility of rejoicing in the days under the sun still exists for them.

[208]It is in this sense that the dead "know nothing" (v. 5). This is not a metaphysical statement about the question of afterlife but a practical assertion that their days under the sun are over.

30. Transition (9:11-12)

[11]I have seen something else under the sun:
The race is not to the swift
or the battle to the strong,
nor does food come to the wise
or wealth to the brilliant
or favor to the learned;
but time and chance happen to them all.

[12]Moreover, no man knows when his hour will come:
As fish are caught in a cruel net,
or birds are taken in a snare,
so men are trapped by evil times
that fall unexpectedly upon them.

9:11-12 This text is transitional. It looks back to previous statements about death when it speaks of the snare that ultimately overtakes us, but it also looks ahead to the following passage, in which wisdom offers no certainty of success in the political realm.

We are all victims of time and chance. In so saying, the Teacher is not abandoning his earlier position that the will of God determines all; he is merely looking at the arbitrary nature of life from a human rather than theological perspective. Merit is not always rewarded, and the world can be unfair. Wisdom, skill, and hard work can promote but not guarantee success.[209] In v. 12 the time and chance that overtakes humans is death itself. It catches one unexpectedly, like a trap, and there is no escape. When the trap has closed, any opportunity to enjoy life is over.

31. On Politics (9:13–10:17)

[13]I also saw under the sun this example of wisdom that greatly impressed me: [14]There was once a small city with only a few people in it. And a powerful king came against it, surrounded it and built huge siegeworks against it. [15]Now there lived in that city a man poor but wise, and he saved the city by his wisdom. But nobody remembered that poor man. [16]So I said, "Wisdom is better than strength." But the poor man's wisdom is despised, and his words are no longer heeded.

[17]The quiet words of the wise are more to be heeded
than the shouts of a ruler of fools.
[18]Wisdom is better than weapons of war,
but one sinner destroys much good.

---

[209]Fox (*Qohelet*, 260) properly observes that v. 11 "does not mean that the swift never win, but that . . . they do not *necessarily* win."

1As dead flies give perfume a bad smell,
so a little folly outweighs wisdom and honor.
2The heart of the wise inclines to the right,
but the heart of the fool to the left.
3Even as he walks along the road,
the fool lacks sense
and shows everyone how stupid he is.
4If a ruler's anger rises against you,
do not leave your post;
calmness can lay great errors to rest.

5There is an evil I have seen under the sun,
the sort of error that arises from a ruler:
6Fools are put in many high positions,
while the rich occupy the low ones.
7I have seen slaves on horseback,
while princes go on foot like slaves.

8Whoever digs a pit may fall into it;
whoever breaks through a wall may be bitten by a snake.
9Whoever quarries stones may be injured by them;
whoever splits logs may be endangered by them.

10If the ax is dull
and its edge unsharpened,
more strength is needed
but skill will bring success.

11If a snake bites before it is charmed,
there is no profit for the charmer.

12Words from a wise man's mouth are gracious,
but a fool is consumed by his own lips.
13At the beginning his words are folly;
at the end they are wicked madness—
14and the fool multiplies words.

No one knows what is coming—
who can tell him what will happen after him?

15A fool's work wearies him;
he does not know the way to town.

16Woe to you, O land whose king was a servant
and whose princes feast in the morning.
17Blessed are you, O land whose king is of noble birth
and whose princes eat at a proper time—
for strength and not for drunkenness.

This collection of proverbs, anecdotes, and observations all center on a common theme: the impulsive nature of political power. The political world is one of uncertainty and flux. More than that, it has incompetence and folly to spare.

9:13-16 Whether the poor man delivered[210] the city by diplomacy or military strategy is not the issue. The point is that the city owed its survival to him, but he received no reward or lasting respect. Wisdom is sought out only in desperate times; otherwise, only those who have wealth or power are in a position to demand public attention.

9:17–10:1 Ecclesiastes 9:17–10:1 should be punctuated as follows: "The quiet words of the wise are more to be heeded than the shouts of a ruler of fools; wisdom is better than weapons of war. But one sinner destroys much good: As dead flies . . . " In other words, there should be a major break after "war" in v. 18, and "But . . . good" leads into the proverbs of 10:1. The whole has a chiastic pattern.

Proverb A	9:17
Lesson of Proverb A	9:18a
Lesson of Proverb B	9:18b
Proverb B	10:1

The whole also has a point-counterpoint pattern.

Point:	Wisdom is better than the sheer exercise of political power (9:17-18a).
Counterpoint:	Wisdom often gets lost in the political process (9:18b–10:1).

9:17-18a In 9:17-18a wisdom carries more authority than brute political force (v. 17; "ruler of fools" is not just a ruler surrounded by fools but a ruler who is himself foolish). His "shouting" stands for the violent use of authority. Wisdom thus provides better security to a community than military strength, the ultimate form of violent political power (v. 18a).

9:18b–10:1 Nevertheless, 9:18b–10:1 counters that a little folly ("sin") cancels out a great deal of wisdom just as a few dead flies make a fine ointment disgusting.[211] In this context the meaning is that a foolish counselor is a danger to the state.[212] Even so, the Teacher is not at this point complaining that the wise are simply ignored. He says that even when a great deal of wisdom is present, things somehow get fouled up by a little folly.

---

[210]Taking וּמִלַּט in an indicative sense rather than in a potential sense ("and he could have saved"), contrary to Crenshaw, *Ecclesiastes*, 166-67. See Gordis, *Koheleth*, 311-12, and Fox, *Qohelet*, 263.

[211]יַבְאִישׁ יַבִּיעַ, lit. "causes to stink, causes to ferment." Cf. BHS note. It is probably best to read גְּבִיעַ, "cup, bowl," for יַבִּיעַ and take יַבְאִישׁ metaphorically as "make [something] irksome/disgusting." Thus, "Dead flies make a bowl of perfumer's ointment disgusting."

[212]The verses in this context are not isolated gnomic sayings on life in general but specific warnings to those who must choose among competing advisors in the political world. Cf. Garrett, "Qoheleth," 173-77.

10:2-7 The folly of a fool is generally self-evident (vv. 2-3); nevertheless, kings often make the mistake of promoting such men to positions of power (vv. 5-7); note the change to personal reflection (third level discourse). Faced with the impulsive and often irrational behavior of rulers, the wise counselor must stand by his post even in the face of the king's wrath over some offense and in so doing turn aside the king's anger (v. 4; cf. 8:1,3).[213] He must patiently await the downfall of the fool and his own vindication. In v. 2 "right" and "left" refer to behavior that is, respectively, skillful or inept. In vv. 6-7 "fools/slaves" and "rich/princes" describe not actual social status (cf. 9:13-16) but moral character: the "fools" and "slaves" are those unworthy of advancement, and the "rich" and "princes" are people of noble character.[214]

From this point on, the rest of the book is traditional wisdom sayings (second level discourse) except for the historical note (first level discourse) of 12:8-10.

10:8-11 This text is made up of two pairs of aphorisms that are again applied to the world of the political counselors. The first pair (vv. 8-9) concern the dangers and instabilities of political life; the second pair (vv. 10-11) deal with the timely application of wisdom to specific problems. Also the four verses are arranged as a chiasmus: "snake" links v. 8 to v. 11 as "ax" and "splitting logs" link vv. 9-10.

Verse 8 draws on the familiar axiom that those who plot evil against others often have their plans backfire on them.[215] This gives some comfort to the just counselor who is competing for royal favor against a scheming climber. But v. 9 throws in a dash of hard realism: even those who are engaged in legitimate activity, such as quarrying or wood cutting, can be hurt in the process. The significance is that those who try to serve fairly and justly may see their efforts blow up in their faces.

These caveats notwithstanding, the wise counselor generally can avert the disasters of vv. 8-9 if he exercises preparation (v. 10)[216] and foresight (v. 11). By so doing, he avoids both wasted effort (v. 10) and personal danger (v. 11).

10:12-15 The most important thing a counselor has to offer his king is his words. The good counselor offers words that are "gracious" (i.e.,

---

[213] מַרְפֵּא is not merely *calmness* but the ability to soothe or calm—in this case, to calm the king's anger. Cf. Fox, *Qohelet*, 266-67.

[214] Whybray (*Ecclesiastes*, 152) compares the *Admonitions of Ipuwer* (ANET, 441-44) and notes that the exaltation of unworthy characters was taken as a sign that society was falling apart.

[215] See Ps 7:15; Prov 26:27.

[216] In 10:10b וְיִתְרוֹן הַכְשֵׁיר חָכְמָה should be treated as a broken construct chain and rendered "but the advantage of wisdom is success." See A. Frendo, "The 'Broken Construct Chain' in Qoh 10,10b," *Bib* 62 (1981): 544-55. Note, however, that construct chains are usually broken only by pronominal suffixes, locative ה, or the like.

both just and well spoken) whereas the evil counselor ruins himself as his advice moves from simple folly to sheer madness (vv. 12-13). The fool also spews out far too many words (v. 14a). This verbosity arises from too high a regard for his own opinions. The wise counselor, however, knows that he cannot predict the future (v. 14b,c) and thus tempers his remarks with restraint and humility.

Verse 15 should be translated, "The effort of fools wearies him who does not know the way to town."[217] In other words, the advice of foolish counselors is so bad that they cannot even give simple directions. Their long-winded explanations only wear out the confused traveler. How much worse to take their counsel in affairs of state.

10:16-17 These verses conclude the Teacher's political meditations. Once again "servant"[218] (v. 16) and "noble" (v. 17) refer to the moral character of the king more than to his genealogy (cf. 4:13). If the king and his administrators view their power as an opportunity for self-indulgence, the nation is lost. If, however, the king and his administration are just and devoted to their duty, the nation is safe.

32. Transition (10:18-20)

18If a man is lazy, the rafters sag;
if his hands are idle, the house leaks.

19A feast is made for laughter,
and wine makes life merry,
but money is the answer for everything.

20Do not revile the king even in your thoughts,
or curse the rich in your bedroom,
because a bird of the air may carry your words,
and a bird on the wing may report what you say.

10:18-20 These verses move us from the Teacher's final political comments to his final remarks on wealth (11:1-6). As such they relate to both discussions. The proverb of v. 18 can obviously apply equally well to the administration of the whole state and the private economy of one's household. Verse 19 should be rendered, "People prepare food for pleasure, and wine makes life joyful, but money pays for both."[219] The point

---

[217]אֲשֶׁר לֹא־יָדַע is a true relative clause, "who does not know." אֲשֶׁר should not be rendered "because" (or simply omitted, as in the NIV). The antecedent to אֲשֶׁר is the pronoun suffix on תְּיַגְּעֶנּוּ ("she wearies him"). The subject of תְּיַגְּעֶנּוּ is הַכְּסִילִים, here regarded as a feminine noun (cf. *BDB*, 765). The plural הַכְּסִילִים ("the fools") makes clear that the one who is "wearied" (singular pronoun suffix) is not הַכְּסִילִים but someone else (i.e., the one who needs directions).

[218]נַעַר ("boy") may refer to emotional immaturity.

[219]See Whybray, *Ecclesiastes*, 157; Gordis, *Koheleth*, 328; Whitley, *Koheleth*, 90; and Crenshaw, *Ecclesiastes*, 177.

is that at least some money is essential for enjoying life, and steps must therefore be taken to insure that the economy (be it national or personal) is sound.

In v. 20 it is possible that the phrase "in your thoughts" should be rendered "among your friends."[220] In either case it counsels the reader to give due deference to both kings (i.e., political power) and the wealthy (i.e., economic power). With this the transition is complete, and the Teacher moves into his concluding remarks on financial prudence.

33. On Wealth (11:1-6)

1Cast your bread upon the waters,
for after many days you will find it again.
2Give portions to seven, yes to eight,
for you do not know what disaster may come upon the land.

3If clouds are full of water,
they pour rain upon the earth.
Whether a tree falls to the south or to the north,
in the place where it falls, there will it lie.
4Whoever watches the wind will not plant;
whoever looks at the clouds will not reap.

5As you do not know the path of the wind,
or how the body is formed in a mother's womb,
so you cannot understand the work of God,
the Maker of all things.

6Sow your seed in the morning,
and at evening let not your hands be idle,
for you do not know which will succeed,
whether this or that,
or whether both will do equally well.

The Teacher concludes his admonitions on wealth with the advice that one should diversify investments. This may seem a prosaic closure to all his meditations over wealth, yet it is in character. The Teacher sees two great dangers connected to the making of money. The one is to become consumed with work and the quest for wealth, but the other is to fall into poverty (and the suffering it entails) through laziness or misfortune. He therefore counsels a safe and sane approach to financial security. It is not a program to get rich quick, but it will save one from many sleepless nights.

---

[220] See M. J. Dahood, "Canaanite Words in Qoheleth 10,20," *Bib* 46 (1965): 210-12. Dahood argues on the basis of Akkadian texts from Ras Shamra. His rendition makes better exegetical sense, but the evidence is not fully compelling.

11:1-2 This is not an exhortation to charity but advice on investments.[221] To cast bread upon the waters is to engage in commercial enterprises involving overseas trade (cf. 1 Kgs 9:26-28; 10:22). Eventually the investment will pay off. "Seven" and "eight" represent a wide diversity of investments. Such diversification is necessary because it affords protection against unforeseen calamity in one or two of the enterprises. An English equivalent is, "Don't put all your eggs in one basket."

11:3-4 These two verses form a chiasmus (vv. 3a,4b: clouds; vv. 3b,4a: falling tree/wind). Verse 3 speaks of a storm and means that it is inevitable that disasters sometimes will occur. "If clouds are full" means that when the time for such a calamity comes, it cannot be avoided. The proverb about trees falling simply means that whatever will happen (i.e., the inevitable) will happen.[222] Verse 4, on the other hand, says that one cannot use the possibility of misfortune as an excuse for inactivity. Someone who is forever afraid of storms will never get around to working his field. The Teacher in effect says, "Just face the fact that things may go wrong, but get out there and do your work anyway."

11:5-6 The Teacher uses the mystery of life to drive home the point that since people are ignorant of God's will and ways, they may as well leave all things in his hands. Verse 5 should be translated, "Just as you do not know how the breath of life enters the fetus in the womb of the pregnant woman, so you do not know the work of God, who does all."[223] In context this means that since you cannot know that all will go well, do not demand assurance of success before you begin any enterprise.[224] Just as in pregnancy a couple can only trust God that all will turn out well, even so in business enterprises one can only leave the outcome to God. Pregnancy is the supreme example of a human endeavor, the results of which are out of human control. Again, however, the lack of certainty in financial investments indicates the wisdom of diligence and diversification (v. 6).

34. On Death and Contentment (11:7–12:7)

7Light is sweet,
and it pleases the eyes to see the sun.

---

[221]While Ecclesiastes is concerned with oppression, it nowhere else takes up the issue of charitable giving. Also v. 6 confirms that this context concerns personal financial strategy. For a good discussion see Gordis, *Koheleth*, 329-30.

[222]A somewhat analogous English proverb is, "Whichever way the cookie crumbles."

[223]For כַּעֲצָמִים read בַּעֲצָמִים, "in the bones." See BHS note. "Bones," in context, is the fetus. מַה־דֶּרֶךְ, "what is the way of?" here means "how?" (analogous to English usage). The form יַעֲשֶׂה should not be translated "Maker" as though only creation were in view. God's continuing control of events in the world is meant.

[224]The Teacher's choice of the example of life in the womb as proof of the limits of human knowledge may arise from a wordplay on the two meanings of רוּחַ, "wind" and "breath of life."

8However many years a man may live,
let him enjoy them all.
But let him remember the days of darkness,
for they will be many.
Everything to come is meaningless.

9Be happy, young man, while you are young,
and let your heart give you joy in the days of your youth.
Follow the ways of your heart
and whatever your eyes see,
but know that for all these things
God will bring you to judgment.
10So then, banish anxiety from your heart
and cast off the troubles of your body,
for youth and vigor are meaningless.

1Remember your Creator
in the days of your youth,
before the days of trouble come
and the years approach when you will say,
"I find no pleasure in them"—
2before the sun and the light
and the moon and the stars grow dark,
and the clouds return after the rain;
3when the keepers of the house tremble,
and the strong men stoop,
when the grinders cease because they are few,
and those looking through the windows grow dim;
4when the doors to the street are closed
and the sound of grinding fades;
when men rise up at the sound of birds,
but all their songs grow faint;
5when men are afraid of heights
and of dangers in the streets;
when the almond tree blossoms
and the grasshopper drags himself along
and desire no longer is stirred.
Then man goes to his eternal home
and mourners go about the streets.

6Remember him—before the silver cord is severed,
or the golden bowl is broken;
before the pitcher is shattered at the spring,
or the wheel broken at the well,
7and the dust returns to the ground it came from,
and the spirit returns to God who gave it.

Appropriately, the last major discourse of Ecclesiastes concerns the grim reality of aging and death and the need to enjoy the life one has under the sun. Nevertheless, this is not a hedonist's creed, for the demand that all be done in the fear of God stands behind and above the whole.

11:7-8 "Light is sweet"[225] means that it is good to be alive. The "days of darkness" (v. 8) are death, not old age. There is no metaphysical speculation here, merely the assertion that the days of one's being dead will far outnumber the days of life under the sun. "Everything to come is *hebel*," similarly, makes no assertion about the nature of Sheol or the question of life after death. "Everything to come" is not the reality after death but the works and events of one's life under the sun (cf. 1:2-11). In other words, "All that you do and everything that happens to you in life will pass away."

11:9-10 The exhortation to follow one's inclinations (v. 9) does not endorse the reckless following of every impulse. Awareness of divine judgment turns the pursuit of joy away from crossing over into sins. The meaning is that one should not be weighed down by vexation over the human condition[226] to the degree that carefree happiness is impossible (v. 10). The days of youth and vigor[227] are few.

12:1-7 This final poem, a series of metaphors,[228] exhorts the reader to remember the Creator[229] before the days of age and death set in. Verse 1a is not a *ḥasid* gloss,[230] nor should "your Creator" be emended to "your wife"[231] or the like. Nor is the exhortation to remember the Creator a contradiction to the exhortations to rejoice. Instead we have a warning against mindless self-indulgence and profligacy during the days of one's vigor. To forget the Creator of youth is to invite bitter regrets and an

---

[225]A number of scholars compare Euripedes, *Iphigenia in Aulis* 1.1219: ἡδὺ γὰρ τὸ φῶς ("for the light is so sweet"). Gordis (*Koheleth*, 334) aptly comments: "There is no real likelihood of borrowing, merely a coincidence in the work of two great writers."

[226]וְהָסֵר כַּעַס מִלִּבֶּךָ וְהַעֲבֵר רָעָה מִבְּשָׂרֶךָ is in effect a hendiadys for, "Cast away grief from yourself [over the human condition]." רָעָה is not personal sin here but the trouble and evil that is part and parcel of human life. Even this command, of course, is not absolute: the point is that one should not allow consternation over human ills to consume one, not that one should be stupidly oblivious to human troubles.

[227]וְהַשַּׁחֲרוּת is literally "blackness" (i.e., of hair) as opposed to grey hair.

[228]The poem is not an allegory (cf. Whybray, *Ecclesiastes*, 165), and thus a single, unified picture should not be sought. Some interpreters, such as Fox (*Qohelet*, 305), can be needlessly concerned with petty details, e.g., that in 12:5a, "afraid of heights," the poem moves "from figurative to literal statement." But there is no reason why the poem should not do precisely that. Fox's objection is especially odd since he points out that a Sumerian poem on aging mixes literal and metaphorical statements (pp. 295-96).

[229]The plural form בּוֹרְאֶיךָ is often regarded as a plural of majesty or a result of morphological analogy of the third ה verb. But note also the plural עָשׂוּהוּ in 2:12 (see commentary above).

[230]Barton, *Ecclesiastes*, 185.

[231]Thus Crenshaw, *Ecclesiastes*, 184-85. Crenshaw accepts the emendation of בּוֹרְאֶיךָ to בְּאֵרְךָ, "your well," and on the basis of Prov 5:15 understands this as a metaphor for the wife. Not only is this emendation without any textual or versional support, but it is highly doubtful that the reader could be expected to make the connection to Prov 5:15 Crenshaw proposes. See also the remarks in Eaton, *Ecclesiastes*, 148; Gordis, *Koheleth*, 340; and Whybray, *Ecclesiastes*, 163.

empty existence in old age. To remember the Creator[232] is to follow the path of wisdom and extend the joy of life.

The following metaphors all describe the deterioration of the body as old age comes on. To take these verses as literal references to the decline of one's household and estate is perverse. At the same time, the richness of the language has not been exhausted at the moment one recognizes a particular metaphor's referent. The darkening of the sky and the silence on the street give to the text an atmosphere that is surreal and even apocalyptic.[233]

12:2 The eyes begin to fail. The cloudiness of vision sounds like glaucoma.[234] The picture of clouds "returning after rain" appears to say that the vision does not clear up, in contrast to weather in which, after a downpour, the clouds dissipate and the day is sunny again. Alternative interpretations are that clouds represent troubles that are minor setbacks in youth but major disasters in old age[235] or that the sad, darkened countenance of an old man is in view.[236] These interpretations are imaginative but not compelling. It seems best to take the verse simply to mean that one no longer sees well.

12:3 One cannot take this verse to refer to literal decline of one's household. Aside from the fact that it does not fit well with v. 2 (How would the decline of one's estate darken the sun, moon, and stars?), this interpretation fails even within this single verse. If the "grinders" were literal people (women who grind flour), they would not "cease" but would have to work all the more diligently if they were "few." It hardly makes sense to think of people who look out windows "growing dim."[237] While there may be a metaphor here of a declining estate, it is clearly a metaphor and cannot be read literally.

The "keepers of the house" are the hands, which tremble in old age; and the "strong men" are the major muscle groups of the legs and back. Beyond that, it is impossible to be specific in anatomical details.[238] The "grinders" are teeth, which have ceased to chew food because they are few. Those who look out of windows are again the eyes, although growing

---

[232]The choice of the term "Creator" is not by accident. It both looks back to the creation narrative, which plays so prominent a role in Ecclesiastes, and maintains the perspective of wisdom that a joyful life is found through adherence to the principles built into the creation. context, however, it is best to take "daughters of song" as a reference to the sounds they make and not to the people themselves and being "low" as meaning that they are inaudible (cf. 2 Sam 19:35).

[233]Cf. Fox, *Qohelet*, 281-98.

[234]Thus Crenshaw, *Ecclesiastes*, 185.

[235]Thus D. Kidner, *A Time to Mourn and a Time to Dance: Ecclesiastes and the Way of the World* (Downers Grove: Intervarsity, 1976), 101-2.

[236]The Targums; cf. Gordis, *Koheleth*, 341.

[237]Crenshaw, *Ecclesiastes*, 186; Whybray, *Ecclesiastes*, 164.

[238]See Barton, *Ecclesiastes*, 188, for examples of specific body parts (arms, legs, knees, etc.) interpreters have seen in these details.

"dim" may refer to a lack of sparkle in the eye rather than inability to see well.

12:4 The shutting of doors refers to the ears,[239] as people shut doors when they want to exclude outside noise. Deafness is meant, as indicated by the sounds of grinding and singing fading out.[240] But rising up at the sound of birds alludes to a cruel paradox of old age: one cannot hear well, but one sleeps so lightly that the slightest disturbance is sufficient to take away sleep.[241]

12:5 Fear of heights and danger in the street means that the feebleness of the body takes away accustomed manliness. The metaphor of a declining household is abandoned here. The blossoming of the almond tree is the turning of the hair to white.

The reference to the grasshopper is obscure, but probably it should be rendered, "And the grasshopper becomes heavy,"[242] a hyperbole meaning that even something as light as a grasshopper seems too heavy to lift. Alternatively, it has been taken to refer to either bad joints, swollen ankles, a halting walk, or impotence.[243] The last interpretation is possible in light of the following line.

"And desire no longer is stirred" paraphrases the Hebrew.[244] Apparently loss of sexual desire is meant. The Targum paraphrases this more directly as, "You will cease from sexual intercourse."[245] An alternative interpretation is that the line should be rendered, "The caperberry bears fruit."[246] This would imply that the blossoming of the almond and fruit-bearing of the caperberry are to be taken literally with the meaning that while nature is renewed every year, the human body simply grows older

[239]As indicated by the dual form דְּלָתַיִם.

[240]וְיִשַּׁחוּ כָּל־בְּנוֹת הַשִּׁיר, "and all the daughters of song are made low," is subject to various interpretations. Some take it to mean that the old man no longer sings well. Fox (*Qohelet*, 304-5) sees here a reference to professional mourners who bow low as they lament. In

[241]Other interpretations fail to satisfy. For example, Kidner (*A Time to Mourn*, 103) takes it to mean that one no longer partakes of the cheerfulness of life, but that can hardly be the meaning of one rising at the sound of a bird.

[242]The Vg reads *inpinguabitur lucusta* ("and the grasshopper shall be fattened"), probably following the LXX καὶ παχυνθῇ ἡ ἀκρίς. Thus some ancient interpreters have taken it to refer to some body part growing fat (thighs or ankles), but a grasshopper may be a hyperbolic assertion that even the lightest things are hard to stoop and pick up.

[243]See Barton, *Ecclesiastes*, 190, and Gordis, *Koheleth*, 345, for examples from the history of exegesis here.

[244]וְתָפֵר הָאֲבִיּוֹנָה means "and the caperberry bursts forth/destroys/fails." Probably the verb should be taken as the hiphil of פרר, here used intransitively to mean "fail." Caperberry was apparently an aphrodisiac, and its failure meant the loss of sexual desire or ability. No evidence for the aphrodisiac qualities of the caper appears prior to the medieval Jewish commentaries, however; and this interpretation is not certain.

[245]Gordis, *Koheleth*, 346.

[246]Taking the verb to be an unusual form of פרה, "to bear fruit."

and weaker. This interpretation requires an anomalous translation of the Hebrew, however, and is not to be followed.[247]

After all this, the body having failed, *ʾādām* goes to his eternal home (the grave), and mourners go about in the street.[248]

12:6 The picture is of a spring or cistern from which one draws the water of life.[249] The obvious meaning is that death has come.

12:7 "Dust" alludes to Gen 2:7 and 3:19. This is the Teacher's final meditation on the fall. The return of the spirit to God refers to death. All life comes from God.

35. Conclusion (12:8-14)

8"Meaningless! Meaningless!" says the Teacher.
"Everything is meaningless!"

9Not only was the Teacher wise, but also he imparted knowledge to the people. He pondered and searched out and set in order many proverbs. 10The Teacher searched to find just the right words, and what he wrote was upright and true.

11The words of the wise are like goads, their collected sayings like firmly embedded nails—given by one Shepherd. 12Be warned, my son, of anything in addition to them. Of making many books there is no end, and much study wearies the body.

13Now all has been heard;
here is the conclusion of the matter:
Fear God and keep his commandments,
for this is the whole [duty] of man.
14For God will bring every deed into judgment,
including every hidden thing,
whether it is good or evil.

12:8 The theme of the book (1:2) is reaffirmed. Everything done under the sun is fleeting and therefore, in the last analysis, meaningless.

247Whybray (*Ecclesiastes*, 167) mentions but does not advocate this interpretation. Loader (*Ecclesiastes*, 131) prefers this interpretation, however, and takes "the grasshopper grows fat" (LXX) to mean that insects, in contrast to old people, have abundant food and are revitalized. Fox (*Qohelet*, 305-6) interprets the verse similarly but emends חָגָב ("locust") to חָצָב ("sea onion" [Mishnaic Hebrew]) and takes it as another example of the renewal of nature.

248Notwithstanding Fox's determined efforts to find references to a funeral in this passage (*Qohelet*, 280-310), this is the only explicit reference to such in the entire text, and it should not be regarded as determinative for the interpretation of the whole. To the contrary, vv. 1-5a,b describe the old age of a man, and vv. 5c-7 describe his death. Verse 5c only gives a passing reference to a funeral.

249For an alternative interpretation, see J. E. Burns ("The Imagery of Eccles 12 6a," *JBL* 84 [1965]: 428-30), who sees here a "silver fillet" and a "golden mixing bowl," both indicative of "feasting and conviviality" that end at death. His argument is not compelling.

12:9-10 The role of Solomon as teacher is reaffirmed. Following his example, teachers must go ahead of pupils to seek out the truth and so convey it to their pupils. In addition, a teacher seeks to make his or her words as palatable as possible and teaches in a way that communicates well.

12:11 The value of wisdom is set over against the tendency to excessive study on the part of the wise. A pastoral metaphor governs v. 11. "Goads" refer to the pointed sticks used to keep cattle moving in the right direction and so serve to represent moral guidance and stimulus in human affairs. All true wisdom comes from the "one Shepherd" (God);[250] again the choice of metaphor is deliberately pastoral. The comparison of "collected sayings"[251] to "embedded nails" would seem to mix the metaphor and introduce a picture of that which makes something fixed and immovable, a symbol of the stabilizing and sure character of wise teachings. Alternatively, the nail might be embedded in the goad and thus continue the pastoral image.[252]

12:12 This verse in the NIV appears to warn the reader against the study of any teachings beyond the true (canonical?) wisdom, but this would be reading too much into the Hebrew text. A more probable translation is: "Beyond all this,[253] my son, be advised: Of making many books there is no end." The contrast is not between the study of canonical versus noncanonical wisdom but between failure to appreciate wisdom on the one hand and excessive zeal for study on the other.

12:13-14 The summary and conclusion of the whole work is now offered: "Fear God and keep his commandments, for this is the whole of humanity." To obey God is to be truly human.[254] Throughout his book the Teacher has investigated the situation of *ʾādām*. Now, surprisingly, he affirms that the whole of humanity consists not in its mortality or ignorance but in its dependence on God. And yet the conclusion is not surprising. It not only flows naturally from all that has gone before but is the book's final look at Gen 2–3. Humanity sought to become like God in disobeying him, but instead they lost the one thing that made them truly human.

---

[250]It is doubtful that Solomon is meant here.

[251]The phrase בַּעֲלֵי אֲסֻפּוֹת is obscure and has given rise to much speculation, but the chiastic structure implies that its meaning is similar to דִּבְרֵי חֲכָמִים. See especially Delitzsch, *Ecclesiastes*, 433-34.

[252]Thus Fox, *Qohelet*, 324-25.

[253]See Gordis, *Koheleth*, 354, and Whybray, *Ecclesiastes*, 173.

[254]כִּי־זֶה כָּל־הָאָדָם is not "this is the whole [duty] of man," or "for this every man should do" (C. Ginsburg, *Coheleth*, 477-78), or "for this [concerns] every man" (Fox, *Qohelet*, 310, 329). It means "this is the whole of man." הָאָדָם, like the traditional use of the English "man," refers to all of humanity corporately and to the characteristics of humanity as they exist in individual women and men. כֹּל followed by a definite, singular noun means "the whole of X," as in Gen 2:2,13; Exod 14:20; Deut 4:29; and esp. Num 12:3; 16:29; and Judg 16:17.

Some have considered these verses the work of a pious epilogist, but this conclusion is not warranted. The use of first level (vv. 9-10) and second level (vv. 11-14) discourse has many parallels throughout the book; and the language, style, and sentiments are not unlike those found earlier in the book. More than that, treating the conclusion as a secondary epilogue, either as a pious gloss or as part of an emerging canon consciousness,[255] decapitates the entire work. Everything Ecclesiastes has affirmed up to this point—the sovereign freedom of God, the limits of human wisdom, thoughts on the use and abuse of wealth and power, and the brevity and absolute contingency of human life—all lead to the command to fear God. To excise the conclusion is to throw away that which binds together all the separate strands of the Teacher's thought. It arises from a failure to think like the Teacher, so to speak.

For us the "meaninglessness" of life which the Teacher so ruthlessly exposes would seem to lead to despair or nihilism; for him it is an incitement to true piety. The insignificance of all that is done under the sun leaves him awestruck and silent before God. His inability to control or predict the future provokes him to dependence on God. The futility of attempting to secure his future through wisdom or acts of religion (e.g., making vows) leads him not to impiety but to an understanding of the true nature of obedient trust.

Seen in this light, to "keep his commandments" is not to behave with the self-satisfied arrogance of religious presumption, nor is it a nod to piety from an otherwise impious book. Rather, it is the deepest expression of humble acceptance of what it means to be a human before God. Solomon as the Teacher, in his address to his aristocratic colleagues, has anticipated perhaps the deepest mystery of the gospel: The just shall live by faith (Hab 2:4; Rom 1:16-17; Gal 3:11; Heb 10:38).

[255]See G. T. Sheppard, "The Epilogue to Qoheleth as Theological Commentary," *CBQ* 39 (1977): 182-89. Cf. Fox, *Qohelet*, 320-21.

Song of Songs

INTRODUCTION OUTLINE

1. Name
2. Date and Authorship
3. Interpretation
    (1) The Allegorical Interpretation
    (2) The Dramatic Interpretation
        The Two-Character Drama
        The Three-Character Drama
    (3) The Historical Interpretation
    (4) The Cultic Interpretation
    (5) The Funerary Interpretation
    (6) The Wedding Interpretation
    (7) The Love Song Interpretation
4. Genre
5. Canonicity
6. Literary Method
    (1) Literary Forms in Ancient Love Poetry
        The Admiration Song
        The Song of Yearning
        The Arrival Song
        The Invitation
        The Prayer for Success in Love
    (2) The Motifs of Song of Songs
        Lovesickness
        The Door
        The Gazelle or Stag
        The Kiss
        The Breasts
        The Authority Figure
        The Garden or Vineyard
        The Theft or Entrapment of the Heart
        Horses and Chariots
        Limbs Described as Precious Metals
        Song of Songs and Other ANE Parallels

7. Unity and Structure of the Song
8. Theology of Song of Songs
9. Summary

INTRODUCTION

1. Name

Among English readers, this book is known by three names: The Song of Solomon, The Song of Songs, and Canticles (the latter is derived from the Vg). The Hebrew title, given in 1:1, is "The Song of Songs [i.e., *the finest of songs*] which is Solomon's." In the Hebrew canon it is among the five *Megilloth*, the books read by the Jews at various holidays. These include Ruth (Pentecost), Song of Songs (Passover), Ecclesiastes (Tabernacles), Lamentations (anniversary of the fall of Jerusalem or occasions of mourning), and Esther (Purim). Evidence for use of Song of Songs as a Passover scroll only dates from the eighth century A.D.;[1] however, that certainly was not its original purpose.

2. Date and Authorship

The title seems to indicate Solomonic authorship, but alternative interpretations of the phrase "of Solomon"[2] have been proposed. It could indicate authorship ("by Solomon") or be a dedication "to Solomon." Some say it may mean "in the style of Solomon."[3] But no clear analogy for interpreting the Hebrew *lamed* as "in the style of" exists.[4] The use of the possessive *lamed* as a term for authorship (*lamed auctoris*) is common and most probably correct,[5] but if "for Solomon" is the adopted translation, it could imply that it was composed by a court musician.

Some have dated the book very late on the basis of Persian and Greek loan words, Aramaic influence, and certain Hebrew forms alleged to be late. An example is the word for "palanquin" (3:9), said to be based on a Greek original. The word may in fact not be Greek but a derivative from ancient Sanskrit.[6] The Hebrew word for "orchard" (4:13) is said to be

---

[1]G. Fohrer, *Introduction to the Old Testament*, trans. D. Green (Nashville: Abingdon, 1968), 300.

[2]לִשְׁלֹמֹה.

[3]Thus R. K. Harrison, *Old Testament Introduction* (Grand Rapids: Eerdmans, 1969), 1049; and W. S. LaSor, D. A. Hubbard, and F. W. Bush, *Old Testament Survey* (Grand Rapids: Eerdmans, 1982), 601.

[4]One would rather expect some use of the preposition כְּ to express this meaning on the analogy of its use in certain psalm superscripts. Cf. Pss 8:1; 9:1; 22:1.

[5]See R. E. Murphy, *The Song of Songs* (Minneapolis: Fortress, 1990), 119.

[6]The Hebrew word is אַפִּרְיוֹן, and the alleged Greek original is φορεῖον. The Sanskrit word that may be behind both words is *paryanka*. This suggestion appears in R. Gordis, *The*

based on a Persian if not a Greek original.[7] Again, however, this approach is misleading since Sanskrit and Assyrian analogies have been found.[8]

Alternative interpretations of alleged Grecisms are also possible. The vocabulary of frequently sung folk music often changes in the course of time, and the Song of Songs may also have experienced such revision.[9] If so, its present vocabulary would provide no reliable information regarding the original date of composition. In addition, some words once thought to have been borrowed *from* Greek now appear to have been borrowed *by* the Greeks.[10]

The "Aramaisms" of Song of Songs include the Hebrew terms for "to guard" (1:6) and "winter" (2:11). This vocabulary may in fact be an indication of northern provenance.[11] At any rate, as Pope notes, "Aramaic is as old as Hebrew and the dialectology of Northwest Semitic gets more complicated as our data increase."[12] In addition, as Walker has pointed out, further research has often shown "Aramaisms" to be words of archaic Canaanite (Ugaritic) origin.[13]

The most frequently cited example of "late" Hebrew in Song of Songs is its common use of an allegedly later form of the relative pronoun.[14] In fact, however, the use of one relative pronoun over another provides no reliable gauge at all for when the Song was written.[15]

Linguistic evidence is not conclusive. Attempts to date the book from vocabulary and grammar are inherently weak because of our limited knowledge of the history of the Hebrew language.[16] When compared to

---

Song of Songs and Lamentations (New York: KTAV, 1954), 20-21. It is supported by Harrison, *Old Testament*, 1050, and G. Archer, *A Survey of Old Testament Introduction* (Chicago: Moody, 1974), 490.

[7]The Hebrew is פַּרְדֵּס, the Persian is *pairi-daēza*, and the Greek is παραδείσος.

[8]Archer, *Survey*, 490.

[9]Cf. M. H. Pope, *Song of Songs*, AB (New York: Doubleday, 1977), 26.

[10]Pope, *Song*, 34. An example is כֹּפֶר, "henna" (Song 1:14; 4:13; 7:12).

[11]The term for "to guard" is נָטַר, and the term for "winter" is סְתָו. See Archer, *Survey*, 490.

[12]Pope, *Song*, 33-34.

[13]L. L. Walker, "Notes on Higher Criticism and the Dating of Biblical Hebrew," in *A Tribute to Gleason Archer* (Chicago: Moody, 1986), 41. Cf. Pope, *Song*, 33-34.

[14]The Song tends to use שֶׁ rather than אֲשֶׁר. See, for example, the use of this argument in F. Landy, *Paradoxes of Paradise: Identity and Difference in the Song of Songs* (Sheffield: Almond, 1983), 18.

[15]אֲשֶׁר is the standard relative pronoun in biblical Hebrew, but שֶׁ became more common in postbiblical Hebrew. שֶׁ is cognate to the Akkadian *sha* (third millennium), to the Ugaritic *d* and *ḏ*, Canaanite *z*, Aramaic *d*, and Arabic *ḏu*. It also appears in some old Hebrew texts (e.g., Judg 5). Cf. Pope, *Song* 33-34, and Archer, *Survey*, 490. שֶׁ is in no sense a distinctively late term. More than that, it is remarkable that the two works that most frequently use שֶׁ are Song of Songs and Ecclesiastes, which suggests a common origin (as the Bible explicitly asserts).

[16]For a survey of the history of Hebrew, see E. Y. Kutscher, *A History of the Hebrew Language*, ed. R. Kutscher (Leiden: Brill, 1982).

vast quantities of Greek documents that have survived from all the dialects and periods of antiquity, extant Hebrew literature is meager indeed. Assertions about the history and dialects of Hebrew are tentative, to say the least. In addition, the possibility that the present text of Song of Songs has been revised complicates further the possibility of dating the text on linguistic grounds.[17]

One rarely explored issue in discussions of the date of Song of Songs is the similarity between the biblical book and Egyptian love poetry of ca. 1300–1100 B.C.[18] A number of these poems have been recovered; the best example is the love song in seven stanzas found in Papyrus Chester Beatty I. These poems are remarkably like Song of Songs. Common formal elements and common literary motifs (see discussion below) strongly indicate that the biblical work was written by someone who was familiar with Egyptian poetry and who lived when the motifs common to both collections were current and appreciated. Indeed, the Song of Songs is most reasonably interpreted as being in the same genre as the Egyptian poetry.

This again agrees with the supposition of Solomonic authorship since he would have had sufficient knowledge of Egyptian literature to compose a love song in this style. Members of his court, however, may also have possessed such knowledge. On the other hand, it is difficult to see how an obscure Jewish songwriter in the Levant, working almost a millennium after this kind of love poetry was produced in Egypt, could have written a work of this type.[19] Curiously, however, some scholars are willing to sac-

[17]Cf. G. Carr, *The Song of Solomon*, TOTC (Downers Grove: InterVarsity, 1984), 18.

[18]Scholars are of course well aware of the parallels. See J. B. White, *A Study of the Language of Love in the Song of Songs and Ancient Egyptian Love Poetry* (Missoula, Mont.: Scholar's Press, 1978).

[19]M. V. Fox's *The Song of Songs and the Ancient Egyptian Love Songs* (Madison: University of Wisconsin Press, 1985) is the most thorough study to date that compares Song of Songs to Egyptian love poetry. Curiously, however, Fox dates Song of Songs to the postexilic period strictly on the basis of lexical data. He then argues that the Egyptian love poetry found its way into Palestine during the Ramesside Empire and that Song of Songs, written roughly in the same genre, was produced a thousand years later. He claims that the persistence of the sonnet form in Western poetry is an analogy that helps explain how the love poetry genre could have survived so long in the Levant (pp. 186-93). There are several flaws in this reasoning. First, it is peculiar to hypothesize with no concrete evidence the Ramesside period as a time of lasting literary influence when the Bible already asserts that the Solomonic period was the time of such influence. Second, it is hard to see how this genre could have persisted for a thousand years in the Levant with hardly a literary trace of having been there and then suddenly burst forth in full flower in the Song. Third, the analogy to the sonnet form is artificial since the sonnet clearly persisted as an art form through the centuries of its use (although current attempts to write sonnets would be rightly termed "archaizing," and there is no reason to suppose that the Song is a deliberately archaized work). Again there is no evidence that the Egyptian love poetry genre was maintained as an art form; to the contrary, we are left with a thousand-year hiatus. This cannot be regarded a reasonable hypothesis. Landy (*Paradoxes*, 18-33) also holds

rifice the obvious implication of Egyptian influence on the Song rather than concede its logical implication, that the Song was written in the united monarchy period.[20]

Because of the many references to places in the north, some scholars have argued that the book originated in the northern monarchy. These place names include Sharon, Lebanon, Hermon, Damascus, and Carmel. On the other hand, the book does not manifest a provincially northern outlook.[21] In addition, the book also mentions southern locales (Jerusalem, Engedi), as well as places in the Transjordan (Heshbon, Gilead). If anything, Song of Songs can be said to have a "pan-Israelite" outlook that includes all the major regions of the nation at its greatest extent.[22] As Segal observes, "Such an extended horizon for a Jerusalem poet suits best the age of Solomon whose rule extended far beyond the confines of the land of Israel."[23]

A particularly significant occurrence of a place name is that of Tirzah in 6:4, where it is set in parallel to Jerusalem. Tirzah was a leading city of the northern part of the nation and capital of the Northern Kingdom until Omri (reigned ca. 885–874 B.C.) built Samaria. The parallelism in 6:4 implies that Tirzah, at the time of composition, was still the chief city of the north.[24] Unless one is willing to beg the question by asserting that the reference is deliberate archaizing, the implication is that Song of Songs antedates Omri.

Other internal evidence also lends support to Solomonic authorship for the book. Carr notes that "single word parallelism" (2:15; 6:8), a feature of late second millennium poetry, is evidence of an early date for the book.[25] Solomon's reputation as both poet and naturalist (1 Kgs 4:32-33) agrees well with both the literary quality of the Song and the obvious familiarity of its author with the flora and fauna of Israel. C. Rabin argues

---

to a "very late date" (p. 18) for the Song, although he relies heavily upon the Egyptian material as a model for the interpretation of the Song (pp. 21-4) and concedes that parallels to Hellenistic poetry are superficial and few in number (p. 26).

[20]Cf. White, *Study*, 153: "It would be unwarranted *due to problems of chronology and cultural interchange* [emphasis added] to propose that the Song of Songs is *literally dependent* [emphasis original] on the ancient Egyptian love lyrics." It would appear that the presupposition of a late date overrules evidence for literary dependence, even though White spends the better part of a dissertation demonstrating parallels between the two.

[21]LaSor et al., *Old Testament*, 602-3.

[22]R. H. Pfeiffer contends that the geographic diversity of the book is due simply to the poet's imagination (*Introduction to the Old Testament* [New York: Harper and Row, 1941], 713). On the contrary, it appears that these places were familiar and accessible to the poet.

[23]M. H. Segal, "The Song of Songs," *VT* 12 (1962): 483.

[24]It is probable that Tirzah became the capital after the split because it was already the chief city in the north. Thus Fox's argument that this could not have been written during the united monarchy is invalid (*Song*, 187).

[25]Carr, *Song*, 18.

that the references to exotic spices and imports indicate commercial relations with India, which implies a Solomonic date.[26]

In addition, Segal points out that the atmosphere of luxury and wealth in the song agrees better with the Solomonic period than with any other. Only then did Jerusalem possess an abundance of spices, perfumes, and luxuries, as well as "rods of gold set with chrysolite," "polished ivory decorated with sapphires," and "pillars of marble set on bases of pure gold" (Song 5:14-15). He also argues that the thousand shields in David's tower (Song 4:4) may be the gold shields looted by Shishak (1 Kgs 10:16-17; 14:26).[27]

Of course, one can argue that these are only similes and that they do not prove that the writer actually lived in an age when such things were common.[28] It is doubtful, however, that a poet would use imagery, described in such vivid detail, that was outside his own frame of reference. When a poet does venture to use a metaphor that is beyond his personal experience, that metaphor is apt to be of a general nature and ridden with cliché (e.g., "as white as snow" or "as brave as a lion"). Certainly this is not the case in Song of Songs.

In summary, nothing in the book demands a late date. The book presents itself as of the Solomonic period, and this is in accord with both its diversity of geographic references and the possible influence of northern dialect in its "Aramaisms." After Solomon and the division of the kingdom, such a pan-Israelite perspective would not be likely. The atmosphere of luxury and wealth also supports Solomonic dating.

3. Interpretation

No other book of the Bible (except perhaps Revelation) suffers under so many radically different interpretations as the Song of Songs. Indeed, Fohrer has correctly commented that the "history of interpretation of the Song of Solomon is no feather in the cap of biblical exegesis."[29] The major approaches are as follows.[30]

---

[26]C. Rabin, "The Song of Songs and Tamil Poetry," *SR* 3 (1973): 205-19. One need not support all of Rabin's theory, especially the idea that the Song is influenced by Tamil poetry, to accept the plausibility of this point.

[27]Segal, "The Song of Songs," 481-83.

[28]As does Fox, *Song*, 187.

[29]Fohrer, *Introduction*, 300.

[30]For a good survey of major trends in the history of the interpretation of the Song, see M. H. Pope, "Metastases in Canonical Shapes of the Super Song," ed. G. M. Tucker, D. L. Petersen, and R. R. Wilson, *Canon, Theology, and Old Testament Interpretation* (Philadelphia: Fortress, 1988), 312-28.

(1) The Allegorical Interpretation

From early times both Christians and Jews have proposed allegorical interpretations of the Song of Songs. Jews have taken it to be an allegory of the love between Yahweh and Israel, and Christians have regarded it as a song of the love between Christ and the church. Many variations of allegorization exist among both groups.

Examples of allegorizing interpretations among the Jews are found in the Mishna, the Talmud, and the Targum on the book.[31] The Targum, for example, interprets the book in five movements as an allegory of Israelite history. These are (1 [1:2–3:6]) the exodus, Sinai, and conquest; (2 [3:7–5:1]) the Solomonic temple; (3 [5:2–6:1]) Israel's sin and exile; (4 [6:2–7:11]) the return and rebuilding of the temple; and (5 [7:12–8:14]) the dispersion in the Roman Empire and expectation of the Messiah. The Targum reached its present form in the seventh or eighth century and is to some degree a polemic meant to counter Christian exegesis.[32] One (among many) alternative Jewish allegorizations of the song was that of D. I. Abravanel (sixteenth century), who regarded it as Solomon's song of his love for wisdom. Thus only the bride was allegorized.[33] Ibn Ezra interpreted 7:2 in a somewhat analogous fashion: "Your navel" was taken as a reference to the Great Sanhedrin, "blended wine" was the law, and "Your waist is a mound of wheat" was taken to allude to the Little Sanhedrin.[34]

For Christians allegorization may seem to gain support from the New Testament metaphor of the church as the bride of Christ (Eph 5:22-33; Rev 18:23-24), although in fact the New Testament never interprets the Song of Songs in this way. The first manifestation of the Christian allegorizing tradition is in the commentary by Hippolytus of Rome (d. 235), now only partially extant.[35] Jerome, Augustine, and above all Origen stand in the tradition of interpreting Song of Songs allegorically. Subsequent luminaries in this tradition include Gregory the Great and the Venerable Bede. Typical allegorizations are that the kisses (1:2) are the word of God, the dark skin of the girl (1:5) is sin, her breasts (7:7) are the church's nurturing doctrine, her two lips (4:11) are law and gospel, and the "army with banners" (6:4) is the church as the enemy of Satan. But countless variations can be found.

---

[31]Harrison, *Old Testament Introduction*, 1052.

[32]This interpretation of the Targum is based on R. Loewe, "Apologetic Motifs in the Targum on the Song of Songs," in A. Altmann, ed., *Biblical Motifs: Origins and Transformations* (Brandeis University, 1966), 159-96.

[33]Pope, *Song*, 110.

[34]Cited in H. H. Rowley, "Interpretation of the Song of Songs," in *The Servant of the Lord and Other Essays* (London: Lutterworth, 1952), 193.

[35]Cf. the discussion in Murphy, *Song*, 14-15.

Martin Luther was unwilling to follow the extravagant allegorism of the medieval church and rightly noted that "it takes no effort to invent [allegories]."[36] He therefore interpreted the Song of Songs more moderately as a Solomonic song of praise for Israel's deliverance. Nevertheless, many of his notes to the Song follow traditional allegorical interpretations.[37]

Calvin also abandoned his normal grammatical-historical mode of interpretation in the face of the Song of Songs.[38] In this he was followed by the Puritans.[39] J. Cotton produced a major allegorizing commentary from the Puritan tradition.[40]

Some commentaries, somewhat like the Targum, see the Song of Songs as an allegorical history of redemption. T. Brightman divided the song into two parts: 1:1–4:6, the true church from David to the death of Christ, and 4:7–8:14, from A.D. 34 to the second advent. Johannes Cocceius saw it as a history of the church that particularly emphasized the Protestant Reformation.[41]

Traditional Roman Catholic commentaries have often attempted to interpret the lady of the Song as the Virgin Mary and so turn the work into a text of Mary veneration.[42] In one interpretation, for example, Song 6:4 presents Mary as beautiful in her holiness, like Jerusalem in that peace between God and man came through her, and awesome in that she was surrounded by a troop of angels.[43] Recent Roman Catholic interpreters, however, have turned away from this mode of allegorization.[44] A recent sustained effort in behalf of an allegorical interpretation is that of A. Robert.[45]

---

[36]*Luther's Works* (St. Louis: Concordia, 1972), 15:200.

[37]E.g., "kisses of his mouth" (1:2) = the word of God, "dark skin" (1:5) = the sinfulness of the church, "winter is past" (2:11) = heresies, etc. See *Luther's Works*, 15:196-264.

[38]Calvin contributed no exposition of Song of Songs, and references to it in the *Institutes* are few. But he allegorized 5:3 as repentance in *Institutes* III. 16.4: "'I have washed my feet,' says the believing soul according to Solomon, 'how shall I defile them anew?'" (trans. F. L. Battles, *Institutes*, LCC [Philadelphia: Westminster, 1960], 20:802).

[39]J. Flavel (1628–1691), for example, opens his meditation on Song 8:6 with the words, "This book is a sacred allegory," and he attributes our failure to understand it to lack of familiarity with its "figures of speech" and deficiency of spiritual insight (*The Works of John Flavel* [1820; reprint, Edinburgh: The Banner of Truth Trust, 1982], 6:450).

[40]J. Cotton, *A Brief Exposition with Practical Observations upon the Whole Book of Canticles* (1655; reprint, New York: Arno Books, 1972).

[41]Pope, *Song*, 128-29, and Rowley, "Song," 200.

[42]This approach was developed by Rupert of Deutz; see Murphy, *Song*, 24-25.

[43]The interpretation is found in R. F. Littledale, *A Commentary on the Song of Song. From Ancient and Medieval Sources* (1869), cited in Pope, *Song*, 563. See also Rowley, "Song" 195-96. P. Patterson (*Song of Solomon* [Chicago: Moody, 1986], 19) refers to such interpretations as "farfetched."

[44]Cf. Pope, *Song*, 188-92.

[45]A. Robert, R. Tournay, and A. Feuillet, *Le Cantique des Cantiques: traduction et commentaire*, Ebib (1963). Many examples of Robert's interpretation can be found in the citations in Pope, *Song*.

A curiosity is that the Song of Songs became a favorite book of the most militant ascetics, such as Origen and Bernard of Clairvaux. Origen's commentary on the Song covered a full ten volumes (now only partially extant),[46] and Bernard preached eighty-six sermons (around 170,000 Latin words!) on the first two chapters of the Song.[47] The picture of monks and ascetics pouring over a book of love poetry and claiming to find in it the most sublime philosophy is intriguing of itself.[48]

The book in no way implies that it is describing the covenantal love between God and his people. Elsewhere in the Bible, as well as in other literature, an allegorical intent is signaled by the use of fantastic imagery or obvious allusions. The allegory of Jotham contains talking trees (Judg 9:7-15). Christian allegory includes such items as the "Slough of Despond" and "Mr. Worldly Wiseman."[49] In the Song of Songs, however, fantasy of this kind as well as references to major elements in the covenant history of Israel (e.g., the exodus) are entirely absent; they can only be manufactured through extravagant allegorizing *on the part of the interpreter.* Clear allusions to Christ are similarly missing without resort to reading those ideas into the text, and none of the New Testament writers suggest a connection.

Allegorization is in its origin and philosophical basis neither a Jewish nor a Christian phenomenon. It began among pagan teachers who were embarrassed at the immoral behavior of the gods and heroes of classical mythology as they appear in Homer and other accounts. Through allegory they were able to utilize the myths in education and portray the apparently crude stories as veiled discussions of philosophic truth. Among the

---

[46]Available in English in Origen, *The Song of Songs Commentary and Homilies*, trans. R. P. Lawson (London: Longmans, Green, and Co., 1957). For Origen the Song primarily concerns the relationship between God and the human soul. To cite one example from Origen, his commentary on Song 1:6 (Book 2.3) interprets the implied mother of the girl as the Heavenly Jerusalem and her brothers as the apostles, who struggled to win the Gentiles (symbolized by the girl) away from paganism. For a sympathetic treatment of Origen's method, see Murphy, *Song*, 16-21. Even Murphy notes, however, that Origen is "conspicuously indebted to Platonic thought" (p. 20).

[47]For a digest of Bernard's sermons, see *Saint Bernard on the Song of Songs*, trans. and ed. A Religious of C.S.M.V. (London: A. R. Mowbray, 1952). A good example of his method is his sermon on 1:2 (pp. 24-31), in which he sees (1) the incarnation of the Word, (2) the graces of self-control and penitence, (3) the soul's burning love for God, and (4) the Holy Spirit as God's kiss toward us. Bernard's sermons have power and clarity that come through even to the modern reader and which I would in no way seek to disparage. Even so, this does not vindicate his method. No doubt many an exegete has sat under preaching that he could acknowledge as both beautiful and profound even though aware that the preacher was misusing the text.

[48]Murphy (*Song*, 21) observes that from the late patristic period through the Middle Ages, Christian interpreters wrote more on the Song than on any other OT book.

[49]Cf. Carr, *Song*, 23.

earliest pagan allegorists were Pherecydes of Syros (fl. 550 B.C.) and Theogenes of Rhegium (fl. 525 B.C.).

The philosophic basis of allegorism is in the dualism of Neoplatonic and Gnostic psychology. In this system the mind or soul, the higher nature of humanity, was thought to be imprisoned in the physical body with its appetites for food and sex. The goal of true philosophy was to free the mind from its bondage to these appetites to enable it to partake fully of the spiritual life. The methods by which this liberation could occur ranged from asceticism to complete indulgence. The Gnostics enthusiastically embraced this understanding of mind and body, and some urged that married couples, in order to achieve spiritual liberation, renounce sexual relations[50] (or, conversely, embraced libertine sexuality).

This perception of reality stands in opposition to the biblical perspective. Creation, as the work of God, is explicitly called good, and no bifurcation of human nature is implied. Sinfulness inhabits the whole personality; it is not the result of the mind being brought down by the body. The Israelites never glorified celibacy as a mark of holiness or set it forth as a requirement for priestly or prophetic service.[51] In the New Testament celibacy is recommended only as a temporary measure to provide more time for the service of Christ, not as a path to sanctification. The marriage bed is holy (Heb 13:4).

The Neoplatonic notion that the outer, visible world is a mirror to the inner, spiritual world (a concept baptized by Origen) is also misleading. While giving the appearance of merely *using* the natural things of life (e.g., sexual love) as symbols that lead us in our inner, spiritual pilgrimage to God, this notion in fact often negates and condemns them as unprofitable and dangerous. In so doing, it forces the devout to vacate a major part of their own existence and so condemns them to a cognitive dissonance in which wholeness of life—a prerequisite of maturity—is impossible. The female body above all is denounced as intrinsically "worldly" in the worst sense.

Allegorical interpretation, therefore, is not intrinsic to biblical thinking but is an alien method to interpret the text out of regard for philosophic assumptions that are themselves unbiblical.[52] Notwithstanding the sup-

[50]Pope, *Song*, 115.

[51]The command that Jeremiah not marry (16:2) is exceptional and is given not on the grounds that it would somehow lessen his holiness but is because of the impending crisis.

[52]The text most commonly alleged to validate allegorical hermeneutics is Gal 4:21-31, where Paul used the births of Ishmael and Isaac and their respective mothers as ἀλληγορούμενα (*allegorized figures*, v. 24). Despite Paul's use of the term ἀλληγορέω, however, he did not engage in the kind of allegorism advocated by the Alexandrian school and their followers. Cf. L. Goppelt, *Typos: The Typological Interpretation of the Old Testament in the New* (Grand Rapids: Eerdmans, 1982), 139-40: "But only certain aspects of [Paul's] exposition come

port given allegorism by many champions of orthodoxy, it is best suited to a Gnostic, not an orthodox, Christianity.

The strongest refutation of the allegorical interpretation of Song of Songs, however, is in the obviously sexual nature of the language. Fairly unambiguous allusions to love play appear in the text (e.g., 5:1). Such language is simply inappropriate as a description of the love between God and his people, other biblical metaphors notwithstanding. The very beginning of the song, "Let him kiss me with the kisses of his mouth," implies that this is not divine-human love. We can hardly imagine Christ describing his love for the church in the terms of 7:7-8.[53] While the Bible does speak of the people of God as his bride, it never indulges in explicitly sexual imagery to describe the relationship.[54]

However good one's intentions may be, sexual language should not be brought into the vocabulary of worship and devotion via allegorism or any other means. The linking of religious adoration to erotic impulses is a mark of paganism and can only be regarded as a dangerous intrusion into the Christian understanding of both life and worship.[55] The two spheres of sexuality and devotion to God should not be confounded or intermingled lest both suffer distortion.

Allegorization is now widely acknowledged to be a false reading of the text,[56] although a few interpreters have in effect tried to reintroduce it through the back door.[57] Such temptations should be resisted. Although

---

close to being allegorical as we conceive of it. His exposition is entirely confined to a typological comparison of historical facts. Moreover, the connection between them is mostly constructed from relationships in redemptive history."

[53]A point already made in C. D. Ginsburg, *The Song of Songs* (1857; reprint, New York: KTAV, 1970), 181: "We earnestly request those who maintain the allegorical interpretation of the Song seriously to reflect whether this verse, and indeed the whole address, can be put into the mouth of Christ as speaking to the Church. Would not our minds recoil with horror were we to hear a Christian using it publicly, or even privately, to illustrate the love of Christ for his Church?"

[54]Contrary to the great Jewish scholar Ibn Ezra, Ezek 16:7-8 does not afford justification for interpreting Song of Songs allegorically. Ezekiel uses the metaphors of Israel as a helpless and wretched infant girl, her growth through puberty, and her marriage to Yahweh; but he does not use a metaphor of love play in the text. Also, of course, Ezekiel explicitly tells the reader that his text is a metaphor of God and Israel; no hint of such a thing appears in Song of Songs.

[55]See also the discussion under the "Theology of Song of Songs."

[56]The demise of the allegorical method is perhaps best illustrated by the shift in R. E. Murphy's perspective. In his early work, "The Structure of Canticle of Canticles," *CBQ* 11 (1949): 381-91, he argues that the Song is "essentially a parable" (p. 381) like Isa 62:5 on the love of Yahweh for his spouse (p. 382). In his later writings he sympathizes with but turns away from such readings.

[57]As in C. H. Bullock, *An Introduction to the Old Testament Poetic Books* (Chicago: Moody, 1979), 232-54; and E. J. Young, *An Introduction to the Old Testament* (Grand Rapids: Eerdmans, 1960), 336. Another example of a hybrid allegorical commentary is B. Dryburgh, *Lessons for Lovers in the Song of Solomon* (New Canaan, Conn.: Keats, 1975). Also

the allegorical interpretation may appear to be pious, anything that draws the reader away from the intended message[58] of the text is destructive.

(2) The Dramatic Interpretation

The Song of Songs is often interpreted in popular conservative literature as a drama telling the story of the love of Solomon for the Shulammite girl. Two distinct interpretations are proposed.

THE TWO-CHARACTER DRAMA. In this interpretation the Song tells the story of the mutual love between Solomon and the Shulammite. This interpretation is very old and was supported by, among others, John Milton.[59] F. Delitzsch developed this interpretation in his commentary.[60] More recently, M. Goulder has argued that the Song is a drama about the marriage of Solomon to a princess.[61] Conservatives who hold to this interpretation generally argue that the woman was Solomon's one true love. An obvious weakness of this interpretation is the difficulty of associating a man with Solomon's reputation (1 Kgs 11:4) with a song of true love.

THE THREE-CHARACTER DRAMA. In this interpretation there are three major characters: Solomon, the Shulammite, and her "shepherd lover." The song tells the story of Solomon's unsuccessful attempt to woo the girl from her true love, the rustic shepherd. The Song of Songs is in this way interpreted as a kind of morality play that proves that true love cannot be dazzled by riches and led away from its true object. First suggested by Ibn Ezra, this interpretation was developed by J. F. Jacobi (1772)[62] and the Jewish scholar Lowisohn (1816) and further by Ewald in 1826;[63] it was subsequently accepted by S. R. Driver[64] and is still maintained by a number of conservative interpreters, such as C. H. Bullock.[65]

---

some have tried to justify the use of allegorization under the umbrella of typology. In fact, however, legitimate biblical typology cannot be meaningfully applied to the Song. Carr (*Song*, 24-32) demonstrates that Ps 45, for which a typological approach is possible, is quite distinct from the Song in its vocabulary and concepts. Alleged "typological" interpretations of the Song are actually allegorical.

[58]Some will object here that to search for the author's intended meaning is futile and even meaningless (the "intentional fallacy"), but consider it to be essential for an evangelical hermeneutic. For a good discussion of this and related issues, see G. R. Osborne, *The Hermeneutical Spiral* (Downers Grove: InterVarsity, 1991), 366-415.

[59]In John Milton's treatise, *The Reason of Church Government Urged against Prelatory*, cited in Pope, *Song*, 35.

[60]F. Delitzsch, *The Song of Songs*, trans. M. G. Easton (reprint ed., Grand Rapids: Eerdmans, n.d.), 8-11. Delitzsch calls the work a "dramatic pastoral" although he admits that the drama did not exist among ancient Semites. He also asserts that the poem "is not a theatrical piece" (p. 8).

[61]M. D. Goulder, *The Song of Fourteen Songs*, JSOTSS 36 (Sheffield: JSOT, 1986).

[62]See Murphy, *Song*, 38.

[63]See Pope, *Song*, 35, 111-12, and Harrison, *Old Testament Introduction*, 1054.

[64]Driver, *Introduction*, 444-47.

[65]Bullock, *Poetic Books*, 232-54.

This approach spoils the aesthetic beauty of the piece in that much of the love poetry is treated as Solomon's attempted seduction. It is also somewhat bizarre in that it asserts that the girl, even in places where she addresses her lover as "you" and invites him to come away with her (e.g., 7:10–8:4), is not addressing "Solomon," who is with her, but the "shepherd," who is absent.[66] This seems to be a case of question begging.

Dramatic interpretations suffer from numerous weaknesses. First and foremost, there is no evidence that the drama, whether historical or fictional, existed as a literary genre in the ancient Levant. It begs the question to assert the Song of Songs is unique in ancient Near Eastern material. The Greeks, of course, developed the drama in the fifth century; but Greek dramatic influence is not discernible in the book, and the Greek dramas are in any case unlike Songs of Songs.

Bullock attempts to avoid this difficulty by classifying Song of Songs as a "lyrical ballad, the narrative of which was known by the original audience but has now been lost."[67] In point of fact, there is no evidence that an "original narrative" ever existed, and again it begs the question to call the Song a ballad. Also Bullock does not supply any examples of this genre contemporary with the Song of Songs.

A second major weakness is that dramatic interpretations must read a great deal of detail into the text. As Rowley observes: "So much has to be read between the lines, and such complicated stage directions have to be supplied, that its critics feel almost as much has to be brought to the book on this interpretation as on the allegorical."[68] Goulder is especially guilty at this point. For example, he arbitrarily reads 1:2-8 as the account of the arrival of the bride. Also, with no clear evidence at all, he declares that the woman of the Song is an Arabian princess. From this he concludes that the Song is a tract written against racism.[69]

At times it is difficult to know who is the speaker of a given line.[70] Of course, it is true that any play would be difficult to unravel if all stage directions and indications of *dramatis personae* were removed, but the text of Song of Songs never implies that it ever was a play or that something like stage directions have been lost. Therefore it is questionable to "reconstruct" them. Carr's comment is worth heeding: "Considerable experience

[66]Bullock (ibid., 252) attempts to resolve this by stating that we can "assume" that Solomon withdraws before the Shulammite's soliloquy. Exegesis, however, should not be driven by assumptions unsupported by the text.

[67]Ibid., 238.

[68]Rowley, "Song," 205. Rowley here specifically refers to the "three-character" interpretation, but the same could be said of any dramatic interpretation.

[69]Goulder, *Song*, 11-14, 75-78.

[70]R. E. Murphy (*Wisdom Literature*, FOTL [Grand Rapids; Eerdmans, 1981], 100) notes that especially difficult texts here include 1:2-4,7-8; 2:7,15; 6:10-12; 7:1-6; 8:51,56-57.

in theatrical production and direction has persuaded me that the Song, as it now stands, is unactable."[71]

Third, no clear conflict or resolution is present in the text. Simply put, it has no story. Any attempt to deduce a plot line or conflict in Song of Songs is purely arbitrary and must be based on either reading action into the story or altering the natural meaning of the lyrics. Bullock, for example, on the basis of 3:11, deduces that not only Solomon but also the Shulammite is wearing a crown and that she is being coerced into a wedding against her wishes.[72] The text implies none of this. Goulder, similarly, in arguing that the Song tells a story, must constantly assign new meanings to the words of the Song to fit his thesis. In 3:1-5, for example, the streets are not streets but the corridors of the palace; the city guards are not city guards but the eunuchs of the harem; and the daughters of Zion are not what the name implies, Jerusalem girls, but the other ladies of Solomon's harem.[73] It is one thing to treat the scenery and language of the Song as metaphorical or symbolic, but it is quite another simply to assign new meanings to words while claiming to adhere to a straightforward interpretation of the text. Without such peculiar handling of the material, however, these and all other attempts at finding a plot line in the Song collapse.

It is not even correct to say, as Murphy does, that Song of Songs is a dialogue.[74] While the two lovers do occasionally address or respond to each other, they are in no sense in genuine dialogue with each other. They are, instead, singing two parts of a duet (with the aid of a chorus). As is common in two-part songs, sometimes the singers address each other and interact directly, but often they do not.

(3) The Historical Interpretation

A number of conservative interpreters combine one of the dramatic interpretations with a historical approach and assert that Song of Songs describes an actual romantic affair from the life of Solomon. The text in no way implies that some historical event is being preserved; such interpretations are more the product of the interpreter's imagination than of the text itself.

One historical interpretation is that of Waterman, who argues that the book tells the story of Solomon's failed attempt to woo Abishag the Shunammite, the girl who warmed David as he lay dying (1 Kgs 1:3-4). Like the "three-character drama," it asserts that he failed and she returned

---

[71]Carr, *Song*, 34.

[72]Bullock, *Poetic Books*, 247.

[73]Goulder, *Song*, 27.

[74]Murphy, *Wisdom Literature*, 100.

to her lover in the north.[75] "Shunammite," however, is not equivalent to "Shulammite,"[76] and this interpretation is founded upon the same kind of assumptions and unusual readings of the text as the dramatic interpretations.

(4) The Cultic Interpretation

This interpretation, proposed by Meek, regards the Song of Songs as erotic literature from the fertility cults associated with Babylonian Tammuz and Canaanite Baal of ancient Near Eastern mythology. The myth cycle concerns the dying of a heroic god in his struggle with a god of darkness and chaos and his resurrection with the help of his lover. The myth was central to the fertility cults, and the language of their texts is often highly erotic. Meek was impressed by similarities between the Song of Songs and the Akkadian hymn list and came to the conclusion that Song of Songs was an expurgated version of Canaanite fertility cult hymnic material.[77]

Meek's positions soon came under the fire of N. Schmidt, who noted that there are no exact parallels between Song of Songs and the Akkadian hymnic material and that the Song gives no hint that it is meant to reawaken the powers of fertility in nature.[78] Meek's thesis is supported by Kramer, except that whereas Meek contends that the original song celebrated a sacred marriage between Yahweh and the goddess, Kramer argues that the original song concerned a sacred marriage between the Israelite king and the goddess (or a representative devotee). Also, Kramer felt no need to contend that the original song contained the dirges for a dying god contained in some of the mythical material.[79]

Pope claims to have found support for the cultic interpretation in the descriptions of the lovers. The man's body is described as if made of precious metals (5:11-15), and the woman's neck is pictured as a tower (4:4).

---

[75]L. Waterman, *The Song of Songs* (Ann Arbor: University of Michigan, 1948). Waterman's thesis is founded on a hypothetical redaction history for the Song and a questionable interpretation of aspects of the history of Solomon's accession. More than that, his position that the Song reflects a hatred of the Davidic dynasty in general and of Solomon in particular is not borne out by the Song unless one is willing to follow Waterman's rather strange interpretations (e.g., that 4:2 is meant to portray Solomon as examining the girl as if she were an animal [p. 41], that 4:4 is meant to make Solomon appear ludicrous [p. 42], that 6:4 serves "only as an excuse in order to exalt the northern capital, Tirzah" [p. 41], and that in 5:10; 6:1; etc., one should understand a proper name "Dodai" instead of the traditional "my beloved" [pp. 19-20, but "your beloved" in 5:9 invalidates this position].

[76]Harrison, *Old Testament Introduction*, 1057.

[77]T. Meek "The Song of Songs and the Fertility Cult," in W. H. Schoff, ed., *The Song of Songs: A Symposium* (Philadelphia: The Commercial Museum, 1924), 48-79.

[78]N. Schmidt, "Is Canticles an Adonis Liturgy?" *JAOS* 46 (1926): 154-64. For a complete review of Meek's position and Schmidt's retort, see Pope, *Song*, 146-51.

[79]S. N. Kramer, *The Sacred Marriage Rite* (Bloomington: Indiana University, 1969), 90-92.

To Pope this suggests that the actual objects of description are the idols of the god and goddess.[80] But it is inappropriate to treat as literal the statement that the man's arms are called rods of gold (5:14). A perusal of the contexts of these verses reveals that most of the language is inappropriate as a description of an idol. The man's eyes are doves (5:12), and the woman's teeth are a flock of sheep (4:2). This is highly metaphoric praise of humans, not literal praise of idols. More recently, Pope has argued that the woman of the poem is a goddess on the grounds that she has such an enormous nose (7:5).[81]

This interpretation suffers from four major weaknesses. First, Song of Songs lacks a number of major motifs associated with the fertility cult. Most important here is the absence of any reference to a dying and rising god.[82] Nor does the Song hint that the sexuality of the couple helps to induce fertility. Second, cultic interpretations are seldom compelling. As Childs notes, "Subtle use of erotic imagery in the biblical poem is far removed from the crass 'explanations' of the book's alleged original meaning."[83] Mythological readings, moreover, are often as forced as allegorical analyses.[84] Third, if Song of Songs were a piece of myth and ritual from the fertility cult, it is difficult to see how it was admitted to the canon.[85]

Fourth, and perhaps most significant, Song of Songs and the fertility cult hymnic material are simply not in the same genre. Song of Songs is not a hymn. Incidental parallels between the love poetry of Song of Songs and the sensual references in cultic texts are instructive in that both came from the ancient Near East, but they are far from being common material. Also the parallels that do exist between the Song and the sacred marriage texts diminish in significance when one recognizes that better parallels to the Song exist in the Egyptian love poetry—poetry that does *not* involve sacred marriage.[86] It is begging the question to assert that all cultic references

---

[80]Pope, *Song*, 465, 548.

[81]Pope, "Metastases," 322-23.

[82]Kramer (*Sacred Marriage*, 91-92) argues that this difficulty is now overcome by the celebratory marriage songs in the Sumerian material.

[83]Childs, *Old Testament*, 573.

[84]E.g., W. F. Albright, "Archaic Survivals in the Text of Canticles," in *Hebrew and Semitic Studies Presented to Godfrey Rolles Driver*, ed. D. W. Thomas and W. D. McHardy (London: Oxford University Press, 1963), 1-7. Interpreting 8:5-7, Albright argues that "the mother of the beloved was a mythical figure, possibly a girl who had escaped to the desert after becoming pregnant by a god" (p. 7)!

[85]On this point and on the matter of a proposed demythologizing redaction of the Song prior to canonization, see especially Rowley, "Song," 221-32.

[86]For example, Kramer (*Sacred Marriage*, 90) believes that the designation of the bride as "sister" is best explained by the application of similar epithets to Ishtar-Inanna. In the Egyptian

were removed from the Song in its redaction.[87]

(5) The Funerary Interpretation

M. Pope, in his massive commentary on the Song of Songs, not only supports the view that the lovers in the song are Baal and his consort but takes the bold step of claiming that the Song was rooted in ancient funerary ritual. He argues that "funeral feasts in the ancient Near East were love feasts celebrated with wine, women and song"[88] and that such may have been the original setting of the Song of Songs.

Pope explores in great detail the debauchery connected to the cult of the dead in the ancient Near East. He points out that dogs often appear in the ritual orgies and does a detailed study of the word *mrzh* ("cultic feast") from biblical and Ugaritic sources.[89] None of this is particularly helpful to his case, however, since neither dogs nor the word *mrzh* occurs in Song of Songs.

For Pope the key text of Song of Songs is 8:6, "For love is as strong as death, its jealousy unyielding as the grave." The theme that only love can frustrate the power of death, he asserts, is the key to the book and the major motif of its function in the funeral cult. But this interpretation is beset with problems.

First of all, "love is as strong as death" does not necessarily imply a funeral setting. To the contrary, death here is a simile that represents the inescapable power of love; like death, it will not release those it has grasped (cf. Eccl 7:26). Gordon has observed that Song of Songs "has nothing to do with death," and it "never raises the question of whether love can triumph over death."[90]

Second, no other reference to funerary or cultic rites appears in the Song. The nearest thing to such an allusion is in 5:1, where spices, honey, wine, and milk are mentioned. Pope calls attention to the fact that these

---

love songs, however, the beloved woman is frequently called "sister." For a discussion of the "secular" nature of both the Song and the Egyptian songs, see Fox, *Song*, 234-43. Even a scholar who wishes to argue that the Egyptian love songs are influenced by Egyptian religion concedes that they are not of themselves religious texts; see V. L. Davis, "Remarks on M. V. Fox's 'The Cairo Love Songs,'" *JAOS* 100 (1981): 111-14.

[87]Kramer (*Sacred Marriage*, 99), after an examination of some of the sacred marriage poetry, tellingly comments that "in this poem there is little that is reminiscent of the 'Song of Songs,' *at least as we have it in our undoubtedly expurgated form*, except for such stylistic features as the brother-sister designation of the lovers and the presence of a chorus of maidens" (emphasis added). But the notion that the Song is in an "expurgated form" is open to question. Cf. Gordis, *Song*, 8.

[88]Pope, *Song*, 228.

[89]Ibid., 211-22.

[90]Review of M. H. Pope, *Song*, by C. H. Gordon, *JAOS* 100 (1980): 355.

ingredients could be used in the anointing of the dead and in libations.[91] It is highly doubtful, however, that such is the intention here; one cannot argue that every mention of such common delicacies and drinks implies a funeral.

(6) The Wedding Interpretation

Some scholars have argued that Song of Songs is a wedding ceremony text. It is argued that in the course of a week-long wedding ceremony, the bride and groom played the roles of queen and king and performed various dances and that songs in praise of the bride or groom (the *wasf*) were sung. Studies of Syrian wedding rituals have been cited as support of this interpretation.[92]

Against this view, some scholars have pointed out that the Shulammite is nowhere called a queen. But it is possible that the name "Shulammite" is a feminine form of "Solomon" (Heb. *šĕlōmô*) and describes the bride as a princess.[93] That is, "Shulammite" may not refer to the girl's hometown but may be a kind of designation of royal status.

Nevertheless, while the parallels drawn from Near Eastern wedding ceremonies have shed light on the book, it is doubtful that the whole book can be interpreted as the text of a wedding ceremony. The book cannot be divided into seven sections corresponding to a ceremony of seven days.[94] While the Song of Songs, or portions of it, may well have been used in ancient times as part of a wedding celebration, that does not appear to be its primary function. Even allowing for exaggeration, much of the language is far too exalted to refer to a peasant wedding ceremony.[95] As Fohrer has commented, the connection to marriage ceremonies cannot be denied, but "neither can the book be interpreted totally from this perspective and called the textbook for an Israelite wedding."[96] While the song does appear to focus on the wedding of the man and woman, that does not mean that it was sung *at* weddings or describes in any detail the ancient Israelite wedding ceremony.

---

[91]Pope, *Song*, 222.

[92]In 1873 J. G. Wetzstein published *Die syrische Dreschtafel* ("The Syrian Threshing-Table") in the *Zeitschrift fur Ethnographie*. He described his experiences observing the wedding ceremony of the Syrians and made comparisons to Song of Songs. His observations, as well as other comments he made in private letters to F. Delitzsch, are summarized in Delitzsch, *Song*, 162-76.

[93]W. H. Schmidt, *Introduction to the Old Testament*, trans. M. J. O'Connell (London: SCM, 1979), 312. Cf. Pope, *Song*, 596-97.

[94]See LaSor, Hubbard, Bush, *Old Testament*, 608.

[95]See Gordis, *Song*, 19.

[96]Fohrer, *Introduction*, 302.

(7) *The Love Song Interpretation*

The best interpretation of Song of Songs is that it is what it appears to be: a love song. This is in fact among the earliest of interpretations, as implied in Rabbi Aqiba's curse on those who sung it frivolously. Josephus considered this interpretation to be self-evident.[97] Theodore of Mopsuestia, of the Antiochene school of literal Bible interpreters, was condemned posthumously in the Fifth Council of Constantinople (553) for holding to this interpretation.[98]

The song is love poetry and should not be interpreted as a historical event. The "Solomon" of the poetry is likely a "poetic symbol." It may seem strange that Solomon, as author, would make himself a poetic symbol for the glory of the bridegroom. That difficulty is acknowledged here, but one must recall that Solomon appears to have taken on the role of the quintessential Eastern monarch, with all the glory and splendor that implies, as a deliberate and self-conscious act (1 Kgs 7:1-12; 9:10–11:3). Therefore Solomon could have set himself in the song as a "poetic symbol" for the splendor of the bridegroom. At the same time, one cannot exclude the possibility that the song was written by a court poet in Solomon's palace; in that case, the use of Solomon as a "poetic symbol" is not only possible but likely. Even if it were penned by a court-poet, however, it would have been "published" with the knowledge and probably direct involvement of the king himself. The text is not a record of historical events in Solomon's life. In love every groom is King Solomon, a shepherd, and even a gazelle; and every bride is a princess and country maiden.

This special status conferred on the man and woman is easier to understand by recognizing them as bride and groom. Several pieces of evidence support this conclusion. First, the dramatic arrival of "Solomon" (3:6-11) is most easily interpreted not as Solomon as a historical figure but as representation of the ideal of the groom. The dramatic appearance of the groom in an ancient Israelite wedding is attested to in Matt 25:6. Second, the processional departure of the man and woman in 6:10-13 is best understood as a ceremonial farewell by a bride and groom. Finally, and most significantly, the man repeatedly refers to the woman as his bride (4:8-12; 5:1). There is no reason to take this in any but its normal sense.[99] At the same time, while the Song concerns a bride and groom, it is not the text of a wedding ceremony.

---

[97]Josephus, *Antiquities* (trans. H. J. Thackeray and R. Marcus [Cambridge: Harvard, 1977]), viii. 7.3.

[98]Fohrer, *Introduction*, 300.

[99]One may object that he also calls her his "sister" in a nonliteral sense. But the use of the terms "brother" and "sister" for one's lover was conventional, as attested to in the Egyptian poetry.

The Song is occasionally called a "collection of love poems," that is, an anthology. This designation is misleading, however; Song of Songs is a single, unified work, as its chiastic structure demonstrates. It is true that Song of Songs at times seems to function without logical transitions between texts,[100] but this is an aspect of its genre. One should not expect the book to conform to modern, more prosaic standards.

A lengthy and somewhat complex song of love, Song of Songs has a number of parallels in the Egyptian love poetry of the Chester Beatty collection. The most strikingly similar work is the poem of seven stanzas from Papyrus Chester Beatty I, in which the two lovers antiphonally sing their parts. Song of Songs is more complex in that it not only has parts for the lovers but also for the "friends," a type of chorus.

It may seem strange to some readers that the Bible should contain love poetry. While the marriage relationship is meant to be a partnership and friendship on the deepest level, that does not mean that the sexual and emotional aspects of love between a man and a woman are themselves unworthy of the Bible's attention. Sexuality and love are fundamental to the human experience; and it is altogether fitting that the Bible, as a book meant to teach the reader how to live a happy and good life, should have something to say in this area.

4. Genre

The Song is unique among the books of the Hebrew Bible in that it alone celebrates sexual love. The covenant between Yahweh and Israel is not in view as it is in the books of the Law and the Prophets. Does this mean it is part of the wisdom corpus? Such a classification seems artificial. The Song of Songs does not teach or explore wisdom after the fashion of Proverbs and Ecclesiastes but celebrates human love.

On the other hand, it has affinities to wisdom literature that should not be overlooked. The very ascription to Solomon is, as Childs notes, strong indication that it belongs to wisdom.[101] Childs also rightly points out that other wisdom material uses sexual language (Prov 7:6ff.; 9:1ff.).[102] The Israelites also made a closer connection between the singing of songs and "wisdom" than modern Occidentals do.[103]

Most important, the function and purpose of wisdom literature must be related to the Song of Songs. Wisdom in the Bible is meant to teach the reader how to live in the world. For this reason politics, personal morality,

---

[100]As noted in Murphy, *Wisdom Literature*, 99.

[101]Childs, *Old Testament*, 573-75.

[102]Childs, *Old Testament*, 575.

[103]See Gordis, *Song*, 14-15. He notes that Jer 9:16 calls professional singers of dirges "wise women."

economics, social behavior, and many other areas of life all come under its teaching. And certainly courtship, sensual love, and marriage cannot be excluded since these areas are among the most basic universals of human experience. The Song of Songs celebrates love, but it also teaches love; in this respect it must be counted as wisdom literature. Nevertheless, among the books of biblical wisdom, it is in a class by itself.

5. Canonicity

The sensuality of the Song of Songs prompted questions among both Jewish and Christian readers about whether it belonged in the canon. Nevertheless, it has firmly held its place in the Bible through the centuries. Rabbi Akiba affirmed the value of the book: "The whole world is not worth the day on which the Song of Songs was given to Israel; all the writings are holy, and the Song of Songs is the holy of holies."[104]

Many assert that the book was allowed into the Canon under the allegorical interpretation.[105] Otherwise, some scholars think, it would never have been admitted. After an analysis of the canonical structure of the book, however, Childs concludes, "There is no sign that the canonical shape of the book ever received an allegorical shaping."[106] His point is well taken. Rather than assert that the allegorical interpretation allowed the book into the canon, it is better to say that the fact that the book was in the canon gave rise to the allegorical interpretation. Certainly no one would dream of interpreting the Song of Songs as an allegory of God and Israel if it were not found in the Bible.

Love and sexuality can be a source of great joy or deep grief and pain. As children become adults and discover their sexuality, and as couples move into marriage and seek to understand each other, it is imperative that they have guidance in this area of life that is so crucial to psychological adjustment. The Bible itself would be incomplete if it only spoke of sexuality in terms of prohibitions and did not give positive instruction to enable the reader to discover the joy of healthy love. Certainly love between man and woman is not the whole of life or even its highest good. The Bible elsewhere emphasizes the vertical relationship between a man or a woman and God as more important than any other. Even so, to regard Song of Songs as unworthy of canonization unless it is allegorized or turned into a historical drama is to deny the crucial importance of cherishing and understanding this area of life. It also reflects a failure to appreciate

---

[104]*M. Yad.* 3:5.

[105]Cf. R. H. Pfeiffer, *Introduction to the Old Testament*, 714: "The *allegorical interpretation*, by discovering a deeper meaning under the plain love poetry, made possible the canonization of the book."

[106]Childs, *Old Testament*, 578.

the place of wisdom literature as a guide to healthy and happy behavior in this world.

6. Literary Method

The reader of the Song of Songs must never forget that this is ancient Near Eastern love poetry and not modern Western love poetry. It uses language in a way that is strange and even offensive to modern standards while natural to the ancient ear and eye. Few modern men would woo the woman of their dreams by telling her that her nose is like a tower (7:4)! Such striking imagery in the description of one's beloved, however, is found not only in the Song of Songs but in other ancient Near Eastern love poetry as well. For example, the seven-stanza love poem from the Papyrus Chester Beatty I (Egypt, New Kingdom period) contains the following description of a young man's beloved: "Upright neck, shining breast,/ Hair true lapis lazuli;/ Arms surpassing gold,/ Fingers like lotus buds."[107]

While the imagery employed in ancient love poetry often places considerable distance between the image and the depicted reality, the early poets achieved a high degree of tenderness and even sensuality without the bald eroticism that sterilizes modern love poetry. Through simile and metaphor, even the strongest and most private of the emotions of sexual love can be expressed in a way that is tasteful, appropriate, and descriptive.

Beyond the profound forcefulness of the metaphors, the Song of Songs also employs a number of poetic devices characteristic of ancient Near Eastern love poetry but not often found in their modern counterparts. One such device is the "poetic symbol," in which the characters take on roles for literary purposes. In Egyptian love poetry, poetic symbols include the man as bird catcher or as door keeper in the woman's home.[108]

In Song of Songs two such poetic symbols are "king" and "shepherd," both of which are applied to the man. The description of the woman as a shepherdess and the term Shulammite may be poetic symbols as well. Whether the song was originally written about a shepherdess is immaterial. The point again is that the experience of love adorns both partners and exalts them in ideal roles.

(1) Literary Forms in Ancient Love Poetry

Love poetry, like much of the literature of the ancient Near East, was dominated by certain literary forms.[109] Here too, as in other form-critical

---

[107]Miriam Lichtheim, *Ancient Egyptian Literature*. 3 vols. Copyright © 1973–1980 Regents of the University of California. Used by permission. 2:182. Hereinafter AEL.

[108]Murphy, *Wisdom Literature*, 102. See AEL 2:190.

[109]The first attempt to categorize the forms of the Song is F. Horst, "Die Formen des althebraischen Liebesiedes," *Orientalistische Studien, Enno Littmann zu Seinem 60. Geburtstag*

analyses, boundaries are not always fixed and rigid; and some texts are not readily classified form-critically (without recourse to artificial designations). Nevertheless, certain formal categories are clear. Among these are the following:[110]

THE ADMIRATION SONG. In this form the lover sings of the wonderful qualities of his or her beloved. Often the physical beauty of the beloved is described, but mental and moral virtues are also the object of praise. Some scholars distinguish between the admiration song and the descriptive song (*wasf*), but this is artificial since description is regularly a part of admiration.[111] Examples of admiration songs are:

> The One, the sister without peer,/ The handsomest of all!/ She looks like the rising morning star/ At the start of a happy year. Shining bright, fair of skin,/ Lovely the look of her eyes, Sweet the speech of her lips,/ She has not a word too much (Papyrus Chester Beatty I).[112]

> Splendid youth who has no peer,/ Brother outstanding in virtues! (Papyrus Chester Beatty I).[113]

Song of Songs has quite a few lengthy admiration songs. Among these are the following:

> My lover is radiant and ruddy,/ outstanding among ten thousand./ His head is purest gold;/ his hair is wavy/ and black as a raven (5:10-16).

> You are beautiful, my darling, as Tirzah,/ lovely as Jerusalem,/ majestic as troops with banners (6:4-9).

THE SONG OF YEARNING. In this form the man or woman sings of his or her desire for the beloved. Schemes to get to the beloved, worries

---

uberrricht (Leiden: Brill, 1935), 43-54; Murphy gives a complete précis of Horst's analysis in *Song*, 60-62.

[110]The following represents my own analysis of formal parallels between the Egyptian love poetry and the Song. For previous studies see White, *Study*, 127-59; *Fox, Song*, 267-94; and Murphy, *Song*, 42-48.

[111]There are of course songs of admiration and description outside of the love poetry of Song of Songs and the Egyptian material cited here, but much of this is either too late to be directly relevant or of altogether different genre. The modern Arabic love songs collected by Stephan and others (cited in Pope, *Song*, 56-66), for example, while illustrative of Near Eastern love poetry and imagery, obviously are too late to have been an influence on Song of Songs. Ugaritic descriptive material, on the other hand, is generally hymnic and not really parallel, on a form-critical basis, to Song of Songs (see the examples cited in Pope, *Song*, 75-76). Where something like love poetry appears in Ugaritic material (e.g., in the description of the girl Hurray in KRT 143-55; cf. Pope, *Song*, 75), the language is still religious ("whose charm is like Anat's charm") and quite unlike Song of Songs. The Sumerian "Message of Ludingir-ra to his Mother" (Pope, *Song*, 70-72), while obviously descriptive, is not love poetry.

[112]AEL 2:182.

[113]Ibid. 2:184.

about obstacles, expressions of sickness and despondency, and appeals to the beloved to return love frequently appear here. Examples are:

> My brother torments my heart with his voice,/ He makes sickness take hold of me;/ He is neighbor to my mother's house, and I cannot go to him! (Papyrus Chester Beatty I).[114]

> My heart devised to see her beauty,/ While sitting down in her house (Papyrus Chester Beatty I).

> O that you came to your sister swiftly!/ Like a swift envoy of the king (Papyrus Chester Beatty I).[115]

Examples of the yearning song also in the Song of Songs are as follows:

> All night long on my bed/ I looked for the one my heart loves;/ I looked for him but did not find him (3:1).

> If only you were to me like a brother,/ who nursed at my mother's breasts!/ Then, if I found you outside,/ I would kiss you,/ and no one would despise me (8:1-2).

THE ARRIVAL SONG. This is a short song that celebrates the coming of the beloved. Examples are:

> My sister has come, my heart exults,/ My arms spread out to embrace her (The Cairo Vase, Ostracon 25218).[116]

> Listen! My lover!/ Look! Here he comes,/ Leaping across the mountains,/ bounding over the hills (Song 2:8).

THE INVITATION. In this song the lover invites the beloved to come away with him/her. It is often a metaphorical invitation to love play. An example is:

> Come away, my lover,/ and be like a gazelle/ or like a young stag/ on the spice laden mountains (Song 8:14).

THE PRAYER FOR SUCCESS IN LOVE. In this form the man or woman prays to a god or goddess either for success in wooing the beloved or in thanks for success already granted. Found several times in Egyptian love poetry, it is noticeably absent from the Bible. Examples are:

> I praise the Golden,[117] I worship her majesty,/ I extol the Lady of Heaven;/ . . . I called to her, she heard my plea,/ She sent my mistress to me (Papyrus Chester Beatty I).[118]

---

[114]Ibid. 2:182-83.
[115]Ibid. 2:186.
[116]Ibid. 2:193.
[117]I.e., Hathor, goddess of love.
[118]AEL 2:184.

> I fare north in the ferry / By the oarsman's stroke, / On my shoulder a bundle of reeds; / I am going to Memphis / To tell Ptah, Lord of Truth / Give me my sister tonight! (Papyrus Harris 500).[119]

The absence of the prayer song from Song of Songs calls for special comment. It does not imply that the Israelites believed that Yahweh was not interested in matters of love and marriage, since Proverbs teaches that it is Yahweh from whom one obtains a good wife (18:22; 19:14). Rather, the orthodox Israelites were unwilling to risk any degradation of their covenant relationship whereby God might be reduced to the level of a love charm. Yahweh is not Aphrodite. It is not that all the emotions of love are by nature impure—wooing is not necessarily the same as seduction—but that the name of God is not to be associated with the unstable and at times flippant mood swings of young love. One must invoke the name of the Lord only with fear and trembling. Also a prayer for success in love, in which one is driven by pure emotion and physical desire, undercuts the wisdom teaching that a man should seek a wife of virtue from God.

No "Individual Psalm of Thanksgiving" deals with romantic interests. God is concerned with love. It is he who, in his providence, guides the good woman to the man who fears him (Prov 19:14; cf. Prov 31:10-31; Eccl 7:26). But he will not be a party to a romantic game.

(2) The Motifs of Song of Songs

Many literary motifs occur in Song of Songs within the various forms described above. These are metaphoric terms, leitmotifs, poetic reference points, literary types, and pieces of stylized imagery that occur repeatedly both in Song of Songs and ancient Egyptian love poetry. A partial list of these motifs is as follows:[120]

LOVESICKNESS. This motif generally occurs in a yearning song. In it the lover claims that he (she) is so filled with longing for the beloved that it has made him (her) ill. Examples are:

> Seven days since I saw my sister, / And sickness invaded me; / I am heavy in all my limbs, / My body has forsaken me (Papyrus Chester Beatty I).[121]

> O daughters of Jerusalem, I charge you— / if you find my lover, / what will you tell him? / Tell him I am faint with love (Song 5:8).

THE DOOR. The image of the door frequently appears in songs of yearning. The door represents both obstacle and opening. At times songs that center on the door that separates the lovers are almost surreal. A particular

---

[119]Ibid. 2:189.

[120]Murphy (*Wisdom Literature*, 102) has a list similar to that which follows here.

[121]AEL 2:185.

submotif that sometimes occurs here is that of frustration. Either the door will not open or when the door is opened the beloved is found to be angry or absent. On the use of this image in the Song, see the commentary.

> I passed by her house in the dark,/ I knocked and no one opened;/ A good night to our doorkeeper,/ Bolt, I will open! (Papyrus Chester Beatty I).[122]

> The mansion of my sister,/ With door in the center of her house,/ Its door-leaves are open,/ The bolt is sprung,/ My sister is angry! (Papyrus Harris 500).[123]

> My lover thrust his hand through the latch-opening,/ my heart began to pound for him/ . . . / I arose to open for my lover,/ . . . / I opened for my lover,/ but my lover had left; he was gone (Song 5:5-6).

THE GAZELLE OR STAG. The man is often called a leaping gazelle or stag by the woman. The motif is sometimes used in the arrival song and sometimes in the invitation song. Occasionally the woman is called a doe. Examples are:

> O that you came to sister swiftly,/ Like a bounding gazelle in the wild (Papyrus Chester Beatty I).[124]

> My lover is like a gazelle or a young stag (Song 2:9).

THE KISS. The kiss, obviously enough, is a frequent motif in love poetry. Sometimes the kiss is combined with the stylization of the beloved as a brother or sister, and it can occur in a song of yearning in which the woman longs to be free to kiss her beloved openly. Examples are:

> Then will I hurry to my brother!/ I will kiss him before his companions,/ I would not weep before them (Papyrus Chester Beatty I).[125]

> If only you were to me like a brother,/ who nursed at my mother's breasts!/ Then, if I found you outside,/ I would kiss you,/ and no one would despise me (Song 8:1).

> Let him kiss me with the kisses of his mouth (Song 1:2).

THE BREASTS. This motif often appears in the song of admiration. Proverbs 5:19, "May her breasts satisfy you always," attests to the tenderness and affection associated with the breasts in the Israelite understanding. Examples are:

> My lover is to me a sachet of myrrh/ resting between my breasts (Song 1:12).

---

[122]Ibid. 2:188.
[123]Ibid. 2:189.
[124]Ibid. 2:187.
[125]Ibid. 2:185.

I am a wall,/and my breasts are like towers./Thus I have become in his eyes/like one bringing contentment (Song 8:10).

THE AUTHORITY FIGURE. Often in the songs of yearning, the lover speaks of her or his frustration at being kept from the beloved by some authority figure. Often it is the mother, but sometimes it is the brothers of the lover. Occasionally civil authorities, such as guards, appear in love poetry. The authority figure stands as an obstacle to the uniting of the lovers. Examples are:

If only my mother knew my heart,/She would have understood by now (Papyrus Chester Beatty I).[126]

The watchmen found me/as they made their rounds in the city./They beat me, they bruised me;/they took away my cloak,/those watchmen of the walls![127] (Song 5:7).

THE GARDEN OR VINEYARD. The delights of a garden, with its fragrances and fruit and vernal images, are a natural motif of love poetry. Sometimes the garden is a metaphor for the woman's body, and it may be used in that way in the invitation song.

I am your sister, your best one;/I belong to you like this plot of ground/That I planted with flowers/And sweet-smelling herbs (Papyrus Harris 500).[128]

Awake, north wind,/and come, south wind!/Blow on my garden,/that its fragrance may spread abroad./Let my lover come into his garden/and taste its choice fruits (Song 4:16).

THE THEFT OR ENTRAPMENT OF THE HEART. Often in songs of yearning the lover speaks of having his or her heart stolen away by the beloved. Examples are:

The voice of the wild goose shrills,/It is caught by its bait;/My love of you pervades me,/I cannot loosen it (Papyrus Harris 500).[129]

You have stolen my heart, my sister, my bride;/with one glance of your eyes,/with one jewel of your necklace (Song 4:9).

---

[126]Ibid. 2:184.

[127]This text is reminiscent of the third stanza of the seven-stanza poem in Papyrus Chester Beatty I. The translation and interpretation of that stanza is controversial; but, following Lichtheim (AEL 2:183), it appears to say that the young man, while trying to get to his beloved, had to avoid the official Mehy and his attendants. Contrast, however, Wilson's interpretation in ANET, 468. The Song, however, uses the concept of the authority figure, symbolized by the night watchmen, in a radically different and creative way, as is elucidated in the commentary.

[128]AEL 2:192.

[129]Ibid. 2:190.

HORSES AND CHARIOTS. Sometimes the man is portrayed as arriving in an entourage with horses and chariots. This motif naturally occurs in an arrival song. The imagery prompts feelings of valor and manly splendor. Examples are:

> All stables are held ready for him,/ He has horses at the stations;/ The chariot is harnessed in its place,/ He may not pause on the road./ When he arrives at his sister's house,/ His heart will jubilate (Papyrus Chester Beatty I).[130]

> Look! It is Solomon's carriage,/ escorted by sixty warriors,/ the noblest of Israel (Song 3:7).

LIMBS DESCRIBED AS PRECIOUS METALS. Gold and silver are frequent metaphors, as are ivory and precious stones. Examples are:

> Arms surpassing gold (Papyrus Chester Beatty I).[131]

> His arms are rods of gold,/ set with chrysolite (Song 5:14).

SONG OF SONGS AND OTHER ANE PARALLELS. The above examples do not imply that the Song of Songs has been influenced *only* by Egyptian poetry. Israelite poetry certainly drew on its Canaanite forebears and on Mesopotamian sources as well.[132] The description of the man in Song 5:15, for example, uses metaphor similar to that in an Akkadian incantation: "Like lapis lazuli I want to cleanse my body,/ Like marble his features should shine,/ Like pure silver, like red gold,/ I want to make clean what is dull."[133] Nevertheless, while the common metaphor indicates the common background of the ancient Near East, Song of Songs is not an incantation. Similarity of metaphor between two pieces does not prove that they are of the same genre or have similar purposes. Also, unlike the Song (and the Egyptian material), the Mesopotamian material tends to be either cultic[134] or graphically erotic.[135]

7. Unity and Structure of the Song

The apparent lack of direction in the Song has caused some scholars to conclude that it is not a single song at all but a collection of several

---

[130]Ibid. 2:186.

[131]Ibid. 2:182.

[132]For a good survey of Sumerian parallels to the Song, see Murphy, *Song*, 48-55. For a good analysis of the possibility of Ugaritic influence, see White, *Study*, 36-44.

[133]Cited in Pope, *Song*, 547. Pope observes that this incantation is for healing sexual impotence.

[134]There are no grounds for maintaining, as a few scholars have done, that the Egyptian love songs are cultic. Cf. White, *Study*, 68.

[135]There are of course exceptions—Mesopotamian songs that are not explicitly erotic or cultic. Cf. "As you let day slip by," cited in Murphy, *Song*, 53.

songs.[136] Both Fox and Murphy, however, demonstrate the weakness of arguments that the Song is an anthology and make compelling cases for the unity of the Song. Fox, for example, points to the high number of repetitious and associative sequences, as well as to the consistent character portrayal, as evidence for the unity of the whole.[137] Murphy, similarly, notes the existence of common refrains, common themes, and common words and phrases.[138]

The unity of the Song does not, however, guarantee that it has a clear or discernible structure, and efforts to discover structural symmetry generally flounder. Perhaps the most valiant effort is that of J. Cheryl Exum, who divides the work into six interlocking "poems."[139] Although her analysis yields valuable insights, inconsistencies have generally left scholars unconvinced.[140] A chiastic analysis by W. Shea, although illuminating, breaks down at several points and thus fails to persuade most scholars.[141]

A more satisfactory analysis is that by R. Alden, who detects not a chiastic structure in the poems of the Song but an arrangement of certain key words and phrases in a chiastic fashion (see chart on the next page). This pattern supports the unity of the Song. More importantly, the center of the chiasmus in 4:16–5:1a, which poetically describes the moment of sexual union between the man and woman, implies that the entire Song, as it were, revolves around this event.[142]

8. Theology of Song of Songs

Karl Barth made perhaps the most profound attempt at a theology of Song of Songs without recourse to allegorism (although he does speak of it as "parable"). In his discussion of the doctrine of creation, Barth draws Gen 2 and Song of Songs together in order to unravel how the Bible, in spite of the corruption of humanity at the fall, maintains the pristine picture of covenant love and sexuality:

---

[136]E.g., Gordis, *Song*, 16-18, and White, *Study*, 163.

[137]Fox, *Song*, 202-22. See also Murphy, *Song*, 76, and the chart of repetitions in Song of Songs in Murphy, *Wisdom Literature*, 99.

[138]R. E. Murphy, "The Unity of the Song of Songs," *VT* 29 (1979); 436-43. See also Murphy, *Song*, 76, and the chart of repetitions in Song of Songs in Murphy, *Wisdom Literature*, 99.

[139]J. C. Exum, "A Literary and Structural Analysis of the Song of Songs," *ZAW* 85 (1973): 47-79.

[140]Cf. Murphy, *Song*, 62-63; Fox, *Song*, 207-10; and Landy, *Paradoxes*, 40.

[141]W. H. Shea, "The Chiastic Structure of the Song of Songs," *ZAW* 92 (1980): 378-96. Cf. Murphy, *Song*, 63-64; and Landy, *Paradoxes*, 40. For yet another but less persuasive chiastic reading, see E. C. Webster, "Pattern in the Song of Songs," *JSOT* 22 (1982): 73-93.

[142]Note that Shea ("Chiastic Structure," 395) also places 4:16–5:1 at the center of the Song. He observes that 4:16 comprises two tricola, and 5:1 comprises three bicola.

- *A* 1:1-4a "Take me away"
  - *B* 1:4b Friends speak
    - *C* 1:5-7 "My own vineyard"
      - *D* 1:8-14 "Breasts," "silver," "we will make"
        - *E* 1:15-2:2 "House"
          - *F* 2:3-7 "His left arm" "daughters of Jerusalem . . . so desires," "apple," "love"
            - *G* 2:8-13 "Fragrance," "come my darling," "blossoming"
              - *H* 2:14-15 "Vineyards," "show me"
                - *I* 2:16-17 "My lover is mine"
                  - *Ja* 3:1-5 "The watchmen found me"
                  - *Jb* 3:6-11 Description of carriage, "gold," "Lebanon," "daughters of Jerusalem"
                  - *Jc* 4:1-7 Description of girl, "Your eyes . . . hair . . . teeth"
                    - *K* 4:8-15 "Myrrh," "spice," "honey," "honeycomb," "wine," "milk"
                      - *L* 4:16 "Into his garden"
                      - *L′* 5:1a "Into my garden"
                    - *K′* 5:1bc "Myrrh," "spice," "honey," "honeycomb," "wine," "milk"
                  - *J′a* 5:2-9 "The watchmen found me"
                  - *J′b* 5:10-6:1 "Gold," "Lebanon," "daughters of Jerusalem"
                  - *J′c* 6:4-11 Description of girl, "Your eyes, . . . hair . . . teeth"
                - *I′* 6:2-3 "My lover is mine"
              - *H′* 6:13-7:9a [10a] "Vines," "wine," "that we me gaze on you"
            - *G′* 7:9b-13 [10b-14] "Fragrance," "come my darling," "blossom"
          - *F′* 8:1-5 "His left arm," "daughters of Jerusalem . . . so desires," "apple," "love"
        - *E′* 8:6-7 "House"
      - *D′* 8:8-9 "Breasts," "silver," "we will build"
    - *C′* 8:10-12 "My own vineyard"
  - *B′* 8:13 "Friends"
- *A′* 8:14 "Come away"

Reproduced by permission of R. L. Alden. The full explanation of the chiastic structuring will be published in Alden's forthcoming commentary.

> In connexion with both passages we may well ask where the authors found the courage—or perhaps we should ask how the redactors of the Canon came to choose these passages whose authors, ignoring the well-known disturbance and corruption in the relationship of the sexes, obviously had the courage—to treat the matter in this way, speaking so bluntly of *eros* and not being content merely with the restrained and in its own way central reference to marriage and posterity. Did they not realise what was involved? Did they not see with what almost hopeless problems the amatory relationship between man and woman is actually burdened? . . . But the author of Gen 2 knew well enough of the ruin of that relationship . . . And we can hardly complain that the rest of the Solomonic literature suffers from illusions regarding the true state of affairs as between man and woman; that it has not seen the abysses and morasses by which the relationship is criss-crossed. . . . [T]he only explanation is that the authors of the creation saga and these love songs had in mind another covenant, stained and spotted, almost unrecognisable in historical reality, and yet concluded, sealed, persisting, and valid.[143]

For Barth, Song of Songs vividly portrays the persistence of the divine grace in spite of all sin and corruption.

Barth brings out an important point. The freedom and openness with which the lovers express their desire for each other is in its own way as great an offense to religion dominated by law as is the Pauline gospel with its rejection of circumcision as being essential for entry into the church.

The Bible, as Barth has well noted, has no illusions about the destructive power of lust—one could hardly find a better statement of this than Prov 7. Marriage and fidelity within marriage are everywhere set forth as the boundaries of sexuality. But Song of Songs, unlike Proverbs, is not a series of warnings on the dangers of sexuality and the need for chastity. It is instead a celebration of the joy and passion of love. Although it in no sense denies the tragedy of sin and the fall, Song of Songs does not go the way of Gnostic asceticism and legal religion and thus assert the creation itself to be an evil thing that must be suppressed, denied, and imprisoned (for that matter, neither does Proverbs).

The religion of the ascetic fears that if the joy of physical love is not condemned as an innate evil, the mind will forget spiritual things and instead plunge into ever deeper corruption. In the same way, it rejects the gospel of salvation by grace through faith on the grounds that it inevitably leads to more sinning "that grace may abound." In its attempt to build a wall around the human soul, legal religion only separates the sinner further from God and gives him or her a false hope of escaping the intermingled yearnings and lusts of the heart.

---

[143]K. Barth, *Church Dogmatics*, III. 1. 313-14.

Biblical faith sees asceticism as it truly is, as both a denial of the goodness of God's creation and as an attempt to conceal the radical nature of human sin behind superficial obedience to the laws of religion. The man and woman of God should no more be slaves to sensuality than they should be gluttons, but the enjoyment of creation and the fulfillment of the drive toward one another is no sin. The united love of the man and woman in Song of Songs is, as Barth perceived, a fulfillment of the creation covenant and a reenactment of the love of the first man and the first woman. It is not a parable; but it is, for the believer, a part of the testimony of the power of grace over sin and the flesh.

The Song presents sexuality as a *good thing protected by marriage and not as an evil thing made permissible by marriage.* The latter attitude has been all too common in Christendom. As H. Gollwitzer has written, "No one church has done better than another; all have operated under the prejudice of a Neoplatonic hostility to the body and to sex."[144]

A neglected point in the study of Song of Songs is that it is not only the similarities but also the *differences* between the Song and ancient Egyptian, Canaanite, and Mesopotamian texts that bring out its meaning. It has already been noted that Song of Songs contains no aphrodisiac prayers for success in love. Also, contrary to the cultic and funerary interpretations, it has no allusions to love play among the gods. It never implies that the sexuality of the couple has any cultic or ritual significance or that their joining promotes the mythical powers of fertility in the renewal of nature.

Simply put, the act of sex is not a religious act. This may seem obvious enough to some, but ancient pagans would have by no means shared this view. The cults of the ancient world, from India to the Mediterranean, promoted sexuality as a ritual of religious devotion. Some medieval Jews also considered marital relations a duty on Sabbath eve.[145] In the modern era recent theological perspectives (particularly radical feminist theology) have sought once again to merge religion and eroticism in a manner unknown in the West since pre-Christian paganism.[146]

None of this, however, is implied in the Song. There the joy of love between man and woman is a wonderful but fleeting pleasure. It has no ritual powers. The effect of this is to make sexual love natural and in fact restrained because it is in its proper sphere. Sexuality falls into its great-

---

[144]H. Gollwitzer, *Song of Love: A Biblical Understanding of Sex*, trans. K. Crim (Philadelphia: Fortress, 1979), 72.

[145]Cf. Pope, *Song*, 158-79.

[146]A programmatic text within this movement might be M. Daly, *Beyond God the Father* (Boston: Beacon, 1973). For an example of an explicit return to paganism within feminist theology, see C. P. Christ, *Laughter of Aphrodite: Reflections on a Journey to the Goddess* (San Francisco: Harper & Row, 1987), especially pp. 176-78 on the religious transcendence of sexuality.

est perversion and excess when it is mythologized and given cosmic significance. For evidence of this, one need look no further than the Mesopotamian and Canaanite texts.

It is in this light that we note that Song of Songs is not stark eroticism but is indeed a highly romantic book. The point is so obvious from the imagery and language of the book that it might be thought hardly worth mentioning, but it is often ignored. Note that the lovers speak to and of each other frequently and in great detail. They relish their pleasure in each other not only with physical action but with carefully composed words. Love is, above all, a matter of the mind and heart and should be declared.

The lesson for the reader is that he or she needs to speak often and openly of his or her joy in the beloved, the spouse. This is, for many lovers, a far more embarrassing revelation of the self than anything that is done with the body. But it is precisely here that the biblical ideal of love is present—in the uniting of the bodies and hearts of the husband and wife in a bond that is as strong as death. Many homes would be happier if men and women would simply *speak* of their love for one another a little more often.

Does the text promote monogamy? A number of scholars have argued that it nowhere refers to marriage; and they insist, in fact, that the couple is unmarried. Yet it is hard to imagine anything more likely to blemish the romantic yearnings of the lovers for each other than the notion that they may have an "open relationship." "I belong to my lover and his desire is for me" (7:10), if it means anything at all, means that the two belong to each other exclusively. More than that, as demonstrated previously, there is adequate evidence to assert that the theme of the Song is the love felt between a man and a woman as they approach and experience their wedding. The ideal of marriage, exclusive love, is everywhere present.

In the same way, the text speaks against other forms of sexual behavior (homosexuality, etc.) not by decree but by example. The Song of Songs portrays how the sexual longings of man and woman ought to be fulfilled.

The romantic unity of man and woman naturally draws us to the question of whether there is also an equality between the man and woman in Song of Songs. Readers have observed that the real central figure of Song of Songs is the woman. She is the principal singer of the Song, and most of the man's lines are taken up in descriptions of her beauty.

For some, therefore, Song of Songs is a statement in behalf of the liberation of women and a beginning of the depatriarchalizing process of calling humanity back to the pristine equality of paradise. One must, however, voice several qualifications. First of all, Song of Songs never takes an advocacy stance regarding the place of women in society. It never implies that a differentiation of roles between the sexes is wrong or in need of change.

Second, it is not clear that the romance and tenderness of Song of Songs is enhanced by a feminist reading. The vigor of the man (e.g., 2:8-9; 3:7-9) and the loveliness and pleasures of the woman (7:6-8) are what endear them to each other. That is not to say that the woman is presented as a pampered hothouse flower (see 1:6), but then again the Bible never asserts this to be an ideal of womanhood (cf. Ruth; Prov 31:10-31). Masculinity and femininity are still distinct traits, however, and they serve to heighten rather than diminish affection between man and woman.

On the other hand, even though the Song of Songs has little to say in the areas of current sexual politics and can hardly be taken as an advocate of unisex roles, it does present man and woman as equal in love. That is, the mutual exchange of affection is not restrained on grounds that the passions of love are unbecoming to a woman or are the exclusive privilege of the man.

This open exchange, moreover, leads to an openness and mutuality in the whole life of the marriage relationship. As in Gen 2 there is a partnership and organic unity between man and woman.

Finally, one may ask if Song of Songs preaches Christ. As argued earlier, the Song does not present us with an allegorical portrait of Christ and the church. It is Christocentric, however, in the same sense that practical teachings of Proverbs and Deuteronomy are Christocentric. Christ is both Lord over the created order and giver of life (Col 1:15-20; John 5:40). God originally pronounced the creation of man and woman "good" and decreed that their union should be the most profound of human relationships (Gen 1:27-31; 2:18-25), and Christ brings this aspect of mortal life to a realization of the creation ideal. Our sexuality and need for a partner is part of our humanity, and in Christ we are most fully and truly human.

It is in the sphere of a new covenant relationship with God in Christ, with transformed attitudes, Spirit-driven enablement, and the awareness of sins forgiven (Jer 31:31-34; Ezek 36:24-30) that husband and wife can find the union of openness and the fullness of blessing God intended (Gen 2:24-25).

9. Summary

The Song of Songs is a song of love written during the Solomonic period. It is neither allegory, drama, hymn, history, nor ceremonial text. Rather, it is a song of love in two parts, the man's and the woman's, assisted by a chorus. Other representatives of the genre of love song are found from Egypt, ca. 1300–1100 B.C., and the Egyptian examples share many elements in common with the Song. The message is that the mutual pleasures of love are good and possible even in this fallen world. The Song is a testimony to the grace of God and a rejection of *both* asceticism and debauchery.

OUTLINE OF THE BOOK

1. Introduction (1:1)
2. Soprano (1:2-4a)
3. Chorus (1:4b)
4. Soprano (1:4c-7)
5. Chorus (1:8)
6. Tenor (1:9-11)
7. Soprano (1:12-14)
8. Tenor (1:15)
9. Soprano (1:16)
10. Tenor (1:17)
11. Soprano (2:1)
12. Tenor (2:2)
13. Soprano (2:3-10a)
14. Tenor (2:10b-15)
15. Soprano (2:16-17)
16. Soprano (3:1-5)
17. Chorus (3:6-11)
18. Tenor (4:1-15)
19. Soprano (4:16)
20. Tenor (5:1a,b)
21. Chorus (5:1c)
22. Soprano (5:2-8)
23. Chorus (5:9)
24. Soprano (5:10-16)
25. Chorus (6:1)
26. Soprano (6:2-3)
27. Tenor (6:4-9)
28. Chorus (6:10)
29. Soprano (6:11-12)
30. Chorus (6:13a)
31. Tenor (6:13b–7:9a)
32. Soprano (7:9b–8:4)
33. Chorus (8:5a)
34. Soprano (8:5b-7)
35. Chorus (8:8-9)
36. Soprano (8:10-12)
37. Tenor (8:13)
38. Soprano (8:14)
39. A Postscript to the Song

OUTLINE OF THE BOOK

1. Introduction (1:1)
2. Soprano (1:2-4a)
3. Chorus (1:4b)
4. Soprano (1:4c-7)
5. Chorus (1:8)
6. Tenor (1:9-11)
7. Soprano (1:12-14)
8. Tenor (1:15)
9. Soprano (1:16)
10. Tenor (1:17)
11. Soprano (2:1)
12. Tenor (2:2)
13. Soprano (2:3-10a)
14. Tenor (2:10b-15)
15. Soprano (2:16-17)
16. Soprano (3:1-5)
17. Chorus (3:6-11)
18. Tenor (4:1-15)
19. Soprano (4:16)
20. Tenor (5:1a,b)
21. Chorus (5:1c)
22. Soprano (5:2-8)
23. Chorus (5:9)
24. Soprano (5:10-16)
25. Chorus (6:1)
26. Soprano (6:2-3)
27. Tenor (6:4-9)
28. Chorus (6:10)
29. Soprano (6:11-12)
30. Chorus (6:13a)
31. Tenor (6:13b–7:9a)
32. Soprano (7:9b–8:4)
33. Chorus (8:5a)
34. Soprano (8:5b-7)
35. Chorus (8:8-9)
36. Soprano (8:10-12)
37. Tenor (8:13)
38. Soprano (8:14)
39. A Postscript to the Song

1. Introduction (1:1)

[1]Solomon's Song of Songs.

1:1 This verse is the title; the song actually begins in v. 2. Unlike the superscripts to many psalms, this verse makes no attempt to tie the Song to any event or person in Solomon's life (contrast, for example, the superscript to Ps 51). From this one might infer that the Israelites had no tradition linking the Song to any historical episode.[1]

In the Song that follows, only three singing parts are evident: a male, a female, and a female chorus. While one could hypothesize that there are more than these three parts (e.g., a male chorus), such a hypothesis is supported by little if any information in the text itself. Some theorize, for example, that 8:8-9 is sung by a male chorus of "brothers," but evidence is lacking. In the absence of any compelling reason to suppose otherwise, it is best to assume that there are only the three basic parts.

The three take turns singing their parts, but they do not follow a consistent sequence. At times it is difficult to tell who is singing a given line or strophe of lyrics because the Hebrew text does not delineate the parts. Usually, however, it is self-evident from the gender of the pronouns used and other explicit details.

In the following comments, I have designated the male part "tenor," the female part "soprano," and the chorus simply as "chorus." The designations "tenor" and "soprano" are obviously arbitrary, but they serve a purpose. They convey the sense that these are *parts of a song* and *not characters in a play or story*. One cannot understand the Song if one does not recognize that it is lyric poetry and not drama.[2]

2. Soprano (1:2-4a)

[2]Let him kiss me with the kisses of his mouth—
for your love is more delightful than wine.
[3]Pleasing is the fragrance of your perfumes;
your name is like perfume poured out.
No wonder the maidens love you!
[4]Take me away with you—let us hurry!
Let the king bring me into his chambers.

---

[1]Cf. R. E. Murphy, *The Song of Songs*, Her (Minneapolis: Fortress, 1990), 120-22.

[2]By "lyric poetry" I refer to poetry that probably was sung to some kind of music, however it was performed in the ancient world. It does not strictly tell a story or follow chronological sequence but uses a series of images, some of them almost surreal, in order to create verbal pictures and convey emotional responses. In classical literature one might contrast the lyric poetry of Pindar with the epic poetry of Homer and the dramatic poetry of Sophocles.

1:2 She desires his kisses.[3] The point of comparison between his lovemaking[4] and wine is twofold: (1) it is sweet upon the lips (the kiss), and (2) it has an intoxicating effect. Note the shift from third to second person, which is common in the Song. Thus the shift back to the third person in v. 4 ("The king has brought me") does not mean that "the king" is someone other than her lover, as in the three-character interpretation.[5]

1:3 The structure of v. 3a indicates that it is a continuation of the comparison in v. 2b. The whole of vv. 2b-3a should be translated: "Your caresses are better than wine,/they are better than the fragrance of your perfumes."[6] His love excites her senses as does fine perfume. Even his name is a source of pleasure (v. 3b),[7] and she considers herself the luckiest of young women that he has chosen her (v. 3c).

1:4a She calls him a king, but this is not to be understood literally; rather it is the language of love. Going to his chambers implies that the wedding night is meant.

3. Chorus (1:4b)

We rejoice and delight in you;
we will praise your love more than wine.

1:4b The woman's friends enhance her appreciation for the man by joining in his praise. It is possible the singer here is still the woman rather than a chorus of women. The ease with which the Song changes person,

---

[3]There is no need to emend נשק ("kiss") to שקה ("give a drink"). Cf. Murphy, *Song*, 125.

[4]דֹּדִים is not love in the abstract but the act of making love. Cf. Prov 7:18; Ezek 16:8 (עֵד דֹּדִים ["time of lovemaking"]); and Ezek 23:17 (מִשְׁכַּב דֹּדִים ["love-bed"]).

[5]Cf. R. Gordis, *The Song of Songs and Lamentations* (New York: KTAV, 1954), 78.

[6]The ל in לְרֵיחַ has occasioned much comment, but it is best to take as emphatic (cf. B. K. Waltke and M. O'Connor, *An Introduction to Biblical Hebrew Syntax* [Winona Lake, Ind.: Eisenbrauns, 1990], 11.2.10h) and as in effect continuing the force of the preceding מִן (Murphy, *Song*, 125). The final טוֹבִים cannot refer to the fragrance, as in the NIV, since that would require a singular predicate adjective in agreement with the noun רֵיחַ. Cf. M. H. Pope, *Song of Songs*, AB (Garden City: Doubleday, 1977), 300. The chiastic structure of the line implies that 2b-3a is to be taken as a unity:

A טוֹבִים דֹּדֶיךָ
B מִיָּיִן
B′ לְרֵיחַ שְׁמָנֶיךָ
A′ טוֹבִים

[7]The meaning of שֶׁמֶן תּוּרַק is uncertain. Often, following the LXX ἐκχεόμενον, the hophal participle מוּרָק is read "poured out" (thus NIV). M. V. Fox (*The Song of Songs and the Ancient Egyptian Love Songs* [Madison: University of Wisconsin, 1985], 98) argues that "poured out" does not enhance the meaning and takes it as a specific type of oil, the "Oil of Turac." But pouring out perfume may allude to perfume extravagantly used for maximum fragrance.

without necessarily a change of singer, has already been observed. It is clear, however, from "How right they are to adore you" (v. 4), parallel to "No wonder the maidens love you" (v. 3),[8] that the text actually speaks of the swooning of *other* women over the man's virility. As such, it is best to regard this line as belonging to a chorus. This brief line introduces the chorus to the audience.

4. Soprano (1:4c-7)

How right they are to adore you!
5Dark am I, yet lovely,
O daughters of Jerusalem,
dark like the tents of Kedar,
like the tent curtains of Solomon.
6Do not stare at me because I am dark,
because I am darkened by the sun.
My mother's sons were angry with me
and made me take care of the vineyards;
my own vineyard I have neglected.
7Tell me, you whom I love, where you graze your flock
and where you rest your sheep at midday.
Why should I be like a veiled woman
beside the flocks of your friends?

1:4c-5 The woman is embarrassed and defensive about her dark skin. In contrast to modern standards of beauty, the ancients in Israel regarded light skin as most attractive. Dark skin identified her as of the laboring class and left her vulnerable to scorn that, as Fox notes, "would originate in social, not racial, prejudices."[9]

"Like the tent curtains of Solomon" is problematic. Some commentators emend the pointing to read "Salma," the name of an Arabian tribe, instead of "Solomon." This has the virtue of creating a parallel to "Kedar," but it is without supporting evidence and in fact obscures the whole point of the line.[10] The two comparisons are set in parallel to the two previous statements about her appearance: She is black, like the tents of Kedar. The tents of the bedouin are blackened by exposure to the elements and are strong enough to endure the desert climate.[11] On the other hand, she is beautiful

---

[8] עַל־כֵּן עֲלָמוֹת אֲהֵבוּךָ ("therefore girls love you") is parallel to מֵישָׁרִים אֲהֵבוּךָ ("rightly they love you").

[9] Fox, *Song*, 101. The line should thus be translated, "I am black but beautiful," not "*and* beautiful," notwithstanding the extravagant exploration of the latter possibility in Pope, *Song*, 307-18. Cf. Murphy, *Song*, 126.

[10] "Solomon" is supported by the ancient versions.

[11] Gordis, *Song*, 79.

like the tent curtains of Solomon.[12] These curtains, one would assume, were of exquisite craftsmanship.[13] In contrast to the chorus of urban girls, she is both hardened by the elements and yet beautiful.

1:6 She now describes the experiences that gave her dark skin. The reason for the brothers' anger is not given; the only significant point is that she was completely under their domination (thus the motif of the authority figure). She uses a wordplay with "vineyard": because she had to tend the family vineyard, she could not take care of her own "vineyard," meaning her body.[14] Working outside, she was darkened by the sun.[15] She therefore does not have the pampered beauty of urban women of the upper class.

1:7 She now addresses the man. Pastoral imagery is common in love poetry. In asking where he pastures his sheep during the heat of the day, she is asking where she can find him at a time when the sheep would be resting and not demanding his complete attention. She is seeking a rendezvous. The question, "Why should I be like a veiled woman?" means that if she does not know precisely where he is to be found, she will have to put on her veil and go from pasture to pasture looking for her beloved.[16]

5. Chorus (1:8)

8If you do not know, most beautiful of women,
follow the tracks of the sheep
and graze your young goats
by the tents of the shepherds.

1:8 Often taken as the man's answer to her question, v. 8 is anything but a clear set of directions. It could be taken as a mild and even playful

---

[12]Thus the structure of the line is:

A: שְׁחוֹרָה אֲנִי
B: וְנָאוָה
C: בְּנוֹת יְרוּשָׁלָם
A′: כְּאָהֳלֵי קֵדָר
B′: כִּירִיעוֹת שְׁלֹמֹה

[13]Note that יְרִיעָה ("curtain, fabric") is used of the elaborate curtains of the tabernacle in Exod 26.

[14]Other wordplays include that the sun "looked upon" (שׁזף) her, implying that, under the authority of her brothers, she has been looked upon by the sun but not by a man and that the brothers "burned with anger" (חרה, niphal stem) toward her, with an obvious play on the burning effect of the sun on her skin (שׁזף = שׁדף, see note below).

[15]שׁזף generally means "to see," but Murphy (*Song*, 126) points out that it is here equivalent to שׁדף, "burn."

[16]Numerous commentators have drawn attention to the similarity between this and Gen 38:14. The woman may imply that if she veils herself and goes wandering among the flocks and shepherds, she will be thought a prostitute. In any case, there is no need to emend the text. Cf. Pope, *Song*, 330-32, and Murphy, *Song*, 131.

rebuke: "You ought to know[17] where to find me; if not, seek me out where shepherds are found." On the other hand, it could be an invitation to join the community of shepherds with the assurance that she will be one among equals there with him, as opposed to the oppression she felt among her brothers (v. 6).[18] Otherwise, it may simply be a tease on his part.[19] A more satisfactory solution is to read this as not the man's but the chorus's line, as Exum demonstrated.[20] They urge her to find her beloved among the tents of the shepherds. The pastoral language and the "tents" imply a love setting, and the tone may be of mild rebuke. She ought to go where he may be found.

6. Tenor (1:9-11)

[9]I liken you, my darling, to a mare
harnessed to one of the chariots of Pharaoh.
[10]Your cheeks are beautiful with earrings,
your neck with strings of jewels.
[11]We will make you earrings of gold,
studded with silver.

1:9-11 The man is at the same time a rustic shepherd (v. 8) and yet able to give his beloved gold jewelry (v. 11). Again, however, this is not to be pressed literally. Both the pastoral language and the mention of fine jewelry heighten the sense of joy in love. The former conveys the image of that which is natural, and the latter makes the impression that love is of great value and adorns the woman.

Verses 9-11 are a brief admiration song of three bicola. The language is far removed from modern, Western poetry and thus may confuse the modern reader. He is not saying she looks like a horse! The horses that drew the pharaoh's chariots[21] were heavily decorated with ornaments and embroidery. The impression conveyed was one of great beauty combined with regal dignity, and it is this he ascribes to the woman.[22]

---

[17]This may be the implication of the לָךְ added to אִם־לֹא תֵדְעִי. Cf. Fox, *Song*, 103.

[18]Cf. F. Landy, *Paradoxes of Paradise: Identity and Difference in the Song of Songs* (Sheffield: Almond, 1983), 171-75.

[19]Murphy, *Song*, 134.

[20]J. C. Exum, "A Literary and Structural Analysis of the Song of Songs," *ZAW* 85 (1973): 47-79, describes on p. 72 the following chiastic structure in 1:5-11:

A: (vv. 5-6) נָאוָה [woman to daughters];
B: (v. 7) תִּרְעֶה [woman to man];
B′: (v. 8) רְעִי and הָרֹעִים [daughters to woman];
A′: (vv. 9-11) נָאווּ [man to woman].

[21]V. 9 could be rendered, "I liken you, my girlfriend, to a mare in the chariotry of pharaoh." The י in לְסֻסָתִי is not the pronoun suffix but the old genitive ending. See GKC, 90, l-n.

[22]It is doubtful that military imagery is meant here, contrary to Pope, *Song*, 336-41. Cf. Fox, *Song*, 105.

7. Soprano (1:12-14)

12While the king was at his table,
my perfume spread its fragrance.
13My lover is to me a sachet of myrrh
resting between my breasts.
14My lover is to me a cluster of henna blossoms
from the vineyards of En Gedi.

1:12 The woman answers in kind with a song of three bicola. She first calls him "king" and then likens him to aromatic plants. The former is no more to be taken literally than the latter. Her perfume giving off its fragrance in his presence may refer to her arousal as well as to her attractiveness (v. 12).[23]

1:13 This could be rendered more accurately as, "A sachet of myrrh is my lover to me/between my breasts he will sleep." She is saying that she will experience his "fragrance" (both literally and metaphorically) when they sleep together.[24] The image of the man as a small sachet of myrrh between her breasts is striking. He is as it were of diminutive size and overwhelmed by her love when nestled there.[25]

1:14 Semitropical vegetation, including Henna, grew at the oasis of En Gedi on the western shore of the Dead Sea. The idea is of rare fragrances of the highest value brought from afar.

8. Tenor (1:15)

15How beautiful you are, my darling!
Oh, how beautiful!
Your eyes are doves.

1:15 The man responds with an exclamation of admiration. Eyes like doves perhaps means either rounded or tranquil in appearance.

9. Soprano (1:16)

16How handsome you are, my lover!
Oh, how charming!
And our bed is verdant.

1:16 The woman again responds in kind and again refers to the bed[26] (v. 12). "Our bed is verdant" means it is lush and luxurious, like a tree thick with foliage.

---

[23]Fox (*Song*, 106) also suggests that the perfume (lit. "spikenard") may have erotic implications.

[24]לין is not simply to "rest" but to "spend the night."

[25]Cf. Landy, *Paradoxes*, 83.

[26]Gordis (*Song*, 80) suggests that עַרְשֵׂנוּ may mean "our arbor."

10. Tenor (1:17)

This could be taken as a continuation of the woman's section, but it appears that from 1:15–2:2 the man and woman are engaged in rapid exchange of one-verse lines.

17The beams of our house are cedars;
our rafters are firs.

1:17 It was a luxury to have a house paneled with cedar, but this is not an actual house but an arbor of cedar and cypress. Even this has no literal referent but is a highly romanticized vision of the idyllic love setting.

11. Soprano (2:1)

1I am a rose of Sharon,
a lily of the valleys.

2:1 The flowers mentioned here are not the modern namesakes. The "rose of Sharon" probably is a crocus, daffodil, or narcissus. The "lily" refers to a flower of an unknown variety. Fox correctly notes that this is not self-praise but a very modest self-appraisal on her part.[27] She is saying that she is only one of many flowers (i.e., girls).

12. Tenor (2:2)

2Like a lily among thorns
is my darling among the maidens.

2:2 Again the man's evaluation of her worth is far higher than her own. Compared to her, all other women are thorns. His love is exclusive and not distracted by others.

13. Soprano (2:3-10a)

3Like an apple tree among the trees of the forest
is my lover among the young men.
I delight to sit in his shade,
and his fruit is sweet to my taste.
4He has taken me to the banquet hall,
and his banner over me is love.
5Strengthen me with raisins,
refresh me with apples,
for I am faint with love.
6His left arm is under my head,
and his right arm embraces me.

[27]Fox, *Song*, 107.

7Daughters of Jerusalem, I charge you
by the gazelles and by the does of the field:
Do not arouse or awaken love
until it so desires.

8Listen! My lover!
Look! Here he comes,
leaping across the mountains,
bounding over the hills.
9My lover is like a gazelle or a young stag.
Look! There he stands behind our wall,
gazing through the windows,
peering through the lattice.
10My lover spoke and said to me,

2:3 Again she answers in kind (v. 3a) but then extends the praise of his love into vv. 3b-6, gives her first admonition to the Jerusalem girls (v. 7), and announces his arrival (vv. 8-10a). He is "like an apple[28] tree," that is, protective ("shade") and pleasurable ("his fruit").

2:4-6 "Banquet hall" is literally "house of wine."[29] Frequently taken to refer to some special location (a banquet hall, tavern, or shrine), it is often drawn into the debate concerning the original setting of the Song. For some it is the location of a wedding celebration, whereas for others it indicates that the Song deals with sacred fertility rites. The reference to "raisins"[30] is taken by some to support the latter notion (cf. Hos 3:1).[31]

Such interpretations, however, are misguided. It is clear from v. 6 that she is in his embrace; in vv. 4-5 she describes her experience in a series of comparisons. The "house of wine" is, as Fox indicates, simply any building where wine is drunk.[32] As a metaphor it means that he is bringing her to pleasures that are almost intoxicating, and the experience causes her to swoon (v. 5c). His intention (rather than "banner" [v. 4][33]) toward her is love, and she yearns for his love, as implied in, "I have the

[28]There is some doubt about whether תַּפּוּחַ is actually the apple. Fox (*Song*, 107) notes that the wild apple is neither palatable nor indigenous to Palestine and that the cultivated apple is recent. He suggests that this is the apricot. See also G. L. Carr, *The Song of Solomon*, TOTC (Downers Grove: InterVarsity, 1984), 89.

[29]בֵּית הַיָּיִן.

[30]The meaning of אֲשִׁישׁוֹת is uncertain, but "raisin cakes" appears probable. Cf. Pope, *Song*, 380.

[31]Cf. Pope, *Song*, 375-77.

[32]Fox, *Song*, 108.

[33]There is no doubt that דֶּגֶל can mean "banner," but it is almost impossible to ascertain what the metaphor "his banner over me is love" may mean. Several scholars, therefore, connect the word with Akkadian *diglu*, "wish, intention," which fits the present context well. See Gordis, *Song*, 81-2, and Pope, *Song*, 376.

love-sickness."[34] As in the Egyptian material, one who yearns for the love of another often describes himself or herself as sick.

She asks to be placed on a bed of raisins and other fruits. (The translations "strengthen" and "refresh" are possible, but an alternative interpretation, "to lay someone down on a bed," has equal if not greater probability [v. 5].[35] In either case, the object of her desire is not real fruit but his love.) As in 2:3 she associates the pleasures he gives with various fruits.

2:7 Two obvious problems here are (1) why does she make them swear by the gazelles and the does, and (2) what is the meaning of the charge she lays upon them?

The cultic interpretation sees here the use of animals in sexual incantations, as in other ancient texts.[36] But the passage gives no intimation that it is part of a magic spell. Others argue that this is circumlocution for the divine title, God Sabaoth (God Almighty).[37] Direct reference to God seems out of place here, however, especially since the flora and fauna of Israel play such a major role in the book.

In adjuring them by the female gazelles and does, she is drawing a picture of the female as beautiful, vigorous, and sexually active. In the same way, she will describe her beloved as a (male) gazelle or roe in 2:9. The reason for this is in the oath to which she calls the Jerusalem girls.

The charge not to arouse or waken love until it desires has been taken as a request that the Jerusalem girls leave the lovers alone and not awaken them[38] and, alternatively, as a request that the woman be allowed to dream about her lover,[39] but neither is plausible. She tells them not to arouse love itself. The charge is that the girls should not allow themselves

---

[34]This interpretation of כִּי־חוֹלַת אַהֲבָה אָנִי is more suitable than, "I am faint with love," which is periphrastic.

[35]See Fox, *Song*, 108-9. The word סמך means "to lay, rest, or support." Only here does it appear in the piel stem, and the meaning "to cause to lie down" is reasonable. On the other hand, the meaning "to sustain" in the sense of providing food is attested in the qal stem of Gen 27:37. The parallel verb רפד, however, means "to spread out" (piel stem) and is found in Job 17:13, "If I spread out my bed." Thus רַפְּדוּנִי בַּתַּפּוּחִים would mean "Spread me out on apricots." On balance the meaning "to lay (someone) on a bed" seems probable for the verbs. Whichever meaning is preferred, however, the concept is metaphorical—the man's love is likened to delicious fruit—and not literal. The plural imperatives are addressed to no one in particular but are exclamatory.

[36]Pope (*Song*, 386) notes that such animals were sacred to Astarte and cites a Mesopotamian incantation for impotence. But the chant uses the male stag rather than the female gazelle as in our text.

[37]צְבָאוֹת "gazelles" = צְבָאוֹת "(Yahweh) Sabaoth," and אַיְלוֹת "does" = אֱלֹהִים "God." Cf. Fox, *Song*, 110. While I doubt that this is to be taken as a veiled oath in God's name, a play on words may be operating here.

[38]Fox, *Song*, 110.

[39]F. Delitzsch, *The Song of Songs*, trans. M. G. Easton, reprint ed. (Grand Rapids: Eerdmans, n.d.), 46-47.

to be aroused sexually until the proper time and person arrives. The natural joy of sexual awakening is ruined by premature experimentation. Thus it is that she adjures them by the doe and gazelle: for a woman to awaken love before it pleases is to deprive herself of the full experience of romance and sexuality symbolized by these graceful animals.

2:8-10a The vigor and grace of the gazelle[40] or stag is now applied to the man (masculine forms are used here) in this arrival song. His peering through the window is a silent invitation for her to come to him, as is made explicit in v. 10b.

14. Tenor (2:10b-15)

"Arise, my darling,
my beautiful one, and come with me.
11 See! The winter is past;
the rains are over and gone.
12 Flowers appear on the earth;
the season of singing has come,
the cooing of doves
is heard in our land.
13 The fig tree forms its early fruit;
the blossoming vines spread their fragrance.
Arise, come, my darling;
my beautiful one, come with me."
14 My dove in the clefts of the rock,
in the hiding places on the mountainside,
show me your face,
let me hear your voice;
for your voice is sweet,
and your face is lovely.
15 Catch for us the foxes,
the little foxes
that ruin the vineyards,
our vineyards that are in bloom.

His invitation is couched in a marvelous picture of the arrival of springtime. The connection between this season and loveplay is universal.

2:11-13 The beauty of these verses as a portrait of the arrival of spring is universally acknowledged. The translation "season of singing" in v. 12 is uncertain; it could be "time of pruning."[41]

---

[40] Murphy (*Song*, 139) notes that there is a play on the two meanings of צְבִי, "gazelle" and "beauty."

[41] The word זָמִיר is a hapax legomenon and could be related to either of two roots זמר, "to cut" or "to sing." Murphy (*Song*, 138) prefers "pruning."

2:14 The description of her as a dove in the clefts of the rocks suggests that she is inaccessible. This theme will be taken up in several of the man's songs.

2:15 This verse is a major enigma. It is not clear whether the singer is the man or the woman (or both of them or the chorus), and the meaning of the verse is much disputed. Proposed interpretations are: (1) The blossoms are the woman, and the foxes are anything that might hinder her blossoming into full feminine charm. (2) The foxes are anything that might hinder the relationship between the couple and ruin the blossoming of their love.[42] (3) The vineyards are girls, and the foxes are lustful boys who would deflower them. In this interpretation the verse is either a moral warning or a coquettish tease spoken by the woman to the man. She in effect could be saying, "I know what you are up to!"[43] (4) The line is the woman's and should be translated, "Little foxes have seized us," meaning that she is no longer a virgin.[44] (5) The call to catch the foxes in the garden is a call to civilize the wildness and freedom inherent in the sexual experience (the foxes) and domesticate it. The "wild life" of sexuality is integrated into society.[45]

Despite the endless variety of interpretations that have been heaped upon v. 15, I rather doubt that either the "little foxes" or the "vineyard" has a specific referent here. The speaker probably is, as the NIV has it, the man. Prior to v. 16 there is no reason to suppose a change of speaker. More importantly the call to come catch foxes is a natural continuation of his invitation song begun in v. 10b. The diminutive "little" removes any sense that the foxes are a significant threat. The vineyard maintains the atmosphere of romance and love without specifically "symbolizing" anything. What is meaningful is that this is a call to join a chase—a chase that is really a game. The operative metaphor, therefore, is not the foxes or the vineyard but the chase itself. It is the kind of childlike play that young lovers often engage in. The verse thus speaks of the playfulness of love. He is calling her away to a game.

15. Soprano (2:16-17)

16My lover is mine and I am his;
he browses among the lilies.
17Until the day breaks
and the shadows flee,
turn, my lover,
and be like a gazelle

---

[42]Delitzsch, *Song*, 53-54.

[43]Fox, *Song*, 114.

[44]Gordis, *Song*, 83. This is to be rejected on several grounds: (1) the sentiment is quite out of place, (2) the woman does not refer to herself in the plural, and (3) the imperative form in the MT (אֶחֱזוּ) makes sense and need not be emended to the perfect.

[45]See Landy, *Paradoxes*, 240-41.

or like a young stag
on the rugged hills.

The woman concludes the first section of Song of Songs in 2:16-17 and begins part 2 with a separate solo in 3:1-5.

2:16 Both the man and the woman have called her a lily (2:1-2); to browse[46] among the lilies is thus to partake of the pleasures she offers him. The man has already been compared to a stag in 2:9 and is again in 2:17, and the same metaphor is implied here as he is likened to a stag "grazing" upon her.

2:17 "Until the day breaks" is literally "until the day breathes," and some have wondered whether it refers to nightfall or daybreak. Context and the parallel line "and the shadows flee" imply that it is daybreak.[47] Two other difficulties in this verse are the meaning of "turn" (is she telling him to turn toward her or to turn away and flee?) and the question of what referent is implied by the phrase "mountains of Bether" ("rugged hills" is odd and not to be followed).

The phrase "mountains of Bether" may be taken as a proper name or translated as "split mountains."[48] The Vulgate takes it as a proper name,[49] but the LXX renders it "mountains of hollow [places]."[50] The Peshitta reads it as "mountains of spices" on analogy with Song 8:14.[51] In fact, however, whether or not there really was a place called the "Split Mountains" in ancient Israel,[52] the nature of the allusion and the parallel in 4:5-6 indicate that the woman's breasts are meant.[53] At the beginning of the arrival song the man was like a gazelle leaping over mountains, and now, in a subtle shift of the metaphor, he is a gazelle that feeds on the "split mountains."

This implies that "turn" cannot mean "turn away and flee."[54] It makes no sense that she would say such a thing here anyway. The first part of

---

[46]רעה can mean "to shepherd a flock" and thus could be taken here to mean that he leads his flock among the lilies. But the meaning "to browse" or "to feed," i.e., that the man himself is feeding on the lilies, is confirmed by the parallel usage in Song 4:5.

[47]So also Pope, *Song*, 408; Carr, *Song*, 102-3; and Fox, *Song*, 115.

[48]הָרֵי בָתֶר. Cf. BDB, 144, and the NRSV, which render it "cleft mountains."

[49]*montes Bether.*

[50]ὄρη κοιλωμάτων.

[51]The phrase in 8:14 is הָרֵי בְשָׂמִים.

[52]A possibility I rather doubt, despite Fox (*Song*, 116), who attempts to relate the term to Bittir, a village southwest of Jerusalem.

[53]Not, as some have supposed, her vagina (see Pope, *Song*, 410), for which the figure "mountains" is inappropriate.

[54]Fox (*Song*, 115) argues that if "turn to me" were meant, "to me" would have to be explicitly stated; thus he takes it as "turn away." But in this context סב is little more than an auxiliary imperative anyway, almost like the auxiliary use of the imperatives of הלך (cf. 1 Sam 22:18; 2 Sam 18:30). The main imperative is דמה ("to be like"). "Turn, be like" does not imply anything about which *direction* he is to turn, only that he is to *be like* a gazelle.

the Song, a pure celebration of their love, ends with a call for him to enjoy the pleasures she gives.

16. Soprano (3:1-5)

1All night long on my bed
I looked for the one my heart loves;
I looked for him but did not find him.
2I will get up now and go about the city,
through its streets and squares;
I will search for the one my heart loves.
So I looked for him but did not find him.
3The watchmen found me
as they made their rounds in the city.
"Have you seen the one my heart loves?"
4Scarcely had I passed them
when I found the one my heart loves.
I held him and would not let him go
till I had brought him to my mother's house,
to the room of the one who conceived me.
5Daughters of Jerusalem, I charge you
by the gazelles and by the does of the field:
Do not arouse or awaken love
until it so desires.

3:1-5 The interpretation of this passage is difficult. Four approaches are possible: the literal, the cultic, the dream, and the symbolic.

If it is understood literally, it means that she longed for her lover and wandered the streets until she found him. This would seem to indicate that they were not married since he appears to be living elsewhere and she wants to bring him to her mother's house. This difficulty might be overcome by assuming that this is a retrospective look to her days before the wedding, although such an interpretation is unnatural.

The most significant objection to the literal interpretation is the inherent peculiarity of what is described. First, it would be very strange for a girl in ancient Israel to wander the streets at night because she misses her boyfriend. Girls in ancient societies were fairly cloistered. A girl wandering the streets at night might well be taken as a prostitute (Prov 7:10; Hos 2:7). Also it is difficult to see her taking her boyfriend to her mother's house for a sexual liaison (v. 4). A woman was taken into the man's household at marriage. This is not to be understood as outside of marriage since taking the man to her parents' home for that purpose would be unthinkable in Israelite society.[55] As Pope comments, "A maiden (?) who

[55]To be sure, a "mother's house" can be literally just that (Gen 24:28; Ruth 1:8), but the literal meaning is too bizarre to be the intended meaning here.

misses her lover in bed, rises to roam the streets in search of him, and encounters the town guards (who in the parallel passage 5:7 beat her and take off her clothes) seems a dubious candidate for a village bride and the whole episode a questionable theme for a wedding song."[56]

The cultic interpretation here stresses the similarity between the woman's search for the man and the search of Anat for Baal.[57] Such an approach is hardly persuasive. The man has not encountered death and is not even in any danger, and the woman is no goddess. The alleged parallel is very thin.

The dream interpretation asserts that none of what is described is reality but is only a dream.[58] In this reading the dream may represent her fear of losing her beloved. The actual details of the passage, however, are still confusing. Why does she meet the guards? Why does she roam the streets (again, a very odd thing to do) and take her lover to her mother's house? Why, in the parallel sequence (5:2-8), is she beaten and stripped by the guards? To interpret all this as a dream is more of an escape than an exegesis. The real problems of the text are not solved but avoided under the argument that anything can happen in a dream.[59]

It is most likely that the entire sequence is symbolic; in a book as heavily symbolic as Song of Songs, this is not unusual. But what is conveyed in the symbolism?

If it can be assumed that this is a love song of the wedding of a couple, then the song is at this point moving toward the joining of the bride and groom. That being the case, one might expect the content of this text to reflect the woman's sexual desires and fears. The sustained use of sexual metaphor in the Song confirms this approach. The opening line, "Night after night[60] upon my bed[61] I sought[62] him whom my soul loves" affirms that the psychological world of the woman is in view.

This being the case, this portion is best read as a song of the woman's anxiety about the approaching loss of her virginity. Three key symbols are operative here: her wandering in the street in search of him, her meeting the guards of the city, and her desire to take the man to her mother's house.

---

[56]Pope, *Song*, 419.

[57]Cf. ANET, 141, and Pope, *Song*, 419-20.

[58]Thus Delitzsch, *Song*, 57.

[59]Cf. Pope, *Song*, 419.

[60]בַּלֵּילוֹת is best taken as "night after night" rather than "all night long." See Fox, *Song*, 118. Thus it is a prolonged period of anxious desire. Murphy (*Song*, 145), however, argues that it can simply mean "at night."

[61]Carr (*Song*, 105) notes that מִשְׁכָּב is often the love bed, as in Ezek 23:17; Gen 49:4; and Num 31:17ff.

[62]בקשׁ here is sexual desire. See Fox, *Song*, 118.

The wandering in the street is most clearly paralleled in Proverbs, in which both Lady Wisdom and the prostitute roam the streets in search of young men. Both figures desire to entice the young man (Prov 1:20-21; 7:10-13; 8:1-4). The desire to entice is not of itself good or evil since Wisdom herself follows this practice. Therefore, when the girl rises to search for her young man, it represents her desire to entice him as an act of love.

The guardians of the city are in the motif of the authority figure. The "city"[63] refers to the woman herself; she is "lovely as Jerusalem" (6:4).[64] For the woman the guardians can only represent her virginity.

The modern, Western reader may have difficulty in appreciating how significant this was to the ancient Israelite. The law provided, on penalty of death, that a woman must maintain proof that she was a virgin at marriage.[65] A priest could marry only a virgin (Lev 21:13). In commemorating Jephthah's daughter, Judg 11:39 points out that "she was a virgin," and 1 Kgs 1:2-3 specifically mentions that David's servants found a virgin to warm him and that he had no sexual relations with her. The Ammon story notes that Tamar "was a virgin, and *it seemed impossible* for [Ammon] to do anything to her" (2 Sam 13:2, emphasis added). A woman's virginity was very much her protection as well as her master.

The Israelite girl must have approached the day of losing her virginity with considerable anxiety. Song of Songs, because it deals with the emotions of love and the wedding day, naturally deals with this as well.

Verse 3 says that "the guards who encircle the city"[66] found her as she sought her beloved. It is *they* who suddenly come upon *her*. As her mind is drawn with desire for him, she is suddenly conscious that the full expression of her longing is restrained by the barrier her virginity creates. It intrudes upon her longing.

On the other hand, she *asks the guards* where her beloved is. No answer, of course, is given; the point is that she seeks her beloved through the very same authorities who separate her from the beloved. Virginity is an impediment between her and the man, but it is also the key to gaining him. She cannot obtain him without it.

Her determination to take the groom to "her mother's house" corroborates this interpretation. As mentioned earlier, this cannot be taken liter-

---

[63] עִיר is generally a walled city. See Carr, *Song*, 105.

[64] A parallel appears in Isa 62:5-6, in which Jerusalem is called a "bride" (כַּלָּה) and God declares he will set watchmen (שֹׁמְרִים) on her walls. In the Song the woman is called a city with watchmen; in Isaiah the city with watchmen is called a bride.

[65] Apparently the woman had to take a blood-stained sheet from her wedding night and leave it with her parents for safekeeping. See Deut 22:13-21 and compare P. C. Craigie, *The Book of Deuteronomy*, NICOT (Grand Rapids: Eerdmans, 1976), 292-93.

[66] הַשֹּׁמְרִים הַסֹּבְבִים בָּעִיר = the woman as city is guarded by the virginity that "encircles" her.

ally. That being the case, the mother's house, "the room of the one who conceived me," must represent the idea of the womb. This is the room in which all are conceived.[67] The bride is drawing strength from the fact that her mother also has gone through this experience and that indeed she owes her very existence to her mother's surrender of her virginity to her father.

The bride, therefore, has anxieties and misgivings about the loss of her virginity and reflects this in her song. Nevertheless, determined to take the man to herself, she embraces him: She seizes him *and will not let him go* until she has taken him to her "mother's house" (v. 4). Note that she meets him immediately after her encounter with the guards.

She will be able to have her beloved only after she has faced the issue of her virginity and is willing to turn from it to him. She triumphs over her fears and is determined to go through with the surrender of her virginity. Perhaps the point is that the woman who has not faced and dealt with this inner struggle is not prepared for the actual encounter with the marriage bed. The experience itself is described in the parallel song, 5:2-8.

The proverb that says not to arouse love until it desires (v. 5; also 2:7 and 8:4) supports this interpretation. It means that sexual love is to be avoided until the proper time (the wedding night) and the proper person arrive. If either the literal or the dream interpretations are followed, this warning makes no sense here. But in a context of the approach of the loss of virginity, the warning to the friends that they maintain their chastity until the right time comes is entirely appropriate.[68]

17. Chorus (3:6-11)

[6]Who is this coming up from the desert
like a column of smoke,
perfumed with myrrh and incense
made from all the spices of the merchant?
[7]Look! It is Solomon's carriage,
escorted by sixty warriors,
the noblest of Israel,
[8]all of them wearing the sword,
all experienced in battle,
each with his sword at his side,
prepared for the terrors of the night.
[9]King Solomon made for himself the carriage;
he made it of wood from Lebanon.
[10]Its posts he made of silver,
its base of gold.

---

[67]Cf. the discussions of 8:2,5.

[68]Murphy (*Song*, 147) notes that her adjuration implies that "love is not to be trifled with."

Its seat was upholstered with purple,
its interior lovingly inlaid
by the daughters of Jerusalem.
[11]Come out, you daughters of Zion,
and look at King Solomon wearing the crown,
the crown with which his mother crowned him
on the day of his wedding,
the day his heart rejoiced.

The question of who the singer is again arises. There are no grounds for seeing the woman as the singer of this part except that vv. 10-11 address the Jerusalem girls. But this does not establish that this portion cannot belong to the chorus. Although the chorus itself is composed of Jerusalem girls, it does not include *all* the girls of Jerusalem. It is more in character with the rest of the song for the chorus to summon other Jerusalem girls than for the woman herself to be calling excitedly for the chorus to come.

3:6 Another problem is that "this" in "Who is this?" is feminine, and yet the object of attention is apparently Solomon in his palanquin. For this reason Fox argues that v. 6 is sung by the girls when they see the woman coming but that the woman sings vv. 7-11 to draw attention to her beloved.[69] This interpretation is forced. Verses 7-11 obviously answer the question posed in v. 6, and the attempt to separate the verses as having two entirely distinct referents is unnatural. Instead, "Who is this?" is not to be taken to mean, "Who is this woman?" The word "this" is a neutrum[70] and refers to the whole spectacle in view.[71] When they say, "*Who* is this?" instead of "*What* is this?" it alludes to the fact that some person ("Solomon") is obviously at the center of the approaching marvel.

His approach from the wilderness (not "desert"[72]) heightens the dramatic nature of the arrival, as does the phrase "like a column of smoke."[73] "Wilderness" also conveys something of the character of Eden; it is the realm of innocence and purity in contrast to the artificial world of the city. As such it relates to the pastoral theme the book heavily develops. It is difficult to see why the historical Solomon would be arriving from the desert. The somewhat unreal nature of the scene is also

[69]Fox, *Song*, 119-27.

[70]Waltke and O'Connor (*Syntax*, 692) define a "neutrum" as "a grammatical element of vague or broad reference, often in Hebrew a feminine pronoun." The pronoun זאת often serves this function (p. 312).

[71]It is of course possible that זאת anticipates the feminine noun in v. 7 that answers the question of v. 6, מִטָּתוֹ ("his palanquin").

[72]מִדְבָּר; see Carr, *Song*, 108. Pope (*Song*, 424) prefers "steppe."

[73]תִּימְרוֹת is not the same word used for the pillar (עַמּוּד) of cloud that followed the Israelites in the wilderness, and it is doubtful that any connection is intended.

implied in the fact that the girls can apparently smell the perfume on the palanquin while it is still in the distance.

3:7-11 The reference to "Solomon"[74] does not mean that Solomon is the singer of the man's part or a *character* in the song. Instead, the figure of Solomon is a poetic symbol and foil here.[75]

On the one hand, every young man in love is a *Solomon in all his glory.* The portrait of the man making a dramatic arrival is perhaps drawn from a wedding custom, in which a groom makes a grand entry at his wedding feast. Particularly relevant is Matt 25:6, if the custom described there has more ancient roots. In the parable the excitement of the ten virgins at the advent of the groom is reminiscent of the excitement of the Jerusalem girls here. Still, the groom of the Song is no more literally Solomon than he is literally a gazelle or apple tree. Solomon is the royal figure par excellence[76] and is a symbol for the glory that belongs to any groom.

On the other hand, Solomon is also a foil since young lovers really do not need the trappings of glory, as Solomon did; they have each other (see 8:11-12).

The NIV "carriage" (vv. 7,9) translates two different words. The word[77] in v. 7 can mean "bed" but is also used of a bier (2 Sam 3:31) and thus apparently of a palanquin or sedan chair. The word in v. 9 is a major difficulty. Its etymology is unknown,[78] but it appears to be used in parallel with v. 7.[79] Thus the two together refer to a palanquin.

The sixty warriors who guard against the "terrors" of the night (vv. 7-8) is also a difficulty. No meaningful relationship exists between sixty warriors and a wedding night, and thus a literalist interpretation is not helpful. For this reason some suggest that the warriors are something of a magical fetish meant to ward off demons who might invade the wedding

---

[74]Attempts to excise or emend שְׁלֹמֹה in this text are unpersuasive. See Pope, *Song*, 432-33.

[75]Murphy (*Song*, 151) observes that "Solomon is to be interpreted in line with the king fiction that dominates the entire work."

[76]Cf. Carr, *Song*, 109-10.

[77]מִטָּה.

[78]אַפִּרְיוֹן. Fox (*Song*, 125-27) rejects a derivation from the Sanskrit *paryanka* and argues that it is indirectly related to the Greek φορειον, "sedan-chair, litter." Yet on the basis of possible cognates from Targumic and Talmudic Aramaic, and in keeping with his thesis that vv. 7-11 are unrelated to v. 6, he contends that both מִטָּה and אַפִּרְיוֹן refer to a fixed bed rather than a litter. But his linguistic arguments are not compelling, and the poetic image created by his interpretation is too illogical to be persuasive. It is easy to see how the common girls of Jerusalem would be called to see the arrival of Solomon's sedan chair, but it is strange to think of them as called to come inspect his bed. Murphy (*Song*, 149) states that the etymology is uncertain.

[79]The position of Carr (*Song*, 111) that the two words refer to separate objects is unreasonable in context.

night and perhaps kill the groom.[80] Such a reading, however, is out of place; "terrors[81] of the night" is a general term for anything that gives rise to fright during the night and need not be exclusively demonic. The notion that the groom needs special protection is also out of place here.

Instead, the symbol of the sixty warriors is to be regarded as an attribute of the groom. His coming is both regal and splendid, but it is also powerful. He brings protection and strength with him. It is his courage, made concrete in the figure of the sixty warriors, that will protect the woman in the vulnerability of her night of love with him.

The other images in this song—the perfume, the precious metals, the crown—all add to the general portrait of the bridegroom's splendor and need not be thought to have some specific referent. One difficulty, however, is the phrase, "Its interior lovingly inlaid by the daughters of Jerusalem" (v. 10). A better translation of vv. 10c-11a would be, "Its interior is inlaid with love./O Jerusalem girls, come out,/and look, O Zion girls!" Contrary to the NIV, the chiastic structure of the last two lines separates them from "inlaid with love."[82] The phrase "inlaid with love" itself need not be emended[83] or treated adverbially as "lovingly." "Inlaid with love" subtly alludes to the association between "palanquin" and "bed" and hints at the purpose for the groom's approach, the wedding night.[84]

18. Tenor (4:1-15)

1How beautiful you are, my darling!
Oh, how beautiful!
Your eyes behind your veil are doves.
Your hair is like a flock of goats
descending from Mount Gilead.
2Your teeth are like a flock of sheep just shorn,
coming up from the washing.
Each has its twin;
not one of them is alone.

---

[80]For an extended discussion, see Pope, *Song*, 435-40.

[81]פחד is often associated with the fear of God, but there is no reason to associate it with demonic power or indeed with supernatural power generally.

[82]Reading בְּנוֹת יְרוּשָׁלָם צְאֶינָה וּרְאֶינָה בְּנוֹת צִיּוֹן. Pope (*Song*, 446) notes that the *mem* of מִבְּנוֹת can be left with אַהֲבָה as an emphatic enclitic.

[83]Fox (*Song*, 126) emends to אֲבָנִים, "stones." But proof is lacking, and אֲבָנִים is a rather prosaic term to use in this context. Contrast the rich vocabulary of Esth 1:6. If any emendation were to be made, a more probable candidate is that of G. R. Driver ("Supposed Arabisms in the Old Testament," *JBL* 55 [1936]: 111) that the word be rendered "leather" on the basis of an Arabic cognate.

[84]אַהֲבָה ("love") is here an abstract quality and not a concrete object. For this reason there is no need to associate this verse with the "ivory inlay of a love scene from the bed of a king of Ugarit" seen in Pope, *Song*, Plate II.

3Your lips are like a scarlet ribbon;
your mouth is lovely.
Your temples behind your veil
are like the halves of a pomegranate.
4Your neck is like the tower of David,
built with elegance;
on it hang a thousand shields,
all of them shields of warriors.
5Your two breasts are like two fawns,
like twin fawns of a gazelle
that browse among the lilies.
6Until the day breaks
and the shadows flee,
I will go to the mountain of myrrh
and to the hill of incense.
7All beautiful you are, my darling;
there is no flaw in you.

8Come with me from Lebanon, my bride,
come with me from Lebanon.
Descend from the crest of Amana,
from the top of Senir, the summit of Hermon,
from the lions' dens
and the mountain haunts of the leopards.
9You have stolen my heart, my sister, my bride;
you have stolen my heart
with one glance of your eyes,
with one jewel of your necklace.
10How delightful is your love, my sister, my bride!
How much more pleasing is your love than wine,
and the fragrance of your perfume than any spice!
11Your lips drop sweetness as the honeycomb, my bride;
milk and honey are under your tongue.
The fragrance of your garments is like that of Lebanon.
12You are a garden locked up, my sister, my bride;
you are a spring enclosed, a sealed fountain.
13Your plants are an orchard of pomegranates
with choice fruits,
with henna and nard,
14nard and saffron,
calamus and cinnamon,
with every kind of incense tree,
with myrrh and aloes
and all the finest spices.
15You are a garden
fountain,
a well of flowing water
streaming down from Lebanon.

The man's part here is divided into two sections, vv. 1-7,[85] an admiration song, and vv. 8-15, which begin with an invitation but then move on to praise the pleasures of the woman's love. The metaphors of the admiration song seem harsh and unnatural to the modern reader because we take them in too literal a sense. He is not describing so much how *she looks* but how *he feels* when he looks at her. Aspects of the woman's beauty provoke profound emotional responses.

4:1 "Doves" convey a sense of gentleness and tenderness. Fox points out that the cooing of doves may also be implied. Her eyes "communicate."[86] The veil[87] both hides and enhances her beauty. It appears that the veil was worn by aristocratic women and not by peasants, which contradicts the portrait of her in 1:6.[88] Concern for logical consistency in the imagery of the Song, however, is out of place. The figure of her hair being like a flock of goats skipping down[89] Mount Gilead corresponds somewhat to the actual appearance of hair flowing down over a girl's shoulder, but the sense of vitality conveyed and the sustaining of the pastoral ambiance are equally important.

4:2 The obvious message here is that her teeth are white and none are missing. Again, however, the picture of a flock that is clean and healthy (not a single lamb has died) tells us that the woman projects a sense of vigor and purity.[90]

4:3 The mouth is attractive too.[91] The "rosy glow" of her lips and cheeks[92] is not merely beautiful but wholesome; "pomegranate" recalls earlier usages of fruit as sexual metaphor, and the sense of desirable to kiss may be implied.

4:4 Her neck is like the tower of David in that both are statuesque and cause feelings of admiration and wonder. He does not mean that her

---

[85]Note the inclusio formed by יָפָה רַעְיָתִי in vv. 1 and 7.

[86]Fox, *Song*, 129.

[87]צַמָּה is probably "veil" and not "locks," as the KJV has. (See Carr, *Song*, 114.)

[88]See Fox, *Song*, 129.

[89]The meaning of גלשׁ is not established. BDB lists the meaning "sit," which implies that the picture is of a herd in repose on a mountainside. Pope (*Song*, 459) lists possible Egyptian and Ugaritic cognates, however, that indicate it may mean "to skip" or "stream down."

[90]Note also the wordplay in שֶׁכֻּלָּם . . . וְשַׁכֻּלָה.

[91]The phrase וּמִדְבָּרֵיךְ נָאוֶה is surprising on two grounds. First is that it uses מִדְבָּר for "mouth" rather than the much more common פִּי, and second is that it is oddly prosaic. Carr (*Song*, 116) says that מִדְבָּר was chosen *causa metri*, but this is not satisfactory. Fox (*Song*, 130) demonstrates that this is wordplay that could be heard as, "Your wilderness is an oasis" (on the basis of the more common usage for מִדְבָּר, "wilderness"), meaning that even her blemishes only enhance her beauty. Also the use of מִדְבָּר may imply that the words she speaks (cf. דָּבָר "word") and not just the shape of her mouth move him.

[92]רַקָּה probably is "cheek" or perhaps "brow" rather than "temple," which would be covered by hair anyway. See Carr, *Song*, 116; Fox, *Song*, 130; and Pope, *Song*, 464.

neck is outlandishly long.[93] What is striking in this analogy is the military terminology. The picture of a tower of David, Israel's great warrior king, adorned with the shields and weapons[94] of mighty men, cannot but convey a sense of unassailable strength.[95] No man could "conquer" her, and her suitor is awed by the dignity she carries. Her love is a gift; it could never become plunder.

4:5 The portrayal of the breasts as a pair of fawns draws on the sense of tenderness that such delicate animals impart.[96] Besides the obvious fact that there are two, no visual similarity is implied.

4:6-7 At the description of her breasts, the man breaks off from his admiration song and declares his intention to make love to her. His words echo her invitation in 2:17, where she spoke of loving until the break of day and where also the breasts were represented as mountains. His words in v. 6 could be translated, "I will get me to Myrrh Mountain and to Incense Hill!"[97] The naming of two "mountains" is not coincidental after his reference to the two breasts in v. 5.

The determination of the man to enjoy the pleasures of the woman is restrained by the fact that he will not and in fact cannot seize those pleasures by force; she must freely give them. The second part of his song (vv. 8-15), therefore, is an appeal for her to give herself to him in sexual union.

4:8 This verse should be translated: "Come from Lebanon, O bride,/ come from Lebanon, make your way!//Venture[98] from the summit of Amana,/from the summit of Senir and Hermon!//From dens of lions,/ from lairs[99] of leopards!" The words "with me" should not be understood here;[100] she is not *with him*, but he is *calling her to himself*. As in the picture

---

[93]Notwithstanding the notion that Egyptians considered a long neck attractive.

[94]שֶׁלֶט is best taken to mean "military equipment" (see Fox, *Song*, 131). תַּלְפִּיּוֹת is more difficult. It could mean "weaponry," but a better interpretation is "built in layers" from the root לפי. See Pope, *Song*, 467, and Gordis, *Song*, 86.

[95]But a rather farfetched reading is found in K. R. Crim, "'Your Neck Is Like the Tower of David' (The Meaning of a Simile in Song of Solomon 4:4)," *BT* 22 (1971): 70-74. He takes it to mean, "Your neck is like the tower of David,/round and smooth./A thousand famous soldiers/surrender their shields to its beauty" (p. 74).

[96]This sense is heightened by their feeding on lilies; cf. Fox, *Song*, 131. Contrary to Pope (*Song*, 470) this third colon need not be deleted.

[97]No mountains of these names actually existed in ancient Israel. Myrrh and frankincense are not indigenous to Palestine. Similarly, the effort of Delitzsch (*Song*, 78) to link this to the temple mount is unwarranted.

[98]This is not שׁור, "to gaze" but שׁור, "to travel"; BDB, 1003, chooses the meaning "gaze" here, but see Fox, *Song*, 135.

[99]מֵהַרְרֵי ("from the mountains of") should be emended to מֵחֹרֵי ("from the lairs of") because of the parallelism. Cf. the parallel use of מענה and חר with the sense "lion's den" in Nah 2:13.

[100]Read אתי as feminine singular imperative of אתה, "Come!" instead of the MT אִתִּי ("with me"). Cf. the LXX δεῦρο and the Vg *veni*.

of her neck like a warrior's tower (v. 4), he sees her as unassailable. She is high in the mountain peaks of the north and surrounded by prides of lions and leopards. This image is stunning. Pope sees here further proof that the woman is in fact a goddess, citing parallels to the myth of Venus and Adonis (Tammuz).[101] Such a mythical reading of the text is again unnecessary. While there is a goddess-like quality to the woman here—she dwells high on a mountain in the north and has the wild animals at her command—she is no more to be understood as an actual goddess than as a lily or as a garden. As the woman in various texts describes her state of mind, so the man here discloses his own perception of reality: he believes himself helpless and unable to attain her.

4:9 The Hebrew here is ambiguous and perhaps deliberately so. The sense of the verb could be either "you have taken away my heart"[102] in the sense of "I am hopelessly in love with you" or "you have 'heartened' me" in the sense of "you have sexually aroused me."[103] The cases for both meanings are strong, and it may be that both nuances were recognized by the ancient audience. If so, rather than decide between the two, one should read this as a double entendre; that is, the text implies both meanings are intended.

4:10-11 The man praises the pleasures of the woman's caresses.[104] He is not, however, describing his present experience but the object of his desire; his words are an appeal for her to lavish these enchantments on him. The emphasis on the scent of her perfume suggests that experiencing her love involves all the senses. The declaration that her lips and tongue taste like honey and milk describes her kisses. The assertion that her clothes have the fragrance of Lebanon in v. 11c seems odd in light of the parallel in v. 10c. Although "Lebanon" is possible in light of Hos 14:6, emending to "incense" is preferable.[105]

4:12-15 The man now describes his beloved under two metaphors, the locked garden and the sealed fountain. This shows fairly plainly that

---

[101]Pope, *Song*, 475-77.

[102]Taking לִבַּבְתִּנִי as a privative piel stem of לבב. See Delitzsch, *Song*, 81-82.

[103]Pope (*Song*, 479-80) demonstrates on the grounds of Mesopotamian usage that לבב could be taken to mean to arouse a man sexually. Principal evidence for this comes from the use of the term in ritual incantations against impotency. N. M. Waldman ("A Note on Canticles 4:9," *JBL* 89 [1970]: 215-17) argues that לבב means "to rage" and thus "to arouse sexually" on the analogy of the Greek development ὀργή ("wrath") ὀργάω ("to arouse"). See also Carr, *Song*, 120, n.1. Fox (*Song*, 136) rejects this understanding of the verb here on the grounds that the man of the Song shows no concern about his virility. The sexual sense of לבב does not imply that it was only used of men who had been formerly impotent, however, and Fox's rebuttal is not persuasive.

[104]Again דֹּדִים is lovemaking, not love in the abstract.

[105]Emending לְבָנוֹן to לְבֹנָה in parallel with בְּשָׂמִים, 10c. Note that Hos 14:6 is not a true parallel since it is describing Israel metaphorically as a plant, which is not the case in this verse. Cf. also Vg: *odor turis*.

this is an appeal for her to open her pleasures to him. The catalog of exotic spices in this "garden" serves to suggest that the pleasures of the woman's love are abundant and especially that they are varied; he could never grow bored in such a garden. They do not, however, have specified symbolic referents, that is, as parts of the woman's anatomy.[106] The spring of water is a metaphor for sexual love in Prov 5:15-20.

One other aspect of this song is noteworthy. Five times in succession (4:8-12) and once in 5:1 the man calls the woman his bride.[107] It is difficult to deny that this is a couple in the process of consummating their marriage.[108]

19. Soprano (4:16)

16Awake, north wind,
and come, south wind!
Blow on my garden,
that its fragrance may spread abroad.
Let my lover come into his garden
and taste its choice fruits.

4:16 This, with 5:1, is the high point of the Song of Songs. She calls on the winds to make her fragrance drift to her beloved, thus drawing him to herself. Maintaining the metaphor of the garden, she invites him to come and enjoy her love. This is the consummation of their marriage.

20. Tenor (5:1a,b)

1I have come into my garden, my sister, my bride;
I have gathered my myrrh with my spice.
I have eaten my honeycomb and my honey;
I have drunk my wine and my milk.

5:1a,b The man responds. The poetry is discreet and restrained; it conveys the joy of sexual love without vulgarity; at the same time, the meaning is quite clear. The catalog of luxuries here (garden, myrrh, honey, wine, etc.) imply that he has partaken of her pleasures to the full.

---

[106]Contrary to Pope (*Song*, 490-91), who takes שְׁלָחַיִךְ (v. 13) to mean "your groove" (i.e., vagina). While a meaning "channel" for שֶׁלַח is possible, the plural diminishes the force of Pope's arguments. Fox (*Song*, 137) takes "your channels" as metonomy for "your watered fields," which makes sense in context. The rendering "your plants," however, is supported by the use of the root שלח (piel stem) in Ps 80:12 and Jer 17:8.

[107]כַּלָּה, which usually means "bride" (Isa 49:18; 61:10; 62:5; Jer 2:32; 7:34; 16:9; 25:10; 33:11) and sometimes means "daughter-in-law" (Ruth 1:6-8,22). The basic idea seems to be "young wife."

[108]The parallel term "my sister" (אֲחֹתִי, v. 9) is a common term of affection for the girl one loves, as seen in the Egyptian poetry. But there is no evidence that כַּלָּה was used loosely for "girlfriend" or even "fiancée" rather than "bride."

21. Chorus (5:1c)

Eat, O friends, and drink;
drink your fill, O lovers.

5:1c This brief call from the chorus breaks the tension of the previous verses and opens the way for a second solo similar to 3:1-5. The picture of these girls intruding on the couple's lovemaking is jarring only if one forgets that this is a song and not some kind of history or drama. By keeping the genre of this text in mind, one can avoid such outrageous interpretations. The chorus calls on both man and woman to let themselves be intoxicated with love.[109]

22. Soprano (5:2-8)

2 I slept but my heart was awake.
Listen! My lover is knocking:
"Open to me, my sister, my darling,
my dove, my flawless one.
My head is drenched with dew,
my hair with the dampness of the night."
3 I have taken off my robe—
must I put it on again?
I have washed my feet—
must I soil them again?
4 My lover thrust his hand through the latch-opening;
my heart began to pound for him.
5 I arose to open for my lover,
and my hands dripped with myrrh,
my fingers with flowing myrrh,
on the handles of the lock.
6 I opened for my lover,
but my lover had left; he was gone.
My heart sank at his departure.
I looked for him but did not find him.
I called him but he did not answer.
7 The watchmen found me
as they made their rounds in the city.
They beat me, they bruised me;
they took away my cloak,
those watchmen of the walls!
8 O daughters of Jerusalem, I charge you—
if you find my lover,

---

[109] וְשִׁכְרוּ דּוֹדִים. שׁכר is properly "to be drunken," and דּוֹדִים probably should be translated "lovemaking" in agreement with parallel usage in the Song. Thus, "And be drunk with lovemaking!"

what will you tell him?
Tell him I am faint with love.

The magical spell of the previous text is jolted by the violence of the woman's surreal account of her experience in her solo. This passage is obviously parallel to 3:1-5 and must be interpreted accordingly. This is another account of the woman's feelings and perceptions as she goes through her first sexual experience.[110]

On the surface of the narrative, she tells how the man came to her door, she rose to let him in after some hesitancy, saw he was gone, and went out to find him but was "beaten" by the guards.[111] This must be understood as metaphor, however, and double entendres abound. As in 3:1-5 this account focuses on her loss of virginity. A difference, however, is that 3:1-5 is prospective, whereas 5:2-8 describes the actual event, albeit from a psychological and metaphorical perspective.

The sequence of her narrative is as follows: She recalls his entreaties for her to open herself to him (v. 2), which alludes to 4:8-15. After some hesitancy she realizes that she has passed the point of no return (v. 3); she cannot escape the loss of virginity. The moment of her sexual experience has come (vv. 4-5). She suddenly feels abandoned by him (v. 6). She seeks her beloved but is "beaten" by the guards—that is, she loses her virginity (v. 7). She calls on the Jerusalem girls to communicate her need to the man (v. 8). The picture of the guards beating and stripping the woman has something of the character of a rape, and the image of the woman's isolation at the very moment of union is stunning. Her understanding of her loss of virginity to her lover is mixed with feelings of love for him and feelings of deep loss of her life as it once was: she is no longer one of the daughters of Jerusalem.

5:2 She was not dreaming—as in 3:1-5, the "dream" interpretation is meaningless.[112] The opening line, "I slept, but my heart was alert," probably means she was in bed and easily awakened[113] by his words. She first recalls his appeals (instead of "my lover is knocking" read "my lover is entreating"[114]) for her to open to him. The monotonous manner in which she repeats his terms of affection ("my sister, my darling, my dove, my

[110]Exum ("Structural Analysis," 50) comments that 5:2-6c is "an account of coition veiled by the indirection of language."

[111]Murphy (*Song*, 168-69) observes that this section does not contain the *paraklausithyron*, or "lover's lament at the door," found in Egyptian love poetry. I would suggest that the Song takes the metaphor of the door and reworks it for a radically different purpose.

[112]See especially Pope (*Song*, 510-11), who points out that dream interpretations are in fact most unbecoming here and that the book uses no Semitic vocabulary for dreams.

[113]Exum ("Structural Analysis," 61) observes that עור here and in 4:16 probably refers to arousal.

[114]דּוֹפֵק probably means not "knocking" but "entreating"; cf. Fox, *Song*, 143.

flawless one") is slightly sarcastic and arises from the pain this experience has given her. In claiming that his hair is wet, the man is appealing to her to let him in the "house" on the grounds that he is getting soaked outside. All this is metaphor, however; it refers to the urgency of his appeals. One should not understand this as a request to come inside a literal house.

5:3 This verse is often taken to mean that she cannot get up and open the door because she has already gone to bed (on the assumption that v. 2 has an actual house in view). But commentators have long recognized that these reasons for not getting up and opening the door are rather flimsy excuses, and the whole sequence of events, on a literal reading, is bizarre. (1) He asks her to let him in, but she refuses with weak excuses. (2) He tries to force his way in (v. 4), she gets up to let him in (v. 5), but he already has lost interest and gone away (v. 6). (3) She goes after him but gets molested by the guards (v. 7). On such a reading, this sequence is illogical (in that no amount of explaining can account for the lovers' strange actions), offensive (in that the intrusion of literal violence spoils the Song), and meaningless (in that there is no conceivable purpose for all of this).[115] It is difficult to imagine how a young love could survive such a wrenching experience as this, and yet in fact the couple makes no mention of her molestation in subsequent lyrics.

Also in light of the fairly conspicuous reference to their sexual union in 4:16–5:1, the sudden coming and going of the characters here is impossible to understand. The woman's words speak not of going to an actual door but of her confrontation with this moment. We should also note that the bolted door is a self-evident metaphor for virginity in 8:9b, which increases the likelihood that the same meaning obtains here.

In addition, however, I would propose that v. 3 is a double entendre and only superficially relates to the metaphor of the door. Her words, in the context of the wedding night with her groom, constitute her recognition that she has come to the point of sexual experience and cannot evade it. "I have removed my robe" means that she cannot turn back now. "I have washed my feet" means that she has gone indoors and metaphorically committed herself to staying. One does not wash one's feet and then turn around and go back outdoors. She cannot flee into the street, as it were.

5:4 The word translated "latch-opening" is simply "opening,"[116] and there is no evidence that some kind of latch opening is meant.[117] The

[115]Bizarre interpretations of this text abound. For example, S. C. Glickman (*A Song for Lovers* [Downers Grove: InterVarsity, 1976], 62-65) argues that the woman was beaten up by a group of guards even though she was in fact the queen (!), yet that the experience "strengthened her determination to be reconciled to her husband" (p. 65). I rather doubt that a beating would have such a positive effect.

[116]חֹר. The word means "cave" or "hole" in 1 Sam 14:11 and Nah 2:13 (Eng. v. 12). See also Isa 11:8; 42:22.

[117]Cf. Pope, *Song*, 518-19; Fox, *Song*, 144; and Carr, *Song*, 134.

metaphor of the door has almost disappeared in this verse. Insomuch as the word "hand" is used in Hebrew as well as in other Semitic languages for the male member,[118] the meaning of the line as a sexual metaphor is clear.[119] The following line is rendered quite periphrastically in the NIV: "My heart began to pound for him." "My insides were in a frenzy"[120] would be more accurate.

5:5 Myrrh was used as an aphrodisiac (Prov 7:17). Even so, the statement that her hand is drenched with myrrh (an expensive, exotic ointment) is another detail that makes the song unintelligible if taken literally. Gordis argues that she anointed herself before bed,[121] but the text states that she is actually dripping with it.[122] It is better to take this as a continuation of the metaphor of her sexual excitement as she "opens the door" for him.

5:6 She opens to her beloved and finds him gone. The poignancy of this verse—her frantic, futile calling to him—is compelling, but what does it mean? Note that the text does not precisely say that she went out into the street[123] (it is assumed that she did so from v. 7). More to the point, it is her *heart*[124] that went after him. It is not that she is physically alone, but that emotionally and psychologically she suddenly feels herself abandoned.[125] Indeed, the manner in which the man seems to appear and disappear with amazing abruptness here and in 3:1-5 should warn us

---

[118]An example in the Hebrew Bible is Isa 57:8, יָד חָזִית, "You have looked upon the 'hand.' " The Qumran manual of discipline has it a punishable offense for one's "hand" to be exposed (1QS 7:13). יד is so used in Ugaritic text 52:33-35 (see UT 409). F. Delitzsch (*Isaiah*, trans. J. Martin [Grand Rapids: Eerdmans, n.d.], 2:375) notes that Arabic "furnishes several analogies to the obscene use of the word."

[119]The use of מִן in מִן־הַחֹר seems odd, but the same usage is found in Song 2:9, where the man is like a gazelle "gazing in through [מִן] the windows, looking in through [מִן] the lattices." Also Pope (*Song*, 518) notes the parallel uses of מִן and בְּ in Prov 17:23 and 21:14. The view of Gordis (*Song*, 90) that the phrase means "withdraw" places an odd meaning on שׁלח ("to send, to stretch out"; cf. esp. texts where the object is יָד: Gen 3:22; 37:22; Job 28:9—the word never means "withdraw"). Thus the line could be translated, "My lover extended his hand through the opening."

[120]המה means to "murmur, growl, be agitated or in a state of confusion, or to stir."

[121]Gordis, *Song*, 90.

[122]Pope (*Song*, 522-24) notes that classical literature refers to rejected lovers leaving flowers, wine, perfume or the like at the doors of those they sought after, but the details of the song here do not correspond to his analogies. Murphy (*Song*, 171) suggests that the man left myrrh on the bolt as a token of his love, but this contradicts the text even in Murphy's own translation. It plainly states that *her hands* dripped myrrh *onto the bolt*, and not the reverse.

[123]בִּקֵּשׁ does not of itself imply wandering in the streets.

[124]נַפְשִׁי. The expression here should not be taken as merely biological, "I fainted," but as almost that her very life went out to him.

[125]The woman of the first "flower song" of Papyrus Harris 500 similarly fears that she will lose her lover now that she has lain with him. See M. Lichtheim, AEL 2:192.

against a literal interpretation. Bodily he is, to be sure, very present. But she goes through this experience alone.

5:7 As suddenly as the man disappeared, the guards appear. They are called "those who encircle the city"[126] and "the keepers of the walls,"[127] and once again her virginity is meant. They beat her, bruise her, and strip her. No meaningful literal interpretation of this verse has been offered. The event is harsh and inexplicable at this level. Metaphorically, then, it is not any person who assaults her; it is her own virginity. This is an experience in which the man paradoxically has no part.

5:8 She calls upon the Jerusalem girls to help her. Once again the question, What are the Jerusalem girls doing there? is illegitimate. This is a song, not a biography. She asks them to relay a message to her lover that she has the lovesickness.[128] This concerns not so much her physical pain as her need for his love and support.[129] As in 2:5, she wants to be strengthened by his love. The fact that she speaks through the Jerusalem girls (who here serve as the community of women) rather than directly to the man is significant. She is not yet able to grapple with the emotional turmoil of her relationship with the man and needs the support of other women. She perhaps feels that they can empathize with her experience in a way he cannot. In addition, it is important that she calls to the Jerusalem girls who are themselves still virgins. She has not yet reconciled herself to the fact that she is no longer one of them.

23. Chorus (5:9)

[9]How is your beloved better than others,
most beautiful of women?
How is your beloved better than others,
that you charge us so?

5:9 This verse introduces the woman's next solo, in which she praises her beloved's beauty. Nevertheless, the answer of the chorus should not be dismissed as mere transition, for it has a highly significant function in the text. The girls do not respond to her request directly, as in, "Yes, we'll do that." Instead, they pose two questions for her, the first here and the second in 6:2. The first is: What is so special about this man[130] that you

[126]הַסֹּבְבִים בָּעִיר.

[127]שֹׁמְרֵי הַחֹמוֹת.

[128]The use of מַה here is paralleled in Hos 9:14, as Pope (*Song*, 528-29) points out. Gordis (*Song*, 91) also observes that מַה is used as "that" in rhetorical questions. It is not to be taken as a negative, as in Fox, *Song*, 146-47.

[129]If the physical pain of the loss of virginity were meant, one would expect her to speak of an injury or wound (e.g., מַכָּה [a bruise] or פָּצַע [to wound], cf. v. 7).

[130]Lit., "What is your beloved compared to [another] beloved?" L. Waterman (*Song*, 6, 19) gives this verse the anomalous translation, "What is your Dodai compared with David?"

would want us to go to him for you? In doing this, they ask her to come to terms with her love for him.

In surrendering her womanhood to him, she has opened herself to great emotional hurt. She feels isolated and, perhaps, depressed. But the solution to her problem is not to be found in something either they or he can do for her; it is to be found in herself. She must recognize that she gave herself to him for a reason, that she is in fact deeply in love with him. He is, in her eyes, better than all other men.

24. Soprano (5:10-16)

10My lover is radiant and ruddy,
outstanding among ten thousand.
11His head is purest gold;
his hair is wavy
and black as a raven.
12His eyes are like doves
by the water streams,
washed in milk,
mounted like jewels.
13His cheeks are like beds of spice
yielding perfume.
His lips are like lilies
dripping with myrrh.
14His arms are rods of gold
set with chrysolite.
His body is like polished ivory
decorated with sapphires.
15His legs are pillars of marble
set on bases of pure gold.
His appearance is like Lebanon,
choice as its cedars.
16His mouth is sweetness itself;
he is altogether lovely.
This is my lover, this my friend,
O daughters of Jerusalem.

This is an admiration song, the longest in the book sung by the woman in praise of the man. In responding to the Jerusalem girls, she rediscovers her love for him.

His thesis is that this is a historical incident and that the woman prefers "Dodai" to Solomon. דּוֹדֵךְ clearly does not mean "your Dodai" (the use of a pronominal suffix with a proper name would be peculiar anyway). More than that, Waterman's interpretation is built on two gratuitous assumptions: that the Jerusalem girls are Solomon's harem and that they would refer to Solomon as "David."

5:10 The brevity of the introduction sharpens the assertiveness of her love: "He is the best[131] man of all!" she replies. He is radiant and well-tanned,[132] which implies not just good looks but health and vitality.

5:11 His face is like gold not only in that it is tanned but of the highest value to her. The thickness[133] and blackness of his hair speak of his youth: He is neither gray nor bald.

5:12 Judging from 4:1, "eyes like doves" seems to be a stock metaphor. "Washed in milk" may refer to the white of the eye, in which the pupils are like bathing doves.[134] "Mounted like jewels" is a hypothetical translation.[135]

5:13 In describing his cheeks and lips in terms of fragrant spices, she is not referring to their appearance but their effect on her. In particular she seems to have his kisses in mind[136] (the connection between spices and lovemaking is made also in 4:14 and 5:5; cf. 1:2). The translation "yielding perfume" is an emendation of the Masoretic Text, which reads "towers of perfume."[137]

5:14 This description is, as Carr puts it, "purely poetic hyperbole."[138] It is a mistake to try to deduce any sense of what the man looks like from these words. Rather, her words convey her estimation of his value.[139]

5:15 The statue-like description of the man conveys a sense of nobility and strength, and once again the use of precious metals speaks of his worth in her eyes. He obviously does not look like Lebanon; the cedars of Leba-

[131]דָּגוּל apparently is equivalent to the adjective "choice." Cf. the LXX ἐκλελοχισμένος and Vg *electus* and see Murphy, *Song*, 166.

[132]אָדוֹם = "red."

[133]The precise meaning of תַּלְתַּלִּים is unknown, but the gist is clear. The word may mean "heaped up," from תֵּל ("heap"; Gordis, *Song*, 91), or it may be related to Akkadian terminology used of the date palm (Pope, *Song*, 536). Cf. the LXX ἐλάται ("pines or fir trees") and Vg *elatae palmarum* ("tops of the palm trees").

[134]M. D. Goulder (*The Song of Fourteen Songs*, JSOTSS 36 [Sheffield: JSOT Press, 1986], 5) interprets the image of the doves as follows: the dove (tails) are the eyelids, the milk is the iris, and the bathing is the fluttering movement of doves that resembles the batting of the eyes.

[135]Gordis (*Song*, 91) calls such a translation "inept." The piel stem of the verb מלא can be used of setting jewels (Exod 28:17; cf. the noun מִלֻּאָה, "setting"), but it is not at all clear that מִלֵּאת has a similar meaning. The meaning of the phrase is uncertain. See Murphy, *Song*, 166.

[136]Carr, *Song*, 142.

[137]Reading מְגַדְּלוֹת as a piel participle. Fox (*Song*, 148) objects to this on the grounds that the piel is used of persons who cause something to grow and not of places where plants grow, but the ultimate object of the metaphor is after all a man, so some fluidity in the language may be allowed. The LXX has φύουσαι.

[138]Carr, *Song*, 143.

[139]Also, contrary to some, there is no phallic imagery here. The plural "hands" (NIV "arms") establishes that literal hands are meant here. Contrast Goulder (*Song*, 5-6), who takes עֶשֶׁת שֵׁן to mean "tusk of ivory" as a phallic euphemism.

non are proverbial types of majesty and beauty. As in the other admiration songs, she is describing how she feels about him rather than how he looks.

5:16 His mouth being sweet refers doubly to his words and kisses. In affirming so strongly his surpassing worth to the Jerusalem girls, she has all but forgotten the trauma of her loss of virginity. Her love for him has carried her through this rite of passage.

25. Chorus (6:1)

1Where has your lover gone,
most beautiful of women?
Which way did your lover turn,
that we may look for him with you?

6:1 The chorus, following her answer to 5:9, now ask their second question: Where is he? Two important aspects of their question strike the reader. First, the admiration and perhaps envy of the girls toward the woman are evident. Here, as in 1:8 and 5:9, they refer to her as the "most beautiful of women."[140] More than that, their enthusiasm to accompany her and find him is apparent. The implication is that his love for her has elevated her in the eyes of the Jerusalem girls. Second, however, any sense that this is a question concerning his literal whereabouts quickly fades when the woman gives her answer. She uses sexually charged language and essentially says, "He is with me."

26. Soprano (6:2-3)

2My lover has gone down to his garden,
to the beds of spices,
to browse in the gardens
and to gather lilies.
3I am my lover's and my lover is mine;
he browses among the lilies.

6:2-3 She answers that he has gone to "his garden" (that is, he has come to her). As in 4:15–5:1, his going down to his garden refers to his coming to make love to her; and as in 2:1-2, the "lilies" refer to the woman herself. The man is not, as some translations have it, pasturing his flock but grazing like a lamb or gazelle in a pasture (thus NIV "browse").[141] Thus the usage is metaphorical for his lovemaking. In reaffirming that she and her lover belong to each other, she is both asserting the exclusiveness of the

---

[140] הַיָּפָה בַּנָּשִׁים.

[141] The word for flock is not in the text. Also, וְלִלְקֹט ("to gather [lilies]"), parallel to לִרְעוֹת, implies that the meaning is "to graze, browse" and not "to tend sheep."

relationship and further distancing herself from her attachment to the Jerusalem girls and to her maidenhood.

Carr refers to this section as a "curious response" on her part that is difficult to interpret,[142] but it is only difficult because most commentators (Carr included) think that 5:2-8 means that the woman literally went wandering in the streets after her beloved and that her dialogue with the Jerusalem girls describes actual, real-world events rather than her psychological state and emotional development.

27. Tenor (6:4-9)

4You are beautiful, my darling, as Tirzah,
lovely as Jerusalem,
majestic as troops with banners.
5Turn your eyes from me;
they overwhelm me.
Your hair is like a flock of goats
descending from Gilead.
6Your teeth are like a flock of sheep
coming up from the washing.
Each has its twin,
not one of them is alone.
7Your temples behind your veil
are like the halves of a pomegranate.
8Sixty queens there may be,
and eighty concubines,
and virgins beyond number;
9but my dove, my perfect one, is unique,
the only daughter of her mother,
the favorite of the one who bore her.
The maidens saw her and called her blessed;
the queens and concubines praised her.

The man now reaffirms his love for her. Much of what he says is repeated from his admiration song of 4:1-5. In particular 6:5b repeats 4:1c,[143] 6:6 repeats 4:2,[144] and 6:7 repeats 4:3b. While there may be some stock metaphors here, the reason for the near verbatim repetition goes beyond the mere use of poetic formulae. The implication is that his desire for her and admiration of her have not diminished now that he has possessed her sexually. He is not like Amnon, of whom it was said after his rape of Tamar that "his hatred of her was even greater than his former desire for her" (2 Sam 13:15).

---

[142]Carr, *Song*, 145.

[143]But 6:5 has מִן־הַגִּלְעָד where 4:1 has מֵהַר גִּלְעָד.

[144]But 6:6 has הָרְחֵלִים for הַקְּצוּבוֹת in 4:2.

6:4-5a His awe of her is as great as ever; if anything, it has increased. She is compared to Tirzah and Jerusalem, the two greatest cities of the early monarchy,[145] in all their splendor.[146] The meaning is that she inspires awe and wonder in him; and, as in his comparison of her to David's tower, he is still aware that he cannot storm her by force (the walls of the city were its most prominent feature). The request that she turn away her eyes further expresses his sense of her power. She can unnerve him with a single glance.

6:5b-7 As in 4:1-5, the description here is not to be taken literally but metaphysically. He is describing her as a beautiful, desirable woman.

6:8-9 As in 2:2, he declares his beloved to be unique; she is utterly beyond compare. The queens and concubines are included for comparison only; there is no need to take this as a reference to Solomon's harem or hypothesize with Delitzsch that the relatively small (!) numbers reflect a period fairly early in his reign.[147] Queens and princesses are characteristically portrayed as stately and beautiful, and concubines are specifically chosen for their beauty. The increasing numbers (sixty, eighty, a countless multitude) are a typical wisdom technique.[148] A much more homey device is his praise of her as the favorite of her mother. The point is that she endears herself to those who know her best, here brought out by the allusion to her sucking at her mother's breast.

28. Chorus (6:10)

10Who is this that appears like the dawn,
fair as the moon, bright as the sun,
majestic as the stars in procession?

145This serves to establish that the Song dates from this period. The argument that Tirzah was actually not the city but some unknown woman of the ancient world renowned for her beauty is not convincing in light of both the biblical references to the city (1 Kgs 14:17; 15:33; etc.; cf. Gordis, *Song*, 92) and the parallel to Jerusalem in this verse. The argument of Fox (*Song*, 151) that Tirzah was "probably half-legendary by the time the Song was composed" is special pleading. There is no evidence that Tirzah ever obtained legendary status (like Babylon), and there is no clear reason why a late postexilic poet would allude to a city that had long passed its prime as an example of splendor.

146אֲיֻמָּה כַּנִּדְגָּלוֹת is often translated as "awesome as an army with banners." Gordis (*Song*, 93) considers this unlikely and argues from the Akkadian form *dagalu*, "look with astonishment," that the phrase means "[You are] awe-inspiring as these great sights." Fox (*Song*, 152) notes that a denominative of דגל (with the meaning "bannered") would more likely be in the pual stem. Pope (*Song*, 560-62) argues for a meaning "trophies," but his case is weak and is driven by a desire to see mythological allusions in the text. Murphy (*Song*, 174-75) suggests "awe-inspiring as visions," but it is hard to see how this relates to the metaphor of the two cities. Probably Gordis's rendition should be followed.

147Delitzsch, *Song*, 111.

148Note that sixty and eighty are respectively three score and four score, as in the wisdom formula, "For three . . . , even for four."

6:10 The question of who is the singer of this verse could be regarded as unsettled if it were not for the introductory line in 6:9c, which clarifies the role assignment. The man's line, "The girls have seen her and congratulated her," is not mere rhetoric on his part but serves to introduce the chorus. In 3:6-11 they sang an arrival song in praise of the man, and here they do the same for the woman. Also the words, "Who is this?" even as a rhetorical question make little sense in the man's mouth. Rather, the woman is so thoroughly transformed that the girls hardly recognize her.

They describe her beauty as like that of the moon and sun, but they do not use the usual vocabulary for these bodies. The word for "moon"[149] here is related to the word "white" and contrasts with her self-description in 1:5, where she asks the Jerusalem girls not to chide her for her dark skin. She is also said to be like the "dawn"; the word used here is a play on the word in 1:5 for "black."[150] The word for "sun,"[151] which is related to the word for "heat," seems to imply that she is too dazzling to behold. In a Cinderella motif, the woman who was very ordinary is now extraordinary in her beauty and breathtaking to behold.

The NIV rendering, "majestic as the stars in procession," is hypothetical. The Hebrew here is identical to the line translated "majestic as troops with banners" in v. 4.[152]

29. Soprano (6:11-12)

[11]I went down to the grove of nut trees
to look at the new growth in the valley,
to see if the vines had budded
or the pomegranates were in bloom.
[12]Before I realized it,
my desire set me among the royal chariots of my people.

Evidence favors the singer here being the woman: (1) her going down to the garden to see if the vineyards are in bloom seems to be a response to his invitation in 2:10-15, and (2) the singer of v. 12 seems to be set beside a prince, which would imply that the singer is the woman.[153]

6:11 If this verse states that she has responded to the call of her beloved and gone down to the garden (2:10-15), the meaning would be that she has accepted his (sexual) invitation. See also 4:12–5:1, where the woman's body is metaphorically a garden.

---

[149]לְבָנָה.
[150]שַׁחַר is "dawn" here; שְׁחוֹרָה is "black" in 1:5.
[151]חמה.
[152]אֲיֻמָּה כַּנִּדְגָּלוֹת.
[153]The LXX leaves no doubt that the woman sings in v. 11. It adds the line ἐκεῖ δώσω τοὺς μαστούς μου σοί, "There I will give you my breasts."

6:12 This verse is highly obscure, as a perusal of translations will readily disclose.[154] Working with a minimal amount of emendation, a possible rendition is: "I am beside myself[155]/you have set me[156] (among) chariots / a prince is with me."[157] The change of person from second to third ("you . . . a prince") is not unusual; see 1:4. The meaning is that she is overwhelmed by all that has happened to her. To be set among the chariots could refer to a wedding custom (the bride departing with the groom in a triumphal procession). She likens her beloved to a prince. The point is that she is about to leave the Jerusalem girls behind once and for all and enter married life. This interpretation is sustained by the following verse.

30. Chorus (6:13a)

[13]Come back, come back, O Shulammite;
come back, come back, that we may gaze on you!

6:13a The chorus longs to be with her as they realize they are losing her to her beloved.[158] She has passed through the rite of becoming a married woman both physically and emotionally and is no longer one of them. The reference to her as "Shulammite" has given rise to a great deal of speculation. Rather than read this as a gentilic for "woman of Shulem"[159] (there being no town by that name in the Old Testament) or as a reference to a pagan goddess,[160] it is better to take it as a term meaning "the Solomoness."[161] As the man is a "Solomon" (3:7-11), so the woman is a "Solomoness." Fox, however, may be correct in his suggestion that it be translated, "O perfect one."[162] But whether the meaning be "Solomoness" or "perfect one," the expression is not to be taken literally but is high praise given in hyperbole.

[154]For a good summary of options proposed, see Pope, *Song*, 584-91.

[155]Taking לֹא יָדַעְתִּי נַפְשִׁי as an idiom meaning "I have lost all composure." See Job 9:21.

[156]Reading the verb as 2 m.s. rather than 3 f.s.

[157]Reading עִמִּי, "with me," rather than עַמִּי, "my people." Cf. Gen 31:31; 39:7,12,14.

[158]שׁוּב ("to return") does not mean "dance" or "whirl." Cf. Fox, *Song* 157, and Murphy, *Song*, 181.

[159]A common suggestion is that "Shulammite" = "Shunammite" and that Abishag the Shunammite is meant. The similarity between the names should be regarded as coincidental in light of the lack of any clear evidence (esp. from the ancient versions) to support the equation. Cf. Fox, *Song*, 157; Murphy, *Song*, 181; and Pope, *Song*, 597-98.

[160]Pope, *Song*, 600.

[161]The definite article may be used since it is not a true proper name. Pope (*Song*, 597) notes that the Ugaritic designation of Danel's wife as "Lady Dantay" (*dnty*) supports this interpretation.

[162]Fox, *Song*, 157-58.

31. Tenor (6:13b–7:9a)

Why would you gaze on the Shulammite
as on the dance of Mahanaim?
1How beautiful your sandaled feet,
O prince's daughter!
Your graceful legs are like jewels,
the work of a craftsman's hands.
2Your navel is a rounded goblet
that never lacks blended wine.
Your waist is a mound of wheat
encircled by lilies.
3Your breasts are like two fawns,
twins of a gazelle.
4Your neck is like an ivory tower.
Your eyes are the pools of Heshbon
by the gate of Bath Rabbim.
Your nose is like the tower of Lebanon
looking toward Damascus.
5Your head crowns you like Mount Carmel.
Your hair is like royal tapestry;
the king is held captive by its tresses.
6How beautiful you are and how pleasing,
O love, with your delights!
7Your stature is like that of the palm,
and your breasts like clusters of fruit.
8I said, "I will climb the palm tree;
I will take hold of its fruit."
May your breasts be like the clusters of the vine,
the fragrance of your breath like apples,
9and your mouth like the best wine.

He answers the chorus[163] in 6:13b and then moves into another praise of the woman's beauty.

6:13b The meaning of "Mahanaim" is uncertain. It could be taken either as the proper name of the village mentioned in Gen 32:2 (as the NIV implies) or as meaning "two groups" (cf. Gen 32:7). Either way it would refer to the name of some dance known to the ancient Israelites but now lost to us. Fox makes the attractive suggestion that the lines mean, "Why would you gaze at the perfect one / as if she were a camp dancer?"[164] Whichever interpretation is preferred, the meaning is that the

[163]The use of the masculine form תֶּחֱזוּ ("you gaze") does not mean that a group of men is addressed since the Song does not adhere to strict grammatical convention in this regard. See Murphy, *Song*, 181.

[164]Fox, *Song*, 158.

Jerusalem girls should not stare at her or try to keep her to themselves as if she were some kind of entertainment. The text does not imply that anyone is really dancing.

From the general description of the woman in the admiration song, it is difficult to avoid the conclusion that she is described as unclothed (notwithstanding her sandals, v. 1). Once again the man and woman are simultaneously together in roles of the closest intimacy and yet in dialogue with the Jerusalem girls. It is impossible to make sense of any of this if these scenes are thought to represent some kind of story. The arrival of the groom and his departure with his bride, the inner world of the woman's emotional journey, the dialogue with the chorus, and the intimacies of the bedroom are all meant to portray the range of emotions and experiences connected with the wedding night.

7:1 His praise of her beauty moves generally from bottom to top, the reverse of 4:1-5. Sandals are mentioned because they enhance the natural beauty of her feet. The comparison of her thighs (rather than "legs"[165]) to jewels means only that they seem finely crafted; no actual description of their appearance is meant. The vocative "prince's daughter" is, like all other such terms, not to be taken literally.

7:2 The comparison of the navel to a goblet arises from its rounded shape.[166] A goblet that never runs dry is one that can ever satisfy his thirst. Similarly, the comparison of her belly to wheat may allude to the color of her skin, but it also implies that she is metaphorically nourishment for him.[167]

7:3 See 4:5.

7:4 The description of her neck may indicate that she is wearing an ivory necklace; but probably, as in the description of her thighs, it merely means that her neck seems to be highly crafted from the finest materials. Unlike the description of the "tower of David" (4:4), no military metaphor is implied. The comparison of her eyes to pools indicates the depth of beauty found in them. The location of "Bath Rabbim" is unknown, but the name probably is a play on words.[168]

---

[165] יָרֵךְ properly is the thigh, buttocks, or lower abdomen region; it is not the entire leg.

[166] A number of commentators suggest that "navel" is a euphemism for the vulva on the grounds that this meaning better suits the movement of the upward-moving description of the woman's body and parallels Arabic usage. If such is meant, however, it is the secondary aspect of a double entendre; "navel" makes sense as the primary meaning (Carr, *Song*, 157, and Pope, *Song*, 617-18). Being full of mixed wine properly is a function of the cup, not of the woman's "navel" and should not be taken as some kind of strange sexual metaphor. "Wine" is simply a metaphor for pleasures generally, which is what she gives him. Murphy (*Song*, 182) takes it as meaning "valley" and thus a euphemism for the female genitals.

[167] Cf. Fox, *Song*, 158-59.

[168] Fox (*Song*, 160) notes that בַּת־רַבִּים means "daughter of nobles" in parallel to בַּת־נָדִיב, "prince's daughter," in 7:2 (Heb.).

To the Western reader, the description of her nose hardly seems complementary. Pope suggests that Mount Hermon is meant and from that concludes that the woman is in fact a goddess.[169] But whether the "tower of Lebanon" is some actual tower or in fact is Mount Hermon, the point is neither that her nose is large or that she is superhuman. Viewed from a distance, a mountain (or tower) adds symmetry and comeliness to an otherwise nondescript horizon. Her nose complements and sets off her facial beauty.

7:5 An alternative translation of this verse is: "Your head upon you is like crimson,[170]/that is[171]—the hair of your head, it is deep red,[172]/a king is ensnared in your locks!" The man's hair is raven black (5:11); hers is deep red. The metaphor of entrapment is common in love poetry (see Introduction).

7:6 Instead of "with your delights," it is better to read "daughter of delights" (i.e., "delightful woman").[173]

7:7-9a As in 4:5-7, the breasts are the focus of the man's sexual attraction and the stimulus to his desire. He says that her breasts are like clusters of fruit and that he will climb the tree and seize the fruit. The meaning of his metaphor can hardly be missed. The statement that her "breath" is fragrant is problematic since the text actually says "nose," a term not elsewhere used of the breath. It is difficult to understand his speaking of the "fragrance of your nose." In light of the fact that the Ugaritic and Akkadian cognates are also used of the nipple, that would seem to be the meaning here.[174] In saying that her mouth is like wine, he means her kisses (cf. 1:2).

32. Soprano (7:9b–8:4)

May the wine go straight to my lover,
flowing gently over lips and teeth.
10 I belong to my lover,
and his desire is for me.
11 Come, my lover, let us go to the countryside,
let us spend the night in the villages.

---

[169] Pope, *Song*, 626-27.

[170] Reading כַּרְמִיל, "crimson," for כַּרְמֶל, "Carmel." Cf. Gordis, *Song*, 96, and note the parallel to אַרְגָּמָן ("deep red").

[171] Epexegetical וְ; see *IBHS*, 652-53 (39.2.4).

[172] אַרְגָּמָן is a purple-red dye, not "royal tapestry."

[173] Thus בַּת תַּעֲנוּגִים with BHS note b. Aquila reads θυγάτηρ τρυφῶν, "daughter of luxuries." The MT has only a single ת due to haplography.

[174] In UT 52.61 *b*ᵓ*ap dd* means "on the nipple of the breast." See Murphy, *Song*, 183, and Pope, *Song*, 636-37. On the other hand, Pope's evidence that אַף can mean "clitoris" is not convincing. His comparison to 2 Aqht 5.4-8 is especially strained.

12 Let us go early to the vineyards
to see if the vines have budded,
if their blossoms have opened,
and if the pomegranates are in bloom—
there I will give you my love.
13 The mandrakes send out their fragrance,
and at our door is every delicacy,
both new and old,
that I have stored up for you, my lover.

1 If only you were to me like a brother,
who was nursed at my mother's breasts!
Then, if I found you outside,
I would kiss you,
and no one would despise me.
2 I would lead you
and bring you to my mother's house—
she who has taught me.
I would give you spiced wine to drink,
the nectar of my pomegranates.
3 His left arm is under my head
and his right arm embraces me.
4 Daughters of Jerusalem, I charge you:
Do not arouse or awaken love
until it so desires.

7:9b The woman[175] interrupts the man and completes the thought of this verse. The significance of this interruption is apparent when this song is compared to 4:1-15. There too the man moves from an admiration song to a proclamation of his desire for her, but he is in somewhat the position of a supplicant. He is aware that he can only await her gift of herself to him. Here he has scarcely begun to express his desire for her when she interrupts to say that she is his. Previous language equating her with a fortress has disappeared.

The MT is difficult here; it reads, "[The wine is] going directly to my lover / overflowing[176] the lips of sleepers." Two emendations for the final clause are possible, giving the meanings "overflowing my lips and teeth"[177] or "overflowing scarlet lips."[178] Either is satisfactory, but the MT, though difficult, is not impossible. "Sleepers" may serve to mean "lovers." This is

---

[175]The form דּוֹדִי (v. 11, Heb.) is used only by the woman; hence she is the singer here.

[176]Fox (*Song*, 163) notes that דבב (found only here in the Bible) means "flow" or "drip" in Mishnaic Hebrew and that it is cognate to the biblical זוּב.

[177]Reading שְׂפָתַי as a suffixed 1 c.s., "my lips," rather than construct plural, and reading וְשִׁנָּיִם, "and teeth," for יְשֵׁנִים, "sleepers." The LXX: καὶ ὀδοῦσιν. The Vg: *et dentibus*.

[178]A suggestion of Fox, *Song*, 163, reading שָׁנִים, "scarlet," for יְשֵׁנִים, "sleepers."

a case where the apparently more difficult reading is to be preferred.[179] The exchange of pleasure in kissing is meant.

7:10-13 His desire for her is evident from his song, but now she fully belongs to him, as implied in this, her answer to him.

The use of pastoral imagery for the setting and pleasures of lovemaking are well-established in the Song by now and need not surprise us. What is noteworthy is that *she* is now inviting *him* away for love (contrast 2:10-13). In her surrender of her virginity to him, she has become liberated in love so that she now aggressively speaks of love and calls him to herself. It would be a mistake to seek a specific referent for each item mentioned here since this is not an allegory. The overall tone of pleasures in the countryside is more important. At any rate, she clarifies the main point of her words in v. 12, "There I will give you my love." An actual country outing is thus not implied.

Three items in v. 13, however, do call for special notice. The first is the mandrake, a vegetable that from antiquity has been regarded as an aphrodisiac (Gen 30:14-16). While the text does not suggest that the couple will eat mandrakes for their alleged power, the implication of mandrakes giving their fragrance would not be lost on the ancient audience.

Second, the picture of the doors being garlanded with every delicacy of the garden is striking. The reference to the "doors" is to the ambiguity and tension that surrounded the concept of the door in earlier texts, especially 5:2-7. Previously the door was both barrier and way of access, and the opening of the door was fraught with tension and danger (especially for the woman). Now the doors are hung with delicacies, and all the previous tensions have disappeared.

Third, the woman speaks of "new and old" treasures she has for the man. This would imply that as they grow in love they will both repeat familiar pleasures and find new ones as well.

8:1 Her wish that her lover were her brother seems strange to the modern reader. The point is that she wishes she were free to display her affection openly. In the ancient world this would have been impossible for a woman with any man except a father, brother, or other near relative, the kissing of whom would not be construed by the public as a quasi-sexual act. The freedom to kiss in public would not apply to her husband. Thus the wish expressed here *is not sexual* but is a desire to be free to show her love for the groom freely and openly.[180]

---

[179]Cf. Gordis, *Song*, 97.

[180]Fox (*Song*, 166) incorrectly assumes that this proves that the couple "is not betrothed, let alone married." But the open display of affection between the sexes is frowned upon in many societies (e.g., traditional Oriental society) regardless of whether the couple is married.

8:2 The English versions are incorrect and misleading here since "I would lead" implies that this is a continuation of the impossible-to-attain wish of v. 1.[181] The sexual desire to take him to her "mother's house" (which again is euphemism for the female parts) and to give him spiced wine and the "nectar of my pomegranates"[182] is incompatible with the wish that he were her brother. The mood of her words here is not subjunctive but indicative and indeed determined, as shown by the juxtaposition of the two verbs; and it should be translated: "I *will* lead you; I *will* take you to the house of my mother." Since she cannot express her love with a kiss openly, she will express her love much more fully privately. The next phrase, "She who has taught me," could be taken to mean that her mother instructed her in the ways of love, but the text is uncertain.[183] It probably is best to emend it to read "to the room of she who bore me" as in 3:4; 6:9; and 8:5.[184] Taken thus, it parallels "my mother's house" and again is sexual euphemism.

8:3-4 See 2:6-7.[185]

32. Chorus (8:5a)

[5]Who is this coming up from the desert
leaning on her lover?

8:5a The opening words of the chorus are identical to their words in 3:6a, the change being that they now focus attention on the woman who is with the "charioteer"[186] and not on the man himself. She has become the object of their attention and admiration. Her leaning[187] upon him presents an attitude of trust and ease, which further suggests that the anxiety of 5:2-9 has ended.

34. Soprano (8:5b-7)

Under the apple tree I roused you;
there your mother conceived you,
there she who was in labor gave you birth.

---

[181]This would be expressed with the *wqtl* (perfect tense with "waw consecutive") rather than by the simple imperfect tense. Cf. Waltke and O'Connor, *Syntax*, 32.2.1d.

[182]Perhaps a euphemism for her breasts.

[183]Actually, "you will teach me" would be a better translation of תְּלַמְּדֵנִי here.

[184]Pope, *Song*, 659. Cf. the LXX, εἰς ταμίειον τῆς συλλαβούσης με.

[185]מָה in 8:4 is perhaps equivalent to אִם in 2:7 (GKC 137b n.l). Alternatively, it may simply be emended (BHS note).

[186]Assuming on the analogy of 3:6ff. that the couple is portrayed as in a chariot or carriage of some sort.

[187]מִתְרַפֶּקֶת is a hapax legomenon in the Hebrew Bible, but the meaning "to lean" has support in other Semitic languages. Cf. *BDB* and Murphy, *Song*, 191.

[6]Place me like a seal over your heart,
like a seal on your arm;
for love is as strong as death,
its jealousy unyielding as the grave.
It burns like blazing fire,
like a mighty flame.
[7]Many waters cannot quench love;
rivers cannot wash it away.
If one were to give
all the wealth of his house for love,
it would be utterly scorned.

8:5b She is not saying that the man's mother actually conceived and gave birth to him under an apple tree. She calls her beloved an apple tree in 2:3, and thus the figure of his mother being "under the apple tree" means that his mother was with his father. Similarly, the place where his mother conceived and gave birth to him refers to the female parts. The usage is analogous to the "house of my mother" in v. 2. The woman means that she and he are now participating in the same act by which the man himself was given life. It is "there" that she aroused him.

8:6 She attests to the absolute devotion of a couple in the love they feel for each other. As in much love poetry, the love is perceived to be eternal. The seals upon the heart and arm symbolize both possession and unbreakable devotion. Love is as strong as death in the sense that its power cannot be resisted. It never releases those whom it has once seized. Even so, the introduction of death and the grave to this context surprises the reader. Even in the ecstasy of love the couple is aware that this too is transitory. Hence the wish is often expressed in love songs that the joy of love could go on forever. Perhaps, if love is as strong as death, it may in some sense transcend death.[188]

The parallel line should be rendered, "Passion is as fierce as the grave." The word "jealousy" is not an apt translation since the English term, in a context of love, implies suspicion of faithlessness on the part of the other. The Hebrew term often refers to this kind of jealousy, but it is not limited to this meaning.[189] Also it is not strictly a sexual passion but rather a strongly emotional attachment to another. This attachment is possessive and exclusive, as in the "passion" of the Lord for Israel. Just as the grave swallows down men and women, so the passion of love, when it has taken a prisoner, never lets him or her go. This does not mean, however, that one is gripped by suspicion that the beloved is faithless.

---

[188]But Murphy (*Song*, 197) comments: "Love is compared to Death as regards strength, but it is not presented as being locked in battle with Death." His point is well taken.

[189]Contrary to Fox (*Song*, 169), who says that קִנְאָה always refers to jealousy. See Job 5:2; Ps 119:139; Prov 14:30; Isa 37:32; 42:13.

Verse 6c could be rendered either, "Its arrow[190] is a burning arrow, [like] lightning"[191] or, "Its flame[192] is a flame of fire, the very hottest fire."[193] The former rendering describes love like one of Cupid's arrows—it strikes and slays its unsuspecting victim. The latter rendering describes love as a flame that is both powerful and eternal. In light of the following line, "Many waters cannot quench love" (v. 7), the latter is to be preferred.

8:7 The comparison of love to a flood alludes to its overwhelming power. In the Old Testament flood waters are the proverbial example of primordial power and thus represent the chaotic passions of love. The point that true love cannot be bought anticipates v. 11, where Solomon serves as a foil to the woman's gift of love.

35. Chorus (8:8-9)

8We have a young sister,
and her breasts are not yet grown.
What shall we do for our sister
for the day she is spoken for?
9If she is a wall,
we will build towers of silver on her.
If she is a door,
we will enclose her with panels of cedar.

8:8-9 Some commentators assign these lines to the woman's brothers on the grounds that they form an inclusio with the reference to the brothers in 1:6. As far as one can tell, however, the brothers have no singing part anywhere else in the Song, and it is odd to have them enter at this point. It is better simply to regard the chorus of Jerusalem girls as the singers here,[194] as indicated by the plural.[195]

The chorus desires that their young sister remain chaste until the proper time for love arrives. Commentators have often noted that this

---

[190]Taking רֶשֶׁף to mean "arrow" on the analogy of Ps 76:4, where רִשְׁפֵי קָשֶׁת = "arrow." But the usage in Ps 76:4 probably is metaphorical with the literal meaning being "flames of the bow" (cf. *BDB*, 958). As such it lends slender support to the view that רֶשֶׁף by itself means "arrow." In Job 5:7 רֶשֶׁף appears to mean "spark" (cf. LXX of Song 8:6, περίπτερα πυρός). In Ps 78:48, however, רֶשֶׁף appears to refer to lightning, which reinforces the interpretation of this line as a description of arrow-like bolts of lightning.

[191]Taking שַׁלְהֶבֶתְיָה, literally "fire of Yah[weh]," to refer to lightning. See Goulder, *Song*, 65-66.

[192]Taking רֶשֶׁף simply as "flame." Cf. the Vg, *lampades ignis.*

[193]Taking שַׁלְהֶבֶתְיָה, "fire of Yah[weh]," as a superlative meaning "the hottest fire." Cf. Gordis, *Song*, 99, and Murphy, *Song*, 191-92.

[194]See Exum, "Structural Analysis," 75-76.

[195]Even more arbitrary is the view of Gordis (*Song*, 99-100) that this part belongs to the "suitors."

verse seems to have no connection with its context,[196] but it probably is an answer to the repeated warnings of the woman that the Jerusalem girls not "arouse love" too soon (e.g., 8:4).

The language used here confirms that the imagery of 3:1-5 and 5:2-7 describes the woman's loss of virginity. The little sister of this text is young (as indicated by her small breasts, v. 8[197]), but "if she is a wall" (v. 9) does *not* refer to her undeveloped breasts even though there is an obvious visual link between a young girl's chest and a wall (otherwise there would be no need for the conditional "if"). The parallel line, "if she is a door," implies that something other than lack of breasts is meant.

In 3:3 and 5:7 the guards, whom we took to refer to her virginity, are "those who go about the walls." In 5:4-6 the image of the door describes the woman's loss of virginity. Here the chorus intends to build battle towers[198] on the "wall" and bar[199] the "door" with cedar planks. In both cases the meaning is that they will take steps to preserve her virginity until the proper time arrives. One should note that the two alternatives ("if she is a wall/a door") should not be taken as antithetical statements about the younger sister's personal morality (as if "wall" = virtuous but "door" = unchaste). Both wall and door[200] are to be understood as barriers representing virginity. The lines present an alternative pair of metaphors for the same thing, virginity.

The materials that bar access to the little girl are of high quality (silver and cedar). This implies that their custody of her will not be harsh or cruel (as would be insinuated by "iron" or the like).

36. Soprano (8:10-12)

[10]I am a wall,
and my breasts are like towers.
Thus I have become in his eyes
like one bringing contentment.

---

[196]Cf. Murphy, *Song*, 198. Goulder (*Song*, 66) thinks that the relatives of a young girl are refusing the offer of a suitor who attempts to buy their sister (v. 7).

[197]Literally, "She has no breasts." Thus the little sister is not the woman of the Song, since the woman plainly does have developed breasts (7:7). This further implies that the singers of these verses are simply the chorus and not the brothers of the woman of the Song. To read these as the brothers' lines with the "little sister" being the woman herself leads to tortured interpretation, as exemplified in Murphy, *Song*, 198-99.

[198]טִירָה = "battlement, enclosure."

[199]צוּר means "to confine or enclose," and in the context of a door it means "to bar." It does not mean to "panel," which makes no sense in this context. It is difficult to imagine why one would panel a door.

[200]Fox (*Song*, 172) rightly observes that word here is דֶּלֶת, which bars entry, and not פֶּתַח, which is open access.

[11]Solomon had a vineyard in Baal Hamon;
he let out his vineyard to tenants.
Each was to bring for its fruit
a thousand shekels of silver.
[12]But my own vineyard is mine to give;
the thousand shekels are for you, O Solomon,
and two hundred are for those who tend its fruit.

8:10 The woman makes a wordplay on the metaphor of the girl as a "wall." I, too, am a wall, she says, but my breasts are its "towers."[201] In other words, she has reached sexual maturity. The following line, "I have become in his eyes[202] like one finding peace,"[203] continues the wordplay. She no longer needs to defend her virginity against the male aggressor who would storm the walls. She, the female, and her lover, the male, are at peace. Instead of battle towers to *defend* her, she has breasts that *adorn* her beauty in his eyes.

8:11 Contrary to some commentators, the woman, not the man, is the singer.[204] The verse obviously parallels 1:6, in which the woman complains that her brothers forced her to work their vineyards and that she was unable to care for her own.[205] The focal point of contrast between the two verses is caring for one's own vineyard as opposed to tending someone else's. In 1:6 she had to look after her brothers' interests at the expense of her own; in 8:11-12 Solomon is detached from his vineyards and merely sees them as a source of revenue. Others do the actual tending of the vines. The mention of large sums of money may also allude to 8:7, where she makes the point that love cannot be bought at any price.

The verse begins by stating that Solomon had a vineyard at Baal Hamon, a place-name[206] meaning "Lord of abundance." Commentators often note that the thousand shekels Solomon received from his vineyard may be a cryptic reference to Solomon's three hundred concubines and seven hundred wives (1 Kgs 11:3). The point would be that the love

---

[201]Note the change to מִגְדָּל, which is not necessarily a battle tower, in contrast to טִירָה, which is a battle tower.

[202]The emendation of Fox (*Song*, 173) to "in your eyes" is unfounded.

[203]Not simply "contentment." In this context, in which there is a play on the notion of the towers on the wall, a military metaphor, the primary sense of *peace* is meant for שָׁלוֹם.

[204]E.g., Fox, *Song*, 174. He argues that v. 12a does not mean, "But my own vineyard is mine to give" but, "My vineyard is before me." He argues that it makes no sense for the woman to speak of "my vineyard before me" since prior usage implies that she herself is the vineyard. But לְפָנָי here means "is at my disposal," a usage confirmed in Gen 13:9; 20:15; etc.; cf. especially Gen 24:51. Also, while the vineyard may in some sense be the woman's body, *metaphorically* it is a vineyard and thus "before" her.

[205]Note especially the use of כַּרְמִי שֶׁלִּי in 8:12 and 1:6, as well as the use of the verb נטר in both texts. By contrast, 8:8-9 has no parallels to 1:6.

[206]The place itself may be fictitious, although Jdt 8:3 mentions a certain Balamon.

between the man and the woman is better than the sexual extravagance of Solomon. A difficulty here is the reference to the two hundred shekels that go to the keepers of the vineyard. Some have taken this as a joke at Solomon's expense meaning that he was not quite able to keep all the women of the harem to himself—some of the "fruit" went to the keepers![207] Insomuch as the harem keepers were characteristically eunuchs, however, this interpretation is doubtful. Solomon is a poetic foil in this text, but not in the superficial manner of this interpretation.

While the "thousand" does suggest Solomon's harem, the numerical correspondence may be coincidental, and in any case the precise figure is irrelevant; what matters is that it is a fantastically large sum. Solomon is able to have others do all the work in his vineyards and yet make five times the profit of those who actually do the labor. The price Solomon pays for this is detachment from the actual life of working the vineyard. As such he cannot fully appreciate the pleasures the vineyard can give. For him the whole arrangement is financial and in fact artificial. The brothers of the woman, similarly, separated themselves from the vineyard when they consigned her to tend them.

8:12 Now, however, the woman is free to care for her own vineyard. It is hers and is at her disposal.[208] As one who tends her own vineyard, she does not experience life through surrogates, nor does she regard the vineyard simply as profit. The "vineyard" is thus not specifically her body, nor is it specifically a metaphor for love, although both are implied. Rather, the vineyard is the freedom she has found in her love for the man. She knows her vineyard, she tends it, and she cares for it. For Solomon wealth and women alike were possessions; for her the relationship she has established is personal, intimate, and nurturing. She is the keeper of the vineyard.

37. Tenor (8:13)

13You who dwell in the gardens
with friends in attendance,
let me hear your voice!

8:13 The woman "dwells in the gardens" in the sense described in 4:12-14; that is, she is a source of every kind of pleasure. The "friends" who listen to the woman's voice are masculine; hence the chorus is not meant. The same term is used in 1:7,[209] where the friends are the other shepherds. This may imply that she has moved out of her old world—the world of her brothers and of the Jerusalem girls—and has entered his.

---

[207]Cf. Murphy, *Song*, 200, and Fox, *Song*, 175.

[208]Thus the emphatic pleonasm כַּרְמִי שֶׁלִּי לְפָנָי ("my vineyard which is mine is at my disposal").

[209]חָבֵר.

"Friends pay heed to your voice," however, simply means that all attention is fixed on her. He regards her as the center of attention because that is what she is to him. As a final confirmation of her value as a person, he calls on her to speak. She is not confined to silence, as though she were a possession, but is fully free and fully a partner.

38. Soprano (8:14)

14Come away, my lover,
and be like a gazelle
or like a young stag
on the spice-laden mountains.

8:14 She calls the man away with her.[210] The "spice-laden mountains" are her breasts but probably refer to the pleasures of love in general. The call for him to depart with her is an apt closure to the Song. Their life together has begun.

39. A Postscript to the Song

In this commentary I have repeatedly stressed that this is a Song and not a play and that many details of the Song must be read metaphorically rather than literally. At this point, having examined the whole of the Song, it is necessary to take a retrospective look at the whole in order to grasp what the Song really is.

At the very beginning of the Song, "Let him kiss me," we are already in the context of the couple's desire for love. All the images of gazelles, gardens, shepherds, and royal processions are meant to convey the pleasure, the natural joy, and the glory that this experience entails. The Jerusalem girls assist in bringing out these emotions.[211] No implication is meant that a newlywed couple would really converse with Jerusalem girls, least of all in the privacy of their wedding night.

The only storyline is that a couple in love marry and have their honeymoon and the bride loses her virginity. This hardly qualifies as a "story."

---

[210]Murphy (*Song*, 194) notes that ברח, "to bolt, flee," does not mean that he should leave her. It is equivalent to שׁוּב ("turn") in 2:17. Fox (*Song*, 176) argues that "with me" would have to be explicit if that were meant, but the idea of "fleeing" is implicit in the metaphor of a gazelle turning to bolt away; it does not actually mean that the man is running from anyone. Some have also suggested that ברח, "to bolt," may have the erotic implications from its cognate noun בְּרִיחַ ("a bolt of a door"), as Fox himself notes. See also Pope, *Song*, 697-98, and cf. Exod 36:33.

[211]Cf. Murphy, *Song*, 84: "From the outset, then, the Daughters function primarily as a foil for the woman's own reflections. They may be likened to an onstage audience or chorus, perhaps present throughout but only rarely speaking, to whom she relates her experiences of love and the lessons she has learned."

Many songs, in fact, do not have a complete plot and storyline. What is meaningful, however, is the psychological and emotional exploration of all that this entails.

It is not surprising that the Song is for the most part given from the woman's perspective. It is she who has to go through the trauma of a rite of passage; the man's rite of passage, insomuch as he has one, is all of pleasure. Her love for him is challenged and emerges triumphant, and her experience makes her the richer and the stronger. She begins as a virtual slave, tending the vineyards of her brothers (1:6), and ends the Song tending her own vineyard (8:12). At the beginning she defends her dark skin before the Jerusalem girls (1:6), but near the end they describe her as being fair as the moon and radiant as the sun (6:10). At the beginning she is aware of how the other girls admire her beloved (1:3), but at the end he notices how his friends admire her (8:13).

The place of this text as wisdom is apparent (see Introduction). It prepares the reader for the joy as well as trauma of love. It readies the woman for marriage and gives the man an added cause to appreciate and admire his bride. It is also a celebration of the woman's love, both as a gift she gives the man and as a signification of her own value and character. It is the Song of love victorious over pain. Love *is* as strong as death and passion as unyielding as the grave.

Selected Subject Index[1]

[1]Indexes were prepared by Lanese Dockery.

Person Index

Selected Scripture Index